THE EARTH AROUND US

THE EARTH AROUND US

Maintaining a Livable Planet

Jill S. Schneiderman
Editor

W. H. FREEMAN AND COMPANY
New York

Interior design by Cambraia (Magalhães) Fernandes

page 18: Excerpt from *Annals of the Former World* by John McPhee. © 1998 by John McPhee. Reprinted by permission of Farrar, Straus & Giroux, Inc.
page 112: Excerpt from *Eight Little Piggies* by Stephen Jay Gould. © 1993 by Stephen Jay Gould. Reprinted by permission of Stephen Jay Gould.

Library of Congress Cataloging-in-Publication Data
Schneiderman, Jill S.
    The earth around us: Maintaining a livable planet / edited by Jill S. Schneiderman.
        p.   cm.
    Includes bibliographical references and index.
    ISBN 0-7167-3397-8
    1. Environmental sciences. 2. Nature—Effect of human beings on. I. Title.
GE105 .S325 2000
333.7—dc21   99-057152

Printed in the United States of America

First printing 2000

W. H. Freeman and Company
41 Madison Avenue, New York, NY 10010
Houndmills, Basingstoke RG21 6XS, England

For Meg, whose generous spirit makes everything possible; and for Caleb, who embodies hope for the future

CONTENTS

PREFACE

When Rachel Carson—scientist, writer, activist—accepted the National Book Award for *The Sea Around Us*, she commented, "But this notion, that 'science' is something that belongs in a separate compartment of its own, apart from everyday life, is one that I should like to challenge. We live in a scientific age; yet we assume that knowledge is the prerogative of only a small number of human beings, isolated and priestlike in their laboratories. This is not true. The materials of science are the materials of life itself. Science is part of the reality of living; it is the what, the how, and the why of everything in our experience."[1] This book, *The Earth Around Us*, honors that sentiment. Throughout its pages, it brings to its readers the scientific understanding of the consequences of human activity on Earth.

Some of the thirty-one essays that constitute this book offer poetic accounts of human thinking about our Earth. Others provide direct and accessible stories of human actions and their aftermath on the planet. In all cases the essays in *The Earth Around Us* encompass a unique resource, a collection of writings by society's foremost scientist-writers, whose goal is to empower its readers by giving them access to scientific information that will bear directly on the ability of *Homo sapiens* to secure a sustainable future on planet Earth. Here readers will glean the perspectives of visionary geoscientists who contemplate Earth's history and the place of humans in it. If the future of humanity is to be environmentally tenable, the public must contemplate these viewpoints.

Scientists articulate their working concepts to the reading public all too infrequently. Authors of essays in *The Earth Around Us* affirm the ability of scientists to communicate relevant science in a clear and engaging fashion, and they enthusiastically embrace their responsibility to do so. The result is a book of lively essays that will captivate readers desiring basic knowledge that can be used to balance human actions within Earth's natural system.

According to environmental activist and writer Robert Gottlieb, a key element in Rachel Carson's argument in her book *Silent Spring* was that science and specialized technical knowledge were separated from public input[2] and that this separation was linked to, in Carson's words, "an era dominated by industry, in which the right to make money, at whatever cost to others, is seldom challenged."[3] In a recent review of John M. Donahue's and Barbara Rose Johnston's *Water, Culture, and Power: Local Struggles in a Global Context*, Gottlieb also comments that a forceful and effective critic of a proposed dam outside of Phoenix, Arizona, was successful precisely because of her ability to "challenge the technical and financial aspects of the project."[4] Surely, science alone cannot fix all the environmental disturbances that humans create. Problems in the physical world are multifaceted; solutions to them will require consideration of ethics and policy as well as judgment informed by cultural, political, social, and historical context. In some cases, to solve the problems that we have induced through the application of scientific principles will necessitate technologies that do not yet exist. Nonetheless, a scientifically aware public, one that knows the ABCs of the earth system, will be able to hold accountable others who act in ignorance of Earth's essential character. By adjusting the compass of our thinking about the natural world, *The Earth Around Us* enables readers to think, speak, and act from knowledge.

The book comprises seven parts, each of which I introduce briefly with a description of the main theme. The book's first section gives readers a sense of Earth's time and history as well as the place of people in it. Part II, "Scientific Judgments and Ethical Considerations," divulges the nature of scientific inquiry about Earth and prompts readers to meditate on reconfigured values that might sustain human life on the planet. The third segment of the book explores a new set of "resources" that we must preserve if life is to persist here: forests, soils, ground and surface waters, and coasts. In the fourth portion, essayists tell true stories about construction projects that defy geological sense. As a hopeful counterpoint to them, the essays in Part V detail geologically aware, innovative thought and action where people have had to respond to environmental challenges. In the sixth part, authors take up issues of planetary change on a global scale—in particular, alterations to the atmosphere. In an effort to spur creative thinking for an environmentally sound and decent future, essayists writing in the final portion of *The Earth Around Us* express philosophies meant to inspire humans to think outside their quotidian existence.

This book is akin to a chorus of voices. Each part can be encountered alone or in relation to the others. Readers can enjoy the essays in any order they choose because each piece of written work was crafted individually. However, the constituent essays form an integrated aggregate that takes the reader on a journey toward prescience about humanity's environmental future. Ultimately, the book is an enticing set of true stories with geological themes. Together the essays make a strong case for the centrality of earth science to environmental sustainability.

In the dystopic future envisioned by poet and novelist Marge Piercy in her book *He, She and It*, the heroine Shira describes listening to a lecture "about two billion people who had starved to death in the Famine, when the ocean rose over rice paddies and breadbaskets of the delta countries like Bangladesh and Egypt, when the Great Plains dried up and blew away in dust storms that darkened the skies and brought early winter, when the deserts of Africa and the new desert of the Amazon spread month by month."[5] Lest this *really* be our future, every person on this planet must come to appreciate the capacity of humans to act as geological agents at nongeological rates.

We humans are coming up against the limits of Earth's ability to provide for us. We have used Earth's resources as if the planet were a bottomless cornucopia. Our consumption of nonrenewable fuel resources has led to global warming, deforestation, and desertification. We've impounded water behind dams to generate hydroelectricity without regard for the destruction of upstream wetlands and other habitats. Our desire for picture-perfect fruits and vegetables out of season has led to widespread use of pesticides and herbicides that have infiltrated our soils and groundwater. Our consumption of goods with little concern for the waste we generate has led to overflowing garbage dumps often constructed on the lands of people forced out of economic necessity to take in the waste of other people. These same landfills sometimes have been constructed without concern for the fluctuating depths of water tables so that leaks have polluted water supplies. We cannot continue to act this way without substantial risk to people and other living things.

All members of the global community must garner a solid working knowledge of our home, this planet. Earth's components—the atmosphere, hydrosphere, biosphere and solid earth—forever interact. When humans deliberately or inadvertently intervene in the natural system, the planet responds. We must learn to anticipate the effects of our actions. I hope this book will help anyone concerned about our planet's ability to support us to understand Earth's history and processes that ground our environmental problems. In the search for a life-sustaining future, geological knowledge is central.

As an epigraph to *Silent Spring*, Rachel Carson quoted writer E. B. White: "I am pessimistic about the human race because it is too ingenious for its own good. Our approach to nature is to beat it into submission. We would stand a better chance of survival if we accommodated ourselves to this planet and viewed it appreciatively instead of skeptically and dictatorially."[6] Unlike White, I am an optimist. A public that understands and appreciates our kaleidoscopic Earth can guide communicative scientists and responsible leaders across the globe so that we live attuned to the Earth's natural system of which we are a part.

ACKNOWLEDGMENTS

I am grateful to members of the geological community whose enthusiasm for the idea behind this project turned my thoughts into this volume of lively essays. The authors' willingness to write original essays for the book even before I obtained a contract for its publication speaks to their profound commitment to the principles that motivate the project. That commitment along with their cooperation has made it possible for me to complete this work. I thank them all: Ronald Amundson, David Applegate, Victor Baker, Jay Banner, Paul Bierman, Marcia Bjørnerud, Ed Buchwald, David Bush, Paul Doss, Thomas Downham, Gordon Eaton, James Evans, George Fischer, Wilfrid Gill, Johan Gottgens, Rosa Gwinn, Robin Hornung, Susan Werner Kieffer, Allison Macfarlane, Scudder Mackey, Catheryn Manduca, Kirsten Menking, Tamara Nameroff, William Neal, Naomi Oreskes, Jeffrey Payne, Orrin Pilkey, Lauret Savoy, Jack Sharp, Virginia Ashby Sharpe, Jill Singer, Steven Stanley, Meg Stewart, Frederick Swanson, and E-an Zen. Also, I thank Stephen Jay Gould and John McPhee for agreeing graciously to have their earlier writing included in this book. Since my days as a graduate student, unique geoscientists in the larger scientific community have inspired and encouraged me to think across disciplines, an endeavor that has surely led to this volume. For this I am indebted intellectually to Gail Ashley, Maria Luisa Crawford, Stephen Jay Gould, Susan Kieffer, Ursula Marvin, Craig Schiffries, James Skehan, S. J., Brian J. Skinner, H. Catherine Skinner, and E-an Zen.

My colleagues in the department of geology and geography, the environmental studies program, the women's studies program, and the dean of studies office at Vassar College have provided cheer and assistance. My students Latia Bowles, Jennifer Cunningham, Maria de la luz Garcia, China Krieker, Thomas Pyun, Laura Ramos, Carolyn Schneyer, and Elizabeth Foster White ably assisted the research for the essays I wrote for this book. I appreciate the sabbatical funds from Vassar that allowed me to work almost exclusively on this project for four months during 1998 and the assistance of librarians at the college. A grant from the National Science Foundation's division of undergraduate education under the direction of Robert Ridky and Dorothy Stout also supported this work, particularly my thinking on the subject of environmental justice. I also thank friends and colleagues Mary Barnett, Robert Brigham, Alexandra Chasin, Monica Church, Ilene Cutler, Gordon Eaton, Erica Flapan, Janet Gray, Adrienne Harrell, Karen Havholm, Robin Hornung, Paula Lockshon, Bruce Loeffler, Ann McHugh, Dorothy Merritts, Jannay Morrow, Judith Nichols, Clare O'Brien, Dan Peck, Debbie Pineiro, Sheila Pinkel, Susan Ratnoff, Vivian Rothstein, Craig Schiffres, Jim Skehan, Brian and Catherine Skinner, Marilyn

Suiter, Robert Suter, Pat Wallace, and Diane Zucker for their advice and support. I owe special thanks to Susan Stocker for the "story starters" that helped form the preface and to Virginia Ashby Sharpe, coauthor, coteacher, and companion in writing and thinking.

Holly Hodder, originally at W. H. Freeman and Company, now at Columbia University Press, has been an energetic and engaged editor. Her ability to share my vision and pace have sustained me in many ways. Erika Goldman, Georgia Lee Hadler, and Melissa Wallerstein at W. H. Freeman have shepherded this manuscript skillfully through the publication process. Jodi Simpson meticulously copyedited the final manuscript.

My family has tolerated the long hours of work that have taken me away from the usual fun we have together. Caleb J. S. Schneiderman, at one and a half years of age, has shown the patience of a geologist. I also thank Jonathan Schneiderman and Jackie Skiff for their encouragement and shared excitement for my work. My abiding appreciation goes to my parents, Alvin and Myrna Schneiderman, who provided the opportunities that opened my eyes to the natural world and moved me toward a passion for the Earth. They have given me unconditional support and unlimited babysitting, without which I would have been unable to complete this work. Finally, I thank Meg Stewart, muse and confidant, for seeing this project to its successful end.

CONTRIBUTORS

Ronald Amundson is interested in the ways that soils record environmental information and how the information may be used to understand past environmental conditions on Earth. A professor of pedology (soil science) in the division of ecosystem sciences at the University of California at Berkeley, he studies the role of soils in the global carbon cycle and the effect of humans on this process.

While pursuing a bachelor's degree in geology from Yale University and a Ph.D. in that subject from the Massachusetts Institute of Technology, **David Applegate** conducted field research on federal lands in California, Idaho, Montana, and Washington. This sparked his interest in public land issues. Currently, he is director of government affairs at the American Geological Institute in Alexandria, Virginia. During the 104th Congress, he worked with the Senate Committee on Energy and Natural Resources as the American Geophysical Union's congressional science fellow and also as a professional staff member for the minority party.

The interests of **Victor R. Baker** focus on geomorphology—the study of forces that affect the shape of landscapes. In particular, he studies the flow of ancient rivers, the effects of floods on land shape, and the forces that have sculpted the surfaces of Mars and Venus. He also pursues work on the history and philosophy of the earth sciences. Vic's written work includes examinations of the significance of earth and environmental sciences to public policy issues. He is Regents professor and head of the department of hydrology and water resources at The University of Arizona. In 1998 he was president of the Geological Society of America.

Born and raised in New York City, **Jay L. Banner** was an undergraduate at the University of Pennsylvania. Midway through his college career, Jay switched from chemistry to geology so that he could spend time outside and still do science. He studies carbonate rocks (those that precipitated out of seawater) and aquifers (conduits of water through rocks) so that he can understand the evolution of groundwater, surface water, and the oceans. The effects of urbanization on aquifers particularly concern him. He is presently an associate professor in the department of geological sciences at the University of Texas at Austin.

Paul R. Bierman is a geologist and associate professor at the University of Vermont in Burlington. His research focuses on the erosion of rock, the movement of sediment, the interaction of people with geology, and the rates at which the surface of the Earth changes. When he is not collecting samples in the Namibian, Australian, and Mojave deserts, Paul is working with his students trenching river and hillslope sediments in the humid Northeast. In recent years he received the Geological Society of America's young scientist award for his promising research on glaciers and climate.

A structural geologist (someone who studies the breaking and bending of rocks), **Marcia G. Bjørnerud** wandered into the field for aesthetic reasons—the beauty of deformed rocks—and stayed. She is interested in how scientific depictions of nature both influence and reflect popular cultural beliefs. She has worked extensively in the high arctic (Svalbard, Ellesmere Island), where Earth's simultaneous fierceness and fragility are in evidence everywhere. She is associate professor of geology at Lawrence University in Appleton, Wisconsin.

Caryl Edward Buchwald, Lloyd McBride professor of environmental studies in the geology department at Carleton College in Northfield, Minnesota, teaches introductory and advanced courses in geology as well as a seminar on wilderness. He also directs the college's natural history program. With degrees in geology from Union College, Syracuse University, and the University of Kansas, Ed has concentrated on surface water studies, assessments of human impacts on the environment, and science education. Ed's work includes many years of service on Minnesota's state environmental regulatory boards. In 1994 he was selected "Citizen of the Academy" by the American Association for Higher Education.

Storm process and coastal hazards are the work of **David M. Bush.** A member of the National Academy of Sciences post-disaster field study team for both Hurricane Gilbert and Hurricane Hugo, he appreciates the power and dynamism of coastal processes. With a Ph.D. in geology from Duke University and postdoctoral work with the program for the study of developed shorelines at Duke, Dave focuses on hazards along coasts, maps risks, and works to mitigate property damage along much of the Atlantic and the Gulf of Mexico seaboards and the Caribbean. He is coauthor of *Living With the Puerto Rico Shore, Living With the South Carolina Coast, The North Carolina Shore and Its Barrier Islands,* and the forthcoming *Living by the Rules of the Sea.* He is assistant professor of geology at the State University of West Georgia in Carrollton.

Paul K. Doss teaches courses in environmental geology, physical geology, wetland science, and hydrogeology at the University of Southern Indiana in Evansville. Paul studies physical and geochemical processes within the hydrologic cycle, investigates the impacts of industrial landfills on water quality, and attends to the earth science needs of public policymakers and secondary and elementary school educators. He takes seriously the role of citizen-geologist and so has served on municipal comprehensive planning and conservation committees. He is currently a member of the natural resources committee at Wesselman Woods Nature Preserve, an old-growth forest in Evansville, Indiana. He has also worked as a hydrogeologist with the U.S. Geological Survey and the National Park Service.

Thomas F. Downham II, is a clinical associate professor of dermatology at Wayne State University School of Medicine in Michigan. For the last 25 years, he has practiced dermatology and taught medical students and residents about the subject. Concerned about the implications of a degraded and unhealthful environment for human existence on Earth, Tom's research since 1989 has focused on the health effects of ultraviolet radiation in relation to global ozone depletion.

A geologist turned administrator, **Gordon P. Eaton** lives on Whidbey Island in northern Puget Sound, Washington. Gordie has steered at least two of the major institutions of earth science in this country: he was the twelfth director of the U.S.

Geological Survey and before that, the director of Columbia University's Lamont-Doherty Earth Observatory. Committed to education as well as science, in earlier years he was provost of Texas A&M University and president of Iowa State University. When he was making what he refers to as "an honest living," most of his geological work—like that of some of his predecessors at the U.S. Geological Survey—focused on geology of the western United States, a region he first came to love at the ripe old age of nine.

James E. Evans teaches sedimentology, hydrogeology, and mechanics of fluid motion in the geology department at Bowling Green State University. His coauthored work on the IVEX Dam and Reservoir for this book is part of an interdisciplinary effort to understand and characterize sediment flows along the coast of Lake Erie and in adjacent watersheds. Jim strives to understand historical changes in the region and develop new solutions to environmental problems there.

Like many geologists captivated by the grandeur of Earth's creations, **George W. Fisher** has studied the rocks that compose mountain belts in an effort to understand how they formed. His recent work links the earth sciences to issues of sustainability and human health, and to the moral, ethical, and theological dimensions of those issues. A professor of earth and planetary sciences at The Johns Hopkins University, George is also the deputy director of the program of dialogue regarding science, ethics, and religion at the American Association for the Advancement of Science.

Wilfrid M. Gill works as a hydrogeologist in the southwestern United States, a portion of this country in dire need of assistance from scientists who appreciate natural constraints to growth in arid areas. Bill earned a master's degree in geology from Bowling Green State University.

As a limnologist in the department of biology at the University of Toledo, **Johan F. Gottgens** studies lake processes. In particular, he studies biomanipulation of aquatic ecosystems and lake and reservoir management.

Stephen Jay Gould teaches geology, history of science, and biology at Harvard University and New York University. He has received many awards—among them the National Book Award, the National Book Critic's Circle Award, and a MacArthur Foundation grant. His most recent books include *Wonderful Life, Dinosaur in a Haystack, Questioning the Millennium,* and *Leonardo's Mountain of Clams and the Diet of Worms.* Among his classic works are *The Mismeasure of Man* and *Time's Arrow, Time's Cycle: Myth and Metaphor in the Discovery of Geological Time.*

Fossil beds that form the falls of the Ohio River in her native Louisville, Kentucky gave **Rosa E. Gwinn** her first exposure to geology. As an undergraduate geology major at Harvard and graduate student at Brown University, she immersed herself in the study of the chemical behavior of volcanic magmas. Rosa chose ultimately to apply herself to understanding the chemical behavior of contaminants near the Earth's surface. She now works for a major environmental consulting firm in Bethesda, Maryland, as an environmental geochemist especially trying to resolve problems of contamination at Superfund sites.

Dermatologist **Robin L. Hornung** earned a bachelor's degree in geology at Yale University and then pursued a career in medicine at the same institution. Combining her interests in the environment, dermatology, and public health, she conducts research on skin cancer prevention. Robin obtained her clinical training in dermatology at Duke University Medical Center and followed this with fellowships in general preventive medicine and public health at the University of North Carolina-Chapel Hill. She now serves as the cochair of the National Council of Sun Protection, Ozone Depletion, and the Ultraviolet Index for the National Association of Physicians for the Environment and is an assistant professor at the University of Washington Medical School in Seattle.

Among various subjects, **Susan Werner Kieffer** has studied meteorite impacts, volcanism on Earth and other planets, shock-wave physics, and hydraulics of river flow. Aspects of these processes have led her to work closely with mathematicians and apply techniques developed for geology to environmental and medical problems. A MacArthur Foundation fellow, Sue founded Kieffer & Woo, Inc., a research and development company that specializes in nonlinear earth processes and data analysis. She also steers the nonprofit Kieffer Institute for Development of Science-Based Education, which is developing a science- and World Wide Web-based integrated curriculum for at-risk K-through-12 students.

Allison Macfarlane concerns herself with the issues surrounding high-level nuclear waste. With a Bunting fellowship from Radcliffe College, she scrutinized the potential problems associated with disposal of high-level radioactive waste at Yucca Mountain, Nevada. Currently she is a Social Science Research Council-MacArthur Foundation fellow in international peace and security at the Belfer Center for science and international affairs at Harvard University. Allison received her Ph.D. in geology from the Massachusetts Institute of Technology in 1992 and has taught geology, environmental science, and women's studies at George Mason University.

At the Ohio Geological Survey, **Scudder D. Mackey** supervises the Lake Erie geology project. His research focuses on sediment transport and erosion along coasts, restoration of lake wetlands, and river processes.

Cathryn A. Manduca tries to infuse students and citizens with the excitement of exploring how the Earth works and to convey the importance of this understanding for decisions at all scales. She does this both as a member of the Olmsted County environmental commission (she was chair of the commission in 1998) and as coordinator of the Keck geology consortium—a group of undergraduate liberal arts geology departments that offers geologic research opportunities for students and faculty and works to improve geoscience education at their schools. Cathy has a Ph.D. in geology from the California Institute of Technology.

John McPhee is a staff writer for *The New Yorker*. He lives and works in Princeton, New Jersey. *Annals of the Former World*, his comprehensive work on the geology of North America, won a Pulitzer Prize in 1999. Some of his previous books—several bestsellers—include *Encounters with the Archdruid, Coming into the Country,*

Basin and Range, In Suspect Terrain, Rising from the Plains, and *The Control of Nature.*

Kirsten M. Menking grew up hunting for fossils in Kansas. Her childhood experiences led to a lifelong fascination with geology and a love of the outdoors. Growing up in Kansas also led her to a great interest in weather and climate. She has managed to fuse these passions by studying the history of climate as it is recorded by geological processes. Kirsten has studied lake sediments from California, New Mexico, and New York to reconstruct the changes in temperature and precipitation that have occurred in these areas over the last several tens of thousands of years. She is a coauthor of *Environmental Geology: An Earth System Science Approach.* She is an assistant professor of geology at Vassar College in Poughkeepsie, New York.

Trained as an oceanographer, **Tamara Nameroff** wrote her essay for this book while serving as the climate task force coordinator for the President's Council on Sustainable Development. Before this appointment, she helped interpret environmental and natural resource policy for a United States senator as the Geological Society of America's 1996–1997 congressional science fellow. Tamara started her professional career as a water quality specialist at an industrial facility.

William J. Neal has conducted investigations of coastal processes for more than 20 years. A professor of geology at Grand Valley State University in Allendale, Michigan, in 1993 he received the American Geological Institute's award for outstanding contributions to public understanding of geology. With Orrin Pilkey, Bill is coeditor of Duke University Press' *Living with the Shore* series.

Naomi Oreskes is a geologist and historian of science who worries about how scientists know the things they know—or *think* they know. Her early experiences as a field geologist searching for mineral deposits in Australia led her to question the reasons for the diminished status of field work in geological research. As a historian of science, she tries to understand the intellectual preferences and predilections of scientists in historical and cultural terms. An associate professor of history of science at the University of California at San Diego, Naomi has written most recently *The Rejection of Continental Drift: Theory and Method in American Earth Science.*

As deputy director of the National Oceanic and Atmospheric Administration's coastal services center in Charleston, South Carolina, **Jeffrey L. Payne** helps set U.S. policy regarding its coasts—an important job because more than half of the U.S. population lives along our nation's shorelines. Jeff's seven years of prior experience working for NOAA in Washington, D.C., the Office of Management and Budget in the executive office of the President, and on Capitol Hill as a congressional science and engineering fellow inform the coastal policy decisions he makes today. Jeff earned his Ph.D. in marine geophysics from Texas A&M University and has spent time at sea conducting marine and coastal research.

Orrin H. Pilkey appreciates barrier beaches, and his research helps him and others understand their nature. In particular, he examines shoreface processes, scrutinizes the viability of beach nourishment plans as a solution to beach erosion, and reviews critically mathematical models used by others to predict beach behavior. Orrin is a James B. Duke professor of geology and director of the program for the study of developed shorelines at Duke University. He received the Francis Shepard award for excellence in marine geology from the Geological Society of America and served on that society's committee on public policy. With Bill Neal, he is coeditor of Duke University Press' *Living with the Shore* series. He is the author of *The Beaches Are Moving* and *The Corps and the Shore*.

Ideas and stories of lands have stirred **Lauret E. Savoy's** imagination and interest since childhood. They were the threads that linked her undergraduate studies in studio art (landscape photography and painting), history (American studies), and, ultimately, geology. As an associate professor in geology and geography at Mount Holyoke College, her current research and teaching interests focus on the "reading" and interpretation of natural landscapes and environments in western North America. More specifically, she pursues two major directions in environmental history—geological analysis of ancient environmental change and interdisciplinary study of human environmental history and ideas of landscape.

Concerned about the welfare of human beings and other living things on this planet, **Jill S. Schneiderman** applies her geological knowledge in order to understand the processes that will help create livable conditions on Earth. Jill's idea for this book came from her desire to help all people understand that earth science is crucial to our ability to enable human beings to live sustainably on this planet in the future. Her scientific research focuses on sediments in rivers and deltas—in particular, the Catskill Mountain watersheds and the Nile and Yangtze deltas. As a science advisor to the democratic leader of the U.S. Senate during the 104th Congress, she worked on environmental issues. She teaches courses on earth history and uses explorations of concepts of justice as a paradigm for studies of the physical environment. She is an associate professor of geology in the geology and geography department at Vassar College.

In Texas, where **John M. Sharp, Jr.** is a professor of geology at the University at Austin, "water is for fighting." That is, water is among the most precious resources, and its use and distribution in Texas can be a contentious subject. With the help of geoscientists, however, Jack contends that if we manage our water carefully we will be able to meet economic and societal needs today and in the future. As a hydrogeologist, he studies a wide array of hydrologic processes ranging from bacterial and chemical processes that alter the surfaces of rock fractures to fluid and heat flow in sedimentary basins such as the Gulf of Mexico.

Virginia Ashby Sharpe is a philosopher and deputy director at the Hastings Center in Garrison, New York and specializes in health care ethics and environmental philosophy. In her work in both areas, she is interested in illuminating the ways in which norms and values express themselves in individual action and public policy. She is also committed to identifying and promoting values necessary for sustainable human and natural communities. She is the author of *Medical Harm: Historical, Conceptual, and Ethical Dimensions of Iatrogenic Illness*.

Jill K. Singer is a sedimentologist and professor at Buffalo State College in Buffalo, New York. Her teaching and research focus on the physical processes of sediment transport. As a local environmental activist, she uses her geological background to address environmental problems, often involving her students in local environmental research projects. For five years, she chaired Erie County's environmental management council and currently is an active member of the Friends of the Buffalo River, an organization concerned with issues surrounding the restoration of a local river. In both the classroom and the community, Jill strives to convey the importance of protecting and restoring our local environmental resources.

Paleontologist **Steven M. Stanley** became interested in geology as a boy, while living along the Chagrin River in Ohio. In college, intellectual excitement about organic evolution impelled him toward his current career. Most of his field work has focused on marine mollusks, but his theoretical research on rates and patterns of evolution has entailed a variety of life forms, from single-celled creatures to human ancestors. Recently, he has been studying the history of life in the context of past environmental change; Steve's textbook, *Earth System History*, reflects this multidisciplinary approach. He is a professor in the department of earth and planetary sciences at Johns Hopkins University. He is also coauthor with David Raup of *Principles of Paleontology*.

Meg E. Stewart is a geologist who has made maps of active faults and other rock structures in the desert southwestern United States. In the eastern United States her interest in environmental contamination and remediation led her to work on problems of pollution in the New York–New Jersey Harbor as a consultant at a major environmental firm. Presently, Meg provides technical support to students and faculty in the Geographic Information Systems (GIS) Computer Laboratory in the department of geology and geography at Vassar College and uses GIS to answer a multitude of land use questions. She also teaches environmental science at Dutchess Community College.

Frederick J. Swanson is a geologist who works in forests. As head of the Long-Term Ecological Research program sponsored by the National Science Foundation at the H. J. Andrews Experimental Forest in western Oregon, Fred has worked closely with forest and stream ecologists to study unmanaged and managed forest watersheds. As ecosystem team leader with the U.S. Forest Service at the Pacific Northwest Research Station in Corvallis, Oregon, he examines especially the interactions of geomorphic (surface-shaping) processes, landforms, and biotic properties of ecosystems.

For many years as a geologist at the U.S. Geological Survey, **E-an Zen** studied Appalachian and Rocky Mountain geology, the origin of metamorphic and igneous rocks, and the processes that shape bedrock river channels. Since then, as an adjunct professor of geology at the University of Maryland, E-an has turned his attention to aspects of global and societal concern among them—K-through-12 science education, human rights, ethics in science, and preservation of the Earth as a habitat against the effects of human fouling. He is a member of the U.S. National Academy of Sciences and a former president of the Geological Society of America.

THE EARTH AROUND US

Part I

RECORDS OF TIME AND HISTORY

Life must be lived amidst that which was made before. Every landscape is an accumulation. The past endures. —Donald W. Meinig

The Earth has a vast history, of which humans are a part. Traces of events that characterize Earth's history lurk amidst landscapes—they convey a context for human existence, they mark our absence or presence. Astute observers can read the record of past events but also must proceed with caution, for human historical context affects human perceptions. The essays that follow build one on the other to give the reader a sense of Earth's time and history as well as the place of people in it.

In the first essay, Susan Kieffer reflects on the rare and the routine among geological events—meteorite impacts, floods, volcanic eruptions, and earthquakes—that affect individuals and civilizations. Then, John McPhee unearths the "abyss of time" in the intellectual rovings of eighteenth- and nineteenth-century naturalists. Lauret Savoy explores the effects of human perceptions and actions on North American terranes from the desert Southwest to midcontinent prairies and grasslands. And finally, Paul Bierman paints a history of natural and human-induced change on a Vermont landscape.

In the aggregate, these essays reveal the simultaneously fleeting yet substantial nature of human participation in Earth's history.

1

Geology: The Bifocal Science

Susan Werner Kieffer

R̲are events seem to be fodder for Hollywood megamovies such as *Volcano, Twister, Dante's Peak, Deep Impact,* and *Armageddon.* However, consideration of the possibility and consequences of such events occupies almost no time in our personal thinking, nor much of a fraction of most community budgets. Major infrastructure sectors, such as power generation and waste disposal facilities, also fail to have resources set aside for such events. But the occurrence of even one rare event can have catastrophic consequences for the planet, for living species, for economies, and for technology.

Bifocal lenses allow people with vision problems to see both near and far objects. In geology, a view of rare events far away in space and time gives us the ability and perspective to focus on their possible occurrence and impact in our nearby space and in current and future times. We will use the bifocal capacity of geology to look into the distant past and deep Earth to focus on rare, but possible, events that could affect human civilization. As we go through examples of such events, we should keep asking: How can we bring rare, nonintuitive events into our collective consciousness and into our planning for future generations? Even in cases where we have 7,000 years of human records—such as the history of the Nile River system—supplemented by a body of geological knowledge that spans an even longer time, do we dare think that we know all the possible behaviors of a geological system or the consequences of our perturbations on it? The bifocal view of geology clearly tells us not to be so arrogant.

WHAT IS RARE?

The word *rare* can be used in the context of space ("spatially rare") or time ("temporally rare"). In the context of space, rare means "thinly distributed over an area," or "widely spaced," often with the implication of having unusual value because of the uncommonness. In the context of time, rare means "occurring infrequently," or "uncommon." Both space and time definitions have implications that depend on the perception of the person describing an event and on the circumstances of lives, economies, cultures, and communication. We also find that there is an interconnectedness between events that are rare in space and those that are rare in time, as I will show in a number of examples.

Consider first the nature of rareness in space. People who have few opportunities to travel will discover with delight new geography and will tend to think that some new sight is rare because it has seldom, or never, occurred in their own experiences. For example, when I moved from Pennsylvania to the Rocky Mountains and then to the Southwest, I was totally unprepared for the high rugged mountains or for the beautiful cacti that I saw. I was overwhelmed by these "rare" mountains and flora, for I had no context for judging the commonness or rareness of what I was seeing. After living in the Southwest for many years, cacti were common and hardwood forests, wetlands, or coastal estuaries seemed rare.

A world traveler will have a perspective on the rareness of various spatial features on the Earth different from that of a local dweller. The traveler will be inclined to say, "Oh, this feature in Asia reminds me of that one in the United States," or "This is amazingly like that." Thus, when the world traveler says that something in our natural world is rare, the meaning can be quite different from that of exactly the same words spoken by the local traveler.

Geologists tend to be world travelers because of the nature of our science. Thus, our perspective on spatially rare features should carry different weight than the perspective of someone who has not traveled so widely. For example, the travels of geologists tend to make them deeply and personally aware of the mushrooming population of the planet—every major city that we visit is growing faster than its infrastructure. Television may carry this message into individual homes, but people who do not travel and personally experience the population changes may think that the situations portrayed are rare. The world traveler, however, will argue that the city–population–infrastructure problem is common, and may even go further and advocate that the problem is so common that it represents a crisis to be solved.

The same comparison holds with respect to time. A young person will relish new experiences as unique and rare. An elder, however, may appear jaded, having lived through many of those new experiences several times. It takes something truly unique to surprise an elder.

How do these perspectives on space and time extend to geology? Geologists are both the world travelers and the elders of the planet. We see the planet in three spatial dimensions and also across the fourth dimension of time. Just as the person who looks through bifocal lenses can see both far and near objects, our science allows us to look at the evolution of our planet at many scales of space and throughout all of geologic and astronomical time. We can think of geology as looking at the world through both a magnifying glass and a microscope. Because of the nature of our science, we can define the terms *common* and *rare* on many different scales of space and time.

For example, what is common and what is rare on the time scale of a billion years, which is the relevant scale for the formation of planets? What is common and what is rare on the time scale of a million years, which is the time scale for the formation of many of the fuel resources that we humans care about? What is common and what is rare on the time scale of a thousand years, which is the time scale we consider when dealing with natural hazards to human civilization and culture? What is common and what is rare on the time scale of a century, which represents three human generations, parent, child, and grandchild? What is common and what is rare on the time scale of a few decades, the life of an individual? What is common and what is rare on the time scale of a few weeks or years—the time scale of teenagers?

On the time scale of a billion years, formation of stars and galaxies is common. However, according to our knowledge at this time, formation of whole universes is rare. Currently, we also think that the formation of planets and other life forms is rare, but our data on this subject are changing rapidly because of improvements in observational techniques. Spatially, these phenomena may also be rare because of the special circumstances required for their formation. Thus, rarity is interconnected spatially and temporally in these processes.

On the time scale of a million years, formation of sedimentary, igneous, and metamorphic rocks is common. Formation of oil, gas, and coal deposits may be rare on this time scale because of particular requirements of large deposits of organic matter combined with highly specific pressure and temperature conditions. Formation of precious metal deposits is probably a common and ongoing process at this time scale, but these deposits are spatially rare.

On the time scale of thousands of years, small volcanic eruptions may be common, but big events that destroy a whole volcanic mountain may be rare because a long time is required to replenish the heat and mass that cause such an event. Likewise, small and medium earthquakes may be common, but large ones that destroy whole cities, nations, or civilizations may be rare because of the long time needed to accumulate strain that is released by the big earthquakes. Spatially, earthquakes and volcanic eruptions are restricted to special parts of the planet because of processes now well explained by the unifying theory of plate tectonics, and their commonness or rarity is determined by the circumstances of supply of strain or of energy and heat at specific locations.

On the time scale of centuries, shooting stars are common, but big meteorite impacts are rare. And, whereas the effects of a big meteorite impact may be global, the craters formed even by large impacts are small compared with the scale of the Earth.

On the time scale of weeks and years, small or medium changes in river flow may be common, but floods that drain an entire watershed during an exceptionally strong El Niño or La Niña event may be rare.

Clearly, conclusions like these depend on our state of knowledge. Not only scientific techniques but also time, communication, and culture play roles in how we perceive "rarity."

In the time domain, the nature of human experience is to consider as common, not rare, those events that occur in one's lifetime. Beyond this, we have the capacity to absorb anecdotal knowledge from our parents, our grandparents, and perhaps our great-grandparents. But, in societies with written rather than strictly oral traditions, knowledge from more remote times becomes intellectual rather than intuitive.

Assuming that the lives of an individual, her parents, and grandparents span a century, events that occur once per century seem to be common because of the family memories. Events that occur on certain time scales are given the names that reflect their statistical likelihoods: "the annual flood," "the hundred-year drought," or "the thousand-year forest fire." Up to intervals of about a century, these events are part of familiar, intuitive experience. In many places, government plans for zoning and response to hazards exist for these time scales. Nevertheless, financial and political factors often result in poor plans. Every year, floods devastate homes built on well-known floodplains, hurricanes destroy fragile houses in areas that are known to experience frequent hurricanes, and waves destroy structures improperly constructed on coastal beaches. These losses arise despite our certain knowledge that these events will occur. The "annual spring flood" may be small for a few years, or big for a few years, but it will occur in the spring. The more serious problem is that there will be larger spring floods over time scales of centuries or millennia, and these rare events are neither intuitive nor easily predicted.

Although rare events are rare, they do happen. Our lives are short; the term of influence of elected politicians is even shorter. Nevertheless, one or more of those "rare" events may happen during our lives, or during some politician's "watch." Obviously, individuals and communities might benefit from a satisfactory, and practical, definition of *rare*. So might groups charged with protecting the public, for these agencies need to be able to predict and to define the hazards and their consequences. Scientific research and monitoring groups, such as the U.S. Geological Survey and the National Center for Atmospheric Research, study and try to understand these events. Even nongeological agencies, such as the Centers for Disease Control in the United States, will benefit from geological evidence about rare events, such as climate change, because of the response of living organisms to these changes. Service agencies, such as the Red Cross and the Federal Emergency Management Agency, that respond to crises brought on by natural phenomena need to know what to expect from and how to respond to crises. Likewise, insurance companies care about a suitable definition of *rare* because they mediate the cost between insurance premiums and payouts.

With this introduction and perspective, let's focus on the concept of "rare" at the time scale of human civilization—thousands to tens of thousands of years. What is common and what is rare? Four examples, viewed at different scales of space and time, bring into focus the issue of rarity over thousands to tens of thousands of years and its relevance to our present and future periods. As we consider these scenarios, we should ask: How can we bring nonintuitive events into people's individual and collective consciousness?

Meteorite Impacts

Most humans probably see a few "shooting stars" in a lifetime. The observation may be in the context of a romantic tryst in the mountains, a small observatory built by a friend or institution, or a nightly newscast. We assimilate shooting stars as part of our individual human experience, in the sense that we "expect" to see them. Therefore, although not common, shooting stars are not rare to most of us.

However, consider the few percent of the human population that do not see shooting stars—perhaps because of perennially bad weather or because of city light pollution. To people living under these conditions, shooting stars are not merely uncommon, they are "rare" or even "unknown." The little and common events do not reside in the individual's consciousness, so there is no basis for extrapolating them into the larger collective consciousness. Superstitions may be rooted in such a condition, that is, a lack of knowledge of common events on which to extrapolate to predictions about larger and rarer events.

If we see shooting stars and understand what causes them, then we have some basis for understanding that bigger shooting stars may exist. With scientific measurements, we find that the shooting stars are caused by meteorites that are the size of a sand grain or a small pea and enter the Earth's atmosphere. We might wonder what would happen if they did not burn up in the atmosphere but landed on Earth, which they would do if they were bigger. In fact, some meteorites do land here; and some of them end up in laboratories, either because some rock collector recognizes an unusual rock on the ground or because these rocks actually disrupt someone's life by falling through roofs, landing in a herd of cattle while a farmer watches, or dropping onto cars.

When meteorites land on the Earth, they make depressions called impact craters. We can go into the field—geology slang for going out into the world and making measurements—and look at various young and old craters, measure their ages, make estimates of the size of the meteorite that caused a particular crater, and infer the frequency with which meteorites of various sizes hit the Earth.[1] A famous small crater less than a half-mile across is Meteor Crater, Arizona, formed by the impact of an iron meteorite about 50,000 years ago. This impact probably caused local effects over northern Arizona. An important large crater about 62 miles in diameter is Chicxulub, on the Yucatan Peninsula in Mexico. This crater was formed about 65 million years ago.[2] The impact at Chicxulub affected the whole planet, causing the extinction of many species, including dinosaurs. By studying the numbers, sizes, and ages of craters on the

Earth and other planets, geologists in the field of planetary sciences are able to make measurements and models of how often meteoroids of different sizes impact the Earth.

We also can go to observatories and measure the numbers of comets and Earth-crossing asteroids that are currently in the vicinity of our solar system.[3] These measurements give us other reference points for our statistics on the frequency of impacts of various sizes.

For example, several meteoroids the size of grapefruits will hit us in an average year. One meteoroid the size of half of a football field will impact every 50,000 years and make a crater about the size of Meteor Crater. A meteoroid a mile in diameter will impact us every few hundred thousand years; it will cause civilization-threatening consequences. A meteoroid with a six-mile diameter will hit us every hundred million years, making a crater the size of Chicxulub and producing global consequences.

We can use these statistics to predict the probability of an impact over any given time frame—for example, we can say that the chance that you will die as a consequence of a meteoroid impact is almost the same as the chance that you will meet your end in the crash of a passenger aircraft: 1 in 20,000. However, we cannot predict exactly when or where an impact might occur until we actually see an object heading on a trajectory toward us. As more measurements on the trajectory and the size of the object are obtained, our ability to predict the consequences of an impact would improve. We would certainly experience different consequences if a crater like Meteor Crater were formed in New York City, or in the Arizona desert, or in the ocean.

Weighing the probability and the possible consequences of impact is a challenge that earth and planetary scientists face. For this problem, the lenses we use are literally as large as the telescopes that aid our search for meteoroids and as small as the microscopes that allow us to examine them in detail.

Floods

Whether about the Mississippi River in the United States, the Red River that crosses the border between the United States and Canada, or the Yangtze River in China, stories of flooding rivers are much in the news. Prior to the time when massive dam projects were initiated in the twentieth century, people in these regions and even desert dwellers in the southwestern United States or along the Nile in Egypt could observe seasonal fluctuations in the discharge of their nearby river. Spring floods, gully washes, flash floods, winter freezes, and ice jams were part of community knowledge.

Even if you lived near a very small creek, as I did when I was a child, you saw the variations seasonally and annually. Much to my parents' annoyance, the Fisher Creek, normally a small trickle that I could easily hop over, typically overflowed its banks about two blocks upstream from our house in the spring and wound its way downstream by taking a right angle bend through our basement. This small creek discharged into the larger Conewango Creek. When the Conewango flooded in the spring—which, of course, it did every year—we students inevitably delighted in a few extra vacation days because the county had unwisely placed the junior high school on the floodplain. Even with a good collective conscience about the seasonal and annual behavior of this small river system, city zoning laws did not, and typically do not, prevent considerable expense and damage due to the floods. Political and economic pressures prevail over geological evidence and collective wisdom.

The massive dam projects that began in the early twentieth century on nearly every river in the United States, and in many other countries, have greatly modified our individual and collective consciousness about flooding. Many people who live downstream of dams see no annual variations in water discharge because the reservoirs behind the dams buffer the seasonal, and even decade-scale, variations. These large dams have had a massive impact in places like Egypt, where a chain of dams culminating in the High Aswan Dam changed the behavior of the Nile; and in the United States, where a series of dams has altered the behavior of the Colorado River system. When the Three Gorges Dam is completed along the Yangtze River in China, there will inevitably be similar great effects. What does history tell us of the effects? And, what does history *not* tell us?

Probably more than any other factor, the Nile was responsible for the great civilization of ancient Egypt. It's history is well documented both historically and geologically.[4] The longest river on the African continent, the Nile flows north into the Mediterranean Sea. Where it meets the sea, the Nile has deposited sediment in the shape of a Greek letter delta. The beginning of Egyptian civilization coincided with the first emergence of the Nile Delta. The annual cycles of discharge of the Nile produced fertile lands along the river floodplains and on the delta. These conditions supported the great Egyptian civilization that began 7,000 to 8,000 years ago.

However, natural annual fluctuations in discharge produced unpredictable flood or famine conditions, so, even during early cultural phases, humans tried to control the fluctuations. The Dynastic period, starting approximately 5,050 years before the present, began at a time when the climate in Egypt became extremely arid and the discharge on the Nile was sufficiently reduced that simple irrigation could be developed to allow year-round cultivation of crops. For 5,000 years, the Nile was slowly modified by human influence; but this modification greatly accelerated in the nineteenth century with the building of the Aswan dams—a series of increasingly high dams started in 1889 and finished when the High Dam was completed in 1970.[5] Lake Nasser formed by the ponding of the Nile behind this last dam.

The Aswan dams control the annual floods that used to cause damage along the floodplain, increase areas that can be cultivated for perennial crops, allow more industrialization by providing about half of Egypt's power supply, and improve navigation conditions on the Nile because they keep water levels fairly constant. Because of the growing population of Egypt, these advantages cannot be ignored.

However, serious disadvantages are also associated with the dams: The cultural disturbance to create the Aswan High Dam was large—almost 90,000 people had to be relocated and many artifacts were lost or had to be moved. The formation of Lake Nasser has induced earthquakes in a previously aseismic region.[6] Seepage and evaporation cause a loss of about 15 percent of the water in the Nile system. And sediments have been filling the reservoir and decreasing its storage capacity, although the High Dam is still expected to have a life of 500 years.

In turn, storage of sediments behind the dam deprives the river of those sediments downstream. So, instead of depositing sediments, the river erodes its banks. Even though the river carries this eroded sediment further downstream toward the delta, it deposits very little material on the delta relative to the amounts deposited in the past. The balance between deposition of sediments and erosion of the delta by coastal processes and subsidence has been upset, and the delta has changed from a constructive regime to a destructive one. Wetlands in the northern part of the delta are being destroyed or reduced, thereby causing ecosystems to be degraded.[7]

Human influence is magnified by these altered conditions along the Nile. Farmers have been forced to use artificial fertilizers because natural fertilizers are no longer replenished by annual floods. Lands that are newly irrigated by the stored and diverted waters do not drain well. Minerals from the fertilizers and salt are accumulating because of evaporation, and these enter the food chain in potentially toxic levels.

Waste of both nonhuman and human origins is concentrated because of the lack of drainage. The accumulation of human waste is an especially serious problem where villages are closely spaced. These conditions have led to the resurgence of diseases. For example, the parasitic disease schistosomiasis, a condition associated with snails that live in the stagnant waters of the new canal and lagoon system, is affecting a greater number of individuals than in the past. These disease threats could become a serious problem because about 95 percent of Egypt's population lives within a dozen miles of the Nile.

These changes in the Nile have influenced even the large Mediterranean Sea. Loss of silt and algae from the Nile caused the disappearance of a major sardine resource from the Mediterranean, and the change in discharge has affected the Mediterranean shrimp population.

The history of the modification of the Nile spans 7,000 years and gives us a perspective that we can apply to other rivers and dam projects. At the present time, the largest hydroelectric project in history is the construction of the Three Gorges Dam on the Yangtze River in China. At the time of the writing of this book, a diversion channel has already been constructed to route the Yangtze around the dam construction site. The dam is scheduled to be completed between 2009 and 2013. When filled, the lake behind the dam will flood about 1,200 square miles. For comparison, Lake Powell behind Glen Canyon Dam covers about 250 square miles, and Lake Nasser behind the Aswan Dam covers nearly 2,000 square miles. By the time the reservoir behind the Three Gorges Dam is filled, over 1,000,000 people will have been relocated and 13 cities, 140 towns, more than 1,300 villages, 650 factories, and hundreds of the world's most ancient archeological ruins—some more than 6,000 years old—will be covered with water.

Internal and international controversy over this dam is strong. The disastrous floods of 1998 in China that killed more than 2,500 people, flooded 22,000,000 acres of farmland, and destroyed nearly 3,000,000 homes did not lessen this controversy. Proponents of the dam claim that the project will stop similar flood disasters in the future. Opponents claim the opposite, largely because much of the flooding comes from rivers below the dam and because money for flood control levies on these rivers has been diverted to the Three Gorges project.

The advantages and problems of the Aswan and Three Gorges dams occur in various forms with large dams all over the world. Logically and rationally, we should be able to anticipate similar effects and should not associate with them the word *rare* when we consider any other large dam. Do we think that, just because we have 7,000 years of records, we know all the possible consequences and there will be no "rare" events to surprise us? Geology tells us very clearly not to be so arrogant—there is much that we may not know.

And so we come to the story of a wave—an unusual wave—in the Colorado River system, a waterway that originates in the Rocky Mountains.[8] From nearly its source to its end, the Colorado River is dammed by the Davis, Parker, Glen Canyon, and Hoover dams (to name the most well known). Probably the most controversial among them has been the Glen Canyon Dam, located near the Arizona–Utah border. Glen Canyon Dam retains a large reservoir, Lake Powell, which releases water into the part of the Colorado River that flows through the Grand Canyon. Originally built for two main purposes—to store and distribute water to seven western states and Mexico and to generate electricity for peak power requirements on the western power grid system—it now must be managed to have minimal impact on the environment. The incompatible nature of these multiple objectives has made management of the dam very complicated. For example, the reservoir must be kept as full as possible to conserve water for distribution according to treaty agreements; yet the water must be released at rates demanded by peak power requirements in faraway cities such as Phoenix and Los Angeles. These required storage and release patterns often do help to preserve and regenerate species of aquatic flora and fauna and to replenish soil nutrients.

Prior to the completion of the dam, the discharge of the Colorado River varied between about 4,000 cubic feet per second (cfs) and approximately 100,000 cfs annually, with century-scale floods known to have reached about 400,000 cfs. After the dam was completed in 1966, the discharge was controlled by the engineers and varied between about 4,000 cfs and about 30,000 cfs. Hence, the peak discharges were only about one-third the volume of typical annual floods and were much smaller than decade-, century-, or millennial-scale floods. Until 1983, Lake Powell retained all the water that would have gone into the large annual floods through the Grand Canyon because it had not filled to its operational level.

The Colorado River system was essentially unexplored until 100 years ago; and even when the Glen Canyon Dam was built, relatively few people had been through the river canyons. The sport of river-running through the 200 miles of spectacular terrain in the Grand Canyon developed rapidly into a tourist industry during the years when the discharges were controlled by the dam; and probably it was enhanced by the relative predictability of the discharges. The intuitions of the river guides, their passengers, and the scientists were formed by phenomena observed at these relatively modest discharges. We knew that the famous "rapids of the Colorado" were always at locations where there were side-canyon tributaries and that floods down these tributaries episodically delivered large boulders from the tributaries into the bed of the Colorado River. Waves formed around these rocks in the riverbed at low discharges, and the rocky regions with their waves were the rapids. These waves were the major challenges, as well as part of the fun, of rafting navigation. River guides, who accumulated the most experience and knowledge of the river, observed that the waves disappeared as discharges increased because the water became deep relative to the height of the obstacles that formed the waves. The river terminology was that the waves "washed out." At the highest discharges characteristic of the operation of Glen Canyon Dam during those years, the river became fast and turbulent but relatively free of problem waves.

The "rare" event occurred in 1983 about 90 miles downstream from the Glen Canyon Dam, with great human and financial cost. In 1983, just when Lake Powell was filled "to the brim," an unusually rapid snowmelt occurred in the Rocky Mountains. That no volume was left in Lake Powell to accommodate this water posed a serious danger downstream because the Glen Canyon Dam might fail to contain it. Sheets of plywood four feet by eight feet were added on top of Glen Canyon Dam to accommodate some of the extra water by raising the level of Lake Powell temporarily. Nevertheless, it also became necessary to open the emergency bypass systems and spillways. Within a period of several days, discharges below the dam increased to over 90,000 cfs.

For the 20 years that Lake Powell had been filling, river guides and scientists had never seen this type of discharge. The guides assumed that they would be rafting on a turbulent, but relatively waveless, river. This assumption held true for about the first 90 miles of river below the dam, but not at a place called Crystal Rapids. Here, the waves did not wash out; instead, an unforeseen and new type of wave formed. This wave reached 20 feet in height and spanned the entire navigable part of the river. Numerous people were injured before the National Park Service was able to temporarily stop all river-running.

The formation of the wave was caused by another "rare" event that had happened after completion of the dam but before any high discharges were needed. Large flash floods down the tributaries of the Colorado occur roughly once per century. And in 1968, just two years after completion of the dam, one of these century-scale floods roared down Crystal Creek, carrying boulders and debris that constricted the Colorado River to about one-quarter of its typical width. Overnight, Crystal Rapids, which had been a mere piffle not even mentioned in the exploration journals of the geologist–explorer John Wesley Powell, became one of the most formidable rapids on the Colorado.

There are many tributaries draining into the Colorado; and over hundreds of thousands of years, they all have had multiple flash floods that formed debris fans.[9] But over the same time scale, these debris fans have been eroded back by the large floods on the Colorado. Small annual floods have eroded the debris fans back a small distance, medium size century-scale floods have cut the fans back further, and the peak floods—perhaps every few millennia— have pushed them back even further. Typically, most debris fans are old enough to have been reworked by the largest floods typical of the Colorado, and they are eroded back so that the river keeps about half its normal width where it passes by them.

Between the time of its formation in 1968 and the flood of 1983, the debris fan at Crystal Creek had never been exposed to flooding, not even an annual flood, to say nothing of a hundred-year or a thousand-year flood. So, the river was unusually constricted there. We could say that this condition was both spatially and temporally rare within this stretch of the river. A "rare" wave formed during the 1983 flood because the river was so unusually constricted by this new debris fan. As a qualitative analogy, think about the problem of running water through a hose, which normally only gets stepped on by people or dogs but suddenly gets stepped on by an elephant. At Crystal Rapids, the debris constriction was akin to the elephant problem. The water could only get through the constriction by dramatically changing its flow conditions, and a standing wave was the result of this change in conditions. (Technically, the transition was from supercritical to subcritical flow; and the far more appropriate analogy is supersonic to subsonic deceleration of an aircraft, rather than the elephant on a hose.) This wave was not the typical wave formed by a single rock or a large submerged obstacle; it was a wave formed by the overall geometric shape of the river at that location. That single flood of 1983 eroded back the Crystal Creek debris fan considerably, but the river is still more constricted there than at most other debris fans, and Crystal Rapids remains a formidable boating obstacle to river rafters because of this constriction. It will never become a "normal" river rapid as long as Glen Canyon Dam operates at its current capacity because it will never experience a peak flood.

The rafting community, engineers who managed the dam, administrators of the Grand Canyon National Park, and scientists had a collective view of the river that was based on a few decades of observation—extended to a century for those who studied the journals of the explorers of the Colorado. However, there was no immediate understanding, prediction capability, or planned response to conditions that exceeded those which were usual for that short period of time. Now that we have seen and experienced this previously rare event, it does not seem surprising to the scientists who understand it. Thus, we can add this wave behavior to our 7,000-year-old body of knowledge about the effect of large dams on river systems.

Our view of the effect of dams on natural systems is actually longer than 7,000 years because we can study the effect that natural blockages, such as landslides or lava flows, have on river systems. However, even though we humans can view all this knowledge from the distant past through our bifocal lenses, we have not brought that understanding clearly into focus on our near and current problems. It is not clear how the "memory" of rare events is or will be passed on institutionally—we typically do not plan adequately, even for more common events. In the case of the Colorado River, guides and boating companies come and go and the individual experience of 1983 will be lost, or retained only by diminished storytelling. Scientific papers are published and get lost in volumes of information. Reports are filed in institutions and disappear onto shelves. Managers and even institutional structures change. This story is repeated on other river systems. How do we preserve and expand the memory and management recommendations for these events, that is, how do we implement action based on a bifocal view?

Volcanoes

The way we live with and react to volcanic eruptions also illustrates well the problem of understanding the probability and consequences of rare events. People who live near active volcanoes develop an understanding and intuition about their normal behavior. Hawaiians are used to frequent but relatively mild eruptions of Kilauea and Mauna Loa, eruptions in which one can generally walk, or at least jog, away from the slowly advancing viscous liquid magma. Yet, in 1790, there was a rare explosion and volcanic blast from Kilauea in which soldiers of Keoua crossing a desert region with their families and cattle were suffocated and burned, and Keoua capitulated to King Kamehameha. Footprints of these doomed people can still be seen in the deposits from this eruption. A smaller, but similar eruption in May 1924 killed a person at the Hawaii Volcano Observatory.[10] These were rare events by Hawaiian standards.

Unlike Hawaiians, people living in the Japan archipelago are used to frequent and much more violent volcanic eruptions. Their "common" eruptions resemble the Hawaiian eruptions of 1790 and 1924. Some schoolchildren routinely wear hard hats to go to and from home and school because of the rain of falling ash and rocks! Yet these daily conditions are mild compared with events that have occurred in the past few thousand years. Mount Fuji, although presently quiescent, erupted 13 times between AD 781 and 1707; and the last eruption in 1707 was violent enough to cover the area of present-day Tokyo, which is 60 miles from Fuji, with an inch of ash. On July 15, 1888, with almost no warning, Bandai-san blasted out its northern flank in a rapid series of violent explosions, sending steam and rock debris down steep slopes at about 50 miles per hour, burying seven villages, and killing 461 people.[11] Twenty-two thousand years ago, an ash flow, called the Ito flow, traveled "over hill and dale" for 45 miles, climbing over topographic obstacles as high as 2,000 feet.[12]

People in the American Northwest were used to living with their beautiful, but not particularly active volcanoes, until Mount St. Helens erupted violently on the eighteenth of May in 1980. Although that eruption was the largest in the Northwest since its settlement by Europeans, we now know that it was a very small eruption compared with those from similar sized volcanoes.[13] Crater Lake, in Oregon, was formed by the decimation of Mount Mazama—a Mount Rainier-type of volcano—only 7,000 years ago, when civilization was emerging along the Nile. As recently as 800 years ago, there was still active volcanic activity under the lake. Seattle, at the base of Mount Rainier, would be devastated by such eruptions.

An eruption of a very similar type of volcano at Novarupta in Alaska on June 6, 1912 spewed almost five cubic miles of magma out of the volcano and transported a total of nine to ten cubic miles of magma and rock down into a valley, forming the still fuming "Valley of Ten Thousand Smokes." This event took only 60 hours and was the largest eruption in the twentieth century. The ash deposits in the Valley of Ten Thousand Smokes—called ignimbrites—are the most extensive historical deposits of that kind, but the geological record shows that ignimbrites can cover thousands of square miles of land. Such eruptions are rare, but we certainly have active volcanoes that have the potential to produce them. Volcanologists are challenged to try to understand what the precursors to such rare and large events might be and how we should respond to them.

Certainly, the eruption of Mount St. Helens elevated the collective consciousness of the residents of the Pacific Northwest to the potential for much more violent eruptions. But how deep is that awareness? Twenty-three thousand people—three-quarters of the people in the single village of Armero—were killed in one horrific night on November 13, 1985 by mud and debris flows down Nevado del Ruiz volcano in Colombia. How real does that fact seem to those of us living at the base of such volcanoes all around the Pacific Ocean? How many of us are aware that that eruption was well predicted by scientists and that the deaths resulted solely from political choices? Decisions to respond to rare events are extremely difficult: Evacuation of a population under the threat of a volcanic eruption that subsequently does not occur causes human dislocations and economic problems. Yet decisions not to evacuate under a threat that develops into an event cost lives, land, and property.

These volcano stories show the connection between rarity in space and time. Volcanoes are spatially rare, occurring only in specific settings that we now understand in terms of the framework of plate tectonics. They occur at lithospheric plate boundaries—the cracks that separate the Earth's crust into a few large pieces—where one plate of the crust descends under another plate; they occur at plate boundaries where plates are being pulled apart; and they occur within plates under certain anomalous conditions. However, they cover a relatively small portion of the Earth's surface and are therefore spatially rare. Large eruptions are rare in time because volcanoes need to recharge heat in order to melt rock and form magma that will erupt. Some volcanoes recharge and erupt in a relatively balanced way, producing the Hawaiian type of volcanism. Others store their recharging magma for a very long time and release it in one or a few huge eruptions.

Our understanding of volcanic behavior has grown enormously over the past few decades for several reasons. Growing populations, and modern satellites, witness eruptions of volcanoes that were previously in uninhabited areas. Modern communication allows this information to be spread globally. Our bifocal lenses now range from billions of human eyes to the strongest of satellite lenses and these certainly help us solve the problems associated with understanding spatial rarity. The post-1960s view of the Earth in terms of plate tectonics theory gives us a framework to understand the locations as well as chemistry, volatility, and explosivity of certain types of volcanoes. And, modern sophisticated supercomputer models of volcanic processes, as well as rapidly changing ideas of how to make predictions in complex systems, allow us to enhance our understanding of physical processes and our prediction capabilities, as well as our knowledge of the limitations of those capabilities.

Earthquakes

Earthquakes are rare spatially but not always restricted to plate boundaries. In hindsight, I'm not surprised that the very first night I was in Pasadena, California, near the boundary between the Pacific and North American plates, I woke up, not because my alarm went off, but because it slid off the table onto the floor. However, I was quite astonished to be rocked in my office chair—near Toronto, Canada—in 1998 by an earthquake near the Ohio–Pennsylvania border—definitely not near a plate boundary.

Californians are used to earthquakes of various magnitudes, and they have a good institutional memory of the 1906 San Francisco earthquake, as well as the more recent earthquakes at Loma Preta (1989), Landers (1992), and Northridge (1994). They also are alert to earthquakes of various magnitudes around the world, including secondary effects such as fires, mudslides, and tsunamis.

However, do Californians have a concept of what could really happen in truly "rare" but possible events? Does knowledge of either the Armenian earthquake of December 7, 1988, in which 25,000 people were killed, or the major earthquake that struck near Izmit, Turkey on August 17, 1999 affect our individual or institutional actions, or is it simply not imaginable that such devastation is possible, even in highly engineered cities? Furthermore, geoscientists now recognize that the strain on large faults may not be released in a single earthquake alone or in a single earthquake followed by minor aftershocks; instead, release may cause a series of relatively large earthquakes as a fault is "unzipped." Events such as these are called earthquake "sequences" or "storms."

Compelling evidence indicates that major civilizations have been severely affected by earthquakes and earthquake storms.[14] One such civilization was that of the Aegean and eastern Mediterranean areas circa 1225–1175 BC, the end of the Late Bronze Age. Why did the Bronze Age end so abruptly—over a period of only about 50 years?

Extremely complex plate tectonics characterize the eastern Mediterranean region—major fault lines have created the topography that has governed the evolution of civilizations through trade routes and earthquakes on those faults have destroyed those very same civilizations. Some earthquake sequences have occurred in this region in historical times. A sequence along the Anatolian Fault occurred during the 30-year period from 1939 to 1967 as strain that had accumulated over 200 quiet years was progressively released. A storm of more than 80 years duration was reported as having occurred along the same fault from AD 967 to 1050, during which time more than 20 earthquakes of damaging to destructive magnitude occurred.[15] A 30-year period of earthquakes between AD 350 and 380, following a quiet period of about 300 years, resulted in damage to sites in Israel, Cyprus, Turkey, Crete, Corinth, Reggio Calabria, Sicily, and northern Libya.[16]

Robert Drews, professor of history and classics at Vanderbilt University, compiled a map of 47 Aegean and eastern Mediterranean sites destroyed in a 50-year period at the end of the Late Bronze Age, including historically famous sites such as Mycennae, Tiryns, Midea, Thebes, Pylos, Kynos, Troy, and Megiddo.[17] According to biblical history, much of this destruction was due to battles, but for some of these sites, there is no independent evidence of battles. When superposed on a map of earthquake intensities in this region, these sites fall along the zones of high-intensity shaking. Drews recognized the possibility of earthquakes as a cause. In fact, earthquake storms disrupted many of these cities over a prolonged, but short, period of time. The destruction of buildings and people affected trade, induced economic hardship, and weakened defenses, situations leading to attacks and uprisings. Clearly, physical events led inexorably to political, social, and economic "systems collapse" in the Aegean and eastern Mediterranean at the end of the Late Bronze Age.

Over four millennia, these storms might be considered "rare." But geology's view through a bifocal lens aimed at ancient archeology suggests that such events do occur—they have occurred often enough that we should expect them in current times. In our modern interconnected world, there are many ways in which a system collapse might be triggered. As we observe the global financial chaos of 1998 caused by the "economic Asian flu," we can only ponder what could happen if Tokyo were devastated in the near future by either a volcanic eruption or an earthquake? What if one or more of the many volcanoes in populous Indonesia has one of its millennial-scale eruptions? Or, what if Mount Ranier took out Seattle and Microsoft just before the millennium?

These four examples illustrate the bifocal perspective that a geological gaze can provide—parallel views of distant and near spaces and times. With it, we can observe the Earth's surface and its depths and look back in time. We can bring that vision to bear on present problems around the Earth and those in the foreseeable future. With this way of considering the world, geological knowledge can elucidate the problems of our physical environment that impact people and other living things inhabiting it.

Although most people may never gain an intuitive familiarity with rare events, we can bring rare events into our collective consciousness by recognizing the nature of the world immediately surrounding us. Once we achieve general consciousness about the possibility of rare events, we can discuss their social, legal, political, scientific, technological, and economic implications. But people must appreciate that some predictions may be relatively good, or in some instances even very good, whereas others may have very large uncertainties.

Nonetheless, rare events will happen—the great focal length of geology's bifocal lens tells us so. Rare occurrences will continue to shape human and natural history. We will help ourselves and others if we grasp this perspective.

2

Set Piece on Geologic Time from *Annals of the Former World*

John McPhee

nterstate 80, in its complete traverse of the North American continent, goes through much open space and three tunnels. As it happens, one tunnel passes through young rock, another through middle-aged rock, and the third through rock that is fairly old, at least with respect to the rock now on earth which has not long since been recycled. At Green River, Wyoming, the road goes under a remnant of the bed of a good-sized Cenozoic lake. The tunnel through Yerba Buena Island, in San Francisco Bay, is in sandstones and shales of the Mesozoic. And in Carlin Canyon, in Nevada, the road makes a neat pair of holes in Paleozoic rock. This all but leaves the false impression that an academic geologist chose the sites—and now, as we approached the tunnel at Carlin Canyon, Deffeyes became so evidently excited that one might have thought he had done so himself. "Yewee zink bogawa!" he said as the pickup rounded a curve and the tunnel appeared in view. I glanced at him, and then followed his gaze to the slope above the tunnel, and failed to see there in the junipers and the rubble what it was that could cause this professor to break out in such language. He did not slow up. He had been here before. He drove through the westbound tube, came out into daylight, and, pointing to the right, said, "Shazam!" He stopped on the shoulder, and we admired the scene. The Humboldt River, blue and full, was flowing toward us, with panes of white ice at its edges, sage and green meadow beside it, and dry russet uplands rising behind. I said I thought that was lovely. He said yes, it was lovely indeed, it was one of the loveliest angular unconformities I was ever likely to see.

The river turned in our direction after bending by a wall of its canyon, and the wall had eroded so unevenly that a prominent remnant now stood on its own as a steep six-hundred-foot hill. It made a mammary silhouette against the sky. My mind worked its way through that image, but still I was not seeing what Deffeyes was seeing. Finally, I took it in. More junipers and rubble and minor creases of erosion had helped withhold the story from my eye. The hill, structurally, consisted of two distinct rock formations, awry to each other, awry to the gyroscope of the earth—just stuck together there like two artistic impulses in a pointedly haphazard collage. Both formations were of stratified rock, sedimentary rock, put down originally in and beside the sea, where they had lain, initially, flat. But now the strata of the upper part of the hill were dipping more than sixty degrees, and the strata of the lower part of the hill were standing almost straight up on end. It was as if, through an error in demolition, one urban building had collapsed upon another. In order to account for that hillside, Deffeyes was saying, you had to build a mountain range, destroy it, and then build a second set of mountains in the same place, and then for the most part destroy them. You would first have had the rock of the lower strata lying flat—a conglomerate with small bright pebbles like effervescent bubbles in a matrix red as wine. Then the forces that had compressed the region and produced mountains would have tilted the red conglomerate, not to the vertical, where it stood now, but to something like forty-five degrees. That mountain range wore away—from peaks to hills to nubbins and on down to nothing much but a horizontal line, the bevelled surface of slanting strata, eventually covered by a sea. In the water, the new sediment of the upper formation would have accumulated gradually upon that surface, and, later, the forces building a fresh mountain range would have shoved, lifted, and rotated the whole package to something close to its present position, with its lower strata nearly vertical and its upper strata aslant. Here in Carlin Canyon, basin-and-range faulting, when it eventually came along, had not much affected the local structure, further tilting the package only two or three degrees.

Clearly, if you were going to change a scene, and change it again and again, you would need adequate time. To make the rock of that lower formation and then tilt it up and wear it down and deposit sediment on it to form the rock above would require an immense quantity of time, an amount that was expressed in the clean, sharp line that divided the formations—the angular unconformity itself. You could place a finger on that line and touch forty million years. The lower formation, called Tonka, formed in middle Mississippian time. The upper formation, called Strathearn, was deposited forty million years afterward, in late Pennsylvanian time. Cambrian, Ordovician, Silurian, Devonian, Mississippian, Pennsylvanian, Permian, Triassic, Jurassic, Cretaceous, Paleocene, Eocene, Oligocene, Miocene, Pliocene, Pleistocene . . . . In the long roll call of the geologic systems and series, those formations—those discrete depositional events, those forty million years—were next-door neighbors on the scale of time. The rock of the lower half of that hill dated to three hundred and thirty million years ago, in the Mississippian, and the rock above the unconformity dated to two hundred and ninety million years ago, in the Pennsylvanian. If you were to lift your arms and spread them wide and hold them straight out to either side and think of the distance from fingertips to fingertips as representing the earth's entire history, then you would have all the principal events in that hillside in the middle of the palm of one hand.

It was an angular unconformity in Scotland—exposed in a riverbank at Jedburgh, near the border, exposed as well in a wave-scoured headland where the Lammermuir Hills intersect the North Sea—that helped to bring the history of the earth, as people had understood it, out of theological metaphor and into the perspectives of actual time. This happened toward the end of the eighteenth century, signalling a revolution that would be quieter, slower, and of another order than the ones that were contemporary in America and France. According to conventional wisdom at the time, the earth was between five thousand and six thousand years old. An Irish archbishop (James Ussher), counting generations in his favorite book, figured this out in the century before. Ussher actually dated the earth, saying that it was created in 4004 BC. The Irish, as any Oxbridge don would know, are imprecise, and shortly after the publication of Ussher's *Annales Veteris et Novi Testamenti* the Vice-Chancellor of Cambridge University bestirred himself to refine the calculations. He confirmed the year. The Holy Trinity had indeed created the earth in 4004 BC— and they had done so, reported the Vice-Chancellor, on October 26th, at 9 AM. His name was Lightfoot. Geologists today will give parties on the twenty-sixth of October. Some of these parties begin on the twenty-fifth and end at nine in the morning.

It was also conventional wisdom toward the end of the eighteenth century that sedimentary rock had been laid down in Noah's Flood. Marine fossils in mountains were creatures that had got there during the Flood. To be sure, not everyone had always believed this. Leonardo, for example, had noticed fossil clams in the Apennines and, taking into account the distance to the Adriatic Sea, had said, in effect, that it must have been a talented clam that could travel a hundred miles in forty days. Herodotus had seen the Nile Delta—and he had seen in its accumulation unguessable millennia. G. L. L. de Buffon, in 1749 (the year of *Tom Jones*), began publishing his forty-four-volume *Histoire Naturelle,* in which he said that the earth had emerged hot from the sun seventy-five thousand years before. There had been, in short, assorted versions of the Big Picture. But the scientific hypothesis that overwhelmingly prevailed at the time of Bunker Hill was neptunism—the aqueous origins of the visible world. Neptunism had become a systematized physiognomy of the earth, carried forward to the *n*th degree by a German academic mineralogist who published very little but whose teaching was so renowned that his interpretation of the earth was taught as received fact at Oxford and Cambridge, Turin and Leyden, Harvard, Princeton, and Yale. His name was Abraham Gottlob Werner. He taught at Freiberg Mining Academy. He had never been outside Saxony. Extrapolation was his means of world travel. He believed in "universal formations." The rock of Saxony was, beyond a doubt, by extension the rock of Peru. He believed that rock of every kind—all of what is now classified as igneous, sedimentary, and

2 Set Piece on Geologic Time

metamorphic—had precipitated out of solution in a globe-engulfing sea. Granite and serpentine, schist and gneiss had precipitated first and were thus "primitive" rocks, the cores and summits of mountains. "Transitional" rocks (slate, for example) had been deposited underwater on high mountain slopes in tilting beds. As the great sea fell and the mountains dried in the sun, "secondary" rocks (sandstone, coal, basalt, and more) were deposited flat in waters above the piedmont. And while the sea kept withdrawing, "alluvial" rock—the "tertiary," as it was sometimes called—was established on what now are coastal plains. That was the earth's surface as it was formed and had remained. There was no hint of where the water went. Werner was gifted with such rhetorical grace that he could successfully omit such details. He could gesture toward the Saxon hills—toward great pyramids of basalt that held castles in the air—and say, without immediate fear of contradiction, "I hold that no basalt is volcanic." He could dismiss volcanism itself as the surface effect of spontaneous combustion of coal. His ideas may now seem risible in direct proportion to their amazing circulation, but that is characteristic more often than not of the lurching progress of science. Those who laugh loudest laugh next. And some contemporary geologists discern in Werner the lineal antecedence of what has come to be known as black-box geology—people in white coats spending summer days in basements watching million-dollar consoles that flash like northern lights—for Werner's "first sketch of a classification of rocks shows by its meagreness how slender at that time was his practical acquaintance with rocks in the field." The words are Sir Archibald Geikie's, and they appeared in 1905 in a book called *The Founders of Geology.* Geikie, director general of the Geological Survey of Great Britain and Ireland, was an accomplished geologist who seems to have dipped in ink the sharp end of his hammer. In summary, he said of Werner, "Through the loyal devotion of his pupils, he was elevated even in his lifetime into the position of a kind of scientific pope, whose decisions were final on any subject regarding which he chose to pronounce them . . . . Tracing in the arrangement of the rocks of the earth's crust the history of an original oceanic envelope, finding in the masses of granite, gneiss, and mica-schist the earliest precipitations from that ocean, and recognising the successive alterations in the constitution of the water as witnessed by the series of geological formations, Werner launched upon the world a bold conception which might well fascinate many a listener to whom the laws of chemistry and physics, even as then understood, were but little known." Moreover, Werner's earth was compatible with Genesis and was thus not unpleasing to the Pope himself. When Werner's pupils, as they spread through the world, encountered reasoning that ran contrary to Werner's, pictures that failed to resemble his picture, they described all these heresies as "visionary fabrics"—including James Hutton's *Theory of the Earth; or, an Investigation of the Laws Observable in the Composition, Dissolution, and Restoration of Land Upon the Globe,* which was first presented before the Royal Society of Edinburgh at its March and April meetings in 1785.

Hutton was a medical doctor who gave up medicine when he was twenty-four and became a farmer who at the age of forty-two retired from the farm. Wherever he had been, he had found himself drawn to riverbeds and cutbanks, ditches and borrow pits, coastal outcrops and upland cliffs; and if he saw black shining cherts in the white chalks of Norfolk, fossil clams in the Cheviot Hills, he wondered why they were there. He had become preoccupied with the operations of the earth, and he was beginning to discern a gradual and repetitive process measured out in dynamic cycles. Instead of attempting to imagine how the earth may have appeared at its vague and unobservable beginning, Hutton thought about the earth as it was; and what he did permit his imagination to do was to work its way from the present moment backward and forward through time. By studying rock as it existed, he thought he could see what it had once been and what it might become. He moved to Edinburgh, with its geologically dramatic setting, and lived below Arthur's Seat and the Salisbury Crags, remnants of what had once been molten rock. It was impossible to accept those battlement hills precipitating in a sea. Hutton had a small fortune, and did not have to distract himself for food. He increased his comfort when he invested in a company that made sal ammoniac from collected soot of the city. He performed experiments—in chemistry, mainly. He extracted table salt from a zeolite. But for the most part—over something like fifteen years—he concentrated his daily study on the building of his theory.

Growing barley on his farm in Berwickshire, he had perceived slow destruction watching streams carry soil to the sea. It occurred to him that if streams were to do that through enough time there would be no land on which to farm. So there must be in the world a source of new soil. It would come from above—that was to say, from high terrain—and be made by rain and frost slowly reducing mountains, which in stages would be ground down from boulders to cobbles to pebbles to sand to silt to mud by a ridge-to-ocean system of dendritic streams. Rivers would carry their burden to the sea, but along the way they would set it down, as fertile plains. The Amazon had brought off the Andes half a continent of plains. Rivers, especially in flood, again and again would pick up the load, to give it up ultimately in depths of still water. There, in layers, the mud, silt, sand, and pebbles would pile up until they reached a depth where heat and pressure could cause them to become consolidated, fused, indurated, lithified—rock. The story could hardly end there. If it did, then the surface of the earth would have long since worn smooth and be some sort of global swamp. "Old continents are wearing away," he decided, "and new continents forming in the bottom of the sea." There were fossil marine creatures in high places. They had not got up there in a flood. Something had lifted the rock out of the sea and folded it up as mountains. One had only to ponder volcanoes and hot springs to sense that there was a great deal of heat within the earth—much exceeding what could ever be produced by an odd seam of spontaneously burning coal—and that not only could high heat soften up rock and change it into other forms of rock, it could apparently move whole regions of the crustal package and bend them and break them and elevate them far above the sea.

Granite also seemed to Hutton to be a product of great heat and in no sense a precipitate that somehow grew in water. Granite was not, in a sequential sense, primitive rock. It appeared to him to have come bursting upward in a hot fluid state to lift the country above it and to squirt itself thick and thin into preexisting formations. No one had so much as imagined this before. Basalt was no precipitate, either. In Hutton's description, it had once been molten, exhibiting "the liquefying power and expansive force of subterranean fire." Hutton's insight was phenomenal but not infallible. He saw marble as having once been lava, when in fact it is limestone cooked under pressure in place.

Item by item, as the picture coalesced, Hutton did not keep it entirely to himself. He routinely spent his evenings in conversation with friends, among them Joseph Black, the chemist, whose responses may have served as a sort of fixed foot to the wide-swinging arcs of Hutton's speculations—about the probable effect on certain materials of varying ratios of temperature and pressure, about the story of the forming of rock. Hutton was an impulsive, highly creative thinker. Black was deliberate and critical. Black had a judgmental look, a lean and sombre look. Hutton had dark eyes that flashed with humor under a far-gone hairline and an oolitic forehead full of stored information. Black is regarded as the discoverer of carbon dioxide. He is one of the great figures in the history of chemistry. Hutton and Black were among the founders of an institution called the Oyster Club, where they whiled away an evening a week with their preferred companions—Adam Smith, David Hume, John Playfair, John Clerk, Robert Adam, Adam Ferguson, and, when they were in town, visitors from near and far such as James Watt and Benjamin Franklin. Franklin called these people "a set of as truly great men . . . as have ever appeared in any Age or Country." The period has since been described as the Scottish Enlightenment, but for the moment it was only described as the Oyster Club. Hutton, who drank nothing, was a veritable cup running over with enthusiasm for the achievements of his friends. When Watt came to town to report distinct progress with his steam engine, Hutton reacted with so much pleasure that one might have thought he was building the thing himself. While the others busied themselves with their economics, their architecture, art, mathematics, and physics, their naval tactics and ranging philosophies, Hutton shared with them the developing fragments of his picture of the earth, which, in years to come, would gradually remove the human world from a specious position in time in much the way that Copernicus had removed us from a specious position in the universe.

A century after Hutton, a historian would note that "the direct antagonism between science and theology which appeared in Catholicism at the time of the discoveries of Copernicus and Galileo was not seriously felt in Protestantism till geologists began to impugn the Mosaic account of the creation."

The date of the effective beginning of the antagonism was the seventh of March, 1785, when Hutton's theory was addressed to the Royal Society in a reading that in all likelihood began with these words: "The purpose of this Dissertation is to form some estimate with regard to the time the globe of this Earth has existed." The presentation was more or less off the cuff, and ten years would pass before the theory would appear (at great length) in book form. Meanwhile, the Society required that Hutton get together a synopsis of what was read on March 7th and finished on April 4, 1785. The present quotations are from that abstract:

We find reason to conclude, 1st, That the land on which we rest is not simple and original, but that it is a composition, and had been formed by the operation of second causes. 2dly, That before the present land was made there had subsisted a world composed of sea and land, in which were tides and currents, with such operations at the bottom of the sea as now take place. And, Lastly, That while the present land was forming at the bottom of the ocean, the former land maintained plants and animals ... in a similar manner as it is at present. Hence we are led to conclude that the greater part of our land, if not the whole, had been produced by operations natural to this globe; but that in order to make this land a permanent body resisting the operations of the waters two things had been required; 1st, The consolidation of masses formed by collections of loose or incoherent materials; 2dly, The elevation of those consolidated masses from the bottom of the sea, the place where they were collected, to the stations in which they now remain above the level of the ocean . . . .

Having found strata consolidated with every species of substance, it is concluded that strata in general have not been consolidated by means of aqueous solution . . . .

It is supposed that the same power of extreme heat by which every different mineral substance had been brought into a melted state might be capable of producing an expansive force sufficient for elevating the land from the bottom of the ocean to the place it now occupies above the surface of the sea . . . .

A theory is thus formed with regard to a mineral system. In this system, hard and solid bodies are to be formed from soft bodies, from loose or incoherent materials, collected together at the bottom of the sea; and the bottom of the ocean is to be made to change its place ... to be formed into land . . . .

Having thus ascertained a regular system in which the present land of the globe had been first formed at the bottom of the ocean and then raised above the surface of the sea, a question naturally occurs with regard to time; what had been the space of time necessary for accomplishing this great work? . . .

We shall be warranted in drawing the following conclusions; 1st, That it had required an indefinite space of time to have produced the land which now appears; 2dly, *That an equal space had been employed upon the construction of that former land from whence the materials of the present came;* Lastly, *That there is presently laying at the bottom of the ocean the foundation of future land . . . .*

As things appear from the perspective of the twentieth century, James Hutton in those readings became the founder of modern geology. As things appeared to Hutton at the time, he had constructed a theory that to him made eminent sense, he had put himself on the line by agreeing to confide it to the world at large, he had provoked not a few hornets into flight, and now—like the experimental physicists who would one day go off to check on Einstein by photographing the edges of solar eclipses—he had best do some additional travelling to see if he was right. As he would express all this in a chapter heading when he ultimately wrote his book, he needed to see his "Theory confirmed from Observations made on purpose to elucidate the Subject." He went to Galloway. He went to Banffshire. He went to Saltcoats, Skelmorlie, Rumbling Bridge. He went to the Isle of Arran, the Isle of Man, Inchkeith Island in the Firth of Forth. His friend John Clerk sometimes went with him and made line drawings and watercolors of scenes that arrested Hutton's attention. In 1968, a John Clerk with a name too old for Roman numerals found a leather portfolio at his Midlothian estate containing seventy of those drawings, among them some cross-sections of mountains with granite cores. Since it was Hutton's idea that granite was not a "primary" rock but something that had come up into Scotland from below, molten, to intrude itself into the existing schist, there ought to be pieces of schist embedded here and there in the granite. There were. "We may now conclude," Hutton wrote later, "that without seeing granite actually in a fluid state we have every demonstration possible of this fact; that is to say, of granite having been forced to flow in a state of fusion among the strata broken by a subterraneous force, and distorted in every manner and degree."

What called most for demonstration was Hutton's essentially novel and all but incomprehensible sense of time. In 4004 + 1785 years, you would scarcely find the time to make a Ben Nevis, let alone a Gibraltar or the domes of Wales. Hutton had seen Hadrian's Wall running across moor and fen after sixteen hundred winters in Northumberland. Not a great deal had happened to it. The geologic process was evidently slow. To accommodate his theory, all that was required was time, adequate time, time in quantities no mind had yet conceived; and what Hutton needed now was a statement in rock, a graphic example, a breath-stopping view of deep time. There was a formation of "schistus" running through southern Scotland in general propinquity to another formation called Old Red Sandstone. The schistus had obviously been pushed around, and the sandstone was essentially flat. If one could see, somewhere, the two formations touching each other with strata awry, one could not help but see that below the disassembling world lie the ruins of a disassembled world below which lie the ruins of still another world. Having figured out inductively what would one day be called an angular unconformity, Hutton went out to look for one. In a damp country covered with heather, with gorse and bracken, with larches and pines, textbook examples of exposed rock were extremely hard to find. As Hutton would write later, in the prototypical lament of the field geologist, "To a naturalist nothing is indifferent; the humble moss that creeps upon the stone is equally interesting as the lofty pine which so beautifully adorns the valley or the mountain: but to a naturalist who is reading in the face of rocks the annals of a former world, the mossy covering which obstructs his view, and renders undistinguishable the different species of stone, is no less than a serious subject of regret." Hutton's perseverance, though, was more than equal to the irksome vegetation. Near Jedburgh, in the border country, he found his first very good example of an angular unconformity. He was roaming about the region on a visit to a friend when he came upon a stream cutbank where high water had laid bare the flat-lying sandstone and, below it, beds of schistus that were standing straight on end. His friend John Clerk later went out and sketched for Hutton this clear conjunction of three worlds—the oldest at the bottom, its remains tilted upward, the intermediate one a flat collection of indurated sand, and the youngest a landscape full of fences and trees with a phaeton-and-two on a road above the rivercut, driver whipping the steeds, rushing through a moment in the there and then. "I was soon satisfied with regard to this phenomenon," Hutton wrote later, "and rejoiced at my good fortune in stumbling upon an object so interesting to the natural history of the earth, and which I had been long looking for in vain."

What was of interest to the natural history of the earth was that, for all the time they represented, these unconforming formations, these two levels of history, were neighboring steps on a ladder of uncountable rungs. Alive in a world that thought of itself as six thousand years old, a society which had placed in that number the outer limits of its grasp of time, Hutton had no way of knowing that there were seventy million years just in the line that separated the two kinds of rock, and many millions more in the story of each formation—but he sensed something like it, sensed the awesome truth, and as he stood there staring at the riverbank he was seeing it for all mankind.

To confirm what he had observed and to involve further witnesses, he got into a boat the following spring and went along the coast of Berwickshire with John Playfair and young James Hall, of Dunglass. Hutton had surmised from the regional geology that they would come to a place among the terminal cliffs of the Lammermuir Hills where the same formations would touch. They touched, as it turned out, in a headland called Siccar Point, where the strata of the lower formation had been upturned to become vertical columns, on which rested the Old Red Sandstone, like the top of a weather-beaten table. Hutton, when he eventually described the scene, was both gratified and succinct—"a beautiful picture . . . washed bare by the sea." Playfair was lyrical:

*On us who saw these phenomena for the first time, the impression made
will not easily be forgotten. The palpable evidence presented to us, of one of
the most extraordinary and important facts in the natural history of the
earth, gave a reality and substance to those theoretical speculations, which,
however probable, had never till now been directly authenticated by the
testimony of the senses. We often said to ourselves, What clearer evidence
could we have had of the different formation of these rocks, and of the long
interval which separated their formation, had we actually seen them
emerging from the bosom of the deep? We felt ourselves necessarily carried
back to the time when the schistus on which we stood was yet at the bottom
of the sea, and when the sandstone before us was only beginning to be
deposited, in the shape of sand or mud, from the waters of a
superincumbent ocean. An epocha still more remote presented itself, when
even the most ancient of these rocks, instead of standing upright in vertical
beds, lay in horizontal planes at the bottom of the sea, and was not yet
disturbed by that immeasurable force which has burst asunder the solid
pavement of the globe. Revolutions still more remote appeared in the
distance of this extraordinary perspective. The mind seemed to grow giddy
by looking so far into the abyss of time.*

Hutton had told the Royal Society that it was his purpose to "form some
estimate with regard to the time the globe of this Earth has existed." But after
Jedburgh and Siccar Point what estimate could there be? "The world which we
inhabit is composed of the materials not of the earth which was the immediate
predecessor of the present but of the earth which . . . had preceded the land
that was above the surface of the sea while our present land was yet beneath
the water of the ocean," he wrote. "Here are three distinct successive periods of
existence, and each of these is, in our measurement of time, a thing of indefinite duration . . . . The result, therefore, of this physical inquiry is, that we find
no vestige of a beginning, no prospect of an end."

3

Stories of Land, Stories from Land

Lauret E. Savoy

On auto journeys or daytime flights that I have taken across the continent, the lessons of time and place become clearer. Especially viewed from the air on cloudless days, landscape patterns from the East Coast westward over 3,000 miles present condensed narratives of Earth and human histories intricately tied together—histories of ideas as well as actions, histories of change.[1] Forest, field, and urban patchworks of the Northeast give way west of the Appalachian Mountains to lowland agricultural fields and large, meandering rivers that drain the midcontinent. Westward beyond the Mississippi River, the green hazy flatness of this lowland gradually but noticeably becomes the beige and brown Great Plains, a semiarid land broken by telltale signs of irrigated agriculture. In the American Southwest beyond the southern Rocky Mountains, aridity claims the land almost fully, and its character remains clear in rugged canyons and plateaus, mountains and dry basins. Here, the evidence of a human presence seems more isolated, with large tracts of land appearing relatively uninhabited.

These changing and diverse landscapes have shaped human perceptions and influenced their actions. Conversely, and in very different ways, humans have marked and shaped the physical history of the land. Thinking globally, the issues at hand and the stakes are clear. The influence of environment on cultural traditions is ancient. So, too, is the ability of our species to modify physical environments—visible faces of the Earth—on local and regional scales by use of fire, agriculture, settlement, or extraction and use of resources. With rapid population growth and the development of industrial societies over the past two centuries, a dominant human presence and a technologically based capability for environmental alteration have arrived.[2] The types, scales, and rates of environmental changes, many of which have been driven by human forces, are such that we now face challenges of regional to global magnitude, including alterations to biogeochemical cycles, deforestation, desertification, and change.

The fundamental question remains: What is and what should be the relationship of our species to the Earth, locally, regionally, and globally? Whether or not one believes that an answer requires reinterpretation or reordering of human relationships with Earth's environments, decisions about how we should live on the planet must be based on an informed understanding of Earth and environmental systems and of the nature of Earth-human interactions, past and present. Although research across the earth sciences, historical ecology, geography, and environmental history has added to a stock of basic knowledge, there is much left to learn about the nature of environments before human existence, the influences of environments on human thought and activities, and, in turn, the impact of such activities on environments or landscapes.[3] Understanding the interplay of these elements through time is key to our comprehension of the Earth-human experience. By realizing our past more fully, we might better guide ourselves to an environmentally sensible future.

The North American landscape, to my mind, is a record and reminder of physical place, its geological origin, and evolution through time. It is also a record of human engagement with Earth over time—of transitions, of human migration—with the growth and settlement of some groups of people and the dislocation of others. By "reading" the land, we can gain a better sense of place and history, and a link between past, present, and, perhaps, future that might help us identify the meaning of the North American Earth in human experience. Reading the land can also provide a clearer sense of how groups of people encountering the continent have viewed, defined, understood, and used the land differently, and how these differences have contributed to a spectrum of impacts, changing activities, and attitudes.[4] Rather than simple arguments of environmental or cultural determinism, these ideas recognize an interdependence of human and environmental variables on different levels.

This essay presents examples of different types of Euro-American encounters with variable environments of the North American midcontinent and Southwest, regions whose boundaries and identities, as well as physical landscapes, have changed over time. The rich narratives of other cultures (Native American, African-American, Latino, and Asian American), regions, and time periods are as important, but they are beyond the scope of this work.

These narratives could be told from multiple perspectives of the humanities, social sciences, and natural sciences; but none would be complete. To obtain a view of the multiple stories we tell about the Earth, first, in a section entitled "The Land," I lay out the general physiography of the midcontinent and Southwest. Then, to show the origin and influence of ideas on the human environmental history of the continent, in "Stories of Land" I consider examples of how Euro-Americans named, defined, and imagined the midcontinent and Southwest. Finally, "Stories from Land" contains two examples of landscapes that are visible historical records of environmental change and human activity. The first example considers how, from reading clues from the land's distant past, earth and environmental scientists try to decipher ancient environmental changes in the Southwest; it also examines some archeological research on the possible impact of environmental change on prehistoric Native Americans. The second example weighs evidence from midcontinent landscapes of more recent environmental transformation by Euro-American agricultural settlement and land use.

THE LAND

Geologically, the midcontinent between the Appalachian Mountains and the Rocky Mountains is considered a stable platform, a region that, unlike the eastern and western edges of the continent, has not experienced cataclysmic events such as mountain building within hundreds of millions of years. Evidence of this stability includes the region's overall flatness, both at the surface and replayed at depth by horizontal to gently warped sediments and sedimentary rocks. These sands and muds, and sandstones, limestones, and mudstones—of Paleozoic (570 to 245 million years), Mesozoic (245 to 65 million years), and Cenozoic (65 million years to the present) ages—record the former presence of ancient inland seas, the evolution and demise of dinosaurs and other creatures, the decay and erosion of mountains, and most recently, the work of ice-age glaciation.

Ecologically, the midcontinent tends to be grasslands. The 100th meridian of longitude cuts from north to south, a third to half of the way through the Dakotas, Nebraska, and Kansas, and then across western Oklahoma and Texas; it has been considered to mark significant geographical and ecological borders in the midcontinent, as well as what historian Walter Prescott Webb, in his book *The Great Plains*, termed a cultural or "institutional fault."[5] In the United States, the 100th meridian approximately coincides with the 20-inch rainfall line. With low average annual precipitation, the semiarid plains west of this 20-inch rainfall line are subject to drought. The meridian also marks the boundary between tallgrass plains to the east and shortgrass ones to the west. And it equates with 2,000 feet of elevation above sea level, which manifests often as a low "break in plains" where geologically young sediments have eroded from the Rocky Mountains and washed eastward onto the plains.[6]

The humid and subhumid Central Lowland extends eastward from the 100th meridian across the Mississippi River to the Appalachian Mountains. Defined by low elevation and topographic relief, this region is a land of Great Lakes and large rivers emptying into the Mississippi River. West of the Central Lowland, the Great Plains constitute the semiarid region that extends from the 100th meridian to the eastern edge of the Rocky Mountains at more than 5,000 feet of elevation. On the western portion of the Great Plains, significant treed areas become confined to local pockets and corridors along rivers such as the Platte, Arkansas, or Yellowstone. The fanlike dendritic patterns of countless small but erosive, ephemeral streams stand out as breaks and badlands.

Semiarid southwestern plains and breaks, New Mexico. (*Photograph by Lauret E. Savoy*)

Farther to the west, the semiarid and arid Southwest is geologically, topo-
graphically, and ecologically a region of great variety. From the southern Rocky
Mountains in New Mexico to the edge of the Sierra Nevada in California, these
are landscapes of mountains and dry, interior basins; plateaus and deeply
incised canyons; plains; badlands; erosional remnants; and escarpments. They
lie largely in the physiographical provinces known as the Colorado Plateau and
the Basin and Range, which are part of the North American Cordillera—the
system of mountains in the western part of the continent. From the Rocky
Mountains to the Pacific Coast, mountain-building activity in the Cordillera is
geologically recent and still ongoing. Earthquakes and volcanic eruptions still
occur here from time to time, and the steep, rugged landscapes can at once
appear new and fresh, yet ancient and timeless.

Climate, in a sense, links the geological, geographical, and ecological variety of the Southwest, making this a region largely defined by what it lacks in
abundance—Mary Austin's "land of little rain."[7] Limited water and high evaporation rates result from the complex interplay of desert-producing factors: lati-
tudinal position; descending, dry air currents; long rain shadows cast by the
Sierra Nevada and other mountains and high plateaus on air masses brought
by prevailing westerly winds from the Pacific; distance from oceanic moisture
sources; and interacting air masses over the gulfs of California and Mexico. In
these drylands, short grasses yield to sagebrush and desert shrub, pinyon
and juniper woodlands, and plants adapted to aridity. Here, mountains and
high plateaus are isolated and, if high enough, forested islands of moisture.

Eroded badlands and breaks, Blue Mesa, Arizona. (*Photograph by Lauret E. Savoy*)

Erosional remnants, Ute Mountain, southern Colorado. (*Photograph by Lauret E. Savoy*)

Perennial streams are not abundant or typically large, and the two major rivers, the Colorado and Rio Grande, carry waters derived largely from the Rocky Mountains. Biologically, the four major deserts of North America—the Mojave, Great Basin, Sonoran, and Chihuahuan—are found in this dry West.

STORIES OF LAND—A WORLD OF LIVING IDEAS

The landscape is the most immediate medium through which we attempt to convert culturally shared dreams into palpable realities. Our actions in the world, in short, are shaped by the paradigms in our head.—Annette Kolodny[8]

Values, both those that we approve of and those that we don't, have roots as deep as creosote rings, and live as long, and grow as slowly. Every action is an idea before it is an action, and perhaps a feeling before it is an idea, and every idea rests upon other ideas that have preceded it in time.—Wallace Stegner[9]

For any region of Earth, bodies of knowledge exist—from myths to maps to scientific theories—that result from attempts to describe, define, and understand that region. The ways in which humans perceive, evaluate, and use Earth's surface are varied. In "The Beholding Eye," historical geographer Donald Meinig describes ten of many possible perspectives by which different individuals today might view and interpret a particular landscape or region, depending on their background and values.[10] He notes that observers might interpret a landscape as *nature*—noting temporal and spatial insignificance of humans; *habitat*—as human adjustment to nature; *artifact*—as nature altered, with marks of humans everywhere; *system*—as processes contributing to a dynamic interaction; *problem*—reflecting larger social issues that require solutions through social action; *wealth*—in terms of property or monetary value; *ideology*—revealing cultural values and social philosophy; *history*—as a cumulative record of works of humans and nature; *place*—as locality or identity that locations have; and *aesthetic*—a comprehensive abstraction of artistic quality. Of course, these ten interpretations do not exhaust all possibilities, but they demonstrate how perceptions of landscapes are complex. They may be shaped by encounters with landscapes as well as by expectations or preconceptions based on values or the cultural context of a time. Realizing how Euro-Americans saw and imagined land and their relation to it in the midcontinent and Southwest is an important element of the human environmental history of North America; it may begin to give us a sense of the legacy of such ideas today—what British archaeologist and writer Jacquetta Hawkes referred to as the "continued presence of the past."[11]

What of language? Imagine a land without names, a map empty of description. We can say place names such as Platte, Rio Grande, Badlands, or Rocky Mountains easily, almost without thinking. Yet what do we know of how these names came to be or of what they meant to the namer and those who followed? Naming came out of human experience with the land and with different peoples—a rich record to be read.

Before the mid-nineteenth century, the continent's grasslands and deserts were anomalous and unfamiliar to most Europeans and their descendants, whose agrarian lifeways and visual habits developed primarily in the familiar, humid, and forested East. West of the Appalachian Mountains, they found forest-bounded, broad, open grasslands, which were much larger than the clearings, meadows, or Native American fields of the otherwise forested or recently deforested lands to the east. The French term *prairie*, meaning meadowland, was first applied to the vast grasslands of the Mississippi Valley and then expanded more broadly to wide treeless expanses across the Central Lowland.[12] Between 1804 and 1806, in the first, official American scientific expedition to cross the continent, Meriwether Lewis and William Clark used the word *prairie* until the patches of open land turned into seemingly limitless treeless expanses—and then they wrote of "great plains."

As George Stewart, an authority on place names in the United States, notes in *Names on the Land*, in many cases, specific midcontinent place names on maps and in journals of European explorers and trappers are translations, transliterations, clippings, or reshapings of words drawn from languages of Native American peoples encountered.[13] Rivers, landscape features, and specific sites were often named for particular native groups living there, or were modified versions of native place names. Messouri, Ouchage, Maha or Omaha, and Kansa are but a few Native American names that French explorers placed on major rivers to note the presence of those people. One broad, shallow, braided river that crosses the plains was called Ni-bthaska in one native language, "ni" for river and "bthaska" as a reference to its spreading flatness. French explorers in the 1700s translated this name to Riviere Plate, but spelled it Platte. The Platte River, as the named survived, became the prominent lifeline of nineteenth-century overland migration routes such as the Oregon and California trails to the West. And from Ni-bthaska later came the name of the state of Nebraska through which the river flows. According to Stewart, later American explorers such as Lewis and Clark also recorded older names, sometimes in translation so that Roche Jaune, itself possibly a translation of a Minnataree name, became the Yellowstone River.[14]

The midcontinent prairies and plains have taken on many identities and were called, at different times and by different peoples, the land where sky begins, land of the buffalo, Great American Desert, great prairie wilderness, sea of grass, Indian Territory, the frontier, the West, the Midwest, the wheat belt, the Dust Bowl, and garden or breadbasket of the world. Each name reflects a different possible narrative, and a separate attempt to understand that land.

One significant narrative is the story of "desert" encounters. The location and identity of "desert" on the continent changed through the nineteenth century as Euro-Americans in their westward movement encountered different lands through exploration, overland migration, and settlement. We can trace an evolution of the word *desert* as a descriptor of any wild, uninhabited, and uncultivated tract to a term referring to an arid, barren area.[15] In Judeo-

Christian tradition, *desert* did carry the original meaning of wilderness or deserted area, and in the world described by the Bible, desert was associated with arid lands.[16] Historian of the West, Patricia Limerick notes that as the word's use evolved in Europe, its association with emptiness remained. Early English colonists commonly described their "new world" of eastern America as deserted. John Smith wrote of Virginia, "most of this country, though desert, [is] yet exceeding[ly] fertile," and Puritan leader Cotton Mather described New England as a "Squalid, horrid American Desart."[17]

The connection with aridity was partly restored in North America by the nineteenth century as the term *desert* was applied to lands beyond the Appalachian Mountains, first to the subhumid and semiarid grasslands of the midcontinent, and then to the true drylands farther west.[18] The association of these lands with vacancy or emptiness, however, was faulty because neither the East Coast nor the region farther west was uninhabited or unused. By year-long occupation or by seasonal presence and mobility, Native American peoples lived in, used, shaped, and altered these environments through hunting and gathering, agriculture, and burning, long before the arrival of Europeans.

Members of the Coronado expedition in the 1500s and the Lewis and Clark expedition in the first part of the nineteenth century commented on the desert nature of the western plains. Yet, reports from American government-sponsored expeditions across the central and southern plains, led by Zebulon Pike during 1806 and 1807 and Stephen Long between 1819 and 1820, set the terms by which Euro-Americans viewed grasslands west of the Mississippi River; they made the Great American Desert—a land thought unfit for habitation or agriculture—a "reality" in public consciousness for several decades of the nineteenth century:

> *I would not think I had done my country justice did I not give birth to what few lights my examination of those internal deserts has enabled me to acquire. In that vast country of which I speak, we find the soil generally dry and sandy, with gravel . . . . But here a barren soil, parched and dried up for eight months in the year, presents neither moisture nor nutrition sufficient to nourish the timber. These vast plains . . . may become in time as celebrated as the sandy deserts of Africa; for I saw in my route, in various places, tracts of many leagues where the wind had thrown up the sand in all the fanciful form of the ocean's rolling wave, and on which not a speck of vegetable matter existed.*
>
> *But from these immense prairies may arise one great advantage to the United States, viz.: The restriction of our population to some certain limits, and thereby a continuation of the Union. Our citizens being so prone to rambling and extending themselves on the frontiers will, through necessity, be constrained to limit their extent on the west to the borders of the Missouri and Mississippi, while they leave the prairies incapable of cultivation to the wandering and uncivilized aborigines of the country.[19]*

Neither the Pike nor the Long expedition crossed the Rocky Mountains and encountered true aridity, and the idea of much of the midcontinent as a Great American Desert partly shaped the courses of later Euro-American exploratory surveys, agricultural settlement, displacement and removal of Indian peoples, and development of the trans-Mississippi West in the early to mid-nineteenth century.[20] Surface water was scarce on much of the plains, and there was no real means of pumping groundwater at that time. Wood for building and fuel was limited or nonexistent, as were communication and transportation networks. Although not *true* desert, the treeless prairies and plains offered lands that were at odds with conventional Euro-American notions of landscape or the practice of judging the fertility of new lands by the types of growing trees.[21] Thus, in the first half of the nineteenth century, the plains did set limits of sorts to movement and settlement, particularly if one views this idea of desert in the context of the time, and considers Euro-American settlers' mode of living, technology of settlement, and methods of agriculture.[22]

The idea of the Great American Desert was popularized beyond government reports by traveler's accounts, newspaper articles, and literature of the day. According to Limerick, for example, Alexis de Tocqueville wrote of the Great American Desert in *Democracy in America*, an insightful analysis of American politics and culture of the middle nineteenth century. Although he never visited the region, Tocqueville stated with certainty that beyond the Mississippi River, "the sparser the vegetation and the poorer becomes the soil, and everything wilts or dies" and that there "the soil is punctured in a thousand places by primitive rocks sticking out here and there like the bones of a skeleton when sinews and flesh have perished."[23]

Eternal prairie and grass, with occasional groups of trees. [Captain John C.] Frémont prefers this to every other landscape. To me it is as if someone would prefer a book with blank pages to a good story.—Charles Preuss, cartographer[24]

The Great American Desert lost some of its meaning as a barrier to westward migration when transcontinental travel to the Pacific Coast increased, beginning in the 1830s. Overland routes such as the Oregon and California, Santa Fe, and Southern trails gave midcentury Euro-American explorers and emigrants a direct experience with arid lands farther west. After the Civil War, the agricultural front pushed westward onto the Great Plains as settlement moved up the valleys of the Platte and other rivers. Here, the plains that once were the Great American Desert became a destination. Henry Nash Smith, who in *Virgin Land* wrote of the power of such images and ideas of the West, posited that by the late nineteenth century the westward extending "myth of the garden," of an agricultural transformation of the frontier, contended with and reshaped the idea of the Great American Desert.[25] For example, it became a commonly held belief of many, scientists as well as settlers, that crop cultivation and tree planting could modify climate, and thus transform or improve the harsh plains environment for human habitation.

But farther west, beyond the Rocky Mountains, lie what Patricia Limerick has called the deserts of actuality rather than deserts of myth.[26] The south-western drylands were not fully comprehensible to the collective nineteenth-century, Euro-American imagination, because they were, as scholar of English and American literature David Teague notes, lands in which "accustomed modes of geography, agriculture, industry, and commerce did not obtain."[27] Aridity—limited rainfall and uncertain water supplies—as well as the rugged landscape itself placed limits on human activities. Too, in the process of naming, language failed because English words did not exist to describe many arid landscape features; many terms now associated with desert lands— *canyon, mesa, arroyo, playa*—were adopted by Euro-Americans from Spanish and other languages.

Limerick's model of three major phases of Euro-American encounters with southwestern deserts and their attitudes toward this "nature at its extreme" is worth noting. Limerick recognized that a simple classification of attitudes toward desert puts "a thin cloak of simplicity over a mass of complexity," but it does give us a general historical framework within which to consider ideas of, and encounters with, arid lands.[28]

According to Limerick, the first phase of encounters with the desert began with explorers and trappers in the 1820s and continued for decades through the period of overland migration. Then, desert was a threat to life and an ordeal to be endured by those who crossed—to get from one livable place to another such as Oregon or California. Desert was risky, uncooperative, and a betrayer. From 1859 to the turn of the century, mineral discoveries and development of water reclamation and irrigation projects partly "compensated" for the aridity. In this second phase of encounters with the desert, with water projects and irrigation efforts in place, the desert could be reclaimed and in a sense "redeemed." Irrigation fell under the category of conservation, and through 1900, dams, reservoirs, and canals constructed to hold and redistribute water meant conserving this "resource" for more "efficient" use. In this view, a desert managed by conservation principles could become a garden, a farm, a city. By the turn of the century, a growing public aesthetic appreciation of desert lands marks Limerick's third phase—a period when literature and art that recorded and celebrated these lands became popular. According to Limerick, the phases do not succeed each other but overlap. And it was, and is, possible for an indi-vidual or group to hold different attitudes simultaneously, because desert could be viewed in the past or present as a reminder of human vulnerability, a source of commercially useful material, and a satisfying setting, visually or emotionally.

Another point to consider is that, in the Southwest and on the high west-ern plains, aridity and erosion conspired to present a land laid open and bare without the vegetative clothing of the humid East. Here, Earth's anatomy, its composition and structure, and their relationships are more easily observed. In *Man in the Landscape,* human ecologist Paul Shepard considered the evocative power of natural landscapes in the response of westward-bound Euro-Americans to "novel" erosional remnants and angular cliffs and escarpments along the Oregon Trail in 1840s.[29] The isolated spires, buttes, and escarpments along the Platte River in the western plains became structures of ghostly or ruined architecture in journals of overland trappers, soldiers, and emigrants. Numerous observers discovered city buildings, lighthouses, forts, spires, streets, and castles, often in ruins; and many references were made to rocks given names like Chimney, Steamboat, Table, or Courthouse:

> *Encamped today near what I shall call the old castle, which is a great*
> *natural curiosity . . . [it has] the appearance of an old enormous building,*
> *somewhat dilapidated . . . . You unconsciously look around for enclosures*
> *but they are all swept away by the lapse of time—for the inhabitants, but*
> *they have disappeared; all is silent and solitary.*—Reverend Samuel Parker[30]

Yet, within many of the journals are also references to the geological materials, such as sand and limestone, that composed the rocks and to the processes of erosion and passing of time that must have occurred to carve the landscape.

Explorations by late nineteenth-century, government-sponsored, scientific surveyors of canyons, plateaus, mountains, and dry lake beds in the dry West also contributed to the development of ideas on how Earth works. John Wesley Powell, who explored and named the Colorado Plateau region, investigated geological processes and history of the Southwest, the ethnography of Native Americans of the region, and the use of arid lands. He sought to understand large-scale landscape-shaping forces and, with his team of scientists including Grove Karl Gilbert and Clarence Dutton, developed significant new ideas on the work of uplift, erosion, and time. Together they defined and advanced basic principles regarding development and deformation of the Earth's surface and crust. Powell's intense interest in the relationship of people to arid lands resulted in *Report on the Lands of the Arid Region of the United States,* which proposed that viable settlement and land-use strategies in the arid West could not follow the practices of the humid East, that aridity required adaptation for settlement.[31]

By the turn of the century, the southwestern desert also found a voice in writers such as Mary Austin, who was one of the first truly western natural history writers in America. Like John Muir and his writing of the Sierra Nevada, Austin adopted, described, and celebrated the desert as animate at a time when the harshness of the region still repelled many:

> *East and south many an uncounted mile, is the Country of Lost Borders.*
> *Ute, Paiute, Mojave, and Shoshone inhabit its frontiers, and as far into the*
> *heart of it as a man dare go. Not the law, but the land sets the limit. Desert is*
> *the name it wears upon the maps, but the Indian's is the better word. Desert*
> *is a loose term to indicate land that supports no man; whether the land can*

*be bitted and broken to that purpose is not proven. Void of life it never is,
however dry the air and villainous the soil.*

*This is the nature of that country. There are hills, rounded, blunt,
burned, squeezed up out of chaos, chrome and vermilion painted, aspiring
to the snow-line.*

*If one is inclined to wonder at first how so many dwellers came to be in
the loneliest land that ever came out of God's hands, what they do there and
why stay, one does not wonder so much after having lived there. None other
than this long brown land lays such a hold on the affections. The rainbow
hills, the tender bluish mists, the luminous radiance of the spring, have the
lotus charm. They trick the sense of time, so that once inhabiting there you
always mean to go away without quite realizing that you have not done
it.*—Mary Austin[32]

As people think about the world around them, they create and impart
images of the land. The senses of place that an individual or group of people
have change, yet deep roots reflect the values and ideas that inform them.
Reflecting on such stories *of* land—stories of how Euro-Americans have
named, defined, and tried to understand the continent's plains and deserts—
gives us some insight on the origin and influence of ideas on the human environmental history of the continent. But just as important is our understanding
of the American landscape itself as a physical and historical record of environmental change and human activity. These stories *from* land follow.

STORIES FROM LAND—PHYSICAL RECORDS
OF ENVIRONMENTAL CHANGE

Although research in the earth and environmental sciences has pieced
together narratives of ancient and historical environmental changes, there is
still much left to learn about the nature and causes of changing conditions
through time, from small-scale, local ecosystem variations to larger, global
variations such as climate change. Reconstructing past environments or landscapes and how they have changed, and evaluating the impact of change on
modern ecosystems, is a puzzle that requires different types of field and docu-
mentary evidence—from traces left in landscape, including fossils and sedimentary deposits, to written, graphical, and oral records.[33] Determining the
degree to which environmental changes may have resulted from human activities also adds layers of complexity. For example, in dealing with environments
modified or altered by human action, geoscientists face what historical ecologist Emily Russell refers to as an "overlay of causation" or agency that has varied over space and time with changed cultural traditions.[34] Yet, recognizing the
impact of past human activities on the environment and the influence of environmental change on humanity—the dynamic interplay of cultural and physical factors—is a key element to our understanding of, and living in, the world.

Two examples follow that read environmental change from the physical records left on the land. The first example from prehistory considers how climatic changes in the American Southwest have been deciphered from geological and ecological records, and notes the potential link between changes in environmental conditions and prehistoric human events. The second example from the more recent past examines the evidence and impact of historical to contemporary transformations of the midcontinent grasslands by primarily Euro-American agricultural settlement in the past two centuries.

Narrative of Prehistoric Environmental Change

Climate—long-term temperature and precipitation patterns in an area—is a primary environmental system that has influenced the distribution and diversity of life on land. The reconstruction and interpretation of the history of past climates and terrestrial environments, the goal of much research in the earth sciences, adds to our understanding of how the climate system operates and how it might change in the future.

How do we analyze and understand past or ancient climates and environments that existed before meteorological instruments were developed to measure ambient conditions? Instrumental records have covered only a small fraction of Earth's history and provide little information on environmental change through time, particularly geologic or "deep" time, to use writer John McPhee's phrase. In the past few decades, earth scientists have collected numerous records of prehistoric or ancient climate changes from tree rings, pollen, ice cores, and deep-sea sediment cores. However, not all the data from these records are sensitive indicators of abrupt environmental changes because their response to change may take time to register physically. In addition, such data may not translate directly into temperature and precipitation records, and they often do not provide continuous records.[35]

The semiarid to arid American Southwest is an excellent area in which to evaluate climatic change over the recent geological past because slight variations in precipitation and temperature patterns have resulted in distinct ecological changes over large biogeographical regions. The climate changes are recorded as shifts in vegetation patterns, tree-ring widths, the balance between erosion and sedimentation in dry riverbeds, and the size and chemistry of lakes. By using these records, earth scientists have attempted to read the landscape record so as to interpret and create narratives of the region's environmental history and its impact on human events.

Geologists commonly use climate tree rings—seasonal growth bands—to measure a tree's growth year by year and infer past climate. Trees growing on sites where there are no environmental limits to growth typically produce uniformly wide rings, whereas trees growing in areas where environmental stresses such as drought may periodically limit growth processes produce rings that vary in width as a function of the severity of the stress.

The matching of overlapping patterns of growth bands between live trees and older dead wood has led to the establishment of a tree-ring chronology—a calendar of nearly 2,000 years—in the Southwest. Because water is an important limiting environmental factor in this region, the variations in the patterns of growth bands are also a rough record of climate. In a study of tree rings from both old live trees and dead ones from El Malpais National Monument in western New Mexico, earth scientist Henri Grissino-Mayer linked historical rainfall to ancient tree rings to create a year-by-year precipitation record for the past 2,000 years there.[36] This record suggests that the last two centuries, which have witnessed the growth of large-scale irrigated agriculture and urbanization in the Southwest, may have been an unusually wet period for the region. According to this study, even drought episodes of this century may have been wetter than the long-term average from El Malpais. Yet, much additional research is required before we will understand fully the climate history of the Southwest.

In addition to the long environmental record, the human record of occupation in what is now the American Southwest is long and continuous over the past 2,000 years.[37] Prehistoric inhabitants such as the ancestral Pueblo Anasazi people emerged as modern Pueblo people, who remain in this area today: Hopi, Zuni, Acoma, Laguna, and Rio Grande Pueblo groups. To survive and perhaps flourish in a marginal environment with variable climate and unpredictable water resources required adaptive change. Ancestral Pueblo people developed subsistence strategies based largely on agriculture, with maize, squash, and beans as major crops; they supplemented their diets with wild plant foods and game animals.[38]

Tree-ring calendars along with other chronological data have been used to establish the timing of large-scale migrations by ancestral Pueblo people from the Mesa Verde–San Juan River area of Utah, Colorado, New Mexico, and Arizona into the Rio Grande Valley by the end of the thirteenth century. In noting the general coincidence in timing of population movement with climatic change, deduced largely from tree rings, some archaeologists proposed drought as the primary cause of migration.[39] But does the temporal coincidence of cultural or demographic events and drought require direct causality? How important are environmental factors in the understanding of past human–environment relationships, particularly if cultural change can be facilitated or mediated by ideological processes or factors such as worldview, economics, politics, or religion?

More recent paleoenvironmental and archaeological research questioned drought as the primary cause of prehistoric migration and recognized a greater range of environmental factors, including the availability of wood and arable soil, as well as reliable water for irrigation. Some recent models have evaluated how social groups both cause and respond to natural and human-influenced environmental variations of different magnitudes and frequencies, including environmental degradation resulting from long-term land use and occupation.[40] Such models emphasize that the scale of migration or population movement also points to complex sociocultural causes rather than solely environmental causes.

And what of the Pueblo peoples' perspectives? Oral tradition and ethnohistorical records of Pueblo ideology suggest different underlying reasons for the common patterns of migration and resettlement into different areas of the Southwest. Zuni Edmund Ladd points to cultural and "religious" reasons; he states that ancestral Pueblo people traveled, not because of droughts or pestilence, but because they were searching for their "center place" in the world.[41] In addition, themes of movement and hardship are strongly entwined within Pueblo oral narratives. Several origin narratives of different Pueblo groups state that at the very beginning, different groups chose their way of life by selecting among different colored corn. In one Hopi narrative, different groups of Native people chose yellow, red, white, speckled, and flint corn, each implying a distinct type of life. Navajo chose yellow corn, which meant a short life of enjoyment and prosperity.[42] The Hopi, choosing last, picked the short blue corn, and with that a long-lasting life, but one of work and hardship.

The relationships between human behavior and activities and environment are complex, particularly across different cultural traditions. Difficulties in deciphering such relationships between prehistoric native peoples and ancient environments may increase as anthropologists, archeologists, and earth scientists begin to take more multidimensional and multicultural views of the ways in which landscapes and humans interact.

One undeniable fact is that the arid to semiarid southwestern United States is a region characterized by limited water. However, the Southwest today is also a region partly transformed by water reclamation, irrigated agriculture, oasis development, and urbanization. Physical manipulations have attempted to turn some dryland regions into crafted, artificial oases. Also, since the 1940s, uranium mining, nuclear weapons testing, and radioactive waste disposal have turned large parts of the Southwest into an experimental nuclear landscape.[43] But the essential character of the Southwest remains, and aridity ultimately will have the last word on how anyone lives on the land. Given the long-term records of climatic variability, what will the desert experience of the next century be?

Historical Human Marks on the Land

Like the desert Southwest, the midcontinent plains and prairie landscapes record a long history of human use and habitation, from diverse Native American lifeways and subsistence strategies to the Euro-American agricultural transformation of the past two centuries. Few ecosystems on Earth have been changed as rapidly or as extensively as North America's midlatitude grasslands, with vegetation, soil, water, and topography impacted primarily by agricultural land use.[44] Considering the geographical organization of the midcontinent today, we see a remnant of nineteenth- and early twentieth century Euro-American settlement fabric still in existence.

Agricultural settlement progressed from east to west across the tallgrass prairies of the Central Lowland, down a precipitation gradient to drier short-grass Great Plains more susceptible to drought.[45] The tallgrass prairies had fertile soil, fairly level land, and a hot and wet growing season; and plows rapidly broke sod and brought these lands into agricultural production.[46] Occupation of the eastern tallgrass prairies began in the 1820s and generally was limited first to small prairies, or the edges of larger ones, where wood for fuel and building materials, and water were available.[47] Last occupied were the interiors of large prairies that were far from navigable waterways or wood sources. In midcentury, railroad construction began to link these distant, relatively inaccessible grasslands; and by the 1880s, the tallgrass prairies were transformed into the Corn Belt.[48]

The Great Plains were largely settled in the late 1800s through the turn of the century, aided by federal policies that enabled the transfer of public lands into private ownership. In many ways similar to the settlement of prairie land to the east, the Great Plains were parceled into numerous small, independent farms or homesteads, and the farming population grew rapidly until about 1930, despite drought-induced setbacks in the 1890s and 1910s.[49] Soil quality, the presence of eroded badlands or sand hills, and water availability all influenced the extent of cultivation of the high western plains.

Towns in the interior grasslands were initially established along navigable rivers during the era of waterway transportation and commerce. But across the prairie and plains by the middle and late 1800s, the number of cultivated acres correlated strongly with the number of miles of railroad built and the density of the railroad–town network. Many towns located along the westward fanning lacework of railroad lines were built at the time of railroad depots as agricultural marketing or trade points; towns like Abilene and Dodge City, Kansas, also mark where railroad lines intersected north–south cattle trails of the late 1800s.[50] One common town design, still recognizable from air or on land across the midwest today, is the T-shaped pattern: the railroad line, demarcated by grain elevators along the right of way, crosses a main street with its business district and the train depot along the T-intersection.[51]

In summarizing the environmental transformation of the tallgrass prairies, ecological historian Gordon Whitney comments that they were "plowed out, grazed out, and mown out" in less than a century.[52] Prior to European and Euro-American settlement, the Central Lowland was primarily patchwork prairies of deep-rooted tall grasses and adjacent hickory–oak forests or small groves. The lowland, particularly the drier prairies that needed no draining, did not obstruct the plows and other farm machinery. Grazing in the open range of wetter prairies was a common practice, particularly early in the nineteenth century.[53] Whitney points out that many native grasses did not tolerate heavy grazing and trampling as well as introduced nonnative counterparts.[54] Mowing also encouraged the replacement of the grasses. Today, isolated remnants of tallgrass prairies can be found in some old pioneer cemeteries, railroad rights-of-ways, and undeveloped or marginal agricultural areas.

The disappearance of a major natural unit of vegetation from the face of the earth is
an event worthy of causing pause and consideration by any nation . . . .
Once destroyed, it can never be replaced . . . .—John Ernest Weaver[55]

The short grasses of the Great Plains were also extensively replaced by crop cultivation. Buffalo and blue gramma grass, both relatively shallow-rooted
grasses, dominated this region prior to agricultural settlement. Geographer
William Riebsame notes that more than 90 percent of the plains is now farm-
or ranchland; 75 percent of this land is cultivated with wheat as the major crop
and the rest is grazed.[56] Towns and cities, highways and railroad rights-of-ways,
and grassland preserves and refuges account for the less than 10 percent of
land not on farms or ranches.

Several direct and indirect changes have resulted from agricultural practices on the semiarid Great Plains. Wind erosion of bared and cultivated soil
produced large dust storms—the Dust Bowl—especially during drought on
the southern plains in the 1930s. The Soil Conservation Service, now the Natural Resources Conservation Service, originated as a result. Conspicuous rows
of trees found along the edges of fields were planted as windbreaks in an effort
to minimize wind erosion and ameliorate harsh climate.

Irrigated agriculture and resultant impacts on water supply have also
transformed the plains environment in the past several decades. Irrigation of
plains farmland began on a small scale by the late nineteenth century with
windmills locally pumping shallow groundwater. Demand for irrigation, particularly during drought episodes, encouraged widespread groundwater
pumping into this century. Large-scale irrigation by center-pivot and side-roll
sprinkler systems and other methods such as gravity or surface systems grew
after World War II as the technology for deep-well drilling and pumping
improved and as fuel prices for pumping decreased.[57] Center-pivot sprinkler
systems also allowed agricultural production from "marginal" areas.

The primary groundwater source in this region is the Ogallala Formation,
also known as the High Plains Aquifer, a sedimentary rock unit as much as five
million years old. This sand and gravel deposit underlies more than 175,000
square miles of plains from South Dakota to Texas and serves as a water source
to 12 million acres of farmland.[58] It provides about 30 percent of the groundwater used for irrigation in this country.[59] It is unfortunate, but not surprising
given the pace of geological processes, that this aquifer has effectively little or
no ability to recharge itself in the human time frame of years or decades.
Extensive pumping in the past few decades has therefore resulted in drastic
lowering of the water table and depletion of this groundwater reservoir. In
addition, on the dry, windy plains, sprinkler systems and standard irrigation
methods lose Ogallala water to evaporation, runoff, and locally excessive infil-
tration into soil. In response to the mining of the aquifer and increases in
pumping costs, some farmers have turned to alternative methods. Reductions
in irrigated acreage and increased water conservation by use of surge irrigation

or low-pressure and low-energy sprinkler systems have helped to slow the aquifer's depletion.[60]

Other water issues on the plains include the contamination of groundwater supplies and changes in soil chemistry as a result of pesticide and fertilizer use in agriculture, as well as local pollution from the development of oil and gas wells.[61] In addition, water storage and use that have accompanied the urbanization along the western edge of the Great Plains in cities such as Denver have reduced the flow and impacted the ecology of eastward flowing plains rivers that originate in the Rocky Mountains, including the Arkansas, Platte, and Missouri rivers.[62]

There is no question that the midcontinent grasslands have been significantly transformed by Euro-American agricultural settlement and production since the mid-1800s. The question that we now ask is whether such land use, particularly on the semiarid Great Plains, can continue in a sustainable way.

There is much left to consider. As in any narrative, I began and ended arbitrarily. I've discussed little of North American lands as they were before human occupancy and of non-European cultural traditions that have had a substantial presence here. Yet, whether viewed from the air as broad, regional landscape patterns or from the ground as intricate, intimate ecological detail, the evidence of interwoven landscape and human histories appears everywhere on the continent. I've offered only glimpses of how complex and interactive a mosaic these histories are.

Human beings reshape the perceived and the real Earth as they live on it, but as they reshape it, the new forms of Earth influence the way people live. Through complex webs of feedback, the two reshape each other. Human activities have left an imprint on the plains and deserts of the trans-Mississippi West that continues to grow. The drylands and eastern, humid regions also mark those who encountered them in terms of how they see, think about, and use these lands, and how they interpret their histories. Settlement and life on semiarid and arid western lands today continue to spark controversy over "proper" uses of land and water. Witness the continuing water wars and conflicts between urbanization, agriculture, recreation, and preservation, among the multitude of land uses in many western states. Notice, too, the development of nuclear landscapes in some southwestern drylands over the last several decades.

Far too many of us have a limited understanding of the influence of deeply rooted values and ideas on how we think and tell stories about the Earth, and then attempt to live by such stories. Our representations of the world, which are based on myth and fact, wield great power and define in large measure how we interact physically with and use the land. We must now confront the legacies of such ideas and actions—Jacquetta Hawkes's "continued presence of the past."

Is there any reason not to attempt to read and understand land and human histories, and reflect on how they are woven together? Stories *of* land and stories *from* land are part of a world of living ideas—ideas that, in helping us to understand our environmental past more fully, may give us a basic knowledge to choose a clearer path to a livable future.

> *Knowledge . . . becomes meaningful, useful and intelligible as we grasp, not only its content, but also its basis, its implications, its relationship and its limitations. Its coherence and significance lie in its relatedness to the whole of the rest of our human experience.* —Frank Rhodes[63]

4

Henry's Land

Paul R. Bierman

Henry Moultroup is a 70-something Vermont farmer with two new hips and a well-used backhoe, a yellow, 1980-something, Extenda-hoe. He's a soft-spoken man with keen eyes, strong wrinkled hands, and many jobs. When Henry's not cutting trees, moving earth, boiling maple sap, or minding the cows, he's collecting back taxes for the town of Huntington.

Henry and his wife and three of his sons live on and from several hundred acres of rolling land in northwestern Vermont. They are Huntington Valley people. Their house sits on one side of the Huntington Road. Their barn sits on the other. Both sit on a terrace of the Huntington River, a flat stretch of land where the river once flowed, where cows have probably wandered for a hundred summers, and where Henry knows the backhoe will dig through ten feet of river gravel before he'll hit dense blue clay and water.

Theirs is both an old and a young landscape. When you walk the hills behind Henry's home, there is dull, wet, mossy gray schist that shines if you break it. The schist was mud once, just a half-billion years ago, mud at the bottom of a now-vanished ocean. Colliding continents compressed the mud, expelled much of the water, and buried the bits of silt and clay many miles down. At such depths, the rocks were slowly warmed by Earth's internal heat. What was once mud is now rock. As the rocks were heated, minerals stable at Earth's surface became unstable. New minerals grew at the expense of old, aligned in response to the motions of great tectonic plates and the weight of overlying material.

The rock developed a foliation—an alignment of minerals, mostly shiny mica. Now, several hundred million years later, it is the orientation of this foliation that dictates the location of Vermont's Green Mountains. Not only are the mountain ridges of today the result of a continental squeeze 400 million years ago, but the same squeeze helps determine where the groundwater flows and where it doesn't. Mica weathers easily in the humid Northeast, providing a means for water to enter the rock. More water means more weathering. More weathering means more water can enter the rock and so on.

The rock we see at the surface today isn't solid. It is riddled with joints—fractures that resulted from millions of years of tectonic squeezing. These joints are widest at the surface and tend to close up at depth. They are the conduits through which much of our groundwater moves. If you look at photographs taken from airplanes, the same photos used to make topographic contour maps, you can see these joints in the schist. You can trace their pattern across the landscape. Where you see two fractures cross, that is the place to go looking for water.

In Vermont, a rural state, most of the land isn't serviced by public water supplies. Fracture tracing is big business; so is dowsing. The schist is mica-rock to the local well drillers who collect nine dollars for every foot of it they drill in search of water. Often they collect for many feet: two hundred, three hundred, four hundred feet. Water can be surprisingly difficult to find in the hills of Vermont if you do not hit the right fracture.

Drill, come up dry. Dowse, trace fractures, drill again, and if you are lucky, find a quart of water dripping each minute into three thousand dollars of well. Maybe then hydrofrac, using tons of force to split the rock deep below the surface with the hope that fractures will open and allow just enough water to seep into the well bore. With luck, half a gallon a minute will fill a 6-inch wide, 400-foot puncture in a state where 30 to 40 inches of rain and snow falls from the sky almost every year. But it doesn't have to be this difficult. A trip to Waterbury, 20 miles down the interstate, will put you face to face with forty-some-thousand well logs, descriptions of just about every well drilled into Vermont since the early 1980s. You can view them town by town. If you are lucky, you can find the well from which you drink. See how deep it is. See what the driller saw as the rig churned. In all likelihood, you'll also see just how many feet of steel pipe go down from your backyard to the bedrock below.

Geology students from the University of Vermont look at these well records every year: sometimes for classes, sometimes for projects, sometimes just out of curiosity. Every one returns to Burlington surprised. Seventy, eighty, ninety percent of wells in most towns are drilled into rock that gives up its water grudgingly, a quart each minute, maybe a half gallon. But sometimes, just next door to a nearly dry hole is a well that didn't go so deep, a well that the driller stopped in gravel, never pushed on to the rock, cost its owner far less and gives its owner far more. In Underhill, beneath the shadow of Mt. Mansfield, one neighbor could water his lawn all day. His well, open to the gravel 100 feet below his acres, yields 20 gallons a minute. Next door, a 300-foot bedrock well would be dry after an hour of lawn watering.

Why is it that day in and day out, well drillers pound right through 100 feet of clay and then through 10, 20, 30 feet of water-filled gravel so that they can set their steel casing into bedrock? Why not gravel wells? In many valleys, they'll yield 10, 20, 30 gallons a minute. Common knowledge has it that a bedrock well is a good well. It will stay clean. People say, the water in rock wells has been filtered by the sand and gravel above. The water is pure. In some cases and places, this is right. In others, it's not.

Fourteen thousand years ago, the highest mountains in New England were just starting to peek out from a 3,281-mile thick blanket of ice, a blanket that had covered them for ten thousand years or more. As the glacier grew thinner, it was hemmed in by the hills, forced to flow only through the valleys. Think of the waning ice sheet as a frozen river, flowing, but slowly, a conveyor belt moving perhaps several feet each day.

As the climate warmed, the glacier that covered most of northern North America continued to melt away. Over time, the edge of the ice was located further and further north. In places, where there were deep valleys that opened northward, the ice formed a dam hundreds of feet tall. The ice dam held back the water derived from rain and from the melting ice. The valleys became lakes. Into these lakes flowed powerful streams of water choked with sediment. Water rushed off the hillsides, barren of vegetation. Water poured off the melting glaciers, from the surface and from tunnels in the ice. All this water carried sediment, fine clay and silt that tinted the lakes green-gray, coarse sand and gravel that became the aquifers from which water today flows at tens, sometimes hundreds of gallons a minute.

Nature did New England a favor. In many valleys, just after the ice left, gravel spilled from the glaciers into now-vanished lake waters. Slowly, as the ice continued to melt, more clay and silt settled over the gravel, cloaking it in a stiff, dense, almost impermeable blanket, tens, even hundreds of feet thick. Years ago, this glacial-lake clay was the raw material that filled the brickyards of the Connecticut, Hudson, Mohawk, and Hoosic river valleys. The clay of the glaciers' lakes held up mills of the industrial revolution, workers' homes, and capitalists' lavish mansions.

Today, most of the mills are condos but the glacial-lake clay is still important. It shields deep, drinkable groundwater from the hazards of modern industry. In many New England valleys, large rivers flow above 100 feet of clay. The clay is a cap over a thin layer of water-charged gravel at its base. This gravel, once poured off the melting glacier, now holds groundwater under pressure, an artesian aquifer. The clay keeps the pressure in and the pollution out. The clay separates the deep groundwater that once fell as rain on clean forested uplands from shallow groundwater that drained off urban parking lots.

Geologists spend a lot of time and a lot of money looking for clay. They walk streambeds, they poke their heads into gullies, they dig pits with shovels, and when that's not enough they bring in the heavy machinery. Backhoes dig trenches into which geologists scramble. Drill rigs turn bits tens of feet into the earth, bringing back small samples from below our feet. Samples of clay.

Samples of gravel. Samples that many times show that the cheapest place to put a well may be the best place.

But back to the Huntington River. It hasn't flowed past the Moultroup house for a while, before the pyramids were built to be more exact, sometime about 8,000 years ago. We know this because Henry unearthed a log several years back. He was running a new waterline from his spring up the hill to his house on an old river terrace. Maybe the old line wasn't buried quite deeply enough in the warm earth. Maybe it had frozen on one of those still, somewhat glacial, Vermont winter nights when the mercury bottoms out somewhere below zero and the snow squeaks underfoot.

The log, the first of two we unearthed, came from a layer of logs buried long ago by a flood of the Huntington River for which no written record survives. A year later, Henry and his backhoe dug out another one of these logs. Twelve feet below his pasture, pickled in groundwater, the log appeared looking hardly worse for the wear as the backhoe bucket brought it up into warm August sunshine. Using a technique that didn't exist when Henry milked his first cow, we knew the age of the log in just a few weeks.

We dried the wood and sent it overnight across the continent. In Livermore, California, a lab that got its start building bombs, burned a pea-sized piece of Henry's log. It met its end, at 1600°F, sealed in a quartz tube with a little bit of penny-colored copper oxide. For millennia, the wood sat below Henry's pasture. In a day, it was nothing more than a breath of carbon dioxide and water.

The next day, the carbon dioxide was converted into graphite—pure, black carbon—under the skilled hand of a chemist. The graphite, a few specks one could easily mistake for dust, was pounded into a steel target the size of a small bullet and set inside the business end of a once-retired, now-resurrected, particle accelerator. Traveling at a few percent of the speed of light, the carbon atoms were whisked around 160 feet of high-vacuum line, nothing more than a high-tech balance. Every hour, several trillion dollars of electronics weighs several million atoms.

Most carbon atoms weigh 12 or 13 atomic mass units and are stable. They have been around a long time and they will continue to be around a long time, billions of years. A few, very few, carbon atoms are heavier, weighing 14 atomic mass units. These heavy carbon atoms are unstable (radioactive) carbon-14, or radiocarbon. Carbon-14 is made in the atmosphere by cosmic rays, particles we'll never see, but which are all around us. Carbon-14 in the atmosphere ends up in carbon dioxide. Carbon dioxide ends up in plants. That's part of photosynthesis. So, plants are slightly, ever so slightly, radioactive. The same thing can be said of animals that eat the plants.

Living things contain radioactive carbon-14; living plants get it from the atmosphere and animals get it from eating once-living plants. At death, plants cease to respire and animals cease to eat. Without a source to replenish the ever-decaying radiocarbon, the level of carbon-14 radioactivity starts to fade, slowly, imperceptibly. The day a tree became Henry's log, the radiocarbon in its wood, in its bark, in the leaves still clinging to its branches began to decay, spontaneously emitting electrons and becoming nitrogen-14, just another atom of common nitrogen in our atmosphere. After 5,700 years, half the carbon-14 that was in Henry's log when it was a living tree was gone. Wait another 5,700 years, half of what's left would be gone and so on; every 5,700 years, half of what's left is gone. After 40 or 50 thousand years, it would be a challenge to find any carbon-14 in Henry's log.

How do we know how much carbon-14 Henry's log started with? Painstaking work by American chemist Willard F. Libby and his research group at the University of Chicago during the 1940s and 1950s demonstrated that living things contain similar concentrations of carbon-14 and that dating was possible. They started by measuring carbon-14 in sewage gas to show that biological materials include this rare isotope. Then, to prove that all living things contained similar concentrations of carbon-14, they measured biological samples from around the world. Finally, they proved the usefulness of carbon-14 by dating archeological samples of known age. All this work earned Libby a Nobel prize in 1960.

Take a small portion of an ounce of carbon from a tree just felled in a clear-cut, a mouse caught last night in a trap, a lock of freshly cut hair. If you monitored the decaying carbon-14, you would find that all three of these samples would give you the same value, 13.7 disintegrations every minute. Livermore's lab work tells us that Henry's log contained only 38 percent of the carbon-14 you would expect to find in a modern tree. From this, it's an easy calculation and we know that the tree died about 8,000 years ago. It's been that long since the Huntington River flowed where the Moultroup house now stands.

One can't dig just anywhere and find eight–thousand-year-old logs. Most places we've dug on river terraces, we just find gravel, gravel, and more gravel. In the Northeast, preserving wood against the ravages of decay requires keeping it wet, cold, and away from too much oxygen. The best way to do this is to keep it below the water table, out of harm's way. For wood to survive any length of time, it needs to be buried, quickly and deeply.

On Henry's farm, nature found an interesting way to keep wood wet, buried, and preserved. Bury it beneath an alluvial fan. Alluvial fans are a favorite feature of many geologists, quite common in arid regions where they dominate the base of mountain fronts. Each is shaped like an inverted ice-cream cone, sloping away from the point of its cone where its source stream dispatches from the mountains. Some fans in the Southwest are as much as six miles long. They coalesce to form massive bajadas—like skirts around the bases of mountains—that slope gently up to the range front. But in New England, alluvial fans are small, rare, and usually isolated. They've never really been studied. They are very subtle features. Some are just a few yards tall, no more than 50 or 60 yards wide. If the fan isn't in a pasture, it's bound to get lost in the trees.

What's the recipe for a fan? Simple. Take a steep slope, make sure that the soil or rock is well loosened, and add water. Gravity will do the rest, pulling material downslope into small channels, which lead to and merge with bigger channels, and so forth. The water and sediment will keep moving until the downslope force of gravity is no longer strong enough to keep sediment moving downhill. Generally, this happens where steep slopes give way to gentle valley bottoms. There, on the flats, the material will be deposited. The big stuff drops out first. The fine material goes the farthest. The resulting deposit is fan shaped. The sediment is waterborne and the process termed alluvial. Thus, an alluvial fan is formed.

There's an alluvial fan behind Henry's house. It sits on the terrace in a pasture. It's often covered by cows and is fed episodically by flows of water and sediment from the steep slopes above it. Today, trees cover these slopes. My students and I found this, our first fan, five years ago and approached it with some curiosity, some trepidation, and two shovels. Henry laughed and offered the backhoe. He cut our first trench in July 1994. It was 25 feet long, 6 feet deep, and 10 feet wide. When we came back the next day, the trench held two feet of standing water. No wonder we found lots of wood in the walls of that trench, the wood had been soaked for thousands of years.

Over the past half-decade, Henry has opened six backhoe trenches for us on his fan. Among the trenches, there were similarities and differences. Every trench was well stratified, showing layers of sediment deposited by individual floods. Near the steep hillside, the fan material was coarse and thick with gravel. Farther down the fan, other trenches revealed mostly sand and silt and clay. Near the top of every trench, we found sediments that had been well stirred by plowing and contain charcoal, the legacy of clearing the land for farming. At the bottom of each trench, below the base of the fan sediments, we saw river terrace gravel and, often, wood. Between the uppermost material stirred by plowing and the gravels of the ancient Huntington River were several feet of alluvial fan sediment that, as we've learned to translate their stories, begin to tell us a history of slopes, erosion, and storms, stretching back 400 generations. Most important, these fans and their sediments detail a history of human impact, a history that we are doomed to repeat unless we understand it.

The history we are struggling to read is one of erosion. Sediment in the fans was once on the hillsides. Most days, that is where it stayed. Today most fans in New England are inactive. They have been turned into well-vegetated homes for cows, sheep, woodlands, and the occasional dwelling. During the average rainstorm, nothing much happens. But every once in a while, the exception happens. It rains for many days; or on a single day, it rains many inches. Then things get exciting. Water races over slopes, streams churn, landslides move, and alluvial fans grow. We search for these exceptional events in the fans.

Using radiocarbon, we have estimated times in the past when the fans were active, times when we presume that it was wetter or stormier or both. The first of these periods of activity was about 8,000 years ago. Again, about 3,000 years ago, sediment poured off some hillsides. But the most impressive erosion event, ten times bigger than anything that happened over the last 8,000 years, occurred within the last 200 years. It happened when settlers came to Vermont and cleared the forests. The fans provide a dramatic record of this clearance.

Get a shovel and dig into a fan. Chances are the first 10, 15, 20 inches will be pretty dull. Brown sand, a few pieces of charcoal, if you're lucky. But keep digging, because somewhere about 25 inches below the surface, things will change. The sediment will get darker, finer, more moist. In some places, it will be chocolate brown, filled with bits of organic material, rotted leaves, grass, twigs. Keep on digging and the material in your shovel will get redder. Keep digging, you'll be back to brown.

What you have encountered is the old surface of the alluvial fan and the soil that formed there. The soil is well developed, an indication that the fan surface was stable for at least hundreds of years. Trees lived and died, dropped their leaves, left their mark, and then, suddenly, the soil was buried by sediment sluicing off the hillsides above. A student from the University of Vermont dug holes in 22 alluvial fans. He found a soil buried in every one of them, quietly preserved out of sight—a mute testimonial to landscape change wrought inadvertently by Vermont settlers.

In the beginning, whenever we found the buried soil, we'd collect a piece of charcoal from just above it, gather a couple hundred dollars, and get a radiocarbon date. The first date was less than 200 years; the second date was less than 200 years. After our fifth young date, we stopped spending money and accepted the likelihood that whenever we found a well-preserved soil near the surface of a fan, that soil was young. Younger than our country.

So, why the buried soil? What happened within the last couple of hundred years? All the evidence suggests that we did it—well, not exactly us, but our ancestors, the non-Native American settlers who cleared the land, first for small subsistence farms, later for grazing sheep, and finally for timber. In 1770, Vermont was almost entirely covered by forest. By 1870, over 80 percent of the state was cleared land. Today, the majority of Vermont is again covered by trees. The correlation is clear, the trees were cut and sediment poured from the hillsides.

Deep in the bowels of the University of Vermont library are cases of old stereo view cards, cards that Victorian-era friends and lovers must have once passed around to one another. The cards are filed by town, so you can easily see what Burlington or Bennington or Brattleboro looked like with barren slopes. Find the Montpelier section and you can see views of the golden-domed state capital, which today glitters before a backdrop of dark green, tree-covered hillsides. In the middle to late 1800s, the slopes are clear to the ridges. Look closely at the old black-and-white photos; there are landslides and gullies just beyond the capital.

How do we know that eroding slopes are linked closely in time to deforestation? There are several strong arguments. Observations made today in the

Pacific Northwest show that deforestation and road building are very effective means of destabilizing slopes. Or, one can start from the fundamental physics of slope stability and use measured soil strengths to predict what will happen when trees are cut. Curiously, such a model predicts that landslides will follow clear cutting by five to ten years. Why the lag? Because it takes the better part of a decade for roots to rot and lose their strength, strength that helps to hold together soil perched on steep hillsides.

Our best evidence for rapid landscape response to clear-cutting was collected inadvertently by the clear-cutters themselves. Search through any large collection of nineteenth century photographic images and you are bound to find a smoking gun. In the collection of 20,000 or so images at the University of Vermont, there are several pictures of just-cleared fields studded with stumps. In the background of one image, behind an austere-looking farmer, behind his cabin, is a steep hillside. On that slope is a clearly defined landslide. There is a picture of the Clarendon Springs hotel probably taken to preserve memories of a summer holiday. At the hillside beyond the building there are eroding gullies and growing alluvial fans, captured in the act.

In Henry's fan, we found perhaps our most poignant evidence for the rapidity of slope failure after land clearance. Late fall 1997, just after dawn, I was alone making the final measurements along a 35-foot trench, the last of a series of trenches that my students and I have opened in the fan. Earlier, 30 of my introductory geology students had dragged trowels over the surface of the

An unknown Vermonter, sometime after 1867, looks out over newly clear-cut fields in the midst of which is a traditional Vermont cape-style house and gazebo. Beyond the fields of stumps, is a clear-cut hillside where shallow landslides have carried away soil and exposed sediments of glacial Lake Vermont that were deposited 12,000 to 14,000 years ago. The slide scars are evident in the stereo view photograph, Highgate, Vermont. (*Used by permission of the University of Vermont, Bailey Howe Library, Special Collections*)

trench, searching for clues about the past in the moist earth. This was a cold, clear October morning, with frost still clinging to the wilted pasture grass. My trowel worked the west wall of the trench, into a corner not previously well explored. It hit something hard and stopped.

Two minutes later, I was holding in my hand a horseshoe. It had come from the buried soil, 30 inches below the current surface. According to Henry, who had shoed enough horses to know, it didn't come from a draft horse working the fields, but from a riding horse and a small one at that. Who had been riding in the field that day maybe 100, maybe 150 years ago? When did the rider notice that the horse had lost its shoe? Did the same rider return to the field after a storm hit? Did the rider stand out in the deluge, dripping wet and watch water pouring from the slopes as sand and gravel and silt and clay covered the horse's tracks and the lost shoe? Just what did this person think as the once-fertile field was buried by sterile sand and gravel ripped from the slopes above and left as mute meteorological testimony on the fan below.

The flood that buried the soil and the horseshoe came quickly. The geology tells us so. The top of the buried soil is not a smooth surface; rather, it undulates in predictable, sharp-crested waves. These waves are plow furrows, seen on end and frozen in time. They are buried by sand, sand that crept below their crests and filled every void. What we see in the trench walls is a snapshot of a day, maybe a week, but probably not a month, caught some time in the last century.

Trees were felled, their stumps burned or wrenched from the ground by oxen. A farmer plowed the field, breaking the sod. A horse moved across the open land, loosing a shoe. A rainstorm hit and water poured down the slope, carrying sand and silt and clay. The field was buried, the plow marks preserved. The field was never plowed again. It remains today a pasture, its richest soil nearly three feet below the cows.

We know that what happened on Henry's land was commonplace and the effects widespread. On every fan we have studied so far, the rate at which sediment poured off the hillsides increased by tenfold when settlers cleared them. But the sediment didn't stop on the fans and in the fields; it kept going right into the rivers of Vermont, including the Huntington, including the Winooski into which the Huntington drains. We know most about the Winooski River; draining much of Vermont's highlands, it responded dramatically to this flood of debris. The Winooski's flood plains filled with sediment, rising in some places five or six feet in the 1800s, before the river's flow subsided as trees regrew on barren hillslopes and the sediment supply waned. In 1870, at the height of deforestation, a wave of sediment moved down the Winooski River, causing the river's delta to grow dramatically into Lake Champlain. Sediment once covering rural hillslopes now extended the lakeshore. The delta has since returned to its original size; its historic addition beaten away by waves and currents. The sediment is now at the bottom of the lake.

Today, the Moultroup property is woods and fields, woods that used to be fields, and woods that are again becoming fields. The alluvial fans are mostly quiet. There are stone walls in the woods that mark the labors of years gone by. There are skidder tracks where just this fall Henry pulled logs to clear a site so that another one of his children could move home. Now, with winter fast coming to the Huntington Valley, the logs are rapidly becoming firewood. Henry's firewood is rumored to be the best in the valley. He and his sons sell a lot of it.

In Huntington, traces of the past are everywhere at the surface and below. Such is the case for most of Vermont and much of the northeastern United States. Today, New England is mostly forest. But things are changing. Logging is returning to the north woods as trees that were seedlings in the last century now mature. After years of slow growth, Vermont's population has expanded dramatically since the 1960s. Human impact on the landscape is growing again. Wal-Marts have come to Vermont. Trees fall before sprawling suburbs. Bills regulating clear-cuts barely pass the legislature and landowners howl in protest, closing their lands to the time-honored tradition of public access.

The Earth records its history and ours in many ways, we need only be aware and alert enough to understand what it is saying. Geology is a way of looking back and seeing into the past. The hope is that by looking backward, we can see into the future.

Part II

SCIENTIFIC JUDGMENTS
AND ETHICAL CONSIDERATIONS

How might science's views of Earth and nature affect the way humans collectively live on the planet? As scientific ideas about the Earth change, so do our approaches to living with it. Although the informed judgments of science can suggest rational modes of sustainable living, they do not provide the moral imperatives that also must guide us. In "Scientific Judgments and Ethical Considerations," essayists convey the dynamism, uncertainty, and flux that has characterized scientific scrutiny of the Earth and suggest paths for living gently on the planet.

To begin, Marcia Bjørnerud recounts scientific depictions of nature and Earth starting in the late seventeenth century and reveals their influence on our use of Earth's resources. Next, Naomi Oreskes questions the legitimacy of predictions about complex earth processes generated by computer models that want for mathematical understanding, computational power, or data from the natural world. Gordon Eaton articulates a history of the U.S. Geological Survey and sketches a twenty-first-century mission for earth science. Incorporating theology, George Fisher searches for constructive dialogue between science and religion so that intellectual knowledge and moral understanding might become the twin fibers that support a "future worth living." To conclude, Stephen Jay Gould argues that attention to human time scales, not geologic ones, should impel us toward an environmental ethic based on the "golden rule."

Together these essays offer historical and contemporary perspectives to help us formulate an environmentalism informed by science and values.

5

Natural Science, Natural Resources, and the Nature of Nature

Marcia G. Bjørnerud

Is Nature benevolent, malevolent, or neutral? Ultimately comprehensible or infinitely complex? Predictable or chaotic? Robust or fragile? Even though such questions are not the sort that most scientists consciously address, tacit assumptions about the nature of Nature shape the way science is done at any historical moment. Scientific assumptions about the natural world, in turn, influence societal attitudes toward Nature and natural resources. Of course, resource use and allocation are governed by many factors—economic, political, and religious, as well as scientific—and scientific paradigms are themselves entangled with economics, politics, and religion. Nonetheless, it is possible to recognize parallels between evolving scientific depictions of Nature and Earth and the manner in which Western societies have organized and justified resource use over the last 300 years. The purpose of this essay is to consider these historical parallels and speculate about how emerging paradigms in the earth sciences may influence resource management in the next century.

Such an analysis is necessarily done with broad brush strokes; the scientific zeitgeist of one age blends imperceptibly into the next, and the spirits of past ages live on today in an inharmonious postmodernist mix. Still, standing back for a retrospective look, one sees how the infinite, chaotic, and threatening Earth of the pre-eighteenth century gradually became the measurable, mechanical, subjugatable Earth of the nineteenth. The latter view has continued to prevail in the present century, though with increasing emphasis on Earth's fragility and finitude. A new view of Earth is emerging, however—one that partly returns to imagery of the 1700s. This new Earth is once again immeasurable—infinite in its complexity at many scales; chaotic—in the mathematical sense of a nondeterministic system; and indomitable.

CHANGING PERCEPTIONS OF THE NATURE OF NATURE AND NATURAL RESOURCES

	Pre-18th century	18th–19th centuries	20th century	21st century
Geological paradigms:	Catastrophism	Uniformitarianism	Plate tectonics	Gaia; Neo-catastrophism
Political paradigms:		Colonialism	Environmentalism	Globalism
SIZE AND SCOPE	**Infinite Earth** Raw materials are limitless; resource availability is restricted only by human labor and technology.	**Measurable Earth** Earth's form and face have been mapped; minerals have been classified; general patterns of resource occurrence have been characterized.	**Finite Earth** Resources are exhaustible in our lifetimes.	**Fractal Earth** Earth is infinite in its complexity at all scales. Previously unrecognized resources are to be found in the microbial world, the diversity of the rainforest, and the deep sea.
ORDER AND ORGANIZATION	**Chaotic Earth** Earth was shaped by cataclysm; geological phenomena are largely inexplicable except as Divine interventions.	**Mechanical Earth** Earth processes are subject to natural laws and are predictable, cyclical, uniformitarian, and gradual. Understanding these processes allows technological intervention in them, and more efficient exploitation of resources. Continents are fixed. Geology is land based. Geological change is gradual and progressionist.	Continents are mobile. Geology is ocean centered.	**Organic Earth** Earth is chaotic in the modern sense; characterized by interconnected systems, nonlinearity, and multiple stable states. Even if natural laws are known, outcomes may not be predictable. Geological change is punctuated and contingent.
BALANCE OF POWER BETWEEN PEOPLE AND PLANET	**Threatening Earth** Wilderness is the realm of beasts and savages; undeveloped land is wasteland.	**Subjugatable Earth** Earth can be cultivated, mined, and tamed on a global scale for human benefit.	**Fragile Earth** The earth machine can break down if abused by humans.	**Robust Earth** Earth will survive the environmental havoc wreaked by humans, but humans may not.

PRE–EIGHTEENTH-CENTURY EARTH

Catastrophe and Chaos

By the late seventeenth century, the scientific revolution was well under way. Sir Issac Newton had reined in the heavens by tethering them to the same fundamental laws that operate on Earth. But the Earth itself remained untamed. Geology had not yet emerged as a distinct discipline with established premises and practices, and most scientific treatises on the formation of the Earth and its landscapes were baroque variations of the biblical account. The cataclysms that had shaped the Earth were depicted in imaginative detail in works like the illustrated *Sacred Physics*, a synthesis of naive paleontological observations, quasi-scientific reasoning, and biblical literalism by Johann Scheuchzer, a Swiss physician, natural historian, fossil collector, and polymath.[1] To Scheuchzer and others, Earth's present was disjunct from its past. Different rules had applied in primordial times, and in any case, the rules were not necessarily meant to be comprehensible by the human intellect. The forces of Nature were capricious, controlled by the hand of an easily angered—if recently mellowed—God.

Wilderness was considered brutal and monstrous. Mountains were pathological—"carbuncles on the face of the Earth"—a diagnosis very different from the "majesty" attributed to them today.[2] According to *Telluris Theoria Sacra* (*The Sacred Theory of the Earth*), a series of volumes written in the 1680s by influential theologian and natural philosopher Thomas Burnet, mountain ranges and canyons were the scars left on a once perfectly smooth "mundane egg," which cracked and released the Noachian deluge.[3] Burnet's geological assertions appear ludicrous to modern readers and were treated with particular scorn by British geologist Sir Charles Lyell as early as 1830 in his review of theories of the Earth.[4] But as Stephen Jay Gould argues in *Time's Arrow, Time's Cycle*, Burnet's approach was scientific, or at least rationalistic, in that he was attempting to integrate sacred and secular knowledge into a single, internally consistent narrative.[5] To Burnet and his contemporaries, the roughness of Earth's landscape was an expression of, and punishment for, Man's iniquitousness. Given such an interpretation, the appropriate posture for Man to assume toward Nature was a half-penitential, half-fearful cower.

Penurious Plenitude

Within this inclement physical and spiritual landscape, humans were left to fend for themselves. In preindustrial times, the use of animal, vegetable, and mineral commodities (not yet called "resources") was a matter of local contingency rather than systematic exploration and distribution. Without any understanding of the evolution of the landscape or the genesis of ore deposits, discovery and extraction of usable earth materials depended on serendipity. Cultivation of land was one of the few activities through which humans could exert direct control over the type and quantity of goods produced, so agriculture-based social structures became the templates for economic and political systems in western Europe.

John Locke's *Second Treatise of Government* (1689), a germinal document in both British and American political history, articulated the late seventeenth century, agri-biblical vision of "natural" rights to land and other property. In Locke's view, the Earth was a Divine gift to Man, but no Eden. He depicted Nature as a grudging provider,[6] asserting repeatedly that land has no intrinsic value until human toil is invested in it:

> 'Tis labor *then which* puts the greatest part of value upon land, *without which it would scarcely be worth any thing . . . nature and the earth furnished only the almost worthless materials, as in themselves.*[7]

Moreover, Locke argued, it is God's intent that land be developed:

> *God gave the world to men in common; but since he gave it them for their benefit and the greatest conveniences of life they were capable to draw from it, it cannot be supposed he meant it should always remain common and uncultivated.*[8]

And when one man cultivated a plot of land, the society as a whole benefited:

> *He who appropriates land to himself by his labor does not lessen but increases the common stock of mankind. For the provisions serving to the support of human life produced by one acre of enclosed and cultivated land, are . . . ten times more, than those which are yielded by an acre of land of an equal richness, lying waste . . . . And therefore he that encloses land, and has a greater plenty of the conveniences of life from ten acres than he could have from an hundred left to Nature, may truly be said to give ninety acres to mankind.*[9]

Although Earth's gifts could be won only through toil and sweat, they were essentially infinite. Human labor was the sole limitation on resource availability, and humans had a moral and social mandate to cultivate, subdue, and domesticate. The concepts of extinction and exhaustion were not yet in circulation.

EIGHTEENTH- AND NINETEENTH-CENTURY EARTH

Classification

Carolus Linnaeus, the great eighteenth-century Swedish biologist, set the agenda for other branches of natural history by organizing the biological world into an orderly hierarchy in which every organism had a first and last name: a place in the pedigree of Life. The quasi-divine act of naming things is an empowering and satisfying task, and taxonomy (together with a fair amount of taxidermy) became a preoccupation of the emerging natural sciences in the eighteenth and nineteenth centuries. The spirit of the scientific times was embodied in the natural history museums of the Victorian era, bursting with stuffed birds, skeletons, fossils, crystals, and other natural wonders, named and tamed, entombed within glass cases.

In the geological realm, there was so much to classify—rocks, minerals, fossils, landforms, structures, ore deposits, sedimentary basins—that the job continued well into the present century. In the absence of unifying genetic models for the formation of most of these features, classification schemes brought a comforting sense of finitude and fixity to nature's variability. Some geological entities, like minerals, fell easily into well-defined categories, and the great nineteenth-century encyclopedic treatises about them—for example, James Dwight Dana's *Manual of Mineralogy*, first published in 1869—are still in circulation, the most complete compendia of their kinds ever produced.[10] But other geological phenomena resisted ready classification, and the best minds of the time struggled to identify idealized Platonic categories that would impose structure on unruly reality.

Developing a universal nomenclature for ore bodies was a particular priority because of their economic importance, but this proved (and to some extent remains) notoriously difficult. The classification schemes were invariably entangled with idiosyncratic theories of ore genesis based on mineral occurrences in a particular region. In the late eighteenth century, mining academies proliferated across Europe, with particularly vigorous programs in Germany, Sweden, and France. Many of these were headed by a single visionary (e.g., Abraham Gottlob Werner in Freiberg, J. Wallerius in Uppsala, and G. F. Rouelle in Paris), surrounded by disciples who helped to propagate their master's system.[11] Few of these theoretical schemes influenced actual mining practices, however; intuition and experience continued to guide the engineers and assayers who directed work in the mines. In the minds of the true believers, however, the theoretical classification schemes had a reality that transcended the ambiguities of particular natural occurrences, which were viewed as degenerate versions of the archetypes. As in Burnet's schema, Nature fell short of perfection. But Man was no longer culpable for its defects; in fact, he could even rise above them through scientific observation and inference. The European mining academies may have had little effect on the mining industry of their time, but their very existence signaled an important new philosophy: The Earth and its mineral resources are knowable.

Cartography

The epoch of scientific classification coincided with, and reflected, European colonization and settlement of the Americas, Africa, and the southern Pacific. Expeditions were sent forth to document the flora, fauna, and mineral riches of the frontiers. The richly detailed, carefully illustrated notebooks of the 1803–1806 North American expedition by Meriwether Lewis and William Clark represent the best of these officially commissioned reports. In the United

States, federal and state geological surveys were established to assess and map the resources of the nation. These surveys were charged with census taking—counting and accounting, making the infinite, and indefinite, finite.[12]

In the Seventh Annual Report of the Geological Survey to the U.S. Congress in 1888, Director John Wesley Powell, who himself had led a great geological expedition in the American West, wrote of the strategic importance of a new program to create accurate topographic and geological charts of the nation.[13] Powell appreciated the power of maps. Like classification schemes, maps confer to the user a kind of ownership over their subjects. First, maps represent measurement, and to measure is to understand—an equation made plain in the dual meanings of the verb *to fathom*. Second, maps carry the power of images. Maps miniaturize wilderness so that it can be held in the hand and seen in the mind's eye.

Maps and surveys were critical in implementation of the U.S. Homestead Act of 1862 and the General Mining Law of 1872, both based on Locke's principle that anyone who worked a parcel of land was the rightful owner of it.[14] The Homestead Act survived well into the twentieth century (it was repealed in 1977), and the General Mining Law, which remains in effect today, seems destined to persist into the twenty-first. These two federal policies were responsible for some of history's most egregious instances of systemic environmental injustice: the repeated reneging by the U.S. Government on treaties with Native American tribes.[15] Implicit in these policies was an intellectual extension of Locke's value-added principle of property rights: Those who could fathom Nature, name it, and map it, have the right to exploit it. It should be mentioned that aboriginal systems of naming and knowing were not recognized.

The western expansion also resurrected the old Baconian metaphor of Nature as female.[16] The language and images associated with the opening of the frontier are telling: virgin forests, mother lodes, fecund prairies waiting for the plow. Classified and catalogued, measured and mapped, Nature could now be dominated.

Mechanism and Certainty

A very different metaphor for Nature was also gaining ascendancy in nineteenth-century science: Nature as machine.[17] The cyclicity implicit in Scottish geologist James Hutton's doctrine of uniformitarianism resonated with the cogs and flywheels of the age of steam.[18] Although Hutton advocated the oxymoronic phrase "living machine" to describe his vision of a self-renewing, self-repairing Earth, the embarrassing organic adjective was dropped by his followers. The mechanical imagery promised a new level of control over nature.[19] If one could only understand the mechanism, the outcome would be determinable. This view was most confidently advanced by physicist Pierre-Simon Laplace in his 1814 *Essai philosophique sur le probabilités*. He asserted that if all forces and bodies in nature could be accounted for, nothing would be uncertain, and the future, as well as the past, would be present to the eyes.[20]

Later in the nineteenth century, knowledge of the future began to look somewhat less attractive. With the rise of thermodynamics, it became clear that Earth's life span was limited, that eventually its great engine would run down and grind to a halt. Lord Kelvin's famous calculations of the age of the Earth (as young as 20 million years) also implied a finite future, as the Earth evolved inexorably toward thermal equilibrium.[21]

Although Kelvin's calculation has been superseded, his application of equilibrium concepts to the earth system is still followed. The assumption that Nature—substitute "ecosystem," "global climate," or "magma chamber"—is at, close to, or tending progressively toward, some well-defined equilibrium state remains a fundamental philosophical tenet in many geological subdisciplines.[22] The idea probably has its roots in older notions of the "balance of nature,"[23] a concept emphasized by Charles Lyell in 1830:

> It is to the efficacy of this ceaseless discharge of heat, and of solid as well as gaseous matter, that we probably owe the general tranquillity of our globe; for were it not that some kind of equilibrium is established between fresh accessions of heat and its discharge, we might expect perpetual convulsions .... But the circulation of heat from the interior to the surface, is probably regulated like that of water from the continents to the sea, in such a manner that it is only when some obstruction occurs to the regular discharge, that the usual repose of Nature is broken.[24]

Lyell's earth machine was benign and efficient, humming along in a steady state except when something jammed the workings. Even then, normal operation would soon resume, with no lasting effects from the breakdown.

The mechanical model for the Earth has persisted into the present; furthermore, in the middle of this century, the machine gained more moving parts in the form of drifting continents. In most histories of geology, the plate tectonic revolution is depicted as an epiphany, a scientific coming of age, the paradigmatic paradigm shift. It would be absurd to deny the intellectual, and practical, importance of plate tectonics. Economically, for example, tectonic theory provided, at long last, the unifying framework for mineral resources that Werner and others had sought. Yet in terms of underlying metaphor, plate tectonics was only an elaboration on a nineteenth-century theme.

TWENTIETH-CENTURY EARTH

Finitude and Fragility

At the beginning of the nineteenth century, English political economist Thomas Robert Malthus, in his *Essay on the Principle of Population* (1798), had been a solitary voice warning of what today is called unsustainable resource use. Malthus's treatise was widely read, and almost universally criticized, throughout the rest of the century for its "terrible demon . . . ready to stifle the hopes of humanity" and "abominable tenet."[25] German socialist Friedrich

Engels called it a "vile and infamous doctrine . . . repulsive blasphemy against man and nature."[26] Charles Darwin was among the few who took Malthus's work seriously. He realized that the Malthusian concept of superfecundity leading to competition for resources could provide the driving force for evolution by natural selection.[27] Although Darwin emphasized the effect of scarcity on the interactions among organisms, neither he nor most of his contemporaries were particularly concerned with the ultimate finitude and potential depletion of resources. As late as 1883, for example, Darwin's vocal disciple, English biologist Thomas Henry Huxley, asserted his belief that the cod fishery was effectively infinite—that "natural check[s]" would always allow the resource to replenish itself "long before anything like permanent exhaustion has occurred."[28] Malthus's message was more than a century ahead of its time.

As the earth machine continued to whir into the twentieth century, however, it began to show signs of frailty. In the United States, the Dust Bowl of the 1930s was an alarming awakening to how quickly a critical resource could be exhausted. Farmland, which had so recently been robust and abundant, was suddenly sickly and scarce. Soil and water conservation became federal priorities. Resources now became entities to "manage." The cherished illusion of limitless resources could no longer be maintained. But then, the exigencies of World War II and the hysterical consumerism of the 1950s made it possible to embrace the illusion again. The publication of Rachel Carson's *Silent Spring* in 1962 is usually cited as the event marking the public's reawakening to the limits of Nature's resilience.[29] Through the rest of the 1960s and 1970s, the rhetoric of the environmental movement became progressively more pessimistic.

The titles of introductory geology textbooks from the 1970s reveal an almost claustrophobic preoccupation with Earth as a closed system (another nineteenth-century thermodynamic concept) and the adversarial relationship between humans and the Earth: *Man's Finite Earth*; *Earthbound: Minerals, Energy and Man's Future*; *Geology: The Paradox of Earth and Man*.[30] Popular titles were apocalyptic: *The Population Bomb*; *The Limits to Growth*; *Future Shock*.[31] The once bountiful and commodious Earth was suddenly too small:

> *This book is about the clash of evergrowing numbers [of people] with a nongrowing habitat. It deals with the environmental problems caused by runaway population growth on a planet that has unalterable dimensions but fixed or shrinking resources.*[32]

Apollo mission images of Earth as a blue ball floating in space underscored the feeling of finitude:

> *It's so incredibly impressive when you look back at our planet from out there in space and you realize so forcibly that it's a closed system—that we don't have any unlimited resources, that there's only so much air and so much water.*—Edgar Dean Mitchell, Apollo 14 astronaut[33]

Environmental rhetoric of the 1990s remains faithful to this vision:

> *The foundation-stone of radical green politics is the belief that our finite*
> *Earth places limits on industrial growth. This finitude, and the scarcity it*
> *implies, is an article of faith for green ideologues, and it provides the*
> *fundamental framework within which any putative picture of a green*
> *society must be drawn.*[34]

Behind these words is the ancient fear that we will one day wake up to find the cupboards bare. An old and frail Mother Earth will no longer be able to provide for her children.

TWENTY-FIRST-CENTURY EARTH

The New Infinitude

But the apocalypse has been postponed. The global famines predicted in *The Population Bomb* for the 1970s and 1980s did not occur. *The Limits to Growth* forecast depletion of copper and other strategic metals by the early 1990s, but reports of the dearth of these commodities appear to have been greatly exaggerated.[35] In 1980, economist Julian Simon challenged ecologist Paul Ehrlich to a wager about how the prices of five metals would change in the coming decade. Ehrlich anticipated that increasing scarcity would drive prices higher. Simon predicted that prices would decrease, and he won the bet.[36] What happened to finitude?

The Limits to Growth by the Massachusetts Institute of Technology-based wunderkinder in the "Club of Rome"[37] was groundbreaking in its use of systems modeling to grapple with complexly linked entities. The "World Model" at the heart of *Limits,* with its profusion of circles and arrows, was by far the most ambitious attempt at the time to integrate natural, economic, and social variables into a single scheme. Like Burnet's *Sacred Theory of the Earth* nearly three centuries earlier, the World Model was an earnest, if naive, effort to create a single unified vision of Earth. The limitations of *Limits,* some of which were recognized within a year of its publication, arose largely from its faith in the nineteenth-century view that Earth is measurable and mechanical.[38] But the comforting concepts of measurement and mechanism were becoming unexpectedly problematic.

"How long is the coastline of Britain?" the provocative title of a 1967 paper by Benoit Mandelbrot of IBM grounded the new mathematics of fractals in the natural world.[39] If your measuring stick is long, you will miss the firths and embayments, and you will conclude that the coastline is short. As you use shorter and shorter rulers, the coastline stretches. How long will copper last? How many people can Earth support? It depends. If you set the price higher, copper will last a few more decades. If most earthlings become vegetarians, the planet could support another billion. There is always more of what you are looking for if you look closer, if you pay more, if you learn to recycle and eat (only) your vegetables. As Joel E. Cohen, professor of populations at Rockefeller

University and Columbia University, has recently argued, "Ecological limits appear not as ceilings but as trade-offs."[40] The sensitive feedbacks of the global marketplace have made Earth effectively infinite again.

Measuring coastlines may no longer be a sure thing, but appraising the planet might be possible. In an audacious 1997 paper in *Nature*, Robert Costanza and 12 other ecologists and economists from around the world placed the value of the "world's ecosystem services and natural capital" at $33 trillion—about twice the global gross international product. If such an analysis seems crass, it at least has the virtue of using a system of measurement that is universally understood. Costanza and his coauthors concede that the undertaking is at some level absurd:

> The economies of the Earth would grind to a halt without the services of ecological life-support systems, so in one sense their total value to the economy is infinite. However, it can be instructive to estimate the "incremental" . . . value of ecosystem services . . . . We acknowledge that there are many conceptual and empirical problems inherent in producing such an estimate.[41]

The international environmental summit meetings of the 1990s have been based on the premise that the only viable solutions to global environmental problems will be those that harness the power of the global market.[42] This is not to say that environmental decisions should be made strictly on economic grounds, but rather that the "hidden" environmental costs of, for example, fossil fuel combustion or nuclear power generation should be acknowledged in the market. Costanza and his coauthors assert that their analyses have two types of practical application: (1) helping nations and international bodies modify "systems of national accounting to better reflect the value of ecosystem services and natural capital" and (2) appraising governmental or commercial initiatives in which "ecosystem services lost must be weighed against the benefits of a specific project."[43] Arguably, then, the most meaningful environmental measurements are those that can be converted to units of currency—as long as the contingent nature of these monetary "measurements" is recognized.

Earth Regains Its Strength and Spirit

At the same time that Nature was beginning to resist measurement, the earth machine was also showing signs of unpredictable behavior. Like Laplace, many modern scientists have continued to embrace the idea that knowing Nature's "rules"—holding the user's manual—will eventually lead to omniscience. Biologist Edward O. Wilson, for example, has recently described his "conviction, far deeper than a mere working proposition, that the world is orderly and can be explained by a small number of natural laws."[44] But even if the number of laws is small, the number of possible outcomes may be infinite, and order, if it exists, is probably ephemeral. These are the lessons emerging from studies of Earth's climate, for example, which is better characterized by the mathematics of chaos and nonlinear systems than by equilibrium thermodynamics.[45] Cores from ice caps and deep-sea sediments record feverish oscillations in global temperature, catastrophic collapses of massive icesheets, and decade-scale reorganization of heat-transporting ocean currents.[46] Biological evolution of species is no longer a stately march but a series of fits and starts.[47] Contrary to Lyell's view, Nature apparently does not spend most of its time in "repose." Rather, "convulsions" large and small are the norm. What happened to equilibrium?

In some subdisciplines within the natural sciences, it is now common to invoke multiple, rather than unique, equilibrium states, separated by narrow thresholds. In these models, even a relatively small perturbation to an apparently stable system can trigger system-wide reorganization. Worse, the response may be sensitive to the history of the system, the scale of investigation, and the rate, as well as the magnitude, of the perturbation.[48] If it was once placid and domesticated, Nature is now irritable and biting back.

Other scientists have begun to question the validity of ascribing even this qualified kind of equilibrium to natural systems. Anthropologist Paul Rabinow writes:

> *Nature reflects the accumulation of countless accidents, not some hidden harmony. Things might have turned out quite differently. Ecosystems are ever changing, dissolving, transforming, recombining in new forms.*[49]

Jianguo Wu and Orie Loucks, both fervent conservationists, argue that sentimental attachment to the idea of the "balance of nature" has undermined the credibility of environmental policy:

> *The classical equilibrium paradigm in ecology . . . has failed not only because equilibrium conditions are rare in nature, but also because of our past inability to incorporate heterogeneity and scale multiplicity into our quantitative expressions for stability. The theories and models built around these equilibrium and stability principles have misrepresented the foundations of resource management, nature conservation, and environmental protection.*[50]

The earth machine has become too complex for the mechanics to understand. Is it time to acknowledge, with the Romantic poets, that the metaphor of mechanism fails to portray the full richness of Nature? The geosciences appear ready to return to Hutton's half-organic depiction of the Earth as a "living machine." There are surprising similarities between Hutton's late eighteenth century vision and atmospheric chemist James Lovelock's late twentieth century Gaia hypothesis, which places Life at the center of the global climate system and geochemical cycles.[51] Although Gaia has not yet been fully welcomed into the scientific fold, she has already found her way in the back gate in the less controversial guise of "geophysiology."[52] If the manuals for the earth machine have begun to seem useless, perhaps it is because we should be consulting a medical reference instead. In any case, Earth seems to have recovered its strength and spirit. Unfortunately, the prognosis for the human race is less clear.

In many ways, scientific views of Earth have come full circle in 300 years. At the start, we feared the power and magnitude of a capricious and capacious Earth; then passed through a period of childlike self-aggrandizement in which we, like Antoine De Saint-Exupery's *Little Prince*, were masters of a planet that was just the right size for us to explore and conquer. Rather suddenly, we found ourselves surrounded by the wreckage of our careless expeditions, on an Earth that seemed to be shrinking. Finally, we have paused long enough to see infinity once more, in grains of sand and nuclei of cells. We are again humbled in the presence of a venerable old planet that is at once benevolent and malevolent, comprehensible and complex, predictable and chaotic, robust and fragile.

6

Why Believe a Computer?
Models, Measures, and Meaning
in the Natural World

Naomi Oreskes

Doubt is the essence of understanding.—Richard Feynman

or at least three centuries, philosophers have tried to determine what separates science from other forms of human knowledge. In the seventeenth century, Sir Francis Bacon introduced the concept of a "crucial experiment"—a test that would uniquely prove or disprove a scientific idea. By actively challenging our beliefs through crucial experiments and critical observations, Bacon held, we could increase our understanding of the natural world and so improve our lot.[1] History has long since demonstrated that a single test is rarely if ever sufficient to convince anyone of anything, and many experiments appear crucial only in retrospect. Still the idea of crucial experiments has held on, because it speaks to a broader point: Testing is the heart of science. Although there is no foolproof way to define science, testability is the most commonly cited demarcation criterion between scientific theories and other forms of human explanatory effort.[2]

Can computer models be tested? In recent years, there has been an explosive increase in the use of computer simulation models in fields as diverse as economics, aeronautics, cosmology, epidemiology, and forest ecology. Geology is no exception. From geochemistry to hydrology, paleontology to mantle dynamics, computer simulation models are now a standard part of the tool kit of the earth sciences. One of the driving forces behind the increased use of computer models in the earth sciences is their applicability to systems that are too large, too complex, or too far away to study by other means. The example familiar to most readers is global climate change. Most scientists believe that carbon dioxide in the atmosphere from human activities is producing an enhanced greenhouse effect and, in the future, the Earth's average temperature will increase as a result. To predict what these effects will be requires powerful computers that can obtain the solutions to a complex set of differential equations involving large quantities of input data. Other examples include models used to predict the behavior of proposed nuclear waste repository sites, to estimate air pollution emission levels from industrial plants, or to determine the circulation of ocean currents affecting fisheries. These are complex systems that cannot be observed simply nor easily recreated in a laboratory experiment.

In many cases, the predictions generated by computer models are considered as a basis for public policy decisions, and government regulators and agencies may be required by law to establish their trustworthiness. This situation has led to the demand for "verification" or "validation" of these models.[3] Claims about model verification and validation are now routinely found in published scientific literature. Are these claims legitimate? Can a computer model be proved true or false? How can we tell when to believe a computer?

THE PROBLEM OF VERIFICATION

All scientific theory testing involves a fundamental ambiguity: There may be several possible configurations of nature that could produce a given set of observed results. Therefore, any empirical data we collect in support of a theory may also be consistent with alternative explanations. For this reason, many scientists accept the view, first developed by Karl Popper in the 1930s, that scientific theories can be proved false but not true. In Popper's terms, theories can be *falsified*, but not *verified*. If empirical data are inconsistent with the predictions of a theory, then something is amiss and the theory must be modified; but if the predictions come true, it may merely mean that our problems have yet to be encountered. Refutation may be just around the corner. This conclusion holds for all scientific knowledge, whether generated by computers or otherwise.

But the issue is more complicated than Popper allowed. If a prediction fails to cohere with the natural world, there is often no simple way to know where the fault lies. The problem may lie in the theory being tested, but it may also lie in a faulty piece of equipment, a bug in a computer program, or a mistaken background assumption. A famous example is the case of "stellar parallax" in the history of astronomy. Parallax is the changing appearance of an object when viewed from different positions, so that the object appears against different backdrops. (Imagine a girl standing on the beach while you sail past in a boat, heading north. First you see her against the northern sky, later you look back and see her against the southern sky.) When Copernicus proposed his heliocentric model of the universe—that the Earth was moving rather than the heavens—astronomers realized that the phenomenon of parallax offered a means to test the theory. If the Earth moved while the sun and stars stayed fixed, then the apparent position of any particular star should change during the course of the year. The star would be seen first against one backdrop, then against another. But when sixteenth-century astronomers searched for stellar parallax, they found none—and they rejected Copernicus's theory. Implicitly, they assumed that the Earth's orbit was large relative to the distance to the stars and therefore the parallax effect would be significant and their telescopes would be able to detect it. These assumptions turned out to be wrong. Because of the enormous distance to the stars, the parallax effect turns out to be very, very small, and it was not until the twentieth century that telescopes became powerful enough to detect it.[4]

Another example comes from the history of geology. One hundred years ago, the great British physicist Lord Kelvin argued that the Earth could not possibly be as old as geologists thought it was. On the basis of the concept of uniformitarianism—the assumption that presently observable geological processes are representative of Earth's history in general—nineteenth-century geologists concluded that the Earth was probably a few billion years old. Given observable rates of erosion and deposition, it would take that long to produce the known rock record. But when Kelvin calculated the time required for a molten body the size of the Earth to cool to its present temperature, he obtained a maximum of 98 million years and promptly declared the entire science of geology invalid. Any conceptual scheme that implied a billion-year-old Earth was fundamentally flawed, he announced. Pursuing the same logic, he dismissed Charles Darwin's theory of natural selection on the grounds of inadequate time for it to operate.[5] For several decades, Kelvin's result held sway and evolutionists were in nearly full retreat, until the discovery of radioactivity proved Kelvin wrong. For his calculation, Kelvin assumed that the Earth had no additional source of heat. In fact, the decay of radioactive elements within the Earth generated heat, and so the Earth had cooled far more slowly than simple physical principles would otherwise suggest.

In hindsight, it is easy to see where others have gone wrong: Astronomers thought their instruments were better than they were; Kelvin thought his knowledge more complete than it was. It is harder to see the flaws in our own reasoning. (If we could see them, presumably we would correct them.) When computer models are involved, it can be more difficult still, because the systems being modeled are very complex and the embedded assumptions can be very hard to see. How *do* we test computer models?

In the earth sciences, models are often tested by "history matching"—by seeing how well the model matches historical data. Hydrologists, for example, may test a groundwater flow model by running it backward in time and comparing the results with published records of water well levels. Climate models can be tested against weather records. If a model accurately reproduces historical data, modelers commonly claim that the model has been "validated" and can therefore be used to predict the future. However, hydrologist Leonard Konikow and his coworkers at the U.S. Geological Survey have shown that many "validated" models in hydrology fare poorly when extended into the future.[6] Why? The most common reason is that modelers fail to anticipate later changes in the modeled system. A region may experience a particularly wet or dry decade, for example, or an unusual confluence of rare events. Humans may change their behavior in ways that affect the natural system. Lacking a reliable way to predict such occurrences, scientists often build their models as if these changes did not occur at all. In effect, scientists treat the systems they are modeling as though the systems were static. This is not to say that modelers *believe* the systems are static—no earth scientist could imagine any earth system as truly static. Nevertheless, scientists often embed stasis into their models, and it often turns out to be wrong.

These examples give us grounds for humility in our assessment of our own best work, but they also provide grounds for long-range optimism because in all three cases the mistaken background assumptions were eventually recognized. The process of scientific research can be self-correcting as we reexamine old questions and build better equipment and instrumentation. The risk of wrongly believing in a false theory or model may seem academic, and in many cases it is. But it is not academic when scientific knowledge provides a basis for public policy. Then, the veracity of our theories can be a matter of human health and safety and the future of our natural environment.

THE PARADOX OF COMPLEX MODELS: REPRESENTATION VERSUS REFUTABILITY

The development of fast, inexpensive computers has been a boon to the earth sciences because they enable us to study problems that might otherwise remain intractable. Complex earth systems—such as the climate response to increased carbon dioxide, the transport of contaminants through groundwater, or the workings of a forest ecosystem—are difficult to address by traditional scientific methods. An ecosystem cannot be brought into the laboratory; the Earth's climate cannot be the site of controlled experiments. If you had proposed adding carbon dioxide to the Earth's atmosphere to test its effects, the experiment would have been rejected on ethical grounds. Numerical simulation models provide an ethical and pragmatic means to grapple with complex natural systems.

A problem arises, however, when we attempt to test the predictions of complex models against the natural world. In Popper's view, if the predictions of a theory (or model) fail to come true, then the theory must be rejected. But this is not what scientists do. As philosophers Imre Lakatos and Thomas Kuhn emphasized, scientists normally modify their theories in various small ways to accommodate observational discrepancies.[7] Recognizing this, the great chemist and philosopher Pierre Duhem concluded long ago that theories cannot be proved false any more than they can be proved true. In his 1906 essay, "Physical Theory and Experiment," Duhem argued that it is always possible to modify a theory in some manner so as to salvage it in the face of recalcitrant empirical evidence.[8] There is no simple criterion that tells us when we should modify an existing theory and when we should throw it out altogether.

Duhem believed that very simple phenomenological laws, deduced directly from empirical observation, might be refutable. Implicitly, he suggested that the more complex a theory and the instrumentation upon which its empirical support relies, the greater the difficulty of testing it, because the greater the number of parts that can be modified. This suggestion has two consequences. As systems become more complex, it becomes increasingly difficult to determine which part of the system is at fault when something goes wrong. And it becomes increasingly easy to modify a system that is failing in the face of negative evidence.

The implication for computer models is evident. The more sophisticated they become, the more difficult it is to refute them. One can save a complex model from refutation by small adjustments to its components. The constraints provided by laboratory experiments, field study, or theoretical considerations are hardly ever sufficient to define the system completely. Models tested against empirical data can therefore be "fine-tuned" to fit those data. Indeed, this is normal practice: Given a set of observational data, scientists will work on a model until they achieve a fit, a process referred to as calibration. A model that did not match available data would be rejected as false, but a model calibrated to fit available data may also be false.

Given this situation, one can see a justification for the traditional value of simplicity in science: Simpler systems are easier to test. One might therefore strive for simplicity in computer models, and some modelers do. For example, scientists working on artificial intelligence may seek the simplest possible model that can perform a task, such as pilot an aircraft or recognize speech. But these scientists are not trying to create a realistic representation of the human brain in all its complexity. Rather, they are building a system to *do* something. Their goals may be described as *functional* rather than *representational*. Modelers who attempt to represent complex natural systems often eschew simplification as fallacious.

A good example is the development of general circulation models (GCMs) for predicting global climate change. GCMs are computer models that attempt to represent the circulation of the Earth's atmosphere toward the goal of understanding climate patterns and climate change. Early GCMs were conspicuously oversimplified. Computational limitations forced scientists to omit many factors, notably the ability of the world's oceans to take in or give off heat. Simplification was a necessity, but not a virtue. With advances in computation, climate modelers have been able to increase the complexity of their models incrementally. First the oceans were added to GCMs in a static way—as if they were blankets of water that absorbed and radiated heat, but did not move. More powerful computers have lately allowed climate modelers to begin to examine the effects of ocean currents, which may turn out to be critical to understanding the greenhouse effect. Although the latest models are still incomplete, nearly all scientists would say that the addition of oceans is a step in the right direction. Because the Earth's climate is a highly complex system, increased complexity in the models is interpreted as evidence of closer approximation to reality.[9]

The history of GCMs illustrates a general point: For modeling earth systems, simplification often means leaving out available information or ignoring known or suspected processes. In the past, this practice was forced upon modelers by the limits of computational power; it used to be a joke in geology that some computer models took longer to run than the geological processes they were simulating. But the greatly increased speed and decreased cost of computer technology has made it possible to construct models of far greater complexity than most scientists imagined only a few years ago. The benefit of simplicity in model testing is now subordinated to the value of complexity, which is interpreted as evidence of the increased sophistication and therefore presumed realism of the model. The greater the scope of the model—the more ambitious it is—the more this is the case. But the more complex a model, the harder it is to refute. So we face a paradox: The closer a model comes to a full representation of a complex earth system, the harder it is to evaluate it. Put another way, the better the model is from the point of view of the modeler, the harder it is for others to evaluate the model. There is a trade-off between representation and refutability.

HETEROGENEITY AND THE (IN)ACCESSIBILITY OF EMPIRICAL INPUT

Complexity is often discussed in terms of the number of different processes or feedbacks represented in a model, but complexity can also be discussed in terms of the *character* of the empirical input parameters required by it. Scientists often think of empirical parameters in terms of physical properties with definite determinable values, like the atomic weight of an element, the salinity of seawater, or the density of the continental crust. Determining the average salt content of seawater is actually a challenging task, because we live on land and coastal processes affect the salinity of the seawater that we can readily reach. Deltas add fresh water that decreases the local salinity of the ocean; lagoons are sites of evaporation that may increase it. If we go to the open ocean to measure salinity, we still have to account for processes that modify salinity elsewhere, such as melting of polar ice. Nevertheless, there is a definite value for the saltiness of the sea, even if we have to work hard to determine it. But in many models of natural systems, the required empirical input may not have definite values and may not be fully determinable. This point requires explanation.

Many models of natural systems are based on continuum theory, in which a material with heterogeneous parts is treated as if it were a single homogeneous entity: the continuum. A familiar example is a household sponge. At some scale the "sponge" does not exist, it is a composite of solid material and the holes within it. The absorbency of sponges is what philosophers call an "emergent" property: It *emerges* from the interrelation of the solid, the holes, and the fluids with which they are in contact. Or consider another example: raisin bread. We all know what raisin bread is and we know what it tastes like. But cut it into small enough pieces and it no longer exists. Instead, we have a pile of raisins and bits of plain bread. The taste, smell, and feel of raisin bread—indeed, the very existence of raisin bread—are all emergent properties. Modeling based on continuum theory relies on the existence of emergent properties in nature; emergent properties permit scientists to describe complex, variable materials in a simple and tractable way.

An important example in earth science is the concept of permeability—the measure of how readily fluids will flow through a rock. Although we think of rocks as solid, really they are not. All rocks contain holes and fractures that can allow fluids to flow through them. The greater the number, size, and interconnectedness of these holes and fractures, the higher the permeability of the rock. Permeability is a crucial measure in siting nuclear waste repositories and toxic disposal sites, because we rely on the surrounding rocks to prevent toxins from escaping the site. On a microscopic level, however, permeability does not exist. On a microscopic level, rocks are complex aggregates of solid mineral grains with no permeability, and the empty spaces between them that have infinite permeability. In principle, the "true" permeability of a rock might be determined by measuring every mineral grain and the size and shape of every space around it. But to describe this complexity in realistic detail would be a hopeless task. A geologist could spend a lifetime describing the patterns of holes in a single rock outcrop.

Continuum theory provides a way to simplify this problem by treating the rock as a continuous material with a single definite property (namely, permeability) that represents the macroscopic behavior of the overall rock mass. But in making this simplification, fine-scale information is lost. We are deliberately ignoring the details. Is the devil in the details? In most cases, probably not, but there is no way to know until we use the model.

In addition to the loss of information at the subcontinuum scale, there is another problem: The emergent properties of the continuum may themselves be heterogeneous. Some parts of a sponge may be more holey than others; some slices of raisin bread may have more raisins; and some parts of a rock layer may be more permeable. Continuum equations traditionally involve the assignment of a single average value (or sometimes simply varying values) for complexly varying emergent properties. When we take an average value, we lose information about highs and lows. And this may matter a lot, because in many geological environments, the flow of fluids is controlled, not by the average properties of the bulk of the rock mass, but by the local presence of zones of very high permeability. In the Earth, heterogeneity matters. We need to know the variability of rocks surrounding a nuclear waste repository, because local zones of above-average permeability may allow contaminants to escape into the hydrosphere and biosphere. We need to know the extremes of weather that global warming may cause, because our houses are built to withstand ordinary weather; it is the extreme events that do damage to life and property. And we need to know the extremes of possible earthquake magnitudes, because one giant quake can do more damage than scores of small ones. From a human perspective, extremes are often more important than averages.

A response to the problem of heterogeneity is to collect spatially or temporally distributed data on heterogeneous properties. For example, we could study the spatial variability of permeability surrounding a proposed nuclear waste repository, and some scientists have done this. But this approach can only take us so far, because exhaustive local sampling presents the risk of modifying the bulk properties we are trying to measure. The insertion of closely spaced drill holes into a rock unit to determine its permeability may change that permeability. A full description of a heterogeneous physical system cannot be obtained without changing or destroying it.

Because of the heterogeneity of the natural world, uncertainty is inherent in the very nature of the systems we are studying. The required empirical input parameters are fundamentally inaccessible, not because our instruments are not sophisticated enough, our budgets not big enough, or we not clever enough, but because *the data do not exist in the form required by the equations at the scale to which we have access.* And when a system is poorly known, there is always uncertainty over whether our samples are representative. One is caught in a circular argument: To judge whether or not our samples are representative, we need to know the characteristics of the system, but if we knew the characteristics of the system, we would not need to sample it!

The heterogeneity of the natural world ensures that any model that strives for realistic representation must contain a large quantity of empirical input. This returns us to the complexity paradox: The more data we have, the more likely our model is to capture nature's diversity and richness. However, the more data we have, the more complex the model becomes and the less likely it is to be unique—another model of equal complexity but with a different mix of empirical input could have produced the same result.

ACCESS TO MODEL PREDICTIONS

Acknowledging these caveats, one may still argue that once a model is built, using the best available information, it can be tested like any other scientific theory by comparing its output with the natural world. Some models perform extremely well when this type of comparison is done. For example, computer models have been developed to predict the positions of the planets, stars, and other celestial bodies, and these predictions can easily be compared with astronomical observations. As the 1996 collision of Comet Shoemaker-Levy with Jupiter shows, these models are successful: Planetary scientists predicted the location and timing of this collision more than a year in advance.

But models in celestial mechanics are the exception that proves the rule: They represent relatively simple physical systems in which the operative forces can be described by a small number of equations involving variables that can be determined with a high degree of precision. Indeed, the equations involved were solved long before the advent of computers. The programs that do this for us today are a matter of convenience, not necessity. Furthermore, the events predicted by celestial mechanics are readily accessible: They take place all the time and in a repetitive way. Any model that did not accurately locate the planets would be subject to modification in very short order. As Karl Popper once explained, astronomical predictions "are possible only because our solar system is a stationary and repetitive system, and this is so because of the accident that it is isolated from the influence of other mechanical systems by immense regions of empty space and is therefore relatively free of interference from outside. Contrary to popular belief the analysis of such repetitive systems is not typical of natural science. These repetitive systems are special cases where scientific prediction becomes particularly impressive—but that is all."[10]

Most of the world is not like the solar system. The systems earth scientists study are not repetitive; they are not isolated from the influence of other systems; and they are not free from outside interference. Although the planets may seem far away—and physically, of course, they are—on a scientific level they are unusually accessible. Ironically, the predictions we make about the Earth we stand on are far less accessible.

For example, global circulation models must predict the Earth's climate over the next several decades. With adequate funding for scientific research, these predictions can be compared with empirical evidence in the years to come. But what exactly is the relevant empirical evidence? A climate model may predict global average temperature, but how does one *measure* the average temperature of the world? The data that are needed to test the model are *themselves modeled*—various point measurements around the globe must be synthesized into a single number, and scientists have argued over how best to achieve that synthesis. Refined GCMs may produce averages for particular regions of the globe—what modelers call model cells—but temperature is not measured in a model cell any more than it is measured in the world at large; temperature is measured at a point. The gap that exists between empirical input and model parameters is mirrored by a gap between model output and the data that could potentially confirm it.

A second problem, which is perhaps more important, is that policy decisions need to be made now. Many earth scientists and environmentalists argue that we cannot wait to confirm the results of GCMs, because, if we wait, it may be too late to undo the damage wrought. When a model predicts a negative outcome unless action is taken, a dilemma develops: We cannot know in advance whether the predictions are correct, but, if we wait to find out, it may be too late to use that information. The result is that testable predictions may be offered as a basis for decision-making in advance of any actual test results.

Other policy-relevant models make predictions on time frames over which science may no longer exist. For example, models of proposed high-level nuclear waste repository sites must predict repository behavior for the next thousand to ten thousand years. Models of this kind raise a fundamental question about what we mean by prediction. If the history of science is any guide, the cultural institution we call science may not exist ten thousand years hence; and if it does, it will almost certainly be in a form that will be unrecognizable to us. More important is that our work will most likely be unintelligible, perhaps even unrecognizable as science, to our successors. Therefore, even if an intellectual tradition were to exist that identified itself as the successor to our science, it is unlikely that its practitioners would be able to make much sense of the predictions we left for them to confirm or deny. There is no way for us to set up a mechanism to confirm the predictions of models 10,000 years in the future. Even if we could set up such tests, by the time we got the results they would be superfluous. Decisions must be made now on the basis of predictions about a future to which we have no access. Models are a surrogate for access to the future. How good a surrogate they are is an open question.

An obvious solution to this problem is to test models on smaller geographical scales and shorter time frames, and earth scientists do this. But, as the example from hydrologic models shows, a match between model results and present observations is no guarantee that the model will do as well in the future, because natural systems are dynamic and may change in unanticipated ways. As the philosopher Sir Alfred J. Ayer argued in a discussion of David Hume's famous skepticism about prediction, the question is not so much *whether* the future will resemble the past—because all science is premised on the assumption that it will—but *how* it will resemble it.[11] Or, as the Greek philosopher Heraclitus put it, we cannot step twice in the same river.

No model output ever matches the natural world exactly. The question is always whether the match is "good enough"—and this raises two issues, one scientific and one social. On a scientific level, evaluation of model fit always depends on scale. Consider this example of scale dependency: If I state that two sisters are the same height, say, five foot three inches, I implicitly mean the same to the nearest inch. With a finer ruler, I could make a finer distinction; but in matters of height, such fine distinctions rarely worry us. In a computer model, however, scale can be vitally important. Small errors that do not significantly affect model fit under the time frame or geographical scale for which data are available may generate large discrepancies when extrapolated over larger scales. A model that works on a small scale may fail on a large scale. A model that seems to be working at present may go wrong in the future. This fact highlights a key difference between natural and engineering systems: Modern engineers start with computer models, but then they build prototypes and pilot plants. If in the building stage a problem arises that was not predicted by the computer model, it can be remedied. Modern aeronautical designs are developed on computers, but no one ever buys a ticket on a commercial jet before a prototype has been flown for many hours.

The social issue at stake when judging model fit is perhaps the most important of all. To ask whether a fit is adequate is to make a judgment call. If we conclude that a proposed nuclear waste repository will not release "significant" radionuclides into the biosphere, we have implicitly invoked a notion of "significance" that rests in turn on prior judgments of socially, politically, and ethically acceptable levels of environmental impact. The same is true for virtually all models that deal with environmental issues. The literature of numerical modeling is filled with words like "adequate," "acceptable," "reasonable," and "significant," yet rarely is there any attempt to define the basis for these judgments. One reason is obvious: Scientists do not like to talk in these terms. Science, at least in our idealized sense of it, is supposed to be about facts, not judgments. Scientists are not trained to talk about questions of moral value. Yet, at root, all environmental issues involve questions of moral value, and judgment is the basis upon which we stake our moral claims. Computer modeling, like all quantification in science, appeals to our sense of objectivity, but even the most mathematically and computationally sophisticated model will not absolve us of the need for judgment, nor of the need to justify our judgments in human terms.

COMPLEXITY IS THE STRENGTH AND WEAKNESS OF NUMERICAL MODELS

The power of contemporary computers allows earth scientists to examine complex processes and systems—the lithosphere, the oceans, the atmosphere, the flow of groundwater—that are not readily studied by other means. These systems sustain life on Earth; and if we fail to understand them, we endanger not merely the quality of our lives, but ultimately life itself. Theirs is no small contribution, for computer models have helped us gain a better understanding of the Earth's complex life-supporting processes. The ability to represent such systems is the obvious strength of models. Their weakness is that these complex models are nonunique, their predictions may be in error, and the scale of their predictions can make them difficult if not impossible to test. Furthermore—and this is perhaps the most important point of all—we cannot separate our judgment of the adequacy of our models from our judgment of the social and moral consequences of the effects we are trying to model.

When scientists construct laboratory experiments to test a theory, they abstract a portion of the physical world in order to ask certain kinds of questions. Computer modelers do the same thing. Numerical simulations are abstractions of the natural world that allow us to ask certain kinds of questions. Not surprising, modelers sometimes call their work "numerical experiments." The laboratory scientist, in constructing a physical experiment, sacrifices the complexity of the natural world for the tractability of a simplified experimental setup. How serious this sacrifice is depends on the problem at hand and cannot be predetermined. Laboratory experiments have provided crucial tools in the history of science, but they have also misled people. The same duality will no doubt prove true for numerical experiments. In numerical modeling, complexity can be preserved but at the cost of physical and intellectual accessibility. Like the sacrifice of complexity inherent in traditional forms of experimentation, the significance of the loss of accessibility is difficult to judge. Past experience tells us what kinds of problems are tackled effectively in the laboratory; future experience will have to do the same for computer modeling.

The traditional point of contact between a laboratory experiment and the natural world is the experimental outcome; but in numerical models, the main point of contact is the *input*. In principle, models allow for input and synthesis of large quantities of information—and this is a very great strength—but in practice, the availability of data from the natural world has not kept pace with advances in theory and computation. And it can be exceedingly difficult for an outsider to judge the quantity and quality of data in a model. A model may give the impression of being grounded in empirical evidence, yet be largely a theoretical edifice. This reality may be what makes some people uncomfortable with computer models. If the ultimate strength of scientific knowledge is its grounding in empirical phenomena, then we should be uncomfortable if the empirical basis of a model is difficult to ascertain. Modeling may lead to greater rigor in the evaluation of earth processes, but it may also propagate the illusion that things are better known than they really are.

SO WHAT DO WE DO?

All models depend on data; and in the earth sciences, data are collected by direct encounters with the Earth. As our models become increasingly sophisticated, the need for data obtained through human encounters with nature will increase rather than decrease. Field-based empirical evidence is essential if we are to understand the distribution of earth materials that control the flow of fluids in the crust, the patterns of ocean circulation that affect climate on a regional scale, or the weather patterns that determine the dispersal of atmospheric pollutants.

Field evidence also provides a complement to reliance on long-term model predictions. No sensible person would wish to court disaster by ignoring the threat of global warming, but neither would any sensible society wish to spend large sums of money solving a problem that does not exist. Geologists can help to determine the extent of global change by studying its effects in presently observable geological processes. Temperature-sensitive natural geological processes like the calving of glacial ice or the evaporation rates in inland lakes can provide direct evidence of climate change. Study of radioactive elements in natural geological environments can teach us about the likely behavior of these and similar elements in nuclear waste repositories without having to wait ten thousand years.

Perhaps the most important perspective geology and geologists can contribute to environmental debates is historical. Uncertainty surrounds environmental questions because there is much about the Earth that we do not understand. In particular, we do not know whether the changes we are currently witnessing are part of the Earth's natural cycle, the result of human activities, or both. The Earth's climate has cooled and warmed many times in geological history: How can we know for sure whether the changes of the twentieth century are caused by human activities or are merely the latest cycle in the Earth's long record of change? Geology can help to provide an answer, because the rock record is the record of Earth's history. Humans have been keeping weather records for a little more than a century and studying the migration of fluids and elements in the crust for a few decades, but rocks have been recording evidence of these processes for nearly four billion years. Geologists can use the rock record to deepen our understanding of the Earth's natural processes and the ways in which human activities may be transforming them.

Computer models of natural processes may be limited by mathematical understanding, computational power, or data. In recent years, there have been great advances in mathematical treatment of complex systems and staggering advances in computational power. But these have not been matched by comparable advances in data from the natural world. Like any chain of reasoning, computer models are only as strong as their weakest link. Without evidence from the physical world, both as input to models and as a check on them, we run the risk of constructing computational houses of cards. And without discussion of the criteria by which we judge our models, we run the risk of obscuring the profound social issues at stake in the shadows of our edifices of computational prowess.

7

Down to Earth: A Historical Look at Government-Sponsored Geology

Gordon P. Eaton

A mile and a half from my house, at the top of a low coastal bluff looking out through the Strait of Juan de Fuca, there is a thick, tarnished brass disk, three and one-half inches across, embedded in a heavy slab of concrete. Around the upper half of the circumference of this disk are stamped the words *National Ocean Survey*, and below them the word *tidal*, plus some alphanumeric characters required to identify uniquely this particular benchmark in a federal data base. There are hundreds of thousands, if not millions, of permanent brass benchmarks throughout the United States; each defines a carefully and accurately surveyed location required for different purposes, to determine a tide level, to mark the exact corner of a square mile section of public land, or to provide a surveyor with the precise geospatial location of the point of land on which the benchmark was set. These benchmarks carry the stamped label, *U.S. Coast and Geodetic Survey* (another name for the National Ocean Survey), or *U.S. General Land Office Survey*, or *U.S. Department of Interior, Geological Survey*.

Many Geological Survey benchmarks are cemented into rock outcrops on hilltops or mountaintops that command open views of the surrounding countryside. Each constitutes a permanent control point established for the purpose of making a detailed topographic map of the area. Maps of this type are published and sold to the public at nominal cost. Some 57,000 of these detailed topographic quadrangle maps—"topo quads"—were required to chart the 48 contiguous United States, a daunting task that took decades to complete.

Preparing and updating these maps is one of many responsibilities of the U.S. Geological Survey (USGS), an agency established by the United States Congress in 1879. As old as it is, it is still a veritable youngster as such organizations go, for the British Geological Survey (BGS) was created in 1835 and the Geological Survey of Canada came into being in 1842.

In earlier years of the nineteenth century, and in the years between the establishment of the BGS and USGS, a number of pioneering state geological surveys were also created in the United States. They still exist. In fact, by 1879, when the USGS was formed somewhat belatedly, 20 nations had already established geological surveys. They, too, continue to this day. What is it about geology that is universally important to nations and their people?

THE STACCATO EMERGENCE OF U.S. GEOLOGY

That geology figured importantly in the minds of leaders in the United States was first evident in 1803 when Congress appropriated funds for Meriwether Lewis and William Clark's Corps of Discovery. Thirty-one years later, Congress designated funds so that the U.S. Army could prepare a geological map of the country. Evidence of on-and-off interest continued with congressional funding for a U.S.–Mexico Border Survey in 1849 and, then, for a Pacific Railroad Survey in 1853.

Finally, a third of a century after the British Parliament established Great Britain's standing survey, our Congress began to authorize and fund significant examinations of large parts of the western United States, examinations in which geology was a major objective. The value and potential of this science would steep in the minds of Congressmen like fine tea leaves for 45 years before the brew that was to become the USGS was eventually served up, sealing its important role in the United States.

In 1867, Clarence King, a young graduate of Yale University, led the first of four congressionally authorized surveys of the West. Later, he became the first director of the new USGS, the ultimate successor to the regional surveys, and made the USGS a bureau of deliberately practical geology.

A HISTORY OF THE U.S. GEOLOGICAL SURVEY

When Congress established the U.S. Geological Survey, it placed the agency in the Interior Department and charged it with classification of public lands, and examination of the geological structure, mineral resources, and products of the nation. To this day, its name, general mission, and responsibilities remain arguably unchanged. Such simple facts tend to obscure the important truth that both the science of geology and the kaleidoscopic nature of the USGS have changed substantially and continuously with time. For 120 years, the USGS has responded to our evolving circumstances and met the changing needs of the United States.

In the next millennium, our society will confront a set of problems different from those of both the past and the present, problems that earth scientists can tackle because of their understanding of the essential wholeness of earth systems. As the scope of earth science has become interdisciplinary, broadly trained geoscientists are perhaps uniquely qualified to address the great national myriad issues in the future.

Why has continuous change in our federal earth science agency taken place? The answer is that the USGS is a living organism that evolves in concert with changes in its external environment, changes that are at once societal, economic, scientific, and political. Old tasks have assumed less national importance, and new pursuits, ones that require skills different from those previously needed, have moved to the top of the agency's agenda. So it is with the issue of mineral resources. In the past, the USGS emphasized understanding of the origin of mineral resources. Today, the USGS confronts a different set of pressing issues related to global change, conservation, and environmental contamination and degradation, to cite but a few.

Metallic mineral resources mattered greatly to the United States during the Industrial Revolution and throughout the two World Wars. They were the principal subject of the first investigative work of the fledgling USGS under Clarence King's direction. In the last decade or two, however, the rise of the information age, the emergence of an interdependent global marketplace and economy, meaningful and successful attention to the recycling of metals, and the creation and widespread use of synthetic materials have lessened this emphasis. Some of these new synthetic materials have been substituted for metals at very competitive prices. Others exhibit superior performance characteristics.

In addition, there is deep concern for Earth's environment—an environment locally devastated in the past by thoughtless mining and smelting practices. These facts have conjoined to lessen national interest in the production of domestic mineral resources. Nevertheless, the USGS still plays a critical role with regard to mineral resources, but it differs from that of long ago: Earth scientists are needed to remedy problems caused by past mining activities. As issues of environmental remediation assume higher national priority, required scientific skills change the makeup, shape, and orientation of a scientific and technical organization such as the USGS.

The history of the USGS reflects Charles Darwin's assertion that it is not the strongest of a species that survives, nor, perhaps, even the most intelligent, but the one most responsive to the pressures of change. As we know, continuity of a species in the biological world is assured through a reproductive process in which adjustments to the specific requirements of a new environment are tested and weighed, and the appropriate ones selected. It seems that the same is true for the evolution, survival, and continuity of organizations.[1]

Changing Work of the U.S. Geological Survey

Several of the earliest geological investigations in the United States were undertaken in the middle to late nineteenth century to support agriculture, then the principal basis for the country's economy. As agricultural productivity slowly diminished, some thought that perhaps science could help. Also, around the same time, in preparation for road and canal construction, topographic and engineering surveys with geological implications were made. Not long after, the federal government needed an informed basis on which to classify public lands as either agricultural or mineral lands before allowing them to be sold.

By 1859, the value of U.S. industrial products exceeded that of agricultural products and an understanding of mineral resources became paramount. The Industrial Revolution was underway and raw mineral materials were vital to it. Then, in the last part of the nineteenth century, water availability became especially significant as the nation's population grew and expanded into the vast semiarid and arid regions of the west.

Throughout these early years, the science of geology matured and repeatedly contributed in relevant and practical ways to problems of the times. Once established, the USGS played a vital role in that arena. Along the way, however, USGS scientists collected and interpreted observational data and elucidated fundamental earth processes. They therefore advanced fundamental geological knowledge.

By the beginning of the twentieth century, interest in nonmetalliferous mineral resources, including fossil fuels, rose. Although attention to metals continued, much of it focused on what came to be called strategic minerals—those minerals considered important to "national security." The USGS provided the nation with developed expertise on these issues as well as in engineering geology, marine geology, land-resource and environmental studies, water quality and supply, underground storage of radioactive and other hazardous wastes, and natural hazards such as earthquakes, volcanic eruptions, landslides, and floods.

Basic Science and Practical Geology

In the last 100 years or more, palpable tension has existed between what came early to be called basic ("pure") research and practical ("applied") research. Geologists have felt this tension. As the first director of the USGS, Clarence King purposefully emphasized practical research. His successor, John Wesley Powell, a one-armed Union officer from the Civil War and the first white explorer of the Grand Canyon, chose primarily to emphasize basic inquiry. Although both approaches were rational, they elicited different responses in their times, responses reflected in the degree of funding appropriated to the USGS by the Congress. King's approach held greater value for the Congress, and consequently, his USGS enjoyed a greater operating budget than did Powell's.

During Powell's tenure as director of the USGS, Congress became concerned that the work of the Survey had become mostly irrelevant to what they regarded as important national issues. As a result, Congress cut USGS funding to make their point with Powell when he did not respond to their expressions of concern. And for a time late on Powell's watch, matters grew so testy that talk in the mining industry and in the cloak rooms of Congress suggested the return of Clarence King as director of the Survey. That did not happen, but the message from Congress was abundantly clear.

The third director of the USGS, Charles Doolittle Walcott, attempted to explain, achieve, and promote amongst the public a balance between basic and practical research. Walcott emphasized that the Survey existed to serve the practical needs of the nation. He argued, however, that in order to do so, it must also advance basic scientific understanding. In those early days, the science of geology was still a relative infant and the number of its practitioners was small. As a result, limited knowledge constrained the influence of the science.

The Effect of the National Science Foundation

From 1879 to 1950, funds to support geological science came from the Congress and went to the USGS almost exclusively. Earth scientists working as college and university faculty members pursued their passion for geology without the benefit of federal support. However, that changed in 1950 when the National Science Foundation (NSF) was created and scientists across the whole academic community in our country could compete for funds to support their research. What before had been an almost exclusive right of the USGS to federal funds in support of earth science came to be widely shared. Much vital and important geoscience research was now conducted outside the Survey with the support of federal dollars specifically directed elsewhere—and like all nonclassified research in the United States, it was broadly and readily available to all scientists to advance their work.

Less than two decades after the NSF was established, the relative proportion of university geoscientists granted coveted memberships in the National Academy of Sciences grew substantially.[2] As the proportion of university geoscientists in the Academy rose, the proportion of those from the USGS fell. This situation created concern in some circles that the Geological Survey had lost its scientific edge.

In response to the fact that more scientists were successfully engaged in geology, particularly research that was curiosity driven, USGS scientists focused their research efforts in order to advance understanding of a topic related to a specific mission. This shift did not signal the end of fundamental inquiry—basic science—in the USGS. Research at the USGS simply reemphasized specific practical objectives articulated in programs funded by Congress for the direct benefit of the people of the United States.

For the past half-century, substantial contributions to our grasp of earth systems have come from the university community. USGS geoscientists still conduct basic research, but it differs in proportion from that of the past and it varies across the four formal divisions of the Survey, divisions that I describe briefly here. Before we turn to them, however, we need to pause to examine where Walcott's successor took the USGS as director and how the organization changed under his leadership.

The Fourth Director and Recent History

George O. Smith, fourth director of the USGS, served for 23 years, the longest of any director before or since. But for most of his long term in office, Congressional appropriations for the USGS stagnated. In the absence of sufficient direct appropriations from Congress, Smith took advantage of funding opportunities provided by other agencies—especially those available for water resource investigations and topographic mapping. He turned to these opportunities, mindful of his responsibility to maintain the momentum of the Survey and to promote its growth.

One result of Smith's inclination, however was a controversial personnel move—a move occasioned by the establishment of the Land Classification Board, a federal organization newly created to reflect and help implement the policies and actions of the Theodore Roosevelt and William Taft administrations regarding conservation. Smith had USGS scientists transferred from positions of fundamental inquiry in the Survey to the well-funded land classification program. This administrative action motivated some geologists to seek employment elsewhere because they did not regard the land classification work as intellectually demanding or personally interesting. Thus, the USGS pendulum swung toward "customer" needs and away from fundamental inquiry.

Within the USGS today, Smith's directorship is generally not recalled with great admiration for this and other reasons—among them an attempt to run the agency on a more businesslike basis.[3] Although Smith apparently strove to assure organizational coherence and continuity, some chose to see his efforts as purposeful diminishment of the scientific backbone of the Survey. Others believe that, in part, he was suspect because he was appointed director from within the USGS without having first had a significant apprenticeship as a scientist. In deference to long-serving Director Smith, who has never been offered much of it, his actions arguably helped the USGS grow in two areas, water and mapping, despite low funding. Eventually, these fields achieved full status as divisions of the USGS.

In retrospect, what happened to the Survey during Smith's directorship exemplifies the effects of pressure exerted on a federal organization by its external environment. Government science is conducted in a political environment in which the legislative and executive branches play a significant role in "calling the shots"—they assign funds.

During a period following the end of World War II when federal funds were widely available to many government agencies, the USGS was remarkably free to set its own research agenda, with only limited intervention. Not until the 1980s and 1990s did Congress and the President of the United States once again strongly exert their influence on the USGS through limited funding growth and directed funding. The pressure of politics culminated, as we shall see, in 1995 with a threat to abolish the agency.

The alternating emphases on basic science and practical research by the USGS in the first half-century is in no way at odds with the present. From today's perspective of competing national priorities, significant constraints on federal dollars available to science, and pressing issues of the environment— earthquake hazards, declining water quality, wildfire fuel state determination, ecosystem degradation and restoration, and increasing coastal erosion—it appears that the next decade or two will be much like the first few and require the directed attention of earth scientists. Societal concerns and national needs will drive much of the work of USGS scientists. Relevance and practical significance will be once again a yardstick by which the societal value of the agency will be measured.

Today we can see that issues which our country will confront in the twenty-first century differ from those which occupied it in the nineteenth and twentieth centuries. By looking back in time, we can also see that we have been fortunate to have had as part of our federal government an organization that has been flexible enough to adapt to meet the changing needs of our society— the USGS has broadened people's understanding of our physical and now, our biological world, a fact to which we shall return. First, however, we'll look a little more closely at the subjects of mapping and water.

The Growing Importance of Maps and Water

Accurate, detailed maps of the nation have been required throughout a long period of national economic and cultural development. They have been prepared and provided by the USGS. This work led to our capability to characterize the Earth's surface and monitor and analyze some of its resources and aspects of its physical and biological state from space. For example, we can now observe the greenness of vegetation across the country, watch it evolve as seasons develop, recognize plant communities under stress, and oversee the onset of drought or recovery from it. The evolution of the old USGS Topographic Division into today's National Mapping Division has been remarkable; it has rapidly adapted emerging technologies to diverse resultant capacities.

The Water Resources Division represents another success story in the evolution of the USGS. When it comes to the subject of water resources in the United States, most of the nation's scientific and technical understanding over many decades has come from the USGS and the Department of Agriculture. Scientific understanding of our water resources grew from early practical work at the USGS, but development of hydrologic theory did not begin in earnest until the 1960s. Before then, a small handful of USGS research hydrologists gained intellectual prominence as a result of their contributions. Few universities included hydrology programs, and the hydrologic consulting industry had not developed. Even the National Science Foundation had not yet recognized hydrology as a distinct branch of geoscience. Although the situation has changed today, the science that has developed in the last few decades has its origins in the pioneering work of the USGS on water quantity, availability, quality, and use, as well as on floods and droughts. Water is one of our most vital natural resources today and one for which global needs will only grow. Unlike certain metals, no substitute for water is on the horizon, nor will there likely ever be one. Our understanding of this life-giving resource owes much to the USGS.

A Restless Kaleidoscope of Organizational Arrangements

As we have seen, Clarence King emphasized mining geology on his watch as the Survey's first director. He relegated subjects including paleontology and topographic mapping to a role supporting the primary effort, mineral exploration.

King's Survey consisted of only two formal divisions: Mining Geology and General Geology. Future director John Wesley Powell headed the General Geology Division. As change came and growth occurred, the USGS reorganized itself into new configurations and administrative arrangements. But the longer a given set of configurations remained in effect, the harder and higher the walls between units became; this situation resulted in varying degrees of intellectual isolation and lack of communication across divisions of the Survey. Over time, the scientific and technical programs of the USGS evolved so that they were not integrated across divisions and were conducted solely within divisional units.

As director, Powell subdivided General Geology into ten divisions: five concerned with geology and five with paleontology. New and distinctive work began to discern the distribution of forest lands, to facilitate irrigation of arid and semiarid lands, and to provide flood relief for the lower Mississippi River valley. The irrigation efforts, prompted largely by settlement of the Great Plains, included the selection of sites for water storage reservoirs and studies of the extent to which semiarid land might be utilized for irrigated crops. History shows us that it was Powell who started the USGS toward work with Earth's hydrosphere, but Charles Walcott and George Smith pursued it vigorously when each directed the Survey.

The Secretary of the Interior appointed Charles Walcott as Geologist-in-Charge of Geology and Paleontology during the last year of Powell's directorship. And under Walcott's leadership, water resources work began in earnest. He established a Hydrographic Division in 1902, which took its place alongside divisions of Physical and Chemical Research, Geology and Paleontology, and Mining and Mineral Resources. In 1903, he added a division of Alaskan Mineral Resources. Although change was underway, a great deal more was still to come.

When the United States entered World War I in 1917 and George Smith was director of the Survey, he created a division of Military Surveys and transferred a number of scientists in the Topographic Branch[4] to the U.S. Army Corps of

Engineers. After the war, the previously established Land Classification Branch was renamed the Conservation Branch, a name it retained until 1982. Scientists in that division classified public lands according to use, promoted development of mineral deposits on public lands, and worked to protect the public's interests in undeveloped mineral, agricultural, and hydropower resources. The Conservation Branch also supervised mineral lease operations on public lands, work that required mining and petroleum engineers, who worked with geologists, hydrologists, and topographic engineers of the other USGS divisions.

By World War II, the USGS had settled into an organizational arrangement consisting of four branches: Geologic, Water Resources, Topographic, and Conservation. It retained this configuration until the early 1980s. In the meantime, the name of the Topographic Division was changed to that of the National Mapping Division in order to reflect better its significantly expanded responsibilities in geography and remote sensing from space. Still more change came in 1982 when the Secretary of the Interior separated the Survey's Conservation Division into its own agency, the Minerals Management Service. From then until 1996, the USGS consisted of the remaining three divisions.

In 1996, the organizational kaleidoscope was turned once again, this time fairly vigorously by Congress, with my agreement, as the twelfth director of the USGS and that of the Interior Secretary. We moved scientists from the National Biological Service to the USGS to create a new division in the USGS: the Biological Resources Division.

AN ANXIOUS MOMENT—THE 104TH CONGRESS THREATENS TO ABOLISH THE USGS

The Honorable Bruce Babbitt was Secretary of the Interior when I was director of the USGS. At that time, the Republican leadership in Congress was deeply divided about whether to eliminate government biological work accomplished through the National Biological Service. Some legislators believed that the work of that organization was tied to the Endangered Species Act, a law that they abhorred for perceived infringements on private property rights. Other lawmakers believed that the work of the National Biological Service should continue, even if in a different guise. These policymakers approached Secretary Babbitt and me separately about the issue. Secretary Babbitt had created the National Biological Service in the first place and had done so at some political risk because he believed very deeply in its importance to the nation; he was amenable to a solution that would both preserve it in some coherent form and keep it within the Interior Department. As lawmakers held separate discussions with the Secretary, I was asked about the scientific advantages and disadvantages of adding the National Biological Service to the U.S. Geological Survey.

Two years earlier, while at Columbia University as head of the Lamont-Doherty Earth Observatory, I had served on a committee of the National

Research Council charged with designing a national biological survey. I was one of five members of the committee who was not a biologist. As a result of my participation in this work, I endorsed enthusiastically the idea of including the National Biological Service in the USGS. I saw unparalleled scientific opportunities resulting from it. Nonetheless, the newly elected majority in Congress threatened to abolish the USGS. In the end, after much long, nerve-jangling suspense, the USGS did incorporate the National Biological Service.

At the time of this move, the USGS had only a few biologists on its staff— they were part of the Mineral Resources Program of the Geologic Division, because plants had been found to be good geochemical indicators of hidden metal deposits. A few other biologists were part of the National Water Quality Assessment program of the Water Resources Division. With the acquisition of the National Biological Service, the USGS now included an entire division of biologists. Just how well this long-lived agency can adapt to its new circumstance remains to be seen. The long historical record suggests that this latest change, although intellectually profound, will be taken in stride. Most important, the incorporation of the National Biological Service into the U.S. Geological Survey offers an unprecedented opportunity to join geology and biology more fully to define and understand earth systems.

When the 104th Congress threatened to abolish the USGS in late 1994 and early 1995, newly elected lawmakers were eager to reduce the size, scope, and reach of federal government. As a long-standing institution that had grown to look inward as it planned its future, the USGS occupied a conspicuous place on a hit list of allegedly unresponsive or irrelevant agencies that some in Congress wanted to eliminate. Absent concern for or understanding of the potential effect of such a move, these policymakers argued that work of the USGS was basically finished and that elimination of the agency would free federal funds, help lower the federal deficit, and facilitate tax cuts.

Also on the hit list were two other bureaus from the Interior Department, the Bureau of Mines and the National Biological Service. Congress took steps that allowed them virtually to eliminate both these organizations so that neither seems any longer to exist. However, both cases involved sleight of hand— the National Biological Service continues under a new guise and the Bureau of Mines was dissected, with certain parts eliminated and others moved to agencies including the USGS.

After a significant budget and personnel reduction, the National Biological Service sank beneath the waves to reappear as the Biological Resources Division at the dockside of the USGS. The Minerals Information team of the Bureau of Mines relocated to the long-standing Mineral Resources program of the USGS. Ironically, some of the very functions that the Minerals Information team had performed were part of the USGS earlier in the century, demonstrating once again that what goes around, comes around.

The biologists and the minerals information scientists brought new responsibilities to the Survey and altered its mission. Today, the Biological

Resources Division is the size of the National Mapping Division and is only slightly smaller than the Geologic Division. The Water Resources Division, on the other hand, is larger than the other three combined and reflects our nation's growing concern about water resource issues.

The USGS is unique in the world; the geological surveys of many other nations have either never had or have lost mapping and water functions, and none have biological components. A multidisciplinary agency that has changed steadily from the time of its first director, its scientists have worked with those in other federal and state bureaus for decades. These facts were part of the basis for its survival when the Congress threatened to eliminate it. Its demise was averted in substantial part also by its clients', customers', and partners' recognition of the practical and meaningful value of its work. These constituents asked Congress to allow the USGS to continue its work to provide the knowledge, services, and products that they and the general public required. For its part, Survey scientists learned a valuable lesson—that its viability and prosperity ultimately depended on its ability to demonstrate the relevance and significance of its work to society. We also learned that we must work to communicate our findings to a wide audience—one that extends beyond traditional professional and scientific societies. Congress is one of these other audiences—one of the most important, for federally funded science takes place in a political environment. Political priorities dictate the allocation of federal funds, including those in support of science. It is not enough now for talented scientists simply to do outstanding work. They must explain and define science's societal payoffs if they are to continue to be funded.

THE UTILITY OF RESEARCH ORGANIZED AROUND PROBLEMS

The dawn of the last 25 years of the twentieth century saw an organizational format for the USGS that reflected a reductionist approach to earth science—the notion that a whole entity can be understood in terms of its component parts. Reductionism is not without a rational basis in science. It was characteristic of most fields of scientific inquiry throughout the twentieth century and can still be seen in our universities, as well as in the structure of geoscience programs of the National Science Foundation.

At the USGS, boundaries among the three long-standing divisons had grown rigid, and only rarely did a scientist seize an opportunity to work synergistically with colleagues of a different discipline or tackle a problem that transcended organizational domains. The USGS had become a "holding company," with its human and fiscal resources belonging to individual divisions. Programs were not integrated.

Fine structure within the USGS was little different. Individual disciplinary branches of Experimental Geochemistry and Mineralogy, Paleontology and Stratigraphy, Geophysics, Water Quality, Groundwater, and Surface Water existed and, like Caesar's Gaul, geoscientific knowledge and work was divided and pigeonholed. Scientists in different fields of specialization examined problems from within the restrictive domains of their disciplines. Depth, rather than breadth, of study was valued and understanding of a narrow subject was advanced by isolating individual parts of larger problems. Generalists were often denigrated and sometimes unfairly judged to be dilettantes. Solo research efforts were highly regarded and therefore scientific teamwork was uncommon, as can be judged from the great number of single-authored scientific papers of the time.

In this milieu, large investigative problems and contexts were necessarily reduced to isolated parts, the remaining elements of the whole left to others. Often, however, these "others" were unidentified. Rarely did any one scientist address a whole problem. Although perhaps overstated, this model operated despite the Survey's early history with the Congress and the lessons it might have learned. Today much of that is changed.

An example of integrative research done early by USGS scientists comes from the Yellowstone region of northwestern Wyoming. One of the great natural wonders of the North American continent, because of its stunning uniqueness and great beauty it was designated as the world's first national park. Many of its features have long been recognized to be those of active volcanoes in other parts of the world: the presence of fumaroles, hot springs, geysers, minerals deposited at the surface by hot, subterranean waters, and extensive outcrops of lava and ash flows. Clearly, these features are volcanic ones, but there is no obvious volcanic edifice here—no mountain—only a very broad, high plateau. During the 1960s and 1970s, interdisciplinary studies involving USGS geochemists, geophysicists, petrologists, mineralogists, hydrologists, glacial geologists, and field geological mappers revealed and explained the complex relationships between the geological history of the area, the circulation and chemical activity of ground and surface waters, and the origin of the intense heat, an origin that leads occasionally to an almost imperceptible swelling and deflating of the ground surface in parts of the park. It is a highly complex natural system that required the application of many branches of science to understand it. Today we also recognize that there are several highly significant biological stories linked to the geological ones in Yellowstone National Park.

Understanding about our nation's geothermal energy resources owes much to the early work at Yellowstone as well as the work of USGS scientists at Steamboat Springs in western Nevada and The Geysers in northern California. Hot groundwater—water that fell originally as rain or snow and percolated downward—is driven toward the surface in all these areas by a geological source of heat, often a shallow, buried "puddle" of molten rock that geologists call magma. The hot waters are extremely active, altering the minerals present in the rocks through which they flow and depositing new ones in their place and at the surface. The upward movement of this hot water constitutes a form of mass and energy transfer, and the heat energy itself can be "captured" and put to many practical uses, including generation of electricity. Yellowstone National Park and geothermal energy are in many ways synonymous.

In the study of geothermal resources in general and Yellowstone in particular, scientific leaders in the USGS brought together teams of diverse specialists from several scientific disciplines and organizational divisions to address the whole of the major issues. When this work was done, though, the divisions pretty much returned to their old way of doing business—they went their individual ways.

It is somewhat ironic that while Walcott was director of the USGS, he chaired a presidential committee appointed to examine the scientific efforts of the U.S. government in order to enhance the usefulness and economy of scientific work. Walcott was acutely conscious of both the scientific *and* the political success of King's approach to running the Survey, as opposed to that of Powell. Some of the final recommendations of his committee have relevance here. The committee recommended that scientific work sponsored by the government should be restricted primarily to useful purposes—it should be practical; that basic science should be undertaken primarily by private institutions; and, that government research should be organized, not around scientific disciplines, but around a problem.

Nine decades later, after following these recommendations in part but not all, the USGS has embraced these concepts in an explicit and substantial way. It was galvanized to do so by the cocking of a powerful arm whose hand held a lethal bolt of lightning, the same arm and hand that earlier had used a club to get John Wesley Powell's attention: the U.S. Congress and its talk of abolishment.

Today, USGS work focuses on four major themes of an integrated nature: resources, geological and hydrological hazards, environment, and integrated data management and analysis. Beyond our nation's human resources, which most would surely agree are of inestimable value, our water, energy, biota, minerals, and land represent our next most important resources. They play a vital role in sustaining our economic strength and growth. Natural geological and hydrological hazards constitute nonpreventable events that can potentially expose people to death or injury, property loss or damage, and degraded infrastructure. We must learn how to live with them. Human activities have significant adverse impacts on our environment and must be recognized, identified, measured, and finally, mitigated, if we are to preserve a livable future on Earth. Finally, sound information management and analysis can make knowledge available and useful to a broad, diverse audience.

Our society must approach today's highest priority earth science problems from an interdisciplinary perspective, one that capitalizes on an array of scientific skills and technical strengths that are not separated but formally integrated. Addition of the Biological Resources Division to the USGS currently allows the scientific community to integrate the physical and biological field sciences, which together help us understand whole earth systems rather than isolated fragments of those systems.

Coupled with its valuable historical databases and its capability to conduct long-lasting, broad-scale studies of areas of varying geographical dimension, the USGS—now nearly 120 years old—studies the whole of several complex natural systems using teams of diverse specialists. The members of Charles Walcott's committee on the usefulness of government science would doubtless smile because, nearly a century after they first proposed it, practical science is happening widely across the USGS.

THE U.S. GEOLOGICAL SURVEY AND THE NEXT MILLENNIUM

Recently, a cross section of scientists, technicians, and administrators prepared the Survey's first comprehensive strategic plan for future endeavors of the agency. The plan outlines a decadal road map by which to address priority societal concerns. And it articulates the importance of having scientists from different divisions and disciplines work together to address these societal needs.

The Survey's plan calls for the following types of issues to be addressed: water availability and quality, natural hazards, geographical and cartographical information needs, threats of contaminated environments, future land use, biological and nonrenewable resources, and health effects that originate from aberrations in the geological, hydrological, and biological environments. The breadth of earth science makes earth scientists uniquely qualified to tackle problems of our environment, for the problems are complex and intellectually demanding problems of whole systems.

What is the probable shape of the future? It is illustrated by the Mojave Desert Ecosystem Science Program of the USGS—a six-year, integrated, interdisciplinary study of the vulnerability of a desert ecosystem to both natural and human-induced disturbances.[5]

The Mojave program aims to enhance our awareness of the fundamental physical and biological processes necessary to assess ecosystem vulnerability and recoverability. In practical terms, scientists involved in the program hope to help land and biota recover from negative human disturbances. They also hope to derive knowledge that can assist land managers to devise policies and practices that will permit human use of the desert, while, at the same time, protecting and preserving its fragile resources. It is an example of practical science, with underpinnings adapted from fundamental inquiry.

Desert surfaces are inherently fragile, easily damaged entities. Many different uses of the land can disrupt the thin crust that influences the dispersal of plants by wind and protects this landscape from erosion by wind and water. Distribution and species composition of the desert surface, as well as its fragility, is being evaluated as part of this program. Another scientific objective will be to determine the natural variability of this desert ecosystem on several different time scales: years, decades, and centuries. A third objective will be to describe the vegetation of both disturbed and undisturbed sites. The descriptions will be used to construct models that define the physiological mechanisms of vegetation distribution in the desert.

Evidence of system disturbance will be measured in terms of soil compaction, wind and water erosion, and disruption of surface water flows. Soil characteristics (moisture, particle size, chemistry, and mineralogy), vegetation cover types, distribution of vertebrate species, ages of the land surfaces, intensity of rainfall, and frequency of freeze and thaw cycles will be tracked by using a Geographic Information System (GIS), and data will be extended to environmentally similar settings. Remote sensing from both aircraft and space platforms will be investigated for its potential to extrapolate to neighboring areas the local landscape characteristics that have been defined by studies on the ground. Remote sensing will also contribute to the development of a strategy to define the vital signs of the desert ecosystem.

This kind of science should give land managers the tools—maps, digital geospatial databases, and models produced within a GIS—that they will need to look at the ecosystem health of the desert today, as well as that of yesterday and of tomorrow. Results of the Mojave Desert Ecosystem Science Program, like other USGS research, will be available to ordinary citizens, state and local governments, Native American tribes, other bureaus of the Interior Department, and any federal agency that must make informed decisions regarding the management of desert lands. The results of the work should be applicable to desert settings on any continent.

Many fundamental questions will arise as this program progresses and will need to be addressed. The project will produce abundant opportunities for scientific inquiry and papers for the peer-reviewed scientific literature. It exemplifies "practical science."

EARTH SCIENCE: A LOCUS FOR PLANNING FOR THE NEXT CENTURY

The breadth of earth science today is greater than it has ever been; therefore, geology coupled with biology should be regarded logically as one of the most critical areas of science for the twenty-first century. Of course, history will judge how effective this approach turns out to be.

The USGS today provides the nation with timely and reliable information that is used to manage our precious natural resources of water, biota, land, energy, and minerals, minimize loss of life and property during and after the occurrence of inevitable natural disasters, and contribute to a sustainable future through wise economic development. It helps to meet the nation's need for basic geospatial data, including information about our natural resources, that furnish insight and technology to design and support sound management and conservation practices. Also, although natural disasters cannot be prevented, we can lessen their impact substantially through the use of data acquired and interpreted by USGS scientists; such data facilitates meaningful hazard assessments and mitigation planning. In sum, the USGS contributes to our abilities to protect and enhance the quality of life in this country.

As the next millennium begins, we must understand our natural resources in innovative ways, that is, in global, economic, and environmental contexts. This approach differs from that of the past. We also need to anticipate with accuracy the environmental consequences of climate variability, whether natural or induced by humans. We are compelled to define ecosystems more comprehensively and in all their various dimensions—biological, hydrologic, geological, and geospatial—and to elucidate the subtle and not-so-subtle links between human and aquatic health and the hydrologic and geological processes that contribute to them. A burgeoning world population obliges us to grasp fully the problems associated with the isolation of now-staggering amounts of waste we in the United States generate. Innovative management practices must be developed as we keep in mind domestic, commercial, industrial, agricultural, recreational, and ecological uses of resources. In addition to all this, we must advance an information infrastructure that can provide simple access to the data, information, and technology that bear on these important issues of the immediate future. Hand in hand, earth and biological sciences have the capacity to provide a sound scientific framework for working on these issues as no other science has before.

8

Sustainable Living: Common Ground for Geology and Theology

George W. Fisher

We notice the small things first: Another farm is converted to tract housing; Chesapeake oysters are no longer served at a favorite restaurant; suburban lawns are parched by an unaccustomed water shortage. More serious signs appear on the evening news: Honduran villages are decimated in the aftermath of a hurricane; epidemic cholera incubated in abnormally warm coastal waters spreads throughout South America, long cholera free; Earth's population has doubled in the last 45 years and may do so again. Two hundred years after Malthus's *Essay on the Principle of Population* appeared, we again begin to wonder how well Earth can support our grandchildren, and we coin the word *sustainability*.

What does it take to achieve a sustainable way of life? We need to understand how the Earth works—how its individual components, the biosphere, solid earth, atmosphere, and hydrosphere, operate on their own, and how they interact with one another as a system. We need to understand how resources are produced and renewed, how climate is controlled and rainfall distributed. But we need more than scientific understanding. We need the wisdom to make agonizingly difficult choices on issues such as resource allocation, land use, and species diversity. If life is to have meaning beyond mere existence, we will need to think deeply about values, about what makes life meaningful. Questions of wisdom, ethics, and values have generally been grounded in religious or theological thought, and it seems to me inevitable that a serious approach to sustainability must involve a constructive dialogue between science and religion.

Although commonly thought to be incompatible, science and theology have a complex history of interaction, often contentious, but in the end

beneficial to both sides. They must remain in dialogue if we are fully to understand who we are as humans and how we are to behave. In this essay, I will
argue that progress on the issue of sustainable living depends on using both
the intellectual knowledge provided by science and the moral understanding
derived from religion. First I will review the history of interaction between science and religion and the philosophical underpinnings of each in order to
highlight similarities and differences. Then I will show the complementarity of
science and religion by considering how the perspectives of geology[1] and theology can together provide a richer understanding of the issues underlying the
question of sustainability.

SCIENCE AND RELIGION: COMPLEMENTARY WAYS OF KNOWING

Some people would assess the prospects for constructive dialogue between
science and religion as dim. Planetary scientist Carl Sagan apparently spoke for
many scientists and intellectuals when he claimed that "the cosmos is all there
is, and all there ever will be," in effect rendering religion superfluous.[2] On the
religious side, many literalists seem to believe that the creation stories of Genesis are to be taken word for word, that the scientific account of a universe
evolving over billions of years is wrong, and that conversation is simply an
opportunity for polemical attempts at conversion. The media often play up
this contrast and portray science and religion as being in a state of open war-
fare, but the true story is far more interesting.

Historical Relations Between Science and Religion

Human understanding of nature has played a central role in religious thought
as far back as we can see. The ancient Middle Eastern picture of the cosmos
provided the frame on which the authors of Genesis stretched their canvas for
a majestic liturgical portrayal of creation, invoking the visible grandeur of the
cosmos, conveying the goodness they sensed in creation, and depicting their
understanding of life's meaning.[3] A competing picture, also widespread in the
ancient Middle East, claimed that an inferior god had created an inherently
flawed cosmos, one radically opposed to the spiritual element, and that evil
resulted from a struggle between positive and negative cosmic forces. The conflict between those views was largely settled by Augustine (354–430 CE), who
sensed in the stately, predictable motion of the stars proof that creation was
harmonious, and evil a distortion of that essential good.

It is hard to imagine how trust in a rational science could have emerged in
a culture that viewed nature as capricious or untrustworthy, and so theologian
Paul Tillich and others have suggested that Augustine's sense of the harmony in
nature made possible the rationality that led to the Enlightenment, modern
science, and contemporary technology.[4] But this sense of harmony was more
than a naive perception of order in the cosmos. It emerged from Augustine's

inner awareness of the immediacy of God, sensed in something unconditional lying at the core of the human mind,[5] something closely akin to the sense of beauty or elegance that many scientists find so useful in discerning fruitful lines of investigation.[6] So it seems that much of modern Western science is rooted in the rich soil where theological reflection and perceptive observation of nature combined to convince Augustine that nature was indeed good and worthy of trust.

For more than a millennium after Augustine, Earth was thought to lie at the center of the cosmos and the account of creation in Genesis was accepted as a factual account of God's direct role in creation and of subsequent human history. Galileo (1564–1642) and later Newton (1642–1727) revolutionized our view of cosmic mechanics and Earth's location, but they did not directly attack the Genesis account of creation. That version was widely accepted by scholars such as Carolus Linnaeus (1707–1778), Immanuel Kant (1724–1804), and Thomas Jefferson (1743–1826) until well into the nineteenth century. Many viewed the cosmos as an intricate machine, designed and built by a creator, then allowed to run on its own.

The challenge to Genesis finally came from geology. Early in the eighteenth century, James Hutton, John Playfair, and Charles Lyell showed that Earth had evolved through everyday processes operating over an immense span of time, and in 1859 Charles Darwin showed that all biological species had emerged from the operation of natural selection on the endless number of small variations within existing species. These ideas stirred deep controversy, but the turmoil resulted as much from paradigm shifts within the geological and theological communities as it did from conflict between the two camps.[7] Beginning as early as Friedrich Schleiermacher (1768–1834), theological thought began to incorporate the evolutionary view and to see creation as a long, slow process operating through natural laws. Although still thought responsible for creation, God was seen as working through evolution by natural selection instead of by direct intervention. Unlike modern paleontologists,[8] nineteenth-century scientists tended to see evolution as producing ever more "advanced" species. That view led contemporary theologians to propose a theology of progressive human betterment, a view that has continued into the twentieth century in the work of theologians such as Teilhard de Chardin and John Cobb.

The Truth of Science

Although science seems at first to be a purely objective way of perceiving the world, it is more than a naive sensory encounter with reality. Like any intellectual encounter, science is an operation of consciousness as well as perception; nature as understood by science is not nature itself, it is nature as organized by our minds. And because the minds doing the organizing are minds intensively trained in the culture of the discipline and society within which they are operating, all data and all science is to some degree culture dependent.[9] And because all observations are preconditioned by specific models or metaphors, all observations are to some degree theory laden. Beyond that, the self-limitation of science to questions that can be tested means that there is a whole realm of experience that is beyond the purview of science, questions that science finds simply "not interesting."

None of this, of course, is to undercut the validity of science within its proper realm of inquiry. The strength of science is that it enables us to make specific predictions that—within the disciplines and models in which they were conceived—can be rigorously tested. The intricate and detailed picture of nature, both operating at scales of space and time each varying over 40 orders of magnitude and spanning disciplines as different as the generation of Earth's magnetic field and evolution of bacterial DNA, is one of the great monuments to human endeavor.

As great a contribution may be the strong commitment to test hypotheses rigorously and to accept the verdict of well-conceived tests. Perhaps more than any other discipline, science is blessed with the humility to recognize when it is wrong, at least within the recognized limits of scientific inquiry. Calvin insisted that symbols of the divine must contain an element of self-negation lest they be taken literally and so become idols.[10] Science's commitment to testing hypotheses is a comparable constraint and provides a powerful example of the value of humility in all fields of thought.

As impressive and as important as the achievements of science are, however, we must remember its limitations whenever science becomes involved in discussions of social policy. In questions of sustainability, science is essential for its ability to help us understand the consequences of different courses of action. But decisions on which action to take and which set of consequences to accept raise questions of values, and sometimes issues of competing values and grounds for preferring one value system rather than another. On such questions, science has little to contribute. It must be humble enough to acknowledge its limitations and to pay serious attention to the insights of other disciplines, such as the moral insights of theology and philosophy.

The Truth of Faith

The problem of establishing theological truth is more difficult than establishing scientific truth. Tillich developed a helpful approach by beginning with the question of faith and developing ways of reaching the truth of faith.[11] For Tillich, faith does not mean blind belief. Rather, it is a centered act engaging our entire personality, including both our power to reason critically and our gift for affective response. It is an act in which one reaches beyond reason, committed by heart and soul as well as by mind to an *ultimate concern*, a concern that cannot be justified on the basis of reason alone but is nonetheless totally compelling.

The power of Tillich's approach is that faith in his sense is not limited to the religious domain. The passionate commitment of a scientist to finding the truth of nature is also an ultimate concern, perhaps the clearest positive example in the secular domain. That commitment cannot be justified on the basis of reason alone. In the face of sometimes powerful temptations to do otherwise, a scientist's ultimate concern with truth will compel her to challenge her own pet theories, to insist on gathering more data when preliminary results appear to support her view, and resolutely to reject temptations to shortcut the scientific process. When asked to justify her commitment, she can only move beyond reason and follow Martin Luther by affirming, "Here I stand; I can do no other." Faith in that sense is transparently obvious in the work of scientists like T. C. Chamberlain, Albert Einstein, and Barbara McClintock.

The difficulty with faith is that, because it moves beyond reason, it cannot be attained by reason alone. Faith must come through revelation, an experience that grasps us totally—heart, mind, and soul—and demands that we respond. And, because we are human, we often fail to understand and so respond in a distorted way. To arrive at criteria for establishing the truth of faith, Tillich began by noting that any state of ultimate concern has both objective and subjective sides, and that faith must be evaluated from both.[12]

From the objective side, Tillich claimed that faith is true when its content is truly ultimate. It is easy for both secular and religious people to accept values that are far from ultimate, like personal success, social status, wealth, or political power and influence. Ethnic or national identity can also become matters of ultimate concern, often with disastrous results, as in the killing fields of Cambodia, in Nazi Germany, or in the recent disintegration of Yugoslavia. A subtler problem arises because, when we try to convey any truly ultimate concern, especially in its affective dimension, we must rely on symbols and metaphors. And as symbols become identified with a faith, they can easily become objects of faith themselves, rather than mere pointers to deeper truths.[13] In religious terms, these symbols become idols. The result is illustrated all too clearly in the endless conflicts over matters of dogma and doctrine that have divided Western religious denominations. An essential function of any faith community is constantly to test the ultimacy of its faith. We must always remember to look beyond a religious doctrine to see the truth to which the doctrine points.

From the subjective side, Tillich claimed that faith can be said to be true if it expresses an ultimate concern in a way so compelling that we must respond, we must act, and we must express our faith to others. Faith must be more than mere intellectual assent; it must move us to respond, even to change the way that we live. But because in responding to faith we move beyond certainty based on reason, our response is always undertaken in the face of doubt. To claim truth, faith must be so strong that it compels us to respond, act, and communicate despite doubt. But response based on faith is not simply irrational. It is more like the response of a scientist, who senses that her research requires that she spend a sabbatical year abroad learning a new technique, knowing that even this new method may not provide the resolution her work needs, and that the year will surely take a toll on her personal life. As she works through the consequences of her decision while on sabbatical, so a person acting out of religious faith observes and reflects on the consequences of his actions to ensure that they remain compatible with his ultimate concerns. It is just this kind of reflection that moved many religious people to support civil rights and global peace in the past, and it is this kind of reflection that impels some to work for biodiversity and environmental justice today.

In using reason to reflect on faith, however, it is essential to avoid a fundamental misunderstanding of theological truth that is common in both religious and secular communities. In science and in ordinary logic, only one of two opposite claims can be true. For example, if a geologist shows that a limestone was deposited on a tidal flat, it cannot also have formed as a deep marine sediment. But that kind of exclusivity no longer holds in fields where truths must be expressed in terms of symbols and metaphors, because symbols rarely capture the whole of the truth to which they point. Niels Bohr made this point in an oft-quoted statement to the effect that the opposite of a simple truth must be false, but the opposite of a deep truth may well be another deep truth.[14] Theological truths are more often of the "both-and" variety than of the "either-or" sort. Religious people miss this point whenever they claim that, because their religion is true, others must be false. And both scientists and religious thinkers make this mistake when they conclude that, if evolution is a valid description of human development, then God cannot have created us. That conclusion ignores the possibility that God works through natural processes, including evolution, and would be logically correct only if the biblical creation stories are taken literally, a view abandoned by most theologians more than a century ago.

The Intersection Between Science and Theology

This exploration of science and Western theology has shown that the two are more closely connected than is generally thought. Both are rooted in the sense of nature's harmony discerned by Augustine. Both rely on reason. Both are based on faith in an ultimate concern that compels adherents to respond by acting on that faith. Science is committed to learning the truth of nature, wherever it may lead, and theology to hearing an inner call, whatever it may ask. Because faith is always fragile, always subject to doubt and temptation, both have developed communities to train adherents, to nurture them, and to challenge them. Practitioners of both science and theology have succumbed to temptation by settling for values that are less than ultimate or by being trapped by models or doctrines well after they have ceased to be compelling. Each has its journeymen practitioners who have never been willing to plumb the depths of mystery. But each has wise and daring souls who have immersed themselves in those depths and have given us compelling images of science and theology. Each field has grown from contact with the other in the past. I believe that the two must continue to interact if our species is to have a future worth living.

Religious thought must pay serious attention to the knowledge of science lest it become anachronistic.[15] Science must honor its own ultimate concern with truth and pay serious attention to the moral insights of theology on questions of policy, use of technology, or design of controversial experiments.

GEOLOGY AND RELIGION: COMPLEMENTARY VIEWS OF SUSTAINABILITY

The Geological Perspective

A compelling symbol of the twentieth century is the image of Earth from space, as photographed by the Apollo astronauts. It fundamentally changed our views of Earth and of ourselves by demonstrating that the metaphor of the endless frontier no longer applies to our world. In its place, we see a small, self-contained planet, breathtaking in its beauty, an exquisite jewel set against the velvety black immensity of space. As the astronauts explored the Moon, we saw a dry, thirsty land devoid of oxygen or life, a reminder of the pummeling that Earth received from space debris four billion years ago. More recently, remotely controlled probes have shown us the golden halo of Saturn's braided rings, the delicate tracery of turbulence on Jupiter's surface, the immensity of a Martian volcano five times the largest on Earth, and the peculiar scone-shaped lava domes of Venus. But nowhere else have we found an environment that could sustain us. The other planets are too hot or too cold, too poor in the water and oxygen we need or too rich in gases harmful to us. Probably the most important factor is that Earth is the only planet in the solar system where surface temperatures and pressures are in the range where liquid water is stable. We began to realize that the ancient Biblical tale that humans had been created in a fertile, well-watered garden was correct. But the tale was also wrong, for we are still in that garden. And we must learn to care for it.

Looking at the Apollo photographs of our earthly garden, we saw it for the first time as a complex system of rock, soil, and water, veiled by a gossamer-thin layer of air, and inhabited by billions of fellow creatures, large and small. And we began to see that all species on Earth are related by an intricate web of biogeochemical cycles in which all of the chemicals needed for life—carbon, water, calcium, nitrogen, phosphorous, potassium—are recycled in a complex series of chemical and physical processes, nearly all powered by solar energy.[16] Perhaps the most familiar example is photosynthesis, by which plants and animals can exchange oxygen and carbon dioxide with each other. We are all radically dependent upon one another and upon the system itself. Except for the input of solar energy and a few stray meteorites, the earth system is closed and has been for about four billion years.

The origins of the biogeochemical system are lost in the mists of time, but carbon isotopes from carbonate rocks in Greenland are fractionated in a way suggesting that photosynthesis had already begun 3.85 billion years ago and that at least a primitive terrestrial carbon cycle had begun to operate.[17] The age of those rocks (Archean) is almost the same as the time of the "late heavy bombardment" of bodies in the inner solar system by meteorites; and if the interpretation of the isotopic data is correct, life must have jumped into being as soon as it was given a chance. It may even have begun prior to the last early Archean impact, only to be snuffed out and forced to start over.[18]

Today, the carbon cycle regulates the amount of atmospheric carbon dioxide that, along with water vapor and other greenhouse gasses, absorbs infrared radiation emitted by Earth and leads to an average surface temperature of 63°F, just about right for carbon-based life. Without that greenhouse effect, Earth's temperature would be 0°F, and the oceans would be largely covered with sea ice, reflecting more incoming solar radiation and perhaps cooling Earth sufficiently so that life as we know it could never have developed. The greenhouse effect has kept Earth's surface temperature within the relatively narrow range required for life for nearly four billion years, despite the fact that the intensity of solar radiation has increased by approximately 20 percent since life originated, despite the fact that the atmosphere has changed from an early, largely reducing composition to its present oxygen-rich composition, and despite the fact that meteorite impacts radically altered the species mix on Earth at the end of the Cretaceous (66 million years ago) and perhaps at the end of the Permian (245 million years ago).

The details are still unclear, but it seems likely that plate tectonics plays a major role in controlling the long-term carbon dioxide content of the atmosphere and therefore the surface temperature by carrying calcite from the ocean floor into the mantle, where it reacts with quartz to form calcium silicate and releases carbon dioxide into the atmosphere once again. Certainly, plate tectonics was crucial in forming the continental masses near which life probably began and where terrestrial animals with brains like ours could evolve.

The key requirements for a sustainable life system seem to be that Earth is close enough to the sun to allow its temperature to lie in the same range as that of liquid water; that its gravity field is strong enough to retain an atmosphere that imposes a surface pressure in a range that allows liquid water to exist; that its daily rotation is fast enough to prevent diurnal temperature variations from being too extreme; that there is a crust light enough to form large continental masses but thin enough to allow plate tectonics to operate; that the crust contains enough radioactive material to keep the upper mantle hot enough to convect, thereby driving plate tectonics; and, perhaps, that the core is hot enough to facilitate convection within the core as well, thereby generating a strong magnetic field to shield Earth's surface from the solar wind. The temperature requirement is not a very severe limitation—given a solar system, at least one planet must be at about the right distance from the sun to meet this condition. But the other requirements are much more difficult to satisfy. In detail, they depend on precisely which planetesimals collided to form Earth, exactly what the bulk composition of the aggregate was, and precisely how each of those collisions happened during the final stages of planetary accretion about four billion years ago.[19] Even small differences in the trajectories of those colliding planetesimals would have led to a different Earth, quite possibly one unable to sustain life. But even an Earth perfectly attuned to nurturing life might not have produced us. Were it not for the fact that the Mesozoic reptiles were largely eliminated by a meteorite impact 65 million years ago, mammalian evolution might never have gotten underway.

This entire story is shot through with chance events, a situation that has led some scientists to conclude that a creator cannot exist;[20] but chance can equally well be seen as one of the ways that a creator might have chosen to work in the world.[21] The prevalence of chance has led some to claim that the odds against life elsewhere are so enormous that we probably are alone in the universe.[22] Still others point out that the number of suns in the universe is also astronomical, and conclude that repetitions are inevitable.[23] Until we have seen more of the universe, we should perhaps limit ourselves to saying that planets "brimming with awareness"[24] like Earth seem to be rare, and that we are very privileged to be here.

Evolutionary history reinforces this sense of privilege. As newcomers on the scene—the earliest hominids originated approximately 3.5 million years ago, modern humans about 150,000 years ago[25]—it is obvious that we are not essential to the existence of life on Earth. Our position at the top of the food chain implies the same point. Aside from a few bacteria, viruses, and parasites that have learned to live at our expense and some domestic animals that we have bred into dependence, few of our fellow creatures would miss us were we to disappear.

Two main conclusions emerge from this geological perspective: We are totally dependent on the rest of the biosphere and we are privileged to be here. A prudent response would be to walk lightly on Earth so as not to abuse our privilege, and to care for the biosphere so that it can continue to nurture us. To respond intelligently, we need a sense of how vulnerable the system is to our increasing impact and of how urgently we need to reduce that impact.

Assessing the system's vulnerability is difficult. On one level, the system itself is extraordinarily stable. It has continued to sustain life on Earth for nearly four billion years, despite a transition from a predominantly reducing atmosphere to oxidizing conditions,[26] despite at least two meteorite impacts and despite an increase in the intensity of solar radiation. It would clearly be very difficult for us to destroy the system. But the real question is whether we might perturb the system to such an extent that it can no longer sustain our species. Although the system itself has lasted a long time, individual species have not. Of the 500 million to 1 billion species thought to have existed at one time or another, only 2 to 30 million are now alive; 98 percent have become extinct, mostly due to their inability to respond to changes in the system, especially changes in climate.[27] Again, we get a sense of our privilege at being here, and our vulnerability.

We have no clear understanding of precisely what confers survivability on a species, but two aspects seem important. First, generalist species seem to be more adaptable than those that have adjusted to very specific niches.[28] On that criterion, humans would seem to score pretty well; but as we begin to approach Earth's carrying capacity, we severely limit our room for maneuvering in response to change. Second, the stability of local ecosystems seems highly sensitive to functional diversity (the number of species with different functions in the system, rather than the sheer number of species) and to changes in system composition by loss of species with critical functions, introduction of exotic species, fragmentation, and predator decimation.[29] Working to sustain the health of critical ecosystems in those terms may be the most important thing that we can do to preserve an environment that can sustain us.

Assessment of the urgency with which we must act requires careful analysis of the rate of population growth, the resources needed to provide each person an existence that we would regard as worthwhile, and a sense of how many people the planet can support at that level of consumption. A featured session at the 1996 annual meeting of the Ecological Society of America in Providence, Rhode Island, grappled with those questions. Although unable to reach consensus on all issues, the participants did seem to reach general agreement that the central issue in determining Earth's "carrying capacity" is the lifestyle that we have come to expect.[30] Population biologist William Rees, for example, estimated that bringing the developing world up to Canada's lifestyle would require three times Earth's resources. That prospect suggests that, at the least, we should have a sense of moderate urgency to begin the attempt to live within our planetary means, while continuing to work as hard as we can to learn precisely what the limits of the earth system are and how we can live well within them.

The Theological Perspective

For modern theologians, the claim that we are to act as stewards of creation has become almost a truism.[31] That view is strongly supported by the creation stories in Genesis, which tell us that we were put in this garden "to till it and keep it" and that we were given "dominion" over other creatures on Earth. The word *dominion* has been widely misinterpreted to mean that we were given license to use creation at our pleasure, but modern commentators agree that in Hebrew "dominion" carries a sense of responsible stewardship, and confirms our obligation to till *and* keep the Earth.[32]

Moreover, theology has consistently challenged us to go beyond a purely ecological view of sustainability and to acknowledge that authentic human existence requires more than the basic physical needs that the earth system can supply. I suspect that all would agree that a meaningful life should include the freedom to enjoy loving relationships with others and the opportunity to find fulfillment in learning what we are good at and doing it well. To provide those opportunities, our concept of sustainability must be expanded to include a reasonable prospect of continued peace and some confidence that our culture or society will continue to function tomorrow. Modern theology would insist that these conditions can ultimately be met only in a society that values justice and equity.[33]

Others have reached the same conclusion from a purely pragmatic perspective. For example, Barkham[34] has argued that sustainability may well be impossible in the absence of a reasonable degree of equity and that paying attention to the needs of the less fortunate is a matter of enlightened self-interest. He concluded that the high rates of population growth in developing countries, which so many see as the primary threat to sustainability, can be reduced only if those countries are allowed an equable share in Earth's bounty. However, it seems clear that our resource base is not adequate to bring the South into equity with a Northern level of consumption and that equity can be approached only by reducing consumption levels in the North.[35] That argument strongly supports Barkham's claim that "action stemming from enlightened self-interest can only emerge with a sophisticated degree of conscious awareness,"[36] and it is precisely in this area of awareness and motivation that a theological perspective is most helpful and most needed. Genuine altruism is rare in human behavior and can perhaps emerge only in a context that honors and mandates justice for all.

So one message of theology, supported by considerable secular thought, is that we need to work toward sustainability, but a new kind of sustainability, one that goes beyond the mere functioning of the natural system to include an explicit dimension of social justice. Theology would then go on to say that if we accept this concept of sustainability as our ultimate concern, we should feel a compulsion to work for sustainability with all of our hearts, our minds, our souls. Mere agreement with this view of sustainability is not enough; we are called to move beyond assent to an active commitment to work to bring that state into being. Religion is not about doctrine; it is about practice.[37]

But at this point we encounter a problem. Although we recognize that we are radically dependent on the earth system, we are also deeply aware of our ignorance of the details of how the system functions; and although we may agree *that* we must act, we are not at all sure just *how* we should act. Or, more realistically, many of us are confident that *we* know; but to our alarm, we see that well-meaning people disagree—in some cases, profoundly—about what to do. The problem is even more acute when we confront the issue of social justice. Even among those who agree that one of the keys to sustainability is a closer approach to global equity, many disagree about how to move toward equity or about whether equity is even remotely attainable.

And here theology has a second message. It does not matter that we are uncertain about how to proceed or that we doubt whether we can succeed. We must do the best that we can, despite our doubts. And to do that, we need to mobilize more than just our minds. We need to involve our hearts and our souls as well. We must act with care, energy, and deep joy at the almost incredible privilege of being called, of being wanted as partners in the continuing process of creation. Our awareness of that call as privilege may be the deepest message of theology.

For avowedly religious people, the path to involving our hearts and our souls is a familiar one. We pray, or we meditate, or we follow some spiritual practice that allows us to act despite our doubt. For more secular people, the path may lie in different directions. Some may find the courage to act in a deep sense of commitment that emerges from their research. Others may sense it in a quiet walk in a near-primeval forest. However we find that courage, it comes to us through revelation. Here I again find Tillich enormously helpful when he says "revelation can reach [us] only in the form of receiving it, and every reception of it, whether more inwardly religious or more openly secular, is religion, and as religion is always humanly distorted."[38] Both parts of that statement are important. Geology and theology must recognize that sustainability is a profound concern for each and that both perspectives on that concern are needed. And we must all admit that we see truth imperfectly. It is inevitable that we will disagree about how to proceed and that we will be wrong much of the time. In dealing with disagreements, we must remember to do justice, to love kindness, and to follow our star humbly.

A SUSTAINABLE STRATEGY

Geology indicates that we are privileged to be here and that it would be prudent for us to live gently on Earth—to work with some sense of urgency to nurture the ecological system, to try to repair the more serious rifts that we have created in the web of life, and to do our best to avoid making any more. Theology strengthens the imperative to act as earthkeepers and reinforces our sense of humility as response to the privilege of being here. But it goes beyond the mandate of science when it asks that we work to bring about a just and equitable global society and when it urges us to share a deep sense of joy in the work of nurturing the garden and one another.

There is, of course, a danger in using religious belief as a way of motivating behavior, because there are many religions as well as many persons who deny the validity of any religion. Here, too, we must remember Tillich's point, just quoted, that any revelation, whether overtly religious or openly secular, is religion. And it seems to me that here religion must take a leaf from the book of geology, where ecosystems with rich functional diversity appear to be the most long-lived. We must learn to see belief systems as simply different ways of representing a common ultimate concern, one that values life on Earth, with justice, and dignity for all. We must remember that all forms of revelation are distorted by our humanness.

A strategy combining geology and theology is a profoundly challenging one, one that our species has never been able to live up to, although many have long espoused most of its tenets. In effect, it requires that we begin to evolve spiritually rather than just biologically. I'm not at all sure that we can do that. I'm only sure that we must try—and that adopting sustainability with equity as our ultimate concern is a good way of trying.[39]

9

The Golden Rule: A Proper Scale for Our Environmental Crisis

Stephen Jay Gould

P atience enjoys a long pedigree of favor. Chaucer pronounced it "an heigh vertu, certeyn" ("The Franklin's Tale"), while the New Testament had already made a motto of the Old Testament's most famous embodiment: "Ye have heard of the patience of Job" (James 5:11). Yet some cases seem so extended in diligence and time that another factor beyond sheer endurance must lie behind the wait. When Alberich, having lost the Ring of the Niebelungen fully three operas ago, shows up in Act 2 of *Götterdämmerung* to advise his son Hagen on strategies for recovery, we can hardly suppress a flicker of admiration for this otherwise unlovable character. (I happen to adore Wagner, but I do recognize that a wait through nearly all of the Ring cycle would be, to certain unenlightened folks, the very definition of eternity in Hades.)

Patience of this magnitude usually involves a deep understanding of a fundamental principle, central to my own profession of geology but all too rarely grasped in daily life—the effects of scale. Phenomena unfold on their own appropriate scales of space and time and may be invisible in our myopic world of dimensions assessed by comparison with human height and times metered by human lifespans. So much of accumulating importance at earthly scales— the results of geological erosion, evolutionary changes in lineages—is invisible by the measuring rod of a human life. So much that matters to particles in the microscopic world of molecules—the history of a dust grain subject to Brownian motion, the fate of shrunken people in *Fantastic Voyage* or *Inner Space*— either averages out to stability at our scale or simply stands below our limits of perception.

It takes a particular kind of genius or deep understanding to transcend this most pervasive of all conceptual biases and to capture a phenomenon by grasping a proper scale beyond the measuring rods of our own world. Alberich and Wotan know that pursuit of the Ring is dynastic or generational, not personal. William of Baskerville (in Umberto Eco's *Name of the Rose*) solves his medieval mystery because he alone understands that, in the perspective of centuries, the convulsive events of his own day (the dispute between papacies of Rome and Avignon) will be forgotten, while the only surviving copy of a book by Aristotle may influence millennia. Architects of medieval cathedrals had to frame satisfaction on scales beyond their own existence, for they could not live to witness the completion of their designs.

May I indulge in a personal anecdote on the subject of scale? I loved to memorize facts as a child, but rebelled at those I deemed unimportant (baseball stats were in, popes of Rome and kings of England out). In sixth grade, I had to memorize the sequence of land acquisitions that built America. I could see the rationale behind learning the Louisiana Purchase and the Mexican Cession, for they added big chunks to our totality. But I remember balking, and publicly challenging the long-suffering Ms. Stack, at the Gadsden Purchase of 1853. Why did I have to know about a sliver of southern Arizona and New Mexico?

Now I am finally hoist on my own petard (blown up by my own noxious charge according to the etymologies). After a lifetime of complete nonimpact by the Gadsden Purchase, I have become unwittingly embroiled in a controversy about a tiny bit of territory within this smallest of American growing points. A little bit of a little bit—so much for effects of scale and the penalties of blithe ignorance.

The case is a classic example of a genre (environmentalists vs. developers) made familiar in recent struggles to save endangered populations—the snail darter of a few years back, the northern spotted owl vs. timber interests. The University of Arizona, with the backing of an international consortium of astronomers, wishes to build a complex of telescopes atop Mount Graham in southeastern Arizona (part of the Gadsden Purchase). But the old-growth spruce–fir habitat on the mountaintop provides the central range for *Tamiasciurus hudsonicus grahamensis,* the Mount Graham Red Squirrel—a distinctive subspecies that lives nowhere else, and that forms the southernmost population of the entire species. The population has already been reduced to some one hundred survivors, and destruction of 125 acres of spruce–fir growth (to build the telescopes) within the 700 or so remaining acres of best habitat might well administer a coup de grâce to this fragile population.

I cannot state an expert opinion on details of this controversy (I have already confessed my ignorance about everything involving the Gadsden Purchase and its legacy). Many questions need to be answered. Is the population already too small to survive in any case? If not, could the population, with proper management, coexist with the telescopes in the remaining habitat?

I do not think that, practically or morally, we can defend a policy of saving every distinctive local population of organisms. I can cite a good rationale for the preservation of species, for each species is a unique and separate natural object that, once lost, can never be reconstituted. But subspecies are distinctive local populations of species with broader geographical ranges. Subspecies are dynamic, interbreedable, and constantly changing; what then are we saving by declaring them all inviolate? Thus, I confess that I do not agree with all arguments advanced by defenders of the Mount Graham Red Squirrel. One leaflet, for example, argues: "The population has been recently shown to have a fixed, homozygous allele which is unique in Western North America." Sorry folks. I will stoutly defend species, but we cannot ask for the preservation of every distinctive gene, unless we find a way to abolish death itself (for many organisms carry unique mutations).

No, I think that for local populations of species with broader ranges, the brief for preservation must be made on a case by case basis, not on a general principle of preservation (lest the environmental movement ultimately lose popular support for trying to freeze a dynamic evolutionary world *in statu quo*). On this proper basis of individual merit, I am entirely persuaded that the Mount Graham Red Squirrel should be protected, for two reasons.

First, the squirrel itself: The Mount Graham Red is an unusually interesting local population within an important species. It is isolated from all other populations and forms the southernmost extreme of the species's range. Such peripheral populations, living in marginal habitats, are of special interest to students of evolution.

Second, the habitat: Environmentalists continually face the political reality that support and funding can be won for soft, cuddly, and "attractive" animals, but not for slimy, grubby, and ugly creatures (of potentially greater evolutionary interest and practical significance) or for habitats. This situation had led to the practical concept of "umbrella" or "indicator" species—surrogates for a larger ecological entity worthy of preservation. Thus, the giant panda (really quite a boring and ornery creature despite its good looks) raises money to save the remaining bamboo forests of China (and a plethora of other endangered creatures with no political clout); the northern spotted owl has just rescued some magnificent stands of old-growth giant cedars, Douglas fir, and redwoods (and I say Hosanna); and the Mount Graham Red Squirrel may save a rare and precious habitat of extraordinary evolutionary interest.

The Pinaleno Mountains, reaching 10,720 feet at Mount Graham, are an isolated fault block range separated from others by alluvial and desert valleys that dip to less than 3,000 feet in elevation. The high peaks of the Pinalenos contain an important and unusual fauna for two reasons. First, they harbor a junction of two biogeographic provinces: the Nearctic or northern by way of the Colorado Plateau and the Neotropical or southern via the Mexican Plateau. The Mount Graham Red Squirrel (a northern species) can live this far south because high elevations reproduce the climate and habitat found nearer sea level in the more congenial north. Second, and more important to evolutionists, the old-growth spruce–fir habitats on the high peaks of the Pinalenos are isolated "sky islands"—10,000-year-old remnants of a habitat more widely spread over the region of the Gadsden Purchase during the height of the last ice age. In evolutionary terms, these isolated pieces of habitat are true islands—patches of more northern microclimate surrounded by southern desert. They are functionally equivalent to bits of land in the ocean. Consider the role that islands (like the Galápagos) have played both in developing the concepts of evolutionary theory and in acting as cradles of origin (through isolation) or vestiges of preservation for biological novelties.

Thus, whether or not the telescopes will drive the Mount Graham Red Squirrel to extinction (an unsettled question well outside my area of expertise), the sky islands of the Pinalenos are precious habitats that should not be compromised. Let the Mount Graham Red Squirrel, so worthy of preservation in its own right, also serve as an indicator species for the unique and fragile habitat that it occupies.

But why should I, a confirmed eastern urbanite who has already disclaimed all concern for the Gadsden Purchase, choose to involve myself in the case of the Mount Graham Red Squirrel? The answer, unsurprisingly, is that I have been enlisted—involuntarily and on the wrong side to boot. I am fighting mad, and fighting back.

The June 7, 1990, *Wall Street Journal* ran a pro-development, anti-squirrel opinion piece by Michael D. Copeland (identified as "executive director of the Political Economy Research Center in Bozeman, Montana") under the patently absurd title: "No Red Squirrels? Mother Nature May Be Better Off." (I can at least grasp, while still rejecting, the claim that nature would be no worse off if the squirrels died, but I am utterly befuddled at how anyone could devise an argument that the squirrels inflict a positive harm upon the mother of us all!) In any case, Mr. Copeland misunderstood my writings in formulating a supposedly scientific argument for his position.

Now scarcely a day goes by when I do not read a misrepresentation of my views (usually by creationists, racists, or football fans, in order of frequency). My response to nearly all misquotation is the effective retort of preference: utter silence. (Honorable intellectual disagreement should always be addressed; misquotation should be ignored, when possible and politically practical). I make an exception in this case because Copeland cited me in the service of a classic false argument—the standard, almost canonical misuse of my profession of paleontology in debates about extinction. We have been enlisted again and again, in opposition to our actual opinions and in support of attitudes that most of us regard as anathema, to uphold arguments by developers about the irrelevance (or even, in this case, the benevolence) of modern anthropogenic extinction. This standard error is a classic example of failure to understand the importance of scale—and thus I return to the premise and structure of my introductory paragraphs (did you really think that I waffled on so long about scale only so I could talk about the Gadsden Purchase?).

Paleontologists do discuss the inevitability of extinction for all species—in the long run, and on the broad scale of geological time. We are fond of saying that 99 percent or more of all species that ever lived are now extinct. (My colleague Dave Raup often opens talks on extinction with a zinging one-liner: "To a first approximation, all species are extinct.") We do therefore identify extinction as the normal fate of species. We also talk a lot—more of late since new data have made the field so exciting—about mass extinctions that punctuate the history of life from time to time. We do discuss the issue of eventual "recovery" from the effects of these extinctions, in the sense that life does rebuild or surpass its former diversity several million years after a great dying. Finally, we do allow that mass extinctions break up stable faunas and, in this sense, permit or even foster evolutionary innovations well down the road (including the dominance of mammals and the eventual origin of humans, following the death of dinosaurs).

From these statements about extinction in the fullness of geological time (on scales of millions of years), some apologists for development have argued that extinction at any scale (even of local populations within years or decades) poses no biological worry but, on the contrary, must be viewed as a comfortable part of an inevitable natural order. Or so Copeland states:

> *Suppose we lost a species. How devastating would that be? "Mass extinctions have been recorded since the dawn of paleontology," writes Harvard paleontologist Stephen Gould . . . . The most severe of these occurred approximately 250 million years ago . . . with an estimated 96 percent extinction of species, says Mr. Gould . . . . There is general agreement among scientists that today's species represent a small proportion of all those that have ever existed—probably less than 1 percent. This means that more than 99 percent of all species ever living have become extinct.*

From these facts, largely irrelevant to red squirrels on Mount Graham, Copeland makes inferences about the benevolence of extinction in general (though the argument only applies to geological scales):

> *Yet, in spite of these extinctions, both Mr. Gould and University of Chicago paleontologist Jack Sepkoski say that the actual number of living species has probably increased over time. [True, but not as a result of mass extinctions, despite Copeland's next sentence.] The "niches" created by extinctions provide an opportunity for a vigorous development of new species . . . . Thus, evolutionary history appears to have been characterized by millions of species extinctions and subsequent increases in species numbers. Indeed, by attempting to preserve species living on the brink of extinction, we may be wasting time, effort and money on animals that will disappear over time, regardless of our efforts.*

But all will "disappear over time, regardless of our efforts"—millions of years from now for most species if we don't interfere. The mean lifespan of marine invertebrate species lies between 5 and 10 million years; terrestrial vertebrate species turn over more rapidly, but still average in the low millions. By contrast, *Homo sapiens* may be only 200,000 years old or so and may enjoy a considerable future if we don't self-destruct. Similarly, recovery from mass extinction takes its natural measure in millions of years—as much as 10 million or more for fully rekindled diversity after major catastrophic events.

These are the natural time scales of evolution and geology on our planet. But what can such vastness possibly mean for our legitimately parochial interest in ourselves, our ethnic groups, our nations, our cultural traditions, our blood lines? Of what conceivable significance to us is the prospect of recovery from mass extinction 10 million years down the road if our entire species, not to mention our personal lineage, has so little prospect of surviving that long?

Capacity for recovery at geological scales has no bearing whatever upon the meaning of extinction today. We are not protecting Mount Graham Red Squirrels because we fear for global stability in a distant future not likely to include us. We are trying to preserve populations and environments because the comfort and decency of our present lives, and those of fellow species that share our planet, depend upon such stability. Mass extinctions may not threaten distant futures, but they are decidedly unpleasant for species caught in the throes of their power. At the appropriate scale of our lives, we are just a species in the midst of such a moment. And to say that we should let the squirrels go (at our immediate scale) because all species eventually die (at geological scales) makes about as much sense as arguing that we shouldn't treat an easily curable childhood infection because all humans are ultimately and inevitably mortal. I love geological time—a wondrous and expansive notion that sets the foundation of my chosen profession—but such vastness is not the proper scale of my personal life.

The same issue of scale underlies the main contribution that my profession of paleontology might make to our larger search for an environmental ethic. This decade, a prelude to the millennium, is widely and correctly viewed as a turning point that will lead either to environmental perdition or stabilization. We have fouled local nests before and driven regional faunas to extinction, but we were never able to unleash planetary effects before this century's concern with nuclear fallout, ozone holes, and putative global warming. In this context, we are searching for proper themes and language to express our environmental worries.

I don't know that paleontology has a great deal to offer, but I would advance one geological insight to combat a well-meaning, but seriously flawed (and all too common), position and to focus attention on the right issue at the proper scale. Two linked arguments are often promoted as a basis for an environmental ethic:

1. We live on a fragile planet now subject to permanent derailment and disruption by human intervention;
2. Humans must learn to act as stewards for this threatened world.

Such views, however well intentioned, are rooted in the old sin of pride and exaggerated self-importance. We are one among millions of species, stewards of nothing. By what argument could we, arising just a geological microsecond ago, become responsible for the affairs of a world 4.5 billion years old, teeming with life that has been evolving and diversifying for at least three-quarters of this immense span? Nature does not exist for us, had no idea we were coming, and doesn't give a damn about us. Omar Khayyam was right in all but his crimped view of the earth as battered, when he made his brilliant comparison of our world to an eastern hotel:

> Think, in this battered caravanserai
> Whose portals are alternate night and day,
> How sultan after sultan with his pomp
> Abode his destined hour, and went his way.

This assertion of ultimate impotence could be countered if we, despite our late arrival, now held power over the planet's future. But we don't, despite popular misperception of our might. We are virtually powerless over the earth at our planet's own geological timescale. All the megatonnage in all our nuclear arsenals yields but one ten-thousandth the power of the 10-kilometer asteroid that might have triggered the Cretaceous mass extinction. Yet the earth survived that larger shock and, in wiping out dinosaurs, paved a road for the evolution of large mammals, including humans. We fear global warming, yet even the most radical model yields an earth far cooler than many happy and prosperous times of a prehuman past. We can surely destroy ourselves, and take many other species with us, but we can barely dent bacterial diversity and will surely not remove many million species of insects and mites. On geological scales, our planet will take good care of itself and let time clear the impact of any human malfeasance.

People who do not appreciate the fundamental principle of appropriate scales often misread such an argument as a claim that we may therefore cease to worry about environmental deterioration, just as Copeland argued falsely that we need not fret about extinction. But I raise the same counterargument. We cannot threaten at geological scales, but such vastness has no impact upon us. We have a legitimately parochial interest in our own lives, the happiness and prosperity of our children, the suffering of our fellows. The planet will recover from nuclear holocaust, but we will be killed and maimed by billions, and our cultures will perish. The earth will prosper if polar icecaps melt under a global greenhouse, but most of our major cities, built at sea level as ports and harbors, will founder, and changing agricultural patterns will uproot our populations.

We must squarely face an unpleasant historical fact. The conservation movement was born, in large part, as an elitist attempt by wealthy social leaders to preserve wilderness as a domain for patrician leisure and contemplation (against the image, so to speak, of poor immigrants traipsing in hordes through the woods with their Sunday picnic baskets). We have never entirely shaken this legacy of environmentalism as something opposed to immediate human needs, particularly of the impoverished and unfortunate. But the Third World expands and contains most of the pristine habitat that we yearn to preserve. Environmental movements cannot prevail until they convince people that clean air and water, solar power, recycling, and reforestation are best solutions (as they are) for human needs at human scales—and not for impossibly distant planetary futures.

I have a decidedly unradical suggestion to make about an appropriate environmental ethic—one rooted, with this entire essay, in the issue of appropriate human scale vs. the majesty, but irrelevance, of geological time. I have never been much attracted to the Kantian categorical imperative in searching for an ethic—to moral laws that are absolute and unconditional, and do not involve any ulterior motive or end. The world is too complex and sloppy for such uncompromising attitudes (and God help us if we embrace the wrong principle and then fight wars, kill, and maim in our absolute certainty). I prefer the messier "hypothetical imperatives" that invoke desire, negotiation, and reciprocity. Of these "lesser," but altogether wiser and deeper principles, one has stood out for its independent derivation, with different words but to the same effect, in culture after culture. I imagine that our various societies grope towards this principle because structural stability (and basic decency necessary for any tolerable life) demand such a maxim. Christians call this principle the "golden rule"; Plato, Hillel, and Confucius knew the same maxim by other names. I cannot think of a better principle based on enlightened self-interest. If we all treated others as we wish to be treated ourselves, then decency and stability would have to prevail.

I suggest that we execute such a pact with our planet. She holds all the cards, and has immense power over us—so such a compact, which we desperately need but she does not at her own timescale, would be a blessing for us and an indulgence for her. We had better sign the papers while she is still willing to make a deal. If we treat her nicely, she will keep us going for a while. If we scratch her, she will bleed, kick us out, bandage up, and go about her business at her own scale. Poor Richard told us that "necessity never made a good bargain," but the earth is kinder than human agents in the "art of the deal." She will uphold her end; we must now go and do likewise.

Editor's note: Though two court injunctions had previously prevented removal of old-growth trees on Mount Graham, in 1996 the Justice Department intervened in the controversy. It permitted tree removal and construction to begin on the University of Arizona's complex of telescopes atop Mount Graham. Those people who would protect the old-growth forest continue to urge the National Aeronautics and Space Administration (NASA) to withhold funds from the project.

Part III

RESOURCES RECONFIGURED

In a traditional litany of important resources, oil, gas, metals, and minerals usually came first. No more. Preoccupation with the materials of industrial development has given way to concern for additional resources that we cannot refurbish easily in a human lifetime. Expansive public lands, verdant forests, rich soils, quality ground and surface waters, and healthy coasts have assumed prominence on today's agenda.

In "Resources Reconfigured," David Applegate surveys U.S. public lands and traces geology's evolving role in their use. Then, from his vantage point beside the trees and streams of the H. J. Andrews Experimental Forest, Fred Swanson celebrates the long-term, beneficial scientific investigations at this Pacific Northwest idyll. From California's Great Central Valley to South Dakota's remnant tallgrass prairies, Ronald Amundson ruminates on something as common, but no less as threatened, as the soil beneath our feet. Jack Sharp and Jay Banner explain the origin and complexities of southern Texas's bountiful water source, the Edwards aquifer. Jill Schneiderman chronicles the history of New York City's water supply as a model for other metropolitan areas. Finally, Jeffrey Payne delivers a warning about overbuilding and overpopulating along the coasts, as well as taking for granted the bounty of the world's oceans.

The twenty-first century beckons humanity to approach it delicately, to stay attuned to our fragile place in this earth system.

10

Ruling the Range: Managing the Public's Resources

David Applegate

Support for preservation of pristine federal lands can be traced back to 1864, when President Abraham Lincoln signed a bill granting the Yosemite Valley and the Mariposa Grove of Big Trees to the new state of California with the proviso that they be held "for public use, resort, and recreation" and that they "be inalienable for all time." In 1872, even as it passed the mining law to encourage development of mineral resources, Congress passed legislation to mandate that the headwaters of the Yellowstone River be "dedicated and set apart as a public park or pleasuring ground for the benefit and enjoyment of the people." The legislation also provided "for the preservation, from injury or spoliation, of all timber, mineral deposits, natural curiosities, or wonders within said park, and their retention in their natural condition." Thus, Yellowstone became the first national park. At the time, the famous geologist and explorer Ferdinand V. Hayden proclaimed it "a tribute from our legislators to science."[1]

The national parks were created to preserve and protect natural resources and to provide for public recreation. Except in a few special cases, resource development is prohibited, and development versus conservation battles fought over federal public lands elsewhere do not occur on national park lands. What's more, one quarter of the 374 parks, monuments, and preserves that make up today's national park system were created solely for their geological qualities. But even though geological wonders have been responsible for the creation of parks, geologists have had only limited roles in park management because we are wrongly viewed as being interested only in resource issues narrowly defined. Even in the most geologically spectacular parks, such as Grand Canyon National Park, few geologists are available to train interpreters, develop educational materials, or provide resource and hazard assessments.

Consequently, visitors to these parks do not have easy access to the full picture of the land.

The future livability of this planet depends on the care with which we manage our lands and its resources today. This observation is especially relevant to all public lands—those owned and managed by governments on behalf of their citizens. In the United States, over a quarter of the country is held in trust by the federal government. These federal public lands represent a collective inheritance for future generations of citizens. Their careful management requires the best available scientific information brought together to form a view of the landscape as a complex and highly interconnected system.

Today, the federal agencies that manage public lands have adopted a strategy based on maintaining healthy ecosystems in order to preserve biodiversity and developing the land's resources responsibly. Such an approach to the whole requires *biological* disciplines such as ecology, pathology, and entomology. It also requires *geological* disciplines of soil science and hydrology in order to understand the physical framework that sustains diverse plant and animal life. Although highly relevant to understanding and promoting ecosystem health, geology's role is often limited by policymakers' perceptions that the science is rooted in mineral and energy resource extraction. Ironically, geology's long and distinguished service in developing the resources used to build this country may present the greatest obstacle to its broader application today.

Throughout its history, the United States has relied on public lands to sustain its prosperity. Resources contained on or under these lands—timber, grasses, minerals, and water—provided the means to expand economically and territorially and served as a source of opportunity for generations of citizens. The evolution of federal land policy can be characterized as a gradual shift away from unrestrained development of commodity resources toward greater management of those resources based on a conservation ethic. It has also been characterized by moves toward a value system based on environmental protection and preservation of noncommodity resources.

Development and settlement of federal land were the dominant interests in our nation's first century. Laws such as the Homestead Act of 1862 and the General Mining Act of 1872 were passed by Congress to encourage settlement of the nation's interior and to facilitate extraction of mineral, energy, and other resources to power the burgeoning Industrial Revolution. As the century progressed, people recognized that the resources of public lands, however vast, could be exhausted and should be conserved for future use. The sentiment that rapid development threatened landscapes of unique scenic beauty, which should be protected and preserved intact, accompanied the awareness of limits to resources. These two distinct interests in conservation and preservation represent a second set of principles that have come to dominate management of public lands in place of unfettered development. During the last decades of the twentieth-century, the environmental movement has dramatically shifted the way we look at the land and adjusted the focus of management toward the protection of ecosystems and biodiversity.

This essay seeks to articulate geology's evolving role in managing federal public lands. Geologists have provided scientific information about these lands since the earliest days of the republic when the first task was to explore and identify just what was out there. Geology has been associated most closely with this phase of federal land policy and with the infrastructure development and agriculture that fostered the nation's early growth. Although energy and mineral extraction will continue as long as the United States remains a resource-dependent nation, low prices and strict environmental regulations have limited their scope on federal lands. That in turn has marginalized geology's traditional role in federal land management.

But, geology must be rewoven into the fabric of public land management. Policymakers and the public need to recognize that geology is essential to achieving fine-tuned comprehension of the environment we wish to protect. Although the focus of this essay is on managing federal public lands, the changing role of geology applies equally to public lands held by states, tribes, and local governments and to privately owned lands.

WHAT ARE PUBLIC LANDS?

For a nation that is the leading capitalist economy in the world and one in which private ownership is paramount, it may seem ironic that the largest landowner is the federal government. The irony is limited, however, when one considers that much of the land is in public hands quite simply because nobody wanted to buy it. Throughout the late eighteenth and nineteenth centuries, a series of laws that promoted settlement and development accompanied territorial expansion. It was not until the second half of the nineteenth century that interest in conservation and preservation began to take hold.

In 1781, two years before the end of the Revolutionary War, the original 13 states ratified the Articles of Confederation, thereby giving the federal government title to all the lands between the Appalachian Mountains and the Mississippi River. Six years later, the Constitution gave Congress the power to "dispose of and make all needful Rules and Regulations" concerning the territories. The cession of the western lands was critical to the survival of the fledgling central government, which, saddled with significant Revolutionary War debt, used sales of those lands to pay off its creditors. Western lands were also seen, particularly by Thomas Jefferson, as the key to establishing his ideal of an agrarian democracy, giving landless people the opportunity to become independent farmers.

From that original cession, the eastern states never lost a sense that they should share in the benefits stemming from the western lands, which they viewed as national public property belonging to all citizens. In contrast, the western states—carved from the public domain—came to view the land as

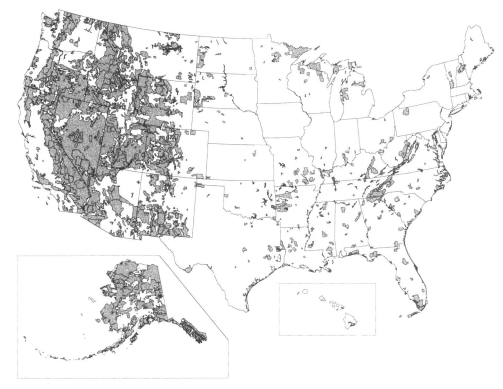

Map of the United States showing federal lands (shaded) in 1999. (*Used by permission of the U.S. Geological Survey; prepared by Harry Allan*)

rightfully theirs. This difference of opinion created the politics of longitude, East versus West, that define the debate over federal lands today.

Over 1.7 billion of the nation's total 2.3 billion acres have been part of the public domain at one time, including the Territory of Alaska, the states of Florida, Alabama, and Mississippi, and all states lying north of the Ohio River and west of the Mississippi River (except Texas, which joined the union as a formerly sovereign nation). Beginning with Ohio in 1802, each of these states had to agree not to interfere with the disposition of federal lands within their borders—that was the price of entry into the union. In return, each new state received land grants for schools and internal improvements as well as a portion of the receipts from land sales. Over one billion acres were eventually sold or given to states, Native American tribes, and private citizens. Today, the federal public lands constitute nearly 650 million acres, or 28 percent of the nation's total land area (not including the offshore outer continental shelf). The bulk of these lands are in the western states, and in many of those, the federal government owns over half the state. The percentage of federal ownership is highest in Nevada, where 86 percent of the land is owned by Uncle Sam.

The Department of the Interior manages federal lands through its Bureau of Land Management (BLM) with 264 million acres, Fish and Wildlife Service (FWS) with 94 million acres, and National Park Service (NPS) with 77 million acres. The U.S. Forest Service in the Department of Agriculture manages over 190 million acres of national forests and grasslands. All but 1 million of the remaining 21 million acres of federal lands are managed by the Departments of Defense and Energy for national security purposes.

The BLM manages what is left of the original public domain, lands never purchased or reserved. Lands managed by the other agencies either were reserved from the original public domain for specific purposes or were purchased. The FWS manages its lands with a focus on the protection of fish and wildlife habitat. The NPS focuses on preservation and protection of lands that are of scenic, scientific, archeological, cultural, or historical value. Managed for a variety of uses and constituting the bulk of federal lands, Forest Service and BLM lands are the principal focus of this essay. They are the lands upon which the opposing interests of development and conservation most often clash and consequently where land managers mostly need the credibility of a strong scientific underpinning for decisions.

GEOLOGY AND RESOURCE DEVELOPMENT

From its inception, the federal government sought to dispose of public lands. Consequently, geology took on an important role from the start because of the need to survey and characterize federal land assets. The first technical need was for boundary surveys, and geological surveys soon followed. During the first half of the nineteenth century, geologists were hired primarily to classify mineral-bearing lands and ascertain their value. David Dale Owens, one of the leading American geologists of the mid-nineteenth century, described this role well in the form of a rhetorical question: "Is it not incumbent on every country and every state of this Union, to adopt measures calculated, first to develop their resources in the various raw materials necessary for their welfare and progress, and having done so, to direct public attention to their stores of mineral wealth?"[2] In the 1850s, Owens convinced several state legislatures that such activities were indeed necessary and thus helped create a number of state geological surveys.

After the Louisiana Purchase in 1802, a century of territorial expansion began. Geology is closely associated with the western exploration that accompanied this age. The great explorer Meriwether Lewis was carefully instructed in mineral identification and other geological skills before undertaking his expedition to the Pacific, so that he might report on potential mineral resources. In the 1850s, geologists accompanied exploration parties that sought a railroad route to the Pacific, an early example of geology's ongoing role in the development of transportation routes. The first federal survey for which geology was the principal focus was authorized in 1867 to explore the land along the fortieth parallel—the latitude of present-day Denver—through which the first transcontinental railroad was to be built. Clarence King, who later became the first director of the U.S. Geological Survey (USGS), was the geologist in charge. He recognized a turning point for geology "when the science ceased to be dragged in the dust of rapid exploration and took a commanding position in the professional work of the country."[3] King's survey was undertaken "to examine and describe the geological structure, geographical condition and natural resources"[4] of the region west of the 105th meridian. Its first published report focused on the mining potential along the route. That same year, the commissioner of the General Land Office (predecessor of BLM), Joseph S. Wilson, stated: "The proper development of the geological characteristics and mineral wealth of the country is a matter of the highest concern to our people."[5]

Following news of the California gold strike in December of 1848, President James Polk asked Congress to provide for a geological and mineralogical examination of the gold-bearing region. Such an examination would support measures "to preserve the mineral lands, especially such as contain the precious metals, for the use of the United States; or, if brought into market, to separate them from the farming lands and dispose of them in such manner as to secure a large return of money to the treasury, and at the same time lead to the development of their wealth by individual proprietors and purchasers."[6] When the Department of the Interior was created several months later, its first Secretary, Thomas Ewing, asserted that government had a scientific role to play: "It is also due to those who become the lessees or purchasers of the mines that they should be furnished by the government with such scientific aid and directions as may enable them to conduct their operations not only to the advantage of the treasury, but also with convenience and profit to themselves."[7]

Ewing's statement acknowledged that, in the absence of scientific input, the gold diggers would mine the deposits in an inefficient and wasteful manner and compromise the sustained availability of the resource. Indeed, geology was widely viewed as a key to more efficient development in the mining districts. The need for a continuous flow of resources to fire the economic expansion of the Industrial Revolution drove the federal government for the first time to spend public money on scientific investigations.

Although much of the geological study of the western lands was devoted to and funded for practical purposes, geologists were often equally interested in fundamental scientific questions that these awesome landscapes posed. The lack of support for what we now think of as curiosity-driven research was lamented by the academicians of the day. In 1875, J. D. Whitney of Harvard University noted that federal interest in geology was limited to its connection with the development of mineral resources. He complained that "little has ever been done by any government to encourage scientific research where there was not some pretty direct practical result to be attained."[8] Pennsylvania State Geologist J. Peter Lesley asserted the following year that geology had become "slave to the economy; a guide to the treasures of force; a fosterer of the comfort of the mass of mankind; the fee'd expert of the Iron Manufacture; and a respected friend of the money-makers."[9]

A SHIFT TOWARD CONSERVATION
AND ENVIRONMENTAL PROTECTION

Toward the end of the nineteenth century, laws designed to urge development and settlement through sales of the federal lands gave way to laws that reflected a new policy, one that set aside federal lands in order to promote resource conservation and protection. The sale of land to private citizens was no longer the primary focus of land management. Instead, the goal was to retain land, improve its management, and generate revenue through leases and royalties.

These changes reflected the fact that Jefferson's ideal agrarian democracy failed as the nation became industrialized. Easterners became more concerned that the laws designed to reward the homesteader and the prospector also allowed large timber and mining companies to reap tremendous profits with little return to the federal coffers. In their wake, the large companies left significant environmental degradation and spoiled landscapes. Champions of conservation like Theodore Roosevelt saw these companies as capitalist despoilers and argued that government must step in and regulate their activities. On an island in the Potomac River just outside Washington, a memorial to Roosevelt includes the following quotation engraved in a giant marble tablet: "The nation behaves well if it treats the natural resources as assets which it must turn over to the next generation increased and not impaired in value." As opposed as Roosevelt was to unrestrained development, however, his other words at the same memorial make clear his sentiment: "Conservation means development as much as it does protection."

The Forest Reserve Act of 1891 gave the president the power to set aside and manage timber resources on federal lands. The first wildlife refuges were established in 1903, and the Forest Service was created two years later. The Antiquities Act of 1906 provided for the protection of natural and cultural resources. The Mineral Leasing Act of 1920 narrowed the scope of the 1872 Mining Law to hardrock minerals (gold and copper) and shifted other minerals (including the industrial minerals, aggregate, coal, and petroleum) to a leasing system. This shift allowed the same kind of resource management approach as that used for timber.

The change in goals from disposal to retention and long-term management was completed in 1976 with the passage of the Federal Land Policy and Management Act (FLPMA). This landmark legislation repealed the homestead laws, declaring that "it is the policy of the United States that the public lands be retained in federal ownership." The legislation also required that "the public lands be managed in a manner that will protect the quality of scientific, scenic, historical, ecological, environmental, air and atmospheric, water resource, and archeological values; that, where appropriate, will preserve and protect certain public lands in their natural condition; that will provide food and habitat for fish and wildlife and domestic animals; and that will provide for outdoor recreation and human occupancy and use." Even the BLM lands now were, in a sense, reserved.

Enactment of these various laws reflected a growing realization that resources were finite. From the beginning of this long road toward reasonable standards for environmental protection, science, and particularly geology, emerged as the key to rational management. In an 1864 book entitled *Man and Nature; or, Physical Geography as Modified by Human Action*, U.S. Ambassador to Italy, George Perkins Marsh, argued that humans were making the Earth uninhabitable and expressed the hope that geological, hydrographic, and topographic surveys would supply the facts "to reason upon all the relations of action and reaction between man and external nature."[10]

ENVIRONMENTAL PROTECTION COMES OF AGE

With roots going back to John Muir and early efforts to create national parks, the environmental movement of the 1960s had a radically different view of public lands and especially of what constituted natural resources. Instead of focusing on the wise management of commodity resources such as timber, minerals, and oil, environmentalists were much more interested in protecting a different set of natural resources including wildlife, wilderness, clean water, recreation, and aesthetic values. Inspired to action by sources such as Rachel Carson's *Silent Spring* and the construction of Glen Canyon Dam on the Colorado River, the movement reflected a varied spectrum of discontent with the status quo. Environmental statutes passed in the ensuing years include the Wilderness Act of 1964, the Wild and Scenic Rivers Act of 1968, the Clean Air Act of 1970, the National Environmental Policy Act of 1970, the Clean Water Act of 1972, and the Endangered Species Act of 1973.

These statutes have by no means put an end to development, but they have dramatically narrowed its scope. In 1968, nearly 75 percent of all federal lands were open to mineral exploration and development under the 1872 Mining Law. By 1974, nearly 75 percent of these lands were excluded from such development, a percentage that has stayed much the same since then.[11] For those lands that remained open to development, the new environmental laws required land management agencies to focus not simply on conserving resources but also on minimizing impacts on the landscape as a whole. In that respect, the most far-reaching of the new laws is the National Environmental Policy Act (NEPA), which requires the preparation of environmental impact assessments for major federal actions. Under NEPA, land management agencies must develop management plans and institute environmental restrictions on land use.

On the face of it, geology's traditional resource assessment role would seem to be compatible with the increased need for management plans and environmental assessments. Despite the growing concern for the environment, resource extraction remained one of the multiple uses of federal lands. Even the Wilderness Act of 1964, designed to withdraw federal land from access to resource exploration, specifies that wilderness lands are to be "surveyed on a planned, recurring basis . . . to determine the mineral values, if any, that may be present." In practice, however, such studies are rare because they are perceived as the first step toward future development.

With energy and mineral resource assessments a required but isolated component of management plans, the geological input into these plans was now also contained. The exception now focuses on the collection of minerals data associated with cleanup of abandoned mine lands, an activity directly tied to environmental priorities. If geology is to provide valuable advice for public land management, it must be relevant not just to society's need for resources but also to our equally strong need to protect our physical and biological environment. For that to happen, geology must move beyond its traditional role and become an integral part of a broader assessment of the landscape and what it may bear. Fortunately, the new paradigm of land use management, based on ecosystems, is ideally suited to support such a role.

GEOLOGY AND ECOSYSTEM MANAGEMENT

The Forest Service defines ecosystem management as "the integration of ecological, economic, and social factors on public lands to best meet current and future needs of people and the environment."[12] The goal is to apply a wholistic approach to natural resource management rather than to focus on individual resources or lands. Ecosystem management looks at an entire landscape and its position in the larger environment, including human impacts, to help achieve sustainable use of all resources. As Forest Service Chief Michael Dombeck told Congress in 1997: "Clearly, we must deliver sustainable supplies of wood fiber for American homes, forage for livestock and minerals and energy that help support healthy economies, but the health of the land must be our first priority. Failing this, nothing else we do really matters."[13] The Forest Service officially adopted this approach in 1992, and BLM adopted it soon thereafter. Now all land management agencies use an ecosystem-based approach.

Under traditional multiple-use management, science was applied directly to the resource in question. Hence, geology was almost exclusively focused on mineral and energy resources. Under ecosystem-based management, plans must consider all resources—both living and nonliving—within an ecosystem and evaluate their effects on one another in order to maintain a healthy ecosystem and provide for present and future needs. And, the scientific information must be integrated as well.

A strong scientific foundation is critical to the success of an ecosystem-based approach, a fact not lost on land managers. A 1996 BLM strategic plan states: "We must enhance our use of existing scientific research and acquire new knowledge if we are to realize our vision of productive, healthy ecosystems on the public lands and sustain vital natural resources over the long term."[14] That document also articulates the BLM's goals for scientific research on the overall health of the land: define critical baseline information; identify and evaluate long-term trends; and predict direct, indirect, and cumulative effects of natural processes and human activities.

The nature of the science needed to reach these goals and understand ecosystems depends on how one defines the term *ecosystem*. The BLM Forest Service has adopted the following definition: "Living organisms interacting with each other and with their physical environment."[15] Such a definition gives a central role to biological information, but it also requires geological information on the physical framework of the biological systems. Geological materials and processes control the type and availability of mineral nutrients, the acidity of soils, and availability and quality of water resources—important factors for sustaining life in ecosystems. Rock chemistry and physical conditions provide chemical elements and affect the physical character of soil. Rocks are the original source of chemical elements that compose biological species. Landforms are the result of geological processes that modify geological materials. Geology also has a considerable effect on how steeply rivers flow downstream, the spacing of stream riffles and pools, and how groundwater recharges itself—all factors that affect watershed health.[16]

Retired U.S. Forest Service geologist Stuart Hughes, a vocal proponent of geology's role in ecosystem management, has argued that "Life cannot exist if chemicals from rocks are not weathered and modified for the biosphere. Physical aspects of geology create niches that favor one adaptive species over another. A consequence of these niches is biodiversity, and it is a rallying cry for those committed to preserving the largest possible variety in the biological gene pool."[17] He has cited a variety of geological controls on species habitat as well as the critical role of groundwater and flooding in the maintenance of ecosystem health.

New cartographical technology makes integration of information across disciplines much easier than in the past. With the development of Geographic Information Systems (GIS), land managers can view integrated thematic maps with multiple layers that show the relationship between geology, soils, ground and surface waters, vegetation, and species distributions. Many of the ecoregion boundaries used for land planning are based on vegetation or climate patterns that closely correlate with geological maps.[18]

Biologists use GIS technology to overlay vegetation and species occurrence data layers on maps showing land use restrictions. Known as gap analysis, this technique makes it possible to identify gaps where areas with significant biodiversity have been left unprotected. Conversely, it can also identify protected areas that have little importance in terms of biodiversity, where restrictions can be relaxed. Incorporating geological data layers can help strengthen gap analysis, for example, by identifying nutrient sources or soil characteristics conducive to future habitat growth.

The Role of the U.S. Geological Survey

As the science agency for the Department of the Interior, the U.S. Geological Survey (USGS) plays a critical role in providing scientific support for Interior's land management agencies as well as for the Forest Service. The congressionally mandated integration of the National Biological Service into the USGS in 1996 provided a singular opportunity for greater collaboration between earth and life scientists on ecosystem problems. Reflecting that opportunity, one of the six key science goals in the USGS Geologic Division's newly released science plan is to establish the geological framework for ecosystem structure and function.

The plan states that "the living resources of ecosystems have a spatial organization imposed upon them by the geologic framework of the region and that geologic processes (for example, sediment transport, soil formation, groundwater flow) significantly influence ecosystem evolution and vitality on time scales of days to decades. Moreover, the geologic record contains valuable clues to the structure, history, and behavior of ecosystems."[19] The plan commits USGS geologists to "work with biologists, ecologists, hydrologists, and chemists to characterize the geologic framework and hydrologic cycle of ecosystems and to identify the geological and geochemical processes critical to ecosystem structure, function, and restoration. The temporal focus will be on time scales of agricultural, industrial, and urban development to provide the scientific understanding necessary for management of ecosystem health, sustainability, and restoration."[20]

Geologists can provide a wealth of information needed to manage ecosystems, including maps of surficial and shallow-subsurface geology, models of geological and geochemical processes that affect ecosystem functions, geochemical baseline data for metals and other contaminants, rates of faunal and floral change during recent geological history determined from paleontological and geochemical studies, and assessments of fundamental geological fluxes that affect ecosystem dynamics. For example, in the Mojave Desert of California, USGS geologists use the decay of radioactive elements to determine the age of the desert surface. Over time, hard algal crusts develop on desert soils, acting as a protective layer. Where the crusts are young or recently disturbed, the soils are more susceptible to erosion by wind or water, which in turn can affect the stability of the desert ecosystems supported by those soils. Also, in semiarid regions such as the western Great Plains, riparian zones adjacent to streams and rivers are some of the most productive and biologically diverse ecosystems in the country. Along the Platte River in Nebraska, geologists study the effects of changing sediment loads in the river due to heightened erosion from overgrazing and clear-cut forestry. Resulting changes in the shape and condition of the river banks have a tremendous impact on the plants and animals that live there. And in southern Florida, rapid population growth and agricultural development have produced significant changes to the Everglades ecosystem. There geologists use geochemical signatures of modern sediments to determine whether inputs of mercury, sulfur, and phosphorus are from natural or agricultural sources. By studying older sediments, geoscientists can determine the historical background levels of such elements prior to human intervention. By understanding natural as opposed to human effects, geologists can help managers determine which remediation techniques will be effective.

Geology in the Land Management Agencies

Although efforts by the USGS to increase the visibility of geology in ecosystem management are commendable, they are ultimately limited by a lack of day-to-day contact between geologists and land managers, particularly at the level of individual forests, parks, and ranges. Land management agencies employ few geologists themselves, and those that do engage geologists in traditional resource assessment activities. Geologists in these agencies want to incorporate their work into ecosystem management but find their efforts limited by their highly focused range of expertise. In 1994, the BLM's mineral specialists developed a still-unreleased draft report on the geological component of ecosystems and ecosystem management. Although the report argues that geology is the bedrock of ecosystems and outlines the many ways that geology affects ecosystems, its focus is limited to the effects of mineral extraction on the long-term sustainability of ecosystems. The report is nonetheless an important step in the right direction.

By far the most ambitious application of ecosystem management is the ongoing Interior Columbia Basin Ecosystem Management Project, jointly undertaken by BLM and the Forest Service. The project covers an area the size of France: 145 million acres stretching east from the Cascade Mountains to the continental divide and including portions of seven states. Its goal is to collect scientific information for the entire basin as the basis for comprehensive land management strategies that address forest health problems, declining salmon populations, and a variety of land use conflicts.

The project's summary of scientific findings includes an extensive section on the physical environment. It states that erosion, sediment transport, and deposition are the most relevant geological processes to the region's ecosystems. The summary refers to soils as an "ecologically rich and active zone" that regulates biologic productivity, hydrologic flow rates, and site stability.[21] It also recognizes geological controls on soils, such as glaciation and source material. For example, the ash-rich soils surrounding the ancient and still active volcanoes in the Cascade Range are very productive but are highly susceptible to compaction from grazing, mining, and logging activities. Once compacted, they lose their ability to absorb water and create higher runoff and sediment erosion rates that can cause clogged streams. Maps generated as part of the scientific assessment show the close relationship between ecosystem distribution and geological parameters such as bedrock type, glaciation, soil characteristics, and precipitation rates. One study conducted as part of the assessment mapped the distribution of bat species based on the occurrence of cave-forming limestone rocks that yielded suitable structures for bat habitat.

TOWARD A SUSTAINABLE FUTURE

The ultimate goal of any land management strategy is to attain sustainability of natural resources; and in a sense, it always has been. What has changed is our conception of what constitutes those natural resources. Teddy Roosevelt's admonition—to treat natural resources as assets that we must turn over to the next generation increased and not impaired in value—is equally valid today. However, the assets to be left to future generations now include clean air, clean water, wild scenery, backcountry recreational opportunities, and free-flowing streams. These new assets have not replaced our nation's need for commodity resources, and thus successful land management must balance a considerable array of conflicting needs and interests.

The situation is further complicated by multiple interests within the federal government. In any given watershed in the American West, the Bureau of Reclamation has responsibility to maintain dams, one of the Department of Energy's power marketing administrations generates and distributes electricity from those dams, the U.S. Fish and Wildlife Service enforces the Endangered Species Act, the Environmental Protection Agency secures standards of air and water quality, the regional Forest Service office must meet annual logging targets and accommodate thousands of yearly recreational visitors, and the Bureau of Land Management manages grazing, mining, and a host of other uses of its lands. Each of these agencies is engaged in projects mandated by the same government, a situation that inevitably produces conflicts.

In the face of these multiple competing interests, an ecosystem-based approach to land management reminds us that the health of the land must be our first priority. For ecosystem management to succeed, it must be based on a credible scientific foundation. Credibility in turn demands the broadest possible spectrum of input from the many scientific disciplines pertaining to the environment, both natural and human. In this context, the quality of work performed by land managers and policymakers will be limited if the broad purview of geology goes unrecognized.

The current situation is both a problem and a challenge for scientists and citizens alike. Any individual who uses federal lands has a stake in seeing land management informed by the most complete scientific data and analysis available. Citizens should demand that such information be the baseline requirement for management decisions. Scientists from different disciplines must learn to collaborate with one another, and they must talk to land managers as well as policymakers in Washington to convey effectively their management needs and then help those same policymakers identify how science can help to meet those needs.

Land management agencies need to broaden their in-house geological expertise and learn to take better advantage of what the USGS has to offer. Soil scientists and hydrologists may be the key link between the geologists and biologists, studying the interface where the rock-derived nutrients and groundwater become available to plants and animals. Linking these disciplines can produce the integrated scientific information required for sound management.

By adapting to changing times, geologists can make as substantial a contribution to land management in the next century as it has in the past two. What must not change is the commitment to provide the best possible scientific information in support of a rational and sustainable land use policy.

11

Rocks, Paper, Soils, Trees: The View from an Experimental Forest

Frederick J. Swanson

Erika, a scientist who had built a career on studies of the northern spotted owl, silently surveyed a tall, old-growth forest in the Oregon Cascade Mountains. This cold, rainy, winter's day in 1999 fueled reflections on her studies here as a graduate student in the 1970s, when the owl was the subject of no more than minor academic interest. In the intervening two decades, this owl species had become central to an environmental war over the balance of wood production and protection of remaining old-growth forests. In a series of legal skirmishes, the timber cut on the vast area of federal lands in the region was reduced to a small fraction of levels cut in the 1980s. Extensive reserve systems were established to protect the owl and hundreds of other species. Coming from a family of loggers, the many dimensions of this battle—overly simplified as "owl versus jobs"—have a very personal impact on Erika. She is well aware that each participant in the battle has distinctive answers to the questions, "What is a forest? How should it be managed?"

Today Erika has come back to this experimental forest to think about an issue that is very old. Recent flooding renewed centuries-long debate about effects of forest cutting and roads on the magnitude of these floods and the amount of sediment in drinking water. But recent social and scientific developments frame this old issue in a more complex manner than ever before: How should we manage dynamic forest ecosystems and watersheds to sustain high-quality drinking water, as well as protect habitat of native species and provide wood fiber for our use? As in the "owl wars," scientists have been asked to present results of their studies, particularly findings from highly interdisciplinary work in experimental forests, such as this. Why do we care about the health of forests and well-functioning watersheds?

As so many people are aware now—especially in the Pacific Northwest—forests are a nexus of interactions among earth, water, atmosphere, and human society. Healthy forests supply wood products but may also provide important ecological services. They regulate stream flow and water quality, offer homes to innumerable organisms of known and undiscovered values, and even influence global climate. Forests constitute an enormous reserve of carbon on our planet. Trees and other vegetation in forests take in carbon dioxide from the atmosphere and give off oxygen. The fixed carbon may be stored for long periods of time in plant matter or soil, before decomposition or fire releases it to circulate once again through the atmosphere or hydrosphere. When we cut forests, we remove from the earth system functioning organisms that can mitigate global warming caused by excessive amounts of carbon dioxide and other gases in the atmosphere.

Interactions of forests with the hydrosphere and the Earth's soil and near-surface bedrock are multifold. Forests pump liquid water from the soil and exhale it to the atmosphere as water vapor. In some environments, trees capture fine water droplets from passing fog and clouds, bringing nearly three feet of water to sites that would not receive this moisture without them. Forest vegetation tightly regulates the flow of chemical elements from precipitation or from breakdown of underlying bedrock. In steep, mountainous areas, forests blanket the soil with a thick, protective layer of organic litter. Tree root systems anchor the soil in place, reducing the potential for landslides. The rate of soil erosion by landslides and water runoff can increase following soil disturbance from logging and other land uses, giving testimony to the watershed protection services provided by intact forests. Water quality in downstream areas can be degraded, if erosion rates exceed normal levels. Much of the nation's drinking water comes from streams and rivers draining forested headwaters, so we have good reason to maintain healthy forests.

Our appreciation of the roles of forests in this intricate web of interactions has evolved slowly.[1] In the Pacific Northwest of the nineteenth century, forests stood in the way of progress. Over much of the twentieth century, forests represented planks waiting to be made into houses and other structures. Foresters and scientists working for the U.S. Forest Service, industry, and universities wanted simply to maximize production of wood. Several developments in the late twentieth century set the stage for dramatic change in our relationship with forests of this region. Environmental concern grew, represented in part by landmarks such as Earth Day and passage of the Endangered Species Act. At the same time, geologists and biologists worked together to gain a broader and deeper comprehension of how ecosystems and watersheds function. These important studies took place in a small number of sites across the country where interdisciplinary groups conducted long-term research that has profoundly influenced land use policy.

The H. J. Andrews Experimental Forest in the Cascade Mountains of Oregon is one of these special sites. The 16,000-acre Andrews Forest is characteristic of old-growth conifer forests, steep hillsides, and cold, clear streams of the Cascades. Here long-term ecosystem research has allowed earth scientists to detect, define, and resolve important environmental problems; it has provided technical guidance for development of sustainable approaches to management of forests, streams, and watersheds. Research at the Andrews Forest is done by geologists, ecologists, and their students who share a strong commitment to learning about this compelling landscape. Some of these scientists work for the U.S. Forest Service in its Pacific Northwest Research Station, and others work for Oregon State University as well as other educational institutions. Working closely with land managers of the Willamette National Forest, scientists translate research findings into new approaches to sustainable land use. The long-term ecosystem research conducted at the Andrews Forest, in which I participate, excellently displays the roles of earth sciences in forest ecosystem research—the subject of this essay.

Since its designation as an experimental forest in 1948, the Andrews has been home to hundreds of studies of hydrology, ecology, and forest geomorphology—examination of the Earth's surface forms and the processes that sculpt them. These investigations occupy the realms of both basic science and science applied to natural resource management. Of course, the Andrews Forest is not the only one of its kind in the United States. We are fortunate to have a national network of similar long-term ecosystem research sites, that helps us to understand better the interactions of geology and ecology in a variety of ecosystems, ranging from Arctic tundra and Antarctic dry valleys to the urban ecosystems of Baltimore and Phoenix. Hubbard Brook and Luquillo Experimental Forests in New Hampshire and Puerto Rico, respectively, are examples of other forested sites like Andrews among the 21 Long-Term Ecological Research (LTER) sites that the National Science Foundation funds. Additionally, there is an international network of LTER-like sites and a UNESCO-sponsored network of Biosphere Reserves, which collectively provide examples of the major ecosystems of our planet. Scientists from around the globe jointly conduct studies across sites within these networks, and their interdisciplinary, socially relevant work contributes to broad application of scientific results.

The earth sciences began to take a prominent role in ecosystem research at Andrews Forest during experimental watershed studies initiated in the 1950s. In these studies, hydrologists and soil scientists teamed with ecologists studying plant communities and nutrient cycling to examine effects of forest cutting and road construction on stream flow, water quality, and soil erosion. This work on areas of forest that ranged in size from 25 to 250 acres examined short-term effects as they occurred in the watershed. However, the accumulated information now spans more than 40 years.

My own involvement began in 1972 when I mapped the geology of the Andrews Forest as part of an international effort to understand the workings of the major types of terrestrial ecosystems of the globe. I was eager to take part in interdisciplinary studies with colleagues in ecology. It is unfortunate, but not surprising, that the time scales we were interested in did not match; the youngest rocks I was mapping were 3.5 million years old—geologically young—but the ecologists were studying biological processes that operated at time steps from minutes to, at most, a few years. With the luxury of time to work together, however, we gradually developed overlapping time and space scales of shared interest. We found common ground in our forest as we tried to understand how ecosystems operate over large areas, on the order of more than 10,000 acres, and over long periods of times, many centuries. Such large areas and swatches of time encompass major wildfires, windstorms, landslides, and floods, all of which have profound effects on ecosystems and hydrologic systems. The long-lived conifer trees record in their growth rings a 500- to 1000-year history of forest development as well as the effects of these kinds of catastrophic disturbances. Also, these great spans of space and time are very relevant for examining the effects of forest land use on soil productivity, biological diversity, and watershed conditions.

I and my colleagues from the U.S. Geological Survey and the U.S. Forest Service developed the study of forest geomorphology. That is, we were interested in landforms as the physical stage on which forest and associated stream ecosystems operate, and we looked at geomorphic processes as agents of ecological change and of movement of soil sediment and nutrients through the forest and streams. We were strongly influenced by the fascinating work that John Hack, a noted geomorphologist with the U.S. Geological Survey, and John Goodlett, who had extensive experience studying forest–soil relations in New England, conducted in the Appalachian Mountains.[2] Working together, they found that soil and vegetation differ greatly between stream bottoms and ridges and that a major downpour dramatically disturbed streamside vegetation, even in this geologically stable Appalachian landscape. As geologists, we were excited at the prospect of working in the steep, wet, geologically unstable, heavily forested landscapes of the Pacific Northwest, which are part of the tectonically active Pacific Rim. To our minds, the themes of forest geomorphology pioneered by Hack and Goodlett would be even more dramatically expressed here.

Research at the Andrews Forest over the past three decades has followed several lines of development in forest geomorphology, each of which has led us to appreciate the dynamic character of forest and stream ecosystems. Some key pieces of this story include investigations of how soil and sediment move through watersheds[3] and roles of vegetation and land use in controlling this movement,[4] especially during floods.[5] The links between geological and ecological worlds are built on knowledge of the interactions between forests and streams[6]—particularly the effects of woody debris in stream systems,[7] and the influences of land surface form on ecological processes.[8] All this work has had tremendous implications for the management of these ecosystems and watersheds.[9] Let me sketch some examples.

Geologists who study forest geomorphology have adopted the systems-oriented thinking of scientists who study hydrology and nutrient cycling in order to characterize the movement and storage of soil and sediment, including organic matter, through watersheds. This work, termed sediment budget and routing studies, seeks to document the amount, types, and paths of sediment moving through a particular watershed and the relative contributions of various geological processes to the total amount of sediment coming from that watershed. In the realm of forest geomorphology, an important question concerns the distinctive effects of vegetation on paths of soil and sediment as they travel through a watershed. For example, strong tree roots can minimize small landslides, wind-toppling of trees can trigger soil movement by turning up root systems, and logjams can store sediment and thereby affect water quality in downstream areas.

These studies have revealed new lessons about natural and managed watersheds. Past ecological studies of the cycling of soil and nutrients through watersheds have focused on the subtle, daily removal of elements dissolved in stream water. However, geological studies of sediment budgets show that the convulsive movement of soil and sediment by landslides, although previously missing from ecological analyses, is a major way that materials are removed from forested ecosystems in steep, slide-prone landscapes. Removal of forest cover can increase landslide frequency for a decade or two, as well as increase the rates of other erosion processes. And landslides do more than transport soil and sediment; they severely disturb plants, animals, and their habitat.

If the only aim of watershed managers was to ease the passage of water and sediment through stream systems, their job would be simple. Today, management of watersheds and ecosystems demands that we find useful balances between geological and ecological worlds, and between simplicity and complexity. The history of work on coarse woody debris in forested streams illustrates the challenge of finding a good balance. In the early years of research on the Andrews Forest ecosystem, geomorphologists and stream ecologists examined effects of coarse woody debris on sediment routing, stream channel shape, and aquatic habitat. Previous investigators had ignored big wood in streams for the simple reason that is was inconvenient to study. That is, big wood decomposes very slowly and moves infrequently. In fact, on the time scale of a typical research grant or thesis project, a large, dead tree changes very little.

By the mid-1970s, however, the geomorphic, ecological, and land management issues surrounding woody debris in streams of the Pacific Northwest demanded attention. At that time, a debate raged over leaving wood in streams or taking it out, and there was little distinction between natural wood and wood derived from logging operations. Up until the 1960s, loggers left large amounts of logging debris in streams. Generally small pieces, this material was highly mobile in floods and could worsen damage to bridges, buildings, and streamside vegetation during floods. Fisheries biologists were concerned that tight-knit logjams composed of logging debris could block passage of migrating fish, like salmon. So wood in streams got a bad name. But studies in natural stream systems of the Andrews Forest gave a different picture. Undisturbed, forested streams commonly contained a wide size-range of woody debris—from the very small to massive logs that were less likely to be carried away by high water flow during storms. Investigators observed fish swimming upstream around or through the natural, loose-knit, logjams during periods of high water flow. In fact, the habitat complexity created by logs in streams continues to provide refuge for fish and other organisms during floods.[10] Woody debris in streams also traps sediment, slowing its movement downstream and providing diverse habitats, including spawning beds for fish.

These findings helped us realize that, in forested areas, we must keep *logging* debris out of streams, maintain *natural* woody debris, and manage streamside regions to provide a continuous supply of woody debris with a natural size distribution. As a result of this research, it is now common practice to design streamside forest zones based on future wood supply to the streams. It is also considered good practice to place woody debris in streams to restore habitat complexity where natural levels of woody debris have been reduced by flooding or removal of fallen logs and standing trees.

As with any theme addressed through long-term research, our thinking about dynamics and functions of woody debris in streams and studies of those functions have evolved over time. This evolution has occurred through both gradual accumulation of knowledge, such as lessons from annual tracking of over 2000 numbered logs in study streams, and in the rush of learning that occurs during a major flood event as we watch 100-foot-long logs float down a stream for the first time in careers that span more than two decades. Because of these observations, we have begun to study mobile wood, its styles of transport, and its effects on streamside vegetation. Floating wood can topple streamside vegetation when carried along on a swift current, bumping into standing trees. So, while big wood in streams has many obvious ecological benefits, it is also an agent of disturbance.

Disturbance is not a common term in the language of geomorphology, but it is widely used in ecology. Perhaps life scientists recognize disturbances because processes like landslides can destroy the subject a life scientist studies. To a geologist, however, a landform-producing process is not viewed as a disturbance. In part, as a result of the involvement of geologists in ecosystem research in recent decades, all scientists more fully appreciate the beneficial aspects of disturbance processes. Many species depend on disturbance events to help them regenerate. Seed dispersal, germination, creation of seedbeds and light conditions favorable for growth are all made possible by disturbances that change the form of the landscape; fire and severe wind in upland habitats and floods and landslides passing through stream networks create landscapes that constitute a shifting mosaic of areas in various stages of recovery after disturbance events.

Understanding the natural disturbance regime of a landscape—the frequency, severity, and spatial patterns of disturbance—is a critical ingredient in appreciating the structure and function of both native and managed ecosystems. The types, ages, and arrangements of plant communities, for example, tell us when and where disturbances have previously occurred in the forest. Also, different types of forest management alter the disturbance regime of a landscape. Intensive plantation forestry and fire suppression, for example, change the frequency, severity, spatial pattern, and type of disturbances that might occur. Forests once prone to fire—ironically a rejuvenating event for some forests—may become crowded, ill, and subject to disease when fire is excluded. Clearly, disturbance processes are integral components of ecosystems.

Scientists and land managers at the Andrews Forest have noted this and have developed landscape management plans based on appreciation of the historical disturbance regimes and range of ecosystem conditions in forests.[11] For example, geological information tells us which areas of the forest are highly susceptible to landslides.[12] As a result, we can avoid human aggravation of naturally unstable areas, and allow natural processes, such as the movement of large woody debris to streams by landsliding, to proceed. We can use information about forest fire history to determine which portion of a forest to leave on a site and which portion to remove for wood products. Thus, we distribute our own disturbances across the landscape in a conscientious manner. This approach complements the conservation biology approach to landscape management, which is based solely on the habitat and dispersal needs of selected species. Science-based management can blend these perspectives on the biosphere, near-surface sediment and rocks, and hydrosphere with a firm grounding in the history of the landscape. Currently we are testing this new, geologically aware approach that uses historical disturbance regime information in a 55,000-acre "adaptive management" area in the hopes that it will enable us to manage better our forests and watersheds.

These sketches about development of concepts and information about sediment paths and budgets, woody debris in streams, and disturbance regimes in landscapes show the results of creative, interdisciplinary research on forest ecosystems and watersheds that includes the critical knowledge of earth science. Earth scientists in particular bring to these studies long-term historical perspective and familiarity with large spatial scales. These perspectives are essential for dealing with today's difficult natural resource issues.

In over a quarter-century of work at the Andrews Forest, I have learned some useful lessons about long-term ecosystem research and its value to society. First, scientists, land managers, policymakers, and the public have essential and distinctive roles in deciding how we will manage our nation's forests and watersheds. Second, it is difficult to anticipate which scientific findings will have great social impact. The work on old-growth forests and northern spotted owls at the Andrews Forest in the 1970s was considered by some to be esoteric and therefore of no societal value. Yet a decade later, this research contributed to major shifts in our perceptions of the nation's forest resources and effected changes in how we manage this resource. Our views of these regional and national changes have been shaped strongly by hundreds of field trips to the Andrews Forest, where examples of basic research and alternative land management systems are discussed critically with people who hold very different perspectives on these management issues. And, scientists have done more than simply publish scientific papers on this issue in peer-reviewed journals; a key paper on the nature of old-growth forests published in the so-called gray literature as a Forest Service General Technical Report[13] was intellectually accessible to anyone interested in the story.

In research at the Andrews Forest, it has been important to balance persistence in sustained long-term studies with attention to major science and societal issues of the day. Good, long-term data are extremely valuable and can be used to address new questions with new techniques. But, frequently it is also important to reevaluate and prove the relevance of such long-term studies to current issues. Well-targeted, short-term studies can help build the link between information in long-term data sets and current questions. Over the course of 40 years of study in the experimental watershed, for example, concerns have shifted successively from the effects of forest cutting on drinking water quality to soil erosion, flooding, and low stream flows as they affect species habitat. Once again, there is great concern about drinking water quality after a major flood in 1996 triggered high turbidity levels. The growing record of watershed conditions and performance over time has allowed us to address old questions with an expanded data record and to ask new questions, such as, How do revegetation patterns affect watershed hydrology and water quality? The answers are complex; but in the simplest terms, a healthy forest, even one establishing itself just a few decades after severe disturbance, can substantially limit the magnitude of floods and soil erosion.

Scientific work at the H. J. Andrews Experimental Forest has been exciting and rewarding in itself, but the sense of accomplishment has been magnified greatly by realizing that discoveries there have helped society better understand these ecosystems and watersheds, which it so enjoys and on which it depends. Geology, although it encompasses vast scales of time and space, contributes perspective and knowledge relevant to our most current issues and sets the historical foundation for practicing good care and stewardship of the natural world.

12

Are Soils Endangered?

Ronald Amundson

We might say that the earth has a spirit of growth; that its flesh is the soil—Leonardo da Vinci

Just over 125 years ago, John Wesley Powell captivated the nation with his nautical exploration of the canyons of the Green and Colorado Rivers. During the trip, he suffered boat wrecks, fire, near starvation, and the loss of three members of his party to an attack, in what appears to be a case of mistaken identity, by Native Americans. Years later, Powell noted with amusement that

> On my return from the first exploration of the canyons of the Colorado, I found that our journey had been the theme of much newspaper writing. A story of disaster had been circulated, with many particulars of hardship and tragedy, so that it was currently believed throughout the United States that all the members of the party were lost save one. A good friend of mine had gathered a great number of obituary notices, and it was interesting and rather flattering to me to discover the high esteem in which I have been held by the people of the United States.[1]

I think we all now recognize how quickly we are changing the Earth, but occasionally we need benchmarks and reminders to grasp its magnitude. Last summer, my wife, infant son, and I loosely followed part of Powell's route in the air-conditioned, four-wheel drive fashion of today's typical Western traveler. In Colorado, reclining in a deck chair alongside the heated swimming pool at the Grand Lake Lodge, I reread Powell's description of the scene:

> The Grand River [now called the Colorado] has its source in the Rocky Mountains, five or six miles west of Long's Peak. A group of little alpine lakes, that receive their waters from perpetual snowbanks, discharge into a

common reservoir known as Grand Lake, a beautiful sheet of water. Its quiet surface reflects towering cliffs and crags of granite on its eastern shore, and stately pines and firs stand on its western margin.[2]

Later in our journey, as we dined on a breakfast of omelets, hotcakes, and fresh fruit in the Lodge on the North Rim of the Grand Canyon, the crisis that Powell faced just a few miles away only a century before, the departure of three members of his band, resonated in my mind:

At last daylight comes and we have breakfast without a word being said about the future. The meal is as solemn as a funeral. After breakfast I ask the three men if they still think it best to leave us. The elder Howland thinks it is, and Dunn agrees with him. The younger Howland tries to persuade them to go on with the party; failing in which, he decides to go with his brother.[3]

Finally, as we sped homeward through the runaway Las Vegas megalopolis, I thought of Powell's band as they emerged from the torrent of the Canyon waters a few miles to the east:

The relief from danger and the joy of success are great. When he who has been chained by wounds to a hospital cot until his canvas tent seems like a dungeon cell, until the groans of those who lie about tortured with probe and knife are piled up, a weight of horror on his ears that he cannot throw off, cannot forget, and until the stench of festering wounds and anaesthetic drugs has filled the air with its loathsome burthen—when he at last goes out into the open field, what a world he sees! How beautiful the sky, how bright the sunshine, what "floods of delirious music" pour from the throats of birds, how sweet the fragrance of earth and tree and blossom![4]

I am a pedologist—an earth scientist who focuses on the origin and distribution of soils. Lately, what has most occupied my mind as I cross the United States landscape is the magnitude of what we have done to soils, in just a blink of time, and what it really means to those of my generation, and to those who are yet to come.

Sitting in front of the screen of my computer, thinking about da Vinci's analogy, I cannot help but notice my hands, now well into their fifth decade of existence. In many ways, my hands reflect the end of a typical academician's semester, pale and lacking any discernible sign of physical labor or effort. Yet, other marks such as scars, wrinkles, and fading calluses belie a more rigorous past: two decades spent as the son of a South Dakota farmer and nearly 20 years engaged in frequent, and physical, field research projects around the world.

The flesh of my hands is a dynamic, functioning organ that also bears a record, albeit incomplete and imperfect, of my history. I do not know what da Vinci really thought about the implications of his analogy, now 500 years old, but it rings with greater truth as we begin to recognize the importance of soil as an organ of the Earth: a key to our past and our future on this planet.

We think of soil as the brown earth exposed in plowed fields, construction sites, and gardens—but it is much more. Soils are living, breathing, historical entities that cover the Earth's surface. Although clearly important for agriculture, they have broader significance to our society. The burning of fossil fuel is largely thought to be the culprit of the growing carbon dioxide in our atmosphere. Yet, each year, soil adds plenty of carbon dioxide to the atmosphere, second only to the oceans, which add the most. Soil microorganisms respire, converting oxygen and organic substances to carbon dioxide. The amount of carbon that soils "breathe" into the atmosphere each year as carbon dioxide is about the same as that in a mountain of coal about ten cubic miles in size, or about ten times that injected into the atmosphere each year by all our industrial uses combined. The carbon dioxide released from soil comes from the breakdown of soil humus—the stuff that makes most soil surfaces dark brown or black—by microbes and other organisms. In a perfectly balanced world, each year plants will add as much carbon back to the soil as leaves and roots as that lost by microbial degradation of humus. However, because of human activity, we no longer live in a world that exists in this natural state of ongoing balance.

In the nineteenth century, the carbon dioxide content of the atmosphere began to increase measurably, long before fossil fuel consumption reached its present alarming rate. Earth scientists now know that this buildup of atmospheric carbon dioxide was the result of a large-scale conversion of prairies and woodlands in the United States and Europe to farmland. The conversion to farmland speeded up the microbial decomposition of soil humus, thereby causing the release of carbon dioxide from soils at a rate that outstripped inputs back to the soil from agricultural crops. Today, our presumed ever-warming world may also produce insidious effects on the amount of carbon dioxide that soils add to the atmosphere. My colleague, Susan Trumbore, a geochemist at the University of California at Irvine, has determined that for each $0.9°F$ increase in global temperature, soil microorganisms will accelerate their metabolism and produce an additional amount of carbon dioxide from decomposition of soil humus that will be roughly equal to a year's worth of global fossil fuel burning.[5] Clearly, soils are the dynamic and very temperamental flesh of the Earth's surface—agitate them and they cough up carbon dioxide at such a rate that it dwarfs many of our other activities.

Across the Earth, soils vary greatly in age, but most are at least 10,000 years old and many approach millions of years in age. When exposed to the elements over geologic time, they acquire physical and chemical features peculiar to the bedrock and climate of the region. Given the variety of rocks and climatic conditions on the Earth's surface, it should not be surprising that there is an almost unlimited variety of soil types. The most visible way that soils reflect their age and environment is through the changes in soil color and texture that one observes with greater depth from the surface. Such variations are called "horizons." Walk by a construction site, or take the more rigorous approach and dig yourself a six foot deep trench, and notice the gradual changes: dark browns at the soil surface are caused by the humus added by plants; reddish browns a foot or two below the ground surface are caused by iron minerals formed by chemical changes in the bedrock. These soil horizons rest on fresh, unaltered rock or sediment seen at the bottom of the trench.

Although some of the soils on the Earth's surface are quite old, they don't survive forever. It commonly escapes our attention during our brief human existence, but the crust of the Earth is inexorably subjected to upheaval. At regular intervals over the past two million years, parts of the Earth have been scoured by ice, water, and wind, and other portions have been buried under the debris created by these processes. The land surface buried by this debris includes the soil, which is transformed from a surficial "living" soil to a buried paleosol or *"fossil soil,"* a term used by the geoscientist Greg Retallack of the University of Oregon.

In the early 1980s, Thure Cerling, a geochemist at the University of Utah, recognized that chemical properties of soils, including their isotopic compositions, directly reflected the vegetation that grew at specific sites. He and his colleagues showed that grasslands, which now cover nearly 25 percent of the Earth's surface, may have evolved roughly eight million years ago—just a blink of an eye ago in geologic time.[6] My colleagues and I have begun recently to study the isotope chemistry of very old "living" soils around the world and are beginning to tease information from them about the "lost worlds" that they have witnessed in their long journey into our present day.

On the High Plains of Wyoming, in the shadow of the Wind River and Owl Creek Ranges, are a series of river terraces, or geological stair steps, leading away from the Wind River floodplain toward the mountain fronts. A climb up these steps is a journey back through geologic time, each step leading to a landscape hundreds of thousands of years older than the previous step. Oliver Chadwick, a soil scientist at the University of California, Santa Barbara, and I have recognized that the soils on each of these terraces can reveal, through their isotope geochemistry, a unique tale of the past. We have learned through oxygen isotopes in the soil minerals that rainfall from past summer monsoons of the Great Plains once extended as far as this high, cool desert.[7] We are presently working with the geochemists Ken Ludwig and Warren Sharp at the Berkeley geochronology center to use the radiogenic isotope composition of these soils to tell more precisely how old they are.

Recent discoveries also show that soil helps to control the composition of the air and the chemistry of our waters in our present world. We are only beginning to recognize the multitude of ways in which soil achieves these functions. But, just as we learn more about how soils function, soils are disappearing from the Earth's surface at a rate that will likely parallel our growing population. Why should we concern ourselves with the loss of soil, particularly undisturbed soil? As a matter of interest, soils record the history of the Earth's land surface over the past tens of thousands to millions of years. As a matter of livability, unique soil types may serve as potential natural resources just as biodiversity does. As a matter of survival, soils may provide processes that make the habitation of our planet possible.

I believe that there are two major reasons why the Earth's soil record is getting lost. First, we pave cultivated soils at an increasingly alarming rate. Thirty-five years ago, as a young student in my one-room rural grade school, the dangers of the loss of farmland to food production were apparent. Yet, it seems that this knowledge has had little effect on the way my generation does business. In central California where I live, it is not untypical for houses to cost $400,000 or more. Less expensive housing is available at the cost of a long commute to housing developments that were once agricultural communities, often 75 to 100 miles from the downtown San Francisco work center. The American Farmland Trust, a private organization devoted to the preservation of prime farmland, projects in its report *Farming on the Edge*[8] that nearly a third of the Great Central Valley of California, an area almost entirely in cropland and now the most productive agricultural region in the United States, will be paved suburban land by the middle of the next century.

Possibly even more disturbing than the loss of cultivated soils to suburbanization is our loss of previously undisturbed soils—and one of the most unique previously undisturbed soils exists in California's Great Central Valley. About a quarter of a million years ago, glaciers that covered the upper regions of the Sierra Nevada mountain range melted in harmony with a global glacial thaw. Meltwater from this massive mountain range, which cascaded into the Great Central Valley to the west, carried vast quantities of finely ground rock—called glacial flour—and spread it out across the valley floor in a thin layer covering more than 500,000 acres. Since that time, the sediment has been exposed to the elements and has developed one of the most unique soils in the United States, a soil called the San Joaquin series by the U.S. Department of Agriculture. Rainwater slowly moving through the soil has reacted with minerals in the glacial flour and has produced brilliant red colors, large amounts of clay, and a silica-cemented "hardpan" that lies about three feet below the land surface. This hardpan—sometimes a characteristic feature of soils that form in Mediterranean climates—greets the unsuspecting farmer or homeowner who would plant trees or install a septic system. How did this hardpan form? During soil formation, the element silicon is released by the chemical breakdown of minerals in the sediment through the action of water and organic acids. The silicon moves downward with slowly percolating water until, during the dry summer months, it is finally deposited as a thin mineral film that coats sand and silt grains. Thousands of years of this annual geochemical ritual finally leaves the lower layers of the soil engulfed in a silicon cement, commonly known as opal. Water and plant roots are unable to move through these cemented layers except in occasional cracks and fissures.

The hardpan of the San Joaquin has inspired poetry, prose, and some unusual approaches to architecture. Near downtown Fresno, California, well below the traffic and strip malls, lies the Forestiere Underground Gardens. Started in 1906 by Baldasare Forestiere, who labored with a pick and shovel to penetrate the hardpan, the garden includes a series of rooms that run 12 to 25 feet below the Earth's surface, among them bedrooms, a kitchen, a ballroom, and an auto tunnel. Listed in the National Register of Historic Places, the gardens attract up to 15,000 visitors each year. In a work of fiction in *The New Yorker* inspired by the real garden and gardener, writer T. Coraghessan Boyle chronicled the life of an Italian immigrant, also known as Baldasare Forestiere, whose fate in love led him to labor below the ground. Of Baldasare's first experience with the San Joaquin soil, Boyle wrote:

> *It was some day of the following week when Baldasare began digging . . . . He wanted the well to be right in front of the shack, beneath the tree where his house would one day stand, but he knew enough about water to know that it wouldn't be as easy as that. He spent a whole morning searching the immediate area, tracing dry watercourses, observing the way the hill under his shack and the one beside it abutted each other . . . until finally . . . he pitched his shovel into the soil.*
>
> > *Two feet down he hit the hardpan. It didn't disconcert him, not at all— he never dreamed it would extend over all the seventy acres.*[9]

In 1997, a class of middle school children from Madera, California, convinced the California state legislature to proclaim the San Joaquin soil the official "State Soil of California." To enable the bill to pass the contentious California Assembly, a rider was attached to ensure that the designation as "State Soil" included no protective status. To most Californians, this technicality likely has little significance. However, as a soil scientist, I am greatly concerned whether there will be any of the San Joaquin soil left for future Baldasares–or for school-children. At the turn of the century, agriculturalists attacked the San Joaquin soil with dynamite and horse-drawn land levelers. Today, the San Joaquin soil is altered by far more effective means, including laser-guided land levelers and Caterpillar-drawn plows that extend to five feet or more in depth. The result of this assault is that it is now a challenge to locate pristine tracts of San Joaquin soil for classes of students or for research projects. The editors of the *San Francisco Examiner* could not resist a humorous jab at both the newly designated State Soil and its lack of protection:

> *In an open invitation to earthy puns and a soiled reputation, the state Senate voted 33–1 the other day to designate the silty loam of the San Joaquin Valley as the Official State Dirt.*
>
> > *This is not a dirty joke . . . .*

Glory doesn't come along every day for dirt.
    Thus it seems impolite to add that much of the valley's once-dusty
topsoil is imprudently loaded with chemical cocktails ... and soaked in
canal water imported from the mountain rivers of Northern California.
        Let's just hope that the Official State Dirt doesn't emulate the Official State
Animal, the grizzly bear, which hasn't been seen in California since 1913.[10]

Why *should* we preserve soils and maintain a diversity of soil types around the world? If we allow ourselves the liberty to view soils as a living, functional organ of the planet, we can use some of the same arguments used on behalf of preserving biodiversity. In their paper "Biodiversity Studies: Science and Policy," biologists Paul Ehrlich and Edward O. Wilson proposed ethical, aesthetic, and economic reasons to preserve biodiversity;[11] these all apply to soils.

Although humans are but one of millions of species on Earth, we affect the chemistry and physical properties of the planet and, subsequently, the fate of most other species. We have a moral obligation to minimize our effect on Earth's other inhabitants and their habitats. Harvard University geologist and essayist Stephen Jay Gould casts this obligation after the biblical tenet "Do unto others . . ." and calls it the ecological "golden rule."[12] Gould argues that we should adhere to this golden rule for the sake of self-preservation rather than because of altruism. He points out that if we agitate the planet enough, humans may be destroyed, but the Earth, with enormous spans of geologic time on its side, will recover and record our brief existence in a thin sedimentary stratum. If we bury prime farmland under asphalt, or push agricultural development further into forests or remaining grasslands, we do not live according to the golden rule.

My late predecessor at Berkeley, Hans Jenny, dazzled audiences from Berkeley to the Vatican with illustrated lectures on the role of soil in landscape painting. As Hans fondly argued, artists chose subjects of aesthetic value, and because they painted soils, soils must have beauty. When asked during an interview about his appreciation of the aesthetics of soil, Hans replied:

Soil appeals to my senses. I like to dig in it and work it with my hands. I
enjoy doing the soil texture feel test with my fingers or kneading a clay soil,
which is a short step from ceramics or sculpture.
    Soil has a pleasant smell. I like to sit on bare, sun-drenched ground
and take in the fragrance of the soil. As yet, neither touch nor smell
sensations have been accorded aesthetic recognition, but colors delight
painters, photographers, and writers, as well as you and me.
    In loess country, plowed fields on slopes show wide bands of attractive
color gradations from dark browns to light yellows, caused by erosion of the
surface soil. Warm brownish colors characterize fields and roofs in
Cézanne's landscape paintings of southern France, and radiant red soils of
the tropics dominate the canvasses of Gauguin and Portinari. Soil profiles
viewed in pits may reveal vivid color and structure patterns of layers of
horizons. I have seen so many delicate shapes, forms, and colors in soil
profiles that, to me, soils are beautiful.[13]

Soil color owes much of its character to the climate. Cool northern climates induce chemical processes which produce minerals confined to grays and tans; while the warm, sunny Mediterranean and tropical climates produce minerals in a profusion of reds, ochres, chestnuts, and terracottas. Vincent van Gogh, shortly before his death, confided in a letter to his brother Theo that:

> *Unfortunately, there are no vineyards here, but for that, I should have time for nothing else this autumn. On the other hand, the olive trees are very characteristic, I'm struggling to catch them. They are old silver. Sometimes with blue in them. Sometime greenish, bronze, fading white, above a soil which is yellow, pink, violet-tinted or orange, to dull red ochre, very difficult though. Very difficult. But that suits me.*[14]

Soils have an obvious economic value, particularly from an agricultural perspective. However, unused soil holds potential economic value beyond agricultural uses. Presently we know little about the geographical distribution of soil microorganisms and their metabolic capabilities. Yet, it is from the soil that some of the great success stories in the development of antibiotics have come. In his wonderful book, *Dirt: The Ecstatic Skin of the Earth*, Bill Logan relates that the Nobel prize in medicine of 1952 was awarded to Selman Waksman, soil microbiologist at Rutgers University, for the discovery of streptomycin. This discovery reportedly stemmed from a question asked over coffee in his lab: "Why is it, when you bury a diseased body in the ground, that this earth is not poisoned?"[15] The answer, of course, was because soil contains an array of natural antibiotics produced by the thousands of various soil microorganisms. Later in his life, Waksman recalled his first research project as a young graduate student, research that formed the basis for his subsequent achievements and acclaim:

> *I . . . selected as a subject for my thesis a problem dealing with the bacterial population of the soil . . . . I decided that a survey of the distribution of the bacteria in different soil types, at different depths and in different seasons of the year, would yield the desired experimental data . . . . I immediately proceeded to dig several ditches, to a depth of thirty inches . . . . Little did I dream at that time that there was gold in those ditches, in the form of microbes, many of which had never been seen before by the human eye.*[16]

On visits back to my home in eastern South Dakota, I sometimes stand on the highest hill on my mother's farm and look out across corn and soybean fields that span seemingly endlessly in all directions. In the loft of our barn are momentos of a very different but recent past: buffalo skulls, stone hammers, and arrowheads. Where has the tallgrass prairie, with its dark humus-rich soils, gone? My colleague Larry Tieszen, a biologist at Augustana College, has spent years scouring eastern South Dakota for pristine tracts of this prairie, with its dusky red grasses that once reached such heights that homesteading mothers worried about losing their children in the grassy forest. One of Larry's study sites is only three miles from my mother's farm, a few square yards of grassland on the crest of a hill, surrounded on all sides by a burr oak woodland. Trees and nonnative plants are encroaching from all sides as I watch this prairie relic diminish in size with the passing years.

In her novel, *My Antonia*, set on the Nebraska plains, Willa Cather wrote of the reduction of the tallgrass prairie to the confines of scattered pioneer cemeteries:

> *Years afterward, when . . . the red grass had been ploughed under and under until it had almost disappeared from the prairie; . . . [the] grave was still there, . . . with its tall red grass that was never mowed, . . . like a little island; . . . I never came upon the place without emotion, and in all that country it was the spot most dear to me . . . . Never a tired driver passed the wooden cross, I am sure, without wishing well to the sleeper.*[17]

While I know that the character of the soil under the rows of corn differs greatly from that under the rich mat of perennial grasses on the hilltop, I look at the soil maps produced by the U.S. Department of Agriculture and find that both sites are considered to have the same soil. In other words, soils are mapped as what they were before being converted to agriculture, not what they now are—a pale, domesticated version of their former selves. It is difficult to convince politicians, or even my colleagues, that certain soil types, such as those that once spread across the plains, are becoming rare, because the soil maps indicate abundance. Some scientists have begun to recognize that many cultivated and irrigated soils must be reclassified and distinguished from uncultivated ones. This shift in perspective is important in preservation efforts, for as Charles Darwin noted in *On the Origin of Species*, "Rarity, as geology tells us, is the precursor to extinction,"[18] a concept now accepted by society when biological rarity is discussed.

Landscapes and soils once considered commonplace and disposable are now being reduced to scattered landscape fragments. Compounding this problem is the fact that unlike rare living species, soils do not reproduce and are likely to be the result of singular circumstances that occurred over the full course of millions of years. We are appalled when a 3,000-year-old tree is cut down, but our culture generally applauds the ingenuity of developers who can transform a 300,000-year-old soil with its hardpan into a golf course or housing tract.

Can ethical, aesthetic, and economic as well as scientific arguments for preservation of soils convince us to shift our attitudes and change our actions? In the end, if a movement to preserve natural landscapes and soils does occur, it may be something far more intuitive and ineffable that motivates us. My wise colleague, Professor Jenny, once was asked, "Does the soil have a right to be protected for any reason other than that based on what is best for humans?" Hans replied:

Society grants human beings the right to exist regardless of whether we are useful or not. The same privilege has been extended to a few endangered plant and animal species. I wish society would grant the same right to soil . . . . Today, the idea of stewardship of land is pitted against the belief in soil exploitation for personal gain and [the belief] that soil is merely an economic commodity in the marketplace . . . . I place natural soils and ecosystems, the nature museums, on par with art museums, . . . college and temples.[19]

In the past few years, an unprecedented series of rainy summers has been a boon to farmers in my mother's corner of South Dakota. These rains have also, for the first time in my life, produced springs in a few of my mother's fields, drowning out small patches of the corn and soybeans. In place of these crops, much to my astonishment, a profusion of cattails, sedges, and wild flowers have erupted—vegetative poltergeists from the prairie past. The seeds of these plants have lain dormant in the soil these past 100 years, awaiting this moment to reassert themselves, and to remind us of the shadow world that patiently waits should we depart.

From some distant vantage point, hundreds of millions of years from now, the geological record will tell the tale of the tenure of *Homo sapiens*. Will the record, told in the language of fossil soils and plants, be a brief one, with eroded and disturbed soils suggesting a global cataclysmic event? Or, will the record be much longer, and will the fossil plants and soils be far richer and diversified, suggesting that this bipedal organism coexisted with a diversified environment for an impressive span of time? Geology has allowed us to peer backward, deep into the chasm of time, in order to learn lessons that will guide us into the future, should we be wise enough to heed that retrospective gaze.

Sometime, about two and a half million years ago on a savanna that is now east Africa, an early species of the genus *Homo* likely fashioned a few stone tools, forever altering our relationship with nature. The shapes and uses of these tools slowly changed with time until, just a few thousands of years ago, a dizzying profusion of metal, glass, and plastic supplanted them. The passage of time has weakened the genetic and cultural threads that connect us to our African predecessor. Yet, in our frenzied world, confronted with diminishing natural resources brought about by our technological precociousness and aware of the power of tools and technology never imagined by our hominoid ancestors, we must again ask ourselves a question that was likely first posed somewhere on that arid plain: "How shall I choose to use this?"

13

The Edwards Aquifer: Water for Thirsty Texans

John M. Sharp, Jr. and Jay L. Banner

Water is our most precious natural resource. Without drinkable water, civilization and life as we know it would cease to exist. In the drier parts of the planet, the presence of reliable sources of drinkable water dictates where and how we live. This is true, for instance, in central, southern, and western Texas.

As one drives up Interstate 37 from the bays, estuaries, beaches, and sand dunes of Port Aransas on the Gulf of Mexico into southern and central Texas, one travels through a subtle variety of landscapes. Near the coast, the land is quite flat and the climate is subtropical. Ship channels in Corpus Christi reveal the varied industry of the area as passing oil tankers dwarf fishing boats. Driving north, one passes gently rolling farmland and cattle range of the Coastal Plain into the Blackland Prairie. The fertile soils of these provinces are developed on sands, silts, and clays that were deposited from rivers and the shallow Gulf of Mexico, whose shoreline migrated with changing sea level over the past 140 million years.

Farther inland, as one reaches San Antonio in central Texas, the climate becomes drier, and western counties experience semiarid conditions, with less than 20 inches of rainfall each year. The landscape becomes hilly as one passes over the few hundred feet of elevation of the Balcones Escarpment, which was produced by faulting in the Earth's crust 15 to 20 million years ago. Standing on the escarpment looking south and east, one gazes out on the Blackland Prairie. To the north stretches the more rugged Edwards Plateau, which is built by flat-lying limestone strata that are dissected by streams. On this plateau, there is sufficient rainfall to support some agriculture and cattle ranching; it hosts a rural, low population-density economy. Along the base of the escarpment are the region's major cities and towns, including San Antonio and Austin. More

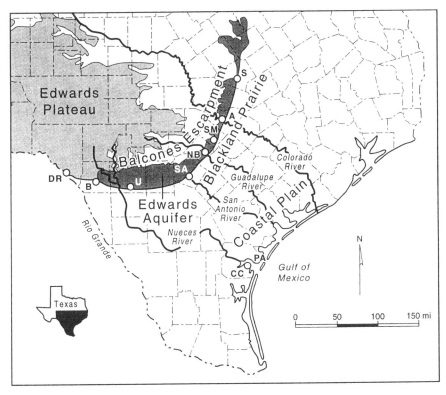

Southern and central Texas, showing the location of the Edwards Aquifer and the Edwards Plateau. Cities and towns are identified by letters: Del Rio (DR), Brackettville (B), Uvalde (U), San Antonio (SA), New Braunfels (NB), San Marcos (SM), Austin (A), Salado (S), Corpus Christi (CC), and Port Arkansas (PA).

than fortuity caused humans to congregate here. Cities and industries require dependable, large volumes of water, and springs feed larger streams along the base of the escarpment. Water is present there because of the region's unique geology, its configuration of rocks and faults. The limestones and associated strata that transmit water to and from the surface compose the Edwards Aquifer, the source of water for the region. The streams, springs, and aquifer are ultimately fed by rainfall from storms.

Rainstorms occur when warm, moist tropical air from the Gulf of Mexico encounters cooler, drier air as it moves northward or as it moves over and is lifted by the Balcones Escarpment in central Texas. Some of the most intense rainfalls in U.S. history have occurred along this escarpment. For example, 38 inches of rain fell in 24 hours near the town of Thrall in 1921. High temperatures and long periods between such storms, however, cause significant dry spells. Studies of historical records show that prolonged dry periods leading to drought are also part of the natural climatic cycle here.

From Del Rio on the Mexican border, east through Brackettville, Uvalde, San Antonio, New Braunfels, San Marcos, and Austin, to Salado, each city is located where major springs issue from the Edwards Aquifer. The aquifer's springs provided a reliable source of fresh water in a region where both river flow and rainfall vary considerably. The obvious relief that the cool spring waters and surrounding dense, wooded vegetation must have brought to early inhabitants of this area was emphasized during the summer of 1998, when the region experienced 26 consecutive days with temperatures of 99°F or higher. Early settlements bordering the Edwards Plateau along the Balcones Escarpment relied on these fresh water sources, and fierce conflicts between Confederates, Comanches, Apaches, Kickapoos, European immigrants, and desperados were influenced by the hydrogeology of the area.[1] Until large reservoirs were constructed in the twentieth century, the major cities developed around the springs and utilized their waters. We still use the springs for water obtained from wells drilled into the Edwards Aquifer. In fact, over two million people, including residents of the city of San Antonio, still get their drinking water from the Edwards. The spring systems and the streams that issue from them are also vital to the culture of these areas. Although some springs have gone dry, parks and recreational areas in the cities center on the springs.

Rapid development and population growth are now occurring in this area. Demand for water has grown and is expected to escalate dramatically. Fueled by a growing technology industry, a varied recreational and cultural landscape, wide-open spaces, fresh air, and mild winters, the population of the general Austin–San Antonio area is projected to double by the year 2025. Will the Edwards Aquifer be able to sustain the water needs of this growing population? Will we be able to develop and enact adequate management and use plans that will conserve water and protect its quality? Or, will we have struggles over water, as our forebears had?

ANATOMY OF AN AQUIFER

Aquifer means "water bearer" in Latin. The term is commonly mentioned in the modern media and therefore a precise definition of aquifers matters for a number of reasons. For instance, a "sole source aquifer" has a certain legal status because there are no viable alternative sources of water where that aquifer exists. Also many aquifers have been degraded or contaminated by human activity and must be cleaned up by the responsible party. Geologists define an aquifer as a body of geological material, such as sand, soil, or rock that yields usable amounts of adequate quality water to wells or springs. An aquifer must have holes in it to hold the water; that is, it must be porous, like a sponge. The pores must also be big enough and interconnected sufficiently to allow water to flow easily through the sand, soil, or rock. The extent of connectivity of the pores is called permeability. Not all geological materials have ample porosity, enough permeability, or satisfactory water quality to form an aquifer. The

Edwards, however, is an exceptional aquifer as a result of the way it was developed over the course of 100 million years.

Today, several hundred feet of carbonate rocks make up the Edwards Aquifer. Carbonates refer to rocks, such as limestones or dolostones, or other sedimentary deposits that are composed mainly of the minerals calcite, aragonite, or dolomite. During the early Cretaceous Period, approximately 100 million years ago, the sediments that would eventually be compressed to form the carbonate rocks were formed on an ancient shallow-water marine shelf. The setting was probably similar to that of the Florida Keys, the Bahamas, and the Arabian Gulf in which carbonate deposits accumulate today. Deposition during the Cretaceous occurred during a time when global sea level was so high that the ancestral Gulf of Mexico flooded into central Texas and much of central North America. The deposits that formed during this time period contained reefs that were dominated by clams, called rudistids, that had unusually shaped shells. Fossils of these now-extinct clams and a variety of other clams, snails, sea urchins, algae, and small one-celled organisms called foraminifera are common in some beds—or stratigraphic layers—within the Edwards Aquifer. Occasionally, the tops of some beds are marked by the track-ways of dinosaurs that trod through the muddy sediment. Some soft-bodied, shrimplike organisms left their mark in the sediments in the form of burrows, which reveal the foraging and dwelling environments of these creatures. In the sediments, pathways with different porosities and permeabilities were created by these burrows and by the spaces between fossils.

Sea levels fluctuated during the Cretaceous, so at times of low sea level these marine sediments were exposed to the atmosphere. During times of exposure and periodic rainfall, some fossil shells were dissolved, and small caves and other dissolution features formed before the seas again covered the rocks. Occasionally, tidal flats and shallow lagoons of vast extent formed and beds of soluble minerals, such as gypsum, formed by evaporation of seawater. At other times, the seas were deep enough to allow great coiled ammonites and mosasaurs to swim above the sediments. Today, the layer of rock above the Edwards Aquifer is the Del Rio clay. This rock was formed by the compression of volcanic ash that settled in quiet waters. The permeability of Del Rio clay is so low that, wherever the clay is present, water cannot flow through it, either into or out of the aquifer. The Del Rio clay serves to confine the aquifer. Where the aquifer rocks are exposed to the land surface, the aquifer is said to be a water-table aquifer, or to be unconfined. The presence or absence of the Del Rio clay has important hydrologic and land use implications for people of this region, because a well drilled into a confined aquifer usually is less susceptible to contamination.

Some 45 million years after the end of the Cretaceous Period of high sea level and carbonate and clay deposition, the Edwards Aquifer rocks were fractured, faulted, and exposed to rainfall and erosion at the Earth's surface as a result of the faulting that produced the Balcones Escarpment. The soluble rocks again began to dissolve. Nodules of gypsum and other soluble minerals were dissolved, and the porosity of the rocks that contained the nodules increased. In addition to the porosity and permeability created by the original pores between and within fossils and burrows in the Edwards strata, rainfall that infiltrated the Edwards enhanced preexisting pathways of permeability—zones of dissolved gypsum, original pores, fault-induced fractures, and horizontal breaks (known to geologists as bedding planes) that separate rock strata. These pathways sped up dissolution of the carbonate rocks. Advanced dissolution formed conduits and caves that often are found aligned along the fractures and bedding planes. These dissolution features give the Edwards Aquifer its tremendous permeability. As a result of the faulting and uplift, streams cut down through the limestone, the water table was lowered, and caves were drained. Today, rainfall percolates down through soils and carbonate rocks, dissolves some of the carbonate minerals, drips into the caves, and slowly deposits calcite in the form of stalactites, stalagmites, and flowstones, which are collectively called speleothems.

In a general sense, the Edwards Aquifer is simple. Water gets into it from the rainfall percolation process just described. In addition, "losing" streams—those which flow over carbonate outcrops and sink into the stream bed—add water to the aquifer. However, this process only happens in the permeable rocks exposed in the unconfined zone; otherwise, the overlying Del Rio clay

Dissolution features in the Edwards Aquifer. The large pores were produced by dissolution of portions of the rock layer; these pores often follow patterns of preexisting shells or burrows of marine organisms that occurred in the original sediment deposited more than 65 million years ago. (*Photograph by John M. Sharp*)

stops percolation. The Edwards differs from most aquifers in that most of the water—almost 80 percent—that gets into—or recharges—the aquifer is from losing streams. Water flowing in stream channels sinks into cracks or sinkholes, so recharge is locally restricted and, therefore, unevenly distributed.

The Edwards Aquifer is shaped like a crescent moon, with its concave side facing to the northwest. It ends to the north because there the Cretaceous carbonate rocks that form the aquifer have been eroded away. The southern boundary of the aquifer is termed the bad-water zone, because there the water in the aquifer is too salty to be used as drinking water. This salinity is natural and does not result from human activities. In the regions of the aquifer near San Antonio and Austin, salty brines migrate up from compacting sediments in the subsurface under the Gulf of Mexico. Near the Rio Grande, saltiness occurs simply because the groundwater dissolves soluble minerals in the aquifer, especially gypsum, along its flow path and introduces mineral salts into the system. There is considerable concern that saltwater from the bad-water zone will migrate into the aquifer and increase its saltiness. However, monitoring has shown that the position of the bad-water zone has been quite stable, even in times of drought.[2] This stability exists because the rocks in the bad-water zone have substantially lower permeability than most of the rocks of the aquifer, because high flow rates in the aquifer push saltier waters south, and because the bad-water zone abuts relatively impermeable, crushed rocks along a fault.

Groundwater flow in the Edwards Aquifer runs mostly along fractures or dissolution zones that are oriented along the Balcones Escarpment. Also, like landscapes carrying surface water, aquifers can have divides. The Continental Divide separates the surface waters that flow to the Pacific Ocean from those that flow to the Atlantic. Every river or stream has its own particular divides. Groundwater divides separate groundwater that flows to one natural outlet from groundwater that flows to another outlet. Groundwater cannot flow across a divide, just as surface waters cannot flow over the Continental Divide. The Edwards Aquifer contains three divides, which separate the aquifer into three distinct groundwater flow regions. From each of these, water leaves the aquifer at big springs or wells. The largest and most politically sensitive segment of the Edwards Aquifer is that which encompasses the largest area and includes the city of San Antonio. This segment of the aquifer provides the majority of water for municipal and agricultural purposes.

COMPETING DEMANDS FOR AQUIFER WATER

Competition for the water from the Edwards Aquifer is intense. The greatest users of water pumped from the aquifer are municipalities and agriculture; they use 89 percent of aquifer waters. Individual wells for domestic use and industry pump the remainder. There are, however, important uses of Edwards waters that depend on the natural spring outflows.

Water from the Edwards Aquifer is desirable because it is uncontaminated, has low salinity, and is very cheap to produce. Such a rapidly urbanizing environment, however, challenges our ability to maintain both water quantity and water quality. Construction of roads, parking lots, and buildings impact water quality because the increase in impervious cover (i.e., pavement) decreases the filtering and water retention capacity of the landscape. In addition, the greater residential and industrial activity above the aquifer produces more chemical and particulate waste. This pollution is a special concern in limestone aquifers such as the Edwards whose enhanced porosity and permeability allow wastes to spread rapidly as groundwater flows along conduits. Few alternative water sources for the region exist, and they will be very expensive to access.

Although few farmers in Texas irrigate their land, any water used for irrigation represents consumptive use. That is, water is not returned to the streams or groundwater, but instead goes into the atmosphere via plant respiration. Another agricultural use is aquaculture. The largest naturally flowing well in the world, at 40,000 gallons per minute, taps the Edwards Aquifer—it was once used to fill ponds for farming catfish.

In Texas, groundwater belongs to the landowner, who can use as much as desired as long as it is used in a "reasonable" manner, as defined by the courts. When criticized for their high water use, farmers have rightly pointed out that growing food benefits people, whereas lawn irrigation, the largest use of water in cities, is wasteful. As our cities grow rapidly, and as residential grass lawns replace native plant species adapted to the semiarid climate, the amount of water used for keeping grass green will continue to grow at a prodigious rate.

The natural spring systems provide important recreational and social amenities for the municipalities that cluster around them. Major urban parks are often built adjacent to the springs, and they host water sports, bathing, fishing, and hiking. To lose natural spring flows, as has already occurred for the San Antonio and San Pedro Springs in San Antonio, is both undesirable and politically unpopular.

Flows from the streams that cross the carbonate rocks of the aquifer or issue from its springs supply downstream users on the Colorado, Guadalupe, San Antonio, and Nueces Rivers. Residents of Corpus Christi as well as residents of smaller cities and farms along these streams rely on these surface waters for their water needs. Anglers, boaters, and campers also make use of these streams between the springs and the Gulf of Mexico. Finally, flows of fresh waters into the bays of the Gulf are needed to maintain the populations of shrimp and other aquatic species.

An incredibly diverse fauna exists within the Edwards Aquifer, including two species of blind catfish and the Texas blind salamander—*Typhomolge rathbuni*, a federally listed endangered species. Several small aquatic organisms live only in the vicinity of the big springs issuing from the Edwards Aquifer. Other species listed as endangered are fish found in Comal, Barton, and San Marcos Springs—the fountain darter (*Etheostoma fonticola*) and the

San Marcos gambusia (*Gambusei georgei*); salamanders—the Barton Springs salamander (*Eurycea sosorum*) and the San Marcos Springs salamander (*Eurycea nana*); and Texas wild rice (*Zinzania texana*). The San Marcos gambusia, however, has not been observed for almost ten years. Several other aquatic species, such as the riffle beetle in Comal Springs (*Heterelmis comalensis*), are potential candidates for the endangered species list. These species are sensitive indicators of the health of the ecosystems in which they live. Federal laws prohibit any actions that might harm or threaten to harm listed species. Clearly, if humans continue to draw heavily from the aquifer, we will decrease spring flows or dry up the spring systems, and thereby eliminate several species.

The case of the Barton Springs salamander has engendered a curious juxtaposition of many interests. These contending parties include people who wish to build homes in the contributing and recharge zones that feed the springs; those who are concerned about the effects of such development on the habitat of the endangered salamander; those who are concerned about the quality of spring water that feeds a giant pool, which at a comfortable temperature of 68°F allows people to swim in it year-round; and those who wish to bathe in parts of the springs that are now fenced off to protect salamander habitats. Even a seemingly simple task such as cleaning the pool has spawned debate regarding the effects (on water quality and habitat) of lowering the pool level and of different methods to remove algae from rocks in the pool.

These varied demands have created numerous political conflicts, because the use of Edwards Aquifer waters is important economically, socially, and ethically. We desire affordable, good-quality water to meet our needs and to stimulate economic growth. We require water for growing crops, for aquaculture, and for livestock. We want continued spring flows to maintain the parks that cluster around the springs and to rejuvenate and sustain endangered species. At the same time, stream flows must remain viable to meet the needs of downstream users. We need fresh water inflows to the Gulf of Mexico in order to support important habitats there. We also hope for inexpensive solutions to the water situation that are acceptable to almost everyone and that do not require massive bureaucracy, government controls, or loss of personal freedom. However, because of past and projected economic growth in the area, it is clear that the aquifer will be greatly strained and may not be able to meet all these requirements.

As described earlier, recharge of the groundwater carried by the Edwards Aquifer occurs through rainfall and the flow of losing streams. Recharge is not uniform, because it depends mostly on leakage from streams that, in turn, have flows dependent on highly variable rainfall. In addition, the aquifer does not respond instantaneously to variations in recharge, nor does it respond immediately to the pumping of water for the multiple uses mentioned. The historical record shows that an extended drought occurred during the late 1940s and early 1950s and caused the Edwards Aquifer to experience low rates of recharge. Since 1956, however, recharge rates have been relatively high. Also, since the late 1950s, population has grown in regions that draw on the Edwards. It is not surprising then, that the amount of water pumped from the aquifer in the last half of the twentieth century has grown steadily—except during wet periods, which minimize the need to use aquifer water for crop irrigation and watering of lawns. However, what will happen when climatic conditions similar to those of the late 1940s and early 1950s recur?

Clearly, when drier conditions recur, someone will have to go without water. Who will it be? Who should it be? Can we by our actions today avoid these choices tomorrow?

OPTIONS

To meet future water resource needs in southern and central Texas, we must increase supplies of water, decrease water demand, and manage water resources more efficiently. Of course, the traditional way to meet higher demand for water is to find additional supplies. For most American cities in the past century, this approach has meant building surface water reservoirs and pipelines. Fortunately or unfortunately, depending on one's perspective, there are few major potential reservoir sites in this part of Texas because there are few deep valleys to dam and few large streams to fill the reservoirs. Therefore, imported surface water would have to come from a considerable distance—perhaps from eastern Texas—and at a huge expense. Long-distance import of water pumped from other aquifers might be possible, but the potential effect on these aquifers and their users still needs study. Small local reservoirs would help the situation, but in drought years such reservoirs may not fill. Enhanced recharge along the losing streams will help. Enhanced recharge could come from dams in streams that cross the Edwards Plateau, whereby water released from the dams could maintain flow in streams that recharge the aquifer. It is logical to pursue this option, although this approach also will not be effective during droughts. It can be developed on a staged and relatively low-cost basis, but enhanced recharge of the Edwards has met with resistance from downstream users who fear that their supplies will be diminished. Removal of salt from Gulf of Mexico seawater—desalination—would also supply additional water to users of the Edwards, but the costs of developing the infrastructure for this process are very high.

An alternative solution would allow dual distribution systems that could perhaps help to increase water availability. Low-quality water resources from deeper aquifers or recycled sewage waters could be used to meet some requirements. Simple rainwater harvesting systems in residences and businesses for low-quality uses have not been widely explored. And, until there is incentive for people and businesses to implement such plans, there will be no demand for and, therefore, no readily available dual distribution systems. Furthermore, when we consider ways to increase our water supply, we must be aware of the effects of manipulations on our landscape. None of our reconfigurations will be without serious consequence, as shown by the history of California's water wars.[3]

Obviously, we must also try to decrease the demand for water from the aquifer. Although curtailed industrial and residential growth is not likely, water conservation and price increases in the cost of water could have long-term positive effects. Municipalities could charge higher rates for "cosmetic" water uses such as lawn watering. A family of four, for example, could pay a higher rate for water it uses above a predetermined amount estimated to be reasonable for a family of this size. Crafting a public policy along these lines may be politically unpopular, but so will not having enough water to go around. Clearly, water conservation practices must be implemented, yet these alone are unlikely to solve the problem.

Just as water conservation practices can help us use water pumped out of the ground more efficiently, there may be ways to use the aquifer more wisely. Conjunctive use of aquifer water with surface waters would permit us to use either surface or groundwater resources in a manner that could ensure maximum efficiency. For instance, we could use groundwater when stream flows are low and switch to surface water when stream flows are high. Conjunctive use, however, will not solve critical problems when droughts happen. If we knew more details about the aquifer, we might be able to design a pumping strategy to minimize adverse affects on spring flows. Which area or zone of the aquifer will yield the most water with the minimal adverse effects? Can we perhaps augment spring flow?[4] Can we take water from one portion of the Edwards Aquifer and reinject it near the springs so that we can continue to use the aquifer during droughts when its use is most important? Finally, can we design our water treatment and distribution systems so as to maximize their efficiencies? When considering these options, we must always be aware of the limitations of engineered solutions in the face of certain geological realities.

WHAT DO WE NEED TO LEARN AND WHAT IS THE ROLE OF GEOLOGISTS?

We must understand better how the Edwards Aquifer works. To make the best use of this precious natural resource, geological studies can offer some of the insights needed to improve our knowledge of how the aquifer works today, how it has operated in the past, and how it might function in the future.

We need a more in-depth understanding of the aquifer's geology, including the alignment and distribution of fractures, to predict the effects of enhanced recharge and development. We need to develop models that allow us to predict responses to pumping, recharge, and potential contamination. We need to know where the aquifer's zones of greatest porosity and permeability are and how these zones are connected to be able to pump water inexpensively and efficiently. We would like to know where to put industrial facilities so that they will not contaminate the aquifer when they leak. We will require geological knowledge on a far more detailed basis than we have ever needed it before.

Geological studies can also offer the added perspective of time. This enhanced approach can give insight into long-term changes in climate that may have occurred in the region. Historical records of rainfall only go back 60 years. Is this long enough to decipher longer-term trends in climate that may have affected the aquifer and may affect it in the future? What do these records portend for the long-term survivability of the region's endangered species?

The news media highlighted warnings of floods from the El Niño climatic event predicted in the summer of 1997. The event in the following fall and winter proved to be the second largest on record and had significant impact in regions such as southern California. Texas experienced only moderately higher than average rainfall, and this was followed by unusually dry and hot conditions in the summer of 1998. The high temperature and lack of rainfall led the U.S. Department of Agriculture to designate all 254 counties in Texas as agricultural disaster areas. Droughts have been and will continue to be part of the natural climatic cycle of central Texas. It will be necessary to deal with drought conditions as well as the projected increased demands on the aquifer that will occur even in the absence of drought. A combination of scientific efforts might improve our capabilities to project the likelihood of droughts. We must build comprehensive records of past climate change, study shorter-term changes in present atmospheric and earth surface conditions by using the growing technological capabilities of space-based observations, and improve computer model simulations of future climate change.

Although available records for central Texas indicate regular, periodic climatic changes, there are not enough data to know whether the climatic changes have a predictable pattern, what the extremes are, and how the climate varies regionally over time. Are the patterns observed in the 60 years of historical measurement, such as rainfall and temperature, superimposed on longer-term trends? Are there more sudden or extreme climatic events than those observed historically?[5] Geological records of environmental change, such as those found in vegetation and in cave and stream deposits, offer a view of this longer term.

Records of seasonal rainfall variations over the past 300 years in Texas are preserved in the changing thickness of tree rings found in climate-sensitive post oak trees.[6] These tree-ring patterns indicate that the last 60 years of historical records are representative of the periodicity of drought over the past 300 years. The tree rings also show that the severity of the 1950s drought has not been exceeded since 1698 and that the approximate frequency of such extreme episodes may be about once per century.

Are there any glimpses to be found into how climate changed on the Edwards Plateau prior to 1698? A sequence of sediments found in Hall's Cave on the Edwards Plateau reveals the deposition of sediment, plants, pollen, and animals that had been washed, blown, and carried into the cave. The record covers the past 16,000 years and reveals a number of lines of evidence about how the environment above the cave changed during that time.[7] For example, changes through this sequence in the proportions of fossils of the drought-tolerant desert shrew (*Notiosorex crawfordi*) and the non–drought-tolerant least shrew (*Cryptotis parva*) show changes in rainfall. The absence of prairie dogs, which require thick soils for their burrows, in the younger part of the sequence reflects a significant loss of soil in the last 8,000 years. The evidence in the sequence indicates that the drought-prone conditions that we are presently experiencing on the Edwards Plateau have persisted for the past 1,000 years. Unfortunately, century-scale changes are still difficult to resolve. However, new research on calcite speleothems from caves in the Edwards Plateau has the potential to provide high precision, long time-scale records (from decades to millennia) of environmental change. Chemical analysis of microscopic layers of mineral growth in the speleothems is being used to determine the ages of the layers as well as clues to how water flow and possibly climate shifted in this region during growth of the layers.[8]

As is the case with all aquifers, the Edwards is a unique resource because of the geological processes that created it. These processes include the accumulation of marine organisms that originally formed the sediment, the crustal upheavals that faulted and cracked the rocks, and the action of streams that cut through them and influenced the development of caverns. To maximize our understanding of the ability of this resource to serve our growing needs, we need to advance our application of geological studies to the Edwards Aquifer. We need projections based on trends of past natural variability and on models for future population growth, urbanization, rainfall, temperature, and land use. There is much that we do not know about the effects of urbanization on water abundance, water quality, and ecosystems. Gathering this information will require integration of principles used by geologists, climatologists, urban planners, hydrogeologists, and biologists, and the attention of policymakers. Add in the potential effects of atmospheric warming due to anthropogenic greenhouse gas emissions and it is clear that a policy that waits until the eleventh hour to address these issues is a policy that is too risky to follow for the next generation of Texans. We must have geological and hydrological research on the Edwards and other aquifers before the next crisis necessitates political, economic, and legal action. The long-term view of geology offers us the unique perspective to understand how the Edwards Aquifer was built, how it functions now, and how it might function in the future.[9]

14

From the Catskills to Canal Street: New York City's Water Supply

Jill S. Schneiderman

To watch Roman Polanski's *China-town* or read Marc Reisner's *Cadillac Desert*, one might think that Los Angeles, California, was the only metropolis that went to extreme—and corrupt—measures to procure water for its growing population. But New York City's water supply has a history nearly as Byzantine as that of Los Angeles, and it is one that began earlier in the history of this country. As early as 1832, in the face of burgeoning population growth, New York City looked miles outside its own borders for a source of "pure and wholesome" water.[1] Themes that arose during the seventeenth, eighteenth, nineteenth and early twentieth centuries as a result of New York City's water supply needs have resurfaced today in the historic watershed agreement signed in 1997 between the City and upstate New York communities. Conflicts about individual property rights and collective action for the protection of many have sounded across the mountains and valleys that are the source of the City's water more than 100 miles away. Past geological events and current geological processes connect the issues raised then and now. The unique configuration of bedrock geology and glacial history of the Catskill Mountains and Delaware River valley have allowed this region of upstate New York to supply the City with the highest quality water enjoyed by any metropolitan area in the United States, "the champagne of drinking water" as it has been called by a series of City mayors. However, human activities in the upstate watersheds have the capacity to degrade or protect the quality of water that can be obtained from the Catskill Mountains. Such actions can also disrupt or enhance the livelihoods of rural residents of this region.

HISTORY

Around 1625, during New York City's earliest years, the 300 or so residents of the place then known as New Amsterdam, got their water from springs, streams, and ponds. As population grew, residents dug private wells south of Wall Street, where porous and permeable sediments—grains with connected spaces between them—allowed water to flow easily.[2] But Manhattan Island, wedged between the Hudson and East rivers and protruding into New York Harbor, is close to sea level; so, fresh water extracted from wells became salty as a result of seawater seeping up through the bottoms of wells. By the middle of the eighteenth century, the infamous Aaron Burr's Manhattan Company, later to become the Chase Manhattan Bank, used wooden mains to distribute water from a reservoir on Chambers Street to one-third of the population of the City.[3] Nonetheless, even after the first public well was dug in 1671, wastes drained into open gutters and contaminated the City's water supply. Yellow fever and cholera epidemics plagued the City's residents both at the end of the eighteenth and at the beginning of the nineteenth centuries.[4]

Clearly, the City needed to find a clean and reliable source of water for its residents. In 1832, City officials commissioned Colonel DeWitt Clinton, a civil engineer, to develop a plan to do just that. As a solution, he suggested a dam on the Croton River north of the City and an aqueduct from the resultant Croton Reservoir—located in what is now Westchester County—along which water could be drawn to the City.[5] Although accomplished by 1842, the City's growing population consumed this water faster than it could be supplied, and droughts in the latter half of the nineteenth century exacerbated the problem. Reservoirs in Central Park and other parts of the City were insufficient to supply residents with the 500 million gallons of water a day that they used by 1900, an amount of water that if released down Fifth Avenue would be three feet deep.[6]

The Manufacturers' Association of Brooklyn, a place not yet incorporated into New York City, began to explore other options for its water supply.[7] Spurred by an 1886 article in *Scientific American* that suggested the Esopus Creek in the Catskill Mountains of Ulster County as a reasonable source of water, investigations by consultants to the Association suggested that the Catskill Mountains indeed held potential for the purpose.[8] By 1899, New York City was a metropolis of more than three million people formed from the incorporated boroughs of Brooklyn, Queens, Staten Island, the Bronx, and Manhattan; it badly needed an additional water supply.[9] Nervous that their land might be appropriated for its water, residents of Dutchess and Rockland counties passed legislation to forbid such action by New York City.[10] Rather than fight the law, the City considered other options.

Water from the Hudson River was an obvious potential source. But during the mid-nineteenth century, industrial expansion of ports along the Hudson such as Kingston, Poughkeepsie, and Newburgh involved shipbuilding;

NEW YORK CITY WATER SUPPLY.—PROPOSED GATE HOUSE FOR NEW AQUEDUCT AT 135TH ST. AND CONVENT AVE.—[See page 326.]

Scientific American 1886. (*Used by permission*)

NEW YORK CITY WATER SUPPLY.—VALVE CHAMBER IN GATE HOUSE, CENTRAL PARK RESERVOIR.

Scientific American 1886. (*Used by permission*)

transportation of lumber, grain, cement, brick, and bluestone; textile production; iron mining and smelting; machine and tool manufacturing; and tanning. As a result of these activities along the Hudson's shores, the water was deemed too polluted to be useful. The Adirondack Mountains and the Great Lakes were also considered as sources of water for the City but seemed too distant.

Geology dictated to New York City Water Board geologist Charles P. Berkey and engineers John Freeman and J. Waldo Smith that Olive Bridge along the Esopus Creek in the Catskill Mountains should be the site of the Ashokan Dam. There an impermeable blanket of sediments left by once present glaciers covered the underlying bedrock, an unfractured mass of rock; the presence of both relatively impermeable sediment and solid bedrock assured engineers that water impounded behind the dam would not flow down and out of the reservoir.[11] And the force of gravity alone would feed water from the elevated reservoir created by the dam along an aqueduct to the City, which is near sea level.

In 1906, as New York City prepared to retrieve water from the Catskills, it set up a watershed police force to protect upstate residents and keep peace in segregated labor camps as European immigrants, especially Italians, North American whites, and African-American workers from the south built the Ashokan Dam and the Catskill Aqueduct.[12] As quoted by writer Bob Steuding in his history of the Ashokan Dam, *The Last of the Handmade Dams,* Sergeants Carmody and Ocker, former Board of Water Supply police officers reported,

> *Ten thousand men, mostly unskilled laborers, and a wild and desperate lot, dumped suddenly into an unpoliced district, can work a lot of havoc. In 1907 they turned the peaceful Wallkill Valley and Catskill regions of New York State into a roaring camp that echoed to their drunken songs and seethed with banditry, outlawry and murder. Though the brawls and orgies were confined, for the most part, to the workmen's camps, not infrequently men stole away to rob and pillage the isolated farm houses in the district. For ten bloody years the natives lived in constant fear of their lives.[13]*

As Steuding comments, these recollections of a "Catskill Reign of Terror" may seem a bit exaggerated, but at the height of the work, 377 patrolmen did arrest more than 1,500 people; most convictions, however, came from acts committed in towns neighboring the construction site rather than at the labor camps themselves.[14] That the construction project was overseen by James O. Winston, son of a colonel in the Confederate Army who at the site rode in a chauffeured limousine costing $13,000, reflected the state of employer–worker relations of the time. Employers faced few restrictions regarding wages and living costs, and unorganized workers and their families were relatively unprotected.[15] Rights of workers and, as we will see, those of permanent upstate residents, were clearly secondary to the goal of building the great dam and supplying water for the growing metropolis.

Creation of the Ashokan Reservoir would displace approximately 2,000 local residents. Yet to the minds of some state and city leaders, this was a small sacrifice to sustain the fastest growing city in the most populous state, "the melting pot and entrance of immigrants, the first city to be electrified, the site of such engineering wonders as the Brooklyn Bridge, the Statue of Liberty and Trinity Church."[16] In fact, in its enthusiasm for the project, the New York City Board of Water Supply undertook preliminary surveys in anticipation of the construction project as much as eight months before the State Water Commission approved the project. Such premature actions belied the attitudes of downstaters and their lawyers, who saw Ulster County residents as country bumpkins and sanctioned brazen behavior toward locals—one old, gray-haired farmer in 1976 recalled how "City surveyors" cut down his mother's prize rose bushes without requesting permission.[17]

During this time, voices from rural areas were barely heard, as this was the Progressive Era—a time marked by great powers of industrial interests in shaping the industrial city. What's more, in the 1904 presidential elections, Theodore Roosevelt had defeated Alton B. Parker, a rural gentleman farmer from Ulster County. From the White House, Roosevelt commandeered an expansive public works movement in line with his policies of resource development, all meant to increase and sustain the resources of the United States and the industries that depended on them.[18] Celebrated as a time of great economic expansion, industrial growth, and urban reconfiguration, the sentiments of rural landowners hardly mattered in the corridors of state and federal government. Such difficulties for rural landowners on the East Coast foreshadowed the difficulties that Job Harriman, leader of the Los Angeles Socialist Party, and other opponents of the Los Angeles Aqueduct would have in questioning whether the Los Angeles area could support an unending cycle of expansion based on the concept of an unlimited water supply.[19] On both coasts during the early twentieth century, rural issues took a back seat to those of urban growth.

Ever since the City went to upstate communities in the early part of the twentieth century, residents resented the bullying they endured from the downstate metropolis. Recounting Bessie Bishop's recollection of the City's condemnation of her home, Bishop's granddaughter Camilla Calhoun wrote:

> *No one seemed to consider the anguish imposed on the inhabitants of the valley who had lived there for generations and were connected to the land in a way which few urban dwellers understand. "How can they be allowed to take our home?" was the question my grandmother continuously asked her father Ephraim Bishop.*[20]

A law enacted in 1905 permitted the City to take possession of a parcel of land along with the homes and other buildings on it at just ten days notice. As compensation, the City would pay to a local bank half the assessed value of the property. In those days, assessed values were low and property which had a sale value of $5,000 might be assessed for $500; it would therefore yield only $250 to its former owner.[21] Foreshadowing the agreement that would come more than 80 years later, early twentieth century inhabitants of the region demanded payment for the loss of income from businesses, wages, real estate value, and diversion of stream water from their lands.[22] Claims hearings dragged on for years. Watchmakers, blacksmiths, doctors, photographers, printers, and cobblers, owners of boarding houses, general stores, wagon shops, barbershops, laundries, mills, liveries, millenaries, and quarries, ultimately received no more than one-quarter of the amounts they claimed.

Perhaps even more disturbing to some residents was the required disinterment of thousands of bodies buried in local cemeteries that would soon be at the bottom of the Ashokan Reservoir. An illustrated pamphlet published in 1909 stated that even "the dead will not . . . be permitted to rest."[23] Steuding recounts the words of Kingston *Daily Freeman* columnist Ella Lockwood Loomis during the final days of old Ashokan: "People who knew every foot of this section find themselves lost when they go to Brown's Station and Olive City; with all the land cleared and the houses gone, they have to inquire their way around . . . . No one really realized what the blotting out of a village meant—until now . . . . Very few buildings are left now to be burned. The trees are all cut down and the village fading as a dream."[24] Although the legacy of Ashokan in New York City was good water, upstate it produced nothing but bad feelings.

In 1913, the Ashokan Dam was completed. Creating a reservoir with a 40-mile shoreline and a 12 square mile surface area, 128 billion gallons of water were impounded behind the dam, an amount that was thought to be enough to "float two flotillas of President Roosevelt's world famous naval ships."[25] The Catskill Aqueduct, which flows beneath the Hudson River at a crossing between Storm King and Breakneck mountains, was completed in 1915. By 1917, all of New York City's boroughs received water from the Ashokan Reservoir.

Before long, however, the City outgrew the Ashokan's supply and planned to build another reservoir. In the town of Gilboa, the City bought up land along Schoharie Creek.[26] They flooded the valley to create the Schoharie Reservoir and shore up the City's water assets. From the Schoharie Reservoir, water traveled to the Esopus Creek by way of the 18-mile Shandaken Tunnel, which, in 1928 when it was completed, was the longest continuous tunnel in the world.[27] From there, it reached the Ashokan Reservoir and eventually made its way to the City along the Catskill Aqueduct.

By 1931, New York City's nearly seven million residents consumed 42 million gallons of water a day. As a result, the City decided to reach for water beyond the watersheds of the Esopus and Schoharie creeks, the land areas over which they and their tributaries flow, into that of the Delaware River. Over objections from the state of New Jersey which, in addition to Pennsylvania, also taps water from the Delaware River watershed, the U.S. Supreme Court allowed New York City to proceed with plans to develop what is now called the Catskill–Delaware water system. Then, throughout the 1940s, 1950s, and 1960s, New York City paid for the construction of a series of reservoirs—Neversink,

Rondout, Pepacton, and Cannonsville—from which water flowed along the newly created Delaware Aqueduct to the City.[28]

Today a network of nineteen reservoirs in an almost 2,000 square mile watershed that extends 125 miles north and west of New York City stores 550 billion gallons of water. From it, the New York City water system supplies 1.4 billion gallons daily to approximately nine million New Yorkers.[29] That is approximately 156 gallons per person every day. The current-day reservoirs are connected to allow exchange of water from one reservoir to another and can accommodate droughts in some watersheds and excess water in others. Principles similar to those of the classic system of ancient Rome allow gravity to deliver almost all the total water supplied to New York City. Remarkably, water

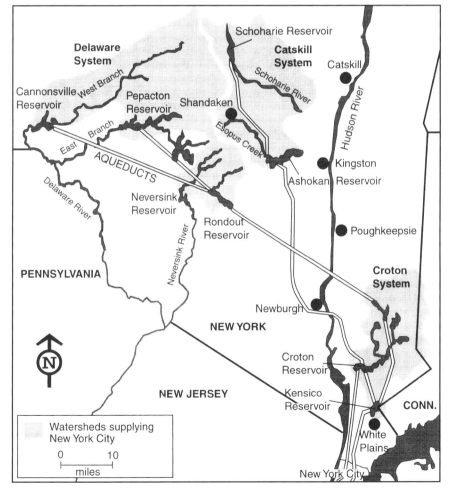

New York City residents receive their water from a series of reservoirs and aqueducts east (Croton system) and west (Catskill and Delaware systems) of the Hudson River.

only needs to be pumped during times of excessive drought. This situation keeps the cost of water in New York City relatively insensitive to fluctuations in the cost of power. Today, water quantity is only occasionally a problem. Water quality, however, is a different issue.

Only 10 percent of the City's daily water comes from the Croton watershed; the remaining 90 percent arrives from the watersheds west of the Hudson River.[30] The geological character of these relatively distant watersheds and the activities of a relatively few individuals within them has profound effects on the water quality of millions of people.

GEOLOGY, HUMAN ACTIONS, AND WATER QUALITY

Geological reality led writer Camilla Calhoun to remark that, "The great expanse of Ashokan water appears, when full, like a natural crater lake nestled in the Catskill valley."[31] In terms of its geomorphology—that is, the shape of the Earth's surface—the land beneath the Ashokan Reservoir suggests itself as a proper place for a lake of sorts. Although not volcanic in nature, the Ashokan Reservoir occupies a spot prepared for it by glaciers that arrived from further north a few million years ago. Glaciers ground and gouged the land. They pushed up piles of rock debris. One pile of rock debris—called a moraine— plugged a bowl-shaped space carved by a glacier, and a vast glacial lake accumulated behind it.[32] Really, Ashokan is a perfect place to put a reservoir because, as geology tells us, one was there once before.

In general, the high quality of water that comes from the Catskill Mountains stems directly from such geological history of the region which dictates the composition and structure of rocks that occur there. The Catskills formed approximately 400 million years ago, after two continents collided and pushed up the Acadian Mountains.[33] As the mountains eroded, rivers carried the sediments derived from them down into a shallow sea, where they were deposited as muds and sands. As the thickness of these sediments grew over time, additional sandy and gravelly sediments carried by the rivers were deposited in a delta that protruded above the surface of the sea. Such a situation exists today as a result of the collision of India with Asia, which has produced the Himalayas; the Ganges and Brahmaputra rivers transport sediments eroded from these mountains downstream into the Bay of Bengal, where they form the Ganges delta. Similarly, compressed and consolidated, the muds, sands, and gravels deposited by streams on the delta formed the shales, sandstones, and conglomerates that make up the Catskill Mountain strata today. The composition of these rocks is fortunate, for they do not contain substantial amounts of certain inorganic elements that would adversely affect the geochemistry of water running over and through them.

Rainwater and snow fall to the ground as relatively pure substances. That is, they contain mostly hydrogen and oxygen. However, when water derived from rain and snow flows over the land surface and percolates into soil and sediment, its composition changes as a result of its interactions with gases and solids. For example, carbon dioxide gas, accumulated in soils and pores between sediment, reacts with water to form a weak acid. Solutions that are even weakly acidic dissolve solids and pick up elements that are in them. If carbonate rocks—those made up of calcium, magnesium, carbon, and oxygen— are present, weakly acidic water dissolves the rock and takes with it the calcium and magnesium. These two elements make water "hard;" that is, calcium- and magnesium-rich water tends to form mineral deposits in pipes and on other surfaces that it contacts and prevents soap from forming lather. Although some limestone occurs in the Catskill Mountains, most often it does not make up the surface or shallow subsurface over and through which water travels. Most water from the Catskills is "soft"—it lathers easily. Similarly, rocks with abundant iron or manganese yield water that leaves rusty or black stains and those with sulfide minerals, which contain ionic sulfur, produce well water with a characteristic "rotten egg" smell or taste. Catskill Mountain shales, sandstones, and gravels tend not to contain these elements, so water that travels over and through them remains relatively pure.

Why do Catskill Mountain rocks contain few of these potential impurities? Simply, these shales, sandstones, and gravels are the result of erosion of a mountain chain. Only the toughest and most abundant minerals survive the journey from mountains down to sea level. Quartz survives because it is hard and relatively unreactive, and feldspar, because there is so much of it. In fact, quartz and feldspar make up the bulk of the Catskill sediments. And because quartz and feldspar, the two most abundant minerals of continents, are composed of silicon and oxygen, and sodium, potassium, aluminum, silicon, and oxygen respectively, they contain almost nothing that will change the chemistry of water.

Glaciation of the Catskill Mountains, beginning approximately two million years ago, has also contributed to its clean water. Pushed from the north by accumulating ice and snow, glaciers overran the Catskill Mountains. They disrupted soils and sediment and crushed and carried southward large and small boulders. During geologically momentary interglacials—those intermittent periods of warmth—meltwater from the glaciers widely distributed sediment that the glaciers brought with them.[34] Gravels and sands deposited in meltwater streams now cover much of the older Catskill shales, sandstones, and gravels that originated 400 million years ago. This geological history is fortunate indeed because materials such as sand and gravel that have high permeability—the ability to transmit water through pores—filter out some biological contaminants that may be carried along with the water flowing through them. So, coliform bacteria and other pathogens from improperly functioning sewage treatment plants, septic tanks, or barnyards that contaminate water get removed during the natural process of groundwater flow.[35]

The underlying structure of the older gravels, sandstone, and shale enhances this filtering effect. Flat, repetitive layers of sandstones and shales in the Catskills have produced a "stair-step" topography—shale makes up the risers and sandstone makes up the treads of the "stairs." As a result, almost all of the water that flows over the land surface in the Catskills percolates down into and through cleansing sandstone before it flows into the reservoirs that collect it.

Many of the watersheds in the Catskill portion of the water system are part of New York's Catskill State Park. The Delaware portion of the system is likewise sparsely developed except for agricultural districts and a few population centers. With 47,000 people living in the watersheds west of the Hudson River compared to perhaps 350,000 living in the watersheds east of it, activities that degrade water quality have been less likely to occur in the Catskill–Delaware system than in the Croton system.[36] Development and population growth west of the Hudson, however, have the potential to affect the geochemistry of that region's relatively clean water supply.

Agriculture, the daily activities of people, and to a lesser extent industry have begun to threaten Catskill–Delaware waters. Residues from pesticides and herbicides used in agriculture pollute surface and groundwater. Parasites such as cryptosporidium come from dairy farms. Excess nitrogen and phosphorus also present in animal wastes and synthetic fertilizers cause eutrophication— the buildup of algae and other organisms in water. Logging also seems to increase the amount of nitrogen in streams and thus causes organism-rich waters.[37] Forestry and farming produce sediment pollution, the input of unnaturally vast amounts of small particles broken from larger rocks into streams and reservoirs. Sediment pollution makes water murky and unpleasant to bathe in or drink. High amounts of sediment in streams reduce the light available to aquatic plants, cover the food supplies and nests of fish, and degrade the ecosystem. Extra sediment in streams accumulates rapidly behind dams, fills up reservoirs, and diminishes a dam's holding capacity.[38]

As a result of fossil fuel combustion, normally neutral snow and rainwater in the Catskills has become acidic. Because higher acidity mobilizes metals, metallic items that we have discarded in landfills or stream valleys now react with acidic water. That water picks up and carries with it metal ions such as lead, arsenic, copper, zinc, and aluminum, all of which can be toxic to humans and aquatic life. Additionally, the recent greater acidity of rainwater in the watershed compromises the neutral quality of reservoir water.[39] Also because of suburbanization and industrialization, we use thousands of synthetic and organic compounds, despite the fact that many are hazardous to human health and aquatic life, even in low concentrations.[40]

Sewage treatment plants associated with towns, hospitals, and industries, along with aging septic systems, can introduce bacteria into water. We add chlorine to water supplies to kill coliform and other bacteria, but chlorine can also react with humic acid derived from soil to form trihalomethanes. These compounds may be carcinogenic.[41]

Outbreaks of waterborne diseases and chemical contamination of water supplies across the United States moved the federal government to pass the Safe Drinking Water Act of 1974. This legislation required the U.S. Environmental Protection Agency to determine which contaminants endangered public health and to set the maximum allowable amounts of those contaminants in public water supplies. Aided by federal funds, states enforced the drinking water rules and supervised the nation's water suppliers, who were directed to monitor their water for contaminants and treat the water to meet the standards. The law made tap water safer from bacteria, sediment, and other traditional contaminants; but by 1985, the EPA had set standards for only 25 pollutants. Concerned that chemicals were tainting public water systems in many parts of the country, Congress amended the Safe Drinking Water Act in 1986; it enjoined the EPA to set standards for 83 chemicals in three years and obliged water suppliers to monitor systems for unregulated contaminants. Most significant for New York City's water supply was a provision in the Act that forced public water systems fed by rivers or other surface water sources to be filtered or otherwise protected.[42]

NEW YORK CITY'S WATERSHED AGREEMENT WITH UPSTATE COMMUNITIES

The completion of the Cannonsville Reservoir in 1967 marked the last time that New York City would expand its reach into new watersheds. Although the City would continue to use water from these distant watersheds, the more-than-100-year history of co-optation of water from outside its limits had come to a close. Left in place as a result of the history was the Board of Water Supply police force. Protecting dams, gatehouses, and other property of the water system, it operated under a set of antiquated regulations—revamped only in 1953—that included rules for managing "two seat privies."[43] With growing technology in the 1960s and 1970s, the rules proved useless for guiding behavior in the watershed. Consequently, members of the force arrested no one for polluting the waters. Furthermore, with the construction of the Catskill–Delaware dams and reservoirs completed, the City largely ignored problems of degrading infrastructure such as bridges and roads in the watersheds and had less of a presence in upstate communities than it had previously. As a result, while harboring past resentments, watershed residents operated on their lands as they pleased. Unfortunately for them, they were not entitled to do so. Throughout most of the twentieth century, a 1911 law that had remained in place gave the City the legal right to dictate what should be allowable and forbidden activities within watersheds that feed its water supply.[44]

Activities of inhabitants and industries in the watersheds became an issue in 1989 when the U.S. Environmental Protection Agency discovered rising levels of contaminants in the City's water supply. Following the stipulations of the Safe Drinking Water Act amendments of 1986, the EPA ordered the City to develop a plan by the end of 1993 to protect its watersheds. If it did not, the City would need to filter its water to reduce the contamination by microbial pathogens.[45] Currently, New York is the only city in the United States with a population of more than one million that does not filter its water supply, because the natural filtering properties of New York City's watersheds had long been considered ample protection.[46] On at least two occasions in 1990 and 1994, the City tried to make more stringent the 1953 regulations on activities that could be undertaken in the watersheds. It also came up with a plan to upgrade septic systems and purchase land to serve as buffer zones around the reservoirs and streams that feed them. As a result, the EPA granted the city a three-year extension to carry out its plan. But given the long and troubled history, upstate residents railed against the prospect of land acquisition and the new rules the City proposed.

Of course, developers in Putnam and Westchester counties, wealthy counties north of the City, and east of the Hudson in the Croton Reservoir watersheds complained most loudly. They filed lawsuits saying that their property had been devalued without recompense because New York City had begun to reinforce the long-ignored regulations for sewage treatment and stormwater drainage. For example, the regulations forbid the construction of household septic tanks and asphalt parking lots. One developer, representative of others, filed suit because the City objected to a housing development he proposed on the basis that his land was too steep for the septic systems he had planned; the City maintained that the steep topography would send inadequately treated water into streams feeding the watershed. Others claimed that the proposed new rules would make it prohibitively expensive to build new businesses and homes and would deter the resurgent economy.[47]

West of the Hudson in the Catskill and Delaware watersheds, farmers scorned the City's new proposed requirements. The City's Department of Environmental Protection perceived farms as contributors to a significant portion of the unwanted nutrients and intestinal parasites that have threatened water quality in recent years. Consequently, the proposed regulations would not permit farmers to spread fertilizer or store manure within 500 feet of any spring or stream. However, in Delaware County, almost every barn has been built next to a stream because, in the past, streams were convenient places to temporarily store milk from dairy cows.[48] Although this had been the situation since the turn of the century, the new environmentalism that was a legacy of the 1970s, dictated more stringent limits on pollution as reflected by federal, state, and city regulations.

Because of the dense population in the Croton watershed, the city agreed to build a $600 million filtration plant for that water system.[49] But the City wanted desperately to avoid building a plant to filter waters from the Catskill and Delaware watersheds. Its still debated cost has been estimated to range from four to eight billion dollars. Because the City owns less that ten percent of land in its watershed, the City's Department of Environmental Protection recognized the importance of getting watershed residents west of the Hudson to cooperate on a watershed protection plan.

In 1997, after almost two years of delicate negotiations, the City signed an agreement with the State that was approved later by the federal Environmental Protection Agency.[50] As stipulated in the agreement, New York City will spend $1.2 billion over ten years to safeguard the quality of water coming from the Catskill–Delaware system. Of that money, it will spend up to $260 million to buy up to 355,000 acres as a buffer against development and its concomitant pollution. It has allocated almost $400 million for water quality protection and partnership programs: to clean up several hundred dairy farms, to improve treatment of waste water flowing into reservoirs from sewage plants, to replace old septic systems, and to spur environmentally sound economic development. Money will be spent on programs to monitor ambient conditions in the watershed and to study the effects of various farming and forestry practices on water quality. And as important, the watershed agreement stipulates a host of new rules by which the City will regulate myriad activities in the watershed. They include stringent requirements on the construction and operation of wastewater treatment plants, as well as prohibitions and restrictions on new septic systems, hazardous substance and petroleum storage tanks, roads, and roofs. If after five years the EPA determines that water quality is still in jeopardy, then the City might be required to construct a filtration plant to protect water quality.[51]

Critics of the watershed agreement maintain that the plan does not create adequate water quality safeguards. They fear that in the long run, a massive plant will need to be built to filter Catskill–Delaware water; motivated especially by fiscal concerns, they fret that more money ultimately will have been spent than if the city had simply built a filtration plant in the first place.[52] Other skeptics contend that corrective and protective measures alone in the watershed will never protect water quality and that they must be done together with filtration. Regardless of whether these concerns turn out to be correct, we must never rely exclusively on technological fixes; human beings must learn to live more delicately as part of a complex earth system.

A lawyer for an environmental group involved in the negotiations suggested that the watershed agreement included significant loopholes because "the closed-door talks leading to the watershed plan were too often focused on political and legal issues, and not often enough on *chemistry and biology* [italics added]."[53] Although he may be right that science did not play a big enough role in figuring details of the plan, he missed the fact that geology is among the sciences that matter most to the City's water quality.

The rocks that make up the mountains and valleys of the watersheds west of the Hudson are responsible for the relatively clean water that flows over and through them unperturbed by the activities of people. The configuration of glacial deposits and streams has allowed us to construct the dams and aqueducts that provide volumes of clean water for the City. But good, clean water originates from the interactions of air, water, sediments, and living organisms.

The interplay of these four components of the earth system, particularly as affected by human actions, regulates the composition of the water on which we depend. Geologists' familiarity with the history and complexity of the earth system allows us to purvey sensible proposals to help humans live harmoniously as part of it.

> *Schoolchildren often ask about the cities they believe are hidden beneath Ashokan's waters, as if they had their own local legend of a mountain Atlantis in mind. They never fail to ask about the church steeple which some friend has heard someone else has seen rising from the depths like the Loch Ness monster. The old Stone Road in the East Basin, looking something like an ancient Roman way, surfaces from time to time in periods of drought, such as the summer of 1985, as do abandoned foundations and bluestone quarries . . . . The 18 inch wide, 4 to 5 foot long slabs of bluestone laid end to end are incised with deep grooves cut to hold the iron wheels of the heavily-loaded bluestone wagons. Near this road are also the markings of the last glacier. These glacial striations look as if some giant mountain lion had raked its paws across the once soft, wet rock.*[54]

These relics of both the human and geological past stand as a reminder that "what goes around, comes around." Geological events cycle; human ones need not. Unlike the solution to New York City's water supply problem forced upon Catskill residents in the earliest part of the twentieth century, the agreement forged near the close of that century depended on fragile trust and the need to provide clean water for the future. Rural residents and city dwellers recognized that they occupied geographically disparate portions of an interconnected whole; they chose to value the resource that the Catskills offer and establish a delicate alliance that acknowledges the reality of human's tenuous existence as part of the earth system. This choice should be a model for others.

15

Sustaining Healthy Coasts

Jeffrey L. Payne

The 1998 tropical storm season in the western hemisphere was one of the most devastating in history. On one day in August, forecasters tracked four storms simultaneously, and 9 of the 14 storms that occurred during the official season became hurricanes. Storms spawned in the Atlantic Ocean that year were responsible for more than 11,000 deaths. Thousands of people were displaced from their homes, and island nations and coastal communities throughout the Caribbean and Latin America were wrecked.

One of the primary reasons for this tremendous level of human loss and destruction is that communities located close to sea level are highly vulnerable to storms. Vulnerability is not only a function of being in harms way but also a measure of the capacity of coastal communities to understand and prepare for high-risk events. During the 1998 tropical storm season, the greatest losses occurred in Nicaragua and Honduras, where rainfall from Hurricane Mitch caused massive landslides that buried thousands of people. In 1999, similar destruction occurred in Venezuela. In these instances, a better understanding of how the coastal and mountain geology of Nicaragua, Honduras, and Venezuela respond to persistent and drenching rain might have led to improved community planning and reduced vulnerability.

Although hurricanes are one of the more remarkable facts of life in the coastal zone, coastal areas and their populations are actually subject to a wide variety of influences and trends that can affect the quality of human life. America's coasts, where colonial settlement first began and then filtered westward, are rapidly becoming the focus of renewed expansion. People are streaming to coastal areas in record numbers, drawn by surging job markets, unique recreational advantages, and lifestyle choices. This attractive, yet fragile fringe of land and water presently is home to more than half of all U.S. citizens, and coastal counties are growing at a rate that exceeds that of inland counties. The impact of this growth on natural and human systems is significant, and our ability to balance economic and environmental concerns will determine the future quality of life in the coastal zone. Multiple stresses due to population growth and development are acting to modify the fabric of coasts, as indicated by changes in water and air quality, natural habitat, living marine resources, land character, and socioeconomic conditions. At the same time, improved comprehension of the critical linkages between human and natural systems is helping to influence those changes in behavior needed to ensure sustainable coastal communities, such as reducing the vulnerability of populations affected by extreme weather events.

The careful study of the relationship of humans to their environment, termed ecology, is increasingly meaningful as population continues to grow and natural resources are tapped to fuel this growth. Coastal areas are particularly susceptible to degradation and the overexploitation of the very resources that humans depend on both for survival and for economic gain. This essay highlights trends in the coastal and ocean environment, and examines the important relationships among human and natural earth systems.

CHANGING DEMOGRAPHICS AND THE CHALLENGE OF SUSTAINABILITY

U.S. coastlines have long been an attractive place to live, work, and play. The coastal zone can be defined in multiple ways but is generally regarded as the narrow band of coastal counties and adjacent bays, harbors, estuaries, and oceans. Current U.S. seagoing jurisdiction is 200 nautical miles from the coast, but it is the nearshore portion of this 200-mile Exclusive Economic Zone that generally is of greatest ecological concern. In addition, it is important to recognize that most watersheds funnel down to the coasts, carrying the products of a vast interior reach. These products tend to both enrich and degrade coastal environments, ranging from the deposition of fertile sediments along rivers and deltas to the transport of pollutants into sensitive bays and estuaries where fish and other organisms dwell.

Coastal counties are the most densely populated and developed in the United States, yet they account for only about 17 percent of the contiguous land area. More than half (about 53 percent) of the population resides here, and current trends indicate that over 1.3 million people will continue to move to the coastal zone each year. The rate of growth along coasts is greater than for that of the nation as a whole. Certain states like Florida and California, which have experienced strong growth along their coastlines in recent years, are expected to continue to expand in population well into the next century.[1]

The growing human presence in the coastal zone drives an economic engine that produces more than one-third of the nation's gross national product. Ports and harbors are bustling centers of commerce, with over 95 percent of U.S. international trade, by weight, arriving and departing by ship.[2] More and more people, both U.S. citizens and foreign visitors, come to coastal areas expressly for recreation and retirement, including the many millions involved in popular recreational fishing and other water-based activities. Commercial fisheries annually produce more than $3 billion in revenue to those people in this industry and generate over ten times that amount in total economic activity nationally.[3]

Commensurate with population growth and economic development in coastal zones is the need to maintain healthy ecosystems and to avoid cumulative environmental degradation. Perhaps the greatest challenge of designing sustainable communities will be to achieve a balance among these mutually desirable, yet often competing goals. Demands for potable water, living space, safety from natural disturbances, human and industrial waste treatment, transportation, food, energy production, and business and service accommodations, all result in the utilization, and sometimes degradation, of natural resources. The resulting stresses can quickly overwhelm the carrying capacity of natural systems, as well as the supporting physical infrastructures that we design.

Shellfish beds in certain areas of the country, for example, have been closed repeatedly during some or all of recent harvest seasons because of water quality concerns. Shellfish are sedentary filter feeders that can concentrate bacteria and harmful pathogens in their tissues. These pathogens often originate from human sewage and from livestock and wildlife organic waste. In 1992, beaches were closed or advisories issued against swimming on almost 3,000 occasions because of this kind of pollution.[4]

Coastal habitats, especially wetlands, are essential to over 75 percent of the total commercial landings and to more than 80 percent of the recreational catch of fish and shellfish.[5] Despite their biological and economic importance, the cumulative effects of pollution, habitat loss, and overfishing have contributed to dramatic reductions in the abundance and diversity of coastal fish and other species. Sea turtles, many species of which are now protected under the Endangered Species Act, compete with humans for nesting space on beaches and fall prey to commercial fishing operations. Restoration plans have been developed for turtles to increase their probability of survival, but the pressures of habitat loss and competition with humans continue to jeopardize restoration efforts.

Recognizing that we need action to mitigate the impacts of population growth on land use, some states and communities are incorporating restrictions on development in sensitive areas and are developing new areas with clustered "set-asides" of open spaces and parks. However, land use planning is only one component in the toolkit needed to address the wide range of consequences of human activities in the coastal zone. Improved understanding of the way coastal and ocean systems function, coupled with an ability to predict the responses of earth systems to human activities, are also important keys to sustainable development and the informed management of natural resources for the long-term benefit of everyone. In addition, natural systems have a strong influence on human safety and quality of life. An important part of the challenge of sustainability will be to design and build disaster-resistant or flexible communities that incorporate concerns about risk and vulnerability.

COASTAL AND OCEAN ISSUES AND IMPLICATIONS

A recent report of the H. J. Heinz III Center for Science, Economics and the Environment, identified three principal obstacles to achieving integrated management that balances the use and conservation of ocean and coastal resources.[6] The report found that (1) the nation has underinvested in the physical and technological infrastructure necessary for the efficient use of oceans and coasts; (2) the national and international institutions and mechanisms for governing and managing ocean and coastal areas and resources are often fragmented and have conflicting mandates; and (3) insufficient effort has been devoted to developing and applying the knowledge necessary for wise management.

In addition to these overarching obstacles, major issues affecting the future development of sustainable coastal communities include water quality, habitat and species conservation, hazard mitigation, and the effective use of cost-benefit analysis. Individuals in government, the private sector, academia, and environmental organizations are trying to develop policies and programs to address these issues and find solutions. The strength of these solutions will depend on the integrity of underlying scientific, economic, and social information. Improved understanding could lead us toward informed decisions and consensus, and away from the traditional avenues of conflict and litigation.

Indeed, one purpose of the International Year of the Ocean—1998—was to raise public awareness of the value of oceans and coasts, and promote learning from past experiences in managing the oceans and their resources. During the summer of 1998, President Clinton announced a series of initiatives designed to reinvigorate the national interest and investment in oceans and coasts, including new funding for science, education, and management needs.

Water Quality

One of our most critical future natural resource management issues is water—its availability, abundance, purity, and use. Water sustains living coastal and ocean resources, ensures safe recreation and seafood, and underpins economic vitality. It is the defining characteristic of coastal regions, where the rivers meet the sea, and the ecosystems change over a relatively short distance from fresh to brackish to highly saline conditions. The Chesapeake Bay is an example of a large and complex estuary and bay system that supports multiple habitats and changes in physical and chemical characteristics. Organisms like those found in the Chesapeake are also found in other estuaries and bays, but they thrive only in very particular conditions of salinity, temperature, and water depth and quality. Large populations of commercially important shellfish, crab, and finfish spend all or part of their lives in estuarine and nearshore environments, and are susceptible to fluctuations in water quality. Trace metals and chemicals that result from human activities have dramatically affected the health of coastal and marine species. Public seafood safety advisories are routinely issued for certain shellfish species and fishing grounds. Clean water—crucial to the effective functioning of ecosystems—is clearly an essential component of healthy habitats, and yet it is often compromised.

Over the last several decades, federal, state, and local regulatory efforts have focused on controlling point-source discharges of pollutants into streams, lakes, and ocean waters. Point sources are manageable in that the type and source, or point of origin, of the pollutant generally is known and can be monitored, as in those resulting from industrial operations. Regulatory strategies can then be directed to treat the effluent prior to release, or to ensure that discharges stay within acceptable limits. Knowledge about earth processes can aid management strategies. For example, regulators may need to understand and account for a host of variables, including flow rates of pollutants into water bodies or the affinity of sediments for concentrating some chemical compounds. As a result of concerted efforts to manage point-source discharges, waterways have experienced substantial decreases in the type, volume, and concentration of pollutants.

Today, geoscientists and resource managers focus their research, monitoring, and assessment activities on a more diffuse problem termed nonpoint-source pollution—pollution that is generated as a result of runoff from the land or through atmospheric deposition. Nonpoint-source pollution includes excessive erosion and deposition of sediments into streams and the nearshore environment, the introduction of pesticides, fertilizers, and manure from agricultural and livestock operations, and contaminated runoff from highways, streets, and parking lots. Unlike point sources of pollution and their effects, the sources and potential effects of nonpoint-source pollution are generally more difficult to characterize and quantify; in fact, they need to be considered from a regional or watershed perspective. During this decade, coastal states have begun to work closely with federal agencies and other groups to develop and implement nonpoint-source pollution programs. These programs should contribute significantly to cleaner coastal waters.

We need to monitor water quality to determine whether pollution reduction programs are working and to identify new threats to ecosystems. Integrated, watershed-level monitoring systems are few, and the costs of maintaining such systems are considerable. Direct monitoring typically is done in discrete locations for specific purposes, such as addressing local decision needs where the potential for degradation is clear. Monitoring efforts also tend to be fragmented, and factors such as data type, quality, precision, and timing limit scientists' ability to exchange and compare information.

Naturally occurring monitoring opportunities exist, and geoscientists use them to examine ecosystem health. Oysters, which accumulate contaminants in their tissues, are an indicator species for pollution. Fish that have high concentrations of heavy metals or exhibit lesions and other abnormalities also indicate ecosystem conditions. Since 1986, the National Oceanic and Atmospheric Administration (NOAA) has managed the National Status and Trends (NS&T) Program, which monitors marine environmental quality. Data from the continuous monitoring of mussels and oysters under the NS&T Program indicate that concentrations of many synthetic chemicals, such as DDT and PCBs, are declining though their persistence still causes sickness and death.[7] The concentration of cadmium is decreasing as well, but concentrations of other trace metals, such as arsenic and selenium, have stayed nearly constant.[8]

The development of monitoring programs that provide for credible, quantitative risk assessments, especially in individual watersheds, still challenges researchers. However, new techniques and data are emerging that should strengthen our abilities to predict ecosystem health. For example, remote monitoring techniques, including space- and aircraft-based sensors, are being developed to improve our abilities to examine ecosystems. We now employ ocean color sensors to identify and track some oil spills and to determine marine chlorophyll concentrations—an indicator of the presence of marine plants. The ability to determine ocean color, in combination with other variables, will be important for building a system to forecast and track seasonal blooms of harmful algae that can threaten U.S. coastal areas.

Nutrient enrichment of coastal, estuarine, and nearshore waters is an issue of growing importance because of the direct link to human activities. Nutrients such as nitrogen and phosphorus generally support biological productivity. However, excessive nutrient discharges, resulting primarily from changes in landscape use and agricultural management practices, can lead to oxygen depletion, fish and shellfish mortality, harmful algal blooms, and habitat loss. Periods of explosive biological productivity can occur as a result of nutrient overenrichment; and as the large volumes of plant and animal remains sink and decompose, they remove oxygen from the water at rates that exceed recharge from surface waters. When this occurs, and if waters approach a hypoxic (low oxygen) or anoxic (lack of oxygen) state, organisms may incur stress or die off in large numbers. The habitat may remain inhospitable until mixing processes restore oxygen levels in the system. We need improved understanding of the physical, chemical, and biological processes associated with hypoxic episodes to develop predictive techniques and management strategies to minimize potentially harmful effects on ecosystems.

Habitat and Species Conservation

Habitat can be defined simply as the home of an organism or biological community. Adequate habitat, including clean water, is a necessary requirement for life. Although organisms may be displaced from their preferred habitat and still survive, habitat condition is a key factor that determines the viability, abundance, and biodiversity of living coastal and marine groups. Loss of habitat, largely due to human-induced pressures, is often cited as the number one cause of species decline worldwide.

Traditional means of dealing with threatened or endangered species have proceeded on a species-by-species basis. For every species trending toward extinction, a management plan has been developed to protect and restore it. This approach has led to costly and contentious decisions about how best to accomplish the task of restoration. We now appreciate that the health and survival of species is a function of multiple environmental factors throughout the range of the species, including not only habitat but also the relationship among organisms within their habitat. We now apply new concepts of ecosystem management to maximize the environmental integrity of a defined area, usually a watershed. This type of management maintains the health of the entire system by considering all inputs to, and outputs from, the system. And this simple, integrated, and preventative maintenance works to hold down costs in the long run.

A good example of the effects of habitat loss on ecosystem integrity exists in the Pacific Northwest, where the once free-flowing Columbia River supported tremendous runs of salmon and steelhead trout. As the river has been modified and managed over the years to support multiple uses—including hydropower production, irrigation, transportation, forestry, fishing, and recreation—the spawning habitat of salmon has been either largely degraded or completely lost. As a result, the federal government and the states of Washington, Oregon, Montana, and Idaho are working under the mandate of the Endangered Species Act to protect and restore several species of salmon and their associated habitat, both of which are currently threatened with extinction. Both public and private groups are doing this in watersheds of the Columbia River basin—they regulate activities that jeopardize fish survival, restore and create habitat, improve fish passage around dams, and limit the ocean harvest of fish.

For each high-profile habitat issue in the coastal zone that revolves around protected species, there are numerous examples of lower-profile, yet significant habitat degradation and loss. For instance, the slow but steady reduction of green space and wetlands in coastal areas results directly from population growth and competition for industrial, business, residential, and recreational space. Also, exotic—nonindigenous—species have been introduced in recent decades, and many seriously jeopardize habitat integrity and the ability of native species to survive. The nutria, a rodent introduced to the United States from South America, is destroying estuarine wetlands from the Chesapeake Bay to Louisiana and Texas at an alarming rate, transforming emergent marsh to open water. Zebra mussels, introduced originally in the Great Lakes through shipping operations, are another well-known invasive species that alters habitat, competes for food supplies, and costs municipal and industrial operations hundreds of millions of dollars to mitigate.

The identification, functional characterization, preservation, and restoration of coastal and marine habitats are critical to the health of commercial and recreational fisheries. As noted earlier, the majority of commercially important fish species depend on coastal habitats for some or all of their life cycles. Florida's mangrove swamps, California's seagrass beds, and Georgia's tidal marshes are all important habitats that provide food and shelter for a large variety and abundance of organisms. Louisiana's estuaries and marshes, for example, provide young fish, crabs, and shrimp with an ample food supply and protection from predators. Viewed nationwide, these are the types of nurseries that support the development of robust, commercially viable ocean and coastal populations of fish and shellfish.

Although marine corals are living organisms that require their own unique habitat to survive, the reef structures they create also serve as important habitats for diverse and abundant populations of marine organisms. In fact, coral reefs have been likened to the undersea equivalent of our terrestrial rainforests. Reefs provide shelter for many organisms, protect shorelines from wave damage, and draw divers, boaters, and anglers for recreation. But coral reefs are important to us, not only as cultural and biological treasures, but also as indicators of possible global climate change.

Many coral reefs presently are experiencing stress, with dramatic declines observed in recent years, but especially in 1998. Natural factors that affect coral reef health include storms, disease, water temperature changes, predators, sediment loading, and oxygen supply. Human impacts on coral reefs range from direct destruction due to ship accidents, to the more subtle changes in habitat brought about as a result of warming global temperatures or pollution. Because living coral reefs comprise sensitive, special areas, management plans similar to those for fisheries conservation have been developed to ensure their protection and wise use. The Florida Keys National Marine Sanctuary, for instance, was created to preserve the living coral reefs of southern Florida, and it operates under a special management plan that provides for research, education, conservation, and multiple use.

Given the importance of habitat and documented trends of degradation and loss, it is unfortunate that we have achieved only limited success in our attempts to either lessen damage or create new habitat environments. In a successful habitat restoration project, the affected habitat returns to nearly full functionality and quality. This result is difficult to achieve even under optimal circumstances. Sometimes we even manipulate habitats to improve the biological value of a certain area and offset the loss of habitat in another region. On the other hand, in habitat creation projects we establish a new habitat or ecosystem in a place where it did not previously exist.

For example, some salmon and steelhead trout streams along Alaska's Kenai Peninsula have been degraded as a result of the pressures of urban development and recreational fishing. State authorities, working with federal and local groups, have developed and applied techniques to stabilize the eroding banks of rivers in high recreational use areas and have helped to restore the functionality of degraded salmon spawning habitat. In coastal Louisiana, restoration and mitigation projects have helped to offset the effects of oil and gas development and dredging. Louisiana instituted a geological review process to evaluate oil industry proposals for less damaging alternatives to the traditional access canals to site and service platforms that have been cut through vegetated wetlands. By using the alternatives, the oil industry reduced the average area of wetlands affected per well from five acres in 1982 to three acres in 1989.[9] On the East Coast, the state of South Carolina has created new offshore artificial reefs, which are submerged habitats composed typically of synthetic materials that would otherwise be recycled or disposed of in landfills.

To do these things well, we must understand how habitats and ecosystems interrelate in a systematic fashion. Individual protection and restoration efforts in the coastal zone that are conducted in isolation may fail if related parameters, such as the effects of upland or upstream inputs within the watershed, are not taken into account. Restoration projects that successfully stabilize erosion may have little functional biological benefit to species that require a specific type of habitat to survive. Although the science and practice of habitat restoration is inexact, it is important that we understand how to minimize pressures of development and pollution in order to maintain healthy habitat, restore or replace damaged habitat, and create new habitat. This cannot happen absent geological input.

Hazard Mitigation

Disaster costs in the United States due to natural hazards average in the tens of billions of dollars annually. Disasters in the last few years alone have cost approximately $50 billion per year, or about $1 billion per week.[10] Disaster losses are on the rise, in part because people are tending to live in high-risk areas, such as exposed, low-lying coasts. Yet, in only five years, the value of coastal residential and commercial property has nearly doubled. With this movement to, and investment in, coastal areas, more people and property are directly at risk. Communities are now challenged to work actively to strengthen building codes, enhance the public's awareness of coastal hazards, and incorporate hazards risk and vulnerability information into emergency and land use planning.

Coastal hazards that result from natural processes range from discrete and potentially high-impact episodes such as hurricanes, to chronic events such as beach erosion, to drought or flooding related to the uncertain effects of long-term climate change. Severe meteorological events including hurricanes and tropical cyclones produce destructive winds, coastal flooding, storm surge, and shoreline erosion. Hurricanes, although infrequent in occurrence, are responsible for tremendous economic losses, often in concentrated regions. For example, the three costliest hurricanes in U.S. history occurred within the last six years and together produced $32.5 billion in damages.[11] Although hurricane deaths in the United States since the turn of the century have dropped dramatically as a result of improved weather forecasting and community preparedness planning, damages have increased in nearly an inverse relationship. A recently released report by the Worldwatch Institute and Munich Re, the world's largest reinsurer, states that violent weather cost the world a record $89 billion during 1998, more money than was lost from weather-related disasters in all of the 1980s.[12] The report suggests that climate change and deforestation are behind many of 1998's most severe disasters, among them Hurricane Mitch, the flooding of China's Yangtze River, and Bangladesh's most extensive flood of the twentieth century.

Public education and the willingness of the public to trust and act on warning and forecast information are crucial to effective hazard mitigation. The U.S. National Weather Service (NWS) currently measures the accuracy of its predictions of hurricane landfall in terms of miles of shoreline that may need to be evacuated, given 24 hours of notice; it seeks to improve its performance by applying new technology and advanced predictive modeling. Earlier and more accurate predictions of hurricane tracks and intensities could reduce the size of the warning areas that people are advised to evacuate. The NWS estimates that the public's average preparation and evacuation costs for each hurricane event exceed $50 million. Improved predictions can cut that cost by $5 million.[13] More important, the public seriously attends to accurate predictions and this promotes sensible behavior and safety.

Other important natural hazards affect U.S. coastal areas in a strongly regional context. Earthquakes, which are more prevalent on the West Coast and Alaska, can cause serious damage because of the potential for liquefaction of sediments—a loss of sediment structure and integrity usually caused by shaking—typical of many coastal uplands, plains, and beaches. Tsunamis are oceanic waves that usually result from offshore volcanic activity or earthquakes. These uniquely coastal events can produce catastrophic tidal waves and nearshore flooding. The infamous 1964 Alaska earthquake generated a tsunami that resulted in human casualties in Alaska, and extensive damage in Alaska, Hawaii, and along the west coast of the contiguous United States.[14]

Regional differences in coastal geology, combined with the constant effects of winds, tides, storm waves, river flow, and alongshore transport, dictate the amount and severity of erosion that occur along coasts as a result of natural conditions. In addition, human alterations to shorelines, which are meant to stabilize erosion in one area, typically exacerbate erosion rates in an adjacent area by impeding the flow and supply of sediments. The creation and maintenance of navigation channels leads to constant bank erosion, that sometimes requires structural reinforcement. All 30 states bordering an ocean or the Great Lakes have erosion problems, and 26 currently are experiencing net loss of their shores.

In addition to natural hazards, coastal areas are vulnerable to technological hazards, including oil and chemical spills, and biological hazards such as harmful algal blooms—commonly known as red tides. State and federal agencies have invested heavily in research and development to define linkages between the extent and composition of harmful algal blooms in coastal waters, ocean processes, and land use patterns in adjacent watersheds. New remote sensing techniques, combined with improved knowledge of the physical and biological conditions that favor algal blooms, are being used to improve our ability to track and publicize such blooms.

International trade involving the transport of hazardous materials and oil occurs mainly by ship. Ships have doubled in size in the last 50 years, and seagoing commerce has tripled, changes leading to a higher risk of accidents in ports and harbors. From 1980 to 1988, tankers in the United States were involved in 468 groundings, 371 collisions, 97 rammings, 55 fires and explosions, and 95 deaths.[15] Oil and chemical spills destroy marine and coastal wildlife, foul beaches and estuaries, and damage natural habitat. Advanced navigation aids, safer vessels, improved weather information, and integrated contingency planning can all help to reduce the risks of technological hazards in the coastal zone.

Human activities are also creating global-scale changes in our environment that will have an impact on the range and severity of hazards. Well-documented human-induced changes include atmospheric pollution and thinning of the stratospheric ozone layer. In addition, for over three decades of long-term monitoring, NOAA has produced incontestable evidence of greater amounts of carbon dioxide in the atmosphere. In 1995, the United Nations's Intergovernmental Panel on Climate Change (IPCC) released findings indicating that temperature may increase 1.8°F to 6.3°F and sea level may rise 6 to 37 inches by the year 2100.[16] The IPCC report further states that the balance of evidence suggests a discernible human influence on climate change. These global trends will affect both natural processes and human systems in the coastal zone, especially regarding the frequency and severity of weather, and the potential for sea level rise and massive inundation and flooding of low-lying areas. However, as proposed actions to balance anticipated changes are expected to be very costly, the availability and application of scientific information will continue to be the most critical requirement for sound decision making. In fact, one estimate puts the value of reducing climate-related uncertainty in the implementation of policies designed to stabilize anthropogenic (human-induced) greenhouse gas emissions at $100 billion, for the United States alone, between now and the year 2020.[17]

The El Niño-Southern Oscillation in the Pacific Ocean is an excellent example of global climate variability. Temperature and precipitation patterns, changes in ocean circulation, and changes in storm frequency caused by this phenomenon have strong effects on economies, planning, and biological systems. The highly publicized El Niño event of 1997–1998 was responsible for unprecedented coastal flooding, wave action, and erosion along the California coast, leading to massive losses of land and property. Normal ocean temperature and circulation regimes in the Pacific Ocean were also affected, and the changes led to the geographical displacement of fish stocks and additional stress on ecosystems. Recent work in this area by researchers has led to improved ability to determine monthly and seasonal probability outlooks for temperature and rainfall for up to one year in advance. The future ability to provide accurate and systematic regionally tailored forecasts of global climate variability will be of tremendous value for coastal economic and social response planning.

Effective response to hazards must figure prominently in the evolution of sustainable coastal communities. Part of the challenge for geoscientists is to understand and foresee the natural and anthropogenic variations, both now and in the decades to come. As 19 of the 20 most densely populated counties in the United States are coastal counties, a clear understanding of the risk, vulnerability, and economic costs associated with coastal hazards and climate change is also in the best interest of the nation. To assess risk, thorough appreciation of the natural forces that act on the coastline and of the response of the dynamic coastal environment to those forces is essential. Risks must be quantified, and the information used to develop techniques to predict potential impacts of hazard events.

Not only must we define the physical effects of hazards on the coastal environment, we must also assess social and economic impacts. Insufficient scientific information exists concerning coastal vulnerability, and this deficiency complicates the process of making decisions about how to protect economic resources. Vulnerability factors include the underlying geological framework of the coast, the patterns and characteristics of the built environment, and the socioeconomic conditions associated with high-risk areas. A range of societal vulnerability currently exists along coasts, including poorly constructed buildings; an aging transportation, energy, water, and sewer infrastructure; and constricted evacuation routes such as the bridge system connecting the Florida Keys. The risks, vulnerabilities, and costs associated with coastal hazards are poorly defined and quantified. Improved information will enable communities to operate from an objective basis in making coastal resource management and planning decisions.

Use of Cost-Benefit Analysis

The general public's heightened awareness and appreciation of the importance of the environment to human health and quality of life is a relatively recent occurrence. Mounting evidence of global-scale environmental degradation and change has led to multiple international resolutions and the development of mitigation plans on an international basis. The Montreal Protocol, for example, established the internationally agreed-on framework for the reduction and eventual phaseout of human-made substances that deplete stratospheric ozone. Some global-scale models of the long-term response of the total earth system to potential greenhouse warming suggest that sea level rise will be of a magnitude sufficient to inundate large areas of coastline. Reliable scientific information could establish an objective basis by which to measure and interpret the potential for environmental harm or change. However, in practice, we find that the economic and societal costs of mitigating potentially harmful changes may be too high to allow appropriate or timely changes to proceed.

Atmospheric pollution is a fair example of this cost-benefit dilemma. We accept certain, and sometimes unhealthy, levels of polluted air in our cities because the costs of abandoning the fossil fuels that drive our established transportation and energy systems outweigh the potential benefits of switching to relatively cleaner energy sources like solar power. In the same fashion, we build high-density, low-quality structures in coastal areas prone to hurricanes and floods, because the social or economic benefits outweigh the potential for catastrophic loss. In fact, some businesses that otherwise cannot acquire insurance because they choose to locate in high-risk areas can still turn enough profit in the short term to more than offset the costs of rebuilding in the same location following a partial or total loss of property.

In the process of least-cost planning, all factors that may influence the total cost of a project are identified and worked into the cost equation. Typically, businesses identify and pay only those direct costs that are required to produce a product or service, meet regulatory and social obligations, and ensure an acceptable profit margin. Least-cost planning can account for additional factors that businesses or industry may not be required to address—the so-called hidden costs, or externalities. The industrial revolution at the turn of the century demanded cheap energy to fuel growth and profits. The true, long-term environmental costs of burning coal were not factored into early comparisons of energy sources. Coal was relatively inexpensive, readily available, and powerful enough to meet industrial needs. Today, we continue to pay for the legacy of cheap fossil fuels, like coal, through stringent and costly regulations on emissions, mitigation programs (to counter the effects of acid rain on crops and water quality), and higher medical costs related to breathing polluted air. Where human health is concerned, society is usually willing to bear reasonable additional costs, as documented by decisions made several decades ago to reduce emissions from motor vehicles (propelled by fossil fuels) through the installation of catalytic converters.

Issues of cost and benefit can greatly influence the decision making process in the coastal zone. Even though sustainable communities should consider the principles of least-cost planning for evaluating decisions based on net benefits in the long-term, the reality is that short-term economic considerations often control the process and outcomes. In decisions to site industrial plants along rivers and estuaries, regulators will determine, for instance, the acceptable types and volumes of industrial effluents and establish thresholds for dissolved oxygen. These thresholds are established to allow the industrial activity to proceed while providing for an adequate level of environmental protection. However, it is clear that rivers and ecosystems will surely be degraded from preindustrial conditions.

If these types of development decisions are evaluated on a case-by-case basis, and if they ignore or fail to capture the hidden costs and cumulative impacts, then individual decisions may result in unexpected environmental harm, in addition to greater overall costs to society to correct the damage. With the pressure of steadily growing population in the coastal zone, our desire to ensure environmental protection and still allow for continued economic growth, will test both the commitment and the knowledge base of community leaders and the public.

IDEAS FOR COMMUNITIES

To address these challenges, governments and communities can do several things:

- Community leaders, in coordination with other government authorities, private, academic, and nonprofit interests, and the public, should create a vision and long-term plan for sustainability. Such planning depends on the development of a comprehensive knowledge base that can guide decisions given multiple scenarios, and precise cause and effect relationships, both at appropriate ecosystem levels. Through planning, communities should seek to shape coastal development—the look, feel, and functionality of their communities. Relationships with other communities should be assessed and established to support common objectives and to leverage costs and learning. Federal and state governments should provide contextual information and guidance for community-based planning; financial and technical support; and the recognition that solutions to many of the issues that communities face will need to be owned and implemented at the local level.

- People at all levels of leadership should take the responsibility to educate citizens, foster greater participation in the public process, and develop community-based capacities for learning and action. Oftentimes, the public is misinformed, is left uninformed, or is largely apathetic about key decisions that will affect their own well-being and the health of their environment. One of the most underappreciated aspects of addressing issues of ocean and coastal resource management is public education and awareness. Citizens constitute a vast pool of talent, ideas, and volunteer spirit that can help to drive the process of designing and building sustainable communities, while nurturing the environmental stewardship ethic.

- Cooperation and consensus must replace the standard practice of resolving problems and issues through adversity and litigation. Much of the progress in the Pacific Northwest for salmon protection and restoration can be linked to the degree of "buy-in" of all interested groups. Federal authorities have sought to limit the number of Endangered Species Act restrictions that may be forced on states and to encourage states to adopt protection and restoration plans. Federal and state authorities have worked closely with the fishing industry in the Gulf of Mexico and other regions to help protected sea turtles survive in the presence of shrimping operations. Federal and state authorities conduct research and development to find technical solutions and work with industries to determine the means to implement proposed solutions in the real world of fishing. New gear and fishery management practices have dramatically reduced the mortality of sea turtles. The alternative to this cooperation would be to shut down certain fisheries that fail to comply with the requirements of the Endangered Species Act.

- Communities must invest in, and draw knowledge from, scientific findings, environmental and socioeconomic information, and newly developed technical means to solve problems. The natural and human-influenced systems of coastal and ocean environments are complex and challenge scientists to refine knowledge about them. But, remote sensing, Geographic Information Systems, ecological modeling, trend analysis, and risk and vulnerability assessment are a few of the tools that we can employ to improve ecological characterizations and provide a better foundation on which policy can be set.

In all of this, geoscientists are uniquely qualified to explain relevant earth processes, interpret data, recommend approaches, and evaluate results of community and government efforts.

The challenge of building sustainable communities is not unique to the coastal zone. Other parts of the United States must also balance growth, economic vitality, environmental protection, and the conservation of natural resources. However, demographic trends in the coastal zone suggest that communities there must now begin to grapple with the real concerns and impacts of population growth and the utilization of natural resources. Science, technology, and adaptive management strategies must converge to support these economic and social decisions. To sustain healthy coasts, we will need to improve our understanding of coastal geology, coastal and ocean processes, climate variations, the function and value of ecosystems, risk and vulnerability, and the impacts of human activities on natural systems.

Part IV

LOCAL MANIPULATIONS

The adage "civilization exists by geological consent, subject to change without notice" is only half true. Indeed the rhythms of Earth's cycles—within the lithosphere, hydrosphere, biosphere, and atmosphere—together permit our presence on the planet. Yet, as humans try to insist that the Earth function as we direct it, the planet endures and clearly indicates its inexorable ways. As Earth's partner, we must accommodate the natural parameters of our habitat and anticipate regular changes to it.

This set of essays describes ways that humans have persisted in changing the local landscape, only to learn that Earth's natural states tend to prevail. First, Orrin Pilkey and colleagues contrast the migratory tendency of natural beaches with efforts to stabilize them and laud a recent move of North Carolina's Cape Hatteras Lighthouse away from the edge of the sea. Further north, Jill Singer walks the shore along Lake Erie's Lotus Bay to expose the folly of construction projects meant to immobilize beaches and provide boat access to the water. In a discussion of the pursuit of navigable waters in the New York–New Jersey Harbor, Meg Stewart weighs options for disposal of never-ending dredged sediment. Paul Doss concludes with a tour of New England building sites that invites skepticism about the wisdom of well-meaning but geologically uninformed plans for economic development.

In sum, these essays suggest that humans must learn to give—and to work with what nature has provided.

16

Lessons from Lighthouses: Shifting Sands, Coastal Management Strategies, and the Cape Hatteras Lighthouse Controversy

Orrin H. Pilkey, David M. Bush, and William J. Neal

O ne dark and stormy night in 1703, the Eddystone light of fame in song and legend, fell into the sea. Earlier, Henry Winstanley, architect of the lighthouse, assured his workers that the lighthouse would never fail. He had even bragged to the press that he looked forward to experiencing the worst storm in English history from inside the lighthouse. His wish was granted. Winstanley was in the lighthouse when it was felled by the storm, and he perished along with his fellow lighthouse workers. The Eddystone light, like most lighthouses, was built to withstand the mighty natural forces associated with dangerous coasts, but like so many lighthouses before and since, the sea proved more powerful.

Lighthouses are an ancient symbol of guidance to mariners, and engineering marvels as well, but we generally do not associate lighthouses with geology. Yet the success or failure of a lighthouse is closely related to the geology and physical processes of its site. And because lighthouses are among the oldest of coastal structures, they serve as both markers to measure longer-term shoreline retreat (erosion) or advance, and as models of how we view our relationship with nature at the coast. They record the tale of how humans respond to coastal hazards. Their long histories provide lessons about the importance of understanding coastal geology, as well as the best ways to respond to coastal hazards. Sadly, those lessons have gone unheeded by the people who have engaged in the rapid coastal development of the last 50 years.

Any number of lighthouses illustrate coastal problems, but the present Cape Hatteras Lighthouse, in North Carolina is one of the best known. The

Cape Hatteras Lighthouse was built in 1870 and first seriously threatened by shoreline erosion in the 1930s. From that time until 1981, government agencies (i.e., taxpayers) including the National Park Service spent about $15 million on interim protection methods. In the 1960s and 1970s, three groins were built, later destroyed by a storm, and then rebuilt. Nylon sandbags were emplaced in front of the lighthouse. Three unsuccessful beach replenishment projects also were pursued during this time. Many of these shoreline projects, primarily done to protect a U.S. Navy facility located just to the north of the lighthouse, were undertaken with ever-increasing costs. They did not stop the shoreline's retreat. In 1980, when the light was almost lost to a winter storm, the National Park Service began to investigate methods to protect the lighthouse from erosion over the long-term.

The controversy that has swirled around the Cape Hatteras Lighthouse may, at times, seem like the old "we're from Washington and we're here to help" story, or like scientists sticking their noses into local problems. But the story really goes far beyond the Cape Hatteras Lighthouse. The Cape Hatteras Lighthouse is a microcosm of national shoreline policy and controversy. A *Washington Post* article stated "whoever wins the battle of ideas over what to do with the Cape Hatteras Light will . . . set the tone for our response on a national

North Carolina's beautiful Cape Hatteras Lighthouse has warned mariners of the treacherous waters of Diamond Shoals since 1870. Three groins—the southernmost of which is shown here—and the sandbag revetment are part of a several-decades-long fight to hold back the sea. The "right" storm could have removed the lighthouse overnight. The pre-June 15, 1999 position of the lighthouse at the edge of the beach, shown here, is not typical of the building's history during which it sat well back from the beach.

scale to the problem of retreating shores."[1] Decisions about the Cape Hatteras Lighthouse may determine the future of shoreline management policy in the United States. The following pages present the typical experiences of lighthouses, and specifically the Cape Hatteras Lighthouse, to illustrate the controversy over the fate of coastal development in the face of a rising sea level.

COASTAL TYPES AND SHORELINE RETREAT

Lighthouses are located by necessity in high hazard areas either to warn mariners of dangerous reefs, shoals, and headlands or to guide them through difficult navigational channels into harbors and through inlets. Their placement is usually determined by optimizing their visibility, rather than considering the stability of the underlying geology, not unlike the criteria for siting coastal cottages and condominiums to ensure a sea view. Lighthouses set above flood and wave levels, back from the sea, or on stable rocky shores persist. Those on shifting sands or in the zone of storm waves on rocky shores frequently fall victim to the sea. The Roman Pharos atop and well back from the edge of the white cliffs of Dover, England has stood since the first century AD because it was out of harm's way. Many of the lighthouses along the U.S. Atlantic Coast from Long Island, New York to the Florida Keys and around the Gulf Coast are descendants of structures already claimed by shoreline erosion.

Lighthouses on the U.S. West Coast sometimes face another danger—earthquakes. The Santa Barbara, California, Lighthouse was built in 1865 and toppled by a 1925 earthquake. The oldest active light on the West Coast, Point Pinos Light at Monterey, California, was built in 1855. The 1906 earthquake shook it so violently that it needed extensive repairs in 1907.

Barrier Island Coasts and Sea Level Rise

Nineteenth- and twentieth-century Americans built lighthouses equal if not superior to those of the Romans, but the geological setting of the U.S. Atlantic and Gulf coasts is mostly barrier islands, which retreat as sea level rises up a sloping coastal plain. These same barrier islands are some of the most intensely developed coasts in North America and have suffered record-setting property losses in great storms—Hurricane Hugo, 1989, $7 billion; Hurricane Andrew, 1992, $26.5 billion; Hurricane Opal, 1995, $3 billion; Hurricane Fran, 1996, $3.2 billion. Lighthouses in the Florida Keys were built very near sea level and have failed under the full force of hurricane winds and waves—on Sand Key, 1846; Key West, 1846; Loggerhead Key, 1853; Garden Key, 1873; Rebecca Shoal, 1953; Alligator Reef, 1960.

For barrier islands, bluffed coasts, and shorelines of erodible materials, the inexorable retreat of the shoreline undermines the structures built on them.

The first Ponce De Leon Lighthouse, in Florida, was undercut by a storm shortly after its construction in 1835; and by December of the same year, it had toppled into the ocean. Shoreline recession allowed the sea to claim successive lighthouses on Sandy Point, Block Island, Rhode Island, in the 1830s and 1840s. Delaware's Cape Henlopen Lighthouse, built with its base on a sand dune 46 feet above sea level, fell into the sea in 1926 as a result of shoreline retreat. A year later, the Tucker Beach Lighthouse off the southern end of Long Beach Island, New Jersey, fell into the sea as the sand barrier on which it was built continued to erode away.

Many U.S. East Coast lighthouses are now the second structure and in some cases, such as Cape May New Jersey, the third structure, that have replaced a previous one that has fallen. In the 1840s, the Lighthouse Service built two 40-foot towers to replace the original Chatham, Massachusetts, twin towers, threatened by bluff erosion. One tower was claimed by bluff retreat in 1879, and the second in 1888. This destruction required the construction of a third set of towers farther inland; this third set of towers was in the path of the retreating bluff edge again by the 1990s. The same fate befell the Three Sisters of Nauset, which toppled in 1892.

The famous Morris Island Lighthouse in South Carolina, was left standing in the sea in the 1940s as a result of rapid shoreline retreat caused by the construction of the Charleston Harbor jetties built in the late 1890s.[2] Dynamic Sand Island, at the mouth of Mobile Bay in Alabama presents a similar example, but drowning of the lighthouse there is the result of natural island migration. Sand Island migrated west-northwest, leaving the static lighthouse marking the former island position.

Rising sea level affects sounds and estuaries as well as the open-ocean shoreline. The shorelines of Chesapeake Bay, Delaware Bay, the North Carolina sounds, Mobile Bay, and the Georgia estuaries are all retreating, both by inundation and erosion. The present Cape Lookout, North Carolina, Lighthouse is threatened from soundside erosion of the island.

Shoreline erosion is not always the force behind lighthouse decommissioning. The 1884 lighthouse on Anclote Key, western Florida, once near the shore, is now 450 feet inland because of beach accretion, most of which has taken place since about 1960.[3] The steady southward migration of Oregon Inlet, North Carolina, has left the Bodie Island Light more than two miles from the present Oregon Inlet—too far away to help navigators striving to cross the bar of this dangerous inlet. In the course of its migration, this inlet obliterated the location of an earlier lighthouse that had been lost to military action during the Civil War. Confederate forces extinguished the lights along the southeastern and Gulf coasts, either by removing the lights or by destroying the lighthouses. Darkened lights included Cape Lookout and Federal Point, North Carolina; St. Simons Island, Georgia; Hunting Island and Morris Island, South Carolina; and Cape Charles, Virginia. Accidental fires also claimed many of the early lights.

Rocky Shores

Lighthouses based on bedrock are not invulnerable, but their record of endurance surpasses that of lighthouses with their feet on sand or the unconsolidated sediment left by glaciers, which is easily eroded by the sea. Rocky shores are buffeted by storm surge waves and flooding, which sometimes take down lighthouses. One of the earliest was the first Boon Island, Maine, Lighthouse, which was built on the rocky island in 1799 and destroyed in a storm just five years later. The replacement lighthouse fared no better and was lost to a storm in 1831. These losses occurred because the island sits in the path of storm waves that can sweep the island with floodwaters and powerful waves. A 1932 storm is reported to have sent 70-foot waves smashing against the house and tower, and a 1991 storm tossed about 100-pound boulders with ease—the same size material is used in some erosion stabilization structures. Just how big waves become in storms also is illustrated by the Portland Head, Maine, Lighthouse, in which a 1972 storm wave broke a window in the tower 55 feet above sea level.[4] The lesson should be obvious: Structures built in high-energy (hazard) zones are going to experience high energy (hazards)!

The Whaleback Lighthouse stands at the mouth of the Piscataqua River, Portsmouth Harbor, Massachusetts. This 1872 lighthouse was modeled after the famous Eddystone and has withstood the test of time; however, its two predecessors both were victims of storms (1820s and 1868) even though their feet were on bedrock. The second loss was blamed on poor construction, the same reason many modern buildings fail in storms.

Storms also plagued the original Minots Ledge Lighthouse in Massachusetts, from the time of its construction, and it fell during an April storm in 1851, with the loss of two of its keepers. The massive granite replacement tower is built to withstand wave impact, but it suffered damage in a 1978 storm. More recently, the Boston Lighthouse was threatened by Hurricane Bob (1991) and northeasters of the 1990s. Structures built on bedrock are not likely to be undercut by erosion, but they are subject to damage and destruction if located in the zone of waves, flooding, and high winds.

IS SHORELINE ENGINEERING THE SOLUTION?

Lighthouses on sandy, retreating shorelines are historic models of what is in store for all buildings in similar settings. The closer the shore moves to the structure, the greater the chance it will sustain damage or topple completely in a storm. And even if a storm does not take its victim, eventually the sea will by erosional undercutting. During the nineteenth century and most of the twentieth century, a common response to the threat imposed by shoreline retreat has been the attempt to hold the shoreline in place through coastal engineering. There have been numerous attempts at armoring the front of lighthouses, but three examples illustrate the futility of this approach.

The 1864 Cape Charles Lighthouse in Virginia, was constructed on a retreating shoreline; this retreat was recognized at least as early as 1850. By the 1880s, the shoreline was shifting landward at an average rate of 30 feet per year. Congress authorized the construction of three stone jetties—also know as groins—in 1885 to halt the erosion, and four more were added in 1891 because the shoreline was still retreating. The erosion continued despite the engineered structures—or perhaps in part because of the structures—and a new lighthouse, established in 1895, had to be constructed about a mile away from the shoreline.[5] Such groin fields were the engineering choice in the 1880s, and extensive groin fields were used to combat erosion along many shorelines. The Absecon Lighthouse in New Jersey, may be an exception; protective jetties built in the 1870s did fill in with sand and halted the rapid shoreline retreat.

Bulkheading—or seawall construction—is another engineering approach that has had only temporary success. The original Ludlam Beach, New Jersey, Lighthouse was frequently battered by storms, so a bulkhead, was constructed to protect the wood-framed building. In 1914, a storm destroyed the wall; and a decade later, the lighthouse was so badly damaged in a storm that it was closed.

George Washington is said to have ordered the Montauk Point, New York, Lighthouse to be built far enough back from the bluff edge to survive bluff erosion for 200 years. In 1795, the structure was about 300 feet from the edge of the bluff; 200 years later, the bluff's edge had retreated to within less than 60 feet of the building. Rather than abandoning or relocating the now-threatened lighthouse, shoreline engineering was used to combat erosion. In 1971, rock revetments—rock covering the upper beach slope—were constructed, together with terracing and gabion structures, but the sea continued its efforts. The combination of Hurricane Bob and the Halloween northeaster of 1991 ripped away at the structures, and the bluff edge lost another 30 feet. Not to be outdone, the Coast Guard, partially funded by public moneys, built a bigger seawall complex in 1993 and 1994 that totaled over 1,000 feet in length and contained boulders weighing up to 10 tons. The wall will buy time, but the bluff edge will again move toward the lighthouse. Consider the following passage from Ken Kochel's *America's Atlantic Coast Lighthouses,* in reference to Mount Desert Rock, Maine: "In a testimonial to the power of the sea, Maine's Superintendent of Lighthouses reported in 1842 that a storm had moved a 57-ton granite boulder the size of a mobile home onto the island. And to top that one, the same report also mentioned that in another storm the sea moved a 75-ton boulder a distance of 60 feet."[6] In the same locale a 1962 storm wave dropped a four-ton boulder through the roof of the boathouse at the light station. Given these examples, the sea certainly is capable of rearranging very heavy boulders in rock walls and revetments.

Setback, Relocate, or Abandon

The Montauk Point Lighthouse provides an example of how American attitudes toward shoreline retreat have changed with time. George Washington made a good call in the 1790s, for today the light still stands, albeit threatened as the bluff edge recedes closer and closer to the structure. The implied expectation was that in 200 years the light would be abandoned and could fall into the sea; but by the late nineteenth to mid-twentieth centuries, brute-force engineering was in vogue. The lessons of failed seawalls and groin fields were yet to be realized. Unfortunately, that philosophy was widely applied to protect buildings at the expense of America's beaches, and it is still advocated by some, even to "protect" lighthouses.[7]

American lighthouse builders learned very early that their structures often fell victim to the sea, and three response strategies other than relying on engineering structures developed: setback, relocate, or abandon.

Setback. First, shoreline retreat was sometimes factored into the planning —as it was at Montauk Point—so that the sea would not arrive at the doorstep of the light until it was past its lifetime. The problem with setbacks on retreating shorelines is that sooner or later the sea catches up to the building; the problem is delayed, not solved. Several historic lighthouses that are in the water or at the water's edge today were not built in such precarious positions. For example, the 1796 Highland Lighthouse on Cape Cod was originally set back 510 feet from the bluff edge; however, an erosion rate of two feet per year closed the distance to less than 130 feet by 1992. Then the rate seemed to jump, and a series of storms began to gnaw away the bluff face rapidly.

The lesson is that even in states with setback requirements, today's coastal development is not safe over the lifetimes of the buildings and, in fact, may be a setup for very heavy coastal property losses in the future.

Relocate. The second strategy of lighthouse builders should be more adaptable to property owners and regulators: Relocate when threatened by shoreline retreat. As in the case of the Cape Hatteras Lighthouse, some preservationists have forgotten that moving structures to new locations is one of the oldest commonsense responses to natural hazards.[8] Many early lighthouses simply were torn down and replaced when threatened by erosion or damaged by storms, but moving the structure was a common practice early in the history of American lighthouses. The first lighthouse in St. Johns River, Florida was moved inland in 1835, just six years after its construction; and the Amelia Island, Florida, Lighthouse was moved from Georgia's Cumberland Island in 1838–1839. Other examples include an early West Chop brick lighthouse on Martha's Vineyard, Massachusetts, which was moved away from the eroding bluff edge in 1847 and again in 1891; the Prudence Island Lighthouse that was moved from Newport, Rhode Island's, Goat Island to Sandy Point in 1851–1852; the Cape Canaveral Lighthouse (Florida) that was moved one and a quarter miles inland in 1893–1894 when threatened by shoreline retreat; and the Hereford Inlet Lighthouse (New Jersey) that was moved 150 feet inland in 1914 after being damaged by a 1913 storm.

Lighthouses were even designed to be disassembled for relocation. The Hillsboro Inlet Lighthouse (Florida) was built in Chicago and assembled at the 1904 St. Louis Exposition, then disassembled and transported to its Pompano

The Nauset Lighthouse, Eastham, Massachusetts, is shown in the process of being moved on November 16, 1996. (*Courtesy of Shirley Sabin, Nauset Light Preservation Society*)

Beach location (Florida) where it was reconstructed in 1907. The second lighthouse on Hunting Island, South Carolina, was set back a quarter of a mile from the shoreline in 1875; but by the late 1880s, the shoreline was near the structure. Fortunately, it was of a design of the time in which the tower consisted of prefabricated metal plates that could be disassembled, and the lighthouse was moved more than one mile in 1889.

When we consider that sea level is rising, inundation will cause shoreline retreat whether or not accompanied by erosion. The Port Mahon Lighthouse on Delaware Bay illustrates this point because it was moved landward three times over the course of a century in response to the gradual flooding of the low-elevation shoreline. The lesson is that relocating landward is a flexible management philosophy; it is least costly in the long term, and least disruptive to fragile coastal environments and the dynamics of the shoreline. Relocation allows us to have our beach and enjoy it too; the aesthetics and environments we come to enjoy at the shore are conserved for us and future generations.

The technology to move large buildings exists, and the modern relocation of three New England lighthouses provides examples. The 2,000-ton Block Island Southeast Lighthouse, Rhode Island, was moved 245 feet inland in 1993. In 1996, the Cape Cod Highland Lighthouse, noted earlier, was moved 450 feet to a position close to its original distance from the bluff edge. Also in 1996, the Nauset Lighthouse in Eastham, Massachusetts, was moved 300 feet inland from its former location near the edge of a 60-foot high eroding bluff face. If only some property owners in nearby Chatham had been so prudent as to move their houses before they fell into the sea.

Abandon. The final strategy of those responsible for America's lighthouses was abandonment, an approach that has been common for as long as there have been lighthouses. It may seem like an extreme concept, but look at any list of lighthouses and their histories and you'll see that when they were no longer functional as navigation aids, they were either abandoned or, less frequently, dismantled or moved for use elsewhere. For some reason, abandonment is a difficult concept for the modern psyche, but those before us routinely walked away from lighthouses, including ones that were "historic" in their own time. In the recent example of the Nauset Lighthouse, the Coast Guard did not plan to save it; rather the Nauset Light Preservation Society raised the money to move and restore the lighthouse. Should we expect public moneys to be spent in an effort to preserve buildings, in place, on retreating shorelines?

Relearning the Lessons

Relocation and abandonment are strategies that have been applied over and over in the coastal zone. Not only lighthouses, but entire towns, have been moved. The lighthouse on Hog Island, Virginia, was torn down in 1948 and the village abandoned to erosion in modern times. Edingsville, South Carolina (1893), and Diamond City, North Carolina (1899), were abandoned or relocated after hurricanes.

The overall lesson is that when a building site proved inappropriate or when a building failed or outlived its design, it was removed or abandoned. Remember, these structures were designed and built to survive punishment by great storms, yet they were frequently damaged or destroyed. In part, we can attribute such failure to poor siting, especially in barrier island environments where no solid substrate is available for firm foundations. More than one lighthouse settled unevenly, causing tilt that impaired the function of the light. Lighthouses at low elevations on easily eroded sand were undercut, as noted earlier, and subjected to storm-surge flooding and wave impact. If a hurricane can level a mighty structure, built to resist storms, what is the future for any lesser design on a barrier island? Few of today's residents and property owners on barrier islands, however, display the prudence of the lighthouse builders, and they do not comprehend retreat or abandonment. To build back "bigger and better" after a hurricane or northeaster, particularly on a barrier island, defies good sense.

Our perception of the forces of nature are not reinforced by the fact that some of the abandoned lights persist and are now looked on with historical interest, economic value derived from tourism, and some nostalgia. Some communities where lighthouses have washed away raise moneys to construct replicas of the former lights as symbols and tourist attractions. These replicas are symbolic of America's beaches, many of which are now artificial, maintained only by beach nourishment.

"Preserve the Lighthouse" is a sentiment expressed in many communities, and again there are lessons to be learned. How many lighthouse preservations can we fund? How many artificial beaches are taxpayers-at-large willing to subsidize? How many seawalls, groin fields, breakwaters, and similar structures can be permanently maintained in the face of a rising sea level? At what cost? The 1799 Eatons Neck, New York, colonial revival style lighthouse is another tower at the edge of a retreating bluff in the late 1990s. The cost estimate for stabilizing the bluff—a temporary fix—is $10 million. Should it be on the long list of lighthouses in need of saving, and is stabilization or relocation the better option? The Sankaty Head Lighthouse on Nantucket Island, Massachusetts, is also near a bluff's edge that lost close to 40 feet in storms of the early 1990s. As of 1998, a private funding group was waiting to see whether shoreline engineering was going to stop the bluff erosion, rather than proceeding with plans to move the lighthouse. They have ignored the lesson of the Great Point, Nantucket Lighthouse, which was destroyed in a powerful northeaster in 1984.

NOT ALL LIGHTHOUSES ARE CREATED EQUAL

Cape Hatteras Lighthouse

The diagonally striped Cape Hatteras Lighthouse is regarded as the most famous lighthouse in North America, and the symbol of North Carolina. Located on North Carolina's Outer Banks, the Cape Hatteras Lighthouse has long been a beacon for mariners sailing the exceptionally dangerous waters off that cape—waters known as the "Graveyard of the Atlantic." Since 1870, the light has helped warn mariners of the treacherous Diamond Shoals off North Carolina's easternmost point.

Although the lighthouse was built 1,500 feet from the shoreline, the sea has progressively trimmed the front of the barrier island, and the lighthouse has been in danger of being destroyed by the sea for decades. In 1936, when shoreline erosion threatened the lighthouse, the Coast Guard temporarily abandoned it and used a steel-skeleton tower in nearby Buxton Woods. Numerous attempts to armor and restore the shoreline in the area of the light failed. Subsequent severe storm erosion prompted the National Park Service in 1979 to solicit proposals for methods of preserving the light.

Physical setting. Cape Hatteras, like other major capes, is a large, well-developed coastal feature formed by sediment-carrying waves approaching from two directions. Sediment piles up offshore of the capes and forms extensive shallow-water sandy areas called shoals. These shallows—such as Cape Hatteras's Diamond Shoals—can extend some distance offshore, forming hazards for ships.

The shoreline north of Cape Hatteras is generally considered to experience the highest wave energy on the U.S. East Coast south of Maine. This concentration of energy is understood geologically to be due to the narrow width of the continental shelf (20 miles) off this section of the Outer Banks. The narrow

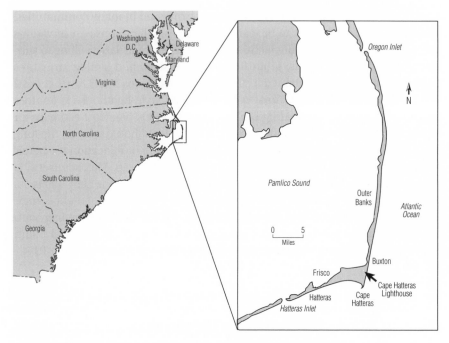

Location of Cape Hatteras, North Carolina. (*Drawing by Amber Taylor*)

shelf minimizes the normal reduction of wave size and energy that is caused by friction as the waves roll across the shallow-shelf waters. By comparison, the relatively low wave energy shoreline of Georgia faces a continental shelf that is 80 miles in width. Continental shelf width controls fundamentally not only average wave energy that strikes a coast, but also tidal influences and potential storm surge. Broad shelves, such as that off Georgia, translate into shallow water; and waves lose energy as they traverse the shallow water. But the shallow water can pile into higher tides and create greater storm surges. Where there are narrow shelves, such as that off Cape Hatteras, less wave energy is lost, and thus larger waves strike the coast. But a narrow shelf is also associated with tides and storm surges that are lower than those associated with wide shelves.

The high wave energy of the Cape Hatteras area is evident as soon as one walks onto the beach from the parking area at the lighthouse. Almost without regard to the day or season, large waves can be seen crashing onshore here, and it is not surprising that Cape Hatteras is a favored surfing spot on the U.S. East Coast. In addition, the windy conditions make this a favorite area of windsurfers.

The Cape Hatteras Lighthouse is in a dangerous physical location. Cape Hatteras juts out into the Atlantic and seems to attract winter storms and hurricanes. Waves approaching the shoreline at an angle push water and sediment along the coast, a process called longshore drift. The dominant direction of longshore drift along the U.S. East Coast is from north to south. Sand flowing down the Outer Banks ultimately ends up on Diamond Shoals. This sand is "permanently" lost from the beach and nearshore system.[9] A U.S. Army Corps of Engineers study for designing a potential seawall around the Cape Hatteras lighthouse summarized the wind, wave, sediment transport, and erosion history for the area.[10] Much of the following information is drawn from that report.

The predominant winds in the Cape Hatteras area, as with most of coastal North Carolina, are from the northeast and southwest. Prevailing winds approach Cape Hatteras from the north-northeast from September to February, then from the southwest from March through August. The annual average wind speed and direction is 11.5 miles per hour from the southwest. The highest winds, however, occur during the peak hurricane season, August through October. Storms are most numerous during the winter storm season, November through April. The highest reported wind speed for Cape Hatteras was 110 miles per hour from the west during the Great Hurricane of September 1944. Over the last half-century, winds above 45 miles per hour occur an average of four times per year.

Detailed wave data are not available for the immediate vicinity of the Cape Hatteras Lighthouse, but they are for Nags Head, only about 50 miles to the north, where the average annual wave height is about three feet, with a period of about 8.6 seconds. Lower wave heights occur between May and August. The largest recorded waves to affect the area—55 feet—occurred during the Ash Wednesday Northeaster of March 1962.

Astronomical tides are semidiurnal in the Cape Hatteras area; in other words, there are two high tides and two low tides each day. The mean tidal range is about 3.5 feet; the spring tidal range is about 4.3 feet. Storms can cause significant deviations from these regular astronomical tidal elevations. Storms are often compared statistically. For example, a storm that has a one percent chance of occurring each year is called a 100-year storm. The 100-year storm in this area could cause a storm surge of 8.5 feet above mean sea level. When such storm surge coincides with the time of high astronomical tide, especially a spring tide, severe flooding occurs.

As a side note, much is made in news reports about the dangerous combination of a hurricane making landfall at high tide. In low tidal range settings, such as Cape Hatteras, low water levels are not significantly different than high water levels. No matter at what point during the tidal cycle a hurricane hits, the water level will be near its mean. On the other hand, in high tidal range settings, there is a significant quantitative difference between high and low water levels. If a storm happens to hit during maximum low water, storm impact will actually be lessened.

As just noted, the predominant direction of longshore transport of sediment in the vicinity of the lighthouse is to the south toward Cape Point—the point of Cape Hatteras. Following the construction of the groin field in 1969, the shoreline accreted within and north of the groins (aided by beach nourishment), whereas south of the groins (downdrift), erosion occurred. The U.S. Army Corps of Engineers study provided very generalized longshore transport estimates, but longshore transport is exceedingly difficult to model mathematically and certainly even harder to measure in nature.[11] Using wave power data and long-term averages, the Corps has claimed that the southerly and northerly sediment transport rates may be on the order of 650,000 cubic yards per year and 300,000 cubic yards per year, respectively, resulting in a net southerly transport of about 350,000 cubic yards per year.

The most widely used longshore sediment transport equation is a relationship known as the "CERC formula"—for Coastal Engineering Research Center—the shortcomings of which have been researched and established.[12] The CERC formula relates total amount of sediment transported in the surf zone to the energy of the moving water. Geologists disagree about the veracity of the equation and about how accurately we can measure the independent variables in the formula. In practice, however, coastal engineers routinely use the equation to predict the volumes of sand moved by longshore currents. The U.S. Army Corps of Engineers presents longshore transport numbers with great certainty. In reality, however, the total volume of longshore sand transport over any time frame—day, week, or decade—has never been measured directly. Crude estimates, based on either the CERC formula or measurements of the amount of sand trapped by jetties at inlets, may be a poor basis on which to predict the sediment budget for the beach in the vicinity of the lighthouse, or the effectiveness of protective engineered structures.

History of erosion. Although the Cape Hatteras shoreline historically has fluctuated back and forth, overall it has translated landward. From the time of the first reliable survey of the shoreline position for the Cape Hatteras area (around 1850) until the present, the shoreline has changed significantly. By comparing the shoreline position plotted on reliable maps and charts, one can see that, in general, the east-facing shoreline north of the Cape has been retreating and the south-facing shoreline west of the Cape has been building seaward or prograding. The actual position and shape of the Cape itself has varied, seeming to undergo cycles of growth and erosion. Sometimes the Cape is more pointed in shape, and sometimes it is more blunted. The point of Cape Hatteras has been moving generally southwestward over time and Cape Point is now over a mile south-southwest of its 1852 position. In the vicinity of the Cape Hatteras Lighthouse, north of Cape Point, shoreline retreat is steadier. The shoreline has moved landward approximately 2,500 feet since 1852. Since around the time of lighthouse construction in 1870, the shoreline has retreated approximately 1,600 feet.

Long-term erosion rates, once based on maps, are now estimated from aerial photographs. Unfortunately, there are no aerial photographs older than about the late 1930s. With aerial photographs, much more accurate shoreline change determinations can be made. The North Carolina Division of Coastal Management (NCDCM) uses these shoreline change maps to determine building setback distances along the coast.[13] The published NCDCM shoreline change rates for the lighthouse area show a trend of retreat—4.5 to 10 feet per year over the past 50 years or so. West of Cape Point, the shoreline is accreting at rates of around 15 feet per year. Of course, these rates are averages, and the Cape Hatteras shoreline fluctuates over time. Recall that the lighthouse was temporarily abandoned in 1936 when the shoreline eroded to within 100 feet of it.

As geologists well know, erosion rates are not constant over time. In fact, the period just before construction of the lighthouse saw the highest erosion rates recorded, at around 33.5 feet per year. Following that rapid retreat, the shoreline erosion rate decreased to a much slower rate to produce an overall retreat rate of around ten feet per year. Erosion rates calculated since the mid-1960s are strongly influenced by the various attempts at erosion control, especially beach nourishment projects and groin construction by the Navy. Since the time the lighthouse was constructed, the overall erosion rate has been about 14.5 feet per year in the vicinity of the light.

A Study in Contrasts

The saga of the Cape Hatteras Lighthouse teaches us many lessons about human nature, coastal hazards, economics, and politics. Contrast the decisions regarding it and South Carolina's Morris Island Lighthouse.

Controversy over whether or not to try to save the Cape Hatteras Lighthouse, and how, has raged for years. Arguments centered around whether to armor the shoreline in an attempt to protect the lighthouse in place, relocate the lighthouse landward, replenish the beach, or do nothing and let the lighthouse fall in when its time came.[14] The Morris Island Lighthouse was never surrounded by such controversy. When the light was near the shore by the late 1930s, the decision was to provide minimum protection and to let nature take its course, rather than spend taxpayer dollars in an attempt to hold back the Atlantic Ocean. The light became stranded offshore a decade later. Perhaps no one thought of it in terms of needing to be "saved." When the Morris Island Lighthouse survived a direct hit from Hurricane Hugo in 1989, it was reported that the Cape Hatteras Lighthouse also could survive a major storm in place and that relocation was not required to save it.[15] Comparing the two lighthouses and saying that what is good for one is good for the other is an oversimplification of the problem. The two buildings, their geological settings, and their engineering settings differ in several ways.

The Cape Hatteras Lighthouse is in a more dangerous physical location than the Morris Island Lighthouse, because of higher average wave energy and more frequent storms. The erosion histories of the two locations also differ. The

Looking to the northeast from Morris Island between 1940 and 1950, one would have seen the Morris Island lighthouse, also known as the Charleston Light, going out to sea. (*Photograph by George W. Johnson from the collection of W. J. Keith*)

Cape Hatteras shore has fluctuated back and forth, although with an overall landward translation of the shoreline.[16] The South Carolina shoreline adjacent to Morris Island has basically just been moving landward.[17] The difference in erosion history illustrates the differing behavior between a cape and a barrier island. Further, the Morris Island Lighthouse, even though it is about a quarter mile offshore, is still in very shallow water. Below a veneer of unconsolidated sediment is a ledge of hard Tertiary rock—as much as 65 million years old—resistant to erosion. Thus, the Morris Island Lighthouse survives in very shallow water because of its geological site on a ledge of persistent rock.

Cape Hatteras is not a highly engineered shoreline. An artificial dune was built along the Outer Banks shoreline in the 1930s. Other than beach replenishment projects and three groins, the shore is unstabilized. Morris Island, however, sits in the sand transport "shadow" of the Charleston Harbor jetties and is greatly affected by shoreline engineering. The jetties interrupt the dominantly southward longshore transport of sand, resulting in severe erosion to the south. Groins at Cape Hatteras have likely helped to protect the Cape Hatteras Lighthouse. Meanwhile, Morris Island is being destroyed by jetties.

The Morris Island Lighthouse today as seen looking approximately south toward Folly Island; Morris Island is out of the picture to the right. (*Courtesy of Gered Lennon*)

Lighthouse design must also be considered. The foundation of the Cape Hatteras Lighthouse is only about seven feet thick, consisting of granite rubble and masonry laid on top of two courses of yellow pine timber.[18] The base of the foundation is actually one foot above sea level. Except for a wall of large nylon sandbags partially encircling the base, the lighthouse foundation is not armored. The result is high potential for storm wave scouring and destruction of the Cape Hatteras Lighthouse by undermining and toppling. In contrast, the base of the foundation of the Morris Island Lighthouse is below sea level and is much more substantial than that of the Cape Hatteras Lighthouse. The Morris Island Lighthouse's foundation consists of piles driven up to 50 feet deep, overlain by two courses of timber encased in concrete. Upon that, a concrete foundation eight feet thick was built, and the brick tower extends upward from there.[19] To protect against potential damage from locally extreme erosion rates, the base of the lighthouse was strengthened in 1938 with a sheet-pile cylindrical wall and a concrete cap.[20] Morris Island Lighthouse's base is obviously much better protected from wave scour than that of the Cape Hatteras Lighthouse and, therefore, much more likely to withstand the fury of storm waves.

In summary, the Cape Hatteras Lighthouse and the Morris Island Lighthouse differ in several significant ways. Coastal-zone managers must take into account all the differences—physical, geological, engineering, and political—when devising shoreline policy.

RESPONSES TO SHORELINE RETREAT: THE CAPE HATTERAS CONTROVERSY

The Cape Hatteras Lighthouse, like other lighthouses along the coast of the Carolinas, provides a range of lessons that go beyond the history of maritime safety and commerce. The original hurricane-resistant construction, lighthouses are markers against which to measure coastal dynamics and how we respond to them, both as individuals and as a society.

When lighthouses are threatened with destruction by the sea—particularly the lighthouse at Cape Hatteras, which is arguably the nation's most recognizable coastal landmark—we must respond. The response to the shoreline retreat that affected much of the Outer Banks by the 1930s, including the lighthouse, was an attempt to engineer nature by lending a well-intentioned hand. Unfortunately, the way barrier islands work was poorly understood at the time. The Civilian Conservation Corps built artificial dunes along the length of the Outer Banks and effectively created a dune dike intended to hold the islands in place. At the time, no one knew that islands migrate. But, when sea level rises, barrier islands do not naturally stay in one place—they survive by migrating. The dune dike blocked the natural cross-island processes by which the islands move landward and upward.

The early stabilization effort was on the right track, however, in that by building dunes, humans were mimicking the natural system. The 1966 beach nourishment project in front of the lighthouse was a harbinger of the "soft" engineering approach that would come to characterize coastal engineering by the end of the century. Unfortunately, the concern for preserving the lighthouse also led to a history of attempts at shore hardening, including the use of groins and seawalls. Between 1978 and 1980, the ocean reached the ruins of the old lighthouse base, washed it into the sea, and moved closer to the present lighthouse.

Shorelines change, inlets migrate, and barrier islands are built by natural processes. Humans may regard these processes as destructive and attempt to block or retard them through coastal engineering. But such geological change goes on inexorably.

Politics of the Lighthouse

Over the past century, federal and state policies have been committed to preserving natural resources and protecting historic landmarks. During this period, geological studies and observations consistently have shown that hard structures at the shoreline, such as seawalls and groins, although temporarily stopping shoreline retreat, actually increase the rate of beach loss. Degradation of the beach occurs as the shoreline continues to retreat just as it did before the wall was built. The beach narrows and eventually disappears as it backs up against the immovable, static wall. In recognition of the great potential for loss of recreational beaches, six states—Maine, Rhode Island, North Carolina, South Carolina, Texas, and Oregon—now outlaw all forms of hard stabilization of shorelines.

Legislation that established the Cape Hatteras National Seashore instructs the National Park Service to provide "for public enjoyment of the area, especially through recreational development, compatible with preservation of the resources."[21] The Park Service is further guided by Executive Order 11593 "to provide leadership in preserving, restoring and maintaining the historic and cultural properties . . . in a spirit of stewardship and trusteeship for future generations"[22] and to direct "policies, plans and programs in such a way that federally owned sites, structures and objects of historical, architectural or archaeological significance are preserved, restored and maintained for the inspiration and benefit of the people."[23]

In accordance with the legislation, the National Park Service in October 1978 published a "Cape Hatteras National Seashore Management Strategy" stating that the National Park Service "will not attempt to stabilize any part of the federally owned shoreline."[24] The National Park Service chose the preservation of beaches over buildings as they decided to let nature take its course on barrier islands under its jurisdiction. It reasoned that to do otherwise would cost inordinate amounts of money for initial construction, maintenance, disaster response, and the inevitable replacements; and furthermore, stabilization structures would certainly damage and destroy the beach. Sensible as it seems, the decision was a profound and controversial one.

The National Park Service also has a proud history of relocating cultural resources to protect them. In fact, a Department of Interior book, *Moving Historic Buildings,* advocates relocation as an alternative when all other solutions fail.[25] What better reason for moving a structure than the migration of a barrier island?

The Cape Hatteras Lighthouse is on the National Register of Historic Places. Many historic structures have been moved, for a variety of reasons. For instance, many historic bridges have been at more than one site. They were dismantled and moved to another river when the first bridge was replaced. Some have been in three or four locations. They are still designated as historic bridges because they are one of a kind; they are unique. Lighthouses also are unique structures whose positions in relation to the ocean matters. When it was first lit in 1870, the Cape Hatteras Lighthouse was, as previously noted, 1,500 feet from the shoreline. It was the opinion of many people involved in the Cape Hatteras Lighthouse controversy that the original relationship between light and shoreline should be restored. Relocation of the lighthouse would restore that relationship and would result in historic site preservation in its truest sense.

To save the Cape Hatteras Lighthouse, the National Park Service in 1980 was directed by the Department of the Interior to find a mode of preservation that would meet three criteria: (1) The lighthouse would be saved; (2) the solution would be permanent; and (3) there would not be major recurring costs. Many solutions were discussed and reviewed.[26]

On December 2, 1980, the National Park Service concluded a preliminary study detailing various methods for preserving the lighthouse. A fair reading of this proposal suggested that relocation was the best alternative for preserving the historic structure. Most cost-effective and permanent of all proposals, relocation was considerably less risky and quicker to implement than was revetment wall construction—it would not compromise the aesthetic properties of the lighthouse and would not destroy the historical context of the lighthouse and surrounding buildings.

Also in 1980, the National Park Service requested that the Army Corps of Engineers evaluate and design the seawall alternative. The Corps's Wilmington, North Carolina, District designed a pentagonal-shaped seawall intended to move out to sea as an island as the shoreline retreated past the lighthouse. Although the initial cost estimate was only $5 million, the long-term cost of maintaining an island on this high-energy coast ranged from $50 to $100 million. In addition, it was recognized that visitors would no longer be able to access the lighthouse easily and that a large storm still could destroy it.

Amazingly, the Army Corps of Engineers's design emerged as the alternative preferred by the National Park Service. Not only did this choice contradict federal and state coastal policies, including the 1978 Park Service decision to halt shoreline armoring, but the selection also contradicted the engineering and cost-analysis studies commissioned by the National Park Service.

In 1985, the Move the Lighthouse Committee, consisting of scientists and engineers, was organized in 1985 by David Fischetti, a Cary, North Carolina, structural engineer. The original aim of the committee was to demonstrate that the National Park Service decision to choose the Army Corps of Engineers' seawall proposal was based on misinformation and confusion of issues, and that the relocation alternative would be preferable on all counts. The committee felt that even though the lighthouse was in danger from coastal erosion and storms, greater peril would result from the proposed seawall construction project.

The Move the Lighthouse Committee successfully stimulated a reevaluation of the options for preserving the light. In fact, money—about $5 million—had already been appropriated by Congress for building the seawall designed by the Army Corps of Engineers. But the Move the Lighthouse Committee overcame the momentum of this federally funded project and convinced decision makers that there might be a better solution.

Controversy erupted and swirled around the lighthouse. An examination of all facts clearly showed that moving the lighthouse was the only solution that satisfied all three criteria of the National Park Service. That conclusion was reached by the Move the Lighthouse Committee in 1986. In 1987, the Committee on Options for Preserving the Cape Hatteras Lighthouse—a committee of the National Academy of Sciences and National Academy of Engineering which had been formed at the request of the National Park Service—reached the same conclusion.[27] In 1989, the National Park Service announced that it now preferred to relocate the lighthouse.

However, an outspoken opponent of moving the lighthouse and a proponent of building up the Cape Hatteras beach, Hugh Morton of Grandfather Mountain, Inc., organized the Save Cape Hatteras Lighthouse Committee, which raised on the order of $500,000 from a campaign directed at North Carolina schoolchildren. Morton used some of that money to emplace Seascape in front of the lighthouse. Seascape—plastic, artificial seaweed intended to reduce wave and current action and thereby cause sand deposition—had twice before been emplaced at the Cape Hatteras shoreline.

Throwing more artificial seaweed at the waves, as Morton proposed, would waste more money and time. Geologists and engineers agreed, virtually unanimously, that artificial seaweed does not build up sand on ocean beaches. Not only did the previous emplacements of Seascape fail to work,[28] the plastic seaweed washed ashore during ongoing, natural seashore changes.[29] In support of Seascape, Morton presented photographs of the shoreline before and after Seascape emplacement to prove its success—but he failed to mention that the shoreline had built out naturally for a short time, mostly in areas where no Seascape was used.

In 1998, Morton arranged for a group of representatives from business, politics, and media to visit Muskegon, Michigan, where erosion control stabilizers, produced by Holmberg Technologies, Inc., had been installed in Lake Michigan. The erosion control stabilizers were described as "speed bumps" that slowed water movement and allowed sand to be deposited. This explanation sounded good to the coastal politicians, who were treated to a great show. However, the impact of the stabilizers on adjacent shores was not addressed during the visit, and the relevance of Lake Michigan "successes" to the high-energy ocean shoreline at Cape Hatteras was not considered. Despite these factors, the contingent returned to North Carolina sold on the technology as a solution to Cape Hatteras erosion.

In 1998, the Save Cape Hatteras Lighthouse Committee sent a letter to newspapers in North Carolina and to several prominent regional newspapers rebutting our and the Army Corps of Engineers's opposition to the use of erosion control stabilizers at Cape Hatteras. The letter pleaded for the use of Holmberg erosion control stabilizers, to work magic on the Hatteras beach. To coastal geologists, however, these beach stabilizers were nothing more than underwater groins consisting of long cloth bags filled with concrete. In response to the Save Cape Hatteras Lighthouse Committee, marine geologists in North Carolina circulated a letter that informed the public about failures of the Holmberg Technologies device and argued that such structures should not be used at Cape Hatteras. On November 14, 1998, Congress appropriated $9 million to move the lighthouse.

Despite subsequent attempts by some to halt the move, the lighthouse was relocated. The move began on June 15, 1999, and the lighthouse reached its

The Cape Hatteras Lighthouse on June 15, 1999, at the beginning of the runway along which it would be moved to its new location approximately one-half mile from the shoreline. (*Photograph by Mike Booher*)

new location on July 9. Eight companies were involved in the heavily planned move. The roadway for the move consisted of gravel 24 inches deep covered by thick steel mats. The lighthouse tower was lifted by 112 heavy jacks to a base of 20 steel beams and moved on seven steel tracks. As one building mover noted, the first few inches of the move were the most difficult. Push jacks were used to move the entire frame and lighthouse at a rate of one foot per hour. (A plan to pull the structure along the rails with cables had been eliminated because of the possibility of sudden jerks and stops.) The maximum rate of lighthouse movement was approximately 300 feet per day. Throughout the move, the structure was heavily monitored by using tilt, acceleration, and strain meters. When it reached its destination the Cape Hatteras Lighthouse had been moved approximately one-half mile from its original location.

If the Cape Hatteras Lighthouse had not been moved, beach stabilization attempts at the lighthouse undoubtedly would have proceeded, the shoreline to the north and south would have continued to erode past the lighthouse, and the bulge of the shoreline at the lighthouse would have become even more pronounced. Eventually, the lighthouse would have been destroyed in an "unusual" storm, and all the money and effort spent to stabilize the shore would have been wasted.

Instead, since the lighthouse has been moved, it is in the same position relative to the shoreline as when it was first constructed, and the shoreline will no longer need to be stabilized. The previously emplaced groins and sandbags will be removed or destroyed by storms, at which time the shoreline will straighten and quickly assume its normal, equilibrium profile and shape. In the end, moving the lighthouse was the only long-term solution for the salvation of this national and state treasure.

In the long debate about the fate of the Cape Hatteras Lighthouse, it was not the unanimous opinion of scientists that the lighthouse should be moved. In fact, some scientists felt that letting the lighthouse fall into the sea would also set an appropriate example of good coastal management. However, the opinion that the lighthouse could not be saved in place was unanimous. In arguing against stabilizing the shoreline to hold the lighthouse in place, scientists successfully provided a leveled playing field for the societal debate. In this appropriate stand, the scientists succeeded.

The primary and most important lesson from the Cape Hatteras Lighthouse example is that we as a nation cannot afford to fight the natural forces of the sea on all of our coasts—there are dozens of lighthouses to be "saved." We must plan an organized retreat from the encroaching sea or alternatively face the expense of vast amounts of money and other resources, only to fail.[30] Geologists and oceanographers recognize the folly of trying to fight the sea and realize that we must learn to live by nature's rules at the shore.[31] Moving the

The Cape Hatteras Lighthouse being moved on seven steel tracks to its destination. (*Photograph by Mike Booher*)

Cape Hatteras Lighthouse has set a bold example for all coastal zone managers to follow. If a lighthouse can be moved, then it is reasonable to accept that other large buildings can be moved. Some would argue that no public money should be spent to move such structures—that we should let them go the way of the Morris Island Lighthouse, to stand or fall into the sea. Lighthouses have historically warned of dangers along coasts; if we heed their beacons now, they will point us toward sensible coastal management strategies for the future.[32]

17

The Follies of Lotus Bay

Jill K. Singer

Ａs a geologist and frequent visitor to Lake Erie's Lotus Bay over the past decade, I have observed the erosive power of Great Lakes storm waves and talked to property owners about building projects along the lake's shores. "You have to fight!" sums up the position taken by many property owners living along Lotus Bay. Implicit in this attitude is the belief that armed with money and the right design, any engineered structure can be made to withstand the force of waves and ice. Despite the fact that Lotus Bay beaches are littered with rubble and steel from a variety of previous projects, property owners appear to disregard past failures. Even long-time residents seem oblivious to wave dynamics and changing lake levels. They attribute the unsuccessful projects of their neighbors to poor design, bad luck, or "freak" weather. Although the challenges of living in coastal areas have been well documented, relatively few beach residents understand coastal processes along lakes and oceans.[1]

In the United States, all 30 states with coastlines—including the states bordering the Great Lakes—are experiencing erosion.[2] The Coastal Zone Management Act passed in 1972 and its 1976 amendments established a national interest in the effective management and protection of the coastal zone; it encouraged states to develop programs to provide good stewardship of their coasts.[3] In New York State, this means that the Department of Environmental Conservation must delineate areas with coastal erosion hazards, and the municipality in which the erosion hazard area occurs must regulate activities in that zone. If the municipality does not meet its obligation, then the county becomes responsible for the regulation. If the county does not meet *its* obligation, the responsibility conveys to the Department of Environmental Conservation.[4] Any person proposing to undertake a regulated activity within a designated erosion hazard area first must obtain a coastal erosion management permit from the Department of Environmental Conservation. New York State requires a permit to construct a new home, modify or add to existing buildings, build or restore erosion protection structures such as bulkheads, jetties, and groins, or excavate, mine, or dredge beach and dune material.

Lotus Bay, a gently curved bay located on the southeastern shore of Lake Erie approximately 30 miles south of Buffalo, New York, falls in the coastal erosion hazard area of the Town of Brant in Erie County, New York.[5] Because neither the Town of Brant nor Erie County have produced regulations for the hazard area, the state must approve and issue coastal erosion management permits for proposed projects in Lotus Bay. Although most of the projects launched by Lotus Bay residents have required permits, in many cases, landowners never consulted the Department of Environmental Conservation. In fact, a number of projects have been completed without permits or with permits issued "after the fact."

Lake Erie's coastal zone, like all the other Great Lakes, is dynamic—waves and storm surges cause erosion and flooding. Times of greatest erosion and flooding coincide with higher lake levels, when waves are able to break close to shore.[6] Pulitzer Prize-winning editorial cartoonist Tom Toles of the *Buffalo News* appreciated this fact—he mixed humor and truth to point out the need for citizens to understand and respect coastal processes in order to protect their property from storm damage. Natural factors such as precipitation, runoff, and evaporation affect the mean water level of Lake Erie. Gauges in most of the lake's major harbors measure its level. Diversions constructed to lower the lake level have only managed to decrease it by about three inches.[7] At present, the lake level at the Buffalo Harbor gauge is 1.5 feet above the lake's average elevation for the period 1918 to 1996.[8]

Lake Erie also experiences major short-term changes in lake level due to storms. Because of the small size, shallow depth, and oblong shape of Lake Erie, the cities of Buffalo, New York, and Toledo, Ohio are particularly vulnerable to dangerous storm surges. And because the long axis of Lake Erie is aligned in the same direction as the prevailing westerly winds and the lake therefore has maximum fetch—open water distance across which the wind blows—strong winds can transport large volumes of water along the lake. The resulting storm surge piles water up at the eastern, Buffalo end of the lake, often within a period of several hours. When the wind subsides, the water reverses direction and flows back down to the western, Toledo end of the lake and gathers there. Lake Erie, because it is very shallow, behaves like a large bathtub—the water sloshes back and forth between Buffalo and Toledo, producing an effect known as a seiche. During storms, lake levels commonly drop several feet in Toledo and rise an equivalent amount in Buffalo. The seiche associated with a storm surge may take several days to dissipate. Seiches are seasonal phenomena; except for unusual years when winters are uncharacteristically mild, ice forms on the lake and its beaches and inhibits storm wave formation, which in turn reduces erosion.

Tom Toles points out the need for citizens to understand coastal processes if they want to protect their property from storm damage. (*Used by permission from The Buffalo News*)

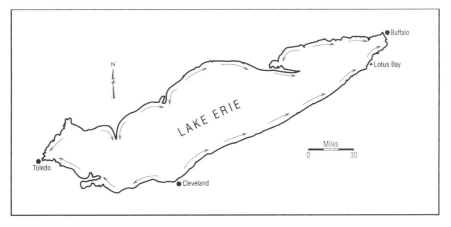

Lotus Bay is located on the southeastern shore of Lake Erie south of Buffalo, New York. The arrows indicate net longshore sand transport directions.

Mile-long Lotus Bay contains a sand and pebble beach and a 15- to 20-foot bluff composed of thin-bedded shales of Devonian age (360–410 million years). Like most Lake Erie beaches, the sediment largely comes from material eroded from the rocky parts of the lake shore and glacial deposits common throughout the area. It also comes from erosion of the bluff itself, which provides the pebbles found on the beach. Cattaraugus Creek, which enters Lake Erie just west of Lotus Bay, also carries sediment to the beaches. Because of the coincident alignment of Lake Erie and the prevailing winds, sediment travels from southwest to northeast along the southeastern shore of the lake.

Exposed to the prevailing westerly winds, Lotus Bay often experiences the large waves and storm surge I've described. Despite its exposed location, Lotus Bay has one of the lowest bluff recession rates along the Lake Erie shore—less than one foot per year—because the beaches absorb much of the wave energy and the bluff shale effectively resists erosion.[9] Fluctuating lake levels, however, affect the width of the Lotus Bay beaches and allow waves to break on the base of bluffs during fall and winter storms. Locals refer to these events as "bank busters," and much of the damage to engineered structures takes place when they occur. Also relevant is the fact that since 1997 lake levels have been above average, and Lotus Bay has lost significant amounts of sand. This loss has further narrowed Lotus Bay beaches and waves now break on the base of bluffs during even minor storms. Newly exposed, previously buried structures—abandoned beach wells and stairs that end above the height of the beach—stand as reminders of the extensive deposition and erosion that have taken place here.

Residents of Lotus Bay have battled Lake Erie for decades. Property owners living there year-round have pursued projects designed to provide them with beach access, water supplies, shoreline protection, or lake entry. However, because these people have consistently underestimated the power of waves and ice as well as the rate of erosion, the structures they have created have not endured. A casual stroll along the bay's shore provides the walker with a view of remnants of failed projects including stairs, boat ramps, docks, beach wells, pump houses, and concrete and boulder walls. The life span of some of these projects has been less than one season, whereas other projects have taken a decade or more to fail. In the end, most projects have succumbed to the power of the waves and winter ice, and the beach is strewn with concrete rubble and scrap steel—a record of human folly.

Most of the houses in Lotus Bay are set back more than 100 feet from the bluff, so present residents are not concerned about the loss of their homes. However, the same bluff that protects their properties also limits access to the beach below. Because of the high bluffs, most property owners have devised some method for beach access. For many, this amounts to a set of stairs leading from the top of the bluff to the beach. Materials used to build the stairs include wood, steel, and concrete. One of the most enduring sets of stairs in

Lotus Bay consists of modified fire escape ladders supported by four eight-inch steel pipes resting on the shale bedrock. But the majority of stairs have not survived the test of time. The most common design involves a platform or deck built on the top of the bluff with fixed or retractable stairs that lead to the beach. After violent storms that occur when property owners either are away or have failed to raise their stairs in time, the lower portion of the stairs are destroyed by large waves. Some of these waves carry entire trees that entered the lake from Cattaraugus Creek or have fallen from the eroding bluffs. Other stairs are twisted or dislodged from their foundations and abandoned by their owners, who then build another set of stairs of similar design. Platforms that support stairs eventually become unstable as a result of bluff recession and ultimately must be reinforced or relocated back from the bluff. Concrete stairs originally embedded in the bluff also become exposed during bluff recession. Ultimately, waves undermine the bluff and cause large sections of stairs to collapse. Property owners seldom remove concrete debris and often incorporate the debris into another set of stairs. Many Lotus Bay residents spend significant amounts of time discussing stair design and the money needed to build, maintain, and reconstruct damaged stairs.

Originally, property owners built and maintained stairways to the beach in order to service beach wells—concrete cisterns (boxes) dug below lake level. Until recently, most Lotus Bay residents relied on beach wells as a source of

Concrete blocks litter the beach as unsightly reminders of past efforts to gain access to the beach. Some property owners incorporate the debris into another set of stairs.

water because water that filled a cistern could be drawn up to a pump house or directly to a residence. Property owners favored beach wells because they provided unlimited quantities of water. But fluctuating lake levels buried cisterns in sand and clogged water intake valves with silt. This situation required excavation of the sand to expose a cistern and allow entry to it to clear the water intake valve. Furthermore, water intake pipes commonly froze during the winter or were severed by shifting shore ice. Until a repair was made and the water supply reestablished, property owners had to transport water from other sources. Finally, pump houses built into an eroding bluff collapsed onto the beach. After collapse, some residents paid thousands of dollars to have holes drilled through the bluff to their homes in order to pump water directly from a beach well. Over time, most property owners abandoned their beach wells and dug ground wells adjacent to their homes. Others used ground wells as a backup when beach wells failed. Today, residents of Lotus Bay no longer need beach wells or pump houses because a municipal water supply system services the area. But all the abandoned beach wells and pump houses remain as reminders of past projects.

Bluff recession rates are relatively low in Lotus Bay. Nevertheless, erosion has concerned many property owners, and they have built walls to minimize bluff recession. Because of the enormous expense, some neighbors have collaborated to share construction costs and maximize the amount of bluff

A former pump house has been converted to a beach house. With continued bluff erosion, the concrete support blocks will be exposed and the house will collapse.

protected. One large-scale effort involved more than 100 limestone blocks of various sizes. The stepped boulder wall was approximately 15 feet high and 150 feet long, and was covered with washed gravel. One neighbor recalled that the cost of the boulder wall exceeded $20,000. Over the years, wave action washed the gravel from behind the blocks and shifted the boulders. Within five years, large sections of the wall slumped onto the beach. Another bluff protection project resembled a concrete bunker, complete with several small high windows to let in light. The structure, which is 15 feet high and 75 feet long and has walls 10 inches thick, reinforces the bluff, provides storage for beach equipment, and houses the pump for a beach well. Because of its size and its protected location within the bay, this structure has held up over time. However, stress cracks are beginning to appear. This structure, painted bright pink, is one of the most aesthetically offensive in the bay and seems to mock nature. However, if the history of other engineered structures in the bay portends the future, "big pink" at some future date will exist only in someone's memory.

Nearly all property owners in Lotus Bay own some kind of boat or water craft. The need to moor and launch these craft has resulted in the construction of docks and boat ramps. But people's ignorance of the destructive power of waves allows fabrication of nonsensical structures. For example, a 100-foot boat dock with a support system composed of steel channel iron and adjustable four-inch steel pipe legs rested on the lake's shale bottom. The dock was covered with two inch by eight inch planks. Installed in the spring of the year, it suffered minor damage during an early storm. To protect the dock from the breaking waves, the owner raised it higher above the water. But then, in calm weather, the owner's boat was two to three feet below the dock, and a ladder was needed to climb down into the boat. The last summer storm of the year completely destroyed the dock—one neighbor recalled that the steel understructure after the storm resembled a child's erector set on the beach. Another neighbor recollected that the wood planks from the dock were strewn like toothpicks for half a mile along the beach. The dock owner lamented the loss but was consoled by the knowledge that an insurance company would pay for the loss.

Another unsuccessful project involved the construction of a combination boat and pump house built into the bluff. A boat launch, composed of four-inch steel pipe connected with steel cross ties, resembled a railroad track and extended approximately 75 feet from the boat house to the water. It survived the first summer. But when the lake froze in winter, the shifting ice destroyed about three-quarters of the steel track. Because the track was connected to the floor of the boat house, the integrity of the boat house was imperiled. Before the boat house suffered further damage, a welder was called to burn the steel pipes and separate them from the boat house. The following spring, realizing that his boat launch was a mangled mess of steel, the owner abandoned the launch and hired a bulldozer operator to pile up beach sand to form a ramp leading from his boat house to the water. The uncompacted sand of the ramp collapsed under the weight of the boat during its first launch. This calamity required yet another bulldozer to pull the boat and trailer out of the sand. After this series of setbacks, the owner wisely chose to store the boat at a marina not five minutes away in nearby Cattaraugus Creek.

Acknowledging the futility of constructed boat docks, some property owners have made bluff cuts in order to launch their boats. Bluff cuts—oriented perpendicular to the shoreline—require the removal of a sloping, wedge-shaped slice of shale bedrock. Some of the first bluff cuts in Lotus Bay were made at places where the bank was less than six feet high. These shallow cuts were also very narrow and barely wide enough to accommodate a boat and trailer. In other parts of the bay, bluff height approaches 20 feet and demands much deeper cuts for lake access. One property owner made a bluff cut ten feet deep and connected it to the beach by a ramp composed of sand and gravel. As a result of erosion by waves, the lower portion of the ramp was constantly in need of replenishment with more sand and gravel—usually with the aid of a bulldozer. Because of the steep angle of descent down the ramp and onto the beach, a bulldozer was also needed to launch boats from this ramp. Recently, to avoid this constant maintenance and with the approval of the Department of Environmental Conservation, this property owner cut completely through the bluff right down to beach level.

Another resident also sought to avoid the constant maintenance of a partial bluff cut. Following his neighbor's example, this individual decided to slice through the bluff on his property but did not request a permit. The owner removed a portion of the 20-foot bluff in front of his house, producing a 25 foot wide gap in the bluff and a 50-foot slope that led from his front lawn to the beach. Much of the shale debris removed during the excavation of the bluff was left as large mounds along the adjacent bank. Shortly after the bluff was cut, an outraged neighbor called state environmental authorities, who then inspected the site. The property owner met with Department of Environmental Conservation personnel and indicated that the project was not yet complete—he intended to build a concrete ramp within the bluff cut. Rather than assess a fine, the state required that he complete a permit application. The permit was approved by the Department of Environmental Conservation, and subsequently the property owner applied for, and was granted, a two-year extension in which to complete the proposed work.

Although I do not feel that any bluff cut is aesthetically pleasing, this massive cut was especially ugly, and the piles of rubble on the adjacent bluff further detracted from the natural beauty of the shoreline. Excessive under any circumstances, the width of this bluff cut seems grossly disproportionate, given that the owner intended to launch only small personal water craft. Because of its great width, the bluff cut acts like a small inlet during storms when water level is high—water flows up into the cut, spreads, slows, and deposits sediment and debris, including large logs, at the base of the cut. Ironically, a bulldozer must frequently clear this bluff cut of debris. Recently, the property owner has constructed a framework of steel reinforcing rods (rebar) by drilling into the underlying shale bedrock and has poured a concrete floor and retaining walls. The lower end of the ramp includes a flared entrance and a gate to keep trespassers out. The boat launch now resembles a concrete underpass without the bridge.

Shortly after the end of the 1997 summer season, another property owner constructed yet another concrete boat ramp where a gravel ramp previously had been sited. What was new was the size of the ramp—20 feet wide, 6 to 10 feet high, and 50 feet long. Also new were the one- to two-ton blocks of concrete stacked on the beach and secured by rebar and concrete. To accommodate varying lake levels, the ramp terminated short of the water and connected to 15 foot long steel tracks that allowed boats to be launched directly into the lake. This structure visually dominated the beach and obstructed the movement of sediment and people. Even during periods of moderate wave action, waves broke over the lower portion of the ramp. The ramp cut off one-third of the bay and isolated a cluster of homes that had shared a common lake access. Anyone who wanted to walk or jog the length of the bay had to scale a four- to five-foot wall of concrete or wade through waist-deep water around the front of the ramp. In the few weeks after the ramp was finished, it became obvious to me that the structure interfered with the longshore transport of sediment—sand and gravel accumulated on the upstream side of the structure and the beach downstream of the structure began to erode rapidly.

From my conversations with several Lotus Bay residents, I realized that I was not alone in my concern about the aesthetic impact of this structure. However, my geological perspective enabled me to identify significant environmental consequences that the bay residents had either overlooked or not considered. I called the New York State Department of Environmental Conservation and articulated my concerns. Remarkably, I was the only person to have called the state about the structure. My inquiries alerted state authorities to the project, which as it turned out, had been conducted without a permit. Following up on my inquiry, I sent photographs and ramp measurements to the state water program specialist. Within two weeks, a state official inspected the site and found that it violated regulatory requirements. Had the property owner applied for a permit, the structure, as designed, would not have been approved. The water program specialist forwarded her recommendations to the legal branch of the Department of Environmental Conservation, and a state attorney met with the property owner. After several months of negotiations, the property owner agreed to remove the ramp. Several pieces of heavy equipment, five days, and perhaps $15,000 were needed to demolish the ramp. Coupled with the cost of construction, this outcome constituted an expensive lesson for the property owner.

This experience has been a small victory, and I derive some satisfaction from it. More important, this situation crystallized for me the challenges inherent in helping people live in balance with earth processes. My conversations

with residents living in Lotus Bay have revealed that most people consider erosion to be "bad." Few residents recognize that erosion is a natural process—
that any development within a coastal zone must accommodate changing lake
levels and acknowledge the destructive power of storm waves. The people with
whom I spoke also were unaware of the constant movement of sediment
throughout the lake and the ability of walls and docks to obstruct that movement. Furthermore, relatively few property owners regularly walk the length of
Lotus Bay, so they don't see the 15 beach wells, 23 sets of stairs, 6 bluff cuts, and
12 pump and boat houses. Although they observed the collapsed structures of
their neighbors, most people did not appreciate the extent to which the natural
beauty of the bay has been diminished by ultimately futile construction projects over the years.

Of all the projects undertaken in Lotus Bay, those that have involved
removal of the bluff for lake access stand apart as the most unnecessary and
geologically shortsighted. Rock that took tens of millions of years to accumulate has been removed, in some instances, with Department of Environmental
Conservation approval, in less than a day by a single property owner. What
would happen if every property owner in the bay filed a permit for a bluff cut?
The resultant shoreline would resemble half a zipper with fragments of the
once continuous bluff interrupted by unsightly cuts—surely a landscape
devoid of natural beauty.

Some have tried to justify bluff cuts on the premise that property owners
are entitled to lake access. However, such arguments fail to consider the rights
of present and future generations to enjoy an unsullied bluff, beach, and lake.
In addition, because the Department of Environmental Conservation reviews
permits on a project-by-project basis, no mechanism exists to evaluate the
cumulative impact of bluff cuts. Such a myopic approach does not consider
the long-term consequences of our actions. It will lead predictably to uneven
erosion and a shoreline that has lost some of its natural protective buffer
against storm waves.

Furthermore, in the permit review process, engineers try to deduce the
structural integrity and longevity of proposed designs. It is unfortunate that
most engineers have had limited, if any, training in geology. Therefore, they
often fail to consider the relationship between the structure and its geological
setting as well as appropriately long time scales. For example, the property
owner who received permission to pour a concrete ramp over shale bedrock
should have been informed that bedrock would be a sufficient base for a ramp.
That water craft were launched successfully for two years before concrete was
added demonstrated that the ramp functioned adequately. Also, what is the
point of building a ramp designed to last 30 years when bluff recession will
separate the bluff and the ramp in 15 years? More than likely, the ramp will be
abandoned, like so many other coastal zone structures, and the property
owner will need to build yet another boat launch.

My conversations with Department of Environmental Conservation officials have helped me appreciate the shortage of field specialists available to monitor the impact of projects on miles of coastline. Review of permit applications consumes most of their time, leaving little for reconnaissance fieldwork—and despite miles of Lake Erie and Lake Ontario coastline, no coastal geologist works in the Buffalo office of the New York State Department of Environmental Conservation. Because residents embark on many projects without a permit, they proceed without valuable expertise. Whereas some property owners may not be aware of their responsibility to request a permit, others simply choose to proceed without permission. For some property owners, the relatively minor fines they subsequently incur are a small price to pay for acting without constraint in the coastal zone. I still find it hard to believe that no one else called the Department of Environmental Conservation about the huge concrete boat ramp I have described. But that reality points to the fact that formal complaints are filed only reluctantly by neighbor against neighbor—even if a project has negative impacts. Also, a substantial number of seasonal residents believe that they should not influence the property rights of full-time residents. It also appears that some neighbors simply do not know whom to call about their concerns. To address some of these problems, lakeshore residents need to understand the government's role in coastal zone management and how it can help to preserve and maintain our coastal resources.

The protection of our coastal zone will require cooperation and shared vision among property owners, residents, developers, and regulating agencies. To accomplish this unified approach, we will need to change our existing regulations and permit review process, increase budgets for enforcement, and educate the general public and elected officials about the long-term consequences of our engineered structures along coastlines. Geologists certainly can provide knowledge about the dynamic processes that continuously modify the coastal landscape—an understanding of which is critical to the project of living sensibly in the central zone. Even though there are no simple guidelines by which to balance the rights of present property owners and those of future generations, one would hope that we can learn from past failures, like many of those in Lotus Bay and countless other places. If we comprehend the shortcomings of our insistent behavior along the coast, we will make better use of our personal energy and limited resources.[10]

18

Dredging to Keep New York–New Jersey Harbor Alive

Meg E. Stewart

The bulk of the water in New York is oily, dirty, and germy. Men on the mud suckers, the big harbor dredges, like to say that you could bottle it and sell it for poison. The bottom of the harbor is dirtier than the water. In most places, it is covered with a blanket of sludge that is composed of silt, sewage, industrial wastes, and clotted oil. The sludge is thickest in the slips along the Hudson, in the flats on the Jersey side of the Upper Bay, and in backwaters such as Newtown Creek, Wallabout Bay, and the Gowanus Canal. In such areas, where it isn't exposed to the full sweep of the tides, it accumulates rapidly.
—Joseph Mitchell, *The Bottom of the Harbor*[1]

Writer Joseph Mitchell's vivid mid-century description of the bottom of the harbor between New York and New Jersey applies today. And, as was true then, contaminated sediment is still dredged from the harbor's navigation channels to enable the unencumbered movement of ship traffic. In the past, harbor mud was dumped in the ocean about six miles offshore. Since 1997, a law signed by President Clinton and the governors of both states has made it illegal to dump dredged "spoils" in the ocean. Almost 50 years after Mitchell directed attention to the problem of contaminated sludge at the harbor's bottom, we must now find a place to put it.

Since the mid-1800s, New York–New Jersey Harbor has been a leading center for shipping and commerce. The chief cargo port on the eastern coast of the United States and the third largest in the nation, it employs almost 200,000 people—a workforce comparable to those of corporations like IBM, Federal Express, and AT&T. Goods that travel through the harbor supply provisions to almost 17 million people in the greater metropolitan area, the mid-Atlantic states, New England, and the Great Lakes region. Petroleum products, food, and textiles come into the port, and a multitude of manufactured items exit it. Such commerce depends on the harbor's navigability.

HISTORY OF THE HARBOR: NATURAL AND UNNATURAL

Glaciation in the Pleistocene, beginning about two million years ago, influenced the depth of New York–New Jersey Harbor and the Hudson River. It also caused the upper harbor to be an estuary; that is, tides greatly influence both the harbor and the rivers that flow into it. During the Pleistocene, a great terminal moraine—a sedimentary deposit that marks the farthest advance of a glacier—stretched east from Staten Island to Long Island and north to Cape Cod. The moraine acted as a dam and contained meltwaters from the glacier, thereby creating large lakes with thick bottom deposits of sand, silt, and clay in what is now the harbor. The glacier itself gouged the valley occupied by the proto-Hudson River; consequently, today's river is more than 100 feet deep in places. Because much of the Earth's water was locked up in snow and ice during the Pleistocene, sea level then was much lower than it is today and the continental shelf—that part of the continent presently below sea level—was exposed. As the Pleistocene ice age came to an end and glaciers retreated, the Hudson River pierced a crack in the moraine; sea level rose and salt water inundated the glacial lakes.[2] Such was the beginning of New York–New Jersey Harbor.

Today along the New Jersey side, the harbor largely comprises tidal and freshwater marshes that are remnants of glacial lakes. On the New York side, because of proximity to the Pleistocene fjord that was the proto-Hudson River, deeper water occurs nearer the shoreline.

The Raritan, Hackensack, Passaic, and Hudson rivers drain into the harbor and carry in their flows millions of cubic yards of sediment each year. This natural geological process keeps the harbor shallow; its average natural depth is only 18 feet. Standard ships require at least a 35-foot depth for unencumbered navigation. So, to accommodate ship traffic, the U.S. Army Corps of Engineers regularly dredges a network of navigation channels throughout the harbor to provide the depth needed by ships. Presently, the Corps maintains more than 240 miles of channels in the port.[3]

Ordinary river flow causes sand and silt to build up in the channels rapidly. An estimated four million cubic yards of it, volumetrically enough to fill both World Trade Towers, accumulate at a rate of about a foot per year and must be removed annually to enable safe navigation.[4] Interruptions to such dredging, even if temporary, affect the local economy. "Any port in a storm," the saying goes; ships without port in New York–New Jersey Harbor change course and dock at competing harbors. Unfortunately, newer ships require a 50-foot water

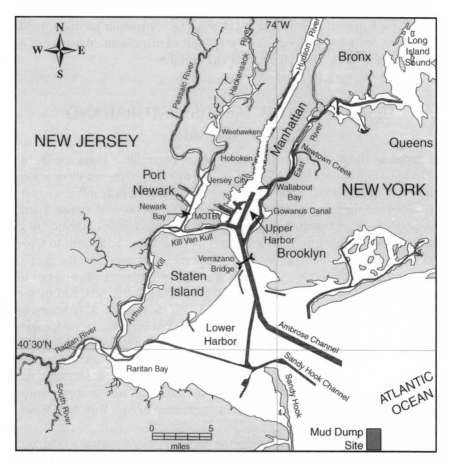

The New York–New Jersey harbor and shipping channels. MOTBY indicates the Military Ocean Terminal, Bayonne, New Jersey. (*Modified from U.S. Army Corps of Engineers, New York District, Dredged Material Management Plan, Interim Report*)

depth and will require deeper navigation channels. More dredged sediment than ever before will need to be disposed of to keep the harbor alive.

From the mid-1800s until 1997, the location of ocean dumping of dredged sediment from the harbor was the New York Bight Dredged Material Disposal Site, also known as the Mud Dump Site. Of course, "official" dumping of dredged sediment at the Mud Dump did not begin until 1888, when Congress directed the Supervisor of New York Harbor to grant permits for the purpose.[5] Six miles east of Sandy Hook, New Jersey, the Mud Dump is located on the continental shelf.

Sediments dredged from the channels contain substantial amounts of chlorinated organic compounds such as dioxin and polychlorinated biphenyls (PCBs)—a sticky, tarlike solvent—as well as heavy metals such as mercury.

According to some estimates, 75 percent of all dredged sediment contains these toxic substances. Most of them originated from industrial activities that have taken place along the harbor and on the banks of rivers that flow into it. For example, General Electric in Fort Edwards, New York, used PCBs in the manufacture of transformers and disposed of their PCB-laden fluid wastes directly into the Hudson River. Because PCBs are heavy, they sink to the bottom of the river and adhere to the surfaces of sediment particles there. Eventually, these contaminated particles move downstream toward the harbor.

In recent years, the location of the Mud Dump Site off the New Jersey coast has caused great ire among New Jersey residents, who felt that they already hosted more than their share of waste, especially from New York. Environmental advocates were fed up with pollutants from the Mud Dump contaminating New Jersey beaches via ocean currents that flow from north to south in this region.

During the 1990s, pressure from New Jersey residents and environmental activists to close the Mud Dump caused Environmental Protection Agency administrator Carole M. Browner, Secretary of Transportation Frederico F. Pena, and Secretary of the Army Togo D. West to suggest an end to dumping at the site.[6] Seeing the urgency of the environmental issue and the importance of thousands of jobs and billions of dollars in shipping to New Jersey and New York, the Clinton Administration worked with the governors of both states to change the situation. The Mud Dump Site eventually will be closed, but prior to closing, federal permits for dredging will be granted more readily so that channels will be clear for the nearest future and ports in the harbor can remain viable at least temporarily. And, the Mud Dump Site can, for a short time, still receive clean dredge sediment. This solution provides time for both states to investigate options for the disposal of contaminated mud dredged from the harbor. Additionally, New York has agreed to investigate ways to reduce the flow of contaminants into the harbor.[7]

Because the new law closes the Mud Dump Site to contaminated sediment and forbids ocean dumping, the Corps must now find other places to dispose of polluted dredge sediment. Millions of cubic yards of contaminated sediment will need to be either trucked away and placed in a landfill or other geochemically isolated location, or cleaned and reused, or left in place to clog the channels. Because of this problem, dredging operations have slowed. In their search for solutions, the Corps would do well to consult with geologists.

A CENTER FOR SHIPPING

In 1524, Giovanni da Verrazano—for whom we have named the bridge between Brooklyn and Staten Island—found verdant shores, calm water, and wooded hillsides in the harbor he referred to as the "Beautiful Lake."[8] In 1609, Henry Hudson sailed the Upper Bay and the river that bears his name. Trade with the indigenous people began shortly thereafter when the Dutch West

India Company was formed. In 1647, a pier was built in the East River, where the water was calm and docks were protected from harsh storms by the glacial deposit that constitutes Long Island. Not until 1775 was the first dock constructed on the Hudson River. After that, shipping began to concentrate on the west side of Manhattan Island, where the naturally deep river and steep banks of the shore were more favorable for docking. Ships docked in New York, dockworkers unloaded them, and goods were transported on land by rail.

However, foreshadowing future problems, in 1860, the ship *Great Eastern* could not dock until high tide, when its 30-foot draft would clear the bottom of the harbor.[9] In 1888, the Federal Rivers and Harbors Act gave the U.S. Army Corps of Engineers responsibility for maintaining all navigable waters in the United States. By 1889, the Corps began to dredge the harbor to create the Ambrose navigation channel.[10] To form the first of the harbor's channels, nearly 55 million cubic yards of sand and gravel were scraped from the bottom of the harbor and dumped out of sight.[11]

For at least 150 years, New York City was a major international port. By the 1960s, however, with the advent of containerized shipping and the rise in significance of truck transport, major shipping facilities in New York–New Jersey Harbor shifted to Port Newark, New Jersey.[12] The lack of quality infrastructure in New York and roadways clogged with cars and trucks made it impossible to handle the volume of goods that needed transport from the harbor to distant towns.

Still, in 1994, New York State exported $34 billion worth of goods globally from the harbor. New Jersey shipped over $13 billion worth of products from the same harbor in 1995. Clearly both New York and New Jersey are major exporting states. In 1995, 120 million tons of cargo came into the harbor and generated over $25 billion in sales for companies in both states. All this harbor commerce creates employment—in New Jersey, 14 percent of all manufacturing jobs depend on the export of products.[13]

On the East Coast, as elsewhere, stiff competition exists for such commerce. Many ports—including Halifax, Nova Scotia; Norfolk, Virginia; and Charleston, South Carolina—are competing actively to become what is known as a hub port, the primary recipient of all shipping lines. From that hub port, a complicated network of freight rail lines, air traffic, and trucking routes will convey products up and down the East Coast as well as across the country. Because shipping is such a boon to the economy, it behooves any port to make sure navigation channels in its harbor stay clear.

A replay of the *Great Eastern*'s docking experience occurred in July 1998 when the *Regina Maersk*—a ship belonging to the largest container shipping company in the world, the Maersk Line—called on Port Newark, New Jersey. Requiring water more than 47 feet deep even when not fully loaded, the *Regina Maersk* needed to wait for high tide to negotiate around Staten Island, through the narrow, shallow channels of the Arthur Kill and the Kill van Kull.[14] The difficulty that the *Regina Maersk* experienced in trying to reach Port Newark represents the future of shipping in New York–New Jersey Harbor, because new ships being built today require deeper waters. Events such as this have caused the Corps of Engineers and the Port Authority of New York and New Jersey, the bistate agency created in 1921 to oversee physical facilities,[15] to assert that channels must be deepened if the port is to compete as a hub.[16]

There is another concern, too. Unless New York–New Jersey Harbor ceases to be a port, inadequate channel maintenance could cause a major environmental catastrophe there. For example, more petroleum products, such as gasoline, jet fuel, and heating oil, are shipped in and out of the port each year than in the next four busiest U.S. oil ports combined. In fact, since 1989, more and more oil tankers have pumped part of their loads into barges just outside the harbor near the Verrazano Bridge because the ships cannot sail directly to the terminals, owing to the sediment-clogged channels.[17] A mishap in this pumping operation is an accident waiting to happen.

DISPOSAL ALTERNATIVES TO OPEN OCEAN DUMPING

Given that open ocean disposal is illegal today and that the health of the New York and New Jersey economies depends on the viability of its harbor ports, the Corps of Engineers must continue to dredge navigation channels and find a method and location for disposing of sediment dredged from the harbor. Because, as with any repository for waste materials, closing of the Mud Dump Site was inevitable, the search for alternatives to ocean dumping has been underway for some time.[18] Solutions considered include landfilling, harbor-bottom pit disposal, island construction, strip-mine filling, and habitat restoration. These alternatives raise numerous issues, among them environmental justice and the magnitude of human needs and desires. Interestingly, no one has suggested that we limit the size of ships that may be built or that may enter the harbor; and, of course, such a solution would only reduce, not eliminate, the volume of dredged sediment needing disposal.

Landfilling

The marshes are doomed. The city has begun to dump garbage on them. It has already filled in hundreds of acres with garbage. Eventually, it will fill in the whole area, and then the Department of Parks will undoubtedly build some proper parks out there, and put in some concrete highways and scatter some concrete benches about . . . sit on these benches and meditate and store up bile. —Joseph Mitchell, *The Bottom of the Harbor*[19]

As Joseph Mitchell indicated, New York City previously took unwanted sediment and used it to fill in wetlands, areas that today we attempt to preserve for their value as water purifiers and wildlife habitat. Such practices are a variation on the traditional mode of disposal for unwanted material—burial in a landfill.

This method could, in theory, be used for the dredged sediment. Once a suitable location is found, a pit would be dug and an impervious lining installed along its bottom and sides. Sediment would be placed in it and covered with an impervious cap. The land could then be used as a park or a building site.

On land and unable to harm sensitive marine organisms, the sediment nevertheless could threaten land-dwelling organisms, including ourselves.[20] Metals, solvents, or other harmful compounds that leak through a faulty lining could enter drinking water supplies. What's more, with land at a premium in the densely populated metropolitan New York–New Jersey area, landfill sites may be hard to find. In fact, with no more room in its landfills, New Jersey currently exports all its municipal solid waste—supposedly nonhazardous garbage—to states including Pennsylvania and Indiana. And because of the NIMBY—not-in-my-backyard—syndrome, no one wants to live near a landfill.

The Corps of Engineers has attempted to identify parcels of land that would be suitable for landfill sites for sediment dredged from the harbor. Using a Geographic Information System (GIS)—a fast and efficient computer application that generates maps of regions fitting specified parameters—the Corps searched for land within two miles of New York–New Jersey Harbor. The two-mile limit made political and economic sense, because no community wants waste that does not geographically belong to it, and two miles would minimize the cost of transporting sediment to the site. The Corps looked for barren land, shrub, forest, pasture, and cropland that was relatively flat and occupied at least 100 acres. It identified 16 potential landfill sites, only three of which turned out to be in New York.

Evaluating the 16 possible sites, the Corps considered the following factors: land use of adjacent property, proximity to transportation routes, property ownership, local zoning, existence of wetlands, soil type, location of nearby public and private water supplies, existence of neighboring habitat for threatened or endangered species, and aquifer locations. Of the 16 sites, two turned out to be existing landfills, one was a public park, and another was the location for planned low-income housing. Obviously, those four sites could not be used. Public antipathy—quite reasonable—to the use of the remaining sites as landfills, caused the Corps to scuttle its plans.[21] Having abandoned the landfill disposal option, the Corps searched for more alternatives.

Harbor-Bottom Pit Disposal

Previous sand-mining operations in the lower harbor have left pockmarks in the harbor bottom. Consequently, another option considered for the disposal of dredged sediment was burial in these harbor-bottom pits. As was true for landfill disposal, this option could provide room for only a finite amount of dredged sediment. But the method could potentially isolate dredged spoil from the biosphere and also could perhaps help to clean up regions in the harbor bottom known to be especially contaminated. If the approach worked, new disposal sites could be dug in the harbor.

For example, the Corps considered digging a series of three pits in Newark Bay to hold approximately five million cubic yards of dredged sediment. In theory, digging operations would first encounter contaminated mud and then reach into clean sand. Both dredged channel sediment and the layer of contaminated mud extracted during the digging would be deposited in the pit. Then, the entire volume of sediment would be covered by the clean sand removed in the digging process. Unfortunately, all this effort would provide a permanent home for only one year's worth of dredged sediment from the harbor. Furthermore, when the Corps and the Port Authority investigated this option more thoroughly, sedimentological and geochemical data showed that the upper sediment layer in Newark Bay was contaminated to a greater depth than they had previously recognized. Disposal of that material along with the dredged channel sediment would have required a much larger pit than first had been imagined.[22]

Still not abandoning the idea of harbor-bottom depressions as potential homes for contaminated dredge spoil, the Corps pushed the notion that pits from previous sand-mining operations would be suitable spots for the disposal of this material. They argued that without the construction time of digging the pit and the need to dispose of additional removed sediment, these sites could be used quickly and at low economic cost. One former sand mine has a capacity of almost 6.5 million cubic yards. However, strong opposition to the use of these sand-mine pits for dredged sediment burial exists because communities of fish reside in the pits, which have become miniature ecosystems.[23] It seemed that there must be some other solution.

Island Construction

The Corps offered another option that they hoped would be considered positively, given the scarcity of land in the New York–New Jersey metropolitan area: island construction. In their view, dredged spoils could be used to manufacture what is known as containment islands in the Lower Harbor. Walls would be built to confine the sediment, and clean sand would be placed over the top to isolate the contaminated dredge material. According to the Corps, islands made of dredged channel sediment are found worldwide—two new airports, Chep Lak Kok in Hong Kong and Kansai in Japan, were constructed on such islands. Of course, in New York and New Jersey, there is little need for a new airport. But the Corps suggested that an island in the harbor could provide a bird habitat, a recreational area, or a space for a prison, power plant, or casino—certainly a motley array of possibilities.[24]

Although such an option might be viable if dredged sediment could be cleaned and isolated from interaction with the Earth's surface sediments and components of the hydrosphere and biosphere, geology tells us that such isolation is unlikely. In fact, the Corps can look to its own errors in replenishing beach sands along the New Jersey coast with sand from the harbor-bottom pits as evidence that water will always move sediments. The Corps must learn that some solutions just cannot be engineered.

INVENTIVE SOLUTIONS

Pennsylvania Mine Reclamation

Looking slightly westward, a unique plan for dredged material disposal is being conceived in an unlikely location and manner. Some resourceful environmental professionals have originated a plan for using dredged sediment in a beneficial, albeit unorthodox, way. They call for using the mud and silt dredged from New York–New Jersey Harbor to seal abandoned coal mines that scar the Pennsylvania countryside.[25]

Pennsylvania, long mined for its rich coal seams, now has more than 14,000 abandoned mines and open pits. Miles-long former strip mines leach more than 100 million gallons of highly acidic water every day. Currently, water that percolates through or runs over iron pyrite—a mineral in coal-mine debris piles—becomes acidic and negatively impacts streams, rivers, and groundwater supplies.[26]

In the mud-into-the-mines disposal option, sediment from the navigation channels would be mixed with ash to harden the soupy sediment so that it could be transported by rail to Pennsylvania. Using a method similar to that employed by the Romans to make the Colosseum, workers would add lime and more ash at the mine sites to make cement from the mud. And like the ancient Colosseum, the cement plugs formed by pouring the mixture into the mines should remain stable for thousands of years. The cement's alkaline properties should buffer acidity from the mines. Furthermore, pollutants in the dredged spoil should remain locked in the cement mixture. The ash-mud cement might also meet environmental standards and could be used for construction fill and landfill cover were it needed for those purposes.

If this option were pursued, Pennsylvania could be the answer to New York's and New Jersey's needs. A seemingly endless stream of dredged sediment could be carted away from the harbor, and the mines could be reclaimed. Although cementing the mines with mud from the harbor could be an economic solution, the environmental cost is uncertain. The mines, and any other site that utilized the cement made from the dredged material, would require regular and careful monitoring over the long term.[27] Geologists with their knowledge of minerals, sediments, and the hydrosphere must be an integral part of any attempt to engineer such a solution.

Habitat Restoration and Urban Revitalization

I prefer to look at the river from the New Jersey side; it is hard to get close to it on the New York side, because of the wall of pier sheds. The best points of vantage are in the riverfront railroad yards in Jersey City, Hoboken, and Weehawken. I used to disregard the "DANGER" and "RAILROAD PROPERTY" and "NO TRESPASSING" signs and walk into these yards and wander around at will. I would go out to the end of one of the railroad piers and sit on the stringpiece and stare at the river for hours, and nobody ever bothered me. —Joseph Mitchell, *The Bottom of the Harbor*[28]

The railroad piers that Mitchell so enjoyed were built by the beginning of the twentieth century on land created from assorted sediment and debris. At that time, tidal marshes along New Jersey's shores were filled in so that, in places like Hoboken and Jersey City where the Hudson is approximately 80 feet deep, people could have access to the river. Boat slips were constructed adjacent to the rail yards so that ships could dock and exchange goods intended for rail transport. One such slip, the Long Slip Canal, was created in Hoboken in 1870 but has not been used for more than 40 years. Its industrial legacy is evident in the metal- and oil-contaminated sediment at the bottom of the slip itself. A place of interest and activity only in the past, it now hosts drainage from sewers. Low oxygen content and lack of circulating fresh water make the waters of the slip inhospitable to marine life. Always a blight on the shore, the slip shares its pollution with the Hudson River when flushing occurs during a major storm or heavy rain. The situation could hardly be worse.

Creative thinkers have suggested that the slip would make a good repository for dredged channel sediment. Indeed, dredged sediment capped with clean cover material could improve this degraded area, because severely contaminated sediment at the bottom of the slip would be buried and diluted by greater volumes of material. Although Long Slip Canal could accommodate only 150,000 cubic yards of dredged sediment—hardly enough to put a dent in the yearly sediment supply from the harbor—other benefits would accrue. Because new housing and hotel space are planned to be built within 500 feet of the slip as part of New Jersey's waterfront revitalization effort, a filled Long Slip Canal would provide more land space as well as an incentive to upgrade sewer outflow lines, to install a walkway, and to improve water circulation and encourage a healthy aquatic habitat.[29] The result, made possible by use of dredged channel sediment, could be revitalized green space with a panoramic view of the Manhattan skyline in an otherwise congested urban city.

In recent years, other harbor-front property has been reclaimed successfully for public and private use. At Battery Park City at the southern tip of Manhattan and Gantry Plaza State Park in Long Island City, Queens, crumbling piers have been renovated for fishing and expired gantry cranes are part of the landscape architecture; these formerly deteriorated sites have been turned into public open space.[30] In other places, such as Port Liberte in Jersey City, developers have purchased waterfront property and built upscale living spaces.[31]

Across the New York–New Jersey metropolitan area, sites similar to Long Slip Canal border the harbor and the rivers that flow into it. A century of industrial and manufacturing activity along the harbor has left many areas contaminated, with no foreseeable positive use. Crumbling and decayed piers are scattered about. But dilapidated pilings are now home to thriving fish and shellfish communities, and some people want to get down to the water's edge. Dredged sediment capped with clean cover material could enliven what has long been abandoned.

ACKNOWLEDGING GEOLOGICAL REALITY

Not long ago the Army Corps of Engineers made a suggestion that any geologist would find mind-boggling. In a 1996 report, Corps engineers suggested that if they could stop sediment from accumulating in harbor navigation channels, they would nearly eliminate the need to dredge them. To that end, the report recommended the following actions: build walls along the sides of some channels; dig basins into which sediment can settle; use mechanical devices to keep sediment from settling to the channel bottom; and realign channels.[32] To an engineer with no knowledge of how the Earth works, these ideas may seem reasonable. However, the only way that sediment will not accumulate in navigation channels is if rivers cease to flow, wind doesn't blow, and the Atlantic Ocean stops circulating. In other words, sediment flow is a natural and inevitable consequence of the dynamic nature of the Earth.

To some minds, continued dredging of existing navigation channels in New York–New Jersey Harbor is inevitable, but geological reality suggests other options. To accommodate ships with larger hulls, deeper waters already existing within the harbor should be considered for use as ports. In Brooklyn's section of the harbor, deep channels lead to currently abandoned piers. Near the Verrazano Bridge off Staten Island, the harbor is 60 feet deep. At the Army's Military Ocean Terminal in Bayonne, New Jersey, large existing cargo areas and docks in deep water are slated to close—they call out for another use.[33] Alternatively, it might be economically and environmentally feasible to take advantage of the great depth of the Hudson River by building a port further upstream at a riverfront town like Newburgh, New York. These geologically savvy port options would take advantage of naturally deep parts of the harbor, require less dredging, and cause fewer negative environmental impacts.

Currently, the vitality of New York–New Jersey Harbor and its ports depends on dredging of navigation channels to accommodate the deep-hulled vessels that represent the future of shipping. With over three million cubic yards of sediment—much of it contaminated with hazardous chemicals— choking the channels yearly and ocean dumping now illegal, sediment disposal options or alternative ports must be found. As every geologist knows, sedimentation into the harbor will not cease; as long as rivers flow, channels will continue to be filled with sand, silt, and mud. As long as point sources of pollution leak into the rivers, the sediment will continue to be contaminated. The shear volume of material makes effective disposal of dredged sediment a seemingly insurmountable task. The relative lack of enthusiasm from residents in either state for hosting contaminated sediments makes the future of the port look bleak. Remediation of the dredged mud in tandem with its use in mine filling or habitat restoration might supply a solution. Geology suggests, however, that the best port in this "storm" should be located in deeper water.

19

An Earth Scientist in City Hall: Geology and Community Planning

Paul K. Doss

t started with a phone call. The city planner asked me to lend my expertise as a geologist to review some recently submitted development plans. Wal-Mart—the national department store chain—was coming to the soon-to-be strip mall on the outskirts of another community in New England. The development was a divisive issue for the community, for on one side were the positive impacts of jobs and economic benefits, and on the other were concerns about the potential harm to the Main Street character of this modest, almost rural, city.

That first phone call from the city planner's office was followed over the years by several others related to wetlands, streams, groundwater quality, and hazards of mass movements such as landslides. The brief and related stories in this essay represent the questions and answers that arise out of typical development and land use issues discussed in city halls. They show how poor planning—not uncommon in towns and cities across the United States—results from inadequate understanding of geological processes. Also, although these descriptions appear to have a beginning and an end, in most cases development questions and decisions linger within city council chambers unless aided by knowledge of our earth system.

PRELUDE: WAL-MART PLANNING

When Wal-Mart applied to the local city planning board to build a retail establishment in town, plans called for the destruction of some wetlands during construction. However, the plans also included efforts to "minimize" the impact of wetland destruction and an attempt to "mitigate" the remaining wetlands. In other words, bulldozers would destroy some acres of wetland in order to construct the buildings and parking lots. But new wetland acreage would be created in order to offset the destruction of the natural wetland on which the Wal-Mart would be built. The mitigated area was slightly greater than the area to be destroyed, so on paper, the city would get a good deal. Clearly, natural resource issues associated with development would dominate consideration of the proposal.

The city fathers and mothers had planned a "walkover." Anyone concerned with the potential construction was invited to visit the proposed development site to examine the existing resource and the plans for change. Most of those invited did attend. The city planner, the chair and members of the city planning board, city council members, attorneys for the developer, members of the city's conservation committee, consultants, and reporters and photographers from the local press all came. It made the front page newspaper in full color the next day.

We held blueprints in our hands as we walked across through the property to be developed. The blueprints showed us the proposed buildings, outlined existing wetlands and drainage patterns, and detailed what the landscape would look like and how it would function hydrologically after the construction was completed. Much of the discussion during the walkover addressed what was there now and what would not be there after construction.

The wetland we walked through that day typified wetland habitat in an urban or suburban area and could be characterized as a medium quality wetland. In terms of flora and fauna, this particular wetland had only moderate species diversity. But this wetland was one of only a few that remained within the community—and it was not rare to see or hear the report of a moose browsing in its shallow water. The wetland also formed part of the headwaters for a stream that flowed through an arboretum, a National Natural Landmark, just a couple of miles downstream. The trees of the arboretum provided the townsfolk ample opportunities for birdwatching, hiking, and solitude. So the wetland area to be destroyed for urban development had direct influence on a natural area downstream, an area that hardly any resident would stand by and allow to be impacted negatively. But those "wetland functions" occur offsite, they are hard to measure, and difficult even to detect, let alone quantify.

WETLANDS, GEOLOGY, AND LAND USE PLANNING

Wetlands are complex ecosystems that share characteristics of upland and aquatic habitats. Their ability to perform ecosystem functions results from the unique configuration of biotic and abiotic components. Vegetation, bacteria, macroinvertebrates, mammals, and birds have a mutually beneficial relationship with the nonliving soil material, groundwater, surface water, and chemical nutrients in wetlands. Wetland vegetation mechanically traps sediment along coasts and rivers; reduces the velocity of floodwaters along stream channels; biologically transmits oxygen to an otherwise anoxic soil; and provides food for waterfowl and other animals. Bacteria form one part of the base of a food chain and behave as water treatment facilities—they remove excess iron and other chemicals from wetland waters. Birds and mammals disperse seeds and continually fertilize and cultivate the substrate. Water in wetlands moves matter and energy throughout the landscape. These and other functions are possible only because of the unique combination of landscape elements in wetlands.

Around the world, wetlands have been underappreciated, and in many places, people have drained and filled them for agriculture and other development. Only recently have societies started to appreciate wetlands as buffers against coastal erosion, important habitats for migrating birds, and effective filters for ground and surface water pollutants. Wholesale destruction of wetlands in the United States has subsided somewhat, and in many places we are attempting to create and restore wetlands.[1] But the truth is that geoscientists, engineers, and the public simply don't understand fully how natural wetlands work. What's more, a great diversity of wetlands exist, and we don't know how they differ in their functions. Consequently, creation or restoration projects often fail as was shown in one study of 40 wetland projects in Florida—only four were deemed successful.[2] Who is going to spend substantial amounts of money to understand fully how a natural wetland operates when it is destined to be destroyed to make room for human development? One typically needs a prototype before making a workable machine. Prototypes show the ways in which an object or a system functions. Natural wetlands are our prototypes—potentially they make it possible for us to reproduce and replace the functions of a specific wetland in a particular location.

For any wetland, particularly one destined for "conversion" or destruction, we must ask: What is the geological setting? What soil types are present? What is the nature of groundwater and surface water movement? What are the chemical characteristics of the wetland? What animal and plant species depend on it? How does the wetland behave differently over the courses of a wet year and a dry year? Most of the questions in this partial list of factors that control any particular wetland ecosystem are left uninvestigated during wetland "replacement." Such unsophisticated wetland replacement is common in community development and construction.

If done well, the buildings and facilities constructed on top of former wetlands would exist in harmony with the newly constructed mitigation wetland. But new construction requires detention ponds—gravel-banked rectangular ponds adjacent to most new building projects. Detention ponds trap newly created urban runoff, water that flows off of the buildings and parking lots. Engineers design these structures to collect and temporarily store urban runoff, with all its road salt, sand, oils, gasoline drippings, and litter. Unfortunately, detention ponds are engineered structures, with blueprints drawn up in an office to describe specific area, depth, inflow points, outflow points, and location. They do not always acknowledge geological reality.

Land for development is costly, and it must be used efficiently. Differences in the perspectives, for example, of a conservation committee member and a developer, often arise out of different definitions of efficiency. Not much money derives from detention ponds and created wetlands. In fact, they are financial liabilities. Because of such liability, developers minimize the acreage dedicated to ponds and created wetlands in construction plans. Most detention areas are built with steep banks because that reduces the total area required for the pond. But how many natural ponds have steep, gravel-lined banks? During the walkover of our local wetland, and in negotiations among the city planner, consultants, and developer in the weeks that followed the walkover, concerned citizens offered suggestions that might improve the development plans; this guidance acknowledged the geological reality of wetlands as best we know it.

Most of the recommended revisions addressed the nature of the designed slope on the pond banks, the plantings for the newly created wetland, and plans for monitoring the success or failure of the wetland mitigation efforts in terms of water quality, water movement, and biodiversity. We discussed the tangible suggestions—reduced slope and more substantial plantings—and to a degree these ideas were incorporated into the final construction plans. However, the more difficult issues—means to evaluate the success or failure of the created wetland and the need for ongoing monitoring of complex factors— were not considered.

Wal-Mart was built, and it clearly has been an economic success. The detention pond was constructed and the mitigation wetland built. There was, however, no comprehensive monitoring of level of success for the newly created wetland. Now—six years after construction—one sees from the access road to the Wal-Mart only a single-species "sea" of cattails, the common disturbance-tolerant wetland plant, and purple loosestrife, the invasive "scourge" of wetlands in the Midwest and the Northeast. Few, if any, people have reported the presence of moose in the wetland.

A PIZZA AFTER SHOPPING?

Along that access road to the Wal-Mart, one now passes another new development site, a Pizza Hut. That establishment was constructed on a foundation of built-up gravel and fill material, within the wetland that was created and restored during the Wal-Mart construction years earlier. If such care was taken earlier to construct a new wetland to replace the one on which the Wal-Mart was built, how could this have happened? Because most municipal planning has an air of crisis management to it, only single questions are answered at a time, and only single problems are allegedly solved. Yet human expansion and development behaves as part of a continuum. When the Wal-Mart was planned and constructed, nothing in the planning process demanded foresight and consideration of what future development might occur in the vicinity. On the same hand, when the new Pizza Hut was planned and constructed, there was no hindsight regarding the prior history of the development site. It did not matter that the exact site for construction of the Pizza Hut had, just a few years earlier, been part of the area designed to mitigate the impacts of the Wal-Mart construction. These issues do not reflect poorly on business owners or developers, they simply identify weaknesses in the current state of community development and land use planning.

A CITY BUILDING PERMIT

A different chapter in this community's development and planning efforts, conceived and written just a few years after the Wal-Mart project, included construction plans that might impact one of the local rivers and its floodplain. The city's sewerage district had submitted a building permit application to construct a storage building on top of fill material, adjacent to one of the two major rivers that flowed through town. The fill material had been disposed of at the site for some undetermined number of years and consisted of waste soil, construction debris, scrap metal, and wood. However, some of the dumping had not been sanctioned, and some unknown, potentially hazardous material had been dumped without authorization. We had a walkover here and observed the waste that had been left behind illegally. We noted that the fill area draped over the river valley and onto a portion of the stream's floodplain. Several metal drums of uncertain origin could be seen sticking out from the fill; the drums were the kind typically used to transport and store solvents, cleansers, or oils. The evidence that the stream was in physical contact with the disposed fill during periods of annual flooding was clear—we could see water-swept vegetation and lodged, floating debris adjacent to it.

The sewerage district readily acknowledged that it was uncertain about the specific nature of the fill material, when it had been dumped, and whether any hazardous materials had been or were leaching from the site. Irony pervades this situation: The sewerage district—a local governmental entity—submitted the permit application, only to find that illegal dumping had occurred at the intended building site. Neither the community, nor the sewerage district, had the funds or time to treat this issue. Nobody will likely ever know what was abandoned there, or if any contamination of floodplain wetlands or the adjacent stream has occurred. The question before the planning board was whether it should approve or deny the application for a building permit. Absent geological interpretation of the site, the board was unable to consider thoroughly the physical ramifications of the proposed construction. The health of the community and its aquatic resources would likely have been improved if the unknown fill had been investigated and, if necessary, remediated.

THE ISSUE OF ZONING

The potential role of an earth scientist in local community planning is large. In some form or another, all questions of development and comprehensive land use planning can and should involve the integration of geological insight. For example, community zoning questions present another problem. Zoning implicitly pits individuals, with their own "guaranteed" freedoms or private property rights, against the needs of the many who constitute a community, whether large or small. Zoning designations are assigned, not only to dictate the types of development that can exist in a given location, but also to control attributes of that development. Communities that have adopted zoning ordinances have designated agricultural, rural residential, low- and high-density residential, light and heavy commercial, and industrial zones. The zoning rules control driveway size, setback limits, utility connections, traffic predictions, and perhaps most important, the nature of land use on specific parcels of earth. Those who make zoning decisions often do not appreciate fully the impacts of land use decisions, many of which are geological. Earth scientists can educate communities and policymakers about the potential long-term effects of particular land use practices and provide advice on zoning.

In the same New England community that I have described, an issue that involved both zoning and unauthorized filling stirred activity in city hall. On the north end of town was another wetland that flanked a small tributary of a large river that runs through town. A high-quality and diverse wetland within the city limits, it was home to Atlantic white cedar, rushes, sedges, waterfowl, wading birds, deer, and moose. Also, the groundwater discharging from this wetland was an important source of the surface water that flowed into the tributary stream. A few years earlier, college students had identified this stream as a spawning area for brook trout and other important fish species. The spawning of brook trout is not a trivial issue here; sport fishing represents a substantial component of the economy in the region. Lots across the street from the wetland were zoned for residential use, but efforts had been underway to rezone much of the area to a category that permitted mixed residential, commercial, and light industrial use. This wetland came to the attention of the planning board because some blatant and illegal filling had occurred at its southern margin, and the part that was filled had shown up as the access-road site of choice on blueprints for a proposed industrial park. Although strongly supported by individuals promoting economic growth—developers maintained that the industrial park would occupy a "corridor" of development that already included an animal shelter, auto repair shop, and self-storage units—numerous local residents vocally opposed the proposed development.

Once again, questions that pertain to development of this site and its impact on a specific type of ecosystem progressed without consideration of earlier construction sites in town. Although only a few more acres of wetland would be impacted at this site, the cumulative effect of Wal-Mart, Pizza Hut, the sewerage district building, and the industrial sites becomes apparent. Wetland scientists have grappled with the problem of cumulative impacts for many years.[3] The accumulated effect of single actions such as individual wetland conversion, disturbance, or destruction is substantial. For example, since the mid-1800s, 98 percent of bottomland hardwood wetland habitat has been lost in southern Illinois.[4] The goals of the Clean Water Act—the federal measure intended to restore and maintain the integrity of the nation's waters—are not being met in some areas, owing in part to the effects of cumulative impacts from permitted disturbance of wetland ecosystems.[5] How would a small community with limited resources, and perhaps limited experience and expertise, grapple with the difficult issue of cumulative impacts on natural resources?

COMPREHENSIVE PLANNING

Many states and communities now enact comprehensive planning strategies and prepare long-range planning documents. In fact, some states have mandated community comprehensive plans. These plans encourage communities to exercise foresight—to think about how development might affect a municipality on a longer time scale. A simple review, however, shows that the primary focus of many plans is economics; plans try to assure economic growth, sustain jobs, and enhance transportation. Comprehensive plans help to identify appropriate areas for growth, including residential, commercial, and industrial development. They also address zoning questions. When business leaders gather to draft a municipal plan, who is present to ask questions that reflect the reality of the earth system? In communities with limited funds, the answer is, "No one." But such questions must be posed and answered. How might communities identify the areas where residential groundwater supplies need to be protected? What might be the cumulative impacts of expansion on natural resources such as wetlands? Where might development be a liability for the community as a result of unforeseen, yet geologically identifiable hazards?

For this New England community, issues that pertained to the public water supply were raised while officials were preparing the city's comprehensive planning document. The two primary concerns were maintenance of high water quality and the ability of the city to provide the water to residents and businesses. The majority of the city receives its water from the publicly designated supplies in a lake approximately 15 miles outside of the city limits. Although the city managers could not improve directly the quality of this body of water, they could support state efforts to do so. Therefore, the community's planning document articulated goals, policies, and strategies to assure the viability of its public water supply.

With most of the city residents connected to a network of municipal water supply lines, the water supply infrastructure was typical of a moderate-sized community. However, pumps that distribute the public water to residents are limited in their capacity. They can only supply areas in the city below a given altitude—270 feet above sea level. Areas at greater elevation cannot be connected to the public water supply. Because of this constraint, discussion of earlier plans to encourage commercial and light industrial development needed to be reconsidered because part of the area chosen by the city for development was higher than 270 feet. The fact that topography limits the public water supply was important in all aspects of planning, because it explicitly delineated the areas where new residences and businesses would be required to drill their own groundwater supply wells. This subject brings us to another near paradox of community planning in need of sound geological input.

Although the planning commission had discussed the need to assure a high-quality public water supply, no one spoke to the need of assuring water quality protection for residents who depended on groundwater. Hundreds of city residents did not benefit from a public water supply and relied on their own, individual domestic groundwater wells. These residents deserved to be afforded the same level of concern and protection for their drinking water. Just as water in the city supply comes from a specific source (the lake outside of town), so too the groundwater in a single family's well comes from some source. That source is the area where infiltrating rainfall and snowmelt saturates the ground to recharge underground water supplies. The flow of that infiltrating water must be unimpeded by barriers such as asphalt and other pavement, and its composition should be protected from contaminants. As it turned out, yet another new area slated for light industrial development was located directly on top of a recharge area for private groundwater supplies. The proposed industrial development site would work against good groundwater quantity and quality.

Wellhead protection involves the design of plans to protect water sources from potential contamination. Such protection limits the types of activities and development in recharge areas of a primary groundwater supply. Recognition of groundwater recharge areas requires knowledge of the geological setting, the interaction of rainfall and snowmelt with topography, and fundamental information on the direction of groundwater movement. Most wellhead protection plans are drawn for large-capacity groundwater wells that provide public water supplies. Such plans did not exist in this community. Here hundreds of city residents, using their own small wells, draw water from beneath land on which paint shops, machine shops, truck garages, and light manufacturing operations were to be built. These types of businesses use and can accidentally spill materials that contaminate water consumed by private citizens for household purposes, including bathing and drinking. The concern for maintaining high water quality does not reflect negatively on any one particular type of business; in fact, members of the comprehensive planning commission wanted to attract light industrial development for the community. However, evidence from a geological investigation volunteered by local college geology students caused the commission to develop and endorse strategies to protect residential groundwater supplies as it protects the public water supply. These policies and strategies included modification of proposed zoning changes in the areas of groundwater recharge. By simply applying a little geological insight, sounder land use plans and zoning modifications were developed.

Hidden in the sea of cattails that remains by the new strip-mall centered around Wal-Mart are a few water-level monitoring sites. They were installed as part of the originally designed plan to examine the health and function of this mitigation wetland. No laws, regulations, or paid employees enforced a monitoring plan or developed a strategy to deal with shortcomings associated with this created wetland. No data documented how the wetland operated after construction. In fact, no data had even been collected for interpretation and evaluation. A cynic might believe that the wetland was created only to meet the criteria for development. And, we still don't hear of any moose returning to this site to browse.

Wetlands have become icons of sorts—they epitomize the conflict between private property rights and environmental quality. That's why wetlands are now often at the center of many development and planning debates. Discussions engage local zoning boards with single farm families in the Midwest who want to drain "prairie potholes"—depressions in fields—that were formed by glaciers and are now wetlands. Federal cases involve the U.S. Environmental Protection Agency, the Army Corps of Engineers, and the Department of Justice.

An important report, released in 1984 by the U.S. Fish and Wildlife Service, describes the status of wetland resources in the United States—over 50 percent of our nation's wetlands have been destroyed since European settlement.[6] In some places, such as Iowa and the Central Valley of California, over 90 percent of original wetland areas have been lost.[7] Between the mid-1950s and mid-1970s, approximately 87 percent of wetland losses was due to draining, ditching, and filling for agricultural purposes.[8] As we enter the millennium, much of that agricultural conversion has been completed, and now the less extensive, yet more visible and contentious urban conversion is commonplace. In an update of the 1984 report, Fish and Wildlife research scientists noted that conversion of wetlands to farmlands has slowed—it has declined to 54 percent of wetland areas destroyed between the 1970s and 1980s.[9] In fact, many previously converted agricultural wetland areas are being restored and returned to natural wetland habitat and ecosystems; this restoration is rooted in our newly found knowledge of the consequences of their demise. Interestingly, much of the agricultural wetland restoration is championed and supported by Ducks Unlimited and the U.S. Fish and Wildlife Service—two organizations interested in viable populations of game birds—together with the U.S. Department of Agriculture, the agency that actively subsidized the initial draining and ditching of agricultural wetlands. It is unfortunate, however, that conversion of urban wetlands, although contentious, is still commonplace.

To be sure, we should put wetlands in their proper context. As a transitional ecosystem—an ecotone—between deepwater habitats and uplands, wetlands are ephemeral features on the landscape. Most of the wetlands that we see in the United States were formed within the last 10,000 years, and they evolve naturally toward self-destruction. That is, wetlands fill in over time. Thus, filling or draining a wetland does not have any lasting impacts on the geological evolution of the landscape.

Generally, however, people don't really care about the long-term geological evolution of the landscape. We want to know what will happen now, tomorrow, next week, or ten years from now. And in that context and on that time frame, we care about healthy water quality, reduction of flood damage, vibrant populations of migratory waterfowl, and, at least to some, plenty of good fish to eat. Wetlands provide these things. And wetlands provide them on the same time frame in which human beings exist.

The same is true for other geological phenomena. Volcanism, that constructive geological process born out of plate tectonics, helps build our continents in the geological time frame, and can destroy societies on a human time frame. The Earth releases its energy as it rearranges the crust, and the resultant earthquakes can wreak havoc on our communities. Recurrent flooding over the long-term shapes our landscape and in many places gives us fertile land, but it also results in catastrophic destruction. Landslides, rockfalls, and other mass movements are manifestations of the Earth's surface striving for equilibrium, trying to get flat. But this viewpoint is unsatisfactory in places such as Malibu, where homeowners have watched their houses destroyed in one of those front-page California mudslides. Coastlines, perhaps the most dynamic geological environment of all, are constantly changing or on the verge of change. Yet when a coast changes itself, which is its "job" after all, it will ultimately take beachfront homes with it. Geology represents the knowledge that allows us to understand how the landscape works and evolves. It allows us to predict how it is going to change during our lifetimes and beyond.

Balancing geological processes with the human time frame is one prerequisite of successful land use and development. The geologist who steps into city hall or planning commission meetings may be able to communicate that balance to decision makers, developers, and the public. Those who are listening must be willing to respect the sometimes hard truth that the Earth may have already made some of its own land use decisions.[10]

Part V

INVENTIVE SOLUTIONS

What examples exist of inventive solutions to tenacious problems associated with human activities on Earth? Do they reflect a truly different attitude to a misperceived human hegemony? These essays show how acknowledgment of inexorable natural processes and technological innovation can provide geoscientists with the methods for remediation of human-induced problems and for remarkable solutions.

At the outset of this part of the book, Jim Evans and colleagues describe how the catastrophic failure of an Ohio dam disclosed historical land use and provided an opportunity to restore wetland habitat. Working a few states west and north, Cathy Manduca deems a unique county-wide geological atlas the essential guide for Minnesotans through the maze of sinkholes, caves, and glacial sediments that affects the area's groundwater quality. Allison Macfarlane queries the suitability of Nevada's Yucca Mountain as a geological repository for high-level radioactive waste and instead justifies safe, temporary storage at the reactor sites that originally generated the nuclear fuel. And at a U.S. Army depot in Utah, Rosa Gwinn nurtures bacterial microbes that metabolize unwanted explosives in soils.

20

From Reservoir to Wetland: The Rise and Fall of an Ohio Dam

James E. Evans, Scudder D. Mackey, Johan F. Gottgens, and Wilfrid M. Gill

T his is a story about the life history of a particular dam and reservoir, the IVEX Corporation Dam, which is located on the Chagrin River in northeastern Ohio. We will trace this history from 1842, when the dam and reservoir were built, to 1994, when the dam failed catastrophically, causing a major flood downstream. Along the way, we want to tell you how the sediment—sand and mud—in the reservoir "speaks" to geologists, telling us important information about changes in the environment over the past 150 years. Finally, we will discuss the decisions made after the dam failed and describe an innovative experiment to remediate a dam and reservoir.

There are over 75,000 dams in the United States, so why select this particular one to study?[1] As we will show you, the IVEX Dam is a wonderful example of the paradox of dams: how an asset became an expensive liability, how priorities and perceptions changed over time, and eventually how creativity and cooperation led to "new solutions"—a constructed environment that strongly resembles the natural environment which existed before the dam was built.

Historically, dams, reservoirs, canals, levees, and other hydraulic structures were the earliest large-scale engineering projects at the dawn of the Industrial Age. The timing of the European settlement of North America was such that these features were often the first public works projects in the United States, and they helped determine the locations of towns, industries, and trade routes. For example, many East Coast cities were built on the "fall line," a line of waterfalls along the flank of the Appalachian Mountains, convenient for hydropower.[2] During the late 1700s and early 1800s, canals were built for transportation, and levees, dikes, dams, and reservoirs were constructed for hydropower, water storage, and flood control. In Ohio, all these activities played a role in the transition from earliest non-Native American settlement in the late 1700s to established commerce and industry by the middle 1800s.

The construction of any dam or reservoir sets into effect significant changes in a river and its watershed. Probably the most important one is how and where the river transports sediment.[3] Geologists have long known that dams and reservoirs create a temporary base level for a fluvial system;[4] in other words, the natural slope of the river from its headwaters to its mouth comes to resemble a series of "stair steps," where the riser of each step is a dam and the tread upstream of each riser is the surface of a reservoir. The changed slope of the river affects the speed and energy of the flowing water, which in turn impacts sediment transport in the watershed. Upstream of the dam, as the water slows down as it enters the reservoir, sediment is deposited in the form of a delta that builds downstream and as fine-grained sediment that settles out in calm water near the dam itself.[5] The filling of the reservoir by sediment is referred to as *capacity loss.* Downstream of the dam, the river flows rapidly and with little sediment in it. As a consequence, sediment is eroded from the bed and banks of the river until it reacquires a normal sediment load.[6] In summary, if you build a dam, you can count on two problems: there will be sediment deposition upstream of the dam (in the reservoir) and erosion downstream from it. In addition to the *physical* problems, biogeochemical ones also occur.[7]

Ways to solve these problems exist, but many solutions are expensive. One solution to capacity loss is to "over-design" the size of the reservoir—that way, it will take many more years for the reservoir to fill, and it will effectively add years to the life of the structure (this is the solution used with many of the largest hydroelectric structures built in the western United States). A second solution is to design the dam so that it does not trap sediment behind (upstream of) it. To accomplish this, one can either use the size, shape, and depth of the reservoir to change water circulation in it or sluice bottom water through the dam.[8] A third solution is to dredge sediment from the reservoir and dispose of it elsewhere—an expensive proposition especially if the sediments in the reservoir have become contaminated.[9]

Old structures, such as the IVEX Dam, are from an era that preceded some of the hydraulic engineering solutions mentioned above. Thus, over its 152-year history, the reservoir continued to fill basically unchecked. When the dam failed in 1994, there had been 86 percent capacity loss—somewhat less than 1 percent per year. This rate of capacity loss is typical for reservoirs from a variety of climatic regions[10] and from other reservoirs in Ohio.[11] Thousands of dams in similar situations, are accidents waiting to happen. Where reservoirs fill up with sediments water has no where to go but up and over the top of a dam.

ANATOMY OF A DAM FAILURE

The Chagrin River

The Chagrin River is located in northeastern Ohio. It's relatively small watershed drains into Lake Erie. The IVEX Dam is located at about the middle of the drainage basin, and two major tributaries (the Aurora Branch and the East

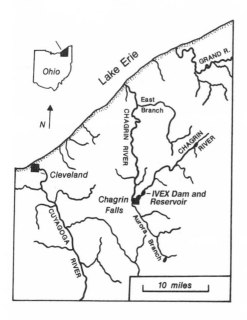

Location of the IVEX Dam and
Reservoir in northeastern Ohio.

Branch) join the river downstream of the dam. The Chagrin River is somewhat
"flashy" and has recorded significant flow events, such as the March 22, 1948,
flood, when discharge was approximately 40 times greater than mean annual
discharge and the river crested at about seven feet above its banks.[12]

The Chagrin River is entrenched into a narrow bedrock valley within which
the floodplain—basically the width of the valley floor—rapidly narrows
upstream. The river has a relatively steep gradient, with numerous rapids and
small waterfalls. Below the IVEX Dam, sand, gravel, or bedrock dominate the
bed and banks of the stream. The steep gradients, narrow floodplains, and
coarse-grained bed and bank materials imply that fine-grained sediments are
efficiently transported through the Chagrin River system, unless they are
trapped behind a dam.

Historical Land Use

The first non-Native American individuals to settle the village of Chagrin Falls
arrived in 1833, a time when the adjacent Cleveland metropolitan area had less
than 1,000 individuals.[13] Settled initially because of its potential for development of hydropower, small wooden dams were constructed immediately to
power saw, grain, and paper mills.[14] In 1842, these initial structures were
replaced by two longer-lived dams, creating the Lower Mill Pond and Upper
Mill Pond (IVEX Reservoir). Hydropower from the IVEX Dam initially powered
a factory that made ax handles from local supplies of wood in the original
dense forests of the region.[15] However, the oldest lithographic print of the
region shows that, by 1846, little of the original forest remained. Destruction of

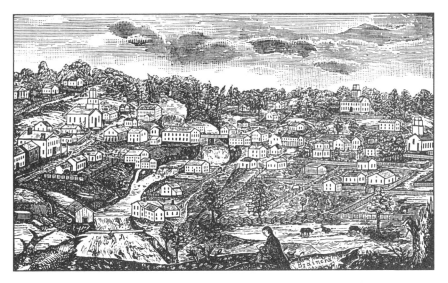

The earliest available lithographic print of the Chagrin Falls area, depicted in 1846, documents deforestation of the watershed. (*From Howe's Historical Collections of Ohio, Volume 1*)

the local forests forced the economy to shift to dairy farming and to woolen mills by 1868. The region's economy stagnated in the late 1800s and early 1900s; farms were abandoned and the land converted to second-growth forests. In fact, throughout Ohio the total acreage of farmland declined by 10 percent during this time.[16] Suburban development related to growth of the Cleveland metropolitan area in the 1950s to 1960s and more recently (late 1980s to early 1990s) has affected the Chagrin Falls region.[17] As a result of this development, the reservoirs have been used exclusively for water supplies, rather than hydropower.

History of the IVEX Dam

The IVEX Dam has regularly produced problems. It partly or completely failed on five separate occasions in its 152-year history. Built as a wooden spar structure in 1842, unattached to the underlying bedrock, it slid and suffered toppling failure within its first year of existence.[18] Rebuilt the same year, the structure evolved into a masonry spillway attached to bedrock on one side of the valley; it was connected to the other side of the valley by an earthen dike. The dam failed again in 1877, emptying the reservoir. Because the owner could not afford to fix it, the reservoir became pasture land until 1890, when repairs were made, and the reservoir refilled. The dam partially failed again in 1913 and 1985, in both cases because high groundwater flow combined with erosion caused higher pressure between the masonry spillway and earthen dike, which was patched with hydraulic cement.[19]

The region surrounding the "pristine" IVEX Dam, circa 1870, shows deforestation of the watershed and partial development of second-growth vegetation. (*Courtesy of Yolita Rausch, Chagrin Falls Historical Society*)

During this time, the ownership of the dam and reservoir changed hands repeatedly, and the use of the structure also changed. Hydropower use of the dam ended in 1926, when the owner—a paper mill—shifted to electricity. The reservoir was then used as a water source for the paper mill. It is possible that upkeep and maintenance of the dam declined somewhat after this.

The safety of a private dam is primarily the owner's responsibility. Although government has been relatively slow to recognize the public safety aspects related to thousands of small, privately owned dams, both federal and state governments now require safety inspections. The Ohio Department of Natural Resources Division of Water, with technical assistance from the U.S. Army Corps of Engineers—the federal agency of jurisdiction—carried out safety inspections of the IVEX Dam. The most recent safety inspection report, in 1987, noted that the IVEX Dam was a "Class 1 Dam"—a large dam capable of causing loss of life or serious damage in the event of failure. It lacked an emergency spillway, was not capable of handling a major flood, and showed signs of enhanced erosion. IVEX Corporation submitted a plan to fix these problems, which was approved by both the Ohio Department of Natural Resources Division of Water and the U.S. Army Corps of Engineers in 1991. However, the IVEX Corporation balked at the cost, considered selling the property, and delayed the repairs—none were in effect when the dam failed.[20]

On August 14, 1994, following an unusually heavy rainfall (5.5 inches in 24 hours), the IVEX Dam failed catastrophically. Prior to failure, flows rose to five feet above the spillway and overtopped the dam itself.[21] It is not clear whether the cause of failure was erosion over the top of the earthen dike, or whether subsurface erosion occurred as a result of the elevated water pressure behind the dam. Regardless, the center of the dam blew out, right where the spillway contacted the earthen dike. Instantly, the reservoir released about ten million gallons of impounded water and sediment, thereby causing extensive flood damage downstream.

If you visited the reservoir just after the flood, as we did, you could have looked upstream through the breach of the dam and seen: (1) the thickness of sediment that had accumulated in the reservoir; (2) erosional grooves cut by the swirling floodwaters within the reservoir as they escaped; (3) large mud-cracks that formed as the reservoir muds dried out; and (4) and large slumps of the poorly consolidated mud into the newly cut channel of the "reborn" Chagrin River, as it immediately adjusted its flow once the dam broke. Also, we might add, you would have wallowed in a lot of mud, which was like quicksand for a number of weeks until it dried out.

We estimated that enough sediment was trapped behind this dam to fill a football stadium 250 feet up into the bleachers. About 13 percent of this sediment was moved out by the floodwaters or soon after, as the Chagrin River recut its channel. Most of these remobilized sediments (about 86 percent)

The IVEX site soon after the dam failed on August 14, 1994. Looking upstream through the breach between the spillway (left) and earthen dike (right), one can see the thick pile of sediment that accumulated in the reservoir. (*Photograph by James E. Evans*)

ended up in Lower Mill Pond a short distance downstream. It is remarkable that the dam responsible for the pond's existence did not fail. If it had, it would have been 1841 all over again—when the Lower Mill Pond Dam failed and entirely destroyed the Village of Chagrin Falls. And remember, this is an "ordinary" dam, neither among the largest nor the smallest of the approximately 75,000 dams in the United States.

THE MUD SPEAKS

Geologists are different from other scientists because of our interest in long-term perspectives. This is actually an important difference. There is great public concern about restoring the natural environment and remediating problems such as pollution. To talk of restoration and remediation presumes you know what the environment *used* to look like, or the baseline to use for comparison. Other scientists sometimes talk about their "extended data sets," by which they mean five or ten years of measurements. To geologists, ten years of data are like blinking while looking at the landscape.

How do you get a long-term perspective? The IVEX Reservoir provides a perfect example. Year after year, layers of sediment accumulated in the reservoir. If we can attach ages to sediment layers, then we can evaluate the timing and pace of specific occurrences. For example, changes in how fast sediment accumulated—the sedimentation rate—might tell us about alterations to the surrounding landscape and approximately when they occurred.[22]

Here are some examples of what we learned when we examined sediment in the IVEX Reservoir. In the new stream cuts across the reservoir, we could find tree stumps from the pre-1842 forest—before the reservoir flooded, killed, and buried the trees. We also found fence posts and other historical artifacts. We could see the layered gravel and sand of the delta filling the reservoir from the upstream end. We could also observe flood layers—alternating coarse- and fine-grained sediment—in the central part of the reservoir. When we took core samples through the reservoir mud, we could view the complete reservoir history: the floodplain muds that were exposed to the atmosphere prior to creation of the reservoir, covered by the muds that were deprived of oxygen when the reservoir was formed; the 1877 flood layer produced when the dam failed; the 1877–1890 soil that developed when the reservoir was a pasture; and subsequent flood layers.[23]

We could also look at the chemistry of the sediments. In one core sample, we measured the amounts of two radioactive isotopes that it contained, lead-210 and cesium-137.[24] The story here is relatively simple. Lead-210, a naturally occurring radioactive material, comes from radon gas in the atmosphere. It settles out of the atmosphere attached to dust particles, landing on all surfaces. Eventually, sediment with lead-210 attached to it is deposited on the bottom of the reservoir and is buried progressively by new sediment. While this goes on, the radioactive lead-210 is decaying, and eventually—after about 150 years—

lead-210 is gone entirely.[25] From the decay rate of lead-210, we can calculate the age of sediment layers, and this number together with the thickness of sediment allows us to calculate sedimentation rates. We can also confirm that the bottom of the reservoir is about 150 years old because the lead-210 vanishes at this level.

Similarly, worldwide nuclear arms testing creates and releases cesium-137, which then travels throughout the entire Earth's atmosphere. Like lead-210, it settles out of the atmosphere with the dust particles to which it is attached. The abundance of cesium-137 at any depth in a core sample of sediments is related to the number and size of nuclear weapons that were tested in a particular year. Historically, 1952 is the age of any sedimentary layer in which cesium-137 first appears. Extensive nuclear weapons testing that occurred in 1957–1958 and 1962–1964 is recorded by high amounts of cesium-137 in sediments deposited during those years. Owing to a moratorium on testing in 1958-1961 and the Limited Test Ban Treaty beginning in 1963, lower amounts of this radioactive material occur in sediments of these ages. Exceptions include slightly higher peaks in 1971 and 1974 because of aboveground testing by non-Treaty nations and in 1985 as a result of the nuclear plant accident at Chernobyl in the former Soviet Union. The method of using cesium-137 to determine the age of layers of sediment is well established.[26] In the Chagrin Reservoir sediments, we found the 1957–1958 cesium-137 peak between the 1954 and 1959 flood horizons and the 1962–1964 peak closely matching the 1964 flood layer.[27]

What did we learn from this? We were able to affix ages to specific layers in the sediment cores, by matching flood layers and other distinctive features to specific flood events and then confirming our deductions by measuring amounts of the lead and cesium isotopes. This approach allowed us to study how sedimentation in the reservoir has changed over time, and how this pattern of changes relates to land use.[28] The results show that rates of sedimentation have changed dramatically over time. High sedimentation rates occurred in the 1840s–1870s, decades that correspond to deforestation in the region. Sedimentation rates were lower during the 1890s–1910s and record abandonment of farms and their reversion to fields and forests. In the middle to late twentieth century, higher sedimentation rates correspond to population increase and suburban growth in the region. This mud tells us how humans have affected the landscape.

ELIMINATION OF THE IVEX DAM

Options for Remediation

After the flood, the IVEX Dam was a wreck—but the site was too hazardous to be left in its damaged condition. Within days of the dam failure, state officials from the Ohio Department of Natural Resources Division of Water visited the site and informed the IVEX Corporation of their legally mandated options: (1) repair the dam so that it could handle another major flood, or (2) remove the dam entirely, which would exempt the site from liability and government supervision. Ultimately, as other interested parties became involved, a third option was proposed.

Rebuilding the dam was the most expensive option considered. Engineers estimated that the repair cost ranged from one to two and a half million dollars, depending on how much of the existing structure could be reused. These estimates did not include costs for remediation of the reservoir, such as dredging sediment to reinvigorate the reservoir's capacity to hold a high volume of water. In sum, the IVEX Corporation judged rebuilding too expensive. However, removal of the dam would also cause problems. First, the IVEX Corporation depended on the dam and reservoir to provide a water supply for its paper mill. Second, the Ohio Geological Survey and other scientists became concerned that, if the dam were removed, the large volume of fine-grained sediments still in the reservoir would move downstream. Such downstream movement of this mud could fill the Lower Mill Pond and cause *it* to fail; the resulting influx of sediment into the Chagrin River would destroy the water quality of this designated State Scenic River and siltation of the gravel stream bed would destroy fisheries habitat.[29] So, the IVEX Corporation was between a dam and a hard place.

The third—and selected—option was to remediate the site as a riparian wetland (a wetland associated with a river). This alternative required several discrete steps. First, the Village of Chagrin Falls agreed to use the municipal water supply to furnish the IVEX Corporation with treated water for its paper mill, provided the corporation transferred ownership of the dam and reservoir to the village. Also, the village agreed that the IVEX Corporation need only pay for the cost of (1) treating paper mill wastewater and (2) necessary additions to the capacity of the municipal water supply system amortized over a mutually agreeable time period. However, these costs were reduced by the fair market value by transferring legal ownership of the dam and reservoir site to the village, less any restoration liability assumed by the village. This agreement was signed, and the land was transferred to the Village of Chagrin Falls in October 1995. As a result, the dam became the village's problem.

The situation was now simplified. Since the village owned the dam and reservoir, and also wanted the reservoir for a park, it could decide to remove the dam. First, wire baskets—filled with rubble created by the dam failure—were used to stabilize the breach and reduce the flow of silt downstream. Later, the entire spillway was removed, thereby creating a rubble rapids. The question now became how best to stabilize the reservoir with its remaining fine-grained sediments. The solution was to create a riparian wetland in its place.

Riparian wetlands remain perennially wet, usually due to seepage from groundwater, but occasionally because of floods along the adjoining river.

The former spillway site shows the rubble rapids created when the masonry spillway was removed. (*Photograph by James E. Evans*)

Consequently, the vegetation in riparian wetlands is a mixture of wetland plants—cattails, bulrushes, grasses, and certain trees and shrubs—with upland forest. The former reservoir sediment would be stabilized initially because it would be physically trapped in a series of small wetland ponds not directly linked to the river and later because the vegetation that grows in wetlands holds sediment in place. Such wetlands also provide significant wildlife habitat.

It is too early to give the final results of this "reservoir to wetland" project on the Chagrin River. However, significant changes have already occurred. The Village of Chagrin Falls hired a consultant to prepare a three-phase land development plan: to create the riparian wetland habitat, to construct park infrastructure (pathways and parking areas), and to develop educational resources including boardwalks, observation areas, and interpretative signs. To create the wetland involves the greatest expense because this transformation requires capping the spillway, installing small ledges with water-level control structures, removing debris, and planting wetland vegetation. The consultant estimated that the entire project would cost $320,000 to $350,000. The Village of Chagrin Falls recently received $100,000 from the Ohio Department of Natural Resources Natureworks Program, which funds habitat restoration projects, and smaller amounts from the U.S. Fish and Wildlife Service for this purpose. The funds have been sufficient to start restoration work while the village seeks additional grants.

It was once "unthinkable" to remove a dam. However, people have begun to reevaluate the cost and benefits of these hydrologic structures. The necessity of repairing or maintaining a dam focuses attention on a feature that may seem to be a part of the natural landscape but really is not. In recent years, several small dams have been removed voluntarily from the Milwaukee River (Wisconsin), and the Federal Energy Regulatory Commission has approved removal of the Edwards Dam on the Kennebec River (Maine). A controversy currently rages about removal of the Elwha and Glines Canyon dams on the Elwha River (Washington).[30] The failure of the IVEX Dam was involuntary, but the same issues were addressed when the decision was made whether to repair it or remove it completely.

We believe that the IVEX Dam is a case study about scientific and public policy issues related to dams. The success of this restoration project can be attributed to several things. One important factor was the willingness of the owners of the dam to negotiate in good faith with the local community—to reach an agreement that benefited all parties. The dilemma for the owners was that the cost to reconstruct the dam was prohibitive, yet they needed the water supply the reservoir provided. The community wanted park land, and they also wanted to retain an important local employer and the resulting tax base. The agreement transferred ownership of the dam and reservoir to the village in exchange for use of the municipal water supply and water treatment facilities. However, in and of itself, this agreement would not have been sufficient, because the village acquired a site that required significant environmental remediation.

At least in part, the Village of Chagrin Falls willingly pursued this agreement—despite the need for significant environmental restoration—because of cooperation between institutions. This cooperation took several forms. First, cooperative scientific research involved state agencies (numerous divisions of the Ohio Department of Natural Resources), several universities, a local high school, and the U.S. Geological Survey. The studies conducted by these organizations helped to evaluate baseline hydrologic and ecological conditions, the magnitude of the damage from the dam failure, and safety considerations. Together they clarified the issues and alternatives at hand. Also very important was the willingness of these agencies and individuals to entertain the riparian wetland option, provide data to support it as a viable concept, and help identify funding sources to implement it.

Finally, financial considerations figured prominently in the case of the IVEX Dam and Reservoir. The Village of Chagrin Falls willingly used funds for the consultant reports needed to develop the riparian wetland project. Other agencies that were not initially involved—such as the Ohio Historic Preservation Office and the Ohio Department of Natural Resources Division of Natural Areas and Preserves and Division of Wildlife—then came forward to provide support and encouragement for the project. All these efforts aided the success of the funding proposals required to implement the project. In the end, with input from earth scientists and cooperation between groups of people with varying interests, a defunct dam and reservoir that could no longer function were used creatively for good purpose.[31]

21

Living with Karst: Maintaining a Clean Water Supply in Olmsted County, Minnesota

Cathryn A. Manduca

Southeastern Minnesota is a rich land with a long tradition of dairy farming, hog production, and corn and soybean cropping. The average passerby would have few clues to the important role bedrock geology plays in everyday life. Perhaps they would notice the advertisements for Mystery and Niagara Caves with underground rivers, pools, and waterfalls; or when flying into the Rochester airport, they might be struck by the odd pattern of round depressions filled with trees. Few would recognize that this part of Minnesota is a fragile environment, where chemical or agricultural spills on the land surface can locally disappear into the ground and contaminate groundwater several miles away in hours or days.

The dangers of water contamination in southeastern Minnesota first received widespread attention in 1939 when eleven cases of typhoid fever and one death were attributed to drinking from a contaminated water supply. Using practices common at the time, a small village was discharging partially treated sewage into one of the area's many small round depressions in the landscape. These depressions—called sinkholes—made convenient places to dispose of a variety of liquid and solid wastes. The sinkholes were not farmable, solid waste was out of sight, and wastewater disappeared into the ground almost instantly. Residents who considered where the wastewater was going most likely believed that it would be purified as it moved slowly through the earth. The Manual of Water Supply Sanitation published at that time by the Minnesota Department of Health was reassuring: "There is a common belief that contamination may seep through the soil for long distances and get into a well in this way, but such is not generally true in Minnesota although it should always be considered a possibility."[1]

The epidemiological investigation following the outbreak of typhoid fever changed this mind-set in southeastern Minnesota forever. Dye introduced into the sinkhole receiving the village's partially treated sewage reappeared within four hours in the farm well where typhoid had first occurred. The dye did not appear in other shallow wells in the area, but typhoid organisms were isolated from water samples taken from a second farm and high concentrations of coliform organisms were measured from a shallow municipal well.[2] As these Minnesotans discovered, water can travel quickly through the subsurface in southeastern Minnesota and may not be purified along the way.

SOUTHEASTERN MINNESOTA'S UNIQUE GEOLOGY

Southeastern Minnesota, like most of central and southern Minnesota, is underlain by Paleozoic sandstones, shales, and limestones that formed from sediments deposited 525 to 445 million years ago when the continent was covered by a shallow sea. Two factors converge to give southeastern Minnesota its special geology. First, the bedrock strata exposed at the surface are carbonate rocks: limestone made primarily of the mineral calcite and a closely related rock called dolostone made primarily of the mineral dolomite. Groundwater seeping through cracks in carbonate rocks can dissolve minerals in the rock to form a network of fractures, fissures, conduits, and sometimes caves. Southeastern Minnesota's sinkholes form when water moving through these fissures removes the overlying soil and causes the ground surface to sag.

Areas where carbonate rocks have been dissolved by groundwater to create underground systems of enlarged cracks, fissures, and caves are called karst.[3] In areas where karst is developed, groundwater does not percolate through rocks and soil like it might through a sponge but moves quickly through fractures. In fact, streams and rivers often disappear in karst terrain, flow underground, and then reemerge at large springs miles away. Parts of southeastern Minnesota have spectacular karst geology.

Southeastern Minnesota is not the only part of Minnesota that has carbonate rocks near the land surface. However, a second factor makes southeastern Minnesota particularly vulnerable to groundwater pollution. Minnesota is famous as the land of 10,000 lakes. These lakes formed during the last ice age, when glaciers extended south from Canada into the upper Midwest. The glaciers acted as a conveyor belt, scraping soil and rock from the northern part of this area and dumping them in the southern part. The piles of glacial sediment act much like bulldozer piles on a big scale, blocking drainage and forming many closed basins that fill to become lakes. In most parts of southern Minnesota, a blanket of sediments, tens to hundreds of feet thick, overlies the Paleozoic carbonate rocks. However, during the last push of glacial ice, an island of land in southeastern Minnesota, northeastern Iowa, and western Wisconsin remained uncovered. This area is relatively free of glacial sediment and is characterized by a lack of lakes—Olmsted County, for instance, has none of Minnesota's 10,000 natural lakes. Instead, water flowing from the melting glaciers drained through southeastern Minnesota, removing sediment and eroding the deep river valleys that characterize the area's topography. As a result, Paleozoic limestone and dolostone often lie exposed at the land surface, without much overlying sediment. The absence of a sediment blanket allows surface water to enter the carbonate rock more easily and promotes the development of karst. Where lack of protective cover and well-developed karst combine, southeastern Minnesota's water supplies are especially vulnerable to contamination.

Southeastern Minnesota has come a long way since 1939 in understanding and protecting its fragile water supply. Immediately after the typhoid fever outbreak, a study of water contamination in the area resulted in new recommendations for well construction and waste disposal, including the recommendation that the practice of discharging wastewater directly into carbonate formations via sinkholes be eliminated.[4] Building on this report, Olmsted County adopted ordinances in the late 1950s that regulated construction of sewage treatment systems and wells in urbanizing areas.[5]

Since that time, geologists have learned a great deal about geological and groundwater conditions in southeastern Minnesota. Geologists from the University of Minnesota and the Department of Natural Resources have studied the development of karst in the area, mapped the distribution of karst features on the surface, and begun to understand the patterns of subsurface water flow. Geologists from the Minnesota Geological Survey have mapped the distribution of limestone and other Paleozoic sedimentary rocks, as well as the distribution and thickness of the glacial sediments.

U.S. Geological Survey hydrogeologists have determined that water flowing through each of the different layers of sedimentary rock in the area behaves differently. Most of the sandstones and carbonate rocks in the area contain lots of water that can flow readily. These layers—called aquifers—are the primary source of the area's drinking water. Other layers in the area, particularly shales (rocks made from clay-rich mud), do not allow significant amounts of water to flow through them. These layers—called confining layers—force water in the sandstone and carbonate aquifers to flow laterally within the aquifer rather than vertically into the confining layer. The interlayered, flat-lying sequence of aquifers and confining layers controls where water flows, where contaminants can enter the groundwater system most easily, and where new water recharges the groundwater system. As the public and policymakers have come to understand the results of these studies, they have developed practices and policies that manage and protect groundwater resources.

APPLYING SCIENCE FOR SAFETY—SITING THE OLMSTED COUNTY KALMAR LANDFILL

Olmsted County, the most populous county in southeastern Minnesota (population 110,000), had an opportunity to test its ability to use geological information to protect groundwater when a new landfill site was required. Improperly sited, constructed, or operated landfills can pose a considerable threat to groundwater supplies. Waste in landfills may contain a variety of toxins, including heavy metals and organic chemicals used in households and manufacturing. These toxins may be picked up by water traveling through the landfill. If this water enters the groundwater system, it can contaminate aquifers used for drinking water supplies.

In the early 1980s, understanding of karst aquifers and the potential for groundwater pollution posed by landfills was sufficient to recognize that the existing Olmsted County landfill posed an unacceptable risk. Sitting directly on exposures of an aquifer used for drinking water, the landfill was located in an area where a number of karst features suggested that spills would quickly enter the aquifer and move rapidly through the subsurface. Thus, in 1983, at the request of the Minnesota Pollution Control Agency, the County initiated a search for a new landfill site.

A task force of citizens, technical experts, county staff, and elected officials was assembled to recommend a new site to Olmsted County commissioners. This group recognized the importance of using the area's geology to minimize the risk of groundwater pollution and decided to make finding a landfill site that afforded adequate protection for the groundwater system a priority. They began by developing a list of criteria that would describe an acceptable location. All land in the county was then tested against these criteria to find the most suitable sites.

Two forms of natural groundwater protection occur in Olmsted County. In some places, a layer of nearly impermeable shale or clay forms a barrier that prevents most water from moving downward into the aquifers used for drinking water. In a few areas, thick piles of sediment, deposited by glaciers and their meltwaters, protect groundwater by filtering surface water as it moves slowly down through the sedimentary particles. Water moving through these sediments travels in thin films and tiny channels. Particles that are large relative to the size of the channels can be mechanically trapped. The large surface area of sediment in contact with the water promotes chemical interaction between the water and sediment. The net result is that the human impact on the composition of the water is reduced. This process is in marked contrast to the relatively rapid movement of water through the karstic carbonate aquifers, where mechanical and chemical processes have little impact.

The task force, with guidance from consulting geologists and engineers, designed siting criteria that would use these natural features to minimize the chance that water from the landfill would contaminate the groundwater aquifer system. An acceptable site was required to have (1) depth to bedrock greater than 100 feet; (2) absence of karst features in the site area and contiguous 160-acre parcels; and (3) presence of an effective confining layer above any aquifer system that might be used for drinking water. The first parameter would help prevent contamination of the groundwater system because it would require a substantial thickness of glacial sediment surrounding the landfill that could serve as a mechanical and chemical filter for any contaminated water that might leak from it. The absence of karst features would minimize the danger that contaminated water could enter and travel quickly throughout the groundwater system. The third criterion, an effective confining layer, would place an impermeable cap between the landfill and potential drinking water aquifers, thereby reducing the chance that water from the landfill could contaminate these aquifers. Sites that did not meet these criteria were removed from consideration.

The data needed to apply the siting criteria county-wide were collected by geologists from the Minnesota Geological Survey and compiled into a series of interpretative maps of the county's geology. A bedrock geology map showed where surface sediments were believed to be underlain by carbonate and where a protective shale layer was present. A map of surficial geology indicated the different kinds of glacial and river deposits overlying bedrock. The thickness of the sediments was shown in a map of depth to bedrock as determined from logs of previously drilled wells. A map of known sinkholes completed the information needed to determine all geologically suitable sites for the landfill, using the task force's criteria.

Using these data and additional siting criteria addressing issues including zoning restrictions, surrounding land use, and state regulations, the task force developed maps showing which land was suitable for the landfill. They located 14 potentially suitable sites, which were investigated more thoroughly. No other land in the county met the task force's criteria.

The task force used a variety of techniques to collect more detailed information about the sites in order to select a smaller number of final candidates. Using a public hearing process, the task force eliminated two sites when new information about karst features was provided by landowners and verified by geologists. Additional field work was combined with aerial photography to make sure that the observable geology met the siting criteria. At this time, other considerations were also taken into account. Sites that were too small, had high visibility, contained more than two existing homes, or were owned by several landowners were all eliminated at this point. The task force zeroed in on four candidate sites for further evaluation.

The final level of investigation combined on-site soil borings and engineering evaluations. Soil borings allowed measurement of the depth to bedrock, type of bedrock, type of sediment overlying bedrock, and the groundwater conditions above the bedrock aquifer at each candidate site. On the basis of this information, one site was eliminated from further consideration because it did not meet the geological criteria. The three remaining sites were ranked on the basis of their hydrogeology, development costs, and several other practical concerns, and a final site was recommended to the County commissioners.

CONVINCING THE PUBLIC

Using geological understanding and data to locate a safe place for a landfill is not enough. Elected officials must approve the selected site. This process means that the public must be convinced that the site is in their best interest. Siting a landfill is often a contentious process. Some citizens recognize that a landfill poses a potential threat to their water quality; others object to the truck traffic involved in dumping; some worry about litter leaving the landfill; and many don't like to look at or listen to the daily operation. All are concerned that their property values will drop and their quality of life will diminish. For all these reasons, landfills often suffer from the "NIMBY" syndrome—the notion that the appropriate site should be not-in-my-backyard.

The landfill siting task force had a strong argument for choosing the selected site, because they used a county-wide screening process based on the need for groundwater protection. The first step in convincing the public was to bring to life the geological history of the county that, on the one hand, made most of the county unsuitable for landfills and, on the other, made one area particularly suitable.

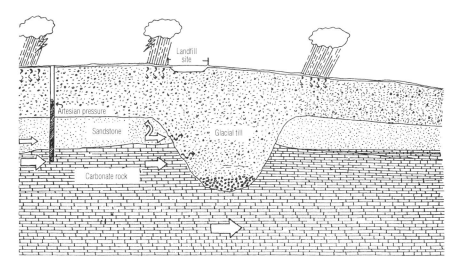

Glacial till fills a preexisting valley and blankets a sandstone and carbonate rock aquifer in the area chosen for siting the Kalmar landfill. Slow movement of precipitation and landfill leachate (small arrows) through the till allows the liquid to be chemically and mechanically filtered as it infiltrates the ground. Also, wells drilled into the aquifer are artesian because water flows easily through the aquifer (large arrows) but when it encounters till, the water slows drastically and creates artesian pressure.

The selected site lay in a part of the county with a unique geological history. Prior to the advance of glaciers into Minnesota in the Pleistocene (1.6 million to 10,000 years ago), an ancient river carved a 300 feet deep valley through this part of the county. The edge of an early glacier was located for a time in and around this valley, and sediment transported by the ice was dumped into the valley and filled it to the brim. After the valley was full, additional sediments were deposited in a blanket over much of the western portion of the county. Subsequently, erosion established the current stream system and removed much of that blanket. However, the new streams do not follow the same path as the ancient river and have left much of the thick section of valley fill intact. These sediments are the thickest in the county and provide the maximum filtering of surface water prior to its entrance into the groundwater system.

The glacial sediments in the ancient valley are rich in fine-grained clay, which makes it difficult for surface water to enter the drinking water aquifer in this area. In the portion of the bedrock valley chosen for the landfill site, wells drilled into the drinking water aquifer are artesian—water rises in the well without pumping—because the clay-rich sediments restrict the upward movement of the drinking water in the lower bedrock aquifer and pressurize it. The artesian nature of these wells verifies that the aquifer is effectively isolated at this location from water in the glacial sediment pile that might be polluted by the landfill, thus decreasing the likelihood of drinking water contamination from a landfill at this site.

A special map showing the sensitivity of the groundwater system to pollution was an important tool for conveying to the public the risks associated with various sites. This map, produced by the Minnesota Geological Survey, uses information on the thickness of materials overlying bedrock, the nature of those materials, the type of bedrock, and the depth to groundwater to estimate how long it would take pollutants to enter the groundwater system. In essence, geologists making this map used the same kind of logic employed in developing the landfill siting criteria to estimate the threat that pollutants spilled on the surface would pose to the groundwater system. The map divides the county into six levels of sensitivity to pollution, ranging from very high (areas where contaminants will almost certainly reach the water table in hours to months) to low (areas where contaminants will require decades or longer to reach the water table). The map is visually very striking in that 82 percent of the county is classified as being in the three highest sensitivity categories—contaminants will reach the water table in minutes to less than a decade. The site selected for use as a landfill is in the only part of the county with a low sensitivity rating that extends more than three square miles.

County officials responsible for presenting information at public hearings on the landfill siting believe that this graphic representation of the relative dangers posed by surface pollutants was critical for convincing the public that the proposed site was in fact the best one. The landfill siting process was successfully completed in 1985, and the Kalmar Landfill opened in 1990.

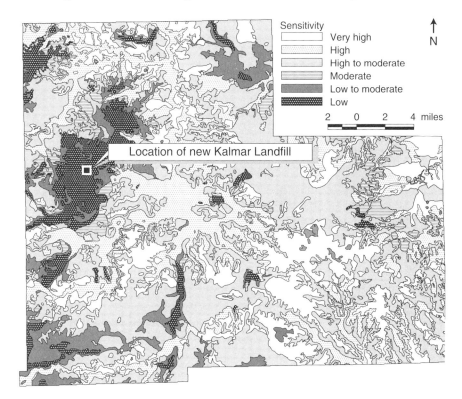

Sensitivity of the groundwater system in Olmsted County to pollution. (*Modified from the Olmsted County Geologic Atlas; courtesy of Olmsted County Planning Department*)

THE GEOLOGICAL ATLAS—AN EVERYDAY TOOL

The maps prepared for the landfill siting process have become an important resource for citizens, policymakers, and staff in Olmsted County. They were augmented and published by the Minnesota Geological Survey in 1988 as the Olmsted County Geologic Atlas and are used daily in county governance.[6] Use varies from visionary—for example, providing information for land use planning decisions—to mundane—data in the atlas are routinely used in making permit decisions for septic fields and determining the specifications for well construction.

In the spring of 1998, the value of this ready geological resource was reemphasized in an unusual emergency: in rural Olmsted County, a cow is thought to have accidentally opened the drain on a storage tank containing feedlot drainage materials.[7] Before the farmer recognized what had happened, approximately 125,000 gallons of liquid containing manure flowed from the tank, down the slope, and into fractured limestone bedrock. The spill was first noticed by a horseback rider along a nearby stream, which, she advised the county, had turned the color of root beer. Minnesota Pollution Control Agency investigators were able to trace the contaminated water to a nearby spring and ultimately to the drained storage tank further upslope. By the time the problem was located, the majority of the manure liquid had disappeared into the groundwater system, raising concern for the safety of drinking water drawn from nearby wells.

State and county officials were able to use maps in the geological atlas to assess the geological setting of the spill. The bedrock hydrogeology map was used to determine the overall flow direction in the aquifer. This map shows the height of the potentiometric surface above sea level—the height to which water would rise in a well. The shape of this surface determines the direction of groundwater flow just as the shape of the Earth's surface determines the direction of surface water flow. Officials used the bedrock hydrogeology map to determine that the flow was dominantly from north to south in the area. Residents in the area surrounding the spill and extending to the south, the anticipated flow direction, were notified of the incident and advised to refrain from drinking well water until the depth and casing in their wells could be evaluated, water tests conducted, and the projected path of contaminants evaluated more thoroughly.

Once the first emergency precautions were taken, officials used the geological atlas to evaluate the overall risk to groundwater. They quickly determined that limestone exposed at the surface was underlain by nearly impermeable shale. This shale was protecting underlying groundwater from contamination and forcing the manure-rich fluid to move laterally. The atlas further indicated that the spill occurred near the edge of a large group of sinkholes. Thus officials had good reason to suspect that groundwater was moving through a well-developed karst system of fissures and channels in this area. Officials interpret that most of the spill moved laterally through the limestone in one or more groundwater channels and discharged within 36 hours to the surface spring. It then flowed into the river drainage system. While not optimal, this outcome from a potentially dangerous spill was a relatively good one for residents.

Familiarity with the geological data allows local government officials frequently to find new applications for the atlas. For example, the City of Rochester, which is the major municipality in the county and has a population of 78,000, is currently embroiled in a controversy over sand and gravel mining, pitting quarry operators and developers against neighboring homeowners. The geological atlas's map of geological resources, which locates sand and gravel deposits and estimates their quality, provides the only data currently available to address this issue.

As these stories show, geological understanding now permeates decision making within the government offices of Olmsted County. It is remarkable to look back to the time when the Minnesota Geological Survey proposed developing the geological atlas to the county. Olmsted County was only the third county in Minnesota to commission such an atlas. Without the prior experience with geological information, many were unsure how it would be used or whether it would be useful. Today, knowing the widespread use the atlas receives, county officials agree that funds used to create the atlas were among the best money they have ever spent. It receives almost daily use, and new applications arise frequently. The information in the atlas provides the framework for organizing and interpreting existing information and for undertaking new studies economically. With the maps in hand, county staff, policymakers, and citizens continue to learn more about the local geology and how it impacts their lives.

CLEAN WATER FOR THE FUTURE

As Olmsted County looks to the future, managing its water resources continues to be both a priority and a challenge. The county now has a plan to protect and manage its water resources, and a water coordinator was added to the staff in 1991. Over the next decade, consolidation in agriculture and particularly the development of larger feedlots will present management challenges and opportunities. Simultaneously, Rochester and its surrounding suburban area are undergoing rapid growth, which is increasing the demands for clean water while contributing to water quality problems.

To keep pace with new questions regarding water resource management, geologists continue to study the groundwater system in Olmsted County. In response to the need for new high-capacity drinking water wells in the City of Rochester, geologists have gathered more detailed information regarding flow in the various sedimentary layers and their capacity for yielding water.[8] To assess the supply of water, a computer model of flow within the aquifer has been developed.[9] These studies are producing greater understanding of exactly where drinking water comes from, and their findings have some major implications for future land use management.

Three different permeable rock formations make up the aquifer that Rochester uses for drinking water. The uppermost rock layer is a sandstone called the St. Peter Formation; the central layers, called the Prairie du Chien Group, are dominated by carbonate rocks; and the bottom layers are a sandstone called the Jordan Formation. There are no thick confining layers between these three formations. As a result, in some areas, the layers may be hydraulically connected, that is, water and any contaminants it contains may be able to move freely from one layer to another. The Prairie du Chien is karstic where it is near the surface, so water entering this portion of the aquifer moves quickly and with minimal filtering. To reduce the risk of contamination, most of Rochester's wells and all newly constructed wells are drawing water from the lowermost portion of the aquifer, the Jordan Formation's sandstone.

Hydrogeological mapping shows that most of the water entering the city's wells originates as surface water in Olmsted County. The potentiometric surface in the drinking water aquifer shows that water entering the aquifer in most of the central part of the county flows toward the basin containing Rochester and the Zumbro River. Water entering the aquifer on the edges of the county flows away from Rochester and out of the county. Thus, for water to reach the city's wells it must enter the drinking water aquifer within the county. This flow pattern is fortunate, because it indicates that the cleanliness of Rochester's drinking water is determined by land use practices and waste handling in Olmsted County, a jurisdiction in which the city has a stake.

There are a number of ways in which surface water can enter the drinking water aquifer and reach the city's wells. In the area surrounding Rochester and in the northern part of the county, the aquifer is exposed at the land surface or is covered only by a thin layer of sediment and soil. In these areas, surface waters, including irrigation water from farms and lawns and runoff from roofs and streets, can enter the drinking water aquifer directly, with minimal filtering. Hydrologic modeling suggests that this process accounts for approximately 35 percent of the water entering the aquifer, with 10 percent coming from the area occupied by the City of Rochester.[10] The city and public utilities are concerned about the quality of water entering the aquifer in this way. They have encouraged a number of studies and continue to develop protective measures. A storm water management plan using vegetated ponds and wetlands to store and treat water is under development as part of this effort.

Current thinking suggests that a process of recharge focused in a narrow zone around Rochester accounts for more than half of the water entering the aquifer. This water is collected in the Galena Group, an overlying karstic, carbonate rock formation exposed near the surface throughout much of the county. A thick formation dominated by shales underlies the Galena Group and prevents groundwater from moving directly downward into the drinking water aquifer. Instead, much of the water in the Galena Group moves laterally until it reaches the Rochester basin. Here, the water spills out into surface sediments and flows just beneath the Earth's surface down over the erosional edge of the shale-rich formations. It may then enter the drinking water aquifer by filtering into the St. Peter Formation (sandstone) or the Prairie du Chien Group (carbonate rock). The process can be envisioned as water that has been confined in a hose (the Galena Group) spilling out of its nozzle (the eroded edge of the aquifer) onto a sponge (the drinking water aquifer). All the discharge from the hose is focused in one place and enters the sponge at the end of the nozzle. Hydrologic modeling suggests that this process accounts for approximately 55 percent of the water entering the aquifer and occurs in a narrow zone on the hillsides surrounding Rochester.

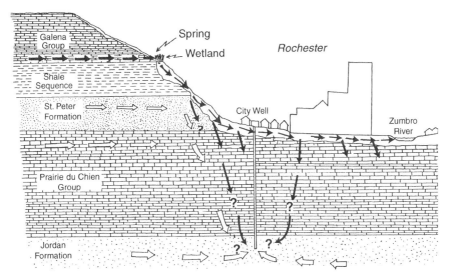

Near Rochester, Minnesota, water (black arrows) flows through the Galena Group, over the confining shale sequence, and into the shallow subsurface on the hillsides surrounding the city. Water enters the permeable St. Peter Formation (sandstone) and Prairie du Chien Group (carbonate rock) and mixes with water from other sources (white arrows) to produce the water supply for the city. Question marks indicate uncertainty as to the precise paths of groundwater flow to the city's wells.

If a large volume of water from the Galena Group is entering the supply area for the city's wells, there may be cause for concern. Because surface waters enter the Galena Group directly with minimal filtering, activities taking place on the land surface, including agriculture, have a major effect on water quality. Water from this aquifer typically has elevated concentrations of a variety of compounds, including nitrates in excess of the drinking water standard. These contaminants indicate the heavy impact of human activities on the water quality and an increased likelihood of contamination by pesticides and other toxins.[11]

Our current level of understanding of the groundwater recharge system is not sufficient to assess accurately the potential impact on Rochester's drinking water supplies. Of primary interest is verification of the amount of water entering the drinking water aquifer from the Galena Group and determining its impact on water quality. What is the prognosis for water quality in the next 10 years, 50 years, or 100 years?

Geologists are taking a variety of approaches to refining understanding of the recharge system. The U.S. Geological Survey currently uses well nests— sets of wells that measure the water pressure in different stratigraphic layers— to determine in detail how water is flowing from the Galena Group into the drinking water aquifer. The ages of water samples collected in this study may also help us understand the rates of water flow and the source of the water.

Other scientists have proposed studying the material properties of the aquifer in the Rochester area to determine whether some of the more critical parameters used in the groundwater flow model are correct. An important next step would be to study the groundwater chemistry in the context of the groundwater flow model. This type of study could form the basis for models of how groundwater quality may evolve in the future.

A second major focus for studies could be to look at how water chemistry changes as water flows from the Galena Group to the lower drinking water aquifer. A wide variety of processes can change the chemistry of groundwater. For example, many organic and inorganic components can be treated or removed from groundwater as it moves slowly through fine-grained sediments or sandstones. If the water is close to the land surface, biological processes are especially effective in breaking down or removing some contaminants. As the water flows near the surface on its path from the upper aquifer to the lower drinking water aquifer, trees and plants may take up many of the impurities in the water, including substantial nitrate, which is a usable plant nutrient. In this way, vegetation on Rochester's hill slopes may play an important role in maintaining a clean water supply for the area.

To assess the impact of water from the Galena Group on the actual drinking water supply, geologists will want to look at how this water moves through the St. Peter-Prairie du Chien-Jordan Aquifer and come to understand the paths it might follow to reach the city's wells. Also of interest are the length of time water from the Galena Group takes to reach the wells and the relative importance of other water sources in supplying the aquifer near the wells.

Geologists have proposed that all these studies be undertaken, and several are underway. However, once again, a good plan for scientific understanding of the problem is not all that is needed to ensure a clean water supply for the future.

TIME PRESSURES

Currently, Rochester is growing rapidly over the zone where water from the Galena Group is thought to spill through the shallow subsurface and into the drinking water aquifer. Construction of new buildings in this area involves removal of some vegetation, disruption of surface sediment and soil and, in some cases, physical modification of the hillsides to create roads and building sites. Many slopes are being mined for sand and crushed rock used in development. Enough is known about the groundwater system to suggest that this area plays an important role in controlling water quality. What strategy should be taken in managing this area? More important, what strategy is politically feasible, given the current level of geological understanding and the rate of growth?

If action is to be taken, then policymakers will need to decide soon how best to manage land use and development on the hillsides surrounding

Rochester. In this context, other questions will become important. Where exactly is the zone where water moves from the Galena Group into the drinking water aquifer and how wide is it? Does this occur everywhere on the hillsides around Rochester or is it concentrated in restricted areas, for example, on the noses of ridges or where streams cut back furthest into the Galena Group? If water quality is improved by vegetation on the hillsides, what kind of vegetation is acceptable? How much is needed? These questions will be answered by policymakers using whatever data are available when they are ready to act. The impact that geological understanding will have in guiding policy depends on the ability of geologists to contribute to this decision-making process. Timing will be very important.

There are good reasons for optimism. So far, it seems that geologists and policymakers will work together to help Rochester and Olmsted County make sound decisions. Recently, scientists from the Minnesota Geological Survey met with staff from the county, the public utility, the Minnesota Pollution Control Agency, and the Department of Natural Resources to design the next steps in their scientific investigations. The meeting was typical of the way the local governmental units do business and exemplified the best of both the scientific and policy-making worlds. Geologists outlined their questions, plans, and ideas. Policymakers identified what data are most needed, how they can be used, and when such information would be too late to impact policy. Through this give and take, all came to understand more about the geological and policy issues, as well as the processes that both groups use to accomplish their work. The future path is uncertain, but we can have confidence in knowing that the right people are talking to one another.

The widespread belief that public education and citizen involvement are fundamental to solving problems in Olmsted County is a second reason for optimism. At every level, people look for opportunities to educate and to work together. For example, the Agricultural Extension Office and the county are working together in several watershed-based educational efforts to help farmers adopt practices that improve surface water and groundwater quality. A task force of citizens, staff, and elected officials recently spent three months learning as much as possible about feedlots in the county and elsewhere as a basis for recommending direction for land use planning and manure management policy.

A citizen's board established in Olmsead County advises the county commissioners on environmental issues. This board allows a number of citizens from a broad spectrum of Olmsted County's agricultural, business, and professional communities to get involved in the environmental decision-making process. At the same time, service on the board provides its members with a first-rate education about environmental problems in the county. The board members can in turn communicate with citizens to expand further public understanding of environmental problems and the decision-making process. The county's educational efforts will pay off in many ways. Perhaps one of them will be that a sufficient number of people will understand the issues surrounding groundwater quality to make appropriate action politically feasible.

In looking back, the people of Olmsted County have learned a great deal about living with karst in the last 60 years. A productive partnership between political leaders, local government staff, and scientists has yielded valuable data that have been used wisely in making a number of important decisions. Most important, an understanding of the area's unique geology and sensitive water supply is widespread among the political leadership and county staff. Educational efforts are increasing the number of citizens who share this understanding: A new sign along a bike path in southeastern Minnesota draws attention to the abundance of round depressions and explains their origin; a rural town boasts that it is the sinkhole capital of the U.S.A.; and beginning in 1999, a new state park interpretive center will help people of all ages understand how underground streams in the park's cave system relate to groundwater movement and drinking water supplies. Perhaps in the future, all will understand the importance of the area's geology to everyday life in southeastern Minnesota.[12]

22

Standoff at Yucca Mountain: High-Level Nuclear Waste in the United States

Allison Macfarlane

I t's a bright spring day in the desert Southwest, sun highlights the white glints of mica in the exposed rock, yellow and pink flowers climb up the sides of the cacti. It's in the low eighties as the sun prepares to reach baking temperatures in the next few months, the moisture of the winter now only a memory. The desert stillness is suddenly broken by a loud, low-pitched hum that grows louder with every minute. The ground begins to tremble, creating small avalanches of pebbles and sand. As the sound grows louder, large rocks become dislodged and the few bewildered lizards quietly sunning themselves scramble for safety. The peace of the desert is completely shattered now by the insistent pounding and quaking of the earth. But no, it's not an earthquake disturbing the quiet of the Nevada desert—or a nuclear test, for that matter, even though our location is within the Nevada Test Site boundary. It's the tunnel boring machine, a 25 foot diameter, 860-ton device, breaking out of a 5 mile long tunnel after three long years of drilling into Yucca Mountain, the potential future home of the nation's most highly radioactive waste.

Not far from the tunnel boring machine, to the east of Yucca Mountain, two geologists extract themselves from a dusty truck to check their equipment. The heat of the day beats down on them as they stride across the rocky desert floor, dressed in shorts, T-shirts, and hiking boots, with packs strapped on their backs. They scramble up the boulders of a sand-colored rock outcropping to see how their Global Positioning System (GPS) equipment, the satellite-based location system, is faring. They arrive to find that the GPS is working fine. It seems to be stable and the battery is working well. Now it's back to the truck and on to the next GPS station, located on the west side of Yucca Mountain. The geologists must travel the routes specified to them by the government officials at the Nevada Test Site, because some areas are off-limits for security and safety reasons associated with the hundreds of nuclear weapons tests conducted there. As a result, it will take them more than an hour to travel to the Western site. Debra, a geology professor, drives, popping a tape of Lyle Lovett into the cassette player—country music is standard for this part of the world. Her companion, Bob, a graduate student, asks, "Why did they decide to store the nuclear waste at Yucca Mountain? Why not just throw it all in one of those bomb craters made from nuclear weapons tests? It's all contaminated already, isn't it?" "That's a good question," Debra responds, "And it's a long story. Let me explain it to you."

Approximately 100 miles northwest of Las Vegas, Yucca Mountain is located within the boundaries of the Nevada Test Site, Nellis Air Force Base, and the Bureau of Land Management. Yucca Mountain itself is actually a low-lying group of hills, that at their highest point reach an altitude of 6,584 feet. The rocks that make up Yucca Mountain and the surrounding area are predominantly tuffs—ancient volcanic ash cemented together by the heat of the eruption and compression over time.

Yucca Mountain is currently the only site in the United States under investigation as a possible mined geological repository for high-level nuclear waste. Such material includes the highly radioactive spent fuel rods from nuclear power reactors and highly radioactive waste materials from the production of nuclear weapons. Another mined geological repository, the Waste Isolation Pilot Project located near Carlsbad, New Mexico, is almost ready to accept less harmful radioactive waste resulting from nuclear weapons production.

The route to a comprehensive management plan for the disposal of nuclear waste in this country has by no means been straight and smooth. The decision to select Yucca Mountain as the nation's potential high-level waste repository was a contentious one—and it isn't finalized yet. The turn of the century will see the outcome of a "viability assessment" of Yucca Mountain as a geological repository, a report that will indicate the existence of roadblocks to the future of the repository. Even if Yucca Mountain passes this test, research over the next few years may still prevent its use as a nuclear waste repository.

So, the question remains unsolved: What should we do with our high-level nuclear waste? Is it up to our generation, the ones who created this mess, to deal with it, or should we wait for possible technological advances in the future that will help solve the problem? The nuclear waste problem involves not only philosophical issues like this one but also technical and intensely political issues. The Yucca Mountain situation provides an excellent example of the contributions geologists can make to an issue of national policy that involves scientific information, but it also illustrates the difficulties regarding such an issue from a solely science-based viewpoint.

HOW DID WE GET INTO THIS MESS?

After the United States dropped atomic weapons on both Hiroshima and Nagasaki (in an effort to end World War II in 1945), it quickly became clear that the energy of an atom's nucleus could be harnessed for electric power generation. A few chemical elements each have a large, unstable nucleus that can split (fission), thereby creating two smaller elements and, in the process, releasing a large amount of energy. Most nuclear energy requires uranium—and a particular kind of uranium, the isotope U-235. (All isotopes of a particular element share the same number of protons but differ in number of neutrons.) The isotope U-235 makes up only 0.7 percent of naturally occurring uranium. The isotope U-238, whose nucleus does not split as readily as that of U-235, forms the majority of naturally occurring uranium. From the late 1950s through the 1970s, the United States built nuclear power plants at a great rate, with many utility companies claiming that the power of the atom would provide energy "too cheap to meter." To produce energy, the reactors required fuel. The same material that powered one of the atomic bombs, uranium is available from mining uranium-rich ores and makes the best fuel for reactors. The nuclear industry enriched mined uranium by increasing its content of the isotope U-235. The enriched product was then pressed into pellets and loaded into zirconium-clad fuel rods.[1]

Because some amount of fissile material remains in used ("spent") nuclear fuel rods, the original 1960s plan to deal with spent fuel, formulated by the utility companies and the U.S. federal government, was to recycle the fuel rods and extract the remaining fissile material. This fissile material consists of the uranium isotope U-235, which is not entirely used up in the reactor as fuel, and the plutonium isotope Pu-239, which is created in the reactor from nuclear reactions; hence, the plan was to extract the uranium and plutonium and reuse it in new fuel for the reactors.

Uranium and plutonium are also the stuff of nuclear weapons. Plutonium, in particular, is desirable because much less plutonium than uranium is needed to make an effective atomic bomb. In addition, the uranium used in some nuclear reactors does not have enough of the isotope U-235 to make a nuclear weapon—most of it consists of the nonfissile isotope U-238. In contrast, most isotopes of plutonium, especially Pu-239, are fissile and can be used in atomic bombs. In other words, there is a fundamental difference between the two elements with respect to recycling.

In the late 1970s, the U.S. government grew concerned about the link between nuclear energy and nuclear weapons. As a result, President Ford in 1976, and later President Carter in 1977, established a policy that would completely change the management of the "back-end," or waste, of the nuclear fuel cycle.[2] These administrations realized that, in recycling spent nuclear fuel rods, uranium and plutonium were being separated out from the rest of the spent fuel and that, in this separated form, they posed a danger. They could potentially be diverted to build nuclear weapons, thus creating a nuclear weapons proliferation risk.

For the most part, these administrations were not worried about diversion of nuclear materials in the United States. They were much more concerned about what might happen in other "less stable" countries where nuclear power plants and spent fuel recycling facilities were not secure. There, it would be possible for terrorists or even the government of the country itself secretly to divert plutonium for use in nuclear weapons. This concern still persists. In fact, in 1974, in a move that prompted the policy, India tested a nuclear weapon it had developed exactly by this method, from plutonium diverted from power reactor fuel. Both Pakistan and Israel have also developed nuclear weapons programs in this way. In an effort to avert such developments in the future, the United States decided to set an example for the rest of the world by establishing a nonproliferation policy whereby commercial nuclear power plants would no longer recycle (or reprocess) their spent nuclear fuel rods. The spent rods would be cooled at the reactor and designated as waste.

The unmistakable consequence of this policy was to create a huge nuclear waste storage problem for the utilities that owned nuclear power plants. Before, when the utilities intended to recycle their spent fuel, they had planned to send their spent fuel away to a recycling facility. In the construction of these power plants, plans for the spent fuel cooling pools had not included the storage of large quantities of spent fuel; no buildup of spent fuel at the plants was ever imagined. With good intentions and the stroke of a pen, the Ford and Carter administrations changed everything. Suddenly, the sheer quantity of high-level waste in the form of spent fuel that the reactors would create over their lifetimes became daunting.

To avert closure of reactors because of a lack of storage space for spent fuel, Congress held hearings on the solutions to the problem of high-level nuclear waste. It found that most options were unfeasible: Shooting the waste into space was expensive and potentially dangerous; storing the waste in the Arctic or the Antarctic was not technically or politically possible; transmutation of radioactive isotopes in an accelerator or reactor relied on unproven technology; and burying the waste in deep-sea muds was politically untenable because such muds are located in international waters. The only option that seemed feasible was geological disposal—either by creating a mined geological repository, a one to four mile deep borehole, or by melting the enclosing rock with the waste. Of all of these options, most countries who planned to dispose of spent fuel within their borders preferred mined geological disposal.

Enactment of the Nuclear Waste Policy Act of 1982 codified into law the plan for a geological repository.[3] This law required that one or more sites be selected; and if the first was located in the West, then the second would be in the East. It called for the opening of the first repository by January 31, 1998, a time that seemed far off in 1982. It established the Nuclear Waste Fund, to be paid into by nuclear utilities, which would cover the cost of developing and operating a geological repository. The Nuclear Waste Policy Act also created a framework to manage the waste. The Department of Energy would oversee the site selection, characterization, and operation. They would apply to the Nuclear Regulatory Commission for a site license, so that there would be a check on the suitability of the site. The Nuclear Regulatory Commission would use environmental standards developed by the Environmental Protection Agency (EPA) to judge site suitability.

By the mid-1980s, nine sites were selected for initial study, but legislation required the Department of Energy rapidly to reduce the number to three. The three chosen sites—the Hanford Site near Richland, Washington, Deaf Smith County in the Texas panhandle, and Yucca Mountain in Nevada—were, not coincidentally, on federally owned land. The final selection would be a politically contentious decision, and the Congressional delegations from Washington, Texas, and Nevada went to work to protect their states. In the end, the final site decision was made by Congress in the 1987 Nuclear Waste Policy Act Amendments.[4]

This legislation made two drastic changes to the original act.[5] First, it established Yucca Mountain as the repository of choice—in Nevada, it is referred to as the "Screw Nevada bill." Second, it abandoned the plan for a second repository in the East. Yucca Mountain would now be the sole high-level nuclear waste repository for the United States if it passed its characterization analysis. Although the political viability of the site already seemed to be decided, the technical viability certainly was not. This issue continues to confront the Department of Energy.

In 1992, Congress again stepped into the nuclear waste fray and discarded the EPA's original human health protection standards for Yucca Mountain.[6] It asked that the EPA redo them, only after the National Academy of Sciences reviewed the original standards and suggested alterations to the currently allowable levels of radiation exposure. Although the Academy's report has long been finished, the EPA has yet to issue new standards for Yucca Mountain. Some policymakers worry that the EPA's new standards may be so stringent that they will be impossible to meet and that, consequently, the repository will never be completed. Antinuclear activists worry that these standards will not be stringent enough and that future local populations will be at grave risk.

In the late 1980s, the date for the opening of the Yucca Mountain repository was revised by the Department of Energy to 2010. At the current rate of progress, it appears that 2010 is optimistic. The lack of apparent progress on the repository project has created frustration among the nuclear utilities and some members of Congress. For others involved in the waste issue, it has become clear that to develop a geological repository that will be leak-proof for 10,000 years to come is a huge job. In their eyes, it is not a project that lends itself well to the legislative wave of the wand.

WHAT'S THE PROBLEM—WHY ISN'T YUCCA MOUNTAIN READY?

The creation of a geological repository to contain the entire country's high-level nuclear waste, in retrospect, is an enormous undertaking. It is, arguably, as difficult as the Manhattan Project, which was responsible for the first nuclear explosions and initiated the source of the waste in the first place. From a simplistic point of view, it should be easy: All that is needed is a dry hole in the ground in an unpopulated area. Yucca Mountain seems to meet the criteria, so what was and is the holdup? Unfortunately, when considered from a closer perspective, it's not an elementary endeavor from either a technical or a political viewpoint.

The main problem lies in the fact that all the requirements for a nuclear waste repository are not yet fully understood. Part of the problem is time. Although we often speak of "nuclear waste disposal," we are not actually talking about elimination of material but about long-term storage. High-level nuclear waste will need to be contained in the chosen repository for geological lengths of time, on the order of 100,000 to over 1,000,000 years—although legislation only stipulates 10,000 years. The radioactive isotopes produced during the operation of a nuclear reactor include "fission products," or lighter, but still radioactive atoms from the splitting of atoms and even heavier radioactive isotopes from reactions in which uranium and other elements absorb a neutron. Both types of reactions may produce long-lived isotopes, those with half-lives—the time over which half of the material decays—greater than a million years. For example, uranium's two main isotopes, U-235 and U-238, have half-lives of 710 million and 4.5 billion years, respectively. A general rule of thumb states that in ten half-lives (7.1 billion and 45 billion years respectively for the uranium isotopes), the material has been reduced to such a small amount that it is considered "gone."[7]

A larger part of the problem has to do with the lack of fit between geology and prediction. Geological science is largely historical in that it looks at the recent or ancient rock record and explains the past behavior of the earth system. One might say that geology is about "postdiction." Unfortunately, what is needed to address the problem of nuclear waste disposal is prediction. Geology so far has predicted little with great accuracy. No earthquake or volcanic event, for example, has ever been predicted with an accuracy of more than a few years. Few people have recognized these limits of geological knowledge; and consequently, unrealistic requirements were made for the Yucca Mountain repository.

Regardless of insufficient geological knowledge, Congress and the Department of Energy selected Yucca Mountain for a few significant reasons. It is in an area that is relatively unpopulated, and there are few identifiable natural resources in the region.[8] Indeed, the federal government already owned the land, so no land battles would have to be fought. Perhaps more significant is the fact that it was adjacent to land already contaminated by radioactivity from the testing of nuclear weapons during the Cold War. The Yucca Mountain location was particularly desirable because it contained the fewest faults and the lowest water table—the depth underground where the rock or soil is saturated with water. The dry conditions promised by a repository at Yucca Mountain were thought to be desirable. Planners believed that there was little chance that the radioactive materials could contaminate the groundwater.

The issue of land ownership turns out to be significantly more complicated than the government and the media have suggested. Actually, the land at Yucca Mountain is claimed by two Native American tribes, the Western Shoshone and the Southern Paiute, who were removed from it in the 1950s when the Department of Defense required the land for nuclear weapons testing.[9] In fact, for these tribes, Yucca Mountain is a holy land. The Western Shoshone in particular have been vocal in proclaiming their disapproval of locating a high-level waste repository on their land. The issue of native lands used as dumping grounds for the nation's nuclear waste is not confined to Yucca Mountain. Two tribes, the Mescalero Apache in New Mexico and the Skull Valley Goshutes in Utah, have actively sought to store nuclear waste on their land, whereas the proposed low-level waste site in Ward Valley, California, is actively opposed by the Mojave tribes.[10]

In general, a repository site should fulfill a few criteria to aid in the primary goal of protecting humans and the environment—present and future—from contamination by radioactive waste. It should be geologically stable for the foreseeable future and be located in an unpopulated area where there is little danger of future human intrusion for natural resources. The hydrology of the repository should minimize water flow past the waste, and the repository rock type and engineered systems should minimize the potential movement of radionuclides from the repository. Yucca Mountain satisfies some, but not all, of those criteria.

The proposed repository is located in an arid region of the country where rainfall is only six inches per year. The water table is extremely low at Yucca Mountain. It resides about 2,000 to 2,500 feet below the ground surface, and the repository level itself will be located about 1,000 feet below the ground surface, 1,000 feet above the water table. The rock formation at the repository level is the Topopah Springs welded tuff. It is a dense rock, high in silica content that was deposited as ash from a volcano and welded together by the heat of the eruption.[11]

At first glance, a dry repository seems to be the best possible situation; but unfortunately, there are a few unexpected issues associated with dry conditions that must be taken into account in repository planning. These have to do with oxidation and reduction. In a dry repository where the waste will be in contact with air, which contains oxygen, the conditions are referred to as oxidizing. In contrast, a wet repository, where waste would be in contact with water, offers reducing conditions. It turns out that a number of materials actually are more apt to break down in an oxidizing environment than in a reducing one. Spent fuel is a good example. Under Yucca Mountain repository conditions, the uranium in spent fuel is expected to oxidize. Just as rust on a car is oxidized metal and is much more likely to break apart, oxidized uranium in spent fuel becomes less stable and breaks down into smaller grain sizes. A decrease in grain size leads to an increase in surface area, leaving more area open to leaching by available groundwater.

By far the largest technical issue facing the Yucca Mountain repository is water transport of radionuclides. When Yucca Mountain was first chosen, it was thought to contain dry horizons perfect for the storage of nuclear waste. Water was thought to move slowly through the mountain, taking hundreds or thousands of years to travel from one spot to the other. These past assumptions about the hydrologic systems at the mountain have recently come into question. What is clear now is that hydrogeology is a young science, and it needs more time to develop before it can be applied with any predictive certainty to a repository situation.

The core of the issue facing Yucca Mountain is radionuclide transport in the far future, a few tens of thousands to a million years or more from now. By that time, the radioactivity of some of the longer-lived radionuclides will reach a maximum. Although Yucca Mountain is a dry environment, it is assumed that 300 to 1,000 years from now small amounts of water will have breached the stainless steel waste containers. When water has gotten into the containers, it will be up to the geology of the repository and any materials filling the space between the waste containers and the bedrock—such as the highly absorbent clay, bentonite—to contain the radioactive material. Will the geology of the repository be able to do its job? This is one of the most pressing unanswered questions facing the repository.

Old models of slow radionuclide transport in the vertical dimension at Yucca Mountain appear to be incorrect. Department of Energy workers recently found the isotopes tritium and chlorine-36 near the repository level in boreholes dug to monitor hydrologic conditions.[12] The majority of both isotopes are produced from the explosion of nuclear weapons; consequently, they make good age-dating tools. High concentrations of these isotopes were not found on Earth prior to the start of nuclear weapons testing in 1945. From 1945 until 1963, during aboveground tests, these isotopes were released into the atmosphere and were transported long distances, only to be returned to land as precipitation. Rainwater is transported down through the soil into the bedrock via fractures and faults, otherwise known as fast water pathways. The borehole data show that water carrying tritium and chlorine-36 was transported over 1,000 feet in depth in about 50 years or less. This is relatively rapid transport in terms of hydrologic systems.

An example of one of the long-term issues facing the repository is the fate of an isotope called neptunium-237. This radionuclide is present in small amounts in spent fuel and has a half-life of 2.1 million years. It is not usually contained by geological materials—especially those at Yucca Mountain—and will travel easily as a dissolved substance if it is released from spent fuel directly into water at the repository level. Consequently, there is a potential that this radioisotope could travel beyond the repository and into the groundwater or future drinking water supply.

Recently discovered uncertainties about radionuclide transport have to do with isotopes such as plutonium-239, cesium-137, and tritium. These isotopes were detected almost a mile from the original site of a 1969 underground nuclear weapons test at the Nevada Test Site, near Yucca Mountain.[13] The transport of plutonium, in particular, such a long distance over such a short time is a surprising and distressing result. Plutonium is known to have low solubility in water—that is, it does not dissolve easily in water. In the past, scientists assumed that if plutonium is exposed to the repository environment, it will not move far from its original location because of its low solubility in groundwater. In the 1990s, research on the transport of plutonium in geological media showed that plutonium can actually move by binding to tiny particles called colloids. These materials, derived either from the surrounding rock or from the waste form itself, are on the order of a few ten-thousandths of an inch or less in size. Thus, if plutonium and other radionuclides bind to colloids, they can be carried long distances. This, in fact, is what the scientists who investigated the Nevada Test Site data concluded was the explanation for the transport of plutonium and other radionuclides.

Another problem associated with radionuclide transport is that of autocatalytic criticality—the possibility that fissile material from spent fuel will migrate to and accumulate in one location in the repository and spontaneously explode, thereby dispersing material into the water supply. The most likely material to create such an explosion is U-235. The amount of U-235 will increase greatly when Pu-239, from both power reactor spent fuel and weapons production, decays over its half-life of 24,100 years to U-235. It turns out that U-235 is also fairly mobile in groundwater, and it could move to and collect in one location. If enough U-235 collects to form a critical mass—the least amount of material needed to create a nuclear chain reaction—then it is possible that a nuclear explosion could occur. Such an explosion would create new water pathways and potentially spread radioactive contamination some distance from the repository. It's not clear whether the effects of such an explosion would contaminate the environment.

Perhaps the second most pressing technical issue at Yucca Mountain has to do with its geological stability. Actually, the Yucca Mountain region is not as stable as it first looked. It is located in the heart of the Basin and Range Province of the western United States, an area that was and still is tectonically active. The majority of recent earthquake activity is located south and west of Yucca Mountain, relatively close to the San Andreas fault system. The Yucca Mountain region itself has experienced seismicity. On 29 June 1992, a magnitude 5.4 earthquake centered on an unknown fault in Little Skull Mountain,

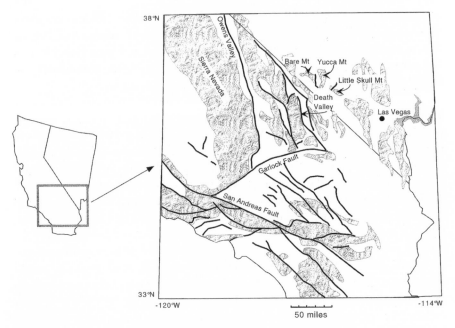

Map of the southwestern Basin and Range Province in California and Nevada, showing the location of Yucca Mountain (actually a low-lying group of hills) east of Death Valley and northwest of Las Vegas. Heavy lines are faults and shaded regions are mountains.

six miles southeast of Yucca Mountain, rocked the area.[14] There are other active major faults in the region also. The length of the mountain runs north–south, parallel to the most potentially hazardous fault in the region, the Bare Mountain fault, located about six miles to the west of Yucca Mountain. There are active faults within the repository itself, the largest of which are the Ghost Dance and Bow Ridge faults.

Faults are not the only threat to the peace of Yucca Mountain; the presence of volcanoes suggests future volcanic activity. Within six miles of the mountain are the Crater Flats volcanic cones, all approximately one million years old. A little further to the south is the infamous Lathrop Wells cone, which has been the source of ample controversy. Some geologists claim that it is as old as 100,000 years, whereas others suggest that it is much younger, on the order of 10,000 years.[15] The probability of future volcanic activity is highly significant to the success of the repository. One does not want a volcanic center to pop up in the middle of the repository, blowing high into the atmosphere all the radioactive material carefully stored there. Geologists have had a difficult time reaching agreement over the probability of future volcanic eruptions near Yucca Mountain. To deal with this disagreement, the Department of Energy convened an event of questionable scientific validity: A number of the geologists who work closely on volcanism in the Yucca Mountain region gathered to debate the probability of future volcanism.

More disturbing than the presence of these faults and volcanoes is the recent suggestion by geologists at the California Institute of Technology and Harvard University that the area may actually be getting *more tectonically active*. On the basis of Global Positioning System surveys of the area over six years, geoscientists have concluded that the crust near Yucca Mountain is stretching at a faster rate than earlier thought.[16] For geologists, stretching results in tearing of the crust, which means more faulting and associated earthquakes. The implications are that the area could become both more seismically and volcanically active over the next few tens of thousands of years. If such a prediction were to come true, the siting of a high-level nuclear waste repository in this area would pose a significant risk to the surrounding environment.

A third major issue facing Yucca Mountain is the possibility of future climate changes in the region and their effect on water transport and the water table. With the dire predictions of global climate change due to the rapid increase of greenhouse gases, it is likely that the arid climate of Yucca Mountain may not always remain so. In fact, it may change sooner rather than later. If the area becomes more humid, then the amount of rainwater transported through the repository may increase dramatically. This change could lead to the transport of radioactive materials at a much faster rate than expected. Another related effect of climate change at Yucca Mountain would be an increase in the level of the water table, which, as mentioned earlier, lies 1,000 feet below the repository horizon. Although studies show that past changes in the water table have been on the order of a few tens of feet, a larger change is possible. A change of 1,000 feet would be extraordinary, however; and most scientists are confident that the water table will not intersect the repository.

Data like that outlined above require us to reexamine our current models of groundwater and radionuclide transport in the unsaturated zone of Yucca Mountain. Previously, predictions of radionuclide transport were based on slow transport models that did not take into account important fracture networks or colloid species that assist water transport of radioactive materials. New research is required to determine the extent of movement of water through the fracture systems at Yucca Mountain. In light of the recent tectonic data, models need to be made of future fracture development at the repository so that we can understand the behavior of future water pathways. Further detailed studies of colloidal transport of radioactive materials are also necessary. Probably one of the best places to conduct such research is the Nevada Test Site, adjacent to Yucca Mountain, which contains similar rocks that are contaminated with a variety of radionuclides. To expedite this process, the federal government needs to allow such research to proceed in the public arena.

To address the technical issues at Yucca Mountain, we need either to redefine our requirements for a geological repository, or we need to be a bit more patient and make a more concerted effort to solve this problem. The best minds in the country, if not the world, were applied to making the first atomic bomb. Why not have innovative thinkers try to solve the problem of nuclear waste disposal? At the moment, only the Department of Energy and its contractors are studying Yucca Mountain. Why not set aside funds to draw in creative geoscientists and other talented scientists to address some of the difficult questions facing a repository at Yucca Mountain? Let's be sure as a nation that we have had the best minds working on this complex problem.

First and foremost, though, we must be patient. We need not rush to find a solution to the problem of high-level nuclear waste. Although cooling pools are nearing full capacity at a few power reactors, technology for on-site dry storage is well known and has been used successfully and safely since the mid-1980s. As a society, we need to define better how well-protected we must be from the waste and decide on the amount of risk we can live with. Geology and other sciences concerned with this problem will never provide us with absolute answers to these questions. Consequently, we must decide what we want science, given its constraints, to provide for us. Why force such a controversial decision at this time? Let us first try to understand the problem thoroughly.

Although there are abundant technical issues that face the proposed Yucca Mountain repository, the larger and more vexing issues tend to be political. In fact, the success or failure of Yucca Mountain rests mostly on the resolution of difficult political issues. First and foremost is the opposition to the repository by the State of Nevada. The governor and the entire congressional delegation have stated their strong opposition to the plan. From Nevada's viewpoint, it has been singled out to handle the entire country's high-level nuclear waste because it has a small Congressional delegation and therefore little power. To residents of the state, this solution seems unjust; the state has no nuclear power reactors to contribute waste of its own.

As high-level nuclear waste legislation has developed throughout the 1980s and 1990s, Nevada's power and compensation have shrunk.[17] In the 1982 Nuclear Waste Policy Act, the state in which the repository was to be sited was to be given a veto on the site, which could be overridden only by Congress. In the 1987 Nuclear Waste Policy Act Amendments, this veto power was removed when Congress designated Yucca Mountain as the sole repository site in the country. Although the legislation required the federal government to provide Nevada with financial and technical assistance, none was provided until the state sued the federal government for it. Consequently, the State of Nevada has fought against the federal government in a fierce battle that actually pits the rights of states against those of the federal government.[18] In response to the federal legislation, Nevada wrote its own legislation, under which it is illegal to store high-level nuclear waste within the state borders. In the end, however, according to some constitutional legal scholars, it is likely that the federal government will have its way. The U.S. government owned the waste site land to begin with, and therefore the state has little basis for a constitutional argument.

Another political battle waiting to be fought is over the transportation of spent fuel from reactors to a geological repository or an interim site. The public is concerned about the safety of nuclear materials, especially nuclear materials that will be transported on roadways in residential communities near schools and homes. A telling example is that of the transport of foreign spent reactor fuel from the Concord Naval Weapons Base near San Francisco, California, to the Idaho National Engineering Laboratory in Idaho Falls, Idaho. Numerous newspaper reports quoted many local residents who expressed outrage and fear at the transportation of nuclear materials on their roadways. Although most scientists would say that transporting gasoline or other such flammable, carcinogenic materials is more hazardous, radioactive materials appear to be akin to deadly biological agents in the public's mind, and in a way they are. Even the Clinton Administration classifies biological weapons as weapons of mass destruction, in the same category as nuclear weapons.

Why do these political problems exist? Partly because the government has not dealt adequately with the public's fear of radiation from nuclear waste. The government's general approach to the public's adverse reactions to the transportation of nuclear waste or the siting of a repository is to provide more information and education, so that the public, once better educated on the topic, will simply fall in line and bend to the will of the federal government. So far, such an approach has not quelled the public's concerns about nuclear waste issues. Nonetheless, the government clings to the idea that it is the lack of education, especially science education, that results in fear of radiation. Clearly, the government needs to listen more carefully to its citizens if such a monumental effort, like the one being conducted at Yucca Mountain, is ever to be successful. In addition, people must learn that we cannot generate such waste with impunity.

CURRENT BATTLES: INTERIM STORAGE LEGISLATION

The most recent iteration of the nuclear waste debate has been played out over the interim storage of spent fuel. With no repository to open by January 31, 1998 (the date specified by the Nuclear Waste Policy Act in 1982) the utilities that own nuclear power plants sued the Department of Energy for contract violation. They felt that the Nuclear Waste Policy Act had provided them with a contract that was clearly going to be violated by the Department of Energy. Members of Congress took up the issue and in 1997 sponsored bills in the House and Senate that would have provided an interim storage site adjacent to Yucca Mountain.[19] Such a centralized interim storage facility was intended to ease the lack of storage space for spent fuel at reactor sites and, in the eyes of the utility companies, would begin to remove the nuclear waste albatross hanging around the neck of the nuclear power industry.

Unfortunately, a centralized interim storage facility attached to Yucca Mountain is not such a simple prospect. The Clinton Administration's position is that an interim facility at Yucca Mountain is only appropriate once Yucca Mountain is actually approved for licensing. The Congressional legislation would have opened a storage facility before Yucca Mountain would be an approved permanent repository. In addition, the Clinton Administration was concerned that directing attention and funding toward an interim site would remove the motivation to continue with a permanent facility, thus creating a "de facto" aboveground permanent storage facility at Yucca Mountain.

There are other reasons for not endorsing an interim storage facility at Yucca Mountain. One is the transportation issue, which has yet to be dealt with in any major fashion in this country. It is not clear that the Department of Energy infrastructure would be capable of large shipments of spent fuel across the country before 2010, let alone be able to deal with the public backlash that would be sure to come. One of the most important considerations in the issue is the fact that the spent fuel is actually safe where it is at the reactors, and it will remain so for at least 100 years to come. These are the conclusions reached by studies released by both the Nuclear Regulatory Commission and the Nuclear Waste Technology Review Board and conducted in the 1990s.[20] When there is no more room for spent fuel storage in the cooling pools at nuclear reactors, the spent fuel can be stored in dry casks on site. Although this option is more costly to nuclear power companies, it is quite safe and will contain the waste until the next century. Consequently, there really is no urgent technical need to move spent fuel to a centralized storage facility. Finally, what is the economic advantage of constructing a large storage facility at Yucca Mountain, a seismically active area, an entire continent away from most of the country's nuclear reactors, only to find 10, 20, or 50 years from now that for some unforeseen reason Yucca Mountain is simply not an appropriate location for a permanent repository?

The interim storage battle will continue to be waged for many years to come until a permanent repository is secured. The actual execution of a project of this magnitude does not occur simply just because it has been legislated to do so—clearly not; otherwise the Yucca Mountain repository would already be accepting waste.

ANOTHER PERSPECTIVE ON THE NUCLEAR WASTE ISSUE

Difficulties in waste disposition are not confined to high-level nuclear waste. Low-level nuclear waste repositories are also experiencing battles over siting and management. This is the case in Ward Valley, California, which is the site of a low-level radioactive waste disposal facility that would store waste generated in California, Arizona, and North and South Dakota. Antinuclear activists, in conjunction with local Native American tribes and a few U.S. Geological Survey geologists, are waging a fierce battle against the site, which they claim will not adequately keep radioactive materials from contaminating the groundwater. As in most of these situations, it's not simply a case of the "antinuclear" folks against the "pronuclear" ones; it's more complicated than is often portrayed by the media. The State of California is partially to blame for this controversy because it allowed a company with an acknowledged history of poor management of low-level radioactive waste dumps—Nuclear Ecology—to characterize and operate the site.

Similarly, the process of high-level waste repository siting is more involved than the simple dichotomy of "us" versus "them." In working toward a repository at Yucca Mountain, much of the process has been controlled and confused by legislation. In many instances, legislation has not facilitated the process of establishing a geological repository. In fact, there appears to be a fundamental flaw in legislating science-based problems: Science does not lend itself well to following the law. Our desire to solve the nuclear waste problem rapidly by justifying proposed solutions with science clashes with the ability of science to *actually* provide such justification. Often, science does not adhere to timetables established in the legislation; it progresses at its own pace.

A fundamental characteristic of the clash between legislation and science is the desire of legislators to govern science. Unfortunately, this does not work. For example, Congress has required that the Yucca Mountain repository contain the radioactive material for 10,000 years following its closure. But the National Academy of Sciences noted that peak risk from some of the radionuclides present in the repository would not occur until at least hundreds of thousands of years from the closure date.[21] One cannot legislate half-lives, which is essentially what this part of the legislation attempts to do.

As another example, a clause in the 1987 Nuclear Waste Policy Act Amendments eliminated all funding for research on repositories within crystalline rocks such as granite.[22] Presumably this line of legislation was included to prevent the siting of a second waste repository on the East Coast of the United States and defied geological reasoning. Unfortunately, it precluded the use of the Climax stock, a granitic rock located at the Nevada Test Site, which would arguably make a more suitable repository than the tuff at Yucca Mountain.[23]

A section of an interim storage bill passed by the Senate in 1998 stated that climate regimes "substantially different from those that have occurred during the previous 100,000 years at the Yucca Mountain site" cannot be considered in characterizing the future performance of a permanent repository there.[24] Consequently, in the face of potentially rapid and large climate change forced by the accumulation of carbon in the atmosphere, scientists are not allowed to consider climate changes 1,000,000, 200,000, or even 100,001 years ago at Yucca Mountain, even if those data suggest that significant changes in the water table could occur at the site if our current climate were to change that drastically. In the face of this, most geologists would throw up their hands in frustration. Congress cannot ask geologists to provide assurances about the integrity of a repository if such scientifically ridiculous requirements are imposed. This situation must change if a repository is to be successful. Certainly, it is the job of Congress to legislate the management structure and operation of repository characterization. But Congress should enlist the help of geologists with the geological problems.

SOLUTIONS FOR THE FUTURE

The question remains, How do we move forward with a solution to the problem of high-level waste disposition? As a nation, we need to agree on the magnitude of the issue and understand that it needs a concerted, unpoliticized effort to solve it. In other words, the desires of interest groups, such as utilities that own nuclear reactors, should not be put above the need to make scientifically sound decisions. More important, we must agree that there is no need to rush to a solution. Technically, the spent fuel is safe where it is, at the reactors that produced it. It will take time for geologists to understand fully the hydrological system, tectonism, and volcanism near Yucca Mountain. To expedite the process and raise the level of the science done at the site, we need to draw in academic geologists to study different aspects of the entire geological system.

To make sure that the repository does in fact open, we need to conduct small-scale experiments with spent fuel at the repository. These experiments will help engineers design the repository and the waste containers and will aid in identifying problems that will be encountered with "real" waste. We must also remain open to the possibility that Yucca Mountain will turn out to be an inappropriate location for the storage of high-level nuclear waste. If so, all is not lost. Valuable data and experience will have been gathered in the attempt to characterize Yucca Mountain, and they can be applied elsewhere.

Finally, it is worthwhile to compare the U.S high-level waste situation with that of other countries. Most European countries have put off a long-term solution. They intend to develop geological repositories but are doing so slowly and carefully, with more conservative schedules than that of the United States. Sweden and France both have interim storage sites, to which spent fuel is transported while it awaits the development of a permanent repository. Neither country has a definite deadline to open a repository though, and both countries are considering geological repositories with conditions that are significantly different from those of Yucca Mountain. Clearly, there are other ways to complete this process and other types of geological regions in which to place the high-level waste.

High-level nuclear waste is an issue with which we as a nation will wrestle for the foreseeable future. In fact, it is possible, if significant global warming occurs, that the United States will become more dependent on nuclear power because that technology does not produce greenhouse gases. If that is so, the increased levels of spent fuel will make it even more imperative that we find a solution to the nuclear waste problem. It is an issue whose solution is clearly rooted in an understanding of geological sciences and the earth system as a whole. By relaxing the legislative requirements on the science, bringing in more geologists to study different aspects of the issue, and holding open, honest discussions with the public in which their concerns are accounted for, the nation will progress toward a solution to the problem presented by nuclear waste.

23

Appetite for Toxins: Bioremediation of Contaminated Soil

Rosa E. Gwinn

$\mathcal{S}$cientific disciplines have converged as people learn more in each of the classically divided disciplines of biology, chemistry, physics, and geology. The boundary between physics and chemistry, for instance, became blurred as technology allowed the observation of chemical activity on the molecular scale. Likewise, as geologists's investigations of chemical processes within the Earth developed, the discipline of geochemistry evolved. A more recent creation is the science of "biogeochemistry"—the study of microbial populations that live within soil and sediments near the Earth's surface. One of the benefits of these microorganisms is their ability to improve the health of the environment. If Earth's soil and sediment becomes contaminated by human activity, native microbial populations can help to clean it, sometimes with only nominal care.

The value of microbes in cleaning the environment was discovered in part by accident and in part through observation. Wastewater engineers knew that by optimizing conditions in which microbes thrive, sewage and petroleum spills would be "eaten." Today, we routinely exploit this microbial capacity when we try to clean up oil spills along coasts. But only as recently as the 1980s did biogeochemists discover that natural microbial populations can eliminate organic contaminants from soil, sediment, and groundwater by eating them. In the language of environmental scientists, this consumption is bioremediation.

Bioremediation is a relatively innovative method for dealing with environmental sites that are contaminated with hazardous materials. A fundamental and apparent contradiction is that the toxins that make a site hazardous to many living things are not toxic to some microbial species. As long ago as 1567, Paracelsus, a Swiss alchemist and physician who has been designated the founder of toxicology, observed: "What is it that is not poison? It is the dose only that makes the poison."[1] In other words, small quantities of a chemical may not be unhealthy, but a large dose may cause negative health effects, even death. A slightly different but related concept is that the nature of a poison also depends on the receptor. For example, the levels of nitrate in water that are safe for some species of plants would cause blood problems in humans if they drank the same water. In this sense, the consumer makes the poison. Bioremediation techniques exploit that toxicological twist. In the right combination, living organisms can metabolize contaminants and, ideally, clean up a site that is hazardous to other parts of the ecosystem.

This essay presents a real-world example of how microbes might help to clean contaminated environments. In particular, I describe how composting is being used to clean up soil at a military facility contaminated with explosives. This promising technology might help undo the damage of contamination caused by military activities throughout the United States and abroad. Because bioremediation exploits natural conditions, it could be called the clean way to clean.

EXPLOSIVES-CONTAMINATED SOILS AT MILITARY DEPOTS

At military facilities throughout the United States and other countries, conventional weapons routinely were disarmed by using water to wash explosives from shells or munitions casings. The use of water reduced the possibility of accidental explosions during the process. However, as a consequence, the water became laden with explosives. To "dispose" of it, the explosives-laden water was pumped into shallow, constructed ponds near the buildings where the washing had taken place. At various military depots, the ponds—also known as washout lagoons—extended over several acres; when full, they contained tens of thousands of gallons of water, pink from the explosives they harbored. As the water evaporated or seeped into the soil beneath the surface and the level of water in the pond subsided, another pulse of water that contained explosives would be pumped into the washout lagoon. Evaporation of each pulse of water left behind layers of pinkish red sediment along the sides and bottom of the washout lagoons. Water that percolated into the sediment beneath the surface at the site carried some of the dissolved explosives with it. As a result of both of these processes—evaporation and water seepage—high concentrations of explosives are present today in the soil and subsurface sediments of washout lagoons at military depots.

Although this practice was acceptable at the time, it is no longer allowed under federal environmental laws. In fact, the Comprehensive Environmental Response, Compensation, and Liability Act (CERCLA), known widely as Superfund, requires that contaminated sites be cleaned—as best we can—in order to minimize the risk they pose to living things.

Geologists, hydrogeologists, and environmental engineers have investi-gated the magnitude and extent of the explosives contamination at some of these sites. To do so, teams of geologists drilled borings in and around the lagoons. They collected samples of the sediment and soil at the surface and below it. Hydrogeologists installed groundwater wells so that they could collect groundwater samples from below the lagoons. The sediment, soil, and water samples were analyzed to determine the amounts and types of explosives they contained; then, these data were plotted on maps of the sites.

Geologists were able to decipher how frequently a lagoon had been used to hold the explosives-laden water by the frequency at which thin, pink-banded layers occurred in the sediments. Each thin layer corresponded to an episode of water disposal in the lagoon. The brighter the pink, the greater the contami-nation. Some sediment layers were nearly red from the very high explosives concentrations in them. By sampling the soils, geologists could determine how far out each lagoon extended, because, beyond the lagoons, the soils were free of explosives. Hydrogeologists could tell from groundwater well samples whether explosives lurked in the groundwater beneath the site and whether the ground water was contaminated and where it was moving.

The study results showed that soils at these facilities were conspicu-ously contaminated and the law required that some form of site cleanup be attempted. None of the concentrations were high enough to cause an explosion—nothing that dramatic. But, in places, the concentrations were unsafe to humans and to animals living at the site. Under Superfund law, sev-eral cleanup alternatives must be evaluated; and on the basis of established criteria, the best option must be pursued.

The chemistry of explosive compounds merits a brief introduction, because most people are not familiar with their nomenclature and chemical structure. Explosives washed out of munitions into the lagoons included trini-trotoluene (TNT), dinitrotoluene (DNT), dinitrobenzene, tetryl, cyclotriameth-ylene trinitramine (Royal Demolition Explosive, RDX), and cyclotetramethyl-ene tetranitramine (High Melting Explosive, HMX). All these explosives are organic compounds, which means that they are composed of carbon, nitrogen, oxygen, and hydrogen. As explosives, they are hazardous to human health in more ways than one. But broken into pieces, these molecules are similar to simpler, less toxic chemicals. For example, nitrate is a nutrient essential for plant metabolism. Under the right conditions, nitrates can be "broken off" of some of these explosives. In fact, all these explosive compounds contain chem-ical complexes that are essential nutrients; but in the explosives, they exist in a form that is not readily usable. Degradation of the complex compounds that make up the explosives into their component molecules seems an attractive alternative method for destroying munitions because the elements they con-tain can be useful organic materials. The challenge of the cleanup is to break down the explosives so that they are neither toxic nor hazardous.

Microbes can break down large organic molecules. As many home garden-ers know, microbes are present naturally in the waste in compost. Compost piles create the right conditions for microbes to disintegrate household or yard waste into usable, nutrient-rich soil. Adding the right amounts of leaves, grass, water, and air can keep a backyard compost pile alive for years. In like manner, biogeochemists have sought ways to simulate good conditions for microbial activity in contaminated soil, to exploit the ability of millions of hungry microbes to break down organic compounds.

Treating contaminants in soil by composting is relatively new; the approach has been applied only in a handful of locations. Composting of explosives-contaminated soil, which naturally contains microbes that may be feasting on the organic matter the soil contains, combines geological, biological, and engineering designs. At hazardous waste sites, the concentrations of explosives in soil may be so high or the population of innate microbes may be so low that degradation of contaminants happens slowly. However, we can add other nutrients to boost microbial activity. The goal is to find the correct mixture of nutrients to add to soil in order to get the organisms to thrive, break down compounds in their feeding, digest the nutrients, and leave behind clean soil.

Scientists and farmers know that robust microbial populations are present in the manure of ruminants—animals that chew again what they have already swallowed, such as cattle, cows, horses, goats, and buffalo. Moreover, the biological activity of these microbes peaks when there is sufficient moisture, abundant oxygen, and a specific ratio of carbon to nitrogen available to the microbes. For example, composting of yard waste works best when one uses plenty of leaves to provide carbon, includes grass to supply nitrogen, adds water, and turns the compost pile regularly to circulate oxygen through it. Unadulterated soil has too few microbes, limited nutrients, inefficient carbon to nitrogen ratios, and insufficient moisture content to promote extensive microbial activity. However, soil composting designs can account for these needs. But they must also incorporate enough of the contaminated soil for it to be worth the expense and effort of treatment.

The U.S. Army has demonstrated that bioremediation technologies can be used to treat soils that are contaminated with explosives.[2] Biological activity from native microorganisms can break down TNT, DNT, RDX, and HMX in soils. From the Army's experiments, it has become clear that bioremediation of explosives must be tailored to the specific site where the contamination exists. Therefore, preliminary studies need to be conducted to develop effective treatment plans at each site.

COMPOSTING AT THE TOOELE ARMY DEPOT, UTAH

Since 1942, the U.S. Army has stored and maintained conventional ammunition at Tooele Army Depot in Tooele, Utah. In 1995, a portion of the depot was designated by the federal government for transfer to private ownership. However, the remaining portion of the depot continues to store, maintain, issue, and dispose of munitions. At the depot, soils at a washout lagoon are contaminated with TNT and RDX. A study of the treatability of soil at the site was completed recently to determine the best way to decontaminate soils at the depot.[3] The study had two stages: a bench-scale test and a pilot-test. In the bench-scale test, 13, 10-gallon containers of compost with different types and amounts of added ingredients—soil amendments—were observed in a field laboratory. The mixtures that worked best to generate effective microbial activity were then duplicated in two 13-cubic-yard pilot-test piles. I describe here the approach and goals of each test and show how, in order to clean up soils contaminated with explosives, bioremediation techniques must create just the right mixture of added ingredients.

To enhance the biodegradation of explosives by composting, contaminated soil from the washout lagoons at Tooele Army Depot was mixed with manure, food waste, and bulking agents. Manure provided abundant microbes. Food waste provided a readily available nutrient source to help the microbes thrive. Bulking agents, such as alfalfa and wood chips, fluffed up the mixture so that oxygen could enter the compost piles. Soil constituted either 20 or 30 percent of the tested mixtures. The studies found that the microbes thrived and broke down explosives when the mixture cooked between 130° and 150°F for at least 20 days. Although hot to the touch, this temperature was ideal for the microbes that consumed explosives.

The composting treatability study at Tooele Army Depot benefited from the results of previous bioremediation composting studies, which had established some basic characteristics of a successful soil composting recipe. The study used locally available amendments because they were inexpensive and readily available. In general, amendments must be tested to determine their nutritional value. Just as fish or eggs have greater nutritional value to human beings than do brownies, some foodstuffs allow microbes to function better by dint of their nutritional value. Local supplies of manure, alfalfa, and wood chips were known to have compositions with good nutritional value for the microbes. Cow manure, like the manure of all ruminants, provides substantial numbers of microbes as well as the carbon to sustain them. Adding chicken manure to the mixture provides high amounts of nitrogen, which are also critical to the success of the composting endeavor. Alfalfa has a beneficial carbon to nitrogen ratio and provides texture to the compost pile. Wood chips fluff and aerate the compost pile and are an economical source of carbon that is moist. These amendments were added to the soil to entice the active microbes to consume the explosives in a frenzy of feeding and thereby utilize the nutrients in the explosives more rapidly than they would have without the additional nutrients.

Previous soil composting studies at sites such as Umatilla Depot in Oregon had showed that potato waste was an excellent primary food source for explosives-eating microbes. We could not use this ingredient at Tooele because potato waste was not available near the Tooele Depot at the time of our treatability study. Instead, we used other (previously untested) vegetable matter—onions, lettuce, and barley for the bench-scale test. In addition, we also tested the benefits of molasses as a soil amendment because it was a readily available source of carbon and moisture at that site.

As a result of the bench-scale tests using onions, lettuce, and barley, we decided to mix lettuce and barley as a food source for the microbes into the bulking materials and manures in the pilot-test piles. A grain, like barley, had never before been used in soil composting. Also unique to the Tooele study, we sprayed molasses onto the pilot-test piles; it increased each pile's moisture content and provided a readily available nutrient source. Our studies showed that the mixture appeared to provide energy to microorganisms in stages: The lettuce was rapidly consumed, barley provided nutrition slowly and evenly, and molasses helped to maintain the temperature of the compost piles for more than 20 days. In the small-volume beds of the bench-scale test, the ability of molasses to boost temperatures was obvious from daily temperature measurements. That observation led us to incorporate molasses into the design of the pilot-test piles.

In the next step of our experimental work, we treated contaminated soil in two separate piles of compost, each approximately 5 feet tall, 16 feet long, and 8 feet wide at their base. Each pile contained soil, cow and chicken manure, lettuce, barley, alfalfa, and wood chips. However, one pile contained more soil than the other, because we were interested in finding the maximum amount of soil that could be added without disturbing the effectiveness of the microbes.

We constructed each compost pile and found that within 24 hours of assembly, the mixture reached the target temperature, which ranged between 130° and 150°F. As noted, we had determined that within this range of temperatures the microbes functioned well. We monitored the compost piles daily to make sure that the desired temperature range was being maintained by the microbial activity. If we found that a pile was too warm or did not have adequate air space, it was turned with a machine that fluffed it. If a pile had cooled below 130°F or was too dry, molasses and water were sprayed on it and mixed in. Each pile stayed warm for 40 days. Because of the thriving microbial population, we needed to add water to the piles daily. The microbes also consumed oxygen efficiently, so we aerated the piles every day as well. On the basis of our daily temperature data, we concluded that the microbes were metabolizing something very energetically, but their effect on the concentrations of explosives in the soils needed to be confirmed through direct measurement.

We measured the amounts of explosives in the compost piles regularly and found that the microbes were indeed digesting these contaminants. In fact, they rapidly reduced the amounts of explosives in the soils to well below the cleanup goals (concentrations below which human health seems not to be threatened). Or course, cleanup goals differ for specific compounds because each substance has different toxic effects. But, remarkably, the average concentration of each type of explosive in the most soil-rich compost pile was reduced to below its specific cleanup goal within ten days. In fact, after 40 days, some explosives concentrations were so low that they could not be detected in laboratory analysis. For instance, at the beginning of our experiments, the most soil-rich compost pile contained 2,000 parts per million of TNT.[4] At the end of the test, its concentration in the compost pile was less than one part per million—a concentration well below the cleanup goal of 94 parts per million.

After 40 days of treatment, the soil and amendments were transformed into a dark, rich, and, most important, nontoxic soil. Although adding the amendments increased the volume of material, the digested compost was only 20 percent greater in volume and had very fine particle size. Much of the material that made up the rejuvenated soil could no longer be visually identified— only occasional barley grains could be seen scattered throughout the soil. After a year of aging to dissipate the ammonia derived from the manure in the soil, we expect that this compost will support some of the most lush plant life seen at the depot.

Based on the extraordinary success of this study and its relatively low cost, it is likely that composting will be used as an innovative solution to clean up explosives-contaminated soil at Tooele and other army depots. It seems, too, that because the rate of degradation of explosives was rapid—as few as ten days to reach cleanup goals—composting can achieve a solution to the problem at these depots rather quickly.

The challenge for the biogeochemist is to apply environmental cleanup approaches in ways that accommodate the particular conditions of a site. Our ability to do so will depend on a thorough understanding of the geology of the soil at a site, the metabolism of the native microbes, and the chemistry of the contaminants. Also, microbial remediation can be used on compounds other than explosives. Much more common, less exotic chemicals such as gasoline and dry cleaning solvents could be digested by microbes. But the types of microbes and the conditions under which they can be coerced to eat such waste differ. Making sense of biogeochemical environments and finding ways to exploit them will allow us to expand our applications of bioremediation to other waste problems.

Part VI

WHOLE EARTH PERTURBATIONS

The Earth's atmosphere, hydrosphere, and lithosphere (air, water, and rocks) know no geographical borders. Together they function as a complex, interconnected system. A change in one part of the system affects all parts of the system—sometimes with dramatic consequences. Natural variability of the Earth's climate system has plunged the entire planet into alternating long periods of icy cold and steamy heat. Previous essays in this book detailed human ability to effect local- and regional-scale change on the landscape. The essays here show that humans may be capable of influencing wider, global-scale change.

In "Ocean Circulation," Steve Stanley narrates a tale of events that carried our planet into the modern ice age some 50,000 years ago, and could catastrophically catapult us right back out of it. From the salt-crusted bed of Owens Lake, California, Kirsten Menking investigates the natural variability in the Earth's climate as a yardstick by which to gauge human-induced climate change. Tamara Nameroff tracks greenhouse gas emissions as a probable culprit of global warming. Finally, linking human and planetary health, physicians Robin Hornung and Thomas Downham scrutinize the consequences of stratospheric ozone depletion.

24

Ocean Circulation: Conveyor of Past and Future Climate

Steven M. Stanley

The geological record tells of Earth's distant past—of mountains rising up and wasting away, of seas flooding continents and receding again, and of distinctive life forms arising and then vanishing to have their places taken by others. Our backward gaze educates and delights us, simply by connecting us with our deep roots, but history for its own sake is not all that geology is about. By studying the distant past, we come to understand how the world around us operates and how future changes wrought by humans may transform our planet and its inhabitants.

Earth's outer shell, together with its oceans and atmosphere, serves as a vast laboratory in which nature conducts experiments on a scale that we cannot faithfully mimic with our own, much simpler physical models and computer programs. Nature's laboratory has been up and running for more than four billion years, and its history has been continually archived through the accumulation of strata and fossils. Although this geological record is far from complete, we can decipher many of its key elements, and the results enlighten us about the functioning of environments and life. What follows is a discussion of one such deciphering. My story is about our global climate: how it has undergone a profound shift within the past few million years and how this vicissitude of the relatively recent geological past informs us about what may happen during the next few decades as human activities alter the natural world.[1]

This story is not confined to the field of geology. It has many geological aspects, some of them involving fossils, but it also entails basic concepts of oceanography and climatology. Such is the multidisciplinary nature of much research in the earth sciences these days. Our planet, its oceans, and its atmosphere interact continuously, and we are finally beginning to treat them as parts of a single system.

We live in an ice age. When I make this statement to an average, well-educated person, the response is disbelief. "I thought that the ice age ended thousands of years ago," is the typical reply. Not so, I explain. What ended was not the ice age but only the most recent glacial maximum, which is to say the most recent interval of glacial expansion. Although we live during an interval of glacial recession for the United States and Europe, an ice cap still blankets nearly all of Greenland; and in about 80,000 years, glaciers are scheduled once again to spread southward to New Jersey and the Alps. We can make this prediction because the ice age that now afflicts the northern hemisphere entails the expansion and contraction of glaciers at regular intervals—intervals dictated by periodic changes in aspects of Earth's rotation both on its axis and in its orbit. These so-called orbital factors change both the amount and the distribution of the solar heat that warms our planet.

Although the glacial fluctuations that result from Earth's orbital motions are environmentally significant, they are nonetheless an epiphenomenon. Far more profound was the global change that plunged the northern hemisphere into the modern ice age to begin with, slightly more than three million years ago—the event that ended a balmy interval and created the cooler climatic conditions that we humans view as normal because our species came into being long after they were in place. These climatic changes brought perennial winter to the northern polar region, where summers had previously been mild, and caused a persistent ice sheet to grow over Greenland, where vegetation had previously cloaked the land. The ice age in which we in North America live is actually best described as the modern ice age of the northern hemisphere, because an ice age that began much earlier in the southern polar region also persists today, and the northern hemisphere itself has experienced other ice ages much further back in Earth's history.

My central topic addresses the cause of this modern ice age of the north, but I will also extract from my explanatory scenario a dire prediction as to what may happen to our planet if we humans do not mend our ways. I will raise the prospect that human-induced environmental change may some decades hence send us plunging precipitously back into the pre-ice age world. The result would be global warming on a scale that scientists have not previously imagined.

A BALMY WORLD BEFORE THE GREAT FREEZING

The northern polar region is the key. Cold in the far north may seem natural from our present perspective, but the top of our planet has actually been bathed in temperate climates during most of the past half-billion years. And so it was before the modern ice age got underway about 3.3 million years ago. During this earlier time, early in the Pliocene Epoch (5.3 up to 1.8 million years ago) when our apelike ancestor nicknamed Lucy and her australopithecine relatives were gamboling about in Africa, the surface of the Dark Continent was even darker than today, because it was moister. Thus, forests and woodlands, which require considerable moisture, were more widespread than they are now, and savannas, which flourish under drier conditions, were less extensive. In fact, back then, many of Earth's terrestrial terrains received more rain than they do today because ocean temperatures were warmer, a condition that led to higher rates of evaporation of surface waters and transport of more moisture to continents. Seas also stood higher relative to continental surfaces than they do now because less of the planet's water was locked up in ice sheets.

Fossils provide abundant evidence of the widespread warmth that preceded the ice age. For example, where shallow seas spread westward beyond Virginia Beach to Petersburg, Virginia, fossils of marine life point to quite mild climates. Although summers there were perhaps no warmer than they are today, winter temperatures were some 9°F higher. Today it is the cold northern polar region that sends frigid air to midlatitudes in winter. Pre-ice age Virginia was obviously spared such icy Arctic blasts. The implication is that the Arctic region was much warmer then than it is today. In fact, there is direct evidence of this condition.

Iceland sits at the juncture between the Arctic and Atlantic oceans. When we understand certain geological indicators, this volcanic island serves as a huge thermometer protruding from the mouth of the Arctic Ocean—a thermometer on which we can read segments of the climatic history of the northern polar region. Rising along the northern shore of Iceland are cliffs of fossiliferous sediment that accumulated in shallow seas shortly before and during the onset of the ice age. Within these strata are so-called tills—gravelly bodies of sediment ploughed up by glaciers early in the history of the ice age. Sediments below the tills give evidence of much warmer climates than those under which glaciers can form. These lower sediments have yielded pollen of ancient coastal land plants that, judging from the requirements of close living relatives, lived in a temperate climate—one that yielded an average annual temperature some 9°F warmer than that of the present.

Fossil shells also abound in the strata of northern Iceland; and at a particular level as one ascends the cliffs, a flood of new species of bivalves, snails, and other forms of marine life appears. Remarkably, these are immigrants of Pacific origins that made their way through the Bering Strait to the Arctic Ocean and through the Arctic to the Atlantic. The most familiar among the Pacific arrivals is the blue mussel, the edible animal that now colonizes rocky shores of the northeastern United States and also Britain, where it is celebrated in the ballad about the vendor singing "Cockles and mussels alive, alive, Oh." The remarkable thing about some of the immigrants that made their way across the polar region is that they cannot tolerate the frigid conditions of the Arctic Ocean today—these are forms assigned to the thermal category for marine life known as cold temperate. Their passage through the Arctic Ocean has been dated at slightly more than 3 million years ago, which tells us that the Arctic at that time had a cold temperate climate. Fossil pollen from North America and Asia tells a similar story. Evergreen forests then grew where tundra now encircles the Arctic. Today, such forests are restricted to more southerly regions where the average July temperature is at least 50°F.

EXTINCTION TELLS OF COOLING

I have spent much time studying the fossil bivalve mollusks—clams, scallops, oysters, and mussels—that inhabited the Atlantic coastal waters of North America during the warm interval that preceded the modern ice age. My interest in this fauna was sparked by the observation that only about 30 percent of its species survive to the present day. This number is less than half the survival percentage for faunas of similar age in California and Japan. In other words, Pacific faunas have been more enduring. Central Florida yields rich fossil mollusk faunas; shells of species that lived slightly before the onset of the ice age are spectacularly preserved, many remaining shiny and some even retaining remnants of color patterns. This region, which is subtropical today, enjoyed a tropical climate before the extinction event. As happens in all marginally tropical regions, some of the species that occupied central Florida just before the ice age were restricted to the tropics, whereas others tolerated cooler conditions. While surveying these species some years ago, I discovered an arresting fact: All the strictly tropical ones were annihilated early in the modern ice age. Every one of the fossil species that survives today ranges well beyond the tropics, around the Gulf Coast to Texas or northward along the Atlantic Coast to the Carolinas. Clearly, the ability to tolerate cool temperatures was the key to survival.

Three great ice caps occupied the land during each glacial maximum of the modern ice age—one centered in eastern Canada, one in Greenland, and one in Scandinavia. These three large ice sheets fringed the North Atlantic Ocean, whereas none bordered the North Pacific. It is easy to see why cooling early in the ice age decimated the North Atlantic marine fauna, whereas the North Pacific fauna was little affected.

WHY AN ICE AGE?

The cause of the modern ice age has long been debated. During much of the last century, an even more fundamental debate raged within the science of geology. The very idea of an ice age seemed at variance with the new uniformitarian view of the planet, which held that all geological features are the products of processes that we can see operating today—volcanic eruptions, for example, and water movements that deposit sand along rivers and beaches, and earthquakes that rend and shift Earth's crust. How could it be that in times past great mountains of ice spread over regions where forests and cities now stand? To many scientists, a less far-fetched mechanism, such as an enormous flood, seemed preferable to account for the transport of boulders far from outcrops of their parent bedrock or for the emplacement of large mounds and sinuous ridges of gravelly sediment.

In time, the glacial hypothesis won out, thanks in part to the discovery in 1852 that ice covered all of Greenland, rather than being confined to its margins. This revelation that a continental ice cap existed in the modern world obviated the uniformitarian objection to the concept of continental glaciation. Then in 1875, geologists discovered scratches in limestone near Berlin that were indistinguishable from ones that had clearly been ground into bedrock in the Swiss Alps by small mountain glaciers. At about the same time, North American geologists traced an irregular rubbly ridge of sediment from Cape Cod to the Pacific Northwest. What could have erected such an extensive structure other than a vast, spreading glacier pushing before it soil, gravel, and boulders ploughed up while it ground southward? Soon geologists universally acknowledged that, quite recently in Earth's history, mountainous glaciers had beset large areas of the northern hemisphere. What followed was more than a century of puzzlement over the cause of this event.

This problem began gnawing at me about two decades ago when I began studying how the sudden chill of the ice age brought an end to the mild climate of eastern North America and wiped out many species of marine life that were ill-adapted to cold winters. Something discouraged me from theorizing about the cause of the ice age, however. This something was the possibility that simple greenhouse cooling was the culprit. The greenhouse effect results from the presence in Earth's atmosphere of certain gases, including carbon dioxide, that trap solar heat like the glass of a greenhouse. It seemed that, just as human burning of fossil fuels intensifies greenhouse warming by releasing carbon dioxide to the atmosphere, some natural change slightly more than three million years ago might have reduced the concentration of carbon dioxide in Earth's atmosphere, diminishing the greenhouse effect enough to cool our planet and trigger the ice age. Then, in 1994, a colleague reported on research ostensibly showing that the concentration of atmospheric carbon dioxide did not decline as the northern hemisphere plunged into the ice age—that greenhouse cooling was not the cause of this profound event. This research has since been discredited, but in 1994 it seemed to compel us to search beyond the greenhouse effect to explain the ice age. Clearly, then, we needed to seek an explanation that entailed changes in circulation patterns of the ocean and atmosphere—changes in the transport of heat, and perhaps moisture, above the solid Earth. Adopting this view, I began to dwell intently on the problem and soon pursued the following line of reasoning.

First, I concluded that a commonly entertained idea must be rejected. This is the notion that the modern ice age of the northern hemisphere began simply because something caused large glaciers to grow. If, for example, precipitation increased, then snow might have accumulated to such great depths over such broad northern regions that its compaction produced large glaciers. The problem here is one of temperature. Before the ice age began, the polar region was much too warm for snow to have persisted at low elevations in summer; and where snow melts in summer, glaciers cannot form. The entire polar region is much colder today than it was shortly before the ice age began; the transition to the colder, modern state is what permitted continental glaciers, including the persistent Greenland ice cap, to grow. In other words, whatever happened to replace the temperate (albeit cold temperate) climate of the far north with the modern Arctic climate was the trigger for the ice age.

The next logical step was to ask what keeps the Arctic region cold today. If we can identify the present refrigeration system and show that it was set in place at the time when the ice age began, then we have an explanation for the ice age.

THE ARCTIC OCEAN IS THE KEY

In the course of geologic time, the Arctic Ocean and the polar atmosphere warm and cool in unison because of their juxtaposition. Because of the high heat capacity of water—that is, its ability to hold heat—we should look to the Arctic Ocean, rather than the polar atmosphere, as the body of fluid that controls the temperature of both. The point is that it takes an enormous mass of air to cool a body of water the size of the Arctic Ocean substantially. On the other hand, a cold Arctic Ocean can easily refrigerate a sizable portion of Earth's atmosphere.

I have come to refer to the upper layer of the Arctic Ocean as the Arctic pond, because it experiences only a weak interchange of water with the Pacific and the Atlantic. The Arctic pond remains cold today because it receives no strong inflow of warm water from the south. It simply assumes the very cold temperature that will characterize any largely isolated body of water in a polar region, where the sun's rays arrive at a low angle. Because of their relative isolation from the rest of the world's oceans, the waters of the Arctic pond are strongly diluted by inflow from large Siberian rivers; thus, they are brackish—or less salty than typical seawater.

Iceland sits near the middle of a broad strait between the Arctic Ocean and the Atlantic. Currents derived from the Gulf Stream carry warm waters northeastward toward this passageway, and they might be expected to flow into the Arctic Ocean, bringing with them much heat. Surprisingly, however, the currents do not continue northward but instead sink to great depths just north of Iceland and double back to the south, eventually surfacing again in the Pacific. By looping downward at the brink of the Arctic Ocean, the Atlantic waters deprive the upper portion of the polar ocean of their warmth. The result is the frigid Arctic pond.

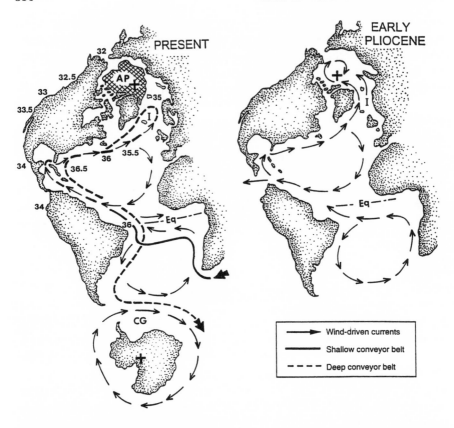

A comparison of northern oceans today and early in the Pliocene Epoch, before the onset of the modern ice age of the northern hemisphere. In the modern world (left), the conveyor belt flow carries surface waters (heavy line) from the Pacific, around the tip of Africa, and through the Caribbean, where they join a wind-driven current (slender arrows) and pass poleward until they sink north of Iceland (I). The submerged conveyor belt waters (dashed line) flow back to the south along a similar course, returning to the Pacific. Largely isolated from the warm Atlantic, the upper waters of the Arctic, which are diluted by river water, form the cold Arctic pond (AP). Numbers in the oceans indicate the salt content of seawater, in parts per thousand; they show that evaporation by the dry trade winds concentrates the conveyor belt waters north of the Equator (Eq), which is why they sink after flowing to the far north, where cooling also increases their density. Pacific waters are less salty, in part because of dilution by water that the trade winds carry across the Isthmus of Panama from the Atlantic. At the other end of the planet, the Circumantarctic Gyre (CG) encircles Antarctica.

Early in Pliocene time (right), before the Isthmus of Panama formed, flow between the Atlantic and Pacific oceans would have kept the waters of these oceans relatively well mixed and similar in salt content. Atlantic waters would not have been dense enough to sink north of Iceland and drive the conveyor belt as they do today, but a wind-driven current would nonetheless have flowed northward through the Atlantic. Being relatively buoyant, the waters of this current should have passed into the Arctic Ocean and warmed it, probably sinking near the North Pole (+) after cooling. The heat that they transported to the Arctic Ocean should have warmed the entire polar region, thereby causing winters here and at middle latitudes to be much warmer than they are today.

THE ROLE OF THE CONVEYOR BELT

The Atlantic waters that descend at the brink of the Arctic Ocean form a segment of the great ribbon of moving water dubbed the oceanic conveyor belt. Waters of the conveyor belt rise up in the middle of the Pacific Ocean and flow westward around the tip of Africa. From there, the conveyor belt flows diagonally across the Atlantic, through the Caribbean, and then poleward. Portions of the conveyor belt, including the segment known as the Gulf Stream, are pushed by the wind, but the main driver of the conveyor belt is its descent north of Iceland under the influence of gravity.

The conveyor belt's waters eventually sink in the north because they have become cool and therefore dense. But this is clearly not the only reason for their descent, because surface waters of the northernmost Pacific are just as cool as those of the northernmost Atlantic, and yet they remain buoyant. A second factor also comes into play: North Atlantic waters are saltier, or more saline, than typical seawater. The high density that causes them to sink and drive the conveyor belt results in part from their cold temperature and in part from their high salt content. They sink in the region where they meet the more buoyant waters at the margin of the Arctic pond.

Because the conveyor belt that deprives the Arctic Ocean of Atlantic warmth owes its existence to the high salinity of the conveyor belt waters, the question that jumps out is whether something may have happened to elevate the salt content of the North Atlantic waters slightly before three million years ago, when the ice age got underway. This would be the event that led to the ice age. To answer this question, we must consider what makes the conveyor belt waters so salty in the North Atlantic region today. Maps depicting the distribution of salinity in this ocean show that the buildup of salt occurs at low latitudes, where the dry trade winds, sweeping westward from the Sahara Desert, evaporate water from the sea surface. Some of the water that the trade winds pick up is dumped in Central America, as monsoon rains, but some of it finds its way to the eastern Pacific Ocean, where it dilutes the surface waters. In other words, the trade winds transfer water from the Atlantic to the Pacific. Thus, as the waters of the conveyor belt pass through the zone of the trade winds, they become more concentrated—more salty. Although these waters become slightly diluted by river water as they move northward, in the area where they descend, just north of Iceland, their salinity remains slightly above the average for seawater.

What might have happened slightly more than three million years ago to initiate the pattern of water movement that makes the Atlantic unusually salty? To answer this question, it is logical to focus on Central America, where the transfer of water to the Pacific takes place. As it turns out, before the ice age began, this region had a very different geographical configuration than it has today. In fact, the Isthmus of Panama did not yet exist. In its place was an oceanic strait connecting the Atlantic and the Pacific. Because of Earth's rotation, winds and currents sweep westward in the equatorial regions of both the Atlantic and the Pacific oceans. When a gap existed between North and South America, the Atlantic equatorial current would have carried saltier-than-normal water of the trade wind belt into the Pacific. Compensating for this exodus of water from the Atlantic would have been a flow of water in the opposite direction—from the Pacific to the Atlantic—deep beneath the ocean's surface. In short, with the two great oceans connected by a sizable strait, their waters would have been relatively well mixed. As a result, their salinities would have been more nearly in balance than they are today; for its part, the Atlantic would have been less saline. All of this had to change when the Isthmus of Panama came into being.

Lo and behold, the modern ice age began at just about the time the isthmus formed. Strange as it may seem, sediment obtained by drilling the floor of the deep sea provides the best means of dating the early stages of the ice age. Cores of deep-sea sediment contain shell-like skeletons of tiny fossil plankton, and the isotopic composition of oxygen in these skeletons records the expansion of glaciers on the land. The basic principles here are easily grasped.

Oxygen comes in two isotopic forms. These are stable isotopes; unlike the radioactive isotopes of some other elements, they do not decay spontaneously. An atom of oxygen-18 contains two more neutrons than an atom of oxygen-16 and is therefore heavier. Water molecules at the surface of the ocean that contain an oxygen-16 atom move into the atmosphere through evaporation more readily than water molecules that contain the heavier isotope, oxygen-18. The result is that the water vapor in clouds that form above the ocean is isotopically lighter than the water below. When such clouds move over a cold landmass and release their moisture as snow, the snow also contains a disproportionately large amount of light oxygen. As a result, when glaciers build up on the land, acting as huge new storage tanks, they sequester from the global hydrologic cycle water that is enriched in oxygen-16. In complementary fashion, the water remaining in the ocean is relatively enriched in heavy oxygen. The result is that organisms that secrete skeletons of calcium carbonate, each molecule of which contains three oxygen atoms, assimilate more heavy oxygen from the surrounding water. When scientists work upward through a deep-sea core, measuring the relative amounts of the two oxygen isotopes in the fossil skeletons of fossil plankton, a pronounced shift toward the heavier isotope generally signals the expansion of glaciers. (Actually, such a shift is magnified by another aspect of skeletal secretion: The relative amount of the heavier isotope incorporated into the skeletons of organisms increases as the temperature of their watery world declines, as it does in many regions at times when glaciers are expanding.)

When the ice age began, oxygen isotopes in seawater began to fluctuate systematically, with reversals occurring every few tens of thousands of years as glacial maxima alternated with glacial minima. A variety of techniques, including dating methods based on the decay of naturally occurring radioactive isotopes, reveal that these fluctuations—and, hence, the ice age—commenced a little more than three million years ago.

The closure of the strait between the Americas cannot be pinned down so precisely in time, in part because it was a somewhat protracted event. The sliver of Earth's crust that now forms the isthmus came into being in the eastern Pacific Ocean millions of years before reaching its present position. It rose up from the floor of the deep sea as an array of volcanic islands. During a regional shifting of vast plates of Earth's outer shell, this group of islands slid eastward to lodge between the Americas. There is geological evidence that the volcanic islands formed a partial barrier more than four million years ago. Fossils, however, reveal that mollusks adapted to shallow water did not become widespread in Panama and Costa Rica until sometime between 3.5 and 3 million years ago; it must have been during this interval that the building of the isthmus was completed. This, then, is when the modern conveyor belt should have been set in motion.

What was the configuration of the Atlantic and Arctic oceans before the Isthmus of Panama wrought its changes? Although the wind-driven Gulf Stream would inevitably have been present, it would have flowed more weakly than today because it lacked the supplemental driving force of the modern conveyor belt. I use the label "modern conveyor belt" because waters may have descended north of Iceland, but closer to the pole than they do today— somewhere in the Arctic Ocean where the waters carried north by the Gulf Stream eventually became cool enough to sink. The key point is that Atlantic waters would not have been dense enough to sink at the brink of the Arctic Ocean, where they do today, and their continued northward flow would have brought much heat to this polar ocean. Here, I believe, is the explanation for the warmth of the pre-ice age Arctic region that we see evidenced by fossil land plants and marine animals.

All this changed when the Isthmus of Panama came into being. The Atlantic Ocean became saltier, and the modern conveyor belt formed, leaving the upper Arctic Ocean only weakly connected to the warm Atlantic and allowing it to cool down in its polar isolation. Here is how we can date the conveyor belt's origin and connect it to that of the isthmus.

The southward-flowing segment of the conveyor belt has deposited sediments in the deep sea, and fossils within these sediments indicate that they began to accumulate slightly before three million years ago. Fossil plankton reveal that the high salinity of the Atlantic—the driving force of the conveyor belt—also appeared at about this time. An isotopic shift toward heavier oxygen in the skeletons of these creatures occurred between four and three million years ago in the Caribbean Sea, along the path of the modern conveyor belt. This region remained warm, however, and large glaciers had not yet grown on northern continents, so the isotopic shift for the Caribbean cannot be attributed to climatic cooling or glacial expansion. The shift must instead have resulted from an entirely different kind of change: increased salinity of Atlantic waters. As we have seen, evaporation preferentially removes isotopically light water molecules from the upper ocean. The shift toward isotopically heavier water in the Caribbean, reflected in the skeletons of plankton, must have resulted from export to the Pacific of the light water that evaporated from the Atlantic. This export was possible only after the strait between North and South America became blocked and the barrier prevented mixing of the two oceans—the Pacific had to retain the water that the trade winds carried to it across the Isthmus of Panama from the Atlantic. The implication is that the Isthmus of Panama became an effective barrier between four and three million years ago. Since that time, the trade winds have transported moisture from the Atlantic to the Pacific, and excessive saltiness of the Atlantic has propelled the conveyor belt.

Support for the scenario I have presented to explain Arctic cooling comes from analogous events at the other end of the world. Early in the age of mammals, about 35 million years ago, climates were very warm at high latitudes on our planet, and then suddenly they cooled. This climatic transition can be traced to events in the vicinity of Antarctica. Then, as now, this continent was centered roughly over the South Pole, but attached to it to form a much larger landmass were South America on the west and Australia on the east. Before the climatic transition, currents from lower latitudes flowed past Antarctica, bathing it in warmth. Then, about 34 million years ago, near the end of the Eocene Epoch (57 million to 34 million years ago), large plates of Earth's upper shell began to move in new ways, breaking South America and Australia away from Antarctica, which was thereby isolated in its polar position. The great counterclockwise currents that cycled through each of the southern oceans—South Atlantic, Indian, and South Pacific—then came to behave like enormous gears, turning another gear in the form of a circular current of water that cycled clockwise around Antarctica. This southern gyre still operates. As happens today, water that became trapped in this gyre must have become increasingly cold as it cycled round and round in its polar location, until its density became so great that it sank to the floor of the deep sea. Then, as now, this cold water spread throughout the deep sea, forming the frigid layer of water at the bottom of the ocean. As this cold gyre formed, it refrigerated Antarctica, triggering the growth of a polar ice cap. Through the transport of its cold waters northward, followed by their upwelling to the surface, the gyre caused climates to cool throughout the world.

This series of events in the south polar region, like the scenario I have described for the north polar region, resulted from movements of Earth's rocky shell. More important, a shared principle lies at the root of each of these reconstructions of a past event of global climatic change: When a sizable body of ocean water becomes largely isolated in a polar region, then that body of water and the atmosphere above it automatically become very cold, and they affect climates throughout the world. (Conversely, a polar region is relatively warm when ocean currents supply it with heat from lower latitudes.) Whereas the isolated body of polar water that formed in the southern hemisphere during the Eocene was a gyre, the one that originated in the northern hemisphere later, during the Pliocene, was a ponded body of water—the uppermost layer of the Arctic Ocean.

The Eocene episode of glaciation and climatic change wrought massive global changes. As oceans cooled, evaporation of their surface waters supplied less moisture to the land; and in the course of several million years, grassy habitats replaced forests in many regions. The result was extinction of many forest-dwelling mammals throughout the world—leaf eaters or animals otherwise dependent on moist, cloistered habitats. The ice age that began later, in the north, caused less extinction of animal life, for two reasons. First, the northern refrigeration system, created by the modern conveyor belt, is weaker than the southern refrigeration system, which is maintained by the current that circles Antarctica. Second, the Antarctic event disrupted a world of remarkably mild, moist climates; the animals adapted to the warmth were these ecologically fragile creatures, ill-fitted to the new, harsher climates. By the time the northern system was set in place, the world had already become what is sometimes dubbed an icehouse world, one that has been pervasively altered by glaciation at one pole. The northern polar system, emplaced more than 30 million years later, simply made things a bit more severe, subjecting many areas at middle and low latitudes to slightly cooler conditions and slightly more pronounced seasonal fluctuations of temperature and precipitation. Of course, Earth's rotational movements have caused climatic conditions to be more severe during glacial maxima of the modern ice age than during glacial minima, such as the one in which we live.

LESSONS FOR THE FUTURE

Might greenhouse warming from our burning of fossil fuels forestall the next glacial maximum? In particular, how might future greenhouse warming affect the conveyor belt, to which I attribute the very existence of the northern ice age? Sad to say, my predictions here are anything but uplifting. Of course, there is debate as to whether greenhouse warming is actually underway. Nonetheless, if we continue to spew carbon dioxide into the atmosphere at an ever-increasing rate, significant global warming will eventually take place—unless northern evergreen forests expand to inhale most of the added carbon dioxide and convert it to plant tissue, or some other as yet unforeseen process compensates for human activities.

Many climatologists predict that if substantial greenhouse warming does occur in the coming centuries, one of the physical casualties may be the oceanic conveyor belt. The idea here is that warmer temperatures in the tropical Atlantic will lead to higher evaporation rates at the ocean surface. This change will enhance an important phenomenon of the present world—the atmospheric transport of moisture to high latitudes, where some of it falls as precipitation. A large increase in precipitation for the northern Atlantic region could dilute the conveyor belt waters to the point where they are no longer dense enough to descend. Thus, the driving force of the conveyor belt would disappear, and along with it, the conveyor belt itself.

Because of heat shed in its direction by the warm waters of the conveyor belt, northern Europe enjoys a remarkably warm climate for its location—the northern half of Germany lies due east of Labrador. It has become conventional in climatological circles to predict that a shutdown of the conveyor belt would plunge Europe into a much colder climate than it experiences today. This view, I argue, is short-sighted. Yes, less heat would be carried northeastward to Europe, but warmer air would flow to Europe from the Arctic. In fact, the entire polar region would heat up considerably—and so, as a consequence, would winters at middle latitudes. This prediction follows from another: Even after future dilution prevents North Atlantic waters from downwelling north of Iceland, a weaker Gulf Stream will remain, driven by wind; failing to sink north of Iceland, the northward flowing waters should continue on into the Arctic Ocean. Even if the inflowing waters become cool enough to sink as they approach the North Pole, they will have transported vast amounts of heat to the Arctic from low latitudes. As these changes get underway, the Arctic Ocean will thaw, and the polar climate will warm. If this chain of events transpires, we will experience global warming on a scale that has not generally been envisioned—we will emerge from the modern ice age.

My apocalyptic scenario is not far-fetched. It parallels one that Knut Aagaard and Lawrence K. Coachman, two experts on Arctic oceanography, advanced as a warning to the Soviet Union in 1975.[2] These American scientists were responding to indications that the Soviets might harness large Siberian rivers, reducing the influx of fresh water to the Arctic Ocean. The surface waters of the Arctic would therefore be left more saline—closer in salt content to typical seawater. Given their increased density, these waters would be more nearly in balance with those of the North Atlantic. Because the North Atlantic waters would not encounter buoyant waters at the brink of the Arctic Ocean, as they do today, the North Atlantic waters would not descend there but would instead flow on into the Arctic, where at some point they would become cold enough to sink. Descent of the Atlantic waters within the Arctic would mix the waters of the polar ocean, eliminating its stratification.

Ironically, relatively warm waters of Atlantic origin flow counterclockwise through the deep Arctic Ocean today. They amount to a subsidiary loop of the conveyor belt, pushing into the polar ocean from the mass of water that descends north of Iceland to drive the conveyor belt. Although warm, this deep water of the Arctic Ocean is quite salty and therefore dense enough to remain below the brackish Arctic pond. Between these two bodies of water and grading into them is an intermediate layer. The lower portion of this intermediate layer is slightly less salty and dense than the loop of conveyor belt water below, so it holds this lower layer in place. The upper portion of the intermediate layer is saltier and denser than the Arctic pond, which therefore floats upon it, so strongly diluted by river water that it can rest on a watery base and so weakly supplied with Atlantic warmth that it remains mostly frozen over.

The layering of today's Arctic Ocean is alarmingly fragile. The intermediate layer that insulates the Arctic pond from the warm Atlantic water below is less than twice as thick as a football field is long, and the Arctic pond itself, which in its frigid isolation refrigerates the entire polar region, is not much deeper than a football field is wide. I believe that if dilution of the upper North Atlantic Ocean allows its warm waters to penetrate deeply into the Arctic before sinking, the modern ice age of the northern hemisphere will come to an end and we will rush headlong back into Pliocene warmth. As temperatures rise around the Arctic Ocean, tundra will give way to evergreen forest, which will further intensify warming by trapping solar heat—a positive feedback. Winters will lose much of their sting, warmer seas will supply more moisture to nearby lands, and forests will invade grassy terrains that receive more rain. More devastating will be the rise of sea level by several feet. Seawater will inundate coastal cities when the Greenland ice cap and other bodies of ice waste away, thereby returning currently immobile water to the ocean.

Of course, we can hope that my scenario will not be tested in the years ahead—that we can manage to avert global warming pronounced enough to push us over the environmental threshold that I have envisioned or across some other, equally disastrous brink that may not yet even come to our attention. Unfortunately, an event of small dimensions on a planetary scale can trigger momentous climatic changes of global proportions. This fact is perhaps the most profound implication of the idea that a spindly little neck of land, by lodging between two great continents, could have set in motion a series of changes in ocean circulation that precipitated the great ice age in which we live.

25

A Record of Climate Change from Owens Lake Sediment

Kirsten M. Menking

Just to the east of California's Sierra Nevada range lies the Owens Valley, a dry landscape of dusty salt flats, alluvial fans, and sagebrush. The valley's spectacular rock formations, in particular, the curiously named Alabama Hills west of the town of Lone Pine, have delighted Hollywood producers for decades with their quintessential western look. Countless spaghetti westerns and car commercials have made use of the deeply weathered granite towers as backdrops. The nooks and crannies in the rocks make excellent sets for gunfights by actors nestled between the boulders; and Movie Road, the aptly named dirt path that winds its way through the spires, provides ample opportunity for sport utility vehicles to test their outdoor mettle before the cinematographer's lens.

Beloved as it is by movie producers, the Owens Valley is a geologist's dream. Faults bound both sides of the valley, allowing it to sink relative to the flanking mountain ranges. Many times in the last few thousand years, rapid movements along these faults have left steep cliffs several feet in height as the valley dropped with a jolt.[1] The semiarid climate ensures that these earthquake features are preserved for thousands of years, thus helping geologists to unravel fault history and, perhaps someday, to predict future earthquakes.

The faults have also acted as conduits for molten rock from the Earth's interior to reach the surface. For approximately the last three million years, lavas have erupted throughout the valley, forming flat-lying flows as well as small volcanoes.[2] The most significant eruption in the region occurred 758,000 years ago, when 130 cubic miles of sticky magma exploded out of the ground, leaving behind an approximately 9 by 21 mile depression known as Long Valley Caldera.[3] Ash from the eruption—called the Bishop Ash after the northern Owens Valley town—blanketed the local environment to a depth of many hundreds of feet.

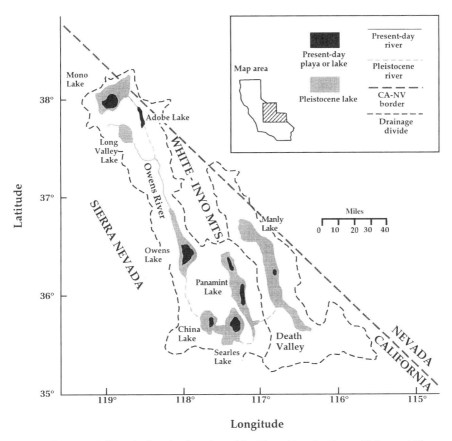

A map of eastern California showing location of the Sierra Nevada, Owens Valley and River, and Owens Lake and surrounding lakes. During the late Pleistocene (approximately 20,000 years ago), Owens Lake overflowed into China Lake. In fact, Owens River water traveled all the way to Death Valley to form Manly Lake.

In addition to its textbook examples of faults and volcanoes, Owens Valley contains clues regarding the history of climate in eastern California over the past million or so years. Geologists working in the Sierra Nevada have found evidence that these mountains were once extensively glaciated. Many of the valleys that feed into Owens are U-shaped troughs and contain rock outcrops covered with long straight scratches, evidence that icy mountain glaciers once inhabited the valleys and that conditions must have been substantially colder and wetter in the past than they are today. The extents of these glaciers can be measured in the deposits they left behind. Called moraines, these piles of sediment—consisting of a mixture of boulders, sand, and tiny clay particles—formed when glaciers melted at their ends, dropping the sediments they carried with them as they flowed down their valleys. When climate warmed and the glaciers melted away completely, the moraines were left behind. By carefully mapping different moraines, geologists discovered that the Sierra Nevada had experienced at least ten separate glacial advances.[4]

In addition to moraines, geologists found other clues that climate in the region used to be much wetter. Owens Lake lies at the southern end of Owens Valley and is fed by the Owens River, which meanders through the valley from its headwaters in the north. The very existence of the lake depends on the faults that bound the valley. For probably the last 9.5 million years, approximately, the valley has been sinking relative to its flanking mountain ranges, becoming a closed basin that traps water and sediment.[5] The southern part of the valley has subsided the most, making it the place where water collects to form a lake. At the turn of the century, Owens Lake extended 105 square miles and was 45 feet deep.[6] All around the lake edge, however, are clues that Owens Lake used to be much larger. This evidence consists of ancient shorelines found at elevations higher than the historic lake level. Looking at these shorelines, geologists realized that the size of Owens Lake changed many times in the past.

Both lake shorelines and moraines are clues that past climate was very different from today's. Neither line of evidence gives a complete history of climatic change, however. If a small glaciation is followed by a larger glaciation, the moraine produced by the smaller event will be wiped out by the larger one. Known to geologists as the "moraine survival problem," this fact ensures that only about a quarter of glaciations are actually recorded in the moraine record. Lake shorelines are also problematic recorders of climatic change. Shorelines represent periods when a lake was at a constant level for a time long enough for waves to do their erosional work. For this reason, rises and falls of the lake surface are not recorded by shorelines.

Luckily, there are geological recorders of climatic change that do operate continuously. Lakes constantly receive water and sediment from their surrounding watersheds, a circumstance making their bottom sediments ideal recorders of the conditions in the local environment. Knowing this, the U.S. Geological Survey embarked on a project in the early 1990s to extract sediments from Owens Lake.[7] Geologists from the Survey hoped to reconstruct the history of lake level changes in Owens Lake, to figure out when glaciations occurred in the Sierra Nevada and to try to link changes in lake level to variations in glacier extent. In so doing, they hoped to find out whether eastern California might one day be in for another glaciation and to derive information about climatic change in the region that could be used to place in context climatic changes that are presently being driven by the activities of humans.

How do geologists use lake sediments to determine that climate has changed? We examine various geological, biological, and chemical tracers in the sediments that respond to changes in climatic parameters like rainfall and temperature. For example, in springtime, as hay fever sufferers well know, the air is full of pollen. This pollen either may be blown directly into a lake or may be washed in via streams. In general, the pollen deposited in a lake reflects the plants in the surrounding watershed. If the composition of the vegetation were to change because of a change in climate, the rain of pollen into the lake would change as well. Different plants have very different ecological requirements. Oaks like much warmer conditions than do spruces. By looking at how the pollen composition has varied over time in Owens Lake sediments, the U.S. Geological Survey scientists hoped to deduce how climate has changed in the watershed.

Another indicator of conditions in the watershed is the type of minerals found in the clay-size fraction of the lake sediments. Clays are tiny particles, much smaller than sand, that are found in soils and other sediments. Glaciers produce many clay-size particles because they drag rocks embedded in their bottom ice over underlying valley floors. The rocks scratch the underlying valley bedrock and are themselves ground down in the process, thereby creating a very fine-grained material called glacial flour. It is this glacial flour that is responsible for making glacial meltwater streams milky in appearance. When glaciers are absent, soils often form in mountain valleys. These soils also contain clay-size particles, but the chemical composition of these particles is usually different from that of the rock from which they formed. Whereas glacial flour consists of finely ground up rock with nearly the same chemical constituents as the rock from which it was produced, soil clays reflect long periods of chemical attack by rainwater and the influence of organic acids from decaying vegetation. By examining the minerals present in the clay-size fraction of Owens Lake sediments, Survey geoscientists hoped to find alternations between glacial flour and soil clays, alternations that would tell when the Sierra Nevada had been glaciated.

The minerals just described are carried to a lake by streams, but minerals can also precipitate—form a solid substance—directly out of lake water, and these crystals give useful information about past conditions in the drainage basin. All the surface waters on Earth contain dissolved compounds derived from the rock and soil over which the water flows. In freshwater lakes with an inlet and an outlet, these dissolved compounds pass through the lake along with the water that is carrying them. In the West, many lakes have no outlet and lose water only by evaporation from their surfaces. As a consequence, the concentration of dissolved compounds in the lake water tends to increase over time, as water continues to bring in new ions—electrically charged elements and molecules—before evaporating away. The ions do not evaporate with the water and instead build up in concentration in the lake. Eventually, the lake water may become so concentrated in various ions that minerals begin to precipitate out of the water, forming crystal sediments on the lake floor. Mineral salts such as calcium carbonate, gypsum, borax, and halite—table salt— are common products of western lakes, many of which have been mined commercially. Cool and wet climates inhibit evaporation and lake waters are perpetually diluted; under these conditions, significant quantities of minerals do not precipitate. Conversely, if climates are warm and dry, evaporation rates may be very high, thus causing widespread salt precipitation.

In addition to mineralogical indicators, lake sediments also contain biological indicators that lake water chemistry and temperature have changed. Single-celled plants called diatoms live in virtually every water body on Earth, but different species are suited to different ecological conditions. Diatoms have very ornate skeletal structures made of silica and each species has a distinctive shape and style, so diatoms are readily identifiable. If information regarding their ecological preferences is known, diatoms in lake sediments can be used to determine how fresh or saline water has been, how warm or cold it has been, indeed, even how turbid or clear it has been.

At Owens Lake, the U.S. Geological Survey scientists hoped to use diatom species and salt mineral fluctuations, among other evidence, to track changes in the size of Owens Lake. From that information, they hoped to deduce changes in climate. For nearly seven weeks in the spring of 1992, I was part of a group of scientists from the Survey and the University of California who drilled into the clays and silts that make up the sedimentary record of Owens Lake.[8] I was a second-year graduate student at the time.

Owens Lake is interesting because its level has changed for reasons other than climate, a fact the Survey would exploit in the drilling process. In the early 1900s, Fred Eaton and William Mulholland, engineers with the Los Angeles City Water Company, conceived of an aqueduct that would transport the meltwaters from the thick Sierran snowpack 240 miles southward to the Los Angeles basin.[9] At the beginning of the twentieth century, the basin was home to only 100,000 people, and the Mediterranean climate was perfect for citrus plantations. The plantations depended on groundwater withdrawals, and Eaton became obsessed with the fact that the Los Angeles Basin was rapidly losing its groundwater supply to overpumping. With its population doubling every few years, the city turned to the Owens Valley as a way to quench its growing thirst. Putting its plan into action, the city of Los Angeles began quietly to buy up ranches on the floor of the valley, thereby securing the water rights.[10] Mulholland's aqueduct, which was completed in 1913, runs the entire length of the Owens Valley, parallel to the Owens River. Creeks that used to flow into the river are now mostly diverted into the aqueduct—a concrete trough that snakes its way across the Mojave Desert. With only a trickle of Owens River water still reaching it every year, Owens Lake rapidly dried up, leaving a thick salt crust behind. This salt crust readily takes to the air with any small amount of wind, giving Owens Valley one of the worst air quality records in the nation.

The desiccation of Owens Lake was not all bad, however, in that the dry surface of the lake bed makes ideal conditions for extracting sediments. Taking sediments from the bottom of a lake can be a very difficult endeavor. Usually, geologists use drilling rigs or coring apparatuses mounted on boats, which must remain fixed in position on a lake surface despite winds and water currents. Seasickness and capsizing are hazards that have to be reckoned with when winds whip up waves on the lake surface. In contrast, at Owens Lake, the dry crust allowed us to drive out onto the lake bed and to set up a drilling rig that remained fixed in place. There was no need to work in a life vest nor any fear of a queasy stomach.

Starting in early April 1992, the Survey drillers set up a drilling rig near the center of the former Owens Lake and cut down through the lake sediments with a hollow tube 15 feet in length and 3 inches in diameter. This tube—called a core barrel—actually consists of two halves that are held together with tape and placed inside another hollow tube—called the drill barrel. The ends of the drill barrel are fitted with sharp teeth that easily cut through the soft lake clays. We geologists waited with anticipation for each new length of sediment to come out of the ever-deepening hole and gazed with tremendous excitement on each section of fresh muck. There is something very exhilarating about being the first person in history to be looking at several hundred thousand-year-old sediments from a particular locale, even if, as in this case, the sediments are mostly monotonous black muds that reek of sulfur, petroleum, and ammonia.

The U.S. Geological Survey drilling team lifts a new length of core out of the ever-deepening hole.

Owens Lake core sediments are largely black muds. Occasionally these muds are interrupted by a deposit of volcanic ash (white layer) or by sandier layers.

A semitrailer rig outfitted with an air conditioning unit became our on-site scientific laboratory. Along one wall of the trailer, we created a workbench on which we could lay out the core tube and sediments. After transferring the sediments to sections of plastic pipe and returning the core tube to the drillers so that they could commence with the next extraction, Survey geologist George Smith described the sediments a half an inch at a time, paying particular attention to grain size, changes in color, presence or absence of fossils, and sediment texture.[11] We hoped that these lines of physical evidence might yield clues about the past conditions within and surrounding the lake. We also took samples from the sediments for various laboratory analyses that would be done in the future. We created a refrigerated core storage area at one end of the trailer by duct-taping up sheets of foamboard insulation to form a fourth wall. As the drilling stretched into June, the core storage area became one of our favorite places to escape the relentless sun of the desert summer.

Graduate student Jonathan Glen brought along a spinner magnetometer, a device used to measure the angle of magnetization of the lake sediments. Earth has a magnetic field that looks very similar to that given off by a large bar magnet. Magnetic field lines, most likely produced by the rotation of Earth's molten iron outer core (at depths of 1,792 to 3,201 miles) around the planet's solid iron inner core (at depths of 3,201 to 3,956 miles), emanate from near the South Pole and wrap around the Earth, reentering it near the north pole. Many times in Earth's history, the magnetic field has reversed polarity, with north becoming south and south becoming north. These flip-flops in the magnetic field are not at all understood, but they may arise from fluid motions within the outer core.

Reversals in the field, which appear to take only a few thousand years to complete, are recorded in magnetic minerals found in volcanic rocks and sediments in much the same way that audio tapes are magnetized by a tape recorder. The last great reversal in magnetic field polarity, the Brunhes-Matuyama reversal, happened ~783,000 years ago.[12] Several smaller near-reversals—called excursions—have occurred since that time. Jonathan used the magnetometer to tell us when we had encountered the Brunhes-Matuyama, ensuring that we had a sedimentary record nearly 800,000 years in length.

For the most part, the sediments making up the upper 650 feet of the Owens Lake core consist of fairly boring-looking black and gray-green mud with occasional sandy units that appear layered or banded in color and/or grain size.[13] There are a few notable exceptions. The first we encountered right at the beginning of the expedition. Directly beneath the approximately 3 feet thick crust of salt formed during the drying up of the lake lies a 13 feet thick layer of oolite, a rock made of tiny spheres of calcium carbonate. Oolite forms in moderately salty lakes that are actively precipitating calcium carbonate. The spheres generally have a nucleus consisting of a small sand grain or piece of shell that is coated in layers of carbonate. Oolite is thought to require fairly shallow water for its formation because the spheres probably pick up their layers by rolling around on the lake floor in response to waves. The presence of oolite beneath the salt crust suggested that the lake had been fairly shallow for some time.

Directly beneath the oolite, the dark muds began. The very fine grain size of the muds combined with their black, green, and gray color—indicative of a low oxygen environment—suggested that we were looking at the remains of a very deep lake. These muds extended to a depth of 650 feet in the core. Occasionally we found a large pebble embedded in them. The pebbles caused great excitement among us because they were evidence that the lake had frozen over, at least partially, at the time the pebble was deposited. Usually, only fine-grained sediments can be transported to the center of a lake because the currents found in lakes are too weak to carry anything larger. Finding a large pebble surrounded by muds then means that the rock must have floated out into the center of the lake on a piece of ice. When the ice melted, the rock fell to the bottom of the lake, becoming a "dropstone." Similar deposits are found all over the North Atlantic from the melting of icebergs. The average air temperature in the Owens Valley during cold winter months is presently about 37°F. If Owens Lake existed today, it would not freeze in winter, because the freezing point for water is 32°F.[14] The dropstones, then, gave us evidence that conditions once were at least 5°F colder in the watershed than today.

Below 650 feet, the sediments changed character dramatically. The dark muds were replaced by layers of sand intermixed with layers of clay and silt. The sandy layers were deposited at times when the lake was fairly shallow, the silts and clays during deeper lake stages. At 980 feet depth, we encountered the

Bishop Ash. Because Owens Lake was so close to the eruption that formed Long Valley Caldera, all the phases of the eruption were captured in the lake sediments. The ash was truly beautiful. At the beginning of the eruption, pink and yellow walnut-sized chunks of pumice—frothy volcanic glass—rained down on the landscape along with snowy white ash. When these deposits fell on land, the heavier pumice fragments were deposited first, the fine ash settling out later. However, in the core, the large pumice fragments are repeatedly found at the top of finer grained ashy sediments. This arrangement suggests that the volcanic sediments fell into standing water.[15] Air bubbles in the pumice fragments took some time to fill with water; thus the large fragments initially floated and took longer to sink than the finer ash. Thereafter, the ash that blanketed the entire landscape was slowly washed into the lake. Current ripples exist in the uppermost section of the ash, defined by thin black laminations in the white sediment. It was only after most of the ash blanket had been removed from the landscape that normal lake sedimentation continued.

In all, the core reached a depth of 1,060 feet below the surface and an age of about 800,000 years. Because most of the lake sediment was simply black mud, physical description of the sediment was not sufficient to reconstruct the history of changes in climate. For this reason, laboratory analyses were necessary. Back at home after the drilling, hundreds of samples were taken from the core and given to different scientists, each of whom performed a specific task on the project. One group dissolved away all of the minerals with strong acids, leaving only the pollen behind.[16] Using a microscope, they carefully identified and counted more than 300 pollen grains per sample and looked at how the percentage abundance of different species varied with depth in the core. Another group examined the remains of organisms that had lived in the lake. Diatoms, mollusks, and fossil fish scales were all painstakingly extracted from the muddy sediments, identified, and counted.[17] Another geologist identified and counted ostracodes, tiny calcium carbonate-secreting crustaceans that live in the lake water and that, like diatoms, mollusks, and fish, are extremely sensitive to lake water temperature and salinity.[18]

Although much of the work done was paleontological, there were also several mineralogical and chemical analyses conducted. I separated the clay-size fraction of the sediments from each sample and then used an instrument that bombards the clay particles with X rays to identify which minerals were present in each sample—clays are too small to be identified with a conventional microscope. I also used a variety of instruments to determine the grain-size distribution of the sediments.[19] Survey geologist Jim Bischoff measured the amount of calcium carbonate present in each sample and also determined the amounts of major elements—calcium, magnesium, potassium, sodium, iron, titanium, chloride, bicarbonate, and sulfate—in each sample.[20]

One of the most important components of a paleoclimate study is the dating of the sediments. Without age control, it is possible to identify climatic cycles, but impossible to say how long they lasted or when certain events last occurred. Three different dating—or geochronologic—methods were used on the Owens Lake sediments. As I've mentioned, Jonathan Glen used a spinner magnetometer to identify the 783,000-year-old Brunhes-Matuyama magnetic reversal. Jonathan also identified the smaller magnetic excursions, whose dates had been determined by earlier work on other lake sediments and volcanic rocks.[21] In addition to the magnetic results, another group of geologists pinned down the age of sediments by using ash layers from various eruptions found throughout the core.[22] Their work—called tephrochronology—uses chemical and microscopic analyses to identify unknown volcanic ashes within a sedimentary sequence. The unknown volcanic ashes are compared with ashes of known age and chemical composition in much the same way that the fingerprints of an unknown criminal are compared with records in the fingerprint library in an FBI crime lab. The third method employed to date the sediments was radiocarbon analysis, which provided dates for the top 35,000 years of the core.[23]

The analyses conducted on the Owens Lake core took several years to complete. Indeed, some studies are still ongoing. The results have been fascinating. The sediments reveal that eastern California has been subjected to very large oscillations in climate over the past 800,000 years. The peak of the last glaciation occurred approximately 20,000 years ago, but this was just the last in a long series of glacial advances that have recurred frequently for at least the last 500,000 years. Moreover, each major glacial advance appears to be matched by an increase in the size of Owens Lake. In fact, Owens Lake repeatedly filled to the level at which it overflowed into adjacent basins. During extremely wet periods, Owens River water probably flowed all the way to Death Valley. The cold, wet periods allowed juniper trees to flourish.[24] These trees were replaced by pines during warmer times, climates that also led to the growth of salt-tolerant diatoms as Owens Lake shrank in size.[25]

Another interesting result of the study has been the discovery of a tremendous drought that occurred sometime in the middle Holocene—the geologic time period that began 10,000 years ago and continues today. Radiocarbon dates at the base of the oolite give an age of 5,100 years.[26] However, the top of the black muds found directly beneath the oolite layer dates to 8,300 years. This finding means that nearly 3,200 years of time are not recorded in the Owens Lake sediments. What could have caused this loss of record? Either Owens Lake dried up completely during the middle Holocene, allowing the soft lake sediments to be blown away by winds, or the lake level fell so low that wind-driven currents in the lake were able to scour the sediment floor. In either case, we know from the date at the base of the oolite that the drought ended 5,100 years ago. Determining the starting year of the drought is not possible with the information we have, because it is impossible to know how deeply wind or water might have eroded the sediment. However, a drought of similar age has been found in many places throughout the Southwest.

In perusing this history of Owens Lake, the reader may ask why it is so important for us to know what climate was like in the past. To answer this question, let's examine a recent climatic event. Between 1986 and 1994, California experienced the worst drought in recorded history. Eight years of below-average rainfall might have seriously disrupted the state's enormous agricultural and industrial economy were it not for water available from the vast reservoirs constructed in the Sierra Nevada in the late 1800s and early 1900s to catch melting snow.[27] With a population of 32 million, California's economy ranks about eighth in the world. It is built on agricultural crops—oranges, strawberries, wine grapes, and artichokes—as well as on high technology, aerospace engineering, tourism, and entertainment. All these industries rely on artificial supplies of water for their continued existence.

Coastal California—including the cities of San Diego, Los Angeles, and San Francisco—is home to 80 percent of the state's population but receives only 15 percent of its precipitation.[28] Most of the rain and snow fall on the Sierra Nevada. As a result, water must be exported hundreds of miles from its point of deposition. The Owens Valley aqueduct is only one of several aqueducts that quench coastal California's thirst. Others siphon water from the Colorado River and the Feather River.[29] In addition, the state stores water in more than 1,200 reservoirs in the mountains.

During the recent drought, strict water rationing was imposed in these cities. Residents were prohibited from watering their lawns and washing their cars; restaurants served water only upon request; hotels and developers of new homes were required to install low-flow shower heads and toilets; and water wasters were fined by water companies for excess use. Despite these provisions, residents looked on with alarm as water levels in the reservoirs continued to drop. Serious discussion was given to constructing desalination plants, such as those used in Saudi Arabia and other arid Middle Eastern countries, to extract drinking water from the ocean. However, as abruptly as it began, the drought ended, leaving many of these plans on hold. Indeed, the drought seems to have faded into distant memory for many people. Unfortunately, geology tells us that this drought will not be the last California will have to endure.

Geologists have found evidence in eastern California of two recent droughts with durations much longer than eight years. For example, tree stumps have been found rooted at the bottom of modern marshes, lakes, and streams in the Sierra Nevada.[30] This finding indicates that these areas were dry long enough for large trees to grow in them before they subsequently refilled with water. Radiocarbon dating of these stumps coupled with counting of tree rings indicates that one drought prior to 1112 AD lasted longer than 200 years and the other, prior to 1350 AD lasted 140 years. Rising water levels drowned these forests as the droughts ended. The drought in the middle Holocene (~8,000–5,000 years ago) recorded in the sediments of Owens Lake was likely longer in duration than either of these. Were such lengthy droughts to occur in modern times, California's economy surely would suffer catastrophically.

A centuries-long drought such as those recorded in eastern California may be responsible for the downfall of the Mayan civilization in Mexico around 750–900 AD. One group of scientists looked at sediments deposited in Lake Chichincanab on the Yucatan Peninsula to determine the history of climate in that region over the last 9,500 years.[31] They found evidence of an extreme drying episode that lasted from 800 to 1000 AD, roughly coincident with the collapse of Mayan civilization. Perhaps this extended drought made food production impossible, a catastrophe leading to famine and migration to more hospitable environments.

Given these examples, it is clear that human societies have a vested interest in studying the climatic and environmental history of their particular home regions as well as that of the Earth as a whole. In particular, it is important for people to understand how past changes in climate led to environmental changes in factors such as water resources and vegetation distribution. If climate changes are found to be cyclical, their recurrence may be predictable, a forecasting ability that would be of great help in land use planning and management. Even if these events are more random in nature—and therefore unpredictable—understanding them can help us develop contingency plans. Thus, in the same way that we today prepare for the next big earthquake, someday we may learn to prepare for the next large drought. The county of Santa Barbara has already done so by constructing a desalination plant to convert seawater to fresh water.[32] The plant is not presently operating, but it is ready for use when droughts return.

Another compelling reason to study the history of climatic change is to try to place human impacts on the climate system into some sort of context. In the last few years, increasing media attention has been given to the phenomenon of global warming, which is thought to be brought about by an increase in greenhouse gas concentrations in the atmosphere. The attention has come about largely because of an apparent change in the frequency of extreme weather events in the last decade. In August of 1992, Hurricane Andrew wreaked havoc in southern Florida. Winds clocked in excess of 170 miles per hour literally tore houses apart. The storm killed 15 people, left 250,000 homeless, and caused nearly $25 billion in property damage.[33] Late spring and early summer of 1993 saw flooding on the Mississippi River the likes of which had never before been recorded. For weeks, storm after storm dumped water in the upper Mississippi drainage basin, saturating the ground and producing enormous volumes of runoff. In St. Louis, Missouri, the Mississippi crested nearly 20 feet above flood stage and remained above its banks for many weeks.[34] Fifty people lost their lives, and thousands of people were displaced from their homes for several weeks to months. In addition, nearly 10,000 homes were totally destroyed.

The summer of 1995 brought searing temperatures to Chicago. A heat wave lasting less than a week led to power outages as people tried to cope with the high temperatures by cranking up their air conditioners. The highest temperature ever recorded in the city—106°F, combined with high humidity to create a heat index temperature of 119°F. Over 700 people, most of them elderly or ill, died from heat stroke or other conditions exacerbated by the hot weather.[35] A similar heat wave occurred in the summer of 1998 in Texas. The state experienced 29 days with temperatures over 100°F. More than 120 deaths were attributed to the heat, as were a minimum of $2.1 billion in agricultural losses.[36]

At the other temperature extreme, a massive blizzard dumped approximately 50 trillion pounds of snow up and down the Atlantic seaboard in early January of 1996, burying many of the nation's largest cities and shattering numerous historical records.[37] New York City, Philadelphia, Boston, Baltimore, Washington, D.C., and many other smaller cities and towns were immobilized for a week or more as state and local agencies struggled to remove the snowdrifts—some as high as 20 feet—that filled every road. As spring arrived, the massive amounts of water discharging from the melting snow caused flooding in many places. In all, the Great Blizzard of 1996 is estimated to have cost the East Coast $7.8 billion in lost commerce, excess expenditures on snow removal, and ensuing floods.

Examples of seemingly bizarre weather events in the last decade are legion—searing heat, monstrous floods, absurdly large blizzards, winds with the strength of tornadoes. The list goes on. Climate change models predict more instability of the climate system as greater levels of greenhouse gases accumulate in the atmosphere.[38] These gases, which include methane, carbon dioxide, chlorofluorocarbons (CFCs), and nitrogen oxides, are very efficient at trapping heat energy given off by Earth's surface, radiating it back to the Earth and warming the planet. Some of these gases have been in the atmosphere nearly since Earth's creation. Others, such as CFCs, are produced solely by humans. Greenhouse gases perform a very vital function for Earth. They are responsible for keeping the planet warm. Without them, Earth's average surface temperature would be about 60°F colder than present, and all water on Earth would be frozen. It would have been very difficult for life to have evolved on Earth in the absence of greenhouse gases. However, since the advent of the industrial revolution, humans have been adding greenhouse gases to the atmosphere, primarily through the combustion of fossil fuels but also through the production of propellants for Styrofoam manufacture (CFCs) and through agriculture—methane produced by rice cultivation and domestic animals. Consequently, the concentrations of some greenhouse gases have risen more than 25 percent in the last century.

As greenhouse gas levels increase, Earth's average temperature is expected to rise. Indeed, instrumental measurements already indicate an increase of about 0.8°F over the last century.[39] With rising temperatures, Earth's hydrologic cycle is predicted to become more active, perhaps leading to a greater incidence of the severe weather events we have witnessed over the past decade.[40] However, skeptics point to events such as the ice ages to prove that climatic change occurred long before humans began adding greenhouse gases to the atmosphere. How can we distinguish between a change in temperature caused by the natural rhythms the Earth has undergone for millions of years and a change brought about by global warming due to increased emissions of greenhouse gases?

Answers to this question can come only from paleoclimatic information. Data from tree rings and ice cores suggest that the last 50 years have been warmer than at any time in the last few hundred to few thousand years. That these 50 years coincide with years of high anthropogenic greenhouse gas emissions may not conclusively prove a link, but juries have convicted criminals on far more circumstantial evidence than this. Furthermore, ice core data have shown that greenhouse gas concentrations and global temperature have varied together in the past 150,000 years.[41] We have no reason to believe that this relationship has changed in modern times. The composition of ice core bubbles has shown that the carbon dioxide concentration of the atmosphere fluctuated between about 180 and 280 parts per million over the last 160,000 years up until the last two centuries. These fluctuations occurred gradually, over tens of thousands of years. In the last two centuries, however, concentrations of carbon dioxide have risen to between 350 and 355 parts per million, a rate of increase unprecedented in recent earth history. Whether ecosystems can keep up with this rapid rate of change remains to be seen.

Through careful examination of tree rings, lake sediment layers, and other evidence, paleoclimatologists have pieced together some of Earth's temperature, precipitation, and storm history over the past 4.6 billion years. We have found that Earth's climate has changed wildly since the planet was born, sometimes for known reasons, but more often for reasons that remain mysterious. Paleoclimatologists have also found that climate swings may be cyclical or random in nature and that they can happen on a variety of time scales, from a handful of years to hundreds of millions of years. The importance of natural variability in climate is beginning to be appreciated, and with this appreciation comes the understanding that humans exist at the mercy of the climate system. Assessing the importance of climatic change to human evolution and history and to our future depends on our ability to determine the nature of climate events—their magnitudes and pace—within the social time frame. Recently, Earth's natural rhythms of climatic change have been joined by human-induced changes. Having a geological perspective on climatic change is critical to our understanding of how human activities may be altering the climate system and of the adjustments we may need to make to cope with future changes. Geological studies such as the one conducted on Owens Lake are part of the continual gathering of evidence needed to put human-induced alterations of the climate system into context.

26

Lessons from the Past for Future Climate

Tamara Nameroff

Maybe people love talking about the weather because it makes us feel connected to our surroundings. Those conversations remind us that, despite our spectacular technological achievements, we are very much subject to nature's whims. An increasing amount of evidence, however, suggests that our actions may be providing some of the fodder for those time-passing conversations. Geoscientists have tied our ever-increasing emissions of greenhouse gases to long-term changes in climate. If our emissions of those gases go unabated, atmospheric concentrations of some greenhouse gases will more than double in the next century, a rate faster than at any time in the last 160,000 years. Continued accumulation of greenhouse gases could cause temperatures to rise higher than anything our planet has seen in 100 million years, with impacts to human habitation, water and food supplies, infectious diseases, ecosystems, urban infrastructure, and floodplain and coastal developments. If the predictions of climate scientists are correct, humanity's potential to alter the climate poses remarkable challenges in terms of both mitigation and adaptation. When our own capacity to alter climate is considered together with nature's ability to effect rapid and significant climate change, developing truly adaptable societies and economies appears to be a formidable task.

Ensconced in climate-controlled buildings in the heart of a big city, it is easy to forget the extent to which human society depends on a stable climate. Climate includes averages and extremes of rainfall, snowfall, temperature, winds and storms, and ocean currents. Climate is not just the magnitude or number of events we experience, but when they happen, as well. The productivity of farms, fisheries, and forests; the livability of our cities in summer and winter; the distributions and abundance of species; and the geography of disease all depend on climate. Likewise, when the climate in some areas doesn't behave as we want, society must pay the costs of engineering environments with structures like sea walls or dikes so that we can live in those places, as well as the property losses and other costs of storms, floods, and sea level rise.

The geological record has important lessons for decision makers today as we try to ensure continued economic growth, social equity, and a healthy environment for ourselves and our descendants. The earth sciences show us how potentially foolhardy it is to pretend that our climate will remain stable in the long term. In their book, *Paleoclimatology*, marine geologist Thomas Crowley and atmospheric scientist Gerald North summarize a wealth of geological evidence that, in the four billion years in which life has existed on Earth, climate has fluctuated dramatically, from ice ages lasting thousands of years to millennia of steamy heat. The rapid and significant natural shifts in climate that happened in the past point to some compelling reasons why we should take steps to reduce the risk of human-induced climate change, as well as insulate ourselves from the impacts of natural climate variability.

The stakes in the climate change debate are enormous. While the calamitous impacts predicted by some scientists might not appear until far in the future, getting serious about reducing greenhouse gas emissions in the near term means we would have to reinvent many of the ways we produce electricity, get to work, build our homes, and manufacture products. Some argue that we should wait for more scientific certainty before acting because the costs of retooling the world economy are significant. Others argue we may already have waited for too long to avoid some costly impacts of a warming world, and further delay ensures future disaster.

THE GREENHOUSE EFFECT AND CLIMATE CHANGE

Given the choice of several neighboring planets, Goldilocks would approve of the Earth. Whereas Venus is boiling and Mars is freezing, Earth is "just right" to support an incredible diversity of life. The Earth's temperature is determined by a balance of incident energy from the sun that warms the planet, less the heat that radiates out from the surface. One of the reasons that all the incoming sunlight is not reflected back into space is because water vapor and other trace gases in the atmosphere—including carbon dioxide, methane, and nitrous oxide—trap infrared radiation emitted from the planet's surface. This natural greenhouse effect keeps the planet about 60°F warmer than it otherwise would be, making the Earth a perfect setting to support life as we know it by providing a blanket of insulation. Because these gases act much like the glass over a greenhouse, they are commonly called greenhouse gases.

Over the last century or so, our emissions of greenhouse gases have increased in near lockstep with industrialization and rapid population growth. Every year, we release more gases into the atmosphere through the combustion of fossil fuels, land use changes, and deforestation than can be absorbed or destroyed by natural processes. Increasing the concentration of any green-house gas—be it carbon dioxide from a cooking fire in Tanzania or nitrous oxide from a fertilizer factory in Italy—increases the ability of the atmosphere to trap heat. And once emitted, these gases stay in the atmosphere for decades to centuries. Because these gases persist for a relatively long time, both the absolute concentration and rate at which those concentrations increase in the atmosphere are important factors in determining the risk of climate change: The effects of today's emissions literally will be felt for generations to come.

HOW GEOSCIENCES INFORM THE CLIMATE DEBATE

One of the keys to understanding future climate is to compare what is happening now with how climate changed in the past. By understanding how climate varied before we started emitting large amounts of greenhouse gases, we gain insight into how nature behaves in the absence of human influence. In turn, we gain insight into the relative magnitude of the stresses we may now be imposing on it.

A network of ground-based and ocean-based sites indicate that average global temperatures have increased 0.5° to 1.1°F since 1880. Increasing the average temperature means that low-probability extreme events of the past become much more common. The National Climatic Data Center of the National Oceanic and Atmospheric Administration predicts that if the average July temperature in Chicago is raised by 5.4°F, the probability that the heat index—a measure that includes humidity and measures overall discomfort—will exceed 120°F sometime during the month increases from 1 in 20 to 1 in 4.[1]

Other indirect evidence also suggests that the climate is warming. Permafrost is melting faster. Many glaciers are receding rapidly. Sea ice is appearing later and melting sooner than it used to. Sea level is rising. And coral "bleaching" events, which happen when the symbiotic organisms are stressed, are being observed more often as ocean temperatures rise.

Climate scientists predict that as the Earth's surface warms, the temperature of the lower atmosphere also should increase. Unfortunately, direct observations of lower atmosphere temperatures do not go back very far. Temperature-recording instruments sent up in weather balloons from the 1960s to the early 1980s show a modest warming trend.[2] An enormous debate has emerged within the scientific community about whether this warming trend has also been observed in more recent data from nine different orbiting satellites, pieced together to form a continuous record from 1979 to the present.

Data from the satellites are used to estimate an average temperature for a region extending from about one to six miles into the atmosphere. Satellites measure microwave radiation from oxygen atoms in the atmosphere. The amount of radiation emitted depends on temperature. To use the microwave radiation data as an indirect or proxy record for atmospheric temperature, scientists calibrate the "radiation thermometer" by determining the mathematical relationship between the amount of radiation measured by the satellites and actual temperature data collected from the balloons. Scientists infer the temperature from the satellite data by using this relationship.

Some scientists have suggested that the satellite data show that the lower atmosphere has cooled.[3] These scientists believe that, because the data are exceedingly precise, have been verified by multiple satellite observations, and have been calibrated against the data collected from the balloon measurements, they provide a better measure of global temperature than the ground-based records do. And because the satellite data show cooling, they reason, concern about human-induced climate change is premature.

Other scientists question this interpretation of the satellite data.[4] Critics of the satellite data have pointed to the relatively short length of the satellite temperature record, as well as the number of assumptions that must be made to calculate temperature from orbit. For example, because satellite orbits change over time, the data must be corrected for the fact that temperature, which varies over the course of the day, is measured at different times for a given location. Corrections must also be made for the changing height of the satellite orbit. Combined with other corrections, critics argue, the number of "fudge factors" needed to estimate temperature trends is so large as to render the data inconclusive. In addition, critics note that the various factors that influence climate, both natural and human-induced, are expected to have different influences on the surface and on the lower atmosphere, so it is not clear whether the satellite- and ground-temperature records are directly comparable. Reconciling the two records has become a high-priority issue for further research and provides an important caution that much remains to be learned about global climate.

Scientific debate during the past few years has attempted to resolve how much of the surface warming observed this century is attributable to human emissions of greenhouse gases. Any human-induced effect on climate will be superimposed on the background "noise" of natural variations in climate. Scientists have discovered that many natural sources can cause the climate to change. For example, on the time scale of greatest interest in terms of the present debate—10 to 1,000 years—solar output, volcanic activity, and changes in interactions between the ocean and the atmosphere such as El Niño all contribute to variability in prevailing patterns of temperature and precipitation. Part of the problem in attributing climate change to human activity is that these natural processes are not yet completely understood. Nevertheless, after an exhaustive review of available research, the Intergovernmental Panel on Climate Change (IPCC)—an international panel of scientists and technical experts sponsored by the United Nations—concluded that the warming trend seen this century is unlikely to be entirely natural in origin.[5]

To put the climate changes that have occurred this century into historical perspective, we must rely on the geological record. Less than 200 years of direct measurements of temperature and rainfall are available, and the reliability of these data decreases as the records go back in time. The challenge for earth scientists has been to figure out how to reconstruct records of temperature, precipitation, and ocean circulation—which themselves leave no trace in the geological record—by using clever proxies for these processes. Small variations in the ratio of oxygen isotopes—atoms of the same element that have different numbers of neutrons in the nucleus—in the calcium carbonate shells of marine organisms can be used to determine how temperature and salinity of surface- and deep-ocean waters changed over thousands of years, as well as how the volume of ice stored in the polar ice sheets varied over time.[6] Long, vertical ice cores recovered from the ice sheets in Greenland and Antarctica record variations in local temperature,[7] global greenhouse gas concentrations,[8] and the dust content of the air.[9] Changing pollen counts in lake sediments reveal how vegetation in the area adjusted over time with shifts in temperature and precipitation.[10] Many other tracers have been developed and ground-tested. Although none is perfect, the fact that multiple tracer studies in particular areas point to the same results gives greater confidence that they are pointing in the right direction.

Temperature variations observed this century are comparable to changes that occurred during the last 1,000 years. Proxy records indicate that climate was relatively stable and that global average temperatures probably fluctuated only about 1.8°F over this time period.[11] This portion of the geological record reveals the sensitivity of human activities to these rather small fluctuations in climate. Increased temperatures in the tenth to thirteenth centuries—the Medieval Warm Period—were enough to make Greenland habitable[12] and allowed several vineyards to be established in England.[13] Return of colder temperatures forced an end to Greenland settlement by 1500.[14] A drop in global temperature of about 0.9°F between 1550 and 1890[15] caused the English vineyards to decline.[16] Not all areas experienced these changes. Temperatures in some locations at that time may have been similar to those of today. In addition, not all areas may have experienced warming at the same point in time.

These millennial-scale climate changes are small when we take a geological view. Changes in the Earth's climate over time scales of tens of thousands of years are dominated by a series of cyclic glaciations. Average global temperature differences between cold and warm periods were as much as 5.4° to 9°F. The slow pulse of the glacial cycle is attributed to small variations in the Earth's orbit around the sun—the so-called Milankovitch effect. These variations alter the seasonal and geographical distribution of sunlight on the planet, which in turn change prevailing regional climate.

Climate changes that occurred on the time scale of tens of thousands of years had profound impacts on the landscape, as well as on human civilization. At the height of the last ice age 23,000 years ago, ice sheets over one mile thick in some places occupied areas now covered by New York City and St. Louis, Missouri.[17] Sea level was lowered more than 300 feet due to the build up of those ice sheets, and this allowed humans to emigrate from Asia to North and South America over the great Bering land bridge.[18]

A high-quality ice core recovered from Antarctica demonstrates that atmospheric concentrations of greenhouse gases and temperature are intimately linked.[19] Because it only takes about one year for the atmosphere to mix completely, bubbles of air trapped in each year's snowfall provide a detailed record of changes in the composition of the atmosphere. As that snow is compressed into ice by growing layers of snow above it, an unbroken record of climate change is locked away. Changes in the ratio of hydrogen isotopes in the ice chronicle variations in regional temperature. The ice core shows that over the last 160,000 years, concentrations of greenhouse gases were significantly lower during cold periods than during interglacial warm times. For example, 23,000 years ago, the concentration of carbon dioxide was about 30 percent lower than it was before the start of the Industrial Revolution. The regional temperature over Antarctica was about 16.2°F cooler when greenhouse gas concentrations were lower. Although the ice core record shows that temperature and greenhouse gases are coupled, it does not show clearly that increases in greenhouse gas concentrations precede increases in temperature. Although carbon dioxide follows temperature very closely during periods of warming, it lags behind temperature changes during periods of cooling.

Reconstructing climates older than 160,000 years is a more uncertain business. From available evidence collected from deep-sea sediment cores, it appears that over the past million years, warm periods such as the one we enjoy today were relatively rare.[20] And if we look back even further, from 2 to 200 million years ago, the geological record suggests that the Earth was much warmer than it is today.[21] When dinosaurs roamed the Earth during the Cretaceous period (136 to 65 million years ago), global temperatures might have been 10.8° to 14.4°F warmer than today. Carbon dioxide concentrations likely were significantly higher, as well.

Although the estimated levels of atmospheric carbon dioxide for these ancient times are uncertain, the amount thought to be present in the air during the Cretaceous is comparable to estimates of the yet-unused amount of coal and other hydrocarbons still locked away in the Earth's depths. We have used only about 5 percent of the available fossil fuel reservoir to date. Barring a radical change in the way we use energy, continued reliance on fossil fuels could mean that people living in 2400–2700 AD could see levels of atmospheric greenhouse gases and temperatures close to those last experienced by *Tyrannosaurus rex*, which lived during a period that probably was as warm as any time in the last billion years.[22]

INTEGRATING THE GEOSCIENCES WITH OTHER SCIENTIFIC TOOLS

While evidence of past climate changes helps illuminate what could happen in the future, it is not a perfect crystal ball. We cannot take any time period in the past as a reliable analogue of what climate might look like in the future because our records are imperfect, which in turn affects our ability to interpret them. The biggest problem is that much of the geological record is smoothed as if by sandpaper. In effect, the "shutter speed" of the available camera frequently is too slow to record fast changes. What results is a sometimes blurred picture of the past. For example, most marine and lake sediments are stirred constantly by animal life. Combined with a relatively slow rate of sediment deposition, the climate signals recorded in the mud reflect changes that may have occurred over several thousand years. Despite these limitations, these proxy records are immensely valuable because they help us place some relative constraints on climate changes that occurred throughout the Earth's history.

With respect to current debates about how much climate might change because of human activity, the value of the geological record is that it can help improve the quality of predictions about future climates. Computer models simulate interactions among ice, sea, land, atmosphere, and sunlight to make predictions of how changing concentrations of atmospheric greenhouse gases might affect climate. Historical data help computer programmers attempt to match their climate models with past conditions. Some argue that if the models can reproduce the past, then it is more likely that they can accurately predict the future.

Despite the wealth of historical data, computer models are far from perfect because the system that scientists are trying to emulate is extraordinarily complex. The models are only as good as the real-world physics on which they are based. And for many parts of the world, the physics is largely guesswork. The models also are limited by the power of computers. Nevertheless, the geological record helps constrain how much temperature and precipitation might have changed in a region, thereby allowing scientists to sort out the relative importance of different physical mechanisms and manifestations of climate change such as rainfall, cloud formation, and ocean circulation. Current models can simulate seasonal variations and climate over thousands of years, leading most scientists to take their overall projections seriously. Using historical data to "tune" the models, the IPCC concluded that by 2100, global average temperatures will increase between 1.8° and 6.5°F if we do nothing to decrease greenhouse gas emissions. To put this change in context, the IPCC's high-end projection of temperature increase in the next 100 years is comparable to the difference in global temperature between the depths of the last ice age and the present.

Another prediction of the climate models is that extreme weather events such as droughts and heavy precipitation could become more common as the climate warms. Cool air holds less water than warm air does, so, as the atmosphere heats up, a possibility exists that when it rains, it will literally pour. Some data suggest that this change in weather patterns may already be underway.[23] In the United States, for example, yearly rainfall has increased nationwide in the last 100 years. In some coastal areas, like Connecticut, it has increased as much as 20 percent. In California and Wyoming, it has fallen by a corresponding amount. The data also suggest that a greater proportion of rain now falls in deluges of two or more inches of rain in a day.[24] These extreme rainfall events can contribute to flooding, erosion, and water quality problems.

Because of limitations in the climate models, projected specific impacts such as the rate, timing, and magnitude of warming in particular locations remains to be determined. On the basis of the body of emerging science on regional impacts of climate change, it is probably safe to say that both good and bad changes could occur, and regional winners and losers will emerge.

The most probable and significant losers are inhabitants of coastal areas. In addition to melting polar ice sheets, higher temperatures cause water to expand. The IPCC predicts that both these factors could contribute to a sea level rise of between 12 and 36 inches in the next century. Rising seas could destroy the viability of some small island states, particularly in cases where the economies of those nations cannot bear the cost of constructing sea walls or relocating inland. Sea walls would do little to help nations in danger of being entirely inundated. Because a significant proportion of the global population lives near coastlines—in the United States about half of the population lives near the coast—shoreline erosion, saltwater intrusion into freshwater supplies, and coastal flooding may also adversely impact those areas. Agricultural disruption due to rising seas may be significant because about one-third of global croplands are in coastal areas.

Natural ecosystems also could suffer, depending on the rate and magnitude of regional changes in climate. Ecosystems have adapted to the steady warming that has occurred since the last ice age, but large and rapid climate changes could be disruptive. Pollen records suggest that temperate forests migrate naturally at approximately 62 miles per century.[25] However, the optimal growing zones for these species could be displaced much more rapidly as a result of temperature changes. Some studies predict that these conditions could be displaced as much as 200 miles for every 4°F of warming. Systems that are already stressed or hemmed in because of human population growth may be particularly affected—there literally could be no place for these species to go. Although climate change is unlikely to decimate vegetation and make land barren, except in limited areas that are now arid and may become even drier, the composition of ecosystems is likely to change as rapidly moving and widely dispersing species—weeds—increase in number and slower-moving species decline and disappear.[26]

Some areas could benefit from a warmer climate. Since 1900, most of the warming that has occurred has been experienced between 40° and 70° north latitude. In the northern United States, for example, the growing season already has lengthened by about one week. As a result of future warming, it could be extended, thereby allowing for more food production—nutrients, pests, and precipitation permitting. Increased carbon dioxide uptake by some types of plants could partially offset some of our greenhouse gas emissions.

But the geological record gives us no reason to assume that climate change will be completely predictable. High-resolution records constructed from Greenland ice core data suggest that climate can "flicker" rapidly between cold and warm modes. During glacial times, a typical leap involved an 11°F change in polar air temperature in the North Atlantic region, a fivefold change in atmospheric dust (a measure of dryness on the continents), and a 20 percent change in the carbon dioxide content of the air.[27] These changes could have occurred over just a few years as a result of changes in North Atlantic circulation. The ice core records demonstrate that climate *can* change abruptly in time. And because some of the climate changes recorded by the ice are regional in nature, the records demonstrate that climate change does not always happen uniformly over the globe. The possibility of "climatic surprises" may be the real danger of climate change, human-induced or natural.

Although a surprise is by definition speculative, numerous examples of abrupt climate change exist in the geological record. On the basis of historical evidence, scientists have suggested that the most likely culprits for causing such a transition probably would be melting of the Arctic ice cap or the West Antarctic ice sheet as a result of increases in temperature; the meltwater could exacerbate sea level rise. Some evidence suggests that these ice sheets have disappeared in the past.[28]

Geochemist Wallace Broecker of Columbia University and paleontologist Steven Stanley have proposed independently that a change in circulation in the North Atlantic could be the Achilles heel of our climate system. Pushed along by the Gulf Stream, the Atlantic "conveyor belt," with the flow of about 100 Amazon Rivers, brings warm water north from the Equator. Evaporation leaves the belt with a higher salt content than the rest of the North Atlantic. The water cools as it heads north. The heat released from the water keeps Europe 10.8° to 14.4°F warmer than it otherwise would be. The now cold and salty water sinks as it approaches Iceland and Greenland, traveling far below the surface in a south-moving return flow. If increased rainfall over the oceans changed the salinity of the northward belt, or if the sea-surface salinity near Iceland and Greenland were lowered because of polar ice cap melting, the Atlantic circulation could change drastically. Shutting off the conveyor belt would almost certainly cool the North Atlantic and its adjacent lands; it is also possible that the effects would be felt worldwide.[29]

Some of these climate "flip-flops" appear to be linked to growth of the continental ice sheets during cold times. Evidence that vast iceberg armadas repeatedly flowed into the sea appears in marine sediments recovered from the North Atlantic as layers of rock fragments from northeastern Canada that are interspersed between clay sediments dating from the late Pleistocene (roughly 60,000 to 12,000 years ago). The weight of the large ice sheets on the northern North American continent may have induced earthquakes that sent these armadas into the North Atlantic.[30] Broecker has estimated that, during the course of the almost 50,000-year glacial period, 20 similar climate shifts occurred.[31] The geological evidence shows that we cannot ignore the possibility of abrupt and rapid climate change in our future.

TOWARD A SUSTAINABLE FUTURE

The evidence of past climate variability coupled with the potential for additional changes in the next century and beyond as a result of our own actions poses a significant challenge to our ability to achieve a sustainable future. Most of our infrastructure and institutional decisions—where to build, where to live, what to leave untouched—assume that past patterns of temperature and precipitation, storm frequency and severity, and sea level are a reasonable surrogate for the future. The body of research demonstrating that climate is capable of very large changes ought to put to rest any argument that these patterns will remain stable, through natural checks and balances, in the face of our increasing emissions of greenhouse gases. Both the predictions of human-induced climate change and evidence of natural swings in climate suggest we must do a better job of planning and preparing for change.

Because it is not our nature to focus on problems that occur over geological time scales—such as the appearance of the next ice age—policies over the next 20 to 100 years likely will focus on the magnitude of human-induced impacts and the effect of natural variability on those forecast changes. Although we don't understand everything about the system, the potential for serious impacts to the well-being of nature and humans in this time frame due to climate change—human-induced or natural—is significant. All the evidence shows that the Earth is a dynamic system that could respond to increasing levels of greenhouse gases in unpredictable ways; it could do so sooner rather than later because of our greenhouse gas emissions. Natural variability of the type experienced over the last 1,000 years could modify the expected effects of increased greenhouse gas concentrations—either masking an underlying warming trend early on or accelerating the rate at which it occurs. From what we know, the effect of natural variability is likely to be smaller than the warming we might expect from human activity.[32] It is this line of reasoning that has led many to call for a serious effort to reduce greenhouse gas emissions worldwide.

Such an approach may not define a complete road map to a sustainable future that takes all the implications of climate change into account. In other words, mitigation is only part of the solution. The effects of greenhouse gases we have already released have not yet completely materialized because oceans delay heating of the atmosphere. Every year, concentrations of greenhouse gases rise as our emissions exceed the ability of forests, oceans, soils, and plants to soak them up. We also need to take into account the slow response time of the system. Any change in emissions trajectories won't have an effect for at least a generation because greenhouse gases stay in the atmosphere for decades to centuries after they are emitted. We need to link our mitigation efforts with adaptive responses in our technology, institutions, regulations, behavior, and economy.

Achieving a future of low greenhouse gas emissions and adapting to new climates in ways that are consistent with our aspirations for economic growth, environmental protection, and social justice will require an holistic approach. This approach could include gradual changes in human behavior and tastes, and new management and regulatory mechanisms that vary with the climate. We can also take steps now to anticipate future climates by adjusting our planning, engineering, and regulatory strategies to take into account the vulnerability of different areas.

One example of this coupled adaptation–mitigation response is found in international efforts to protect the ozone layer. Development of new technologies made it possible to ban production of many substances that harm the ozone layer. In addition to an aggressive timetable to eliminate the production and use of many ozone-depleting chemicals, governments and other organizations helped raise public awareness of the health and environmental impacts of a thinning ozone layer. Although the analogy between ozone and climate protection is not perfect—greenhouse gases are released from a range of sources and climate change will require a much broader array of adaptation measures—these efforts demonstrate that we can apply an integrated approach if we are serious about addressing a global problem.

Developing responses to climate change that put us on a solid course to a sustainable future need not focus exclusively on achieving greenhouse gas emissions reductions. We can protect the climate at the same time we meet other goals for economic growth, environmental protection, and social justice because an array of fiscal, statutory, and regulatory policy tools influence patterns of energy and land use. Even if the purpose of those policies is not to modify the human activities that emit or remove greenhouse gases from the atmosphere or affect our ability to adapt to a changing climate, they may coincidentally advance or hinder our efforts in these matters. Our response to urban sprawl—the rapid growth of metropolitan areas—helps illustrate these linkages. Policies to control urban sprawl in the United States are frequently motivated by desires to protect open space.[33] The climate-related benefits are not usually considered explicitly. More compact development can help lower greenhouse gas emissions by reducing the need for travel in cars and the total distance traveled. Protecting open space for recreation or farming means that trees, soils, and vegetation on that land can continue to remove carbon dioxide from the atmosphere through photosynthesis. Preserving "green space" can also help ensure that plants and animals will have a place to migrate if the local climate changes.

The array of potential economic, environmental, and social impacts associated with climate change also can be minimized by increasing the ability of our society to respond to the kinds of disasters that we must already contend with, and might intensify if the predictions of climate scientists are correct. The degree of adaptation needed from different sectors and in various regions will vary. In some cases, climate change could significantly weaken already fragile systems. For example, prairie pothole wetlands—marshy areas that occupy depressions in the landscape in dry climates with small watershed areas—are very vulnerable to changes in their water supply. These ecosystems are sensitive to changes in snow cover and associated spring runoff, droughts, and increased climate variability. Already strained by losses of at least 50 percent in North America, prairie wetlands yield 50 to 75 percent of all North American waterfowl produced in any year. Any additional stress from rapid climate change (or other factors) could be accommodated only through active programs to protect, enhance, and increase wetland areas in this region.[34] Other systems may be more robust. If climate variability remains the same as at present, adaptive strategies such as a change in sowing dates, the genetic makeup of crops, and crop rotation patterns will continue to offset expected production losses in the agriculture sector in Europe, as long as such strategies are not counteracted by government or other polices.[35] In both of these cases, contingency planning, ecosystem management, and research and development could help increase the resiliency of these systems and minimize the negative impacts of a changing climate.

Some contingency planning efforts already underway could be applicable to a more broadly defined climate change strategy. Following the 1993 floods in the midwestern United States, a multidisciplinary team of experts recommended that the Mississippi River basin floodplain should be managed as a system rather than as a patchwork of individual components. The team also recommended returning some agricultural areas to wetlands, relocating some communities, and improving floodplain management by using better scientific and technical information. Not all the team's recommendations were implemented. However, some communities took the offer of federal assistance to break the cycle of flood-and-rebuild and thereby avoid the future social and economic costs of flooding disasters. Residents of Pattonsburg, Missouri, a small community that was nearly destroyed by the floods, worked with federal agencies charged with implementing the recommendations to move the town—literally—to higher ground. The community seized this opportunity to incorporate concepts and technologies for a more sustainable future at all levels of their relocation scheme, from the physical structure of the new town to economic strategies for redevelopment that include measures that could help them mitigate and respond to the effects of a changing climate. The town's buildings are energy- and resource-efficient, street design is pedestrian-oriented, and the town's layout maximizes southern exposure to each home, giving residents the best opportunity to use passive solar heating to lower their energy needs.[36]

Many states already have taken steps to ensure that growth in the coastal zones and the potential loss of resources will be planned for and managed. The State of Maine, for example, requires removal of development to allow dunes to migrate inward as sea level rises. Other examples of adapting to sea level rise include policies that require development to be set back from the shore by a prescribed distance, standards for infrastructure development, research, and education.

A SUSTAINABLE FUTURE THAT REFLECTS LESSONS FROM THE GEOLOGICAL RECORD

Going back in time to look at how climate has changed teaches us a valuable lesson that we should consider when we set climate policy goals. Natural forces will cause climate to change, irrespective of our actions. Although we can seek to limit human influence on the climate, we must also be prepared for the changes nature can impose on its own. Records of past climates from thousands to millions of years ago provide us with a good reference of the range of possibilities with which human society may one day have to reckon. However, over the time scales that we are best able to plan for—the next 20 to 100 years—the current buildup of greenhouse gases in the atmosphere poses special challenges. Meeting them will require us to think creatively about how to mitigate and adapt to changes that will occur. Designing strong and flexible institutions has important benefits for coping with both human-induced and natural changes in climate. Creating a society that can adapt readily to inevitable change is an important component of both climate policy and a strategy to build a sustainable future. The geosciences can certainly help us achieve these goals.[37]

27

Nature's Sunscreen: Ozone Depletion and the Health of the Whole

Robin L. Hornung and Thomas F. Downham II

If you make an enemy of the Earth, you make an enemy of your own body.—Mayan shaman

Imagine an Earth where there are no tree frogs singing throaty, rhythmic songs throughout a still summer night. Imagine an Earth where the quiet rustling of a tree's leaves in a gentle breeze cannot be heard. Imagine an Earth without plentiful crops of delectable melons to savor on sunny afternoons. Imagine an Earth without magnificent great fish dominating the seas. Imagine an Earth without human beings. Such an Earth existed in the early Cambrian Period over 500 million years ago—it was an Earth without an ozone layer.

About 450 million years ago, the Earth acquired what is today called the ozone layer. This thin layer of the atmosphere is located mainly within the planet's stratosphere, a layer of the atmosphere located approximately 6 to 30 miles above the Earth's surface. The stratosphere sits atop the troposphere, which extends from the Earth's surface to heights between 6 and 11 miles, depending on where it is measured.[1]

The formation of our Earth's ozone layer allowed marine organisms to evolve into land-dwelling creatures, for it protected them from the lethal effects of ultraviolet radiation. Until then, Earth's land surfaces had been inhospitable places for more than 4,000 million years. In geologic time, formation of the ozone layer happened quickly. Yet the consequences of its formation for life and evolution on this planet were profoundly meaningful and persist today.

SOLAR RADIATION

The sun and stars spontaneously emit energy in the form of electromagnetic waves. This radiant energy comprises the electromagnetic spectrum, which is divided into multiple regions according to the wavelength of the electromagnetic waves. From a health perspective, some of the most important electromagnetic energy occurs in the form of infrared, visible, and ultraviolet waves because this radiation reaches the Earth's surface. (X rays and gamma rays do not reach the Earth's surface and therefore do not contribute to biological processes.) Infrared radiation constitutes 40 percent of the radiant energy reaching the Earth's surface. It contributes to warmth because infrared waves—sometimes called heat waves—are produced by hot objects and are absorbed readily by most materials. Infrared radiation keeps life on this planet from freezing—and is not typically associated with health hazards to living things. Visible light—perhaps the most familiar form of electromagnetic waves—is that part of the electromagnetic spectrum that the human eye can detect. Ultraviolet radiation is produced by the sun, and much of it is absorbed by atoms in the stratosphere. It is often used to kill germs—ultraviolet lamps are sometimes placed above grocery store meat counters to reduce spoilage.

Many important and complicated life processes such as photosynthesis, vision, and vitamin D synthesis require visible and ultraviolet radiation. Clearly, life could not exist on Earth without electromagnetic radiation. However, too much exposure to some forms of electromagnetic radiation can have untoward health consequences.

Photobiology is the scientific study of the effects of visible and ultraviolet radiation on living matter. Medical photobiologists refer to short wavelength ultraviolet radiation as UVC or "germicidal radiation." This type of radiation can be lethal to organisms because deoxyribonucleic acid (DNA), ribonucleic acid (RNA), and the proteins of cells absorb these wavelengths and are distorted. "Germicidal lamps" in hospital operating rooms emit UVC and produce a sterile—germ-free—environment for surgery. The Earth's atmosphere screens most UVC so that, unlike longer wavelength ultraviolet radiation, generally it does not reach the Earth's surface. Medium wavelength ultraviolet radiation is called UVB radiation. It *does* penetrate the Earth's atmosphere and causes the bulk of harm to the health of animals—including humans. The shorter the wavelength of the UVB radiation—that is, the more like UVC it becomes—the greater is its potential for harm. The longest wavelength ultraviolet radiation is called UVA or "black light" radiation because, although it causes certain substances to emit fluorescent colors, the human eye cannot see such light under normal conditions. Like UVB radiation, UVA radiation readily reaches the Earth's surface. In fact, more UVA radiation reaches the Earth's surface than UVB radiation, but it is a much weaker form of ultraviolet radiation and therefore less harmful. In the practice of medicine, both UVB and UVA are used in "phototherapy" to treat certain diseases.

The amount of ultraviolet radiation that reaches our biosphere varies with season and latitude. Some of the variation is predictable and due to well-determined factors such as the sun's altitude above the horizon and the annual change in the distance between the Earth and the sun. Geographical location also effects the amount of ultraviolet radiation present at the Earth's surface—measurements of ultraviolet radiation have shown that relatively short wavelength ultraviolet radiation is present at high altitudes (e.g., on top of mountains in the Himalaya) whereas at sea level, only the relatively long wavelength ultraviolet radiation is present.

OZONE IN THE STRATOSPHERE AND TROPOSPHERE

Ozone in the stratosphere is a highly unstable molecule made up of three atoms of oxygen (O_3). It is formed in the stratosphere when ultraviolet rays from the sun split apart oxygen molecules (O_2) and thus produce single oxygen atoms (O)—free oxygen—which are available to combine with molecular oxygen to form ozone.[2] Because ultraviolet radiation is most abundant in the upper atmosphere, the highest concentrations of ozone occur there. A dynamic balance of generation and degradation controls the amount of ozone in the stratosphere.

The atmosphere surrounding the Earth actually contains very small quantities of ozone. If compressed to a pressure equal to the pressure at the Earth's surface, the ozone layer would be less than a quarter of an inch thick. Given this fact, it is quite amazing that ozone in the stratosphere prevents 95 to 99 percent of the sun's ultraviolet radiation from reaching the Earth's surface and absorbs much of the sun's dangerous ultraviolet radiation. Because they are so important to the health of living things, we must understand these processes that sustain or destroy ozone in the stratosphere.

Stratospheric ozone has become known as "good" ozone because of its ability to protect humans from the harmful effects of ultraviolet radiation. In contrast, ozone in the troposphere is often referred to as "bad" ozone because it can cause a variety of adverse effects on living things. Ozone is produced in the troposphere in the following manner. Fuel combustion in automobiles produces a steady supply of nitrogen oxides. Ultraviolet rays from the sun break apart the nitrogen dioxide (NO_2) molecules, thereby releasing free oxygen (O). The free oxygen combines with molecular oxygen—just as it does in the stratosphere—to form ozone. Ozone in the troposphere can cause eye, nose, and throat irritation, eye damage, and breathing problems—including asthma severe enough to require hospitalization. Tropospheric ozone also kills plant tissues; large stands of trees in forests in Europe and around the Los Angeles basin have been killed by ozone pollution in nearby cities.[3] Along with nitrogen oxides and hydrocarbons, ozone is also a component of smog—itself responsible for respiratory problems, reduced visibility, and damage to vegetation.

DESTRUCTION OF STRATOSPHERIC OZONE

In the early 1970s, scientists were concerned that planes flying at high altitudes would damage the stratospheric ozone layer. While studying the composition of the stratosphere, they found that chlorofluorocarbons (CFCs)—a class of synthetic gases that have been used as coolants in air conditioners and refrigerators, propellants in aerosol cans and metered-dose inhalers, and puffing agents in Styrofoam manufacture—released into the atmosphere react with ultraviolet light and form chlorine. Chlorine reacts with ozone to produce molecular oxygen and chlorine monoxide (ClO). The chlorine monoxide reacts with single atoms of oxygen to form more molecular oxygen and release more chlorine. In other words, once chlorine is introduced into the atmosphere by CFCs, it reproduces itself forever. Recognition of this cyclic process alarmed scientists, such as future Nobel prize winners F. Sherwood Rowland and Mario Molina, who in 1974 warned that industrial processes could ultimately destroy ozone in the stratosphere.[4] Although scientists could not yet measure damage to the ozone layer, theoretical evidence for such destruction was compelling. As a result, in the late 1970s, the federal government responded to these warnings—in 1977, Congress passed amendments to the Clean Air Act that authorized the administrator of the Environmental Protection Agency to regulate substances affecting the stratosphere; and in 1978, the Environmental Protection Agency banned the use of CFCs in most aerosols.

In 1985, a group of British scientists who had been monitoring stratospheric ozone levels for 30 years found a significant thinning—or a "hole"—in the ozone layer over the Antarctic. This hole extended over a region that was the size of North America.[5] In this region, ozone concentrations had dropped to as low as five percent of their former levels.[6] They also determined that the hole was seasonal, lasting three months during the Antarctic spring and summer. Then, the National Science Foundation sent a group of researchers to Antarctica later that year, and they ultimately concluded that chlorine chemistry was involved in ozone depletion and that the hole was getting larger.[7] Subsequent studies have determined that the ozone layer has thinned over other parts of the southern hemisphere, such as Australia and New Zealand, and in the northern hemisphere, especially over the North Sea. Ongoing satellite monitoring of the ozone layer provides convincing scientific evidence that the problem is real and that the global trend toward ozone depletion needs to be monitored and carefully considered by policymakers.

By 1987, the scientific community organized a historic international agreement, the Montreal Protocol on Substances That Deplete the Ozone Layer. The document set a strict timetable of step-by-step reductions in CFCs and ozone-depleting substances, leading to a total ban on production by 2000. It has since been amended at meetings in London (1990), Copenhagen (1992), and Montreal (1997) to accelerate the CFC phaseout plan and to limit emissions and eventually phase out use of methyl bromide—a substance used to fumigate soils and crops—which may be responsible for ten percent of the ozone loss so far. Overall, the protocol aims to eliminate emissions of human-made ozone-depleting substances. However, full implementation of the protocol is necessary to achieve a satisfactory recovery of the Earth's protective ozone shield over the next 50 years.

The ozone layer is in a vulnerable state. Although global consumption of CFCs has decreased from its peak in 1988, ozone depletion is still proceeding twice as fast as expected over parts of the northern hemisphere. Ozone-depleting substances in the stratosphere are expected to reach maximum levels before the year 2000; and according to the World Meteorological Organization, the ozone layer will be thinner than ever by 2000 or 2001. Because the life of ozone-depleting substances already in the stratosphere is long, a depleted ozone layer is forecast to remain for at least the next several decades before the amount of ozone in the stratosphere returns to its pre-1960s concentrations.

What does this all mean for ground-level ultraviolet radiation? Evidence suggests that ozone losses of three to six percent in the northern hemisphere render an increase of surface sunburn (UVB) radiation of four to seven percent. In the southern hemisphere, an ozone loss of five percent translates to a six percent increase in surface sunburn radiation.[8] Have we acted too late to prevent widespread harm from a depleted ozone layer?

HEALTH AND BIOLOGICAL EFFECTS OF OZONE DEPLETION

Understanding causes of and mechanisms for ozone depletion can also lead us to comprehend its potential consequences for human health and other biological systems. What can happen with rapid depletion of the ozone layer? The scientific literature contains abundant documentation of the potential harmful effects of ozone depletion. Because the main consequence of a thinning ozone layer is an increase in the amount of ultraviolet radiation that reaches the Earth's surface—specifically UVB radiation—we must examine the consequences of overexposure to it.[9]

The degree of damage that ultraviolet radiation produces in skin, for example, depends on the intensity (dose), the wavelength (UVA or UVB), and the depth of penetration. Exposure to high doses of UVA exposure can cause delayed sunburn (erythema) reactions to tanning. Acute effects on the skin from UVB radiation include sunburn, blister formation, and destruction of the outer protective layer of skin—the epidermis—with or without infection. Chronic skin changes due to both UVA and UVB exposure eventually may cause skin cancer, pigment changes, or ongoing "photoaging." A recent significant study has shown that, after it interacts with UVA, a skin protein changes shape; chronic exposure leads to sustained photoaging.[10] Ongoing studies indicate that newer sunscreens must have components to protect against both UVA and UVB wavelengths in solar radiation.

One of the most prevalent and serious current public health problems is the escalating epidemic of skin cancer. There are three main types of skin cancer: basal cell carcinoma, squamous cell carcinoma, and melanoma. The United Nations Environment Program has estimated that over 2,000,000 basal cell and squamous cell carcinomas (nonmelanoma skin cancers) and 200,000 malignant melanomas occur globally each year. These figures are likely to be an underestimate because in the United States over one million new non-melanoma cancers will be diagnosed this year alone. In the event of a ten percent decrease in stratospheric ozone along with current trends and sun-worship behavior, an additional 300,000 nonmelanoma and 4,500 melanoma skin cancers could be expected worldwide.[11] Skin cancer now represents the most common malignancy in the United States and the world today. In fact, approximately one in five Americans will get skin cancer in her or his lifetime.

The basal cell and squamous cell carcinomas are the most common types of skin cancers. Fortunately, although these cancers make up the majority of all skin cancers, they are the least aggressive. Nevertheless, they can sometimes cause death; but the most serious issue is deformity. These carcinomas easily can cause enough damage to destroy large areas of the skin or other vital structures such as the eyes, ears, and nose. Melanoma, on the other hand, can be an extremely aggressive cancer. Although it makes up only 4 percent of all skin cancers, it causes about 75 percent of all skin cancer-related deaths, and its incidence has been rapidly rising. In 1935, only 1 in 1,500 people developed this type of cancer; now the figure stands at 1 in 87. It is projected that by the year 2000, 1 in 75 Americans will be diagnosed with melanoma.[12]

Significant scientific evidence demonstrates a very strong association between ultraviolet radiation exposure and malignant degeneration in the skin. Now we know that DNA absorbs ultraviolet radiation and that the absorbed energy causes bonds in the molecule to break, thus leading to genetic damage. With this strong cause-and-effect relationship, it makes sense that increases in ultraviolet radiation at the Earth's surface could lead to more incidents of skin cancer. Estimates suggest that a one percent decrease in atmospheric ozone will result in rates of nonmelanoma skin cancer that are two to three percent higher than those of today.[13] Studies of disorders involving the inability of an organism to repair defective DNA have established a clear link between ultraviolet-induced DNA damage and various types of skin cancer.

Another hazard from overexposure to ultraviolet radiation is eye damage. After receiving high doses of ultraviolet radiation, people and animals can develop a temporary clouding of the cornea, often referred to as "snow blindness." More chronic ultraviolet exposures can lead to cataracts, which are permanent changes in the cornea that lead to blindness. Interestingly, there are higher incidences of cataracts found in lower latitudes (near the Equator) and at higher elevations, both areas where ultraviolet radiation intensity is high. About 12 to 15 million people in the world are blind because of cataracts. The World Health Organization has estimated that up to 20 percent of cataracts—or three million per year—could be due to eye exposure to ultraviolet radiation. Recent estimates project that each one percent decrease in stratospheric ozone would cause an increase of half a percent in the number of cataracts caused by solar ultraviolet radiation.[14] The United States government spends over three billion dollars in health care for more than one million cataract operations per year.

There is now significant evidence that ultraviolet radiation can impair an organism's overall immune system—the natural defense system that fights infections and cancers. Laboratory studies have demonstrated significant immune suppression or dysfunction in animals—mice, rats, and guinea pigs—when they are exposed to ultraviolet radiation for protracted periods of time. In humans, it is well known that UVB sunlight triggers certain infections, such as the herpes simplex virus that causes the common cold sore. Ultraviolet radiation not only suppresses the immune response, but in some situations it can actually trigger it, causing hypersensitivity and autoimmune reactions. Specifically, sunlight may trigger an autoimmune disease, such as lupus erythematosus. In a disorder like lupus, after interacting with ultraviolet radiation the body's immune system reacts to its own DNA in the same way it reacts to infections. Specific vital organs in such a situation are targeted for attack by an autoimmune process, and a key part of therapy is protection from solar ultraviolet radiation.

Another substantial concern is that ozone depletion could lead to deleterious worldwide biological effects. A ten percent reduction in stratospheric ozone could lead to ultraviolet radiation exposure that is as much as fifteen to twenty percent higher than at present. This radiation would affect marine phytoplankton, plants, and food crops and disrupt balanced ecosystems. Phytoplankton and plants vary greatly in their sensitivity to UVB radiation. More than half of all agricultural plants tested have demonstrated reduced quality under increased UVB exposure. Many terrestrial plant species have demonstrated lower photosynthetic activity and subsequent reduction in stem and leaf growth when exposed to UVB. Although aquatic phytoplankton have adjusted to equatorial habitats where levels of ultraviolet radiation are over 1,000 times higher than in polar regions, the rapidly thinning and patchy ozone layer may produce challenges to the survival of sensitive Antarctic phytoplankton. Indeed, one large-scale field survey of Antarctic regions showed that there was a 6 to 12 percent drop in phytoplankton productivity during development of the springtime ozone hole.[15] Loss of the plankton biomass may seriously disrupt functional relationships in the finely balanced marine food web.

Also notable is the marked decline in amphibian populations worldwide. Although habitat destruction is likely the predominant cause, evidence suggests that UVB plays a significant role. Much of the decline is occurring at higher altitudes where amphibians lay eggs in shallow, open water. UVB penetration into the water can lead to fungal infections that overwhelm and destroy the amphibian eggs. Increasing UVB radiation could finally damage the DNA and proteins of all living creatures and could thus become a cause of species extinction and loss of biodiversity.[16]

Destruction of stratospheric ozone is one of today's major environmental issues. In fact, some researchers maintain that we are in the middle of an ultraviolet radiation experiment on a global scale. Unlike many other environmental problems that threaten the health of the planet, ozone depletion has received the attention and action of countries worldwide.

However, it is important to think about the Earth as a complete system and to consider perturbations to it. These very serious threats include global warming; habitat destruction and loss of biodiversity; air, water, and soil pollution; and species extinction. Geologic time puts the latter into perspective. Before the rise of *Homo sapiens* on Earth, the average projected life span of any given biological species ranged from one to ten million years.[17] Current extinction rates have led to a predicted life span of 10,000 years for bird and mammal species. This interval is a drop in the bucket of geologic time, yet the consequences may be greater than ever before. At today's rapid rates of species extinction, it is almost certain that this period in Earth's history will be characterized as a time of global mass extinction.

Like animal and human physiology, the Earth's physiology is profoundly complex. Furthermore, these physiologies are linked, because our physical environment is undoubtedly the most important determinant of animal and human health. Humans must develop an ongoing concern for a healthy environment, and we must attempt to solve current and future problems that will threaten our existence in an evolving global environment. But it is only after we come to understand Earth's complex physiology that we will begin to understand the ways we can preserve planetary health, and therefore the health of all living creatures that inhabit this shared space. We must understand the ozone layer as well as other parts of a globally perturbed system to ensure a habitable planet.

Part VII

GLOBAL PERSPECTIVES

How should one end a book whose goal is to invigorate purpose and promote a fresh beginning? These final essays express, albeit in divergent ways, the greater philosophical and humanistic lines of inquiry that geoscience inspires. Which ethical tenets and choices will current and future societies espouse? What will be critical to the survival of the Earth and its inhabitants?

Beyond the traditional bounds of scientific method, Victor Baker lauds the connection between the observer and the observed in geology and presents it as the most natural of the sciences. Jill Schneiderman and Virginia Ashby Sharpe raise the principles of liberty and equality in search of just distribution of environmental risks. E-an Zen writes about the essence of human dignity and explores how the "rivers" of the world's societies can abandon paths of overconsumption and waste production to achieve such dignity. Finally, Ed Buchwald takes the long view of a precarious future and provides us with a way to ascertain the most basic knowledge we need to comprehend and anticipate the challenges sure to confront all of us, and our Earth.

Taken together, the essays contained here should provoke innovative thought—and action.

28

Let Earth Speak!

Victor R. Baker

In his history of earth science, entitled *The Dark Side of the Earth*, British geophysicist and science writer Robert Muir Wood argues that geology reached its intellectual peak around 1900.[1] During the twentieth century, according to Wood, geology's intellectual decline coincided with the rise of modern physics, chemistry, and biology. In the 1960s and 1970s, however, a new earth science developed, replacing anachronistic "geological" concerns and methods with the global view and scientific methodologies of geophysics. Geochemist and science minister of France, Claude Allègre offers somewhat similar views on how much modern geochemical science has supplanted the "mapping mentality" of geology.[2] According to these scholars, rigorous, scientific geophysical, geochemical, and (presumably) geobiological approaches are now replacing the outmoded geological one.

Wood diagnoses the cause of geology's presumed intellectual stagnation: Geology is a science marked by the "failure to separate man's experience from the object he wished to study."[3] Geology, he maintains, has retained its bond with the Earth at a time when mainstream science has become more objective—more detached from the subject matter it isolates in experimental "systems" or explains via computer models.

The modern success of physics, chemistry, and biology would seem in some ways to bolster Wood's arguments. The twentieth century has witnessed spectacular advances in human understanding of the universe, the human body, the nature of matter, and even our own minds. The associated explosion of technology has generated space exploration, the conquest of disease, and phenomenally increased agricultural productivity. Recently, evolutionary biologist Edward O. Wilson has even argued that the highly successful web of causal explanation linking the natural sciences deserves to be extended to the social sciences and humanities.[4] He describes this ideal alignment with the term "consilience," a term he borrowed—and somewhat redefined—from the writings of the Cambridge mineralogist William Whewell.[5]

It is a paradox of our modern time that this immense success of science is being questioned at the very height of its achievement. Even as we search for a new national rationale for science to replace Cold War policies focused on defense, industrial policy, and international prestige, the scientific establishment is being criticized by politicians, the media, and humanist scholars. Science is faulted for its privileged status, cases of fraud and misconduct, its seeming lack of concern to achieve a more humane society, the degraded natural environment, the high stress of the modern technological world, and even for moral decline. As to the possibility of Wilson's consilience of the sciences and humanities, the eminent philosopher Richard Rorty echos the opinion of many humanist scholars when he observes, "it is not clear that our answers to . . . moral . . . questions will be improved by better knowledge of how things work."[6] Both Rorty and Wilson agree that science is knowledge and power; they disagree on the universal application of that knowledge and power.

Scientists can readily prepare logical arguments as to why various criticisms are unfair, untrue, and unrealistic. Before taking satisfaction in such idealism, however, one should note that scientists are subject to the same pragmatic principle that governs other members of a society: It does not matter whether an idea or concern of people is real or not; if people believe it is real, then it will be real in its consequences. The present state of "science literacy" among the potential believers of our society does not give comfort that their reasoned understanding of science will thwart any adverse consequences of current antiscientific trends. Indeed, the rampant and growing science illiteracy may be the single most disturbing trend in a democratic society that has become so technological and science-driven.

THE UNNATURAL NATURE OF MODERN SCIENCE

What do the spokespeople of modern science say about this paradox? Who indeed are the spokespeople? In contrast to the situation 100 years ago, they are not geologists. Science is spoken for by physicists, chemists, and biologists, typically with the physicists confidently explaining how, why, and for what purposes science is done. Physicist Alan Cromer argues that science (physics) involves an "uncommon sense" about the world.[7] This can only be appreciated through rigor and discipline, by learning the facts and often counterintuitive laws of nature. Lewis Wolpert, a distinguished biomedical professor, provides great detail on this "unnatural nature" of modern science, illustrating it with the latest theories and discoveries of molecular biology.[8] The implications of this view for science education, environmental problem solving, and public understanding are ominous. Physicist Morris Shamos concludes that extensive

science literacy is impossible.[9] At best, one should strive for public appreciation of science—presumably to keep the money flowing for its support.
Cromer advocates the rigorous and disciplined inculcation of scientifically
proven facts and methodology, abandoning recent "constructivist" approaches
that allow students to exercise their own common sense.[10] (Ironically, it was the
creation 100 years ago of the supposedly rigorous biology-chemistry-physics
high school curriculum that led up to our present science illiteracy. The argument that it will be reformed by the same failed philosophy is fascinating
indeed.)

These arguments are laden with value judgments about science. Such an
axiology—philosophical theory of values—is ironic in view of the claim by
many analytical philosophers and scientists (speaking as philosophers) that
science is "value free." Although interesting as a metaphysical topic, such
scholasticism ignores the obvious fact that the practice of science has consequences for society, and that these consequences are judged in value-laden
terms. Moreover, in their everyday practice, scientists impose various values or
norms upon themselves as they compete for funding, prestige, and power. Science is conducted by human beings, and all human beings impose and react to
values.

It is fashionable in the logic-chopping of modern philosophy of science to
set up arbitrary divisions for rhetorical advantage when comparing one class of
science with another. Thus, for various unstated presumptions, deductive science is considered superior to inductive; more mathematical to less mathematical; and generalized/predictive to particular/unique or historical. The presumptions leading to this axiology come from norms in the pure sciences.[11]
They also lead to a presumed hierarchy of sciences in which predictive and
experimental sciences that are pure—not applied—occupy the top positions
in a hierarchy, whereas mathematically less sophisticated historical and
descriptive sciences, especially when applied, fill the low positions.[12] Little
wonder then that many geologists aspire to move from their underworld status
to one more similar to that of mathematical physicists.

The relationship of science to society is mutually sustained by a complex
of shared values. However, the inability of the general public to understand science is only matched by the inability of most practicing physical scientists to
understand the social world. For this reason, the shared values of science and
society take the form of "myths." Such myths tie together complex issues and
suppress the need to question the synthesis that they afford. From his experience with science policy, geologist Daniel Sarewitz identifies five myths that
apply to the relationship of science to society, as follows: (1) science provides
infinite benefit to society; (2) any fundamental line of research is as likely to
benefit society as any other; (3) the research system is made ethically pure
through its system of peer review; (4) science provides the objective basis for
societal decisions; and (5) scientific knowledge is a valid end in itself, without
considering its moral and practical consequences in society.[13] But this is the

present state of affairs. Science is spoken for by those who equate it to physics, arguably the least natural of the natural sciences. Its virtues are extolled for public appreciation, sustaining various myths adhered to by a populace mostly unfamiliar with the workings of science and technology. A nasty intellectual argument—the so-called science wars—rages among humanist scholars, relativist social scientists, and self-appointed spokespeople for scientific purity.[14] We are, to paraphrase Dickens, clearly in the best of times, and simultaneously in the worst of times. During such times of crisis, it is well to go back to fundamentals. Might geologists say anything differently about such matters?

GEOLOGICAL SIGNS

Whether one relates to the world scientifically or nonscientifically, that relationship is not direct. It is mediated by observation, experience, and thought. Experience is the undergoing of things generally as they occur in the course of time. Through a sequence of causal connections, the environment also undergoes changes through time, thus constituting a kind of natural experience available to be interpreted by the geologist. Through that interpretation, this natural experience becomes continuous with the thought and experience of the geologist. Ultimately, this continuity of experience, from observed environment to observing geologist, leads to wisdom about what is observed. The nonscientist in society has an experience of encountering both the natural environment and the scientist's characterization of it.

Thought involves some connection to experience, a connection that can be quite formalized, as in the case of science, or less formal and more reliant on common sense, as in the case of the nonscientific public. The obvious framework by which such thought connection occurs in people is language, or more generally, by means of signs. Semiotics—the study of signs—holds that all experience, natural and human, is pervaded by an interpretive structure mediated and sustained by signs.[15] In this structure, signs stand for something—an object—in relationship to something else—an interpretant. An excellent example of such a relationship is the fossilized bone of an extinct dinosaur. The bone stands for the dinosaur. Indeed, it was the past existence of the dinosaur that caused the bone to be a sign of that existence. Now what of the interpretant? The bone is encased in strata that mark the evidence of its relation to other bones, from which the connection to the dinosaur can be realized by a clever paleontologist. The interpretant is that aspect of the sign relationship that connects the bone to its origin. This relationship is virtual in the strata, always having the potential to be realized by a paleontologist.

The interpretant of a sign itself becomes a sign. The geological strata signify both history and processes, and they do this in relation to other strata, which indicate other histories and processes, which lead on and on in endless connections. Similarly, the paleontologist may name or describe the bone in a way that indicates an object—the dinosaur—associated with knowledge triggered in other paleontologists about this relationship (bone-to-dinosaur), which, in turn, will produce other unending associations. Note how this process constitutes an unlimited action of signs. The subjective aspects of thought by paleontologists, the objects of inquiry—dinosaur bones, and their historical and causal connections—are all related through this action of signs.

What is going on here? Is this uncommon sense? Is this an unnatural way of reasoning about the world? There is a logic here, but one less akin to experimental or theoretical physics and more akin to that of the investigator at a murder scene. Consider a detective who finds a small hole in the wall and an embedded lead particle. The detective's observation might serve as the test of the theory—or model—that a gun was used in the crime and that it fired a bullet that made a hole. Of course, other theories could explain these circumstances. Perhaps the gun that fired the bullet was not related to the crime. Viewed as the action of signs, however, the crime theory is not the immediate concern. Instead, the detective is a student of bullet holes, much as Sherlock Holmes was a student of exotic tobacco. It is a rather secure notion that the hole and embedded lead particle provide an index of a process, gunfire. The detective studies this clue—sign—and combines it with other clues, developing a web of interconnecting clues. Eventually, a narrative connecting these clues emerges as the hypothesized solution of the crime.

The model-testing approach of sciences like physics and chemistry is limited to the particular model—or crime theory—in mind.[16] Detectives formulating controlled experiments and testing models are not the stuff of interesting murder mysteries. In contrast, the semiotic approach exemplified by the paleontologist is part of an open process of inquiry that readers of detective stories will recognize immediately. Lest the logic of this analogy seem trivial, I note that the logic of detectives is exactly the same as that of hypothetical reasoning in science. Semioticians Umberto Eco and Thomas Sebeok develop a full analysis of this "logic" through reference to detective stories by Edgar Allan Poe and Conan Doyle.[17]

EARTH LOGIC

Logic is the science of sound reasoning. It is a formal science, in that it concerns how reasoning ought to be done. It is in the philosophical basis of its logic that classical geology parts company with experimental and theoretical physics. Now, the philosophy of logic must seem to be the most obscure of subjects to introduce at this point. Indeed, the very word *trivial* derives from old pejoratives applied to scholastic studies of logic. The topic has led to storied arguments over the number of angels able to alight on the heads of pins.

The prevailing philosophy of logic, going back to English philospher and political economist John Stuart Mill, who was also the intellectual archenemy of William Whewell, is that logic provides a system of names for patterns of inference; there is no reality in these names per se, although the thought systems described by these names may refer to real objects. In scientific application, the thought systems are conventions, and science seeks a correspondence of these thought systems to measured attributes of the real world. It is in the course of controlled experimentation that the thought systems of theories and hypotheses come to mirror the real world. Much of physics and the philosophy of science describing its methods relate to this logical basis.

That the above philosophy of logic—called nominalism—does not apply to geology has much to do with the structure of sign relationships described in the previous section. The paleontologist can only know the connections of thought to dinosaur bones through this web of signs, just as Sherlock Holmes can only solve a mystery through a web of signs (clues) left as past traces of causation. Neither Holmes nor the paleontologist can perform controlled experiments on the whole problem. Both, of course, can and often do perform smaller "experiments" on elements of the whole problem, working out physical or chemical details. However, the eventual solution depends on developing a coherent picture of past connections, rather than performing some key experimental test. Both Holmes and the geologist must take the world as it is.

There is another subtle difference in how logic is applied through our language. This subtlety can be appreciated from a story concerning the great physicist Niels Bohr. A young scientist was asking Bohr about quantum mechanics, a subject for which Bohr was an originator. Quantum mechanics involves the most fundamental behavior of matter and energy, which make up the entire physical world. It is also one of the most successful of all physical theories, in that its counterintuitive predictions have been experimentally verified to an amazing degree. Moreover, no subject better illustrates the "unnatural nature" of science and its "uncommon sense." The young scientist asked Bohr what this great theory of physics told us about what nature is like in reality. Bohr answered, "It is wrong to think that the task of physics is to find out how nature is. Physics concerns what we can say about nature."[18]

For the reasoning of geologists, logic must be a part of the semiotic structure, tied by signs to the natural world. Physicists try to say the best things possible about nature, using a nominalistic logic to make clear, sound, and concise statements. They use mathematics to make many of their statements, because no more clear, sound, and concise form of expression is known. Indeed, British physicist John Ziman defines physics as the "*science* devoted to discovering, developing and refining those aspects of reality that are amenable to mathematical analysis."[19] In contrast, the thought system of geological inquiry does not separate neatly from the object being studied. What Robert Muir Wood termed a "failure" of geology is something actually imbedded into the nature of the reasoning that geologists must do.[20] The experience of geologists is not separate from the object they wish to study.

This is not a trivial issue. It means that geology, unlike physics, does not take the position of being about what geologists can say logically about the

Earth. Geologists must take a logical stance that amounts to a kind of conversation with the Earth, but a conversation in signs analogous to the conversation in clues so familiar in detective stories. Geologists understand this metaphorically, as the great German field geologist Hans Cloos so eloquently put it:

> We decipher the earth's diary that has been left us as a legacy. We read with trained senses and interpret with the tools of disciplined thinking. We translate the earth's language into our own, and enrich the already bright and colorful surface of the present with the knowledge of the inexhaustible abundance of the past.[21]

This is not merely a different methodology from the analytical theorizing and controlled experimentation of physics. This is a completely different point of view. It is certainly not nominalistic logic. For want of a better name, and to highlight its geological expression, I call it earth logic.

HOW EARTH SPEAKS

Generations of young physics students have been admonished to learn their calculus with a quote from Galileo—usually taken out of context. To paraphrase, the book of the universe is written in the symbolic language of mathematics; to read the book of the universe, one must learn this language. Sometimes physics teachers add that one does not actually read calculus from nature, rather the predictions made by using calculus to express physical theories are mirrored in nature. For geologists, mathematics provides a useful tool for explanation, but it does not constitute the language of Earth's text.

Geologists have long applied a commonsense approach in which signs directly represent causative agents and present a great text by which to interpret those agents. This earth text cannot be understood fully via a nominalistic language imposed by human convention. The sign language of geology is partly conveyed through interaction with nature itself. Various landforms, sediments, fossils, and artifacts all constitute the sign language within which geological reasoning occurs. By adopting this approach to science, geologists are led into a process of inquiry that leads them to understand nature's reality. They need not delineate systems to facilitate explanation, using the methods of physics.

There is one major philosophy of reasoning that was built upon a motivation to purge logic of detached and disconnecting nominalistic tendencies—that of the great American polymath Charles S. Peirce. Peirce's life contains many fascinating points, some of which delayed recognition of his philosophical genius.[22] Even more amazing is that this prolific philosopher spent his professional career as an earth scientist, measuring Earth's gravity, and was tutored for six months in paleontology by Louis Agassiz, the great Swiss naturalist and professor at Harvard University whose glacial theory transformed geology. Although his logic has only recently been extensively tied to that of geology,[23] there is considerable evidence[24] that Peirce personally or indirectly influenced the thinking of American geologists Grove Karl Gilbert, T. C. Chamberlin, and William M. Davis, all of whom wrote classic papers on the philosophy of geology between 1880 and 1930.[25]

The realist philosophy of Charles Peirce is a very complex affair, for which good syntheses have only recently appeared.[26] It was Peirce's insight that logic constitutes a formal semiotic. Logic provides valid patterns—forms—for signs, the entities that, according to Peirce, composed all thought. Probably the most important of Peirce's logical insights for geology is his method of retroduction—or abduction, as he also called it. Retroduction involves reasoning from effect to cause, or, to use G. K. Gilbert's terms, from "consequent" to "antecedent."[27] Retroduction is the logic of hypotheses, and Peirce himself noted that geology is the science of hypotheses. Readers familiar with the writings of Gilbert,[28] Chamberlin,[29] and Davis[30] will recognize how this resonates with actual geological practice. I,[31] as well as others,[32] have discussed the logic of retroduction in geology. Very simply put, retroduction is a form of synthetic inference that involves a continuous activity of comparing, connecting, and putting together thoughts and perceptions. Using retroduction, geologists derive hypotheses from nature rather than from the analytical application of elegant theories.

One of the worst mistakes in logic—as well as the most common—according to Peirce, is to confuse retroduction with induction. These are both synthetic forms of reasoning. And the modern philosophy of science deals so exclusively with induction that many people presume that it, together with some deduction, constitutes the method of science. Induction does not generate hypotheses; it can only be used when there is a hypothesis already in mind. In fact, nominalist logicians dismiss the formation of hypotheses as unreal—as a psychological matter involving creative genius. Thus, the most important element of science for geology—the generation of hypotheses—is treated with either bizarre ignorance or benign neglect by most analytical philosophers of science.

The Earth speaks to geologists through its signs. The causal signs—called indices—are objects of interpretation. This interaction through causal signs is what geologists mean when they speak of "reconstructing" the past, although the term seems to beg the question as to who "constructed" the past in the first place.[33] The interpretation is from sign to hypothesis, by way of retroduction. The hypothesis, of course, must be compared to further signs. Its consequences are deduced, and these consequences generate additional observations for comparison. Anomalies in this process draw attention to new and special signs, stimulate more retroduction, and so on. This is the nature of geologists' "conversation" with the Earth.

WHAT TO DO

The noted distinctions in logic that underlie basic geological reasoning imply profound statements about education as well as public understanding of science.[34] For education, we see that science is not limited to "uncommon sense" and "unnatural" inquiry. Rather science includes the most natural mode of commonsense inquiry—retroduction. And the subject that can communicate this mode of inquiry to a society of people generally unfamiliar with science is geology—not physics.

With regard to general understanding about science, the public commonly assumes that conceptual schemes—theories or laws—provide the basis for societal actions. But in practice, we are motivated by perceptions. For example, much of the public—and even many scientists—misunderstand the concept of the "100-year flood." Yet, people can and do understand indices of real floods.[35] Scientists should communicate reality to the public, not abstract concepts.[36] Geologists, using earth logic, have access to that reality.

In a book[37] criticized as "folk wisdom" by advocates of conventional "scientific logic,"[38] geomorphologist Stanley Schumm outlines one of many models for how earth logic might be applied. Schumm compares geological reasoning to a medical diagnosis.[39] He specifically relates the famous method of multiple working hypotheses to differential medical diagnosis, which analyzes complex combinations of symptoms as the cause of disease.[40] Schumm fails to add that the study of symptoms, as far in the past as Galen in Ancient Greece and Hippocrates, is a prime example of inquiry by means of signs.[41] Moreover, the obvious patient for this diagnosis is Earth's great interconnected, self-regulating system, envisioned as the superorganism Gaia by atmospheric chemist James Lovelock.[42]

Although written nearly a century ago, the words of American geologist Herman L. Fairchild remain true today: "Geologists have been too generous in allowing other people to make their philosophy for them."[43] The great opportunity for geology in the next century derives less from its facts and theories about the Earth than from its profoundly naturalistic reasoning. The earth logic of geology likely will continue to be disparaged by advocates of a disconnecting, overly objective purity in scientific reasoning. Many geologists still will be humbled by the writings of philosophers who lack any sense that a science can preserve—very appropriately—its bond to its object of study.[44] They shouldn't be. The retroductive inferences of geology have more to tell us about Earth's real experiences and needs than have any elegant deductions from already known principles, or even than have multitudinous inductions that blindly and objectively classify random samples.

The famous physicist Lord Rutherford once motivated scholars in his laboratory with this view of science—there is only physics; all else is stamp collecting. Despite the uncultured, illogical ignorance of statements such as this, they have long bothered geologists and caused a low self-esteem in the profession. Some have named this affliction "the Kelvin effect" after Lord Kelvin, another physicist who directly disparaged the reasoning processes of geologists.[45]

Geologists have been reluctant to engage in the immense cultural debates that now surround society. I hypothesize that the Kelvin effect and an aversion to considering fundamental beliefs about science are responsible for this reticence. One recent president of the Geological Society of America issued a "call to action," stating, "it is time for [we in] the geosciences to stand up and assert ourselves."[46] But such action requires belief—that basis upon which one acts. Geologists, unlike the physicists described, simply lack a compelling belief in the scientific basis of their own enterprise. Sure, they believe in what they do in the operational sense of conducting their own personal research. They derive great enjoyment from that research—enough to sustain their personal vocation. But here I am referring to the belief that calls one to public action—deep conviction that compels some of our physics colleagues to speak boldly for all science. I am not suggesting that geologists speak for physicists. The statements geologists make about nature will never be as elegant as the models of physicists. What geologists can do is what the blinders of nominalistic logic prevent their fellow scientists from doing. Geologists can, in a very real sense, speak for Earth, rather than to it. They alone have the experience with retroductive logic to read the signs of Earth's text. This is the basis on which geologists can act. It gives them an awesome responsibility and an amazing opportunity. Let Earth speak![47]

29

Geology and Environmental Justice: An Example from Hawaii

Jill S. Schneiderman and Virginia Ashby Sharpe

We face the future fortified only with the lessons we have learned from the past. It is today that we must create the world of the future .... In a very real sense, tomorrow is now. —Eleanor Roosevelt

When native Hawaiian activists Palikapu Dedman, Dr. Noa Emmett Aluli, and Professor Davianna McGregor organized the Pele Defense Fund in 1985, they knew they were in for a long and tough fight. Their opponents, the state government, and private companies, True/Mid-Pacific Geothermal Venture, and later Puna Geothermal Venture, intended to develop geothermal energy sources on the "Big Island" of Hawaii located partially within the Wao Kele O Puna tropical rainforest. Geothermal resources would help supply the state's energy needs—today almost wholly met by oil shipped to its shores. According to the plan, electricity generated by steam from beneath Kilauea volcano on the Big Island would be transferred to the islands of Oahu and Maui by an extensive overland and submarine cable system. Activists objected to the proposal because wells drilled into the volcano desecrated Pele, a deity central to the religious beliefs of native Hawaiians whom they believe the volcano embodies.[1] They also knew that the resultant electricity would be used primarily to power extravagant resorts on Oahu.

The confrontations and litigation that surrounded the geothermal project raise issues of environmental justice—questions of the distribution of the goods and harms associated with impacts on the environment. Understanding the issue of geothermal drilling in Hawaii as a question of environmental justice depends on insights drawn from the geology, the traditional local religion, and the political economy of the region.

THE LIVING VOLCANO: ENERGY, MATTER, SPIRIT

Geothermal energy originates in heat derived from the Earth's interior. Where molten rock (magma) and very hot but still solid rock occur within a few miles of the Earth's surface, groundwater in the pores of that rock becomes heated.[2] When pore water gets hot, it expands, rises, and circulates back toward the surface as hot water or steam. Just as wells are drilled to tap groundwater for public and private water supplies, they can be also drilled into a porous rock layer above a pool of magma to retrieve steam or hot water. As it rises to the Earth's surface, steam then enters pipes constructed to carry it under pressure to a turbine. In the same way that blowing on a pinwheel causes it to turn, pressurized steam spins a turbine, which subsequently powers a generator that converts this mechanical energy into electricity. In conventional energy production, we burn fossil fuels to boil water and create steam that turns the turbines. Regardless of the source of the steam, the electric current travels along power lines to be distributed for private and public use.

Currently, Hawaii imports billions of barrels of oil every year to supply its energy. That activity raises the potential for oil spills. Also, it ultimately leads to the production of greenhouse gases, which have been implicated in global warming. Given the threat of oil spills and atmospheric degradation, the prospect of using local geothermal power might have seemed a welcome one to residents of the state. But the promise of geothermal energy did not look so bright to native Hawaiian activists Dedman, Aluli, and McGregor. Although geothermal energy is often thought to have minor negative environmental impacts in comparison to other energy sources, in June 1991, an "uncontrolled vent incident" at the Puna Geothermal Venture project on the Big Island of Hawaii released gases including hydrogen sulfide, which contribute to acid rain and can be fatal in high concentrations.[3] The blowout at the drilling site caused noise levels reaching 100 decibels, noxious odors, and alarm among residents about future emissions.[4]

And to the native Hawaiians, drilling into the flanks of the active volcano to access its steam was akin to invading the body and extracting the life force of Pele. Anyone who has seen the glowing red lava that has flowed regularly since 1983 from Kilauea's east flank might acknowledge the vital nature of the volcano and appreciate its significance in the native Hawaiian worldview.

Lava oozes from the volcano dependably, because in the framework of plate tectonics, the Big Island sits atop a geological "hot spot." A localized source of heat emanating from the Earth's mantle, a hot spot causes melting of overlying rock and the eruption of lava at the Earth's surface. With each eruption, new lava gets added to Kilauea—the active volcano that makes up the eastern half of the Big Island of Hawaii—and the island grows. In the animistic religion of native Hawaiians, the volcano is a living spirit.

PAST AND PRESENT GEOTHERMAL INITIATIVES IN HAWAII

The idea of using near-surface steam and volcanic hot water as an energy source in Hawaii is not new. In 1881, King David Kalakaua discussed with Thomas Edison the feasibility of using Hawaiian volcanoes to produce electricity to illuminate Hawaii's capital.[5] But geothermal exploration in Hawaii did not begin in earnest until nearly 100 years later. In the late 1970s, the Hawaii state legislature began enacting laws to encourage and assist geothermal development. As a feasibility test, the first geothermal well in Hawaii was drilled in 1976, tapping steam from more than one mile beneath the Earth's surface. In 1982, a three-megawatt generating plant first produced electricity that was sold to the Hawaii Electric Light Company for use by electric customers on the Big Island. This plant operated until 1989.[6]

The success of the feasibility test prompted the State of Hawaii to develop the 500-megawatt Hawaii Geothermal Project. Given the "energy crisis" of the late 1970s and early 1980s, the development of geothermal resources would decrease Hawaii's dependence on imported oil for nearly 90 percent of its electricity needs.[7] The plan called for the construction of a complex of 20 geothermal power plants along Kilauea volcano's eastern flank and the transfer of 500 megawatts of electricity to Oahu, using a 188-mile interisland undersea cable.[8] Described as a "federal-state-private partnership leading toward commercialization," the project was to take place in four phases: assessment of the resource; investigation of the proposed cable system; characterization and verification of the resource; and construction of the commercial geothermal and cable system.[9] Drilling the first geothermal well in Hawaii in 1976 constituted part of phase one. During phase two, a feasibility study financed by the U.S. federal government showed that the submarine cable could be built, but that it would be a formidable engineering challenge where the ocean is deep. Those with knowledge of coastal and marine processes expressed concern that the cable, lined with oil, could be severed by hurricanes, currents, or strong earthquakes.[10]

As part of phase three, 25 commercial-scale wells would be drilled to demonstrate the availability of a geothermal resource that could generate 500 megawatts of energy.[11] To accomplish this phase of the project, private developers—True/Mid-Pacific Geothermal Venture and Puna Geothermal Venture—would contribute $26 million. Also, the U.S. Department of Energy and the state's Scientific Observation (Drill) Hole program would supply $15 million and $9 million, respectively.[12] Success of this phase would make way for the final phase, private construction of the generating plants.

In June 1991, a federal court ruled that the U.S. government could not contribute further funds toward the development of geothermal energy in Hawaii until a full environmental impact statement was prepared. The ruling was based on the National Environmental Policy Act of 1969 (NEPA), which requires the federal government to develop environmental impact statements *before* undertaking major federal actions.[13] Judge David Ezra, who ruled in the case, asserted that the potential environmental, social, and economic effects of the project warranted the completion of an environmental impact statement.[14] In addition, the Sierra Club Legal Defense Fund[15] filed a lawsuit against the state on behalf of a coalition of 12 environmental, cultural, neighborhood, and business groups.[16] The plaintiffs in the lawsuit claimed that, because more than $17 million in state funds had been appropriated for the project since 1986 and no state environmental impact statement had been completed, the state was violating the Hawaii Environmental Policy Act. Modeled after the federal law, the State of Hawaii's Environmental Policy Act also requires that an environmental impact statement be completed before projects are started.[17]

Although much of the objection from the native Hawaiian community living on the Big Island originated from their belief system—that drilling into Kilauea volcano violated respect for Pele—joining efforts with Wao Kele O Puna rainforest activists seemed to provide a more effective route for preventing geothermal development. The 27,000-acre Wao Kele O Puna rainforest is the only lowland tropical rainforest remaining in the United States. Rainforest activists believed it should be valued and preserved because of the genetic resources represented by the diverse species it contains.[18] Scientists at the Pacific Science Congress in Honolulu in June 1991 passed a resolution condemning geothermal development in the rainforest because of the damage it would do to the entire ecosystem, one that included endangered plants and animals.[19] The work of activists and some scientists, which included litigation, boycotts, and rallies on Oahu and the Big Island, led to growing opposition to geothermal development, particularly in the rainforest.

In 1992, as a result of this pressure, the state decided not to pursue the large-scale geothermal/interisland cable project.[20] The withdrawal of all state and federal funding from the proposed project eliminated the legal requirement for environmental impact statements. In addition, the state and Mid-Pacific/True Geothermal abandoned plans to develop geothermal energy in the Wao Kele O Puna rainforest.[21] Instead, the state redefined its geothermal development goals and sought, for the time being, to allow only smaller scale, *privately funded* development to contribute to the energy needs on the Big Island.[22] As a result of this policy shift, Puna Geothermal Venture constructed the state's first and only commercial geothermal plant on privately owned land at the southeastern tip of the Big Island. The 25-megawatt plant began to produce electricity in April 1993.[23] It taps steam at 660°F from a depth of approximately one mile below the eastern flank of Kilauea.[24]

THE ENVIRONMENTAL JUSTICE MOVEMENT

The strategy used by native Hawaiian and other activists to halt the development of geothermal energy on Hawaii echoes concerns of activists throughout the United States and elsewhere, all who consider themselves part of the movement for environmental justice. Environmental justice activists contend that people of color, women, and the poor bear a disproportionate burden of environmental risk, a burden associated with the location of undesirable, polluting technologies and waste disposal facilities in low-income communities and communities of color.[25]

The environmental justice movement has its roots in protests surrounding the 1967 drowning death of an eight-year-old African-American girl in Houston at a garbage dump.[26] Her death sparked student protests at the predominantly African-American Texas Southern University. Demonstrators questioned the location of the garbage dump in the mostly African-American neighborhood of Sunnyside. In fact, related concerns regarding improved working conditions for striking African-American garbage workers was to have been the subject of Reverend Martin Luther King, Jr.'s 1968 speech in Memphis, Tennessee. He was assassinated there before he could address his audience. More than ten years later, in 1979, residents of Northwood Manor, a suburban Houston neighborhood of African-American homeowners, filed a lawsuit against Browning-Ferris Industries, asserting environmental discrimination in the siting of a municipal solid waste landfill in their community. This kind of activism established a link between civil rights and environmental issues, a link that had not been forged previously in the mainstream environmental movement.

Some mark the birth of the environmental justice movement in 1982 in Warren County, North Carolina. An African-American county, this rural location had been selected as the disposal site for 812,000 cubic feet of soil contaminated with polychlorinated biphenyls (PCBs). Although demonstrations did not prevent construction of the landfill, they marked the first time that African-Americans mobilized a national, broad-based effort to oppose what they defined as environmental racism.[27] In 1983, a study by the U.S. General Accounting Office found a strong correlation between the location of off-site hazardous waste landfills and the race and socioeconomic status of surrounding communities in Alabama, Florida, Georgia, Kentucky, Mississippi, North Carolina, South Carolina, and Tennessee.[28] A 1987 study commissioned by the United Church of Christ and the National Association for the Advancement of Colored People corroborated the results of the federal study but found that race, rather than class, was the primary factor affecting decisions regarding the location of waste sites and other polluting technologies.[29]

Subsequent studies in the 1990s have led the federal government to acknowledge that environmental laws, regulations, and policies are not uniformly applied or enforced. In 1994, President Clinton signed an Executive Order on Environmental Justice. It requires collection and interpretation of data on disparate risk and health effects of industrial facilities on communities, identification of impacts of federal environmental programs on affected communities, and interagency coordination to eliminate discriminatory siting of polluting facilities.[30] The order also clarifies the applicability of Title VI of the Civil Rights Act of 1964 by prohibiting discrimination against communities of color and the poor in federally funded environmental programs.

Despite these important developments, the environmental justice movement faces a number of hurdles. First, although mainstream environmental organizations are beginning to broaden their focus, they have been slow to incorporate the concerns of environmental justice into their traditional agendas of wilderness preservation and conservation. Second, the Executive Order of 1994 is not law and therefore may be enforceable only through the term of the Clinton presidency. Third, although the National Environmental Policy Act (NEPA), the most well established environmental regulation in this country, was crafted to "assure for all Americans safe, healthful, productive, and aesthetically and culturally pleasing surroundings," its purpose remains unfulfilled.[31] One reason for this shortfall is the inherent difficulty of quantifying items such as cultural and spiritual values within the Act's required cost-benefit analyses. Fourth, although the Executive Order provided for integration of environmental justice concerns into NEPA, this regulation applies to federally funded projects only. (Recall that, in Hawaii, this regulation has resulted in the withdrawal of federal and state funding from the Hawaii Geothermal Project and has opened the way for private geothermal development—unregulated by NEPA.) Fifth, private industries continue to choose the easiest targets—communities with few resources available to mobilize against the designation of sites for hazardous waste, energy, and similar noxious projects. Sixth, communities confronted with a decision to host an undesirable industry often have few options for economic development and are therefore faced with desperate choices.

The native Hawaiian activists' approach to preventing geothermal development on the Big Island not only reflects the constraints of national policy and the environmental bureaucracies that have grown up around it but also point to native Hawaiians' vulnerability to *private* land use decisions. Despite the fact that they opposed geothermal development—because it violated their religious beliefs and cultural traditions—native Hawaiian activists made a decision for the sake of expediency: They allowed their agenda to be subsumed under that of rainforest protection activists who were backed by the wealth and weight of mainstream environmental organizations such as Rainforest Action Network and the Sierra Club.

THE IDEAL OF JUSTICE

The ideal of justice is as old as human society and has been the subject of some of the world's most profound moral and political thought. From Plato's *Republic* and Aristotle's *Nicomachean Ethics*, from Thomas Hobbes' *Leviathan*, and

John Locke's *Second Treatise on Government*, from John Rawls's *Theory of Justice* to Robert Nozick's *Anarchy, State and Utopia*, theorists have attempted to add substance to Aristotle's basic notion that equals should be treated equally and that unequals may be treated unequally.[32] These theories have recommended various forms of government from aristocracy to libertarian democracy and have, since the Enlightenment (seventeenth through eighteenth centuries), hinged the benefits and protections of government on the rights of citizens deemed equal by virtue of their rationality and human dignity.

In the liberal democracy of the United States, people have basic civil and political rights like freedom of speech, assembly, the right to hold property, to vote, and to hold office. The rights are basic because they guarantee only that individuals may freely—that is, without interference—pursue whatever life goals they choose—so long as they don't interfere with the freedom of others. What these basic rights do not provide, however, is positive entitlement to particular goods—that is, benefits, such as health care, education, food, shelter, or a safe environment. Said differently, the basic rights are negative in the sense that they only require others to leave us alone. Entitlement to particular goods, by contrast, would be a positive right, because it would place a positive obligation on others to provide that good. In this way, the basic rights of a liberal democracy are said to be procedural rather than substantive; they guarantee justice in *processes*, not in *outcomes*. When a liberal democracy *does* establish policies for substantive benefits, such as public education, parks, and museums, it does so through a policy process that is intended to reflect the consent of the governed. Regulating substantive harms is a slightly different matter.

Because an individual's pursuit of liberty cannot run roughshod over the liberty of others—"I am not at liberty to harm you"—the story gets somewhat complicated at this point. Just as our liberal democracy remains neutral about substantive benefits—individuals can pursue freely particular ideas of the good life either by themselves or through contracts—so too it does *not* attempt to fully specify what constitutes a substantive harm (beyond an array of obvious harms such as killing, assault, battery, kidnapping, and trespass). It is by public consensus or through the court system that determinations of substantive harm are made.

It is hard to reach consensus about harm and therefore to establish legitimate limits to liberty. Some activities are not universally regarded as harmful—we need only recall historical attitudes toward slavery, child labor, or wife-beating. In addition, it can be difficult to show absolute cause and effect, that one person or industry's actions definitively causes harm to others—we can think of the link between pornography and rape, television violence and violent behavior, and cigarette smoking and lung cancer, or industrial pollution and disease as examples. Third, to prevent harm to others, we must take positive action rather than simply refrain from obviously damaging activities—that is, we must clean up contaminated ground and take deliberate steps to prevent air and water pollution. When the line between refraining from harm and helping to rectify a problem is blurred, general consensus is difficult to achieve. People don't like being told what they *cannot* do; they especially dislike being told what they *must* do. But, sometimes, in order to prevent or remove harm, prohibitions and actions must be prescribed. This approach is often the case with toxic substances. Finally, some harms are accepted as the price we must pay for things like employment and national security. Cost-benefit analysis (required under NEPA, for example) and cost-effectiveness analysis are two methods used to determine the relationship of cost (or harm) to benefit.[33] This topic brings us to the issue of environmental justice.

Our society has not yet reached agreement on assessing the risks of environmental impacts or determining the acceptability of known harms—for example, carcinogenic pesticides, herbicides, solvents, or nuclear waste. Without agreement, we continue to produce and use these and other substances despite the fact that poor communities and communities of color disproportionately bear the associated environmental costs. Justice offers two possible responses to the question of environmental risk. Our current situation requires individuals or communities to prove that harm has been done to them. Instead of this, we can decide as a nation to require producers to prove that their questionable substances are safe before they can be used.[34] Alternatively, if it is true that there will be some inevitable harms associated with the benefits of industrial production, we must establish a fair way to distribute the risk associated with such production. To understand what fair distribution of risk might entail, we must examine two dominant principles in our society that guide the distribution of goods, rights, and privileges—liberty and equality.

The idea that liberty should be the basis of distribution is a key tenet of libertarianism and free market economics;[35] people are free to expose themselves to an otherwise undesirable risk or harm in exchange for a compensatory benefit. For example, a community may choose to store nuclear waste and expose its members to radiation in exchange for a monetary fee. The assumption behind this view is that individuals should not be stopped from entering into contracts that they choose freely. Another and perhaps more fundamental assumption is that the contracting parties have chosen freely and that the contract is therefore valid. This assumption reflects one of the most dangerous temptations in a society premised on basic equality and liberty of all—the temptation to suppose that the playing field of society actually *is* level, that liberty and equality actually *have* been achieved for all. Disproportionate environmental impacts are only recent evidence of an enduring legacy of prejudice that has justified unequal treatment based on belief in the inherent superiority and inferiority of particular groups of people. Disproportionate environmental impacts reveal that historically disenfranchised groups continue to be denied equal treatment, *despite* our constitutional ideal of equality.

Those who argue that people *freely choose* to host garbage or toxic waste dumps and other undesirable activities on their land forget that these activities *are undesirable* and that communities make these agreements, often for compensation, *out of desperation in the absence of any other options.* As Charles Streadit, president of Houston's Northeast Community Action Group said in regard to the siting of a landfill in his community and the money and jobs that would come with it, "We need all the money we can get to upgrade our school system. But we shouldn't have to be poisoned to get improvements for our children."[36] Historical injustices seriously constrain the present-day choices of those who have experienced systematic discrimination. This fact challenges the working assumption of free market liberalism that liberty—which assumes that choice is free—is the best means to achieve a fair distribution of harms and benefits. However, if we agree that it is patronizing and demeaning to tell desperate people that they "should not pursue their best option for survival because their choices are not really *free*," then we must find a just alternative. To guarantee that our society doesn't systematically place people in a position to make a choice out of desperation is such an alternative. At the very least, this alternative will require that we rethink radically the current manner in which we distribute environmental risks and harms.

As we have just seen, liberty is one principle that can guide distribution. Equality is another. In our contemporary constitutional democracy, the principle of equality means that all persons regardless of sex, race, religion, or national origin are "created equal." If, as Aristotle observed, justice requires that "equals must be treated equally," distinctions of race or sex, for example, are not, therefore, a legitimate basis for differential treatment (except perhaps to redress past wrongs). There is considerable controversy about exactly what constitutes equal treatment and how far government should go to achieve it. Is society equal enough if it guarantees everyone the same opportunities, or should it try to achieve equality of condition? In other words, should equality be a matter of fair procedures only or also of fair outcomes?

When we think about the question of environmental justice, a procedural view of equality requires that all stakeholders should have access to meaningful involvement in plans affecting their communities. A substantive view of equality requires more. It requires that steps be taken to assure that outcomes are fair and that no group is systematically disadvantaged in the actual harms they are exposed to. According to the EPA's definition of environmental justice, fair treatment involves both:

> *Environmental Justice means the fair treatment and meaningful involvement of all people, regardless of race, ethnicity, culture, income or education level with respect to the development, implementation and enforcement of environmental laws, regulations, and policies. Fair treatment means that no population, due to political or economic disempowerment, is forced to shoulder the negative human health and environmental impacts of pollution or other environmental hazards. Meaningful involvement means that all people have an equal opportunity, both procedurally and substantially, to participate in the decision-making process.*[37]

The achievement of fair treatment as articulated by the Environmental Protection Agency would require a "proportionate" distribution of negative environmental effects. Given the moral and legal equality that we share, and the fact that industrial production serves the whole of society, "proportionality" can mean nothing less than the equal distribution of the burdens of production. Under the principle of equality, dumps, waste treatment facilities, power plants, chemical factories, and bus depots would be distributed equally in the communities of whites, blacks, Hispanics, Asians; in urban and rural locations; in communities of the wealthy, the poor, and the middle class. Equality in distribution would check the "NIMBY" (not-in-my-backyard) phenomenon because individuals and communities would not be allowed to buy or trade their way out of exposure to risk. Perhaps if we were all made to share equally in the environmental harms and health risks associated with industrial production, then we would develop the political will to demand that those harms and risks be reduced. The problem here is that achieving such equality would significantly constrain liberty.

How do the twin principles of liberty and equality affect the issue of geothermal drilling on Hawaii? Are native Hawaiians at liberty to choose allowable activities in the Wao Kele O Puna rainforest? Are they treated as equal partners in deliberations regarding energy supplies for Hawaii? To answer these questions and understand the issue of geothermal drilling on Hawaii as one of environmental justice, we must understand some of the changes that have taken place in Hawaii over the last two centuries.

WHAT PRICE PARADISE?

When Captain James Cook, one of the earliest European navigators to chart the location of the Hawaiian islands, came to Hawaii in 1778, between 300,000 and 400,000 native Hawaiians lived on the mid-Pacific island chain. Shortly thereafter in 1792, Captain Vancouver, leader of an English exploring party, also came and remained for a time on the islands. In 1794, two American ships entered the harbor of Honolulu, which subsequently became a favorite port for trading and whaling vessels of many nations.[38] Over the next 100 years, nonnative diseases were introduced—including smallpox, measles, whooping cough, influenza, and venereal disease—and killed almost 90 percent of the population. By 1878, no more than 50,000 native Hawaiians survived on the islands of Hawaii.[39]

The influx of outsiders brought changes to the landscape and its unique ecosystems: Lowland forests were cleared for farming, flightless birds became victims of hunters, and alien insects and plants began to overrun native species. These changes have persistently threatened the native Hawaiian populations that value and use the forests as traditional hunting grounds, as a source of medicine, and for traditional ceremonies. Damage to the forests and surrounding environs has undermined communities because it has degraded the values on which the communities are based.[40] The arrival of Christian missionaries in Hawaii and its annexation as the forty-ninth state in the United States also had profound effects on native Hawaiian culture.

Before contact with Europeans, most formal Hawaiian learning—including cosmology, history, and genealogy—occurred through chants and hulas. This knowledge was recited as oral history by Hawaiian nobility (*ali'i*) during ceremonies.[41] But in 1820, when the first party of Protestant Christian missionaries arrived at the islands from Massachusetts, they condemned the chants and hula. Instead, they introduced writing and English on the islands. These actions reduced demand for the memorized cultural knowledge of the *ali'i*.

During the latter half of the nineteenth century, plantation capitalism expanded on the islands. In 1893, Queen Lili'uokalani, the elder of two sisters who succeeded King Kalakaua, was overthrown, thus ending Hawaiian sovereignty. Then, the American-controlled provisional government banned the use of the Hawaiian language in government offices, courts, and schools. In 1898, the United States annexed Hawaii in what has been called the "last chapter, in the history of the spirit of manifest destiny."[42] Hawaii became the fiftieth state in 1959.[43]

Today native Hawaiians constitute about 19 percent of the total population of the state and have the lowest median family income among all the state's ethnic groups.[44] Typically, many native Hawaiians work two jobs to support families and live in what many Americans would describe as dire poverty. Since the decline of the pineapple and sugar cane industries, many native Hawaiians are factory workers or maids and maintenance workers in the hotel industry—a typical source of jobs for so-called unskilled workers. More than 2,000 native Hawaiians live in rusted cars, tents, or cardboard boxes.[45]

Tourism is the primary source of income in Hawaii. Each year approximately seven million visitors spend as much as $10 billion on the islands at resort complexes.[46] Most native Hawaiians share in the wealth created by tourism only to the extent that they hold menial resort jobs. Furthermore, the land used for the construction of resorts often eradicates Hawaiian archeological sites, including temples, stone carvings, dwellings, and burial grounds. Tourist resorts also destroy the region's rural environments, which provide the means of living for many who dwell in small-scale farming and fishing communities.[47]

For example, in the South Kona district on the west coast of the Big Island, Japan Airlines bought 1540 acres of agricultural land to develop "The Village at Hokukano," a resort that would contain 1,440 luxury home sites, a private member lodge of 100 units, and three nine-hole golf courses, all just about two miles from the National Marine Life Sanctuary at Kealakekua Bay. At South Kona, more than 175 sacred sites and numerous indigenous plant species still used for medicinal purposes would be destroyed by bulldozers. And because a typical eighteen-hole golf course annually uses 50,000 pounds of dry and liquid chemicals—about ten times the amount used by large-scale agriculture—the introduction of thousands of pounds of chemicals poses a risk to the health of local residents as well as terrestrial and marine life.[48] What's more, enormous amounts of energy will be needed to power the resort.

Local residents, including native Hawaiians, are once again united with environmentalists to oppose the proposed resort. Whereas environmentalists may be concerned specifically about the health and well-being of ecosystems, native Hawaiians focus on justice. Should such a resort be built, they will reap little benefit from a development that entails the destruction of their local environment and the desecration of sacred volcanic sites.

To understand questions of development in Hawaii as an issue of justice requires us to think about the fairness of deliberative processes, the limits of property rights, and the distributions of benefits and harms. Because our liberal democracy aspires to guarantee the maximum amount of freedom possible for individuals, it emphasizes justice and fairness in decision-making processes more than justice and fairness in outcomes. Individuals are best able to decide for themselves what is desirable or undesirable and thus should be free to make the best choice.[49] In the context of public policy decision making—decision making at the federal, state, or local level—justice in the *process* of decision making is all important, because it guarantees that representation will be equal and democratic. For example, in government-funded projects that are expected to have environmental impacts, environmental justice requires public participation—and to make the public participation fair, positive steps must be taken to enable the participation of all who want to be involved. This help includes public education, transportation assistance, translated information, and convenient siting and timing of meetings.[50]

When the proposed geothermal drilling projects in Hawaii were scheduled to involve federal and state funding, all the provisions of NEPA were in force, including the need to prepare environmental impact statements and encourage public participation. When the federal and state governments removed themselves from the proposed development, it became a private, commercial venture, and NEPA requirements no longer applied. Why? Because the land was now *privately* owned, and in a liberal democracy, the government only reluctantly regulates private actions on private property unless these actions infringe on the liberties of others.

Just what constitutes the difference between public and private is hotly contested. People fear regulation of private land because it threatens the distinction between private and public. However, the problem with this distinction is that it is irrelevant in the context of the whole earth system—air, water, rocks, and life. In the case of geothermal drilling, spiritual beliefs regarding Pele also transcend the artificial boundaries between private and public.

In other words, where atmosphere, hydrosphere, solid earth, and biosphere are concerned, private action can easily affect the public, including those spiritual values linked to land. Despite the fact that the government does not require NEPA compliance except where federal monies are involved, it has nonetheless acknowledged the permeability of "private" and "public" in defining environmental justice to include the effects of private industrial and commercial operations as well as public activities.[51] If we are to realize environmental justice broadly, courts must continue to expand their understanding of the concepts of nuisance and harm to include environmental effects on health as well as on sacred sites.[52] In this way, public welfare would take precedence over private property rights—and private land use, like public land use, would be accountable to the demands of environmental justice.[53]

The EPA's definition of environmental justice raises another important concern about the meaning of fair distribution. The notion of environmental justice that has evolved in U.S. public policy requires fair distribution only of the *negative* environmental effects of public, industrial, and commercial activities. In a market-based liberal democracy, justice is not thought to require the fair distribution of *benefits*. What we are trying to get at here is not that *people* don't think that justice requires fair distribution of benefits but that the theories of free market capitalism and free market liberalism themselves—the theories on which our society is based—structurally reject the premise that benefits should be distributed fairly. This is one of the deep reasons—embedded in our political theory—why inequalities are said to be "institutionalized." It's not simply that there are individual people who are bigoted or uncharitable, or champions of laissez-faire economics, for example; rather, it is that our political and economic frameworks are set up in such a way that equality is very difficult to achieve.

How then are we to respond when the benefits of geothermal drilling in Hawaii will accrue chiefly to developers of luxury tourist resorts while native Hawaiians continue to live in poverty? In his book *A Theory of Justice*, philosopher John Rawls provides one answer.[54] To take seriously the historical wrongs that continue to disadvantage certain groups, fairness requires that "Social and economic inequalities are to be arranged so that they are . . . to the greatest benefit of the least advantaged."[55] For native Hawaiians, this might mean that development could be regulated so that its benefits accrue predominantly to them until they achieve social and economic equality.

Our capitalist democracy cannot easily accommodate the idea of equal distribution of benefits or goods and cannot be expected to embrace it easily. Responding to the issue of geothermal drilling in Hawaii, we might rely on a less controversial principle, basic to liberal democracy, namely, that it is wrong to harm people against their will for the benefit of others. Because geothermal drilling in Hawaiian volcanoes violates native Hawaiian religious beliefs, it should not be done for the benefit of others.

Yet the problem of an ongoing shortage of fuel sources remains. The continued need for energy resources in Hawaii, and the risks and costs associated with the use of oil, make it necessary to consider other energy options. Here, geology can provide some insights.

DRAWING INSIGHT FROM GEOLOGY

There are a number of ways that geological knowledge might provide insights for informed and fair decision making in Hawaii. Geologists experienced with geothermal energy development can help assess the resource in terms of physical costs and benefits. Especially in Hawaii, any geothermal well and power plant is vulnerable to the ever-present threat of damage from volcanic eruptions or their associated earthquakes. In addition to hot water and steam, geothermal wells release hydrogen sulfide and sulfur dioxide gases. The underground water used to power geothermal plants contains potentially toxic elements and compounds, such as arsenic, boron, mercury, ammonia, and benzene.[56] Geothermal water can also be radioactive. Because of this, disposal of the used water could potentially contaminate local surface water and harm many forms of life. And the land around a geothermal well often sinks after large amounts of fluid are removed. Geothermal plants can generate noise as the pressurized steam rushes up narrow pipes and vents. Finally, geothermal plants have a limited life span—generally, only a few decades—because hot rock conducts heat poorly.[57] Because the water draws its heat from the rocks, they cool over time and it takes longer for water that circulates through them to be heated. In the case of Hawaii, the magma below Kilauea has not disappeared, but it transmits its heat slowly. Although a renewable source of energy, it is not replenished quickly, certainly not at the rate at which humans would use it.[58]

Optimists believe that many of these problems can be addressed with technological innovations. For example, harmful gases can be kept from escaping into the atmosphere and wastewater can be reinjected into the well to help replenish the reservoir, eliminate pollution, and prevent land subsidence.[59]

In Hawaii, knowledge about the earth system points to alternatives to geothermal energy development for sources of power for the islands. Because of its location in the mid-Pacific Ocean, Hawaii contains enormous potential for the use of solar, wind, and ocean thermal energy conversion power as alternatives to fossil fuel use. And because of the presence of industries on the island that utilize vegetation, there is potential for biomass waste as yet another energy source.

Solar Energy

Solar radiation is the most abundant energy source on Earth and, from the human perspective, is inexhaustible as long as the sun shines. The Earth receives as much solar energy in 20 days as is stored in all its fossils fuels.[60] Sunshine is free and it falls to Earth without any mining, drilling, pumping, or disruption of the land. And its use is essentially pollution free because it produces no hazardous solid wastes, no air or water pollution, and no noise. Absorption of sunlight for heat or operation of a solar cell for electricity is a very clean process, although solar electricity has some environmental costs.[61]

Distributed unequally across the globe, solar energy is concentrated along the Earth's middle latitudes, including those occupied by Hawaii. A general problem with its use, however, applies equally everywhere: Abundant solar energy reaches the Earth's surface, but at any one location, it is very diffuse. Therefore, to use large quantities of solar energy to generate electricity, collectors must cover a wide geographical area. Before the sun can be the principal source of electricity anywhere, we need major improvements in efficiency of generation and in storage technology.

Solar energy can, however, also be used to provide heat and hot water through passive systems, those that act like greenhouses—they intercept solar energy, allow it to pass through to indoor surfaces, and convert it to low-temperature heat but they do not allow the heat to readily pass back out. On Hawaii, where temperatures are generally warm, passive solar energy could be used on those islands not prone to cloudy weather; unlike the use of solar energy for electricity generation, the technology exists now and, environmentally, it is relatively cost free.

Wind Energy

On Oahu, the most populated of the Hawaiian islands, the potential for power generated from the very strong and consistent trade winds is substantial. Wind energy can be thought of as a variation of solar energy because winds are ultimately powered by the sun: Air moves in response to differences in pressure, which, in turn, come from differences in surface temperature. Because the sun's rays are more dispersed near the poles than near the Equator, air over equatorial regions such as Hawaii is warmer than that over the Earth's poles. Warm, less dense air rises near the Equator and cool, dense polar air sinks and moves toward the Equator. This movement gives rise to large winds, massive circulating cells of air.

The energy of wind has been used to do work for several thousand years— grinding grain in mills, sailing ships, and lifting water from wells. Today, wind power usually is converted by turbines into electricity and is becoming economically competitive with conventional sources of power. Most approaches to the use of wind energy for commercial generation of electric power involve "wind farms"—concentrations of many windmills in a few especially favorable windy sites. As with the use of solar cells to generate electricity, wind farms require space. Windmills must be spread out or they block one another's wind flow. Spacing them at four windmills per one-half square mile requires about 100 square miles of land to produce energy equivalent to the output of a 1,000-megawatt power plant—one large enough to service a major city such as Chicago. However, the land can be used for other purposes simultaneously. So far, there seem to be few environmental problems associated with wind farms.

However, some people have aesthetic objections to wind farms. Furthermore, where turbines are located along migratory bird routes, birds are killed when they fly into the wind blades. Still, the Hawaii Natural Energy Institute has conducted basic research on wind energy in Hawaii and this includes studies of wind speed variations on power output quality and cost-effective battery storage for wind-generated energy. With a number of industries accessing wind power in the state, this energy source may supply ten percent of it's energy early in the twenty-first century.[62]

Ocean Thermal Energy Conversion

Along some coastal areas, the water deepens quickly. Where this is the case, the temperature difference between warm surface water and colder deep waters holds promise for power generation based on that difference in water temperature. The temperature difference in ocean thermal energy conversion can actually power a generator. The process is surprisingly simple. A fluid whose density changes readily with small temperature changes—ammonia, for example—can be condensed by using cold water from the deep ocean. Once it is pumped to the surface, warm surface water heats the previously chilled, condensed fluid so that it expands to drive a turbine.[63] The island of Oahu has just the right oceanographic conditions for this form of energy conversion. In the 1980s, a small ocean thermal energy conversion project that was operated in Hawaii produced 50 kilowatts of energy. Because this was an experimental endeavor, the electricity was not transmitted to shore but powered a continuously burning light bulb on a float near the village of Mokapu. Although this technology is not at the point where it can be used on a large scale, the Hawaii Natural Energy Institute has helped to refine the technology and it may someday be useful on a larger, commercial scale. Certainly, in suitable physical environments such as island communities, it may provide a partial solution to energy needs.[64]

Biomass

Biomass composed of plant matter and animal waste can be burned for its energy. Because most biomass energy sources are plant materials and because plants need sunlight to grow, this fuel can be thought of as "unfossilized fuel"—fuel derived from living or recent organisms rather than ancient ones.[65]

About one-third of Hawaii's electricity is already provided by biomass, particularly by burning plant waste from macadamia nut and sugar cane processing—wastes that previously were dumped in the ocean or in landfills. Because biomass fuels are burned to release their energy, they unfortunately share the carbon dioxide pollution problems of fossil fuels. Another negative aspect of biomass fuel arises from the need to produce or replenish it on the same time scale as we use it. The pace of this production could cause a loss of organic matter in soil, which is necessary for maintaining soil fertility.[66]

SCIENCE AND VALUES

Information derived from earth science is essential to our understanding of the possible sources of energy for the Hawaiian Islands, but we cannot expect to answer the question of appropriate sources and uses solely by better or more objective scientific insight. Although we need data on the relative efficiency, cost, and drawbacks of various energy sources to determine feasibility, these data cannot tell us what *should* happen in Hawaii or in any other area seeking energy solutions. The question of what *should* happen is a question of political, social, cultural, and ecological values, and the political process by which we debate and prioritize them. Environmental justice not only demands that the political process be open, accessible, and accountable to the voices of minority, low income, and indigenous communities, but also that the values of equality and public welfare occupy the forefront of public and private land use decisions. Since World War II, the United States has led the world in economic development, industrial production, and military buildup, activities that separately and collectively have had devastating environmental effects.[67] At present, minority and low-income communities disproportionately experience these effects—they live with the majority of petrochemical facilities, dump sites, and water hazards in this country. In other words, in terms of its environmental consequences, the expansion of the United States economy has been achieved on the backs of communities marginalized by their race, gender, and income. This is not progress, nor is it an acceptable cost in a country that champions the value of equality.

In Pahoa, 2.5 miles from the Puna geothermal drilling site, native Hawaiian Emily Naeole gathers flowers to make leis, each of which she sells for approximately $20. Living in a shanty on the town's main road, she supports her husband, three young daughters, and an infant son on the meager living her occupation ekes out. In *Broken Rainbow*, an award-winning documentary about the plight of native Hawaiians, she asks, "Who is powerless? Who doesn't have a voice in courts or in general decisions?" She comments, "We are not asked, 'What did you do on this land?' This is Hawaiian ancestral land. We are not telling non-Hawaiians to get out. But American law does give lands to indigenous people and they should have control over their lands." Emily Naeole, like other native Hawaiians opposed to geothermal development on the Big Island, wants cultural and religious traditions to count as costs of development.[68]

The development of industries and activities that are energy intensive in lands where resources to produce that energy are scarce or not technologically well developed usually makes little geological and environmental sense. That the economic and recreational interests of newcomers and visitors frequently override the desires and needs of people long dwelling in such a place is unacceptable. In the interest of sustainability and fairness, we must embrace the notion that humans live within the physical constraints of the environment. If

Eleanor Roosevelt was right when she said "We face the future fortified only with the lessons we have learned from the past," then we know that governments and economies cannot be based on oppression and exploitation.[69] Our job now and for the future is to live in such a way that our activities do not undermine the values on which our democracy is built, or the communities that make up our nation.[70]

30

Stakes, Options, and Some Natural Limits to a Sustainable World

E-an Zen

A COMMON CHALLENGE

*L*et me set the stage for this essay with a metaphor. Suppose I am the guardian for someone who may soon need long-term nursing care for which I cannot pay. As a prudent person, should I count on a medical miracle or on winning a lottery? Should I forget about buying that luxury car and instead buy a long-term care insurance policy?

The Earth as a habitat too needs a long-term care policy, a safety net; and we humans, so sure of our sagacity that we call ourselves *Homo sapiens,* are its only capable guardians.

Concern about the future of the Earth as a place for civil habitation, of course, has a long history. For example, in his essay, "The Tragedy of the Commons," Garrett Hardin suggested that a community threatened by over-crowding and diminishing resources might yet salvage sustainably civil social arrangements by adopting a code of rewards and penalties so designed that self-interest propels communal responsibility; he called this "mutual coercion mutually agreed upon."[1] A tragedy would result, however, if absent such a code of ethics, short-sighted self-interest is free to trample on the common good. During the 30 years since Hardin's paper, world population has nearly doubled, consumerism is on the rise globally, and is applauded by politicians and economists as a sign of an improved world. The tragedy depicted by Hardin seems to be racing, unstoppable, toward its fatal conclusion.

In addition to the desire to leave a civilized society for our descendants, another concern is that those who benefit from living in rich and powerful nations and societies should do their share to ensure social justice on a global scale. This inclination means that the future we envision should include ame-lioration of the exploitation of the environment and resources of the poor soci-eties by the rich.

Considerations such as these have led to the notion of "sustainable devel-opment," an idea widely circulated through a report of the World Commission on Environment and Development and defined as "development that meets the needs of the present without compromising the ability of future genera-tions to meet their own needs."[2] This definition is at once canny and cunning, but what do the words mean? How do we translate good intentions into action that may be politically unpopular?[3] How do we arrive at international and intercultural compacts that can effectively implement Hardin's "mutual coer-cion" that is at the heart of a sustainable world?

Presumably in an attempt to get away from semantic quagmires and from conflicts of perspective, some scholars have shifted their focus onto "sustain-ability transition." According to the National Research Council's Board on Sus-tainable Development, this means "the primary goals of a transition toward sustainability over the next two generations should be to meet the needs of a much larger but stabilizing human population, to sustain the life support sys-tems of the planet, and to substantially reduce hunger and poverty."[4]

This description is much more specific than the definition of "sustainable development" and displays a commendable purpose. However, translation of these good intentions to effective global action is probably no less challenging than attaining a sustainable world itself.

To begin this process of transition, the developed and developing nations must establish a shared view of what constitutes fair and equitable distribution of resources and of how that can be achieved. It remains unclear whether all nations will agree on the criteria for a fair and just human society—a point central to global sustainability.[5] However, when they see that it is in their self-interest to cooperate—that essential ingredient to successful mutual coercion—some national leaders have at least shown verbal statesmanship. This accord has led to the Law of the Sea Regime for that global commons, the Montreal Protocol on chlorofluorocarbon for stratospheric ozone depletion, the Rio Treaty on the global environment, and the Kyoto Compact to reduce carbon dioxide emission. These agreements do not add up to a program for sustainability, but they are notable first steps.

WHAT DO WE WANT TO SUSTAIN, AND WHAT'S AT STAKE

The term *sustainable* must mean a state in which population size, resource stock, food supply, and environmental quality are in balance, for a period that is long relative to what it would take to get us there. This conclusion must be correct because, unless that balanced condition lasts, it would be just a blip on a curve of continued growth.

A viable state of sustainability must be global. It must be established in a materially closed system, through reordering of priorities and habit change, and aided by human ingenuity. What conditions are needed for it to work, and what may be our safety net if it should fail? What constraints might be imposed by nature and by our concept of our relation to nature? What can earth science do to help inform us about the prospects and limits of such a social transformation? And, very important, what role would political and cultural factors that embody the communities' value systems play in our striving for sustainability? Might these factors form a landmine of social strife and resistance, triggered by fear of scarcity and of change, even before the actual depletion of natural resources?

We need to be explicit about what we seek to sustain. I maintain that we must not sustain the current rates of resource consumption and waste production, and we must not sustain the current pace of population growth and the disparity in wealth among nations. We cannot seek sustainable *development*, which is arguably an oxymoron—hereafter I will speak of a sustainable world, society, or future. Instead, we should examine the lifestyle of the vast middle-class of the world, which might provide clues on productive approaches to global sustainability.[6]

We also need to know what is possible. We must answer the following questions: (1) Are there configurations of society that are unacceptable to all civilizations and must be excluded from the roster of potential goals? (2) What would be the burden imposed on the Earth and its resources, including the biosphere and the Earth's physical environment, if the goals of a global society are pegged to the developed world's level of material affluence? Lest we forget, such goals are even now being touted by our lifestyles and by the exhortations of our entrepreneurs and economic and political leaders. Finally, (3) What are the options that must be treasured and preserved by a society that promotes a decent life for its inhabitants, and what are the material bases essential for assuring that these options will be available at a future time and will survive the aforementioned process of sustainability transition?

The scale and complexity of the global future defies accurate prediction, and well-intentioned efforts to forestall potential problems could backfire; the world is complex and poorly understood, and nature's processes are commonly nonlinear—that is, they have unanticipated but important connectedness, so their effects are not simply additive. For example, forecasts of global warming have often been challenged.[7] Past predictions that the world would run out of Earth-based resources or food have been confronted by the bountiful and continued supply of fossil fuel and metals, at least in the more affluent societies, and by successes in plant breeding that have provided rich harvests of rice, wheat, and corn.[8]

Despite these numerous past successes that seem to give the lie to Cassandra's dire predictions,[9] it seems obvious that the combination of population growth and consumerism cannot go on forever.[10] This limit is real despite the claim by scientists and others that science will fix problems of resource use and our environment through ingenuity. Such problems go beyond technical knowledge and fixes; they place demands on the Earth that push the limits posed by laws of thermodynamics. Even though human ingenuity and the elasticity in the natural system have allowed the human-caused global material and energy flow to increase until now, the Earth is a closed system except for the input of solar energy. Sooner or later, we will run out of room for growth.[11] Relying on future inventiveness is the metaphorical equivalent of relying on a timely medical miracle.

We do not know when that moment of saturation will arrive: It may already be here, only waiting to be recognized. Harbingers of the day of reckoning may be the oil embargo of the early 1970s, the Gulf War, triggered by the oil-consuming nations' perceived need to protect their supply, and the collapse of the world's fisheries. Yet few national leaders face these threats to the habitability of the Earth with much sense of urgency: Which U.S. leaders can expect to be reelected if they advocate a no-growth national economy? Yet, if we seriously care about the well-being of our descendants, then we must not assume that human ingenuity will provide the panacea. We who live in affluent societies will have to change our lifestyles; all of us, wherever we live, will have to work together to effect drastic reductions in global procreational fecundity.

Among the world's five most populous nations—China, India, United States, Indonesia, and Brazil—the United States leads in material use and waste production.[12] On a per capita basis, preeminence of the United States is even more striking—our per capita consumption and waste generation is 10 to 15 times those of the other four nations. Put another way, in terms of consumption and waste generation, every child born and brought up in the United States will have an impact that is equivalent to 10 to 15 children in the other nations. If we deplore societies that have ten children per family, how then can we accept with equanimity two-child families in the United States, with their projected life-time consumption?

Most of us probably share a feeling that people of the less developed nations deserve a better quality of life. Decency and equity require that we help them to improve their lot. Better life, to many—especially those who hitherto have done without—means more creature comforts, material goods, and improved social services; for better or for worse, this outcome will mean more demand on resources, and more pollution.

To illustrate this point, suppose the per capita standard of living in China, India, Indonesia, and Brazil is improved. Higher standards of living will cause an increase in the material load on the Earth. To estimate how this improvement would affect the anthropogenic load on the Earth's resources and environment, I have chosen six factors [commerical energy use; three Earth-based metals (aluminum, copper, and steel); two greenhouse gases (carbon dioxide and methane)] as indicators of the expected overall changes on the Earth.

A useful way to measure the resultant change in demand—that is, the changed material load on the Earth—is to begin with the per capita demand: the magnitude of the total demand placed on the Earth by any nation is directly proportional to the size of the national population and to the size of the change in demand. To estimate the change in demand, we can use the ratio of the per capita demand of the sample nation to that of the United States. We designate this ratio by the symbol m. Multiplying m by the ratio of the sample nation's population to that of the United States gives us a factor, f:

$$f = m \times \frac{\text{sample nation's population}}{\text{U.S. population}}$$

If we multiply f for China, India, Indonesia, or Brazil by the actual total U.S. demand, we have calculated the projected national demand when the living standard of that sample nation equals a fraction, m, of that of the United States.

Using data from 1995, the table gives results for an arbitrary value of $m = 0.25$ for China, India, Indonesia, and Brazil—that is, if the per capita standard of living for the four nations is increased to one-quarter of the U.S. per

PROJECTED MATERIAL LOAD ON EARTH
FOR THE UNITED STATES, CHINA, INDIA, INDONESIA, AND BRAZIL

Consumer	f^a	Energy Use[b] (Giga-Gj)[c]	Aluminum (Mt)[c]	Copper (Mt)[c]	Steel (Mt)[c]	Carbon Dioxide[d] (Gt)[c]	Methane[e] (Mt)[c]
United States	—	81.75	5.41	2.64	93.33	4.88	27.00
China (C)	1.160	94.83	6.28	3.10	108.26	5.66	31.32
India (I)	0.888	72.59	4.80	2.37	82.88	4.33	23.98
Indonesia (D)	0.188	15.37	1.02	0.50	17.55	0.92	5.08
Brazil (B)	0.154	12.59	0.83	0.41	14.37	0.75	4.16
Projected sum for C, I, D, B		195.38	12.93	6.38	233.06	11.66	64.54

Source: World Resources Institute, World Resources 1996–1997 (New York: Oxford University Press, 1996).
a. $f = 0.25 \times$ (sample nation's population)/(U.S. population).
b.   Commercial energy use.
c.   Abbreviations of units of measure: Giga-Gj = giga-gigajoules (one billion-billion joules), Mt = megatonnes (one million metric tonnes), Gt = giga-metric tonnes (one billion metric tonnes). For simplicity's sake, I have not included English equivalent units.
d.   Industrial carbon dioxide.
e.   Anthropogenic methane.

capita standard of living for the same time period. The bottom row of the table shows that the total projected material load on the Earth, indicated by the six factors, is more than twice as large as the load imposed in 1995 by the United States alone. So, everything else being equal, the material load on the Earth will increase by an amount that depends on the size of the national populations and on the magnitude of the change in our demands on the Earth.

Despite our imperfect understanding of all the interactions that affect the Earth's ability to sustain us, we can be reasonably sure that we must meet the following conditions: (1) the world population must be stabilized; (2) the per capita consumption of materials and generation of pollutants must be drastically reduced; and (3) the disparity between developed nations (symbolized by the United States) and developing nations must be reduced.

This may be a tall order, perhaps unattainable. However, the consequence of not taking precautionary measures and relying on the hope that things will somehow work out would equate to counting on winning a lottery in order to pay a medical bill. Should we not accept social responsibility for the protection of the future habitability of the Earth? If so, we need an insurance policy, a hedge against a situation that must not be allowed to happen if the human society is to have a viable future.

RELEVANCE OF THE GEOLOGICAL RECORD

The Earth is not a static place; the geological record shows that the physical and ecological environments of the Earth have always been changing.[13] Some changes are slow on a human time scale; others, not necessarily minor, are rapid. Slow rates inferred from the geological record may in part reflect the fact that our chronological mileposts are commonly far apart, so the average rates we deduce on this basis may be much too low.

Changes, both natural and anthropogenic, that may affect the future of the Earth as a habitat are increases in amounts of greenhouse gases, climate change, sea level fluctuations, and ecosystem changes, including large-scale migration or extinction of fauna and flora. Such geological changes are indeed ever-present and inevitable; they provide the needed context to view the future. Runaway growth in human population at the expense of the rest of the ecosystem might be just another geologically insignificant natural event. This, however, does not address a purely human-centered concern: Are we destroying our own future by our profligate ways?

In the geological past, fertile land may have been reduced to desert, sea level rise may have inundated lowland areas, and air temperature may have risen to a point where animal and plant life were destroyed. Nobody was there to protect threatened life species—they died out, evolved, or adapted to different ways of living. As members of "civilized" human society, however, we seek to control and manage our land and its utility. We want to maintain the Earth as a stable living space consistent with our idea of a "comfort zone," modifying the Earth to suit our desires rather than adapting ourselves to it—witness the damming of rivers the world over; the channelization of the Mississippi River on its own delta; the diversions of river flow away from California's Owens Lake, the Aral Sea, and the Nile Delta; or the efforts to "shore up" the beaches on the mid-Atlantic seaboard so that vacation houses may be rebuilt on shifting sand.

This approach is a different proposition from acknowledging that the geological record tells us that we must expect changes. Moreover, aside from the fact that we deem natural changes beyond certain limits unacceptable, we also do not know how large-scale human-induced changes would interact with natural processes, and on what kind of time scale. For example, in two important papers, geochemist Wallace Broecker discussed how anthropogenic carbon dioxide could cause major mode shifts in ocean circulation that would drastically affect the productivity of agricultural land in the circum-Atlantic region.[14] The record of the Holocene Period—the last 10,000 years—shows that such mode changes happened numerous times and that the rate of change could be fast—years to decades—even by human standards.[15] Even if we ignore the rest of our ecosystem and focus only on the well-being of *Homo sapiens,* we will be irresponsible if we do not address how changes in natural conditions, whatever their causes, may affect the future viability of the global habitat.

OPTIONS AS NONRENEWABLE RESOURCES

I take it for granted that we want to leave for our descendants a sustainable opportunity to lead decent, civil lives. Such lives surely must include the possibility of making real choices among alternative ways of living. Thus, a prime objective for a sustainable world must be to preserve and, if possible, to enhance future options. Options are themselves resources, some of which are nonrenewable and are being depleted rapidly by human activities.[16] Options change with human perception of what is possible and what goods and services are available; they are both material and intangible and are anchored in both material and cultural foundations.

What options are essential to assure that a future society will provide a decent life for all, while treading gently on the ecosystem? Every choice has its consequences. For example, if we choose to use up our petroleum resources, then future societies would have to do without this source of energy as well as important petrochemicals, including plastics and many medicines. If we do not take steps to protect the soil of the arable lands, we would be hurting people's dietary habits and health. Converting nonrenewable resources in the ground into capital—lauded as "value added" in conventional economics— would reduce options.

Our land use plans, especially for sensitive niches such as tropical forests, wetlands, riparian systems, and ocean islands, should opt for flexibility and for conditions favorable to ecological diversity. We should consider *how* to sequence our land use so as to maximize options, and *whether* to set aside certain earth resources so that future societies may deal with civilization's emergencies.[17] We should bequeath to our descendants both the opportunity and the wherewithal to review *their* future options in a meaningful way, and this bequest must include a margin of safety for surprises and miscalculations. Last, respect for human dignity, that *sine qua non* for our self-designation as *Homo sapiens,* is also a social option, and a fragile one at that. The sidewalks of Calcutta, the shantytowns of Rio, and the slums of our own inner cities—not to mention the recent global record of governance by mass terror—are testaments to that fragility. If we want to preserve future generations' options to choose social systems that respect human dignity and human rights, then we must preserve the material base for it.

What material goods are required to underpin a given option? What is the relative importance of using the available goods now versus preserving them for future exercise of options? How should we allocate alternative ways to use a given resource, both geopolitically and in terms of the nature of the commodity? These issues need to be addressed, and the sooner the better.

GETTING THERE FROM HERE

Let me change my metaphor. Instead of looking over a long-term care insurance policy, we are now a group of Lilliputians traveling down a rapids-filled river in a bulky and unwieldy raft. Our diminutive size relative to the river prevents us from getting an overview of the channels in the river. Although we know that different passages lead to different strands of the river, some of which provide quieter water and safety from a disastrous overturning, we are unsure of the locations of these desirable strands or the passages leading to them. Indeed, we have not yet fully defined the configuration of the desired quiet strand. So, not only must we make decisions on the run, we must make decisions soon because delays will cause the loss of some passages and quiet strands. We must also steer the unwieldy raft into the passage and the quiet water without major mishap. How, then, should we proceed?

It seems prudent that we have some clear idea of what kinds of sustainable society (which quiet water strands) are acceptable, and that we should study the nature of the river channel and currents so that we can steer the raft safely through the transition. Even though we do not want to preempt the ability of our descendants to make their own choices, including their preferred form of social organization, we must recognize that our decisions and actions, or lack thereof, will affect their choices, so we need to make allowance for that fact when we make our own choices. We must also allow for our miscalculations.

A conceivable sustainable society is one in which the majority of people live in hovels, barely surviving at the subsistence level: Would that be an acceptable goal? Would a habitat that is fully polluted and teeming with sick people be acceptable? Should we tolerate arrangements in which terror and intimidation are the normal way to rule and be ruled? Should we insist that all nation-societies enjoy equitable and equal access to human amenities, or should we accept social and economical disparities across and within national boundaries, as they exist now? How important is it for us to insist that the sustainable society includes respect for human dignity and human rights?

Assuming that we can answer these questions and can choose our goal, we next need to consider how to preserve the options that accompany this choice. The list of options must be complemented and supported by a full appreciation of the required underpinning of material bases.

CHOICES WE NEED TO MAKE

It seems reasonable to base our planning on a realistic size of the future world population—for instance, 12 billion a century from now. We need to anticipate how the population will be distributed, economically and geographically. I believe we already have a reasonable grip on the available nonrenewable earth resources.[18] I think we also have a pretty good idea of the pattern whereby these nonrenewable resources tend to diminish, and some idea of the difficulties in extracting the inaccessible remainders.

Suppose we take the most parsimonious projection as a start, and assume that civil society can be sustained with little or no amenity—say 2,000 kilocalories of daily per capita food intake, hovels for shelter, polluted air and water, and no ecosystem save what is absolutely essential for human survival at this crude level. What would be the demands of this projection on material resource and the environment? This level of survival is perhaps unacceptable for most of us living in the developed world, but it is close to daily reality for millions. Social scientist Alan Durning estimated that about 20 percent of the world population eat an insufficient grain diet and drink unsafe water.[19] Sad to say, even this rock-bottom state of subsistence would be unsustainable if population growth continues unabated.

More than 30 years ago, agriculturalist William Paddock and foreign service officer Paul Paddock asked how an affluent society should respond when it encounters dire poverty in societies where basic human needs such as food are in short supply and require donation from outside. They suggested a triage approach, with the donor societies assigning recipients to different aid categories. Despite economist Julian Simon's offhand dismissal, this deeply troubling issue of balancing national interest, capability, and needs with fairness and justice remains unresolved and could seriously impede an equitable and peaceful sustainability transition.[20]

The planners—social scientists, philosophers, economists, lawyers, natural scientists (especially ecologists and geologists), political leaders, along with the media—will need to get together and consider how to establish a process by which mutual coercion can be defined and accepted. The discussion must include, not only natural resources and environment, but also the social and cultural adjustments that accompany the transition. The planet is small not just in ecological terms, but also in human terms; the connectivity of human and natural constraints should play a major role in our planning for a sustainable future.[21]

The scope of planning may be global, or it may be a mosaic of regional compacts; it could even be based on political scientist Samuel Huntington's "civilizations."[22] However it is done, the resolution will no doubt be dictated in part by the realities of today's national powers and resource distribution and in part by demographic projections; but, I hope, also in part by a robust sense of social and environmental justice and idealism. Every conceivable improvement would require added material resources, some of which may be impossible for certain demographic projections. Decisions on these choices will lead us to different strands of quiet water, and they are ineluctably governed by the availability of earth resources.

These earth resources are often classified as "renewable" and "nonrenewable" depending on whether their time scales for replenishment are human or geologic. We consider clean water and air, timber, soil, and fish stock to be renewable; we think of fossil fuels, ores of metals, and hydroelectric dam sites as nonrenewable. For any sustainable future, the time scales of replenishment must be short, or we must keep to a very low rate of consumption. If the rate of replenishment is long relative to the rate of consumption, then even "renewable" resources become effectively nonrenewable.

Clean water and air, fertile soil, healthy and multispecies stands of timber, robust and sustainable fisheries—these are surely essential for a healthy society; yet all are now under siege because short-term gains have taken precedence over long-term conservation. A high-priority item in planning for a successful sustainability transition must be to point out how to use the renewable resources so that they stay renewable.

Nonrenewable resources, by definition, cannot be extracted in any sustainable way within the life span of human institutions. How to provide future generations with such resources, then, depends on the time scale we want to consider. It seems that a minimum duration worthy of our effort should be eight to ten human generations—say, two centuries. Some of our nonrenewable resources may be effectively exhausted by then, in the sense that the remaining material could be utilized only with investments of energy, capital, and other materials whose values exceed that of the desired resource. To achieve a sustainable future, we must circumvent this major barrier.

Recycling and substitution, using materials and methods that perhaps we have not even thought of, may alleviate this upcoming shortfall. For example, the use of aluminum and titanium as manufacturing materials, and the use of nuclear reactions to generate electric energy, were inconceivable options merely a century ago. However, the efficacy of recycling is ultimately limited by the second law of thermodynamics; every instance of recycling loses some material and requires more energy input, so sooner or later too much energy will need to be put into what we want to get out. Likewise, reliance on the conjectured future emergence of new options, such as the substitution of one material for another, is based on faith; even if it should ultimately prove true, such reliance is akin to counting on a medical miracle for a terminal patient.

EPILOGUE: WORKING FOR OUR COMMON FUTURE

As our Lilliputian travelers brave the rapids, they do have some notion that there may be more than one strand of safe water, and that although no strand has all the desirable attributes, some strands are better than others. Choices must be made: One strand may be "equitable, egalitarian, limited affluence for all," one may be "a world with creature comforts but without human dignity; reign by terror"; yet another may be "subsistence for most, opulence for a few." The rafters know that every strand is accessible from one or more of the anastomosing channels of the river, even if they are not sure which passage is connected to which strand. They also know that the manner of approach to any strand could determine the outcome.

As responsible citizens, should we not urgently discuss where we want to go and agree on the ground rules by which to make our decisions? Can we implement sustainable societies and sustainability transition in the face of social inertia and ignorance, and in the face of geological and biological realities? The four apocalyptic horses and riders of sustainability are not conquest, slaughter, famine, and death; they are crowding, loss of options, marginal subsistence, and loss of human dignity. The horses and riders are reared and fed on unbridled population growth, resource depletion, habitat fouling, and social inertia and selfish intransigence. These factors interact in ways we do not yet fully understand; yet the task of sustainability transition hinges on knowing how to quantitatively counter their effects.

Happily, some leaders now recognize the need to act while there is still time.[23] The international agreements of recent years to conserve the Earth's habitat, even if only partially effective, do signal us to pause and think. These are hopeful signs that Hardin's vision for a social ethic, his "mutual coercion mutually agreed upon," might yet be put into practice. But the grandest of all pacts of mutual coercion, that of coordinated, civilized, and effective planning on population, is not yet within sight. Social custom, religious scruples, value systems, and other factors have so far collectively prevented the world from dealing sensibly and effectively with resource consumption and waste production combined with population growth.

Even blind inaction and indecision on our part will affect available choices for our descendants. Prudence and good stewardship for the living world dictate that we start to chart our future soon, and in rather specific terms. We may or may not yet have the knowledge or wisdom to make all the right choices, but do we at least have the sense of purpose to begin?[24]

31

What Else Should My Neighbor Know?

Caryl Edward Buchwald

A few years ago, geologist Allison R. Palmer wrote a short piece for the predecessor of *Geology Today* wherein he addressed the question: What should my neighbor know?[1] It was Palmer's clever way to get his audience to think about the challenge of spreading geological knowledge beyond the profession of geology, itself, to the greater world. His major thesis was something to this effect, "If you think education is expensive, try ignorance." He pointed out the cost of ignorance in land use planning and water planning. I would like to take up that challenge in a slightly different way and ask the question, "What else does my neighbor need to know to understand the predicaments of an environmentally precarious future?" That is, given that we are all busy living our lives, worrying about income and taxes, children and health, love won and lost, what is the most basic knowledge that we need to have to understand the complexity of modern environmental problems?

I think it mostly boils down to three things that are so unavoidably important that to not know about them is to be profoundly ignorant of the dilemmas that modern people find themselves facing. There are plenty of problems in the world, and almost all of them have centrally important aspects that can be better understood if we can grasp these fundamental issues: (1) Earth's human population, as a whole, continues to grow at a rate unprecedented in world history, or "Exponential arithmetic is not your ordinary arithmetic"; (2) The first and second laws of thermodynamics are still operating and are not likely to be revoked; (3) Everywhere in the world, we are perturbing large-scale biogeochemical cycles without anticipating exactly what effects will result from our actions.

POPULATION

One good source of information about the growth of population in the world and in the United States can be found at a Web site sponsored by the United States Census Bureau.[2] A population "clock" run by the bureau clearly shows some of our best estimates of how many people there are in the United States and the world and why these populations are growing. I downloaded the pop-clock for September 9, 1999, at 1:18:47 PM Eastern Standard Time and found out that the population of the United States was 273,459,155. The component parts of this estimate are based on one birth every 8 seconds, one death every 15 seconds, a gain of one person every 31 seconds when immigration and emigration are added, and a gain of one person every 4,834 seconds when returning U.S. citizens are balanced against those who leave. The net result is an increase in the population of the United States of one person every 10 seconds.

There are a number of interesting things about these component estimates. A large component of growth is from international migrants; but even if the United States were to close its borders there would still be a net increase due to the fact that there is a birth every 8 seconds but a death only every 15 seconds. A teacher I work with draws the analogy of population growth to the filling of a bathtub that is missing the stopper for the drain. If the faucet can put water into the tub at a rate faster than water can drain out, then the tub will continue to fill until it overflows onto the floor. If the input of births exceeds the output of deaths, then population will continue to grow. The rate of growth depends on the birthrate and the death rate.

All of these statistics do not mean much unless we understand how exponential arithmetic works. All of us were taught in elementary school how to do plain, old arithmetic—adding, subtracting, multiplying, and dividing. Those skills are useful in everyday life and are essential in the world of science. However, if we were taught about exponential functions, it was not until algebra classes, and then it probably did not sink in as to how important it was, that is, unless you had a knack for banking or investing. Bankers know a lot about annual percentage rates for financing loans and how the cost of interest on a loan can grow to huge amounts. Bankers sometimes try to hide the fact that for a long-term loan like a mortgage, the total interest payments can easily exceed the initial principle that was borrowed. So it is with population growth.[3] People can quickly multiply into a very large number of women, men, and children.

A nifty trick that I learned about annual percentage rates is that I can estimate the time it takes for a population to double if I divide the number 70 by the annual growth rate.[4] Thus, an annual growth rate of two percent will cause a population to double in 35 years. Twenty dollars invested at three percent per year will double and return 40 dollars in little more than 23 years. An annual growth rate of three percent will cause a human population to double in just about 23 years. What is hard to believe is this—in exponentially growing populations, every time the population doubles, it contains more people than ever existed in that population up until that time! Try it for yourself. Do the numbers: 1, 2, 4, 8, 16, 32, 64, 128, and so on. The number 16 is larger than 1 plus 2 plus 4 plus 8. This is a profoundly important idea, because we must eventually rectify the growth with the use of resources—something about which every geologist can speak.

Of course, to maintain a livable planet, we need to understand the growth of world population and the demands that come with that increase in population. The same Web site that contains the population clock for the United States has a population clock for the world.[5] It shows that the world population for September 8, 1999, at 1:52:23 PM Eastern Standard Time was 6,010,866,199 (more than six billion) people. And a graph of the estimated growth rate of world population shows the annual rate of increase to be about one and one-third percent. Some good news is that the annual percentage rate is expected to continue to decline at least through 2050. But, positive exponential growth continues, and still another graph shows world population to be an expected nine billion people or more by the year 2050.

Those of us who are interested in economic justice of the sort that assumes the rest of the world could live at the North American level of consumption assert that we need to discover and exploit resources at the same exponential population growth rate.

The way I like to think about it is this: If the people in the developing world aspire to live at the consumption level of North Americans and Western Europeans, then we will have to produce enough material things to account for both population growth and the growth in affluence. A detailed look at population growth shows that most of it is occurring in developing countries. Therefore, both population growth and growth in affluence will contribute to very large demands for material goods.

Consider the effect of consumption on the landscape. The amount of land that is dug up and profoundly disturbed by mining today would be minuscule in comparison to the land area disturbed to make and supply people over the globe with new consumer goods. Likewise, if we want the entire world to eat at the level at which most North Americans eat, we will need new agricultural land and improved efficiency so that we can produce and distribute an increasing amount of food each year. By the year 2050, world agricultural output must be 50 percent larger than it is today in order to keep pace with world population. Should people in developing countries change their diets and consume much more meat and total calories than they now do, then the world agricultural output would need to be even greater than an added 50 percent. Given present trends in agriculture, it also means more nitrate fertilizers, more pesticides, more water use, more animal wastes, and more energy consumption.

Another important trend driven by demographic change is the growth of cities. In 1970, a little more than a third of the world's people lived in cities. Now, more than half of all human beings live in cities; and by 2020, most experts think that more than 60 percent of the world's population will be urbanized.[6] When people are concentrated in cities, there is a great need for carefully conceived and developed infrastructure such as water supply, waste disposal, and building-supply resources—things like sand and gravel. When people are concentrated into small areas, the demand for water, as an example, becomes concentrated on the resources at hand. In many parts of the world, there just is not enough water to supply present populations easily, much less even larger populations.[7] Many major cities in the United States find themselves in search of water sources well beyond the city limits. New York City gets its water from vast tracts of land in the distant Catskill Mountains. Denver, Colorado, seeks to use water from adjacent river basins, but that water must be transferred from basin to basin to be used.[8] Los Angeles, California, takes water from the east side of the High Sierras and diverts streams that had once spilled into Mono Lake and the Owens Valley.[9] The development of these cities has made the countryside less habitable because water resources are directed away from rural areas.

With rapid urban growth, there is also a tendency to build on any land that is available, even if it is unsafe.[10] Thus we see people throughout the world living in flood-prone areas, on the sides of steep mountains, and near volcanic hazards. The best land seems to be taken first, and later migrants to the city must make do with marginal lands in areas prone to floods, landslides, and earthquake damage.[11] In the United States, people with financial resources often seek out dangerous mountainsides,[12] coastal zones,[13] and river floodplains[14] in an attempt to escape the city and be closer to nature.

Population has a major impact on limited resources. Two examples from my home state of Minnesota will illustrate this for you. At the northeastern end of Minnesota is the world famous Boundary Waters Canoe Area Wilderness. It is the most heavily used and popular wilderness area in the United States. It consists of hundreds of lakes that can be visited by canoe, provided you are strong enough to carry the canoe across portages from one lake to another. By portaging the canoe, it is possible to go for days on end visiting one lake after another in this remote area. In 1983, it took my college-age son more than five weeks to paddle from one end to the other by himself. He often went days at a time without seeing other canoeists. With the growth of population, primarily in the midwestern states, and the popularity of getting back to nature, this area has become very desirable for wilderness outings. Now it is so frequently used that a system of wilderness permits limiting visitors and requiring special arrangements—group size, camping spots, entry points, restricted fire building—are enforced by the forest rangers of the Superior National Forest. Inevitably, people who like to fish from motor boats have come into conflict with those who prefer the quietude of the paddle. In winter, the conflict is between snowmobile users and nonmotorized recreationists. The disagreements arise principally because wilderness and quietude are scarce resources and are in demand by more and more people. Conflicts seem inevitable.

Similar disputes occur all over my home state—hog farmers polluting the air and water conflict with people who retreat to the country for clean air and water; power boat owners who require immense water surfaces for their noisy, speeding craft conflict with anglers, sailors, and people seeking to enjoy wildlife more quietly.

The lesson seems clear. Population growth and the push for economic parity will demand the use of more natural resources and ever more intense rates of utilization. We will need to be more efficient and more clever about our exploitation of resources if we hope to mitigate some of the impact of growth. Rapid urbanization will exacerbate problems of water supply, clean air, noise, recreation, and other resource availability. Geologists will be called upon to measure those resources and suggest ways to mitigate the impact of their overuse.[15]

LAWS OF THERMODYNAMICS

Many years ago during the so-called Arab oil embargo, I was engaged in conversation with a faculty member at the college where I teach. The colleague asked me why, in the face of the embargo, we did not just synthesize all the oil we needed. I proceeded to explain some of the history of synthetic fuels research and what little I knew of the politics and economics of the situation. The faculty member became quite impatient with my explanation and reiterated the question: "Why don't we just synthesize the oil we need?"

All good teachers try hard to understand the basis of their student's questions, so I asked in reply: "What should we synthesize it from?" The faculty member, thereupon, looked very puzzled and said, "I mean, just synthesize it." At that point, I realized why we did not understand one another. Thermodynamics laws tell us unequivocally that it is impossible to synthesize something out of nothing. We cannot possibly synthesize oil out of nothing; it always takes raw materials to start the process.

Although knowledgeable and quite brilliant in some ways, this person apparently never learned the lessons of the first and second laws of thermodynamics. The first law of thermodynamics boldly states that matter—or energy—can neither be created nor destroyed. It can only be changed from one form to another. It also makes sense to think of matter as being composed of energy; according to Einstein's famous equation, the relationship is $E = mc^2$. The energy (E) available in a mass (m) is proportional to the square of the speed of light (c). The first law says that when atomic energy is used, mass is converted to energy, but nothing new is created nor is anything old destroyed. It is merely a conversion from one to another.

If it is impossible to synthesize fuel from nothing, it must be equally true that we cannot ever throw anything away. Taking trash to the nearest landfill is not a question of disposing of waste. It is simply putting the waste somewhere else. It may undergo some degradation, meaning that the original material—

paper for example—partially dissolves or breaks down to simpler molecules, but it does not disappear in the sense of going from something to nothing. That is the problem with trying to engineer sanitary landfills. Materials generated by consumers and placed in landfills by garbage haulers and dump operators have the potential to escape the confines of the landfill and go somewhere to cause problems. Where I live, there is a fairly high potential for polluting groundwater, so some people think that it is preferable to burn garbage. I hope they do not think that burning garbage makes it disappear. Garbage that is burned is converted to energy and other kinds of matter. The energy can be captured and used creatively to heat buildings in metropolitan areas, but the altered matter is a bit of a problem because it goes out the smokestack and into the air, where it causes air pollution—emissions of sulfur dioxide, hydrochloric acid, and heavy metals. Furthermore, there is still a residue of ash that must be stored somewhere, such as in a "sanitary" landfill. The first law of thermodynamics tells us that we cannot destroy the matter of which the garbage is made. If we are really clever, we might be able to convert it to some things that are not particularly obnoxious, but we cannot destroy it. We cannot throw it away.

My faculty friend needs to know that we cannot create something from nothing. We cannot synthesize things in the sense that my friend understood it, nor can we make nothing out of something. We cannot get rid of garbage by giving it to the landfill. The best we can do is store it for a long, long time and hope that it does not pollute the places where we live.

Geologists have spent a large amount of time and money studying energy and matter conversions. For instance, an intriguing question arises from thinking about the energy balance of Earth and trying to write a budget that will account for all the incoming energy and all the outgoing energy. This is particularly important in the ongoing debate about global warming. The average temperature of Earth is determined by the amount of energy coming to the system versus the amount of energy leaving the system. The amount of energy available from inside the Earth is really quite small when compared with the amount of energy arriving from the sun. The amount leaving Earth is ultimately determined by the temperature of the globe and the ability of Earth to absorb and reflect radiant energy. The higher the average temperature, then the more heat will be lost to outer space. In fact, the rate of heat loss is a function of the difference between the average temperature of Earth and the temperature of outer space. So, if the sun should begin to give off more energy, then Earth's temperature will rise until the rate of heat loss just balances the new rate of heat gain. If the sun's energy level were to decline, then Earth would cool off.

What many people worry about now is what will happen if we change Earth's ability to absorb and reflect radiant energy? If we temporarily alter the way Earth absorbs and reflects radiant energy, then Earth's temperature can change. The first law of thermodynamics teaches us that we can change the rate of heat loss to outer space by changing the composition of the atmosphere and thereby raise the temperature of Earth. The consequences of having more heat energy available are not easy to determine, but an example may suffice to show the challenge. The hydrologic cycle gives a description of the movement of water from the atmosphere onto and into the land and from the land to the oceans and back to the atmosphere. The system is run by energy from the sun, which, through the action of evaporation and uneven heating of the atmosphere, turns liquid water at sea level into water vapor. It enters the atmosphere, reaches great heights, and begins its journey back to the oceans. Because it takes heat energy to evaporate water, a result of global warming is likely to be the acceleration of the evaporative part of the hydrologic cycle. But when and where the evaporation will occur is the subject of intensive research and is still poorly understood in detail. Furthermore, we do not fully understand where the subsequent condensation and precipitation will occur.

The first law of thermodynamics applies to every process and substance that has been studied, and no exceptions to the law have ever been found. In the few cases when we think we have found perpetual motion machines— machines that run forever without energy input—it turns out that our accounting system has been in error. Somewhere we missed counting all the energy and matter involved in the process.

The second law of thermodynamics is subtler and more difficult to grasp and has even been called inscrutable.[16] General statements are hard to formulate. They sound like these—living structures decay, order deteriorates, everything tends to disorder (entropy increases), and growth only occurs at the

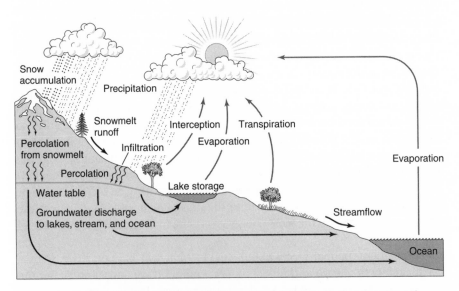

Schematic diagram of the hydrologic cycle. Human activity changes the intensity and duration of movements through the cycle. From Thomas Dunne and Luna B. Leopold, *Water in Environmental Planning* (San Francisco: W. H. Freeman and Company, 1978), 5.

expense of destruction somewhere else. Creating a highly ordered thing like an automobile requires that the landscape of the iron mine become disordered. Coal must be converted to coke before it is used in the steel-making process. The conversion occurs only at great expense. The place where the coal comes from and the air that carries away the waste products in the coke-manufacturing process are degraded. Likewise, the plastics, rubber, copper, paint, glass, and other components of the modern automobile are created only at the expense of disordering the environment where they originated. The second law of thermodynamics says this is inevitable; we cannot be 100 percent efficient at converting matter from one form to another. There is always waste, because we cannot be 100 percent efficient at using energy, either. Entropy for the system inevitably increases.

The second law tells us that geological resources must be limited and nonrenewable. Pessimists look to the present rate of consumption and the growing population and confidently say that we are using up the resources necessary for our industrial base. Optimists almost always point to technological advances as having the potential to save us. Most often technology helps us to substitute one substance for another. So now we build more cars with more and more plastic—derived from petroleum—and aluminum and less and less steel. So we have changed from one potentially nonrenewable resource to another.

The second law also helps us to understand why it is so costly to clean up pollution. The problem arises when pollutants are dispersed into the environment—petroleum in an oil spill at sea, agricultural pesticides in ground water, or ozone-destroying chemicals in the air. An oil spill is essentially a much lower concentration of matter than oil that is still confined to a pipeline or the hold of a ship—or confined naturally in bedrock. Once the oil escapes, there are two problems: oil molecules must be identified, and we must find a cost-effective way to retrieve them. We need to get those molecules back into the pipe or into the ship's hold. The *Exxon Valdez* incident showed us that even when it was relatively easy to locate and identify the oil—for example, on the beaches of Prince Edward Sound, Alaska—it was very difficult to recapture it. In other places, we have tried paper towels, straw, shovels, and other ways to recapture the oil, but it always takes many humans—and people are a valuable resource—who have been trained to identify the oil and how to mop it up.

Likewise, but even more insidious, is the problem of DDT. It is well known by now that DDT, which was used to control insects—I remember being "fogged" with DDT sprays at Scout camp in the mosquito-infested Adirondack Mountains as a boy—has spread through the food web to the most remote parts of the globe. Even penguins in Antarctica have DDT molecules in their fatty tissues. DDT is a very persistent organic compound that seems to resist metabolism by almost all organisms. So, if we want to rid the world of DDT, and more and more that seems like a good idea, we need to find those DDT molecules, identify them properly, and put them back in the spray gun. The amount of energy spent in searching and identifying such molecules is enormous. It is so large that we will, in all likelihood, never be able to retrieve all those errant DDT molecules. The lesson is this: Be very careful about broadly dispersing new chemicals before you understand their effects in the ecosystem. In Minnesota, virtually all the shallow groundwater contains easily measured amounts of corn pesticides, and we do not know what harm they might cause or even what to do about the problem.[17]

Perhaps the most important lesson from the second law of thermodynamics is that of extinction in the biosphere. The laws of thermodynamics also govern the assembly and maintenance of unique genomes. The second law helps us understand that any particular genome is a very complex assemblage of genetic information. If that information is lost because of extinction, it is extremely unlikely that it will be reassembled. Unique genomes represent concentrations of knowledge into highly ordered systems; extinction represents the ultimate loss of that knowledge. No modern biologists I know would predict that new genomes will arise rapidly to replace those we are losing. Geological evidence from mass extinctions at the Permo-Triassic boundary (approximately 250 million years ago) and the Cretaceous-Tertiary boundary (66 million years ago) tells us that it took several millions of years for the biodiversity of Earth to climb back to pre-extinction event levels. Apparently the natural biodiversity of the world cannot be replicated in a short time.[18] My own experience with prairie restoration and that of others with wetland restoration shows how very difficult it is to recreate complex and diverse ecosystems.[19] Our descendants are going to be particularly upset with us if we do little to slow down the mass extinctions that are occurring now.

The laws of thermodynamics viewed this way seem rather depressing. But then, if your objective is to fly, the law of gravity seems depressing, too. The laws of thermodynamics keep us from believing charlatans by helping us to understand the way that the world really works.

HUMANS: A FORCE OF GEOLOGICAL PROPORTION

Earth has a number of large-scale, biogeochemical cycles, which involve the transfer of material and energy from one place to another and from places of storage to places of activity. Human beings are now so numerous and so powerful that our normal, everyday activity perturbs these cycles. Sometimes these perturbations cause huge problems because they disrupt systems that have evolved over millennia and that cannot adjust rapidly to the new set of conditions we have imposed. There are many examples, such as cycles of water, carbon, nitrogen, phosphorus, and sulfur among others, but two illustrate the overall problems. Studying the diagram of the hydrologic cycle makes it possible to see the impact that people have on the movement of water from one place to another. Every arrow in the hydrologic cycle diagram is affected by the activity of people. The impact is very significant. For example, when we build cities, we have a major influence on the places where water can percolate into soils and eventually down into the groundwater system. Roof tops—by design, lawns—because of compaction and their small size, streets, and sidewalks are all quite impervious to water. Good engineers build roadways that drain quickly and have no places for water to puddle. So, instead of percolating into the ground, rainwater flows off into storm sewers and quickly into urban streams. As a result, streams have flash floods when it rains and very low flows when it does not, because the groundwater system does not get replenished and cannot supply enough water to make the streams flow regularly. Erratic flows discourage the formation of equilibrium channels and the needed conditions for the kinds of aquatic organisms that we like. If we had, instead, decided to create a system that was biologically and geologically friendly, we would have figured out how to put the water back in the groundwater system as nature seems to have intended.

A corn field adjacent to my home acts in the same unbalanced way. Essentially no vegetation exists on that field except for part of June, July, August, and September. If all goes well, the farmer removes the crop by October and plows the field. When it rains, there is nothing to protect the soils from the impact of raindrops and little to hold back the water during all the other months of the year. The result, by our own measurements, is a huge proportion of rainfall running off the field, carrying dark-brown soil through a gully on our land and down to the nearby Cannon River. For days after a hard summer rain, the river runs dark brown and is nearly opaque. Not only has the groundwater not been replenished; the rainwater has eroded fertile soil from the field and put it into the river, where it does not belong.

Other parts of the hydrologic cycle are affected by the actions of people. We transfer groundwater to the surface by using wells. We drain wetlands. We dam rivers. We cut forests and reduce transpiration by trees. Our impact on the hydrologic cycle is immense in some areas and not always beneficial.

The carbon cycle is another large-scale biogeochemical cycle that we have perturbed—in this case, on a global basis. Under natural circumstances, carbon moves from the atmosphere to the biosphere to the hydrosphere to the lithosphere (region of soil, sediments and rocks) and back again. Plants take carbon dioxide from the atmosphere and, using photosynthetic processes, combine it with water to produce sugars and oxygen. The carbon has been taken from the atmosphere and incorporated into plant tissue. We and other animals eat the plants, metabolize the tissue by combining it with oxygen, and breathe out a residue of carbon dioxide. Shellfish and other lime-secreting organisms take carbon dioxide out of water, combine it with calcium, and produce their characteristic shells. If the shells are incorporated in the sediment on the bottom of the ocean, then the carbon is moved via the biosphere from the atmosphere to the hydrosphere to the lithosphere. Plants that become

peat, lignite, and coal also move carbon from the atmosphere to the lithosphere. The rate at which things move from one place to another is determined
mostly by temperature and the numbers of plants and animals on Earth.

We have learned to find coal, petroleum, and natural gas deposits, all of
which are warehouses for ancient carbon. We take that carbon and burn it,
thus producing more carbon dioxide that goes back into the atmosphere. The
rate at which we burn coal, petroleum, and natural gas exceeds the rate at
which the remains of shellfish and other animals and plants are added to the
lithosphere. So, in fact, we are rapidly transferring carbon—in the form of carbon dioxide—from its position in rocks to the atmosphere. Well, so what?

For more than 100 years, we have known that carbon dioxide plays a role
in the heat balance of Earth. Carbon dioxide acts as a gatekeeper for forms of
radiant energy. It allows ultraviolet energy into our system but keeps infrared
energy from escaping our system. The result is that, on the short term, we are
changing the energy equation of the atmosphere. We are allowing more energy
to come in than we allow to escape, with the result that Earth will seek a new
equilibrium temperature that is higher than the present temperature.

Coming from Minnesota, where the winters can be very cold and very
long, that does not seem so bad. It does not seem too bad until we try to figure
out what will happen to the amount of rainfall, snowfall, and severe storms
that we might get in the future. It does not seem too bad, that is, until we try to
figure out what will happen to native vegetation that has evolved here under
the present climate. Some people argue that part of Minnesota will become
hotter and drier. That would mean the border between prairie and deciduous
woods—known as Big Woods, here—would move eastward. Deciduous trees
would die out but would not be replaced by prairie because there is no longer a
good seed source for prairie grasses. And it does not appear too bad until we
try to determine what will happen to the soils that also have evolved here
under the present climate. The northern part of the state has very large areas of
peat wetlands—in fact, the largest peat deposits in the lower 48 states. If they
become drier and warmer, they will disappear; and the remaining soils will not
be very good for growing corn and soybeans, the two most important cash
crops in the state. Perhaps the winters will be milder, but there is a distinct possibility that agriculture and native vegetation will both be greatly disrupted.
The point seems to be that we humans are now a geological force of global proportions, creating and running an experiment for which we have little predictive certainty.

Well, there you have it. Here is what my neighbor ought to know about how
Earth works. The population is growing rapidly and becoming urbanized at an
unprecedented scale. As a whole, we seem to misunderstand the lessons of the
laws of thermodynamics—the set of rules governing how energy and matter
behave. We cannot make things out of nothing. We cannot throw things away,
and it is very hard to clean up messes. We have grown so numerous and so

powerful that we are now a geological force of global proportions. We regularly disturb major biogeochemical cycles. Every human being needs to appreciate these three profound ideas. With a future that is environmentally precarious, ignorance of these ideas is just too expensive—its cost could be the livability of our planet.

SOURCE NOTES

Preface

1. Quoted in Paul Brooks, *The House of Life: Rachel Carson at Work* (Boston: Houghton Mifflin, 1972), 127–129.
2. Robert Gottlieb, *Forcing the Spring: The Transformation of the American Environmental Movement* (Washington, DC: Island Press, 1993), 86.
3. Rachel Carson, "Silent Spring-III," *The New Yorker* 38 (30 June 1962): 67.
4. Robert Gottlieb, "A Sense of Place." Review of *Water, Culture, and Power: Local Struggles in a Global Context* by John M. Donahue and Barbara Rose Johnston. *Science* 280 (1998): 1209.
5. Marge Piercy, *He, She and It* (New York: Fawcett Crest, 1991), 41.
6. Rachel Carson, *Silent Spring* (Boston: Houghton Mifflin, 1962).

1   Geology: The Bifocal Science

1. Eugene M. Shoemaker, Ruth F. Wolfe, and Carolyn S. Shoemaker, "Asteroid and Comet Flux in the Neighborhood of Earth," in *Global Catastrophes in Earth History,* Virgil L. Sharpton and Peter D. Ward, eds. Geological Society of America Special Paper 247 (Boulder, CO: Geological Society of America, 1990), 155–170.
2. The "discovery paper" on this topic: Luis W. Alvarez, Walter Alvarez, Frank Asaro, and Helen V. Michel, "Extraterrestrial Cause for the Cretaceous–Tertiary Extinction," *Science* 208 (1980): 1095–1108. The following book reviews recent developments on the subject: Walter Alvarez, *T. rex and the Crater of Doom* (Princeton, NJ: Princeton University Press, 1997).
3. Eugene M. Shoemaker, Paul R. Weissman, and Carolyn S. Shoemaker, "The Flux of Periodic Comets Near the Earth," in *Hazards Due to Comets and Asteroids,* Tom Gehrels, Mildred Shapley Matthews, and A. M. Schumann, eds. (Tucson: University of Arizona Press, 1995).
4. Daniel J. Stanley and Andrew G. Warne, "Nile Delta in Its Destruction Phase," *Journal of Coastal Research* 14 (1998): 794–825. This article provides a recent view of the evolution of the Nile Delta and human history there.
5. Ibid., 807.
6. David W. Simpson, A. Gharib, and R. M. Kebeasy, "Induced Seismicity and Changes in Water Level at Aswan Reservoir, Egypt," *Gerlands Beitraege zur Geophysik* 99 (1990): 191–204.
7. Stanley and Warne, "Nile Delta," 794–825.
8. Susan W. Kieffer, "The 1983 Hydraulic Jump in Crystal Rapid: Implications for River-Running and Geomorphic Evolution in the Grand Canyon," *Journal of Geology* 93 (1985): 385–406.
9. Hal G. Stephens and Eugene M. Shoemaker, *In the Footsteps of John Wesley Powell: An Album of Comparative Photographs of the Green and Colorado Rivers 1871–72 and 1968* (Boulder, CO: Johnson Books, 1972).
10. Thomas A. Jagger, "Volcanic Phenomena of the Eruption (of 1924)," *Monthly Bulletin of the Hawaiian Volcano Observatory* 12 (1924): 45.
11. Howell Williams and Alexander R. McBirney, *Volcanology* (San Francisco: Freeman, Cooper and Company, 1979).
12. Shiego Arimaki and Tad Ui, "The Aira and Ata Pyroclastic Flows and Related Caldera Depressions in Southern Kyushu, Japan," *Bulletin of Volcanology* 29 (1966): 29–47, as cited in Richard V. Fisher and Hans-Ulrich Schmincke, *Pyroclas-*

tic Rocks (Berlin: Springer-Verlag, 1984).

13. Susan W. Kieffer, "Blast Dynamics at Mount St. Helens on 18 May 1980," *Nature* 281 (1981): 568–570.

14. Amos Nur and Hagai Ron, "Armageddon's Earthquakes," *International Geology* 39 (1997): 532–541.

15. Nicholas N. Ambraseys, "Value of Historical Records of Earthquakes," *Nature* 232 (1971): 375–379.

16. Amos Nur and Eric H. Cline, "Plate Tectonics, Earthquake Storms, and Systems Collapse at the End of the Late Bronze Age in the Aegean and Eastern Mediterranean," *Journal of Archeological Research,* in press.

17. Robert Drews, *The End of the Bronze Age* (Princeton, NJ: Princeton University Press, 1993).

3 Stories of Land, Stories from Land

1. Always my guide and companion on any cross-country journey is the beautiful, hand-drawn map of landforms of the United States by Erwin Raisz. This map can be found in Wallace Walter Atwood, *The Physiographic Provinces of North America* (Boston: Blaisdall, 1964).

2. For example, B. L. Turner II, William C. Clark, Robert W. Kates, John F. Richards, Jessica T. Matthews, and William B. Meyer, eds., *The Earth as Transformed by Human Action: Global and Regional Changes in the Biosphere over the Past 300 Years* (Cambridge: Cambridge University Press, 1990).

3. Human activities here are broadly defined as existing within a network of processes, relationships, and systems that are natural (geological and ecological) as well as cultural. See, for example, William Cronon, "A Place for Stories: Nature, History, and Narrative," *Journal of American History* 78 (1992): 1347–1376.

4. For example, see Emily W. B. Russell, *People and the Land Through Time: Linking Ecology and History* (New Haven, CT: Yale University Press, 1997).

5. Walter Prescott Webb, *The Great Plains* (1931; reprinted, Lincoln: University of Nebraska Press, 1981).

6. Charles B. Hunt, *Natural Regions of the United States* (San Francisco: W. H. Freeman and Company, 1974).

7. Mary Austin, *The Land of Little Rain* (1903; reprinted, Albuquerque: University of New Mexico Press, 1974).

8. Annette Kolodny, *The Land Before Her: Fantasy and Experience of the American Frontiers, 1630–1860* (Chapel Hill: University of North Carolina Press, 1984), xii.

9. Wallace Stegner, *Where the Bluebird Sings to the Lemonade Springs: Living and Writing in the West* (New York: Random House, Inc. and Penguin Books, 1992), 117.

10. Donald W. Meinig, "The Beholding Eye: Ten Versions of the Same Scene," *The Interpretation of Ordinary Landscapes: Geographical Essays,* Donald W. Meinig, ed. (New York: Oxford University Press, 1979).

11. Jacquetta Hopkins Hawkes, *A Land* (New York: Random House, 1951), 8.

12. See, for example, George R. Stewart, *Names on the Land: A Historical Account of Place-Naming in the United States*, 3rd Ed. (Boston: Houghton-Mifflin Company, 1967); and Gordon G. Whitney, *From Coastal Wilderness to Fruited Plain: A History of Environmental Change in Temperate North America from 1500 to the Present* (Cambridge: Cambridge University Press, 1994).

13. Stewart, *Names on the Land.*

14. Ibid.

15. For example, David W. Teague, *The Southwest in American Literature and Art: The Rise of a Desert Aesthetic* (Tucson: University of Arizona Press, 1997).

16. See George H. Williams, *Wilderness and Paradise in Christian Thought: The Biblical Experience of the Desert in the History of Christianity and the Paradise Theme in the Theological Ideal of the University* (New York: Harper and Brothers, 1962); and

Patricia N. Limerick, *Desert Passages: Encounters with the American Deserts* (Niwot: University Press of Colorado, 1989).

17. Stewart, *Names on the Land,* 219; Williams, *Wilderness and Paradise in Christian Thought,* 108.

18. Limerick, *Desert Passages.*

19. Zebulon M. Pike, *The Expeditions of Zebulon Montgomery Pike,* Elliott Coues, ed., Vol. 2 (1810; reprinted, New York: Dover Publications, 1987), 524–525.

20. M. J. Bowden, "The Great American Desert in the American Mind: The Historiography of a Geographical Notion," in *Geographies of the Mind,* D. Lowenthal and M. J. Bowden, eds. (New York: Oxford University Press, 1975), 119–147.

21. For example, D. J. Browne, *The Sylva Americana: or, a Description of Forest Trees Indigenous to the United States Practically and Botanically Considered* (Boston: William Hyde and Company, 1832), cited in Whitney, *From Coastal Wilderness to Fruited Plain;* Thomas Pownall, *A Topographical Description of the Dominions of the United States of America* (1776; reprinted, Pittsburgh, PA: University of Pittsburgh Press, 1949); and Henry N. Smith, *Virgin Land: The American West as Symbol and Myth* (Cambridge, MA: Harvard University Press, 1950).

22. William H. Goetzmann, *Exploration and Empire* (New York: Alfred A. Knopf, 1966).

23. Alexis de Tocqueville, *Democracy in America: A New Translation by George Lawrence,* J. P. Mayer, ed. (New York: Doubleday, 1969), 25. See also Limerick, *Desert Passages,* for a discussion of Tocqueville's comments on the "desert."

24. Charles Preuss, *Exploring with Frémont: The Private Diaries of Charles Preuss, Cartographer for John C. Frémont on His First, Second, and Fourth Expeditions to the Far West,* Erwin G. and Elisabeth K. Gudde, trans. (Norman: University of Oklahoma Press, 1958), 5.

25. Smith, *Virgin Land.*

26. Limerick, *Desert Passages.*

27. Teague, *The Southwest in American Literature and Art,* 3.

28. Limerick, *Desert Passages,* 6.

29. Paul Shepard, *Man in the Landscape: A Historic View of the Esthetics of Nature* (New York: Alfred A. Knopf, 1967).

30. From the "Diary of Reverend Samuel Parker, 1835, along the Platte River," cited in Shepard, *Man in the Landscape,* 238.

31. John Wesley Powell, *Report on the Lands of the Arid Region of the United States, with a More Detailed Account of the Lands of Utah* (Washington, DC: Government Printing Office, 1878).

32. Mary Austin, *Land of Little Rain,* 3–4, 16.

33. For example, see Whitney, *From Coastal Wilderness to Fruited Plain;* and Russell, *People and the Land Through Time.*

34. Russell, *People and the Land Through Time.*

35. For example, Raymond Bradley, *Quaternary Paleoclimatology: Methods of Paleoclimate Reconstruction* (Boston: Unwin Hyman, 1985).

36. Henri Grissino-Mayer, "Tree-Ring Reconstructions of Climate and Fire History at El Malpais National Monument, New Mexico," dissertation, University of Arizona, Tucson, 1995.

37. For example, Debra L. Martin, Alan H. Goodman, George J. Armelagos, and Ann L. Magennis, *Black Mesa Anasazi Health: Reconstructing Life from Patterns of Death and Disease,* Southern Illinois University Center for Archeological Investigations Occasional Paper No. 14 (1991); and Linda S. Cordell, *Prehistory of the Southwest,* 2nd Ed. (San Diego: Academic Press, 1998).

38. Stephen Plog, *Ancient People of the American Southwest* (London: Thames and Hudson, 1998).

39. Older studies include Andrew E. Douglas, "The Secret of the Southwest Solved by Talkative Tree Rings," *National Geographic Magazine* 56 (1929): 736–770; and

Emil W. Haury, "Tree Rings—The Archaeologist's Time-Piece," *American Antiquity* 1 (1935): 98–108.

40. For example, Carla R. Van West, *Modeling Prehistoric Agricultural Productivity in Southwestern Colorado: A GIS Approach,* Washington State University, Department of Anthropology Reports of Investigations 67 (1994); and Richard V. N. Ahlstrom, Carla R. Van West, and Jeffrey S. Dean, "Environmental and Chronological Factors in the Mesa Verde–Northern Rio Grande Migration," *Journal of Anthropological Archaeology* 14 (1995): 125–142.

41. Edmund Ladd, "On the Zuni View," in *The Anasazi,* Jerold G. Widdison, ed. (Albuquerque, NM: Southwest Natural and Cultural Heritage Association Press, 1991), 34–36.

42. Harold Courlander, *People of the Short Blue Corn: Tales and Legends of the Hopi Indians* (New York: Henry Holt and Company, 1970).

43. For example, Valerie L. Kuletz, *The Tainted Desert: Environmental and Social Ruin in the American Southwest* (New York: Routledge, 1998).

44. For example, John C. Hudson, "Settlement of the American Grassland," in *The Making of the American Landscape,* Michael Conzen, ed. (Boston: Unwin Hyman, 1980), 169–185; William E. Riebsame, "The United States Great Plains," in *The Earth as Transformed by Human Action,* Turner et al., eds., 561–575; Whitney, *From Coastal Wilderness to Fruited Plain.*

45. Riebsame, "The United States Great Plains."

46. Hunt, *Natural Regions of the United States.*

47. Whitney, *From Coastal Wilderness to Fruited Plain.*

48. Allan G. Bogue, *From Prairie to Cornbelt: Farming on the Illinois and Iowa Prairies in the Nineteenth Century* (Chicago: University of Chicago Press, 1963; reprinted, Ames, IA: Iowa State University Press, 1994); Whitney, *From Coastal Wilderness to Fruited Plain.*

49. Riebsame, "The United States Great Plains"; and Daniel Hillel, *Out of the Earth: Civilization and the Life of Soil* (Berkeley: University of California Press, 1991).

50. Hudson, "Settlement of the American Grassland."

51. Ibid.

52. Whitney, *From Coastal Wilderness to Fruited Plain.*

53. Bogue, *From Prairie to Cornbelt.*

54. Whitney, *From Coastal Wilderness to Fruited Plain.*

55. John E. Weaver, *North American Prairie* (Lincoln, NE: Johnsen Publishing Company, 1954), 325.

56. Riebsame, "The United States Great Plains."

57. Ibid.

58. Harry E. Schwarz, Jacque Emel, William J. Dickens, Peter Rogers, and John Thompson, "Water Quality and Flows," in *The Earth as Transformed by Human Action,* Turner et al., eds., 253–270.

59. Sandra Postel, *Last Oasis: Facing Water Scarcity* (New York: W. W. Norton, 1992).

60. Ibid.

61. Riebsame, "The United States Great Plains;" Schwarz et al., "Water Quality and Flows."

62. Ibid.

63. Frank H. T. Rhodes and Richard O. Stone, *Language of the Earth* (New York: Pergamon Press, 1981), ix.

5   *Natural Science, Natural Resources, and the Nature of Nature*

1. Martin Rudwick, *Scenes from Deep Time* (Chicago: University of Chicago Press, 1992), 4–16.

2. Simon Schama, *Landscape and Memory* (New York: Alfred A. Knopf, 1995), 451.

3. Stephen Jay Gould, *Time's Arrow/Time's Cycle: Myth and Metaphor in the*

Discovery of Geological Time (Cambridge, MA: Harvard University Press, 1987), 30–41.

4. Charles Lyell, *Principles of Geology* (1830; reprinted, Chicago: University of Chicago Press, 1990), 37–38.

5. Gould, *Time's Arrow/Time's Cycle,* 28.

6. Interestingly, Locke betrayed a deep ambivalence about nature. On the one hand, he described a paradisiacal "State of Nature" in which humans coexisted in an environment of mutual respect and good will; on the other hand, Nature itself was depicted as stingy and unforgiving.

7. John Locke, *The Second Treatise of Civil Government: An Essay Concerning the True, Original, Extent and End of Civil Government,* Richard H. Cox, ed. (1689; reprinted, Arlington Heights, IL: Harlan Davidson, 1982), 27–28.

8. Ibid., 21.

9. Ibid., 24.

10. The complete title conveys the ambitiousness of the work: *Manual of Mineralogy, Including Observations on Mines, Rocks, Reduction of Ores, and the Application of the Science to the Arts.*

11. Rachel Laudan, *From Mineralogy to Geology: The Foundations of a Science, 1650–1830* (Chicago: University of Chicago Press, 1987), 47–69, 87–112.

12. Interestingly, as Earth was becoming spatially finite, it became temporally infinite. The Earth could be compassed, but the date of its Creation had retreated into James Hutton's (actually John Playfair's) "abyss of time."

13. John Wesley Powell, *Seventh Annual Report of the Geological Survey to the Two Houses of Congress* (Washington, DC: Government Printing Office, 1888), 3–4.

14. Thomas H. Watkins, "Introduction: Law and Liquidation," *Wilderness* 55.197 (1992): 11–13.

15. See, for example, Ronald Satz, *Chippewa Treaty Rights* (Madison: Wisconsin Academy of Sciences, Arts, and Letters, 1991).

16. Evelyn Fox Keller, *Reflections on Gender and Science* (New Haven, CT: Yale University Press, 1985), 33–42.

17. Gould, *Time's Arrow/Time's Cycle,* 63–66. See also David Abrams, "The Mechanical and the Organic: On the Impact of Metaphor in Science," in *Scientists on Gaia,* Stephen H. Schneider and Penelope J. Boston, eds. (Cambridge, MA: MIT Press, 1992), 66.

18. Uniformitarianism, the assumption that geological processes operating today are the same as those that occurred in the past, underlies all geological inferences.

19. The metaphor of mechanism was well enough established by the early 1800s to spawn the cultural counterreaction of Romanticism, a celebration of all that was wild and amechanistic in nature.

20. Charles C. Gillispie, *Pierre-Simon Laplace (1749–1827): A Life in Exact Science* (Princeton, NJ: Princeton University Press, 1997), 26–27.

21. Joe D. Burchfield, *Lord Kelvin and the Age of the Earth* (Chicago: University of Chicago Press, 1990), 13–14.

22. Quantitative petrology is, for example, rooted in the assumption that equilibrium thermodynamics can be applied meaningfully to igneous and metamorphic systems. Yet, the study of high-temperature rocks would be much more difficult— and far less interesting—if achievement of equilibrium were in fact the norm, because all evidence of past states (compositional zoning, intracrystalline strain, metastable phases) would be erased.

23. Jianguo Wu and Orie L. Loucks, "From Balance of Nature to Hierarchical Patch Dynamics: A Paradigm Shift in Ecology," *The Quarterly Review of Biology* 70 (1995): 440.

24. Lyell, *Principles of Geology,* 470.

25. Quoted in Phillip Appleman, ed., "Introduction," in *Norton Critical Edition of An Essay on the Principle of Population* (New York: W. W. Norton, 1976), xii.

26. Ibid.

27. Ernst Mayr, *One Long Argument: Charles Darwin and the Genesis of Modern Evolutionary Thought* (Cambridge, MA: Harvard University Press, 1991), 84–85.

28. Quoted in Mark Kurlansky, *Cod: A Biography of the Fish That Changed the World* (New York: Walker, 1997), 122.

29. Rachel Carson, *Silent Spring* (Boston: Houghton-Mifflin, 1962).

30. Russell Utgard and Garry McKenzie, *Man's Finite Earth* (Minneapolis, MN: Burgess, 1974); Charles Park, *Earthbound: Minerals, Energy and Man's Future* (San Francisco: Freeman, Cooper and Company, 1975); Keith Young, *Geology: The Paradox of Earth and Man* (Boston: Houghton-Mifflin, 1975).

31. Paul Ehrlich, *The Population Bomb*, 2nd Ed. (New York: Ballantine Books, 1976); Donella Meadows, Dennis L. Meadows, Jorgen Randers, and William Behrens, *The Limits to Growth* (New York: Universe Books, 1972); Alvin Toffler, *Future Shock* (New York: Random House, 1970).

32. John Fagan, *The Earth Environment* (Englewood Cliffs, NJ: Prentice Hall, 1974), 2.

33. Quoted in Park, *Earthbound*, 11.

34. Andrew Dobson, *Green Political Thought* (London: Routledge, 1995), 72.

35. Meadows et al., *The Limits to Growth.*

36. John Tierney, "Betting the Planet," *New York Times Magazine*, 2 Dec 1990, 82.

37. The origin of the name Club of Rome is obscure but apparently arose out of an international meeting on resources and environmental issues held in Rome around 1970. Because the meeting produced the seeds of the book, the authors of *The Limits to Growth* began to call themselves the Club of Rome.

38. H. S. D. Cole, Christopher Freeman, Marie Jahoda, and K. L. R. Pavitt, *Models of Doom: A Critique of The Limits to Growth* (New York: Universe Books, 1973), 14–32.

39. See also Benoit Mandelbrot, *The Fractal Geometry of Nature* (San Francisco: W. H. Freeman and Company, 1983).

40. Quoted by Anne S. Moffatt, "Ecologists Look at the Big Picture," *Science* 273 (1996): 1490.

41. Robert Costanza et al., "The Value of the World's Ecosystem Services and Natural Capital," *Nature* 387 (1997): 253.

42. Hillary French, "Investing in the Future: Harnessing Private Capital Flows for Environmentally Sustainable Development," Worldwatch Paper 139 (Washington, DC: Worldwatch Institute, 1998), 8.

43. Costanza et al., "The Value of the World's Ecosystem Services and Natural Capital," 259.

44. Edward O. Wilson, *Consilience: The Unity of Knowledge* (New York: Alfred A. Knopf, 1998), 4. In an interview in 1990 with Bill Moyers, Evelyn Fox Keller has pointed out the interesting anachronism inherent in the idea of "laws of nature": The metaphor survives from the time when nature was governed by God's edicts.

45. "Chaotic" systems are characterized by extreme sensitivity to starting conditions: Trivial differences in the values of variables at the outset can lead to widely diverging results. Nonlinear systems are those in which cause and effect are not in simple linear proportion to each other. Recognizing that nonlinearity is actually the norm rather than the exception in natural systems, some scientists liken the linear versus nonlinear distinction to categorizing animals as "elephants" and "nonelephants."

46. Wallace Broecker, "Massive Iceberg Discharges as Triggers for Global Climate Change," *Nature* 372 (1994): 421.

47. A 1997 review article by Eldredge et al. traces the evolution of this evolutionary theory: Niles Eldredge, Stephen Jay Gould, Jerry Coyne, and Brian Charlesworth, "On Punctuated Equilibria," *Science* 276 (1997): 338–341.

48. See, for example, Thomas Stocker and Andreas Schmittner, "Influence of CO_2 Emission Rates on the Stability of the Thermohaline Circulation," *Nature* 388

(1997): 862–865, on the possible effects of increasing carbon dioxide emissions on ocean circulation.

49. Paul Rabinow, "Chaos in the Garden," *New York Times Book Review,* 12 November 1995, 61.
50. Wu and Loucks, "From Balance of Nature to Hierarchical Patch Dynamics," 439.
51. James E. Lovelock, *The Ages of Gaia: A Biography of Our Living Earth* (New York: W. W. Norton, 1988), 3–14.
52. Lee Kump, "The Physiology of the Planet," *Nature* 381 (1996): 111.

6   *Why Believe a Computer? Models, Measures, and Meaning in the Natural World*

1. Sir Francis Bacon, *The New Organon* (1620; reprinted, New York: Macmillan Publishing, 1960); Peter Urbach, *Francis Bacon's Philosophy: An Account and a Reappraisal* (LaSalle, IL: Open Court, 1987).
2. Carl G. Hempel, *Philosophy of Natural Science* (Englewood Cliffs, NJ: Prentice Hall, 1966); Sir Karl Popper, *The Logic of Scientific Discovery* (1959; reprinted, New York: Harper & Row, 1968); also see Popper's *Conjectures and Refutations: The Growth of Scientific Knowledge* (1963; reprinted, London: Routledge, 1992).
3. Leonard F. Konikow and John D. Bredehoeft, "Ground-Water Models Cannot Be Validated," *Advances in Water Resources* 15 (1992): 75–83; Naomi Oreskes, Kristin Shrader-Frechette, and Kenneth Belitz, "Verification, Validation, and Confirmation of Numerical Models in the Earth Sciences," *Science* 263 (1994): 641–646; Naomi Oreskes, "Evaluation (Not Validation) of Quantitative Models," *Environmental Health Perspectives* 106.6 (1998): 1453–1460.
4. Thomas S. Kuhn, *The Copernican Revolution* (1957; reprinted, Cambridge, MA: Harvard University Press, 1981).
5. Oreskes, "Evaluation."
6. Leonard F. Konikow, "Predictive Accuracy of a Ground-Water Model: Lessons from a Postaudit," *Ground Water* 24 (1986): 173–184; Leonard F. Konikow and Lindsay A. Swain, "Assessment of Predictive Accuracy of a Model of Artificial Recharge Effects in the Upper Coachella Valley, California," *28th International Geological Congress Selected Papers on Hydrogeology,* H. Hiese, ed. (Hannover: Springer-Verlag, 1990), 433–449; see also Mary P. Anderson and William W. Woessner, "The Role of the Postaudit in Model Validation," *Advances in Water Resources* 15 (1992): 167–173.
7. Thomas S. Kuhn, *The Structure of Scientific Revolutions* (1962; reprinted, Chicago: University of Chicago Press, 1970); Imre Lakatos, "Falsification and the Methodology of Scientific Research Programmes," in *Criticism and the Growth of Knowledge,* Imre Lakatos and Alan Musgrave, eds. (Cambridge: Cambridge University Press, 1970), 91–196.
8. Pierre Duhem, "Physical Theory and Experiment," in *The Aim and Structure of Physical Theory,* Philip P. Wiener, trans. (1954; reprinted, Princeton, NJ: Princeton University Press, 1991).
9. Simon Shackley, Stuart Parkinson, Peter Young, and Brian Wynne, "Uncertainty, Complexity, and Concepts of 'Good Science' in Climate Change Modelling: Are GCMs the Best Tools?" *Climatic Change* 38 (1998): 159–205. For a counterargument, see Stuart Parkinson and Peter Young, "Uncertainty and Sensitivity in Global Carbon Cycle Modelling," *Climate Research* 9 (1998): 157–174.
10. Popper, *Conjectures,* 339–340.
11. Sir Alfred J. Ayer, *Hume* (Oxford: Oxford University Press, 1990), 74.

7   *Down to Earth: An Historical Look at Government-Sponsored Geology*

1. Readers interested in the history of geological inquiry in the United States and the work of the U.S. Geological Survey may consult Mary C. Rabbitt's comprehensive

work, *Minerals, Lands, and Geology for the Common Defence and General Welfare*, vols. 1–3 (Washington, DC: Government Printing Office, 1979, 1980, 1986). Many historical facts recounted here were drawn from this source.
2. Membership in the National Academy of Sciences is intended to recognize intellectual contributions to fundamental scientific knowledge. (Editor's note: Despite the substantial contribution of female scientists to basic scientific knowledge, membership in the National Academy of Sciences is overwhelmingly male.)
3. Smith also proposed that field personnel wear distinctive USGS uniforms. As a result of this short-lived idea, brass buttons intended for the uniforms have become coveted collector's items today.
4. This and other branches were later renamed divisions.
5. This program is one of many underway in the USGS, an organization of some 10,000 employees housed in 400 offices across the country.

8 Sustainable Living: Common Ground for Geology and Theology

1. In this paper I use the term *geology* in something like its original nineteenth-century sense, when it was taken to include the fields that we now call ecology, paleoecology, hydrology, and geomorphology.
2. Carl Sagan, *Cosmos* (New York: Ballantine Books, 1980), 1.
3. Henry Jackson Flanders, Robert W. Crapps, and David A. Smith, *People of the Covenant: An Introduction to the Hebrew Bible* (New York: Oxford University Press, 1996), 97–115.
4. Paul Tillich, *A History of Christian Thought: From Its Judaic and Hellenistic Origins to Existentialism* (New York: Simon & Schuster, 1967), 107.
5. Ibid., 184–194.
6. John Polkinghorne, *Belief in God in an Age of Science* (New Haven, CT: Yale University Press, 1998), 106.
7. Ian G. Barbour, *Religion and Science: Historical and Contemporary Issues* (San Francisco: Harper San Francisco, 1997), 50–74.
8. See, for example, Stephen Jay Gould, *Wonderful Life: The Burgess Shale and the Nature of History* (New York: W. W. Norton and Company, 1989) and *Full House: The Spread of Excellence from Plato to Darwin* (New York: W. W. Norton, 1996).
9. See Evelyn Fox Keller, *Reflections on Gender and Science* (New Haven, CT: Yale University Press, 1985); Thomas S. Kuhn, *The Structure of Scientific Revolutions* (Chicago: University of Chicago Press, 1970).
10. Tillich, *A History of Christian Thought*, 263.
11. Paul Tillich, *Dynamics of Faith* (New York: Harper & Row, 1957).
12. Tillich, *Dynamics of Faith*, 95–98.
13. Tillich, *A History of Christian Thought*, 267.
14. Neils H. D. Bohr, "Essays 1932–1957 on Atomic Physics and Human Knowledge," in *The Philosophical Writings of Neils Bohr*, Vol. 2 (Woodbridge, CT: Ox Bow Press, 1987), 66.
15. Sallie McFague, *The Body of God: An Ecological Theology* (Minneapolis, MN: Fortress Press, 1993).
16. Fred T. Mackenzie, *Our Changing Planet: An Introduction to Earth System Science and Global Environmental Change* (Upper Saddle River, NJ: Prentice Hall, 1998).
17. S. J. Mojzsis, G. Arrhenius, K. D. McKeegan, T. Mark Harrison, A. P. Nutman, and C. L. Friend, "Evidence for Life on Earth Before 3,800 Million Years Ago," *Nature* 384 (1996): 55–59.
18. John M. Hayes, "The Earliest Moments of Life on Earth," *Nature* 384 (1996): 21–22.
19. Stuart R. Taylor, *Solar System Evolution: A New Perspective* (New York: Cambridge University Press, 1992), 287–291.
20. Gould, *Wonderful Life*.

21. Barbour, *Religion and Science,* 237–240.

22. See, for example, Taylor, *Solar System Evolution.*

23. Barbour, *Religion and Science,* 215.

24. Ursula W. Goodenough, *The Sacred Depths of Nature* (New York: Oxford University Press, 1998).

25. Richard Leakey and Roger Lewin, *Origins Reconsidered: In Search of What Makes Us Human* (New York: Doubleday, 1992).

26. Mackenzie, *Our Changing Planet,* 195.

27. Peter D. Stilling, *Introductory Ecology* (Englewood Cliffs, NJ: Prentice Hall, 1992), 79.

28. Ibid., 81.

29. David A. Tillman, Johannes Knops, David Wedlin, Peter Reich, Mark Ritchie, and Evan Siemann, "The Influence of Functional Diversity and Composition on Ecosystem Processes," *Science* 277 (1997): 1300–1302.

30. Anne S. Moffat, "Ecologists Look at the Big Picture," *Science* 273 (1996): 1490.

31. See, for example, McFague, *The Body of God;* Langdon Gilkey, *Nature, Reality and the Sacred: The Nexus of Science and Religion* (Minneapolis, MN: Fortress Press, 1993), 147ff.

32. Walter Brueggemann, *Genesis. Interpretation, A Bible Commentary for Teaching and Preaching* (Atlanta, GA: John Knox Press, 1982), 32.

33. See, for example, Leonardo Boff, *The Lord's Prayer: The Prayer of Integral Liberation* (Maryknoll, NY: Orbis Books, 1983); Robert McAfee Brown, *Theology in a New Key: Responding to Liberation Themes* (Philadelphia, PA: Westminster Press, 1978).

34. J. P. Barkham, "Environmental Needs and Social Justice," *Biodiversity and Conservation* 4 (1995): 857–868.

35. Moffat, "Ecologists Look at the Big Picture."

36. Barkham, "Environmental Needs and Social Justice," 860.

37. Boff, *The Lord's Prayer,* 3.

38. Tillich, *A History of Christian Thought,* 537.

39. Many friends and colleagues have been enormously helpful and supportive of my attempts to learn enough about theology to write this essay, especially Dr. Steven Vicchio of Notre Dame College and St. Mary's Seminary; Dr. John Haught, of Georgetown University; my wife, the Rev. Gretchen van Utt, Pastor of Springfield Presbyterian Church, and Rev. Roger Gench, Pastor of Brown Memorial Presbyterian Church, Park Avenue. On the geology side, I've benefited greatly from conversations with Drs. Bruce Marsh, Steven Stanley, and Katalyn Szlavecz of Johns Hopkins University, and E-an Zen, of the University of Maryland. And my debt to the work of Professors Paul Tillich and Langdon Gilkey is much deeper than the citations in the text can possibly indicate.

10   Ruling the Range: Managing the Public's Resources

1. Quoted in Mary C. Rabbitt, *Minerals, Lands, and Geology for the Common Defence and General Welfare,* Vol. 1 (Washington, DC: Government Printing Office, 1979), 198.

2. Ibid., 115.

3. Ibid., 159.

4. Ibid., 162.

5. Ibid., 161.

6. Ibid., 91.

7. Ibid., 92.

8. Ibid., 223.

9. Ibid., 223.

10. Ibid.,150.

11. L. Courtland Lee, "Lack of Access Makes Mining Law Reform Irrelevant," *American Mining Congress Journal* 280 (1994): 12–17.

12. U.S. Forest Service, "An Approach to Working with Sustainability: Sustainable Development Interdeputy Area Team Discussion Paper Number 4," 17 December 1999, <http://www.fs.fed.us/land/sustain_dev/susdev4.html>.

13. David Unger, *Interior Columbia Basin Ecosystem Management Project,* "Science and Collaborative Stewardship of the Federal Lands: A Partnership Renewed," 17 December 1999, <http://www.icbemp.gov/science/ungerks.htm>.

14. Bureau of Land Management, *A Strategy for Meeting Our Research and Scientific Information Needs* (Washington, DC: Bureau of Land Management, 1996), 2.

15. Merrill R. Kauffman et al., *An Ecological Basis for Ecosystem Management,* General Technical Report RM-246 (Washington, DC: U.S. Forest Service, 1994), 16.

16. See Stuart P. Hughes, "Let's Apply Geology to Ecosystem Management," *Geotimes* 39.3 (1994): 4; and Stuart P. Hughes, "Two Tools for Integrating Geology into Ecosystem Studies," *Environmental Geology* 26 (1995): 246–251.

17. Hughes, "Let's Apply Geology," 4.

18. Hughes, "Let's Apply Geology."

19. Steven R. Bohlen et al., *Geology for a Changing World: A Science Strategy for the Geologic Division of the U.S. Geological Survey, 2000–2010,* Circular 1172 (Reston, VA: U.S. Geological Survey, 1998), 33.

20. Ibid.

21. U.S. Forest Service, *Status of the Interior Columbia Basin: Summary of Scientific Findings* (Washington, DC: Government Printing Office, 1997).

11   Rocks, Paper, Soils, Trees: The View from an Experimental Forest

1. David A. Perry, "The Scientific Basis of Forestry," *Annual Review of Ecology and Systematics* 29 (1998): 435–466.

2. John T. Hack and John C. Goodlett, *Geomorphology and Forest Ecology of a Mountain Region in the Central Appalachians,* U.S. Geological Survey Professional Paper 346 (Reston, VA: U.S. Geological Survey, 1960).

3. Frederick J. Swanson, et al., eds., *Workshop on Sediment Budgets and Routing in Forested Drainage Basins: Proceedings,* GTR PNW-141 (Portland, OR: USDA Forest Service, 1982).

4. Frederick J. Swanson and C. T. Dyrness, "Impact of Clear-Cutting and Road Construction on Soil Erosion by Landslides in the Western Cascade Range, Oregon," *Geology* 3 (1975): 393–396; Swanson et al., *Workshop on Sediment Budgets.*

5. Frederick J. Swanson, S. L. Johnson, Stanley V. Gregory, and S. A. Acker, "Flood Disturbance in a Forested Mountain Landscape," *BioScience* 48 (1998): 681–689.

6. Stanley V. Gregory et al., "An Ecosystem Perspective of Riparian Zones," *BioScience* 41 (1991): 540–551.

7. Mark E. Harmon et al., "Ecology of Coarse Woody Debris in Temperate Ecosystems," *Advances in Ecological Research,* A. MacFadyen and E. D. Ford, eds. (Orlando, FL: Academic Press, 1986), 133–302.

8. Frederick J. Swanson et al., "Landform Effects on Ecosystem Patterns and Processes," *BioScience* 38 (1988): 92–98.

9. John H. Cissel, Frederick J. Swanson, W. A. McKee, and A. L. Burditt., "Using the Past to Plan the Future in the Pacific Northwest," *Journal of Forestry* 92.8 (1994): 30–31, 46.

10. Swanson et al., "Flood Disturbance."

11. Cissel et al., "Using the Past."

12. Swanson and Dyrness, "Impact of Clear-Cutting."

13. Jerry F. Franklin et al., *Ecological Characteristics of Old-Growth Douglas-Fir Forests,* GTR PNW-118 (Portland, OR: USDA Forest Service, 1981).

12   Are Soils Endangered?

1. John Wesley Powell, *The Exploration of the Colorado River and Its Canyons* (1895; reprinted, New York: Dover, 1961), iii.

2. Ibid., 17.
3. Ibid., 280.
4. Ibid., 284.
5. Susan E. Trumbore, Oliver A. Chadwick, and Ronald Amundson, "Rapid Exchange Between Soil Carbon and Atmospheric Carbon Dioxide Driven by Temperature Change," *Science* 272 (1996): 393–396.
6. Thure Cerling, Yang Wang, and Jay Quade, "Expansion of C4 Ecosystems as an Indicator of Global Ecological Change in the Late Miocene," *Nature* 361 (1993): 344–345.
7. Ronald Amundson, Oliver Chadwick, Carol Kendall, Yang Wang, and Michael DeNiro, "Isotopic Evidence for Shifts in Atmospheric Circulation Patterns during the Late Quaternary in Mid-North America," *Geology* 24 (1996): 23–26.
8. Ann A. Sorensen, Richard P. Greene, and Karen Russ, *Farming on the Edge* (Washington, DC: American Farmland Trust, 1997).
9. T. Coraghessan Boyle, "The Underground Gardens," *The New Yorker* 74 (25 May 1998): 103.
10. "Here's the Latest Dirt," *San Francisco Examiner,* 20 April 1997, C-16.
11. Paul R. Ehrlich and Edward O. Wilson, "Biodiversity Studies: Science and Policy," *Science* 253 (1991): 758–762.
12. Stephen Jay Gould, "The Golden Rule: A Proper Scale for Our Environmental Crisis," in *Eight Little Piggies* (New York: W. W. Norton, 1993), 50.
13. Hans Jenny and Kevin Stuart, "My Friend, the Soil," *Journal of Soil and Water Conservation* 39 (May–June 1984): 158.
14. *Vincent. The Life and Death of Vincent van Gogh,* Paul Cox, dir., Roxie Video, 1990.
15. William Bryant Logan, *Dirt: The Ecstatic Skin of the Earth* (New York: Riverhead Books, 1995), 151.
16. Selman A. Waksman, *My Life with the Microbes* (New York: Simon & Schuster, 1954), 209.
17. Willa Cather, *My Antonia* (Boston: Houghton-Mifflin, 1977), 118–119.
18. Charles Darwin, *On the Origin of Species by Means of Natural Selection, or the Preservation of Favoured Races in the Struggle for Life* (1859; reprinted, Cambridge, MA: Harvard University Press, 1964), 109.
19. Jenny and Stuart, "My Friend, the Soil," 161.

13 The Edwards Aquifer: Water for Thirsty Texans

1. Peter R. Rose, *Tribal Conflict and Vengeance in the Frontier Hill Country: An Addendum to Geology, Frontier History, and Wineries, Texas Hill Country,* Field Trip Guidebook for the Society of Independent Professional Earth Scientists 1997 Convention and 34th Annual Meeting (Austin, TX: SIPES, 1997), 64.
2. Daene C. McKinney and John M. Sharp, Jr., "Springflow Augmentation of Comal and San Marcos Springs, Texas: Phase I—Feasibility Study," Center for Research in Water Resources, Technical Report 247 (Austin: University of Texas, 1995).
3. Marc Reisner, *Cadillac Desert: The American West and Its Disappearing Water* (New York: Penguin Books, 1986).
4. McKinney and Sharp, "Springflow Augmentation—Feasibility Study"; Matthew Uliana and John M. Sharp, Jr., "Springflow Augmentation Possibilities at Comal and San Marcos Springs, Edwards Aquifer," *Transactions of the Gulf Coast Association of Geological Societies* 46 (1996), 423.
5. Wallace S. Broecker, "Thermohaline Circulation, the Achilles Heel of Our Climate System: Will Man-Made CO_2 Upset the Current Balance?" *Science* 278 (1997): 1582–1588.
6. David W. Stahle and Malcolm K. Cleveland, "Texas Drought History Reconstructed and Analyzed from 1698 to 1980," *Journal of Climate* 1 (1988): 59–74.
7. Rickard S. Toomey, Michael D. Blum, and Salvatore Valastro, "Late Quaternary Climates and Environments of the Edwards Plateau, Texas," *Global and Planetary Change* 7 (1993): 299–320.

8. MaryLynn Musgrove, Jay L. Banner, and Lawrence E. Mack, "Cave Speleothems as Potential Tracers of Long-Term Variations in Groundwater Flow Routes in a Karst Aquifer, Central Texas, USA," in *Fluid Flow in Carbonates: Interdisciplinary Approaches,* SEPM Research Conference, Programs with Abstracts, 20–24 September 1998 (Tulsa, OK: Society for Sedimentary Research, 1998).

9. We thank our students and colleagues whose research efforts over the years have contributed greatly to the present knowledge of how the Edwards Aquifer works. Chock Woodruff provided helpful comments on an earlier version of this essay. Our research on karst aquifers has been supported by the National Science Foundation (EAR-9526714), the Department of Energy (DE-FG03-97ER14812), and the geology foundation of the University of Texas.

14   *From the Catskills to Canal Street: New York City's Water Supply*

1. Bob Steuding, *The Last of the Handmade Dams: The Story of the Ashokan Reservoir,* Rev. Ed. (Fleischmanns, NY: Purple Mountain Press, 1989), 20.

2. Gerald R. Iwan, "Drinking Water Quality Concerns of New York City, Past and Present," *The Annals of the New York Academy of Sciences* 502 (1987): 186.

3. Steuding, *Last of the Handmade Dams,* 20.

4. Iwan, "Drinking Water Quality," 187.

5. Steuding, *Last of the Handmade Dams,* 20.

6. Ibid., 19.

7. Ibid., 20.

8. R. D. A. Parrott, "The Water Supply of New York City," *Scientific American* 557 (1886): 144.

9. Steuding, *Last of the Handmade Dams,* 21.

10. Ibid., 23.

11. Lazarus White, *The Catskill Water Supply of New York City* (New York: John Wiley, 1913), 77.

12. Steuding, *Last of the Handmade Dams,* 47–50.

13. Quoted in Ibid., 50.

14. Ibid.

15. Ibid., 40.

16. Ibid., 28–29.

17. Ibid., 28.

18. Robert Gottlieb, *Forcing the Spring: The Transformation of the American Environmental Movement* (Washington, DC: Island Press, 1993), 23.

19. Ibid., 29.

20. Camilla Calhoun, *Westchester Land Trust,* "A Town Called Olive: A Perspective on New York City's Water Supply," 12 March 1999, <http://www.westchester-landtrust.org/watershed/olive.html>.

21. Steuding, *Last of the Handmade Dams,* 85.

22. Ibid., 92–96.

23. Quoted in Ibid., 75.

24. Quoted in Ibid., 100.

25. Ibid., 35.

26. Gilboa is perhaps one of the most famous fossil sites in New York State because of the Gilboa fossil forest. Paleontologists discovered it in 1869, when a flood exposed a horizon of rock containing fossil tree trunks along Schoharie Creek. The very early land plants that made up the forest had no leaves or roots but were composed only of wood and had tall trunks. Since their first discovery, 200 fossilized tree trunks have been found near Gilboa, some as a result of the excavation for Schoharie Reservoir. A few of the fossil trees can still be seen today because they were relocated to the perimeter of the valley before it was flooded to make the reservoir. For more information on the Gilboa fossil forest, see Robert Titus,

The Catskills: A Geological Guide (Fleischmanns, NY: Purple Mountain Press, 1993), 96–98.

27. Camilla Calhoun, <http://www.westchesterlandtrust.org/watershed/olive.html>.
28. *City of New York: Department of Environmental Protection,* "New York City's Water Supply System," 14 Mar 1999, <http://www.ci.nyc.ny.us/html/dep/html/history.html>.
29. Ibid.
30. Iwan, "Drinking Water Quality," 184.
31. Camilla Calhoun, <http://www.westchesterlandtrust.org/watershed/olive.html>.
32. Rudolf Ruedeman, "Development of Drainage of Catskills," *American Journal of Science* 23.136 (1932): 337–349.
33. Titus, *The Catskills,* 23.
34. Ibid., 105.
35. Bernard W. Pipkin and Dee Trent, *Geology and the Environment,* 2nd Ed. (Belmont, CA: Wadsworth, 1997), 285.
36. U.S. Environmental Protection Agency, Region 2, *Surface Water Treatment Rule Determination: New York City's Catskill and Delaware Water Supplies,* 30 December 1993 (New York: Environmental Protection Agency, 1993).
37. Andrew Goudie and Heather Viles, *The Earth Transformed* (Malden, MA: Blackwell, 1997), 145–146.
38. Carla Montgomery, *Environmental Geology,* 4th Ed. (Dubuque: Wm. C. Brown, 1995), 364.
39. Dorothy J. Merritts, Andrew De Wet, and Kirsten Menking, *Environmental Geology: An Earth System Science Approach* (New York: W. H. Freeman and Company, 1998), 281.
40. Jill S. Schneiderman, "Golf's Unwanted Runoff," Letter, *New York Times,* 30 June 1999, A22.
41. Iwan, "Drinking Water Quality," 193.
42. Jacqueline Vaughn Switzer, *Environmental Politics: Domestic and Global Dimensions* (New York: St. Martin's Press, 1994) 1, 76.
43. Andrew C. Revkin, "New York Begins Spending to Save City's Reservoirs," *New York Times,* 22 January 1997: A-1ff.
44. Andrew C. Revkin, "Billion-Dollar Plan to Clean New York City Water at Its Source," *New York Times,* 31 August 1997, I-1ff.
45. "Save the Watershed," *New York Times,* 15 May 1994, sec. 1, 14.
46. Andrew C. Revkin, "Watershed Protection Agreement Is Praised," *New York Times,* 11 September 1996, B-2.
47. Joseph Berger, "Life as a Watershed Irks Putnam County," *New York Times,* 5 May 1994, B-1ff.
48. Andrew C. Revkin, "In Unusual Partnership, Farmers Help Safeguard New York Water," *New York Times,* 13 August 1995, I-1ff.
49. John Jordan, "Hearings Scheduled on Rules to Protect Reservoir Systems," *New York Times,* 5 February 1995, WC-13.
50. Andrew C. Revkin, "New York Begins Spending."
51. Andrew C. Revkin, "Billion-Dollar Plan."
52. Richard Perez-Pena, "Accord on Water Supply Is Criticized for Weakness," *New York Times,* 20 October 1996, I-35.
53. Andrew C. Revkin, "Billion-Dollar Plan."
54. Quoted in Steuding, *Last of the Handmade Dams,* 108.

15 Sustaining Healthy Coasts

1. Thomas J. Culliton, *Population: Distribution, Density and Growth,* National Oceanic and Atmospheric Administration, State of the Coast Report, 9 February 1999, <http://state_of_coast.noaa.gov/bulletins/html/pop_01/pop.html>.

2. *Highlights of the U.S. Public Port Industry,* Department of Transportation, Maritime Administration Home Page, 9 February 1999, <http://marad.dot.gov/highlights.html>.

3. National Marine Fisheries Service, *Fisheries of the United States, 1995* (Silver Spring, MD: National Oceanic and Atmospheric Administration, National Marine Fisheries Service, 1996).

4. Pamela Weiant, *Testing the Waters IV: The Unsolved Problem of U.S. Beach Pollution* (New York: Natural Resources Defense Council, 1994).

5. National Marine Fisheries Service, *Habitat Protection Activity Report 1991–1993* (Silver Spring, MD: National Oceanic and Atmospheric Administration, National Marine Fisheries Service, 1994).

6. Charles A. Bookman, ed., *Our Ocean Future: Themes and Issues Concerning the Nation's Stake in the Oceans* (Washington, DC: H. John Heinz III Center for Science, Economics and the Environment, 1998).

7. Sandra Steingraber, *Living Downstream: A Scientist's Personal Investigation of Cancer and the Environment* (New York: Vintage Books, 1998).

8. Tom O'Connor, *Chemical Contaminants in Oysters and Mussels,* National Oceanic and Atmospheric Administration, State of the Coast Report, 9 February 1999, <http://state_of_coast.noaa.gov/bulletins/html/ccom_05/ccom.html>.

9. James W. Good, J. W. Weber, J. W., Charland, J. V. Olson, and K. A. Chapin, *National Coastal Zone Management Effectiveness Study: Protecting Estuaries and Coastal Wetlands,* Final Report to the Office of Ocean and Coastal Resources Management, National Oceanic and Atmospheric Administration, Oregon Seat Grant Special Report PI-98-001 (Corvallis: Oregon State University, 1998).

10. D. James Baker, Phillip Singerman, Gary Bachula, Ray Kammer, and R. Roger Majak, *Out of Harm's Way, FY 2000 Natural Disaster Reduction Initiative* (Washington, DC: U.S. Department of Commerce, 1998).

11. Ibid.

12. "Report Cites Humans for $89B in Weather Damage," *The Post and Courier,* 28 November 1998, A-3.

13. General Accounting Office, Executive Guide, *Effectively Implementing the Government Performance and Results Act* (Washington, DC: Government Printing Office, 1996).

14. Sandy Ward and Catherine Main, *Population at Risk from Natural Hazards,* National Oceanic and Atmospheric Administration, State of the Coast Report, 9 February 1999, <http://state_of_coast.noaa.gov/bulletins/html/par_02/par.html>.

15. Natural Resources Defense Council, *No Safe Harbor; Tanker Safety in America's Ports* (New York: Natural Resources Defense Council, 1990).

16. Intergovernmental Panel on Climate Change, *Climate Change 1995—The Science of Climate Change, Summary for Policymakers and Technical Summary of the Working Group I Report,* (Cambridge: Cambridge University Press, 1996).

17. Alan S. Manne and Richard G. Richels, *Buying Greenhouse Gas Insurance: The Economic Cost of Carbon Dioxide Emission Limits* (Cambridge, MA: MIT Press, 1992).

16   Lessons from Lighthouses: Shifting Sands, Coastal Management Strategies, and the Cape Hatteras Lighthouse Controversy

1. Orrin H. Pilkey, Jr., "Coastal Geology: Don't Stop the Ocean, Move the Light," *Washington Post,* 4 January 1987, C-3ff.

2. Gered Lennon, William J. Neal, Orrin H. Pilkey, Jr., David M. Bush, Matthew Stutz, and Jane Bullock, *Living With the South Carolina Coast* (Durham, NC: Duke University Press, 1996).

3. Richard A. Davis, Jr., and Albert C. Hine, *Quaternary Geology and Sedimentology of*

the Barrier Island and Marshy Coast, West-Central Florida, U.S.A., Field Trip Guidebook T375 (Washington, DC: American Geophysical Union, 1989).

4. Kenneth G. Kochel, *America's Atlantic Coast Lighthouses,* 3rd Ed. (Clearwater, FL: Kenneth Kochel Publishing, 1998), 332.

5. Ibid, 102–103.

6. Ibid., 390.

7. Orrin H. Pilkey, Jr., and Howard L. Wright, III, "Seawalls Versus Beaches," in *The Effects of Seawalls on the Beach,* N. C. Kraus and Orrin H. Pilkey, Jr., eds., *Journal of Coastal Research* Special Issue 4 (1988): 41–64.

8. Cornelia Dean, *Against the Tide: The Battle for America's Beaches* (New York: Columbia University Press, 1999).

9. Jesse E. McNinch, "The Effectiveness of Beach Scraping as a Method of Erosion Control: Topsail Beach, North Carolina," master's thesis, Institute of Marine Science, University of North Carolina at Chapel Hill, 1989.

10. U.S. Army Corps of Engineers, *Seawall and Revetment Design for Long-Term Protection of Cape Hatteras Lighthouse, North Carolina,* prepared by U.S. Army Corps of Engineers, Wilmington District, for the National Park Service, Cape Hatteras National Seashore (Washington, DC: Government Printing Office, 1985).

11. Ibid.

12. E. Robert Thieler, Orrin H. Pilkey, Jr., Robert S. Young, David M. Bush, and Fei Chai, "The Use of Mathematical Models to Predict Beach Behavior: A Critical Review," *Journal of Coastal Research* (in press).

13. North Carolina Division of Coastal Management, *Long-Term Average Annual Shoreline Change Rates Updated Through 1992* (Raleigh: North Carolina Department of Health, Environment and Natural Resources, Division of Coastal Management, 1992).

14. National Research Council Committee on Options for Preserving Cape Hatteras Lighthouse, *Saving Cape Hatteras Lighthouse from the Sea: Options and Policy Implications* (Washington, DC: National Academy Press, 1988).

15. Stephen P. Leatherman and Jakob J. Møller, "Morris Island Lighthouse: A 'Survivor' of Hurricane Hugo," *Shore and Beach* 59 (1991): 11–15.

16. Lennon et al., *Living with the South Carolina Coast.*

17. Orrin H. Pilkey, Jr., William J. Neal, Stanley R. Riggs, Craig A. Webb, David M. Bush, Deborah F. Pilkey, Jane Bullock, and Brian A. Cowan, *The North Carolina Shore and Its Barrier Islands: Restless Ribbons of Sand* (Durham, NC: Duke University Press, 1998).

18. Lorance D. Lisle, "Foundation of the Cape Hatteras Lighthouse," *Shore and Beach* 53 (1985): 29–31.

19. Francis Ross Holland, Jr., *America's Lighthouses: An Illustrated History* (Toronto: General Publishing Company, 1972).

20. Leatherman and Møller, "Morris Island Lighthouse."

21. National Park Service, *Environmental Assessment for the Cape Hatteras Lighthouse Protection Plan,* National Park Service Publication NPS 1902 (Washington, DC: United States Department of the Interior, 1982).

22. Ibid.

23. Ibid.

24. Ibid.

25. John Obed Curtis, *Moving Historic Buildings* (Washington, DC: Government Printing Office, 1979).

26. National Park Service, *Environmental Assessment for the Cape Hatteras Lighthouse Protection Plan;* National Park Service, *Protection Alternatives, Development Concept Plan/Environmental Assessment, Cape Hatteras Lighthouse Complex, Cape Hatteras,* National Park Service Publication NPS D-47, June 1989 Draft (Washington, DC: United States Department of the Interior, 1989).

27. In 1997, a committee of North Carolina State University marine scientists also

came to the same conclusion. See Arthur W. Cooper, Leon E. Danielson, John M. Hanson, Leonard J. Pietrafesa, Paul Z. Zia, and Ellis B. Cowling, *Saving the Cape Hatteras Lighthouse from the Sea, Review and Update of the 1988 National Research Council Report* (Raleigh: North Carolina State University, 1997).

28. Spencer M. Rogers, Jr., *Artificial Seaweed for Shoreline Erosion Control?* University of North Carolina Sea Grant, Publication NCU-T-86-005 (Raleigh: University of North Carolina, 1986); Spencer M. Rogers, Jr., "Artificial Seaweed for Erosion Control," *Shore and Beach* 55 (1987): 19–29.

29. J. W. Forman, *Generalized Monitoring of 'Seascape' Installation at Cape Hatteras Lighthouse, North Carolina,* U.S. Army Corps of Engineers Miscellaneous Paper CERC-86-2 (Washington, DC: Government Printing Office, 1986).

30. James D. Howard, Wallace Kaufman, and Orrin H. Pilkey, Jr., eds., *National Strategy for Beach Preservation,* Proceedings of the Second Skidaway Institute of Oceanography Conference on America's Eroding Shoreline (Savannah, GA: Skidaway Institute of Oceanography, 1985).

31. David M. Bush, Orrin H. Pilkey, Jr., and William J. Neal, *Living by the Rules of the Sea* (Durham, NC: Duke University Press, 1996).

32. The authors would like to thank several people and organizations. Dave Fischetti, founder and president of the Move the Lighthouse Committee, worked tirelessly to save the noble light. Shirley Sabin and the Nauset Light Preservation Society, Eastham, Massachussets, provided background on the Nauset Light. Amber Taylor has, over the years, provided valuable perspective on coastal management issues.

17   The Follies of Lotus Bay

1. Wallace Kaufman and Orrin H. Pilkey, Jr., *The Beaches Are Moving: The Drowning of America's Shoreline* (Durham, NC: Duke University Press, 1983); Eric C. F. Bird, *Beach Management* (New York: John Wiley & Sons, 1996); David M. Bush, Orrin H. Pilkey, Jr., and William J. Neal, *Living by the Rules of the Sea* (Durham, NC: Duke University Press, 1996); R. William G. Carter, ed., *Coastal Environments: An Introduction to the Physical, Ecological and Cultural Systems of Coastlines* (Berkeley, CA: Academic Press, 1988); Charles H. Carter, William J. Neal, William S. Haras, and Orrin H. Pilkey, Jr., *Living with the Lake Erie Shore* (Durham, NC: Duke University Press, 1987).

2. S. Jeffress Williams, Kurt Dodd, and Kathleen Krafft Gohn, *Coasts in Crisis,* U.S. Geological Survey Circular 1075 (Washington, DC: Government Printing Office, 1991), iv.

3. Carter et al., *Living with the Lake Erie Shore,* 187.

4. New York State Department of Environmental Conservation, *Coastal Erosion Management Regulations,* 6 NYCRR Part 505 (Albany: New York State Department of Environmental Conservation: 1988), 1; Carter et al., *Living with the Lake Erie Shore,* 194.

5. *Coastal Erosion Hazard Area Town of Brant,* Map (Albany: New York State Department of Environmental Conservation, 1988).

6. Carter et al., *Living with the Lake Erie Shore,* 21.

7. Ibid., 23.

8. U.S. Army Corps of Engineers, *Monthly Bulletin of Lake Levels for the Great Lakes* (Detroit District: U.S. Army Corps of Engineers, 1998), 3.

9. Carter et al., *Living with the Lake Erie Shore,* 134.

10. I would like to thank Sandy Hooge, Jim Hooge, and Jim Shea, long-time residents of Lotus Bay, for speaking with me about Lotus Bay. They generously shared maps and photos of the bay as well as details of many projects along the lake, only remnants of which remain today. John Grant and John Whitney made invaluable suggestions. I especially appreciate Tom Toles's willingness to "dig" through his files until he located the cartoon used in this essay.

18 Dredging to Keep New York–New Jersey Harbor Alive

1. Joseph Mitchell, *The Bottom of the Harbor* (1951, 1959; reprinted, New York: Modern Library, 1987), 29.
2. Donald Squires and Kevin Bone, "The Beautiful Lake: The Promise of the Natural Systems," in *The New York Waterfront: Evolution and Building Culture of the Port and Harbor,* Kevin Bone, ed. (New York: Monacelli Press, 1997), 16–35.
3. Andrew C. Revkin, "Curbs on Silt Disposal Threaten Port of New York," *New York Times,* 18 March 1996, A-1ff.
4. U.S. Army Corps of Engineers, *Dredged Material Management Plan for the Port of New York and New Jersey: Interim Report, September 1996* (New York: U.S. Army Corps of Engineers, 1996); U.S. Army Corps of Engineers, *Dredged Material Management Plan for the Port of New York and New Jersey: Progress Report, December 1997* (New York: U.S. Army Corps of Engineers, 1997); U.S. Army Corps of Engineers, *Dredged Material Management Plan for the Port of New York and New Jersey: Progress Report, December 1998* (New York: U.S. Army Corps of Engineers, 1998).
5. S. Jeffress Williams, "Geological Effects of Ocean Dumping on the New York Bight Inner Shelf," in *Ocean Dumping and Marine Pollution: Geological Aspects of Waste Disposal at Sea,* H. D. Palmer and M. Grant Gross, eds. (Stroudsburg: Dowden, Hutchinson and Ross, 1979), 51–72.
6. U.S. Environmental Protection Agency, *EPA Site Analysis, Jersey Turnpike Dump No. 5, Jersey City, New Jersey,* TS-PIC-91036, EPA Region II and OERR, July 1991 (New York: Environmental Protection Agency, 1991).
7. John H. Cushman, Jr., "White House Offers Plan for Dredging," *New York Times,* 24 July 1996, B-1; Andrew C. Revkin, "Two Governors Plan Cleanup for Harbor: Trying to Keep Shippers from Leaving New York," *New York Times,* 6 October 1996, A-37.
8. Squires and Bone, "The Beautiful Lake."
9. U.S. Army Corps of Engineers, *Managing Dredged Material* (New York: U.S. Army Corps of Engineers, 1989).
10. Kevin Bone, ed., *The New York Waterfront: Evolution and Building Culture of the Port and Harbor* (New York: Monacelli Press, 1997).
11. U.S. Army Corps of Engineers, *Managing Dredged Material.*
12. Bone, *The New York Waterfront.*
13. Asef Ashar, "Impact of Dredging New York Harbor," *Transportation Quarterly* 51.1 (1997): 45–62; U.S. Army Corps of Engineers, *Dredged Material Management Plan, September 1996.*
14. Many rivers in New York State contain the word or suffix *kill* (creek in Dutch).
15. Bone, *The New York Waterfront.*
16. Andrew C. Revkin, "Supership Carries a Big Message: To Secure Trade, Ports Need Deeper and Safer Channels," *New York Times,* 23 July 1998, B-1.
17. Revkin, "Curbs on Silt."
18. Mitre Corporation, *Proceedings of the New York Dredged Material Disposal Alternatives Workshop, October 11–13,* Mitre Paper M77-114 (New York: U.S. Army Corps of Engineers, 1977); Mitre Corporation, *Disposal of Dredged Material Within the New York District: Volume II—Preliminary Evaluation of Upland Disposal* (New York: U.S. Army Corps of Engineers, 1980); U.S. Army Corps of Engineers, *Locating Upland Disposal Sites for Dredged Material* (New York: U.S. Army Corps of Engineers, 1983); U.S. Army Corps of Engineers, *Locating Upland Disposal Sites for Dredged Material: Progress Report, January 1984* (New York: U.S. Army Corps of Engineers, 1984); U.S. Army Corps of Engineers, *Managing Dredged Material.*
19. Mitchell, *The Bottom of the Harbor,* 47.
20. Revkin, "Curbs on Silt."
21. U.S. Army Corps of Engineers, *Dredged Material Management Plan, September 1996;* U.S. Army Corps of Engineers, *Dredged Material Management Plan, December 1997.*
22. U.S. Army Corps of Engineers, *Dredged Material Management Plan, December 1997.*
23. U.S. Army Corps of Engineers, *Dredged Material Management Plan, September 1996.*

24. Ibid.

25. Andrew C. Revkin, "Mud from Clogged Harbor May Be a Resource in the Rough," *New York Times,* 10 August 1997, A-29.

26. Ibid.

27. Ibid.

28. Mitchell, *The Bottom of the Harbor,* 139.

29. Dennis Hevesi, "On the Hudson: A City Within Jersey City," *New York Times,* 13 September 1998, B-1.

30. Herbert Muschamp, "Where Iron Gives Way to Beauty and Games," *New York Times,* 13 December 1998, AR-35.

31. Hevesi, "On the Hudson."

32. U.S. Army Corps of Engineers, *Dredged Material Management Plan, September 1996.*

33. Revkin, "Curbs on Silt."

19   *An Earth Scientist in City Hall: Geology and Community Planning*

1. William J. Mitsch and James G. Gooselink, *Wetlands,* 2nd Ed. (New York: Van Nostrand Reinhold, 1993), 579.

2. Ibid., 580.

3. James G. Gooselink and Lyndon C. Lee, "Cumulative Impact Assessment in Bottomland Hardwood Forests," *Wetlands* 9 (1989): 95.

4. Ibid., 97.

5. Eric D. Stein and Richard F. Ambrose, "Cumulative Impacts of Section 404 Clean Water Act Permitting on the Riparian Habitat of the Santa Margarita, California Watershed," *Wetlands* 18 (1998): 406.

6. Ralph W. Tiner, U.S. Department of the Interior, U.S. Fish and Wildlife Service, *Wetlands of the United States: Current Status and Trends* (Washington, DC: Government Printing Office, 1984), 29.

7. Ibid., 32.

8. Ibid., 31.

9. Thomas E. Dahl, Craig E. Johnson, and W. E. Frayer, U.S. Department of the Interior, U.S. Fish and Wildlife Service, *Wetlands Status and Trends in the Contermi-nous United States, Mid-1970's to Mid-1980's* (Washington, DC: Government Printing Office, 1991), 2.

10. I thank Sally Roth and Heidi Doss for insightful and helpful reviews of an early draft of this manuscript.

20   *From Reservoir to Wetland: The Rise and Fall of an Ohio Dam*

1. *Water Power: Use and Regulation of a Renewable Resource,* Federal Energy Regulatory Commission, 11 November 1998, <http://www.ferc.fed.us/hydro/docs/ waterpwr.html>.

2. Arthur L. Bloom, *Geomorphology: A Systematic Analysis of Late Cenozoic Landforms* (Upper Saddle River, NJ: Prentice Hall, 1998).

3. Louis C. Gottschalk, "Reservoir Sedimentation," in *Handbook of Applied Hydrology,* V.T. Chow, ed. (New York: McGraw-Hill, 1964), 1–34; J. Roger McHenry, "Reservoir Sedimentation," *Water Resources Bulletin* 10 (1974): 329–337; Robert M. Baxter, "Environmental Effects of Dams and Impoundments," *Annual Review of Ecology and Systematics* 8 (1977): 255–283; Dennis E. Ford, "Reservoir Transport Processes," in *Reservoir Limnology,* Kent W. Thornton, B. L. Kimmel, and F. E. Payne, eds. (New York: John Wiley, 1990), 15–41; Kent W. Thornton, "Sedimentary Processes," in *Reservoir Limnology,* Kent W. Thornton, B. L. Kimmel, and F. E. Payne (New York: John Wiley, 1990), 43–69.

4. Luna B. Leopold, "Land Use and Sediment Yield," in *Man's Role in Changing the Face of the Earth,* W. L. Thomas, ed. (Chicago: University of Chicago Press, 1956), 639–647; Luna B. Leopold, M. Gordon Wolman, and John P. Miller, *Fluvial Processes in Geomorphology* (San Francisco: W. H. Freeman and Company, 1964).

5. Gottschalk, "Reservoir Sedimentation."

6. Kenneth J. Gregory and C. C. Park, "Adjustment of River Channel Capacity Downstream from a Reservoir," *Water Resources Research* 10 (1974): 870–873; Robert Dolan, Alan D. Howard, and Arthur Gallenson, "Man's Impact on the Colorado River in Grand Canyon," *American Scientist* 62 (1974): 392–401; Daryl B. Simons, "Effects of Stream Regulation on Channel Morphology," in *The Ecology of Regulated Streams*, J. V. Ward and J. A. Stanford, ed. (New York: Plenum Publishing, 1979), 95–111; Edward D. Andrews, "Downstream Effects of Flaming Gorge Reservoir on the Green River, Colorado and Utah," *Geological Society of America Bulletin* 97 (1986): 1012–1023.

7. Dolan et al., "Man's Impact"; Baxter, "Environmental Effects of Dams and Impoundments"; Paul Carling, "Implications of Sediment Transport for Instream Flow Modeling of Aquatic Habitat," in *The Ecological Basis for River Management*, D. M. Harper and A. J. D. Ferguson, eds. (Chichester: John Wiley & Sons, 1995), 17–31.

8. Gunnar M. Brune, "Trap Efficiency of Reservoirs," *Transactions of the American Geophysical Union* 34 (1953): 407–418; C. T. Haan, B. J. Barfield, and J. C. Hayes, *Design Hydrology and Sedimentology for Small Catchments* (San Diego: Academic Press, 1994).

9. G. Dennis Cooke, Eugene B. Welch, Spencer A. Peterson, and Peter R. Newroth, *Restoration and Management of Lakes and Reservoirs*, 2nd Ed. (Boca Raton, FL: Lewis Publishers, 1993).

10. F. E. Dendy and W. A. Champion, U.S. Department of Agriculture, Miscellaneous Publication 1362, *Sediment Deposition in United States Reservoirs: Summary of Data Reported Through 1975* (Washington, DC: U.S. Department of Agriculture, 1978); Abdelhadi Lahlou, "The Silting of Moroccan Dams," M. P. Bordas and D. E. Walling, eds., *International Association of Hydrological Sciences* 174 (1988): 71–77.

11. Charles L. Hahn, *Reservoir Sedimentation in Ohio*, Ohio Department of Natural Resources, Division of Water Bulletin 10 (Columbus: Ohio Department of Natural Resources, 1955); Peter L. McCall, John A. Robbins, and Gerald Matisoff, "[137]Cs and [210]Pb Transport and Geochronologies in Urbanized Reservoirs with Rapidly Increasing Sedimentation Rates," *Chemical Geology* 44 (1984): 33–65; James E. Evans, Johan F. Gottgens, Wilfrid M. Gill, Aaron D. Svitana, and Scudder D. Mackey, "Assessing Historical Land-Use Changes Using the Sedimentary Archives from Two Reservoirs in Northern Ohio," *Journal of Soil and Water Conservation* (under review, 1999).

12. Ohio Department of Natural Resources, *Dam Inspection Report: Chase Bag Company—Upper Lake Dam, Cuyahoga County*, File #1313-004 (Columbus: Ohio Department of Natural Resources, 1987); *Streamflow Data: Chagrin River at Station 04209000*, U.S. Geological Survey, 11 November 1998, <http://water.usgs.gov/swr/OH/data>.

13. Francis P. Weisenburger, *The Passing of the Frontier, 1825–1850*, Vol. 3 of *The History of the State of Ohio*, Carl Wittke, ed., (Columbus: Ohio State Archaeological and Historical Society, 1941).

14. C. T. Blakeslee, *The History of Chagrin Falls and Vicinity* (1874; reprinted, Chagrin Falls, OH: Friends of the Chagrin Falls Library, 1969).

15. Robert B. Gordon, *Natural Vegetation of Ohio, at the Time of the Earliest Land Surveys*, map and legend (Columbus: Ohio Biological Survey, 1966); and by the same author, *The Natural Vegetation of Ohio in Pioneer Days* (Columbus: Ohio Biological Survey, 1969); Weisenburger, *The Passing of the Frontier*.

16. Harlow Lindley, *Ohio in the Twentieth Century, 1900–1938*, Vol. 6 of *The History of the State of Ohio*, Carl Wittke, ed., (Columbus: Ohio State Archaeological and Historical Society, 1942).

17. Gerald Pyle, "The Population of Ohio—Past, Present, and Future Distribution," in *Ohio: An American Heartland*, A. G. Noble and A. J. Korsok, eds. *Ohio Geological Survey Bulletin* 65 (1975): 19–26.

18. Blakeslee, *The History of Chagrin Falls.*

19. Ohio Department of Natural Resources, *Dam Inspection Report.*

20. Ken Baka, "Is Lower Dam Safe Now That Upper Dam Broke?" *Chagrin Herald Sun,* 29 September 1994, A-1ff.

21. Written communication from Larry Rohman, IVEX Corporation, to the Ohio Department of Natural Resources, 17 August 1994.

22. Evans et al., "Assessing Historical Land-Use Changes."

23. Ibid.

24. The numbers 210 and 137 correspond to the atomic weights of the specific isotopes of lead and cesium, respectively.

25. Edward D. Goldberg, ed., "Geochronology with ^{210}Pb," in *Radioactive Dating* (Vienna: International Atomic Energy Agency, 1963), 121–131; Jerry C. Ritchie, J. Roger McHenry, and Angela C. Gill, "Dating Recent Sediments," *Limnology and Oceanography* 18 (1973): 254–263; John A. Robbins, "Geochemical and Geophysical Applications of Radioactive Lead," in *Biogeochemistry of Lead in the Environment, Part A,* O. J. Nriagu, ed. (New York: Elsevier, 1978), 285–293; Peter G. Appleby and Frank Oldfield, "The Calculation of [210]Pb Dates Assuming a Constant Rate of Supply of Unsupported ^{210}Pb to the Sediments," *Catena* 5 (1978): 1–18; James E. Evans, Thomas C. Johnson, E. Calvin Alexander, Richard S. Lively, and Steven J. Eisenreich, "Sedimentation Rates and Depositional Processes in Lake Superior from [210]Pb Geochronology," *Journal of Great Lakes Research* 7 (1981): 299–310; Frank Oldfield, Peter G. Appleby, and R. Thompson, "Palaeoecological Studies of Lakes in the Highlands of Papua New Guinea: I. The Chronology of Sedimentation," *Journal of Ecology* 68 (1980): 457–477.

26. Winifred Pennington, R. S. Cambray, and E. M. Fisher, "Observations on Lake Sediments Using Fallout ^{137}Cs as a Tracer," *Nature* 242 (1973): 324–326; Jerry C. Ritchie, P. H. Hawks, and J. Roger McHenry, "Deposition Rates in Valleys Determined Using Fallout Caesium-137," *Geological Society of America Bulletin* 86 (1975); McCall et al., "[137]Cs and [210]Pb Transport." Jerry C. Ritchie and J. Roger McHenry, "Application of Radioactive Cesium-137 for Measuring Soil Erosion and Sediment Accumulation Rates and Patterns: A Review," *Journal of Environmental Quality* 19 (1990): 215–233.

27. Evans et al., "Assessing Historical Land-Use."

28. Ibid.

29. Baka, "Is Lower Dam Safe."

30. Bruce Stoker and Jon M. Harbor, "Dam Removal Methods, Elwha River, Washington," in *Hydraulic Engineering, Proceedings of the National Conference on Hydraulic Engineering,* R. M. Shane, ed. (New York: American Society of Civil Engineers, 1991), 668–673; Blaine Harden, "U.S. Orders Maine Dam Destroyed," *Washington Post,* 26 November 1997, A-1ff; Patrick Joseph, "The Battle of the Dams," *Smithsonian Magazine,* 29.8 (1998), 48–61.

31. We wish to thank those people who have provided some of the information used in this essay, specifically Larry Rohman (IVEX Corporation), Ben Himes and Robert McKay (Village of Chagrin Falls), Yolita Rausch (Chagrin Falls Historical Society), Mark Ogden (Ohio Department of Natural Resources Division of Water), and Harold Schindel (U.S. Geological Survey).

21   Living with Karst: Maintaining a Clean Water Supply in Olmstead County, Minnesota

1. Minnesota Department of Health, Manual of Water Supply Sanitation, 1939.

2. Samuel P. Kingston, "Contamination of Water Supplies in Limestone Formation," *Journal of the American Water Works Association* 356 (1943): 1450–1456.

3. The name derives from the Karst region in Slovenia.

4. Kingston, "Contamination of Water Supplies," 1450.

5. Interoffice Memo received from Richard A. Peter, December 1989.

6. N. H. Balaban, ed., *Geologic Atlas, Olmsted County, Minnesota* (St. Paul: Minnesota Geological Survey, 1988).

7. Richard A. Peter, Interoffice Memo, "Report to Orion Township Board and Residents Regarding Concluding Assessment and Findings on Groundwater Quality and Water Wells in the Vicinity of a Feedlot Drainage Release in Section 16, Orion Township," 15 April 1998.

8. Anthony C. Runkel, *Geologic Investigations Applicable to Ground-water Management, Rochester Metropolitan Area, Minnesota*, Open-File Report 96-1 (St. Paul: Minnesota Geological Survey, 1996).

9. Geoffrey N. Delin, *Hydrogeology and Simulation of Ground-water Flow in the Rochester Area, Southeastern Minnesota, 1987–88*, U.S. Geological Survey Water-Resources Investigations Report 90-4081 (Mounds View, MN: U.S. Geological Survey, 1991); Richard J. Lindgren, *Hydraulic Properties and Ground-water Flow in the St. Peter-Prairie du Chien-Jordan Aquifer, Rochester Area, Southeastern Minnesota*, U.S. Geological Survey Water-Resources Investigations Report 97-4015 (Mounds View, MN: U.S. Geological Survey, 1997).

10. Delin, *Hydrogeology and Simulation of Ground-water Flow.*

11. Robert G. Tipping, *Southeastern Minnesota Regional Groundwater Monitoring Study,* Minnesota Geological Survey Open-File Report 94-1 (St. Paul: Minnesota Geological Survey, 1994).

12. I would like to thank the Olmsted County staff who provided information and reviewed this paper, particularly Mary Callier, Assistant County Administrator; Terry Lee, Water Coordinator; Rich Peter, Director of Environmental Health Services; Mike Cousino, Director of Public Works; Phil Wheeler, Director of Planning; Gene Mossing, Solid Waste Manager; Dennis Siems, Landfill Supervisor; Barbara Huberty, Environmental Analyst; John Harford, Senior Planner; and Geri Maki, Planner. Helpful reviews were provided by Geoff Delin at the U.S. Geological Survey, Tony Runkel at the Minnesota Geological Survey, Calvin Alexander at the University of Minnesota, Jeff Broberg at McGhee and Betts, Tom Clark at the Minnesota Pollution Control Agency, and Jeff Green at the Department of Natural Resources. State and local government officials have been very gracious in allowing me to participate in their meetings to discuss future research in the Rochester area. A special thanks to Tony Hill, South Zumbro Watershed Partnership Coordinator, who turned his artistic talents to creating needed illustrations, and to Olmsted County Planning for creating the figure showing groundwater sensitivity.

22 *Standoff at Yucca Mountain: High-Level Nuclear Waste in the United States*

1. David Bodansky, *Nuclear Energy: Principles, Practices, and Prospects* (Woodbury, NY: American Institute of Physics, 1996); Richard Wolfson, *Nuclear Choices: A Citizen's Guide to Nuclear Technology,* Rev. Ed. (Cambridge, MA: MIT Press, 1993).

2. David A. Lochbaum, *Nuclear Waste Disposal Crisis* (Tulsa, OK: PennWell Books, 1996); Michael B. Gerrard, *Whose Backyard, Whose Risk? Fear and Fairness in Toxic and Nuclear Waste Siting* (Cambridge, MA: MIT Press, 1994).

3. U.S. Congress, House, *Nuclear Waste Policy Act,* Trans. *H.R. 3809,* 98th Congress, 1st session (Washington, DC: Government Printing Office, 1982).

4. Gerrard, *Whose Backyard? Whose Risk?*

5. U.S. Congress, *Budget Reconciliation Act of 1987,* Trans. *Nuclear Waste Policy Act Amendments,* 100th Congress, 1st session (Washington, DC: Government Printing Office, 1987).

6. National Research Council, *Technical Bases for Yucca Mountain Standards* (Washington, DC: National Academy Press, 1995).

7. For comparison, the Earth is approximately 4.5 billion years old. In the case of U-238, ten times the amount of time that has transpired since the Earth first formed

would need to pass before U-238 formed today could be considered "gone" from the environment.

8. National Research Council, *Technical Bases for Yucca Mountains Standards.*
9. Valerie L. Kuletz, *The Tainted Desert: Environmental and Social Ruin in the American West* (New York: Routledge, 1998).
10. Randall Hanson, "From Environmental Bads to Economic Goods: Marketing Nuclear Waste to American Indians," dissertation, University of Minnesota, Minneapolis, 1998.
11. National Research Council, *Technical Bases for Yucca Mountain Standards.*
12. Yucca Mountain Project, "Project Scientists Assess Tritium Traces for Evidence of Fast Routes to Repository," *Of Mountains and Science* Winter (1996): 134, 139.
13. Annie B. Kersting et al., "Migration of Plutonium in Ground Water at the Nevada Test Site," *Nature* 397 (1999): 56–59.
14. Yucca Mountain Project, "Damage to FOC from '92 Quake Less than First Cited," *Of Mountains and Science* Winter (1996): 132–133.
15. Charles B. Connor, "Assessing the Long-Term Volcanic Hazards to the Geologic Disposal of Nuclear Waste," *Technology Today* 16.2 (June 1995): 2–10; S. G. Wells, L. D. McFadden, C. E. Renault, B. M. Crowe, "Geomorphic Assessment of Late Quaternary Volcanism in the Yucca Mountain Area, Southern Nevada: Implications for the Proposed High Level Radioactive Waste Repository," *Geology* 18 (1990): 549–553.
16. Brian Wernicke, James L. Davis, Richard A. Bennett, Pedro Elosegui, Mark J. Abolins, Robert J. Brady, Martha A. House, Nathan A. Niemi, J. Kent Snow, "Anomalous Strain Accumulation in the Yucca Mountain Area, Nevada," *Science* 279 (1998): 2096–2099.
17. Gerrard, *Whose Backyard? Whose Risk?*
18. H. Josef Hebert, "Nevada Nixes Nuclear Waste Storage," *Washington Post,* 3 June 1998.
19. U.S. Congress, Senate, *To Amend the Nuclear Waste Policy Act of 1982,* Trans. S. 104, 105th Congress, 1st session (Washington, DC: Government Printing Office, 1997).
20. Nuclear Regulatory Commission, "Waste Confidence Decision Review," *Federal Register* 55. 81 (1990): 38474–38514; Nuclear Waste Technology Review Board, *Disposal and Storage of Spent Nuclear Fuel—Finding the Right Balance* (Washington, DC: Nuclear Waste Technology Review Board, 1996).
21. National Research Council, *Technical Bases for Yucca Mountain Standards.*
22. U.S. Congress, *Budget Reconciliation Act of 1987.*
23. *Stock* is a geological term for an irregularly shaped mass of igneous rock that has solidified from magma beneath the Earth's surface.
24. U.S. Congress, Senate, *To Amend the Nuclear Waste Policy Act of 1982.*

23   *Appetite for Toxins: Bioremediation of Contaminated Soil*

1. M. Alice Ottoboni, *The Dose Makes the Poison: A Plain Language Guide to Toxicology* (New York: Van Nostrand Reinhold, 1991), 31.
2. Roy F. Weston, Inc., *Windrow Composting Demonstration for Explosives-Contaminated Soils at the Umatilla Depot Activity, Hermiston, Oregon,* prepared under Contract Number DACA31-91-D-0079 for the U.S. Army Environmental Center, Aberdeen Proving Ground, Maryland (Seattle, WA: Roy F. Weston, 1993).
3. Dames & Moore, Inc., *Technical Report: Soil Composting Treatability Study, TNT Washout Facility (SWMU 10), Tooele Army Depot, Tooele, Utah,* prepared under Contract No. DACA31-94-D-0060 for Tooele Army Depot, Utah (Bethesda, MD: Dames & Moore, 1998).
4. One percent is equal to one part per hundred; one part per million is 10,000 times less than that.

24 Ocean Circulation: Conveyor of Past and Future Climate

1. For a more technical account of my ideas on the cause of the modern ice age of the Northern Hemisphere, see Steven M. Stanley, "Presidential Address. New Horizons for Paleontology, with Two Examples: The Rise and Fall of the Supertethys and the Cause of the Modern Ice Age," *Journal of Paleontology* 69 (1995): 999–1007.
2. Knut Aagaard and Lawrence K. Coachman, "Toward an Ice-Free Arctic Ocean," *Eos* 56 (1975): 484–486.

25 A Record of Climate Change from Owens Lake Sediment

1. Alan R. Gillespie, "Quaternary Glaciation and Tectonism in the Southeastern Sierra Nevada, Inyo County, California," dissertation, California Institute of Technology, Pasadena, 1982; Marcus Bursik and Kerry E. Sieh, "Range Front Faulting and Volcanism in the Mono Basin, Eastern California," *Journal of Geophysical Research* 94 (1989): 15587.
2. Paul R. Bierman, Alan Gillespie, Kelin Whipple, and Douglas Clark, "Quaternary Geomorphology and Geochronology of Owens Valley, California: Geological Society of America Field Trip," in *Geological Excursions in Southern California and Mexico,* Michael J. Walawender and Barry B. Hanan, eds. (Boulder, CO: Geological Society of America, 1991), 199–223.
3. David P. Hill, E. Kissling, J. H. Luetgert, and U. Kradolfer, "Constraints on the Upper Crustal Structure of the Long Valley-Mono Craters Volcanic Complex, Eastern California, from Seismic Refraction Measurements," *Journal of Geophysical Research* 90 (1985): 11135–11550; Bierman et al., "Quaternany Geomorphology and Geochronology."
4. Eliot Blackwelder, "Pleistocene Glaciation in the Sierra Nevada and Basin Ranges," *Geological Society of America Bulletin* 42 (1931): 865–922; Robert P. Sharp, "Pleistocene Glaciation, Bridgeport Basin, California," *Geological Society of America Bulletin* 83 (1972): 2233–2260; Clyde Wahrhaftig and Joseph H. Birman, "The Quaternary of the Pacific Mountain System in California," in *The Quaternary of the United States,* Herbert E. Wright, Jr. and David G. Frey, eds. (Princeton, NJ: Princeton University Press, 1965), 299–340; Gillespie, "Quaternary Glaciation and Tectonism."
5. Paul C. Bateman, *Geology and Tungsten Mineralization of the Bishop District, California,* U.S. Geological Survey Professional Paper 470 (Reston, VA: U.S. Geological Survey, 1965).
6. George I. Smith and F. Alayne Street-Perrott, "Pluvial Lakes of the Western United States," in *The Late Quaternary,* Vol. 1 of *Late Quaternary Environments of the United States,* Stephen C. Porter, ed. (Minneapolis: University of Minnesota Press, 1983), 190–212.
7. George I. Smith and James L. Bischoff, "Core OL-92 from Owens Lake: Project Rationale, Geologic Setting, Drilling Procedures, and Summary," in *An 800,000-Year Paleoclimatic Record from Core OL-92, Owens Lake, Southeast California,* Geological Society of America Special Paper 317, George I. Smith and James L. Bischoff, eds. (Boulder, CO: Geological Society of America, 1997), 1–8.
8. The scientists from the U.S. Geological Survey were George Smith and Jim Bischoff; Jonathan Glen and I were involved in the project as graduate students from the University of California at Santa Cruz.
9. Marc Reisner, *Cadillac Desert: The American West and Its Disappearing Water* (New York: Viking 1986).
10. *Cadillac Desert* contains an excellent history of the corruption and greed that accompanied the early settlement of Los Angeles and allowed it to become the second largest city in the nation.
11. George I. Smith, "Stratigraphy, Lithologies, and Sedimentary Structures of

Owens Lake Core OL-92," in Smith and Bischoff, *An 800,000-Year Paleoclimatic Record,* 9–24.

12. Ajoy K. Baksi, Vindell Hsu, Michael O. McWilliams, and Edward Farrar, "^{40}Ar/^{39}Ar Dating of the Brunhes-Matuyama Geomagnetic Field Reversal," *Science* 256 (1992): 356–357.

13. Smith, "Stratigraphy, Lithologies, and Sedimentary Structures."

14. Ibid.

15. Andrei M. Sarna-Wojcicki, Charles E. Meyer, and Elmira Wan, "Age and Correlation of Tephra Layers, Position of the Matuyama-Brunhes Chron Boundary, and Effects of Bishop Ash Eruption on Owens Lake, as Determined from Drill Hole OL-92, Southeast California," in Smith and Bischoff, *An 800,000-Year Paleoclimatic Record,* 79–90.

16. R. J. Litwin, D. P. Adam, N. O. Frederiksen, and W. B. Woolfenden, "An 800,000-Year Pollen Record from Owens Lake, California: Preliminary Analyses," in Smith and Bischoff, *An 800,000-Year Paleoclimatic Record,* 127–142.

17. J. Pratt Bradbury, "A Diatom-Based Paleohydrologic Record of Climate Change for the Past 800 K.Y. from Owens Lake, California," in Smith and Bischoff, *An 800,000-Year Paleoclimatic Record,* 99–112; James R. Firby, Saxon E. Sharpe, Joseph F. Whelan, Gerald R. Smith, and W. Geoffrey Spaulding, "Paleobiotic and Isotopic Analysis of Mollusks, Fish, and Plants from Core OL-92: Indicators for an Open or Closed Lake System," in Smith and Bischoff, *An 800,000-Year Paleoclimatic Record,* 121–125.

18. Claire Carter, "Ostracodes in Owens Lake Core OL-92: Alternation of Saline and Freshwater Forms Through Time," in Smith and Bischoff, *An 800,000-Year Paleoclimatic Record,* 113–119.

19. Kirsten M. Menking, "Climatic Signals in Clay Mineralogy and Grain-Size Variations in Owens Lake Core OL-92, Southeast California," in Smith and Bischoff, *An 800,000-Year Paleoclimatic Record,* 25–36.

20. James L. Bischoff, Jeffrey P. Fitts, and John A. Fitzpatrick, "Responses of Sediment Geochemistry to Climate Change in Owens Lake Sediment: An 800-K.Y. Record of Saline/Fresh Cycles in Core OL-92," in Smith and Bischoff, *An 800,000-Year Paleoclimatic Record,* 37–48.

21. Jonathan M. Glen and Robert S. Coe, "Paleomagnetism and Magnetic Susceptibility of Pleistocene Sediments from Drill Hole OL-92, Owens Lake, California," in Smith and Bischoff, *An 800,000-Year Paleoclimatic Record,* 67–78.

22. Sarna-Wojcicki et al., "Age and Correlation of Tephra Layers."

23. James L. Bischoff, Thomas W. Stafford, Jr., and Meyer Rubin, "A Time–Depth Scale for Owens Lake Sediments of Core OL-92: Radiocarbon Dates and Constant Mass-Accumulation Rate," in Smith and Bischoff, *An 800,000-Year Paleoclimatic Record,* 91–98.

24. Litwin et al., "An 800,000-Year Pollen Record."

25. Bradbury, "A Diatom-Based Paleohydrologic Record."

26. Bischoff, Stafford, and Rubin, "A Time–Depth Scale."

27. Reisner, *Cadillac Desert.*

28. Telephone interview with Maurice Roos, 15 April 1997.

29. Reisner, *Cadillac Desert.*

30. Scott Stine, "Extreme and Persistent Drought in California and Patagonia During Mediaeval Time," *Nature* 369 (1994): 546–549.

31. David A. Hodell, Jason H. Curtis, and Mark Brenner, "Possible Role of Climate in the Collapse of Classic Maya Civilization," *Nature* 375 (1995): 391–394.

32. *Water Supply Overview,* Santa Barbara County Public Works Department, 28 November 1999, <http://www.publicworkssb.org/water/watersources.html>.

33. *Hurricane Andrew,* National Oceanic and Atmospheric Administration, 7 December 1998, <http://www.nhc.noaa.gov/1992andrewpr.html>.

34. *Daily River Stage Along the Mississippi River at St. Louis, Missouri,* Midwestern Climate Center, 12 February 1999, <http://mcc.sws.uiuc.edu/~scott/flood93/hydro/missrs/stlouis.dat>.

35. *1915, 1916, 1955, 1995: Heat Waves,* Chicago Public Library, 11 February 1999, <http://www.chipublib.org/004chicago/disasters/heat_waves.html>.

36. Associated Press, "Heat Toll in Texas Reaches 128," *Dallas Morning News,* 13 August 1998, 35-A; *Summer Sizzle Continues in Texas, Southern Plains,* CNN Interactive, 12 February 1999, <http://cnn.com/US/9808/03/heat.wave.02/index.html>.

37. *Snowfall Summary for the Northeast,* Northeast Regional Climate Center, Cornell University, 12 February 1999, <http://met-www.cit.cornell.edu/snow_records.html>.

38. Intergovernmental Panel on Climate Change, *Climate Change 1995: IPCC Second Assessment Report* (Cambridge: Cambridge University Press, 1995).

39. Thomas J. Crowley and Gerald R. North, *Paleoclimatology* (New York: Oxford University Press, 1991).

40. Intergovernmental Panel on Climate Change, *Climate Change 1995.*

41. C. Lorius, J. Jouzel, D. Raynaud, J. Hansen, and H. Le Treut, "The Ice-Core Record: Climate Sensitivity and Future Greenhouse Warming," *Nature* 347 (1990): 139–145.

26 *Lessons from the Past for Future Climate*

1. Thomas R. Karl, Neville Nicholls, and Jonathan Gregory, "The Coming Climate," *Scientific American* 281.5 (1997): 80.

2. Intergovernmental Panel on Climate Change, *Climate Change 1995: The Science of Climate Change, Summary for Policymakers and Technical Summary of the Working Group I Report* (Cambridge: Cambridge University Press, 1996), 32.

3. See, for example, S. Fred Singer, *Hot Talk, Cold Science: Global Warming's Unfinished Debate* (Oakland, CA: The Independent Institute, 1998), 10.

4. See, for example, J. W. Hurrell and K. E. Trenberth, "Spurious Trends in Satellite MSU Temperatures from Merging Different Satellite Records," *Nature* 386 (1997): 164–167.

5. Intergovernmental Panel on Climate Change, *Climate Change 1995,* 10.

6. Stephen H. Schneider and Randi Londer, *The Coevolution of Climate and Life* (San Francisco: Sierra Club Books, 1984), 44.

7. J. Jouzel, C. Lorius, J. R. Petit, C. Genthon, N. I. Barkov, V. M. Kotlyakov, and V. M. Petrov, "Vostok Ice Core: A Continuous Isotope Temperature Record Over the Last Climatic Cycle (160,000 Years)," *Nature* 329 (1987): 403–407.

8. J. M. Barnola, D. Raynaud, Y. S. Korotkevich, and C. Lorius, "Vostok Ice Core Provides 160,000-Year Record of Atmospheric CO_2," *Nature* 329 (1987): 408–414; GRIP Project Members, "Evidence for General Instability of Past Climate from a 250-K.Y. Ice-Core Record," *Nature* 364 (1993): 203–207.

9. Thomas J. Crowley and Gerald R. North, *Paleoclimatology* (New York: Oxford University Press, 1991), 54.

10. Schneider and Londer, *The Coevolution of Climate and Life,* 49.

11. Thomas J. Crowley, "Remembrance of Things Past: Greenhouse Lessons from the Geologic Record," *Consequences* 2 (1996): 5.

12. Schneider and Londer, *The Coevolution of Climate and Life,* 111.

13. Ibid, 113.

14. Heather Pringle, "Death in Norse Greenland," *Science* 275 (1997): 924–926.

15. Crowley, "Remembrance of Things Past," 5.

16. Schneider and Londer, *The Coevolution of Climate and Life,* 114.

17. Crowley, "Remembrance of Things Past," 6.

18. Scott A. Elias, Susan K. Short, and C. Hans Nelson, "Life and Times of the Bering Land Bridge," *Nature* 382 (1996): 60–63.

19. Barnola et al., "Vostok Ice Core," 408; Jouzel et al., "Vostok Ice Core," 403.

20. Crowley, "Remembrance of Things Past," 7.

21. Ibid, 8.

22. Ibid.

23. Intergovernmental Panel on Climate Change, *Climate Change 1995*, 33.

24. Karl, Nicholls, and Gregory, "The Coming Climate," 81.

25. U.S. Congress, Office of Technology Assessment, *Preparing for an Uncertain Climate*, Vol. 1 (Washington, DC: Government Printing Office, 1993), 94.

26. Ibid.

27. Wallace S. Broecker, "Unpleasant Surprises in the Greenhouse?" *Nature* 328 (1987): 123–126.

28. Crowley and North, *Paleoclimatology*, 259.

29. Wallace S. Broecker, "Thermohaline Circulation, the Achilles Heel of Our Climate System: Will Man-Made CO_2 Upset the Current Balance?" *Science* 278 (1997): 1582–1588; see also Steven M. Stanley, "Presidential Address. New Horizons for Paleontology, with Two Examples: The Rise and Fall of the Supertethys and the Cause of the Modern Ice Age," *Journal of Paleontology* 69 (1995): 999–1007.

30. A. G. Hunt and P. E. Malin, "Possible Triggering of Heinrich Events by Ice-Load-Induced Earthquakes," *Nature* 393 (1998): 155–158.

31. Broecker, "Thermohaline Circulation," 1582.

32. Crowley, "Remembrance of Things Past," 5.

33. Timothy Egan, "The New Politics of Urban Sprawl," *New York Times*, 15 November 1998, A-1ff.

34. David S. Shriner and Roger B. Street, "North America," in *The Regional Impacts of Climate Change: An Assessment of Vulnerability*, Robert T. Watson, Marufu C. Zinyowera and Richard H. Moss, eds. (Cambridge: Cambridge University Press, 1998), 282.

35. Martin Beniston and Richard S. J. Tol, "Europe," in Watson et al., *The Regional Impacts of Climate Change*, 169.

36. President's Council on Sustainable Development, *Sustainable America: A New Consensus for Prosperity, Opportunity, and a Healthy Environment for the Future* (Washington, DC: Government Printing Office, 1996), 98.

37. Mike MacCracken provided insight on the satellite controversy. David Applegate, Stephanie DeVilliers, and Catherine McKalip-Thompson provided helpful comments on earlier drafts of this essay.

27 Nature's Sunscreen: Ozone Depletion and the Health of the Whole

1. Dorothy Merritts, Andrew De Wet, and Kirsten Menking, *Environmental Geology: An Earth System Science Approach* (New York: W. H. Freeman and Company, 1998), 264.

2. Ibid., 265.

3. Ibid., 283.

4. Jacqueline Vaughn Switzer, with Gary Bryner, *Environmental Politics: Domestic and Global Dimensions*, 2nd Ed. (New York: St. Martin's Press, 1998), 226.

5. Susan Solomon, Rolando R. Garcia, F. Sherwood Rowland, and Donald J. Wuebbles, "On Depletion of Antarctic Ozone," *Nature* 321 (1986): 755–758.

6. National Aeronautics and Space Administration, *TOMS (Total Ozone Mapping Spectrometer) Home Page*, 3 October 1998, <http://toms.nasa.gov>.

7. Switzer, *Environmental Politics*, 226.

8. World Meteorological Organization, "Scientific Assessment of Ozone Depletion, 1998: Executive Summary," *World Meteorological Organization Global Ozone Research and Monitoring Project* (Geneva: World Meteorological Organization, 1998).

9. J. R. Herman, "UV-B Increases (1979–92) from Decreases in Total Ozone," *Geophysical Research Letters* 23 (1996): 2117–2120.

10. Kerry M. Hanson and John D. Simon, "Epidermal Trans-Urocanic Acid and the

UV-A Induced Photoaging of the Skin," *Proceedings of the National Academy of Sciences* 95 (1998): 10576–10578.

11. World Meteorological Organization, "Scientific Assessment of Ozone Depletion, 1998."

12. *Health and Environmental Effects of Ultraviolet Radiation,* INTERSUN: The Global UV Project, 28 November 1998, <http://www.who.int/peh-uv/publications/english/who-ehg-95-16.html>.

13. Ibid.

14. Ibid.

15. R. Smith, "Ozone Depletion: Ultraviolet Radiation and Phytoplankton Biology in Antarctic Waters," *Science* 255 (1992): 952.

16. Francesca Grifo and Joshua Rosenthal, eds., *Biodiversity and Human Health* (Washington, DC: Island Press, 1997).

17. Steven M. Stanley, *Earth and Life Through Time,* 2nd Ed. (New York: W. H. Freeman and Company, 1989), 147.

28   *Let Earth Speak!*

1. Robert Muir Wood, *The Dark Side of the Earth* (London: Allen and Unwin, 1985), 1.

2. Claude Allègre, *The Behavior of the Earth* (Cambridge, MA: Harvard University Press, 1988), 22.

3. Wood, *The Dark Side of the Earth,* 7.

4. Edward O. Wilson, *Consilience: The Unity of Knowledge* (New York: Alfred A. Knopf, 1998).

5. Ironically, Whewell is one of the few serious philosophers of science to deal substantively with methodological issues appropriate to geology.

6. Richard R. Rorty, "Against Unity," *Wilson Quarterly* 20 (Winter 1998): 38.

7. Alan Cromer, *Uncommon Sense: The Heretical Nature of Science* (Oxford: Oxford University Press, 1993).

8. Lewis Wolpert, *The Unchanged Nature of Science* (Cambridge, MA: Harvard University Press, 1992).

9. Morris H. Shamos, *The Myth of Scientific Literacy* (New Brunswick, NJ: Rutgers University Press, 1995).

10. Alan Cromer, *Connected Knowledge* (Oxford: Oxford University Press, 1997).

11. Alvin M. Weinberg, "The Axiology of Science," *American Scientist* 58 (1970): 612–617.

12. Walter Alvarez, "The Gentle Art of Scientific Trespassing," *GSA Today* 1 (1991): 29–31, 34.

13. Daniel Sarewitz, *Frontiers of Illusion: Science, Technology, and the Politics of Progress* (Philadelphia, PA: Temple University Press, 1996).

14. For example, Paul R. Gross and Norman Levitt, *Higher Superstition: The Academic Left and Its Quarrels with Science* (Baltimore, MD: Johns Hopkins University Press, 1994).

15. John Deely, *Basics of Semiotics* (Bloomington: Indiana University Press, 1990).

16. In the model-testing approach of science, one formulates a theory or model. One then tests this theory against the 'facts.' If the facts concur with the model, then one knows that the model is not proved wrong. However, one does not know whether the model is correct because this simple test does not tell whether some other model might also predict the same result. If the facts do not concur with the model, then the model is indeed wrong.

17. Umberto Eco and Thomas Sebeok, *The Sign of Three: Dupin, Holmes, Peirce* (Bloomington: Indiana University Press, 1988).

18. Aage Peterson, "The Philosophy of Niels Bohr," in *Niels Bohr: A Centenary Volume,* A. P. French and P. J. Kennedy, eds. (Cambridge, MA: Harvard University Press, 1985), 305.

19. John Ziman, *Reliable Knowledge: An Exploration for the Grounds for Belief in Science* (Cambridge: Cambridge University Press, 1978), 28.

20. Wood, *The Dark Side of the Earth*, 7.
21. Hans Cloos, *Conversation with the Earth* (New York: Alfred A. Knopf, 1953), 4.
22. See, for example, Joseph Brent, *Charles Sanders Peirce: A Life* (Bloomington: Indiana University Press, 1998).
23. See, for example, Wolf von Engelhardt and Jorge Zimmermann, *Theory of Earth Science* (Cambridge: Cambridge University Press, 1988).
24. Victor R. Baker, "The Pragmatic Roots of American Quaternary Geology and Geomorphology," *Geomorphology* 16 (1996): 197–215.
25. See, for example, Claude C. Albritton, Jr., ed., *Philosophy of Geohistory: 1785–1970* (Stroudsburg PA: Dowden, Hutchinson and Ross, 1975).
26. Nathan Houser and Christian Kloesel, *The Essential Peirce*, Vol. 1 (Bloomington: Indiana University Press, 1992), 1; Kenneth L. Ketner, ed., *Reasoning and the Logic of Things* (Cambridge, MA: Harvard University Press, 1992); James J. Liszka, *A General Introduction to the Semeiotic of Charles Sanders Peirce* (Bloomington: Indiana University Press, 1996); Peirce Edition Project, *The Essential Peirce*, Vol. 2 (Bloomington: Indiana University Press, 1998).
27. Grove K. Gilbert, "The Inculcation of Scientific Method by Example," *American Journal of Science* 31 (1886): 286.
28. Grove K. Gilbert, "The Origin of Hypotheses Illustrated by the Discussion of a Topographic Problem," *Science* 3 (1896): 1–13.
29. Thomas C. Chamberlin, "The Method of Multiple Working Hypotheses," *Science* 15 (1890): 92–96; Thomas C. Chamberlin, "The Methods of Earth-Sciences," *Popular Science Monthly* 66 (1904): 66–75.
30. William M. Davis, "The Value of Outrageous Geological Hypotheses," *Science* 63 (1926): 463–468.
31. Victor R. Baker, "Hypotheses and Geomorphological Reasoning," in *The Scientific Nature of Geomorphology*, B. L. Rhoads and C. E. Thoin, eds. (New York: Wiley, 1996), 57–85.
32. Von Engelhardt and Zimmerman, *Theory of Earth Science*.
33. Victor R. Baker, "Discovering Earth's Future in Its Past: Palaeohydrology and Global Environmental Change," in *Global Continental Changes: The Context of Palaeohydrology*, Geological Society Special Publication 115, J. Branson, A. J. Brown, and K. J. Gregory, eds. (London: Geological Society, 1996), 73–83.
34. Victor R. Baker, "Geological Understanding and the Changing Environment," *Transactions of the Gulf Coast Association of Geological Societies* 44 (1994): 13–20.
35. Victor R. Baker, "Geomorphological Understanding of Floods," *Geomorphology* 10 (1994): 139–156.
36. Victor R. Baker, "Hydrological Understanding and Societal Action," *Journal of the American Water Resources Association* 34.4 (1998): 1–7.
37. Stanley A. Schumm, *To Interpret the Earth: Ten Ways to Be Wrong* (Cambridge: Cambridge University Press, 1991).
38. See, for example, Rob Ferguson, "Review of Schumm, S. A., 1991: *To Interpret the Earth*," *Progress in Physical Geography* 16 (1992): 499–500; or Keith S. Richards, "Review of *To Interpret the Earth* by S. A. Schumm," *Earth Surface Processes and Landforms* 17 (1992): 639.
39. Schumm, *To Interpret the Earth*, 14.
40. Chamberlin, "The Method of Multiple Working Hypotheses."
41. Thomas A. Sebeok, "Symptom," in *New Directions in Linguistics and Semiotics*, J. E. Copeland, ed. (Houston, TX: Rice University Press, 1984), 211.
42. James E. Lovelock, *The Ages of Gaia: A Biography of Our Living Earth* (New York: W. W. Norton, 1988).
43. Herman Le Roy Fairchild, "Geology Under the Planetesimal Hypothesis of Earth-Origin (With Discussion)," *Geological Society of America Bulletin* 15 (1904): 261.
44. For a dissenting view on this philosophical position, see Evelyn Fox Keller, *Reflections on Gender and Science* (New Haven, CT: Yale University Press, 1985).

45. Eldridge M. Moores, "Geology and Culture: A Call to Action," *GSA Today* 7.1 (1997): 7–11.
46. Ibid., 11.
47. Joseph Brent helped me understand many aspects of the philosophy of Charles S. Peirce.

29   Geology and Environmental Justice: An Example from Hawaii

1. Pele is a deity in the native Hawaiian pantheon of hundreds, many who take natural forms such as taro, bamboo, sugar cane, coconut, sweet potatoes, lightning, and rain clouds. Pele takes the form of volcanoes. Many native Hawaiians take Pele seriously and bring offerings to her at the rim of Halemaumau crater in Hawaii Volcanoes National Park.
2. Contrary to expectations, volcanic rocks may be quite porous because gas bubbles that escape from molten rock as it cools at the Earth's surface leave behind holes in the rock.
3. Ian Anderson, "Blowout Blights Future of Hawaii's Geothermal Power," *New Scientist* 131.1778 (20 July 1991): 17.
4. Ibid.
5. *Geothermal Fact Sheet,* 29 November 1999, <http://www.state.hi.us/dbedt/ert/geo_hi.html>.
6. Ibid.
7. J. W. Saulsbury and R. M. Reed, *Identifying the Environmental and Cultural Issues Associated with Geothermal Development in Hawaii,* 13 June 1999, <http://www.naep.org/Conference/Abstracts/Saulsbury.abs.html>.
8. Annie Szvetecz, *Coalition Sues State to Stop Hawaii Geothermal Project,* 29 November 1999, <http://forests.org/gopher/america/Hawaii2.txt>.
9. Ibid.
10. Anderson, "Blowout Blights Future."
11. One megawatt equals one million watts.
12. Szvetecz, *Coalition Sues State.*
13. The law was authorized permanently—that is, without expiration date—and created the Council on Environmental Quality.
14. Szvetecz, *Coalition Sues State.*
15. This organization is now the Earth Justice Legal Defense Fund.
16. The plaintiffs included The Wao Kele O Puna Rainforest, Greenpeace USA, and Greenpeace Hawaii, Big Island Rainforest Action Group, Blue Ocean Preservation Society, Citizens for Responsible Energy Development with Aloha Aina, Friends of the Earth, Kapoho Community Association, Oahu Rainforest Action Group, Pahoa Business Association, Pele Defense Fund, Rainforest Action Network, and the Sierra Club.
17. Szvetecz, *Coalition Sues State.*
18. Mark Mardon, "Steamed Up Over Rainforests," *Sierra* 75 (May/June 1990): 80–82.
19. Anderson, "Blowout Blights Future."
20. State of Hawaii, Energy, Resources, and Technology Division, Annotated Bibliography, 1995, 28 March 1999, <http://www.Hawaii.gov/dbedt/ert/bib/bib_geo.html#anchor1804972>.
21. Rainforest Action Newtwork, *Geothermal Suit Settled,* 28 March 1999, <http://www.ra.org/ran/victories/victoryarchives.html>.
22. Saulsbury and Reed, *Identifying the Environmental and Cultural Issues.*
23. Leonard Greer, State of Hawaii, Department of Business, Economic Development & Tourism, 28 March 1999, <http://www.Hawaii.gov/dbedt/ert/hirenw/hir_ch3.html#anchor615853>.
24. Carla Montgomery, *Environmental Geology,* 4th Ed. (Dubuque, IA: Wm. C. Brown, 1995), 321.
25. Some readers may be unfamiliar with the phrase *people of color.* A term preferred

to the word *minority* by many individuals of different races who are active in civil rights and social justice movements, the phrase more accurately describes people of different races who, taken together, are not in the minority across the globe. The phrase *people of color* is particularly appropriate in this discussion because whites constitute only one-third of the population in the State of Hawaii.

26. For an introduction to the environmental justice movement and its roots, from which some of the information in the following paragraphs comes, see Robert D. Bullard, "Environmental Justice for All," in *Unequal Protection: Environmental Justice and Communities of Color,* Robert D. Bullard, ed. (San Francisco: Sierra Club Books, 1994), 3–22.

27. Ibid., 5.

28. Ibid., 6.

29. United Church of Christ Commission for Racial Justice, *Toxic Wastes and Race in the United States: A National Study of the Racial and Socioeconomic Characteristics of Communities with Hazardous Waste Sites* (New York: United Church of Christ, 1987).

30. *Federal Actions to Address Environmental Justice in Minority Populations and Low-Income Populations: Executive Order 12898, February 11, 1994,* 13 June 1999, <http://www.fs.fed.us/land/envjust.html>.

31. Council on Environmental Quality, *NEPA Net,* 29 November 1999, <http:/www.whitehouse.gov/CEQ/>.

32. Terrence Irwin, trans., *Nicomachean Ethics,* by Aristotle (Indianapolis, IN: Hackett, 1985), 1131, a20–25.

33. Mark Sagoff, *The Economy of the Earth* (New York: Cambridge University Press, 1988).

34. See the Wingspread Statement on the Precautionary Principle in Sandra Steingraber, *Living Downstream: A Scientist's Personal Investigation of Cancer and the Environment* (New York: Vintage Books, 1998), 283.

35. Robert Nozick, *Anarchy, State and Utopia* (New York: Basic Books, 1974).

36. Bullard, "Environmental Justice for All," 4–5.

37. Environmental Protection Agency, *Inclusion of Environmental Justice in Comparative Risk Projects,* 29 November 1999, <http://www.epa.gov/opperspd/just/appendix.html>.

38. R. M. Daggett, "Introduction," in *The Legends and Myths of Hawaii,* R. M. Daggett and Terence Barrow, eds. (1972; reprinted, Rutland, VT: Charles E. Tuttle, 1990), 27.

39. John Fischer, *The People of Hawaii: An Introduction,* 29 November 1999, <http://gohawaii.miningco.com/travel/gohawaii/library/weekly/aa011298.html>.

40. John Falconer, "Rx for Hawaii," *American Forests* 99.3–4 (1993): 64.

41. Linda S. Parker, "Review of *Paradise Remade: The Politics of Culture and History in Hawaii," American Historical Review* 99 (April 1994): 631.

42. Sylvester Stevens, *American Expansion in Hawaii 1842–1898* (Harrisburg, PA: Archives Publishing, 1945), 299.

43. Hawaii State Government, *A Brief History of Hawaii,* 29 December 1999, <http://www.hawaii.gov/about/history.htm>.

44. *Broken Rainbow,* Steven Okazaki, dir., Farallon Films, 1992; Fischer, *People of Hawaii.*

45. Ibid.

46. Ibid.

47. Sara Chamberlain, "Golf Endangers Hawai'ian Ecology and Culture," *Earth Island Journal* Summer (1995): 21.

48. Ibid.

49. This tenet is the basic rationale behind religious freedom and the separation of church and state. The state remains neutral regarding religious beliefs so that individuals may choose or reject a faith commitment.

50. Council on Environmental Quality, *Environmental Justice: Guidance Under the National Environmental Policy Act, December 10, 1997,* 13 June 1999, <http://www.whitehouse.gov/CEQ/>.

51. Ibid.
52. *Executive Order 13007 on Indian Sacred Sites, May 24, 1996,* 13 June 1999, <http://es.epa.gov/oeca/ofa/ejepa.html>.
53. See Richard R. B. Powell, "The Relationship Between Property Rights and Civil Rights," *Hastings Law Journal* 15 (1963): 135–152.
54. John Rawls, *A Theory of Justice* (Cambridge, MA: Harvard University Press, 1971).
55. Ibid., 302.
56. Daniel Morgan, "Geothermal Energy—A Fact Sheet," Congressional Research Service, Science Policy Division, 92.109 (1992).
57. This characteristic of rock is familiar to anyone who has turned over a flat, sun-baked rock on a clear but cool day—the surface exposed to the sun is hot to the touch but the underside is cool because the heat will not have traveled far into the rock. In like manner, hot water or steam removed by a geothermal well gets replaced by cool water that needs to be heated before it can be used.
58. Montgomery, *Environmental Geology,* 316.
59. David J. Fishman, "Deep Heat: Geothermal Energy," *Science World* 50.5 (1993): 14.
60. Dorothy J. Merritts, Andrew De Wet, and Kirsten Menking, *Environmental Geology: An Earth System Science Approach* (New York: W. H. Freeman and Company, 1998), 350.
61. Montgomery, *Environmental Geology,* 311.
62. Ibid., 320.
63. Merritts et al., *Environmental Geology,* 355.
64. Bernard W. Pipkin and Dee Trent, *Geology and the Environment,* 2nd Ed. (Belmont, CA: Wadsworth, 1997), 403.
65. Montgomery, *Environmental Geology,* 320.
66. Merritts et al., *Environmental Geology,* 356.
67. Joni Seager, *Earth Follies: Coming to Feminist Terms with the Global Environmental Crisis* (New York: Routledge, 1993).
68. *Broken Rainbow.*
69. Eleanor Roosevelt, *Tomorrow Is Now* (New York: Harper and Row, 1963), xv–xvi.
70. We are grateful to the National Science Foundation, Division of Undergraduate Education, for the grant that allowed us to develop an interdisciplinary course on earth system science and environmental justice at Vassar College (DUE 9653266).

30 *Stakes, Options, and Some Natural Limits to a Sustainable World*

1. Garrett Hardin, "The Tragedy of the Commons," *Science* 162 (1968): 1243–1248.
2. World Commission on Environment and Development, *Our Common Future* (New York: Oxford University Press, 1987), 43.
3. Eric Ashby, "Foreword," in *Environmental Dilemmas, Ethics and Decisions,* R. J. Berry, ed. (London: Chapman & Hall, 1993), xiv.
4. National Research Council, *Our Common Journey* (Washington, DC: National Academy Press, 1999), 4.
5. See Samuel P. Huntington, *The Clash of Civilizations and the Remaking of World Order* (New York: Simon & Schuster, 1996).
6. Alan T. Durning, *How Much Is Enough? The Consumer Society and the Fate of the Earth* (New York: W. W. Norton, 1992); letter received from Kenneth Conca, 1998.
7. For example J. D. Mahlman, "Uncertainties in Projections of Human-Caused Climate Warming," *Science* 278 (1997): 1416–1417; S. Fred Singer, *Hot Talk, Cold Science: Global Warming's Unfinished Debate* (Oakland, CA: The Independent Institute, 1997).
8. William Paddock and Paul Paddock, *Famine 1975! America's Decision: Who Will Survive* (Boston: Little Brown, 1967).
9. For example, see the introduction and conclusion of Julian L. Simon, ed., *The State of Humanity* (Oxford: Blackwell, 1995).

10. Joel E. Cohen, "How Many People Can the Earth Support?" *American Academy of Arts and Sciences Bulletin* LI.4 (1998): 25–39. This article comments on some of the fallacies in such optimism.

11. See Herman E. Daly and John B. Cobb, Jr., *For the Common Good: Redirecting the Economy Toward Community, the Environment, and a Sustainable Future,* 2nd Ed. (Boston: Beacon Press, 1994); Walter L. Youngquist, *GeoDestinies:* The Inevitable Control of Earth Resources Over Nations and Individuals (Portland, OR: National Book Company, 1997).

12. World Resources Institute, *World Resources 1996–1997,* (New York: Oxford University Press, 1996).

13. For example, Evelyn C. Pielou, *After the Ice Age: The Return of Life to Glaciated North America* (Chicago: University of Chicago Press, 1992); William R. Dickinson, "The Times Are Always Changing: The Holocene Saga," *Geological Society of America Bulletin* 107 (1995): 1–7; S. Fred Singer, *Hot Talk, Cold Science.*

14. Wallace S. Broecker, "Thermohaline Circulation, the Achilles Heel of Our Climate System: Will Man-Made CO_2 Upset the Current Balance?" *Science* 278 (1997): 1582–1588; Wallace S. Broecker, "Will Our Ride into the Greenhouse Future Be a Smooth One?" *GSA Today* 7.5 (1996): 1–7.

15. For data and primary sources, see Broecker, "Thermohaline Circulation," 1582; and Gerard C. Bond, William J. Showers, and Maziet Cheseby, "A Pervasive Millennial-Scale Cycle in North Atlantic Holocene and Glacial Climates," *Science* 278 (1997): 1257–1266.

16. E-an Zen, "The Citizen-Geologist: GSA Presidential Address, 1992," *GSA Today* 3.1 (1993): 3.

17. E-an Zen, "Land-Use Planning: One Geologist's Viewpoint," *Environmental Conservation* 10 (1983): 99.

18. See, for example, Youngquist, *GeoDestinies;* James R. Craig, David J. Vaughan, and Brian J. Skinner, *Resources of the Earth* (Englewood Cliffs, NJ: Prentice Hall, 1988).

19. Durning, *How Much Is Enough?* 27.

20. Simon, *The State of Humanity,* 22.

21. Aaron Sachs, "The Other Side of the World: Why Does Anyone Care About Sustainability?" *Worldwatch* 11.3 (1998): 31–38.

22. Huntington, *The Clash of Civilizations.*

23. See, for example, Albert Gore, Jr., *Earth in the Balance* (Boston: Houghton Mifflin, 1992).

24. I have benefited from discussions with Paul B. Barton, Norman Newell, Kenneth Conca, George W. Fisher, Walter R. Hearn, Arthur H. Lachenbruch, Allison R. ("Pete") Palmer, Joel E. Cohen, and Kai N. Lee; Kai inspired the rapids metaphor. I thank Barton, Conca, Lachenbruch, Palmer, Susan W. Kieffer, Brian J. Skinner, Robert W. Kates, and Carroll Ann Hodges for reviewing this manuscript. Conca's insights as a social scientist are especially instructive. Garrett Hardin verified my interpretion of his views; Kates gave permission to quote the National Research Council document. To all of them, my thanks.

31   *What Else Should My Neighbor Know?*

1. Allison R. Palmer, "What Should My Neighbor Know?" *G.S.A. News & Information* 12 (October 1990): 277–279.

2. U.S. Census Bureau, *Popclock,* 9 September 1999, <www.census.gov/main/www/popclock.html>.

3. Joel E. Cohen, *How Many People Can the Earth Support?* (New York: W. W. Norton, 1995).

4. Donella A. Meadows, Dennis C. Meadows, and Jorgen Randers, *Beyond the Limits* (Post Mills, VT: Chelsea Green, 1992).

5. U.S. Census Bureau, *Popclock*.

6. Marcia D. Lowe, "Shaping Cities: The Environmental and Human Dimensions," *Worldwatch Paper* 105 (1991).

7. Peter H. Gleick, ed., *Water in Crisis: A Guide to the World's Fresh Water Resources* (New York: Oxford University Press, 1993).

8. John E. Costa and Victor R. Baker, *Surficial Geology: Building with the Earth* (New York: John Wiley and Sons, 1981).

9. Marc Reisner, *Cadillac Desert: The American West and Its Disappearing Water* (New York: Viking Press, 1986).

10. Nicholas K. Coch, *Geohazards Natural and Human* (Englewood Cliffs, NJ: Prentice Hall, 1995).

11. Edward B. Nuhfer, Richard J. Proctor, and Paul H. Moser, *The Citizen's Guide to Geologic Hazards* (Arvada, CO: American Institute of Professional Geologists, 1993).

12. John McPhee, *The Control of Nature* (New York: Farrar Straus and Giroux, 1989).

13. Orrin H. Pilkey, Jr., and William J. Neal, eds., *Living with the Shore* (Durham, NC: Duke University Press, 1996).

14. Norma T. Moline, "Perception Research and Local Planning: Floods on the Rock River, Illinois," in *Natural Hazards: Local, National, Global,* Gilbert F. White, ed. (New York: Oxford University Press, 1974).

15. Anthony R. Berger, "Environmental Change, Geoindicators, and the Autonomy of Nature," *GSA Today* 8.1 (January 1998): 3–7.

16. Paul R. Ehrlich and Anne H. Ehrlich, *Population, Resources, Environment: Issues in Human Ecology* (San Francisco: W. H. Freeman and Company, 1972).

17. Press release from Minnesota Department of Agriculture and Minnesota Department of Health, "Summary of Water Well Pesticide Surveys," 3 March 1998.

18. Stuart L. Pimm and John H. Lawton, "Planning for Biodiversity," *Science* 279 (1998): 2068–2069.

19. David Malakoff, "Restored Wetlands Flunk Real-World Test," *Science* 280 (1998): 371–372.

Index